Standards for Foreign Language Learning in the 21st Century

This document incorporates the *Standards for Foreign Language Learning: Preparing for the 21st Century*. Initial funding for the development of the standards was provided by the U.S. Department of Education and the National Endowment for the Humanities (Grant No. R211U30004) with additional support from D.C. Heath and Company and EMC Publishing Company.

Printed by Allen Press, Inc.
Lawrence, KS

Copyright 2006
National Standards in Foreign Language Education Project
All rights reserved

The National Standards in Foreign Language Education Project is a collaborative effort of the American Council on the Teaching of Foreign Languages, American Association of Teachers of Arabic, American Association of Teachers of French, American Association of Teachers of German, American Association of Teachers of Italian, American Association of Teachers of Spanish and Portuguese, American Classical League, American Council of Teachers of Russian, Chinese Language Association of Secondary-Elementary Schools/Chinese Language Teachers Association, and the National Council of Japanese Language Teachers/Association of Teachers of Japanese.

Permission to copy or reprint portions of this document should be sought from the project's copyright office at 700 S. Washington St., Suite 210, Alexandria, VA 22314 Phone: 703-894-2900 Fax: 703-894-2905. Permission is routinely granted for educational and classroom use contingent upon appropriate credit being given to the National Standards in Foreign Language Education Project. ISBN: 0-9705798-1-0

Endorsing Organizations

The following organizations support and/or endorse the work of the Student Standards Task Force of the National Standards in Foreign Language Education Project:

- Alabama Association of Foreign Language Teachers
- American Association for Applied Linguistics
- American Association of Teachers of Arabic
- American Association of Teachers of French
- American Association of Teachers of German
- American Association of Teachers of Italian
- American Association of Teachers of Spanish and Portuguese
- American Classical League/American Philological Association Task Force on Standards for Classical Languages
- American Council of Teachers of Russian
- American Council on the Teaching of Foreign Languages
- Arizona Language Association
- California Language Teachers Association
- Central States Conference on the Teaching of Foreign Languages
- Chinese Language Association of Secondary-Elementary Schools
- Colorado Congress of Foreign Language Teachers
- Connecticut Organization of Language Teachers
- Delaware Council on the Teaching of Foreign Languages
- Foreign Language Association of Maine
- Foreign Language Association of Missouri
- Foreign Language Association of North Carolina
- Foreign Language Association of Virginia
- Greater Washington Association of Teachers of Foreign Languages
- Illinois Council on the Teaching of Foreign Languages
- Illinois Foreign Language Teachers' Association
- Joint National Committee for Languages
- Kentucky Council on the Teaching of Foreign Languages
- Massachusetts Foreign Language Association
- Minnesota Council on the Teaching of Languages and Cultures
- Modern Language Association
- Montana Association of Language Teachers
- National Association of District Supervisors of Foreign Languages
- National Association of Self-Instructional Language Programs
- National Council of State Supervisors of Foreign Languages
- National Network for Early Language Learning
- Nevada Language Association
- New Mexico Organization of Language Educators
- New York State Association of Foreign Language Teachers
- Ohio Foreign Language Association
- Oklahoma Foreign Language Teachers Association
- Pacific Northwest Council for Languages
- Pennsylvania State Modern Language Association
- Southern Conference on Language Teaching
- Southwest Conference on Language Teaching
- Teachers of English to Speakers of Other Languages
- Vermont Foreign Language Association
- Wisconsin Association of Foreign Language Teachers
- Wyoming Foreign Language Teachers Association

Table of Contents

ACKNOWLEDGEMENTS — 5

STATEMENT OF PHILOSOPHY — 7

STANDARDS FOR FOREIGN LANGUAGE LEARNING — 9

INTRODUCTION — 11
Foreign Languages and the Educated Citizen — 11
The Development of Standards — 12
The Implications of Standards — 15

LANGUAGE STUDY IN THE UNITED STATES — 17
The Current Status — 17
Program Models from K-16 — 20
Multiple Entry Points and an Extended Sequence of Study — 22
Instructional Approaches — 24
Special Features of Language Study — 25

ABOUT *STANDARDS FOR FOREIGN LANGUAGE LEARNING* — 27
A Brief Word About the Use of "Foreign Language" — 27
Organization and Definitions — 27
How to Use *Standards for Foreign Language Learning* — 28

ORGANIZING PRINCIPLES — 31
Five Cs of Foreign Language Education — 31
The "Weave" of Curricular Elements — 32
The Framework of Communicative Modes — 36

COMMUNICATION: Communicate in Languages Other Than English — 39

CULTURES: Gain Knowledge and Understanding of Other Cultures — 47

CONNECTIONS: Connect With Other Disciplines and Acquire New Information — 53

COMPARISONS: Develop Insight into the Nature of Language and Culture — 57

COMMUNITIES: Participate in Multilingual Communities at Home and Around the World — 63

CONCLUSIONS — 69

LEARNING SCENARIOS — 71

FREQUENTLY ASKED QUESTIONS — 97

APPENDICES — 101
    A: References and Further Reading — 101
    B: Project Personnel — 105

STANDARDS FOR ARABIC LANGUAGE LEARNING — 111

STANDARDS FOR CHINESE LANGUAGE LEARNING — 157

STANDARDS FOR CLASSICAL LANGUAGE LEARNING — 199

STANDARDS FOR THE LEARNING OF FRENCH, K-16 — 243

STANDARDS FOR LEARNING GERMAN — 287

STANDARDS FOR LEARNING ITALIAN — 329

STANDARDS FOR JAPANESE LANGUAGE LEARNING — 369

STANDARDS FOR LEARNING PORTUGUESE — 405

STANDARDS FOR RUSSIAN LANGUAGE LEARNING — 433

STANDARDS FOR LEARNING SPANISH — 475

Acknowledgements

Many organizations and individuals deserve recognition for their intellectual and financial support of the collaborative effort that has resulted in the production of the Standards for Foreign Language Learning. We wish to thank:

▶ the U.S. Department of Education and the National Endowment for the Humanities for committing the funds that provided us with the opportunity to develop standards for the study of the world's languages, which will enable American youth to take their place among multilingual societies;

▶ the program officers at both funding agencies for their constant guidance and support;

▶ the collaborating organizations and Board of Directors for demonstrating the power that professional unity can achieve;

▶ the Advisory Council that brought together individuals in leadership positions in business and industry, government, community organizations, and education to review and endorse these standards as challenging goals for students;

▶ the Task Force members, project staff, and consultants who spent countless hours discussing, evaluating, revising, and creating this document;

▶ state representatives who met with us to inform, to react, and to assure that this document has the power to serve as a beacon for effective programs into the next century;

▶ pilot school participants for helping us balance the challenge and the reach of standards with the possible; and

▶ the Board of Reviewers and the thousands of individuals who intensively examined the drafts of the standards and conscientiously communicated their reactions so that the resulting document reflects an overwhelming consensus of the profession.

June K. Phillips
Project Director

Christine Brown
Task Force Chair

Statement of Philosophy

The following statement was developed by the K-12 Student Standards Task Force as it began work on developing national standards in foreign language learning. From this philosophy, the goals for foreign language education were derived, and all the work in standards setting relates to these concepts.

Language and communication are at the heart of the human experience. The United States must educate students who are equipped linguistically and culturally to communicate successfully in a pluralistic American society and abroad. This imperative envisions a future in which ALL students will develop and maintain proficiency in English and at least one other language, modern or classical. Children who come to school from non-English-speaking backgrounds should also have opportunities to develop further proficiencies in their first language.

Supporting this vision are three assumptions about language and culture, learners of language and culture, and language and culture education:

Competence in more than one language and culture enables people to
- communicate with other people in other cultures in a variety of settings,
- look beyond their customary borders,
- develop insight into their own language and culture,
- act with greater awareness of self, of other cultures, and their own relationship to those cultures,
- gain direct access to additional bodies of knowledge, and
- participate more fully in the global community and marketplace.

All students can be successful language and culture learners, and they
- must have access to language and culture study that is integrated into the entire school experience,
- benefit from the development and maintenance of proficiency in more than one language,
- learn in a variety of ways and settings, and
- acquire proficiency at varied rates.

Language and culture education is part of the core curriculum, and it
- is tied to program models that incorporate effective strategies, assessment procedures, and technologies,
- reflects evolving standards at the national, state, and local levels, and
- develops and enhances basic communication skills and higher order thinking skills.

Standards for Foreign Language Learning

COMMUNICATION
Communicate in Languages Other Than English

Standard 1.1: Students engage in conversations, provide and obtain information, express feelings and emotions, and exchange opinions.

Standard 1.2: Students understand and interpret written and spoken language on a variety of topics.

Standard 1.3: Students present information, concepts, and ideas to an audience of listeners or readers on a variety of topics.

CULTURES
Gain Knowledge and Understanding of Other Cultures

Standard 2.1: Students demonstrate an understanding of the relationship between the practices and perspectives of the culture studied.

Standard 2.2: Students demonstrate an understanding of the relationship between the products and perspectives of the culture studied.

CONNECTIONS
Connect with Other Disciplines and Acquire Information

Standard 3.1: Students reinforce and further their knowledge of other disciplines through the foreign language.

Standard 3.2: Students acquire information and recognize the distinctive viewpoints that are only available through the foreign language and its cultures.

COMPARISONS
Develop Insight into the Nature of Language and Culture

Standard 4.1: Students demonstrate understanding of the nature of language through comparisons of the language studied and their own.

Standard 4.2: Students demonstrate understanding of the concept of culture through comparisons of the cultures studied and their own.

COMMUNITIES
Participate in Multilingual Communities at Home and Around the World

Standard 5.1: Students use the language both within and beyond the school setting.

Standard 5.2: Students show evidence of becoming life-long learners by using the language for personal enjoyment and enrichment.

Introduction

The businessperson, the poet, the emergency room nurse, the diplomat, the scientist, and the teenage computer buff are representative Americans who play diverse roles in life, yet each could present a convincing rationale for the importance of studying a foreign language. Their reasons might range from the realistic to the idealistic, but one simple truth would give substance to them all: to relate in a meaningful way to another human being, one must be able to *communicate*.

From the flowing green lawns and porch swings of rural America to the front stoops of our cities, ours has traditionally been a culture of openness, of passing the time of day with friends who stroll by. But today it is the whole world that is strolling by—coming to our doors to question and discuss, to request our aid, to bring rich gifts. And since the street leads in both directions, we are going out into the wide world to run *our* errands. The neighborhood language of the front porch will no longer serve to transact world business and to make new friends. We must acquire the ability to understand and to be understood in the languages of the worldwide neighborhood.

To study another language and culture gives one the powerful key to successful communication: *knowing how, when, and why, to say what to whom*. All the linguistic and social knowledge required for effective human-to-human interaction is encompassed in those ten words. Formerly, most teaching in foreign language classrooms concentrated on the *how* (grammar) to say *what* (vocabulary). While these components of language remain crucial, the current organizing principle for language study is communication, which also highlights the *why*, the *whom*, and the *when* (the sociolinguistic and cultural aspects of language). The approach to second language instruction found in today's schools is designed to facilitate genuine interaction with others, whether they are on another continent, across town, or within the neighborhood.

> **WE MUST ACQUIRE THE ABILITY TO UNDERSTAND AND BE UNDERSTOOD IN THE LANGUAGES OF THE WORLDWIDE NEIGHBORHOOD.**

FOREIGN LANGUAGES AND THE EDUCATED CITIZEN

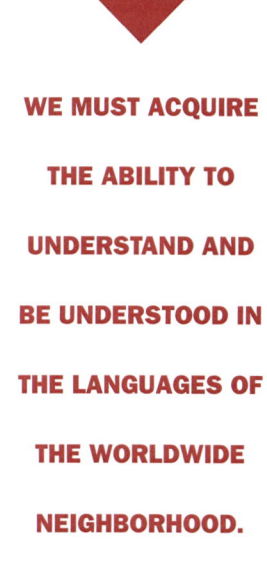

To study another language and culture enhances one's personal education in many ways. It is only in learning a new linguistic system that one acquires an objective view of one's native language. For someone who has never learned a second language, this point is difficult to comprehend; for those who have learned one, it is manifestly clear. The structural bones of one's language, the limits to the range of ideas expressible in that language, the intense interdependence of language and culture—all these concepts become apparent only as second language acquisition takes place. The student becomes aware of the ways in which language speakers adroitly switch levels of discourse as the context of communication changes. The contributions of volume, pitch, speed, and tone of voice to the emotional layers of language become clear. The language learner also realizes that eye contact, facial expression, and gestures play a vital role in enhancing the message that is being conveyed. With these understandings comes a new-found respect for the beauty and grace of others' languages, as well as one's own.

Research studies indicate that the very process of studying another language may give students a cognitive boost which enables them to perform at higher levels in some other subjects. An analysis of data on over 17,000 students who applied for admission to Northeast Missouri State University between 1981-86 revealed that students who had completed a foreign language course in high school tended to have higher scores on the ACT exams in English and math *regardless of their ability level* (Olsen and Brown 1992). This study reinforces the findings of another researcher, who discovered that high school foreign language students perform significantly better on the SAT verbal exam than non-foreign-language students, and that SAT verbal scores increase successively with each half year of foreign language study. In the same study, it was shown that the economic background of foreign language students did not affect performance; students from lower socioeconomic levels who studied foreign languages performed on a par with their more affluent peers (Cooper 1987).

To study another language and culture provides access to literature as it is experienced by the audience for whom it was written. Irony, humor, satire, and other rich textures of prose are revealed at their deepest level only to those familiar with both the language and culture. Similarly, the subtle seasonings which flavor drama and poetry are discernible only to those who know the language of the playwright and the poet.

To study another language and culture increases enormously one's ability to see connections. Since the *content* of a foreign language course deals with history, geography, social studies, science, math, and the fine arts, it is easy for students to develop an interdisciplinary perspective at the same time they are gaining intercultural understandings. Pedagogically, this is enhanced by the methods used to teach foreign languages: the use of images and items from real life for sharpening perception, a wide variety of physical activities and games, involvement in role play and other dramatic activities, the use of music in both receptive and participatory modes, and learning experiences that call for sequencing, memorizing, problem solving as well as both inductive and deductive reasoning. This broad range of language learning strategies appeals to a variety of learning styles and expands the learner's awareness of the many dimensions of his/her own intelligence.

To study another language and culture is to gain an especially rich preparation for the future. It is difficult to imagine a job, a profession, a career, or a leisure activity in the twenty-first century which will not be enhanced by the ability to communicate efficiently and sensitively with others. While it is impossible to foresee which foreign language will be useful at a later point in life, those who have once experienced the process of acquiring a second language have gained language learning skills that make learning another language easier. Possession of the linguistic and cultural insights which come with foreign language study will be a requisite for life as a citizen in the worldwide neighborhood.

THE DEVELOPMENT OF STANDARDS

In 1993, foreign language education became the seventh and final subject area to receive federal funding to develop national standards for students in kindergarten through twelfth

> **THE KEY TO SUCCESSFUL COMMUNICATION: KNOWING HOW, WHEN, AND WHY TO SAY WHAT TO WHOM**

grade. An eleven-member task force, representing a variety of languages, levels of instruction, program models, and geographic regions, was appointed to undertake the enormous task of defining *content standards*—what students should know and be able to do—in foreign language education in grades four, eight, and twelve. These standards are intended to serve as a gauge for excellence, as states and local districts carry out their responsibilities for curriculum in the schools.

The Process

The members of the task force approached the development of standards by examining first what foreign language education should prepare students to do: they identified the broad goals of the discipline. Within each of these areas, they then identified the essential skills and knowledge students would need to acquire by the time they left the twelfth grade. It is these essential skills and knowledge which comprise the standards.

At each stage of development, the task force shared its work with the broader profession. Several drafts were widely disseminated. Task force members gave literally hundreds of presentations and read through many more written comments with each iteration of the draft. All comments were seriously considered, and this document reflects many of the recommended changes.

Subsequent to the publication in 1996 of *Standards for Foreign Language Learning: Preparing for the 21st Century*, the collaboration of the four professional organizations that had sponsored the standards project (American Council on the Teaching of Foreign Languages, American Association of Teachers of French, American Association of Teachers of German, American Association of Teachers of Spanish and Portuguese) was expanded to include seven others: American Association of Teachers of Italian, American Classical League, American Council of Teachers of Russian, Chinese Language Association of Secondary-Elementary Schools/Chinese Language Teachers Association, National Council of Secondary Teachers of Japanese/Association of Teachers of Japanese. These groups pursued the next steps in specifying standards by creating language-specific standards that built upon the original ones, commonly referred to as the "generic" standards. This 1999 edition of standards includes the work of these professional organizations.

Relationship to the ACTFL Proficiency Guidelines

In 1986, the American Council on the Teaching of Foreign Languages (ACTFL) released the ACTFL Proficiency Guidelines. Based on the scale developed for use by the federal government, the guidelines provide a common metric against which to measure performance in speaking, reading, writing, and listening in a second language. The work on proficiency has provided the profession with a common yardstick with which to begin the discussion of performance assessment. These discussions have placed the foreign language profession in an excellent position to develop new kinds of performance-based assessments that reflect the content standards in this document. It is obvious in working with the content standards that they encompass much more than the separate skills format outlined in the proficiency guidelines.

Teachers will recognize the influence of the guidelines within the standards, particularly in the area of communication. However, in keeping with the attempt to create broadly conceived standards, communication is organized around a framework of interpersonal, interpretive, and presentational modes (see pages 32-34), rather than carved into separate skill areas of listening, speaking, reading, and writing. In 1998, ACTFL issued its *Performance Guidelines for K–12 Learners*. These are performance standards that define the "how well" students can be expected to do the "what" from the content standards. The *K–12 Performance Guidelines* set forth characteristics of language users at the various stages or benchmarks of learning and development and are articulated according to the communicative modes: Interpersonal, Interpretive, and Presentational. Most importantly, the standards venture into areas that will bring legitimacy to many important elements of foreign language instruction that have often been viewed as options or add-ons to make the class "more interesting." It is this focus on content (i.e., gaining access to information in a range of areas of inquiry and human activity) that may have the most lasting impact on our students in the future.

Setting Performance Standards for Language Competencies

Individual states and school districts hold the responsibility for determining performance standards for their students. At the same time, the standards document was developed in the context of raising U.S. expectations to those of schools in other nations. Consequently, schools are encouraged to set exit performance standards that go well beyond the minimal usages common in the past. The traditional two-year high school programs produced students whose ability to function in the second language was limited to learned expressions and restrained interactions in oral skills. As long as classroom instruction had provided for direct practice with phrases and situations, students appeared able to respond. When opportunities arose for students to be in a situation where the language was used by representatives of the culture, these same students reverted all too frequently to English because they found the level at which they could speak to be inadequate.

In a foreign language program based on the standards outlined in this document, the key question of what students know and are able to do at any level in their studies entails assessment. The variable of language experience and development will have to be constantly monitored so that students and their teachers have a clear understanding of how they are progressing. Learners often reach plateaus in their performance in one modality or context, and they need some time to work comfortably before venturing again into more demanding culturally appropriate communicative tasks. These are some of the main programmatic variables that must be taken into consideration with the various language goals.

No single continuum of language learning exists for all students. Rather, the progress and performance levels of individual learners at any given time depend on a number of factors, including motivation, learning styles and preferences, age, and language learning experiences, which include the languages the learner speaks and the one being learned. For example, Joseph, studying his first foreign language, may be an active conversationalist who likes to stretch himself to get his meaning across, but he may be a less avid reader who rarely ventures beyond classroom texts. Valerie, who studied French in elementary school, now takes Italian in high school and seeks out opportunities to read. She has become quite adept at comprehending challenging materials, but when in a face-to-face conversation, she limits herself in this language to what she knows she can say well. Tina, whose grandparents speak to her in Spanish, is more advanced than others in her class. Her interest is to improve the range of topics she can discuss and write about so that she can use her Spanish later in her career. Jeff, who learned Cantonese at home and in middle school, is now concentrating on learning to speak Mandarin in high school. Students may be at different stages in different modalities or contexts. Determining learner profiles and setting performance levels that will result in more students exiting school at higher stages of second language competencies is a programmatic responsibility.

Particularly for the extended sequences of study envisioned in this document, it will be important that schools set exit standards for communication that reflect the additional time available as well as the range of goals outlined in the standards. All students with motivation and opportunity to learn should be able to reach a stage that reflects abilities to create with the language, to function effectively in that language in anticipated and expanded contexts, to be flexible enough to negotiate meanings on a variety of topics, to pick up a magazine or book that appeals to age and interest and understand portions of it, and to behave in culturally acceptable ways. Some learners will excel and advance to a stage where their language allows them to have greater choice and control in style and range of situations. The content standards provided in this document begin the discussion upon which to build the performance standards that will assess the stage of competencies students are able to attain in U.S. school settings.

THE IMPLICATIONS OF STANDARDS

The development of standards has galvanized the field of foreign language education. The degree of involvement, and of consensus, among educators at all levels has been unprecedented. In some respects, foreign language education was better prepared than other disciplines to undertake standards development. More than a decade of work on defining competency-based teaching and assessment focused language educators on preparing students who can use the language in meaningful ways, in real life situations. Furthermore, that work generated a dynamic discussion on a compelling rationale for language education for all students.

At the same time, the emphasis on immediate needs often resulted in a curriculum that lacked richness and depth and failed to provide a broad range of experience and knowledge. Standards preparation is forcing attention to the broader view of second language study and competence: what should students know and be able to do—and how well? Clearly, the foreign language standards provide the broader, more complete rationale for foreign language education that we have sought for decades but never managed to capture in words or in concept until now.

Even as the national standards were being published in 1996, the impact was being felt in states and local districts. Standards that build upon the national ones have been developed in a majority of states and, consequently, numerous local districts have reconstructed curriculum to align with them. Some states have initiated assessments tied to selected standards, and growth in elementary programs can be directly tied to the earlier starts advocated in the standards.

National standards establish a new context that defines the central role of foreign language in the learning career of every student. Change will continue to be incremental, but it will accelerate if we succeed in addressing the central issue that sets the stage for the future: the preparation of new teachers of all languages at all levels within our schools. Professional development for practicing teachers will also be crucial, and the message of standards must permeate those learning experiences as well.

Standards have defined the agenda for the next decade—and beyond.

> **THIS IS ONLY THE BEGINNING... STANDARDS HAVE DEFINED THE AGENDA FOR THE NEXT DECADE–AND BEYOND.**

Language Study in the United States

Foreign language programs are thriving at all grade levels in schools throughout the United States. Yet this is not a universal condition, and the opportunity for individual students to develop strong second-language competencies depends greatly on time and place. As the states move forward in adopting stronger standards, they will be looking to expand foreign language programs so that greater numbers of students benefit from longer sequences of instruction in more languages.

THE CURRENT STATUS

The present patchwork quilt of American foreign language curriculum comes in all shapes and sizes. By far, the most common pattern is for schools to introduce foreign language study to ninth graders, and the majority of adolescents enroll for a two-year sequence. That pattern has shifted in many places as states have increased requirements for college admission or for honors diplomas. Most promising is that students themselves recognize the value of another language and choose to progress beyond minimal requirements. In the high schools, enrollments in elective and advanced placement courses are rising. Even with the availability of more advanced courses, beginning a second language in high school does not provide much time for learning to communicate effectively. Students who start earlier have a distinct advantage. Middle schools are now more likely to offer foreign language study than ever before. More significantly, at long last in the United States, we are seeing greater numbers of successful elementary school programs in foreign languages. Young children are learning foreign languages daily in small units of time or more intensively through immersion programs where much of the curriculum is delivered in a second language. Naturally the levels of achievement differ drastically, given such variations.

A Multitude of Languages

The array of languages American students are learning in their schools today might also surprise the general public. Tradition, history, and even availability of certified teachers have rendered French, German, Latin, and Spanish the most commonly studied languages. Yet, in many regions of the country, programs in languages such as Arabic, Chinese, Hebrew, Italian, Japanese, Portuguese, and Russian attract students who choose those languages for purposes that include ties to ethnic or regional backgrounds, early career plans, personal curiosity, or the perceived challenge.

The Classics. As we approach the beginning of the twenty-first century, the study of classical languages maintains a viable position in foreign language programs at the middle school and high school levels in many parts of the United States. Almost 86,000 students of Latin participated in the 1994 National Latin Exam, and the number of Latin students tak-

> BEGINNING A LANGUAGE IN HIGH SCHOOL DOES NOT PROVIDE MUCH TIME FOR LEARNING TO COMMUNICATE EFFECTIVELY. STUDENTS WHO START EARLIER HAVE A DISTINCT ADVANTAGE.

Standards for Foreign Language Learning

ing the Advanced Placement Latin Exams increases each year. The study of Ancient Greek, most commonly available in private schools, also shows increased enrollments based on student entries in the National Greek Exam. The study of classical languages offers students the same benefits as the study of other languages, except that the emphasis on using the language for oral communication is not as significant. The insights into language development, the interaction with ancient civilizations through their literature, and the crosscultural understanding that results from the study of these languages are all compelling reasons for the inclusion of language instruction in the curricula of our schools.

The Less Commonly Taught Languages. The "less commonly taught" languages are paradoxically some of the most commonly spoken languages in the world community. They include Chinese, Arabic, Russian, and Japanese—languages spoken by very large numbers of people. They are the languages of communication among peoples with whom the United States has important relationships in terms of economic ties, strategic interests, and increasing cultural awareness. While speakers of English find certain aspects of these languages (e.g., their writing systems) to be challenging, they are accessible when taught for purposes of communication. Since the time of study required for proficiency in these languages is longer than for other modern languages, it is important to encourage long-sequence programs which begin at the precollege level.

Experience with learning the less commonly taught languages shows that the process of encountering linguistic differences (e.g., the Russian case system, Japanese characters, verbal aspects in Chinese) influences students to become acutely aware of aspects of their own language and of languages in general. As students learn to function in a language like Russian or Chinese, they are also learning strategies for managing the process of language acquisition and for coping with the large variety of language possibilities. Simply put, if studying Russian provokes students to ask whether or not numbers ever have their own "alphabet" or if the past tense requires another set of verb endings, they are learning to see language as an open set of possibilities. The answers to those questions also help them see some of the limitations to those possibilities, as well as the common structures of language.

Diverse Language Learners

At one time, and not so long ago, most second-language learners in high schools belonged to the college-bound group. These students pursued language study mainly because higher education required it. In other countries, citizens saw language learning as essential for all people: for those who went on to pursue a professional or liberal education, for those who more directly entered the work force, for those in service industries, or for those who simply wanted to travel. For many years, Americans used the excuse that there was no necessity for other languages, because their country was vast, and English encompassed a huge populace here and abroad. Telecommunications, market competitiveness, and international living have all changed the dynamic as greater numbers of United States citizens now recognize the power of communicating in another language and of knowing other cultures.

Many school personnel understand that the value of language learning goes beyond the practical benefits of communication. All children profit in their thinking skills by learning how a different language system operates, how languages influence one another, and how different cultures express ideas. Students once shut out of language courses prosper in class-

ALL STUDENTS ARE CAPABLE OF LEARNING OTHER LANGUAGES GIVEN OPPORTUNITIES FOR QUALITY INSTRUCTION.

Standards for Foreign Language Learning

rooms that acknowledge that ALL students are capable of learning other languages given opportunities for quality instruction. Parents and school personnel who observe children in elementary school foreign language instruction cannot identify the college-bound; indeed, they see enthusiastic and successful youngsters enjoying stories or chatting in a second language. In middle schools, students participate in second language learning under a number of program models consistent with current philosophies and approaches for that age group. Earlier starts with language instruction assure greater success for more students.

In many schools around the country, the presence of large groups of students who have home backgrounds in the languages taught at school (e.g., Spanish or Chinese) has led to the establishment of special language courses designed to develop and maintain the language abilities of these students. In Texas, for example, in districts populated by many first, second, and third generation students of Mexican or Central American origin, schools offer both a foreign language track of Spanish courses as well as a track designed for "bilingual" students. Additionally, among many language groups, such as the Chinese, the study and learning of heritage languages are supported in community Saturday programs and schools. In many cases, these groups are exploring the possibility of obtaining academic credit for such study.

Specifically, students who enroll in "foreign" language classes are assumed to belong to one of the following two categories: (1) no home background in languages other than English, or (2) home background in languages other than English. The latter category can be further divided into those who are speakers of languages commonly taught in schools as foreign languages (e.g., Spanish), those who are speakers of languages increasingly taught in schools (e.g., Chinese, Japanese, Russian), and those rarely taught in schools as foreign languages (e.g., Thai, Vietnamese, Hungarian).

Among students with home language backgrounds, varying abilities and proficiencies in the heritage language exist. A summary chart of characteristics of home background students is included below. It illustrates the language development needs facing the language teaching professional with regard to these student characteristics.

> **EARLIER STARTS WITH LANGUAGE INSTRUCTION ASSURE GREATER SUCCESS FOR MORE STUDENTS.**

Figure 1. Characteristics of Home Background Students

Student Characteristics	English Language Development Needs	Heritage/Home Language Development Needs
Second and third generation "bilinguals" schooled exclusively in English in the U.S.	Continued development of age-appropriate English language competencies	Maintenance, retrieval, and/or acquisition of language competencies (e.g., oral productive abilities)
		Transfer of literacy skills developed in English to the home language
		Continued development of age-appropriate competencies in both oral and written modes
First generation immigrant students schooled primarily in the U.S.	Continued development of age-appropriate English language competencies	Development of literacy skills in first language
		Continued development of age-appropriate language competencies in oral mode
Newly arrived immigrant students	Acquisition of oral and written English	Continued development of age-appropriate competencies in both oral and written modes

Students with varying needs all require access to language instruction that will allow them to: (1) maintain existing strengths in the language; (2) develop strengths in areas in which the home background has not provided support; and (3) use the language for reading and writing.

PROGRAM MODELS FROM K-16[1]

Opportunities to learn K-8

Elementary school programs come in many models. Immersion programs are the most intensive, in that all the curricular content is learned in the target language with the exception of language arts in English. In full immersion programs, students spend 60-100 percent of the school day learning subject matter in the target language, which itself becomes acquired. Partial immersion programs tend to do about half of each day in English and half in the target language. Another variety of this model, two-way immersion, can be implemented when native speakers of a language other than English are enrolled in the school; in this model native speakers of the target language and English speakers join together to pursue classroom content in both languages.

FLES (Foreign Languages in Elementary Schools) programs are less intensive than any of the varieties of immersion. These articulated programs specifically teach the target language for designated periods of time; teachers should be competent in the language and certified to teach in the elementary grades. Many present-day FLES programs take on elements of immersion by designing integrated thematic instruction that reinforces the elementary curriculum; this is sometimes called "content-enriched" instruction. FLES programs must have adequate time scheduled in the school day if children are to gain competencies as exemplified by the grade 4 and 8 progress indicators in the standards.

FLEX (Foreign Language Experience or Exploratory) programs also exist in elementary or middle schools. These programs allow students to "sample" several languages prior to students' selection of a language for further study. FLES and FLEX programs may be taught by a target-language-proficient classroom teacher or by a language specialist. Some programs are technology-assisted, and the classroom teacher may not be proficient in the language. Naturally the outcomes achievable under each context will differ.

In the early grades, many language learning programs exist that are of a less formal structure. These include before- or after-school programs taught by advanced high school or college students, parents, or community volunteers with command of the language. Saturday schools often attract heritage or home language students who wish to maintain or improve competencies. These kinds of programs provide opportunities where a curriculum taught within the school day by certified teachers is not yet available.

As more districts adopt elementary programs, it becomes incumbent upon middle school teachers to offer a well articulated continuation that expands upon student achievement of the standards. Variations in middle school scheduling, as well as emerging philosophies for that age student, lead to a wide variety of models such as block scheduling of classes, alternate semester sequences, team teaching, and thematically organized instruction.

---

[1] The material for this section was adapted from the draft version of *Standards for Learning German*.

Some young people may desire to try a new language at the middle school level because they have developed an interest in a part of the world where it is spoken. The middle school should provide for entry into languages that may not have been available earlier. Adolescents who begin a third language have a distinct advantage over those beginning a second. Ideally, they understand words as symbols that represent concepts rather than assuming that words are concepts. As students work toward the Comparisons goal in a second language, they develop insights into how languages operate and these understandings make them quite different learners of a third or fourth language. A broadening of opportunities with middle school and high school programs capitalizes on the general linguistic advantage that comes from extended study and early opportunities.

Programs in Grades 9-12

In high schools, many program models currently exist and new ones will be developed as districts implement instruction in the early grades. Unfortunately, today many students still have their first foreign language experience in high school, but soon that level will be primarily for students who want to learn a third or fourth language. Some of the more common models for extended learning in high schools include:

- Advanced Placement courses that offer the possibility of college credit dependent upon national examination scores and individual college policies;
- International Baccalaureate courses that prepare students for international studies, an international diploma based upon examination, or college credit;
- Concurrent enrollments or language classes conducted in high schools by high school faculty endorsed by a local college or university which grants college credit;
- Content-based advanced courses in a world language that focus on subject matter from another discipline while continuing skill development in the language;
- School-within-a-school models that have a world language as part of a magnet or specific program;
- Academic or magnet schools that focus on language development through a particular discipline (e.g., international marketing, health professions).

In addition, high school students often pursue other settings in which they develop language and culture goals.

- Schools for home-schoolers that bring home-schooled students to a site where they can learn a world language that is added to content that parents can teach
- Saturday school programs that offer language in intensive all-day or half-day sessions
- International schools that enroll children from the U.S. and other nations as represented in a community
- Topic-oriented courses (e.g., conversation, business) that are not part of the regular high school sequence
- Summer camps, week-long/weekend immersion camps
- Exchange programs and study abroad programs during the academic year or in summer

Programs at the Postsecondary Level

Students entering colleges and universities of the 21st century will be competent in second languages and cultures; they will expect to continue studies in those languages, cultures, lit-

> ALL CHILDREN...
> WILL RISE TO MEET
> EXPECTATIONS
> WHEN GOALS ARE
> APPROPRIATELY
> SET AND THE
> CONDITIONS FOR
> LEARNING ARE
> DESIGNED TO
> FOSTER
> ACHIEVEMENT.

eratures, and in other disciplines that draw upon those abilities. Students will desire an array of options beyond that of today's curriculum. Colleges and universities have an exciting challenge to redesign programs in new and innovative ways. Initiatives such as Foreign Languages Across the Curriculum will be able to grow and develop new dimensions since students will be more skillful interpreters and discussants. Tomorrow's students will be able to use world languages in fields ranging from history, philosophy, business, art history, journalism to nursing, engineering, and the sciences. The inclusion of post-secondary programs in the language-specific documents insures a seamless continuity, student-centered articulation and high levels of performance among graduates.

As in the past, however, there will always be students who will wish to begin the study of a new language at the post-secondary level, so institutions will still need to offer basic language instruction. Many colleges and universities are already finding ways of doing this through affiliated centers that focus on beginning instruction in a variety of languages.

Implementing the standards at the postsecondary level presents a unique opportunity for faculty to develop new program options. Students who have achieved proficiency through an extended sequence of study will demand courses and programs that reach to connect with career goals and crosscultural ventures. Many institutions are expanding their language and literature programs into "language studies" that include content courses outside the language department with a focus on interdisciplinary work in politics, history, or economics. Another innovation sure to spread include Bridge Courses and Content Courses. Bridge courses, now often in fifth or sixth semesters, may be appropriate to lower division students who wish to refine their language through subject-related content such as film studies, an historical period, or music history; these courses are taught by language faculty. Content courses tend to be full fledged courses given in German with the greater emphasis on learning the content itself. These may be taught by language or content area specialists.

Finally, we shall see more dual degree programs at colleges and universities as students seek to combine the traditional liberal arts education with a professional field in preparation for a life of work in a global economy. Dual degree programs often combine study or internships abroad so that students gain the cultural, linguistic, and pragmatic job experiences that enable them to become effective citizens of the world.

MULTIPLE ENTRY POINTS AND AN EXTENDED SEQUENCE OF STUDY

The standards set forth here presume that sequential study for an extended period of time is the ideal for achieving the highest levels of performance in the five goal areas, and the progress indicators also assume that instruction has begun in the early grades and continues throughout the secondary years (most of the language-specific documents attached to this edition extend the sequence into college and university programs). For a number of reasons, however, it will be important for schools to provide multiple entry points into the curriculum. The goal of having students experience the study of world languages every year is not intended to limit the choice of language or the opportunity to begin study at predetermined points. We would ill serve learners if the effort to have extended sequences resulted in districts offering only one language.

Multiple entry points accommodate students who transfer among schools, students

> WE WOULD ILL-SERVE LEARNERS IF THE EFFORT TO HAVE EXTENDED SEQUENCES RESULTED IN DISTRICTS OFFERING ONLY ONE LANGUAGE

who develop interests in specific languages during their middle- or high-school years because of career choices or personal motivation, or students who wish to study additional languages (a concept referred to as "language layering"). In early grades, districts may be able to offer only a limited number of languages due to staffing constraints or the size of

Figure 2. Multiple Entry Points and Language Layering

The chart below illustrates the concepts of multiple entry points and language layering. Multiple entry points will vary from district to district depending upon grade configurations (e.g., K-4, K-5, K-6, K-8).

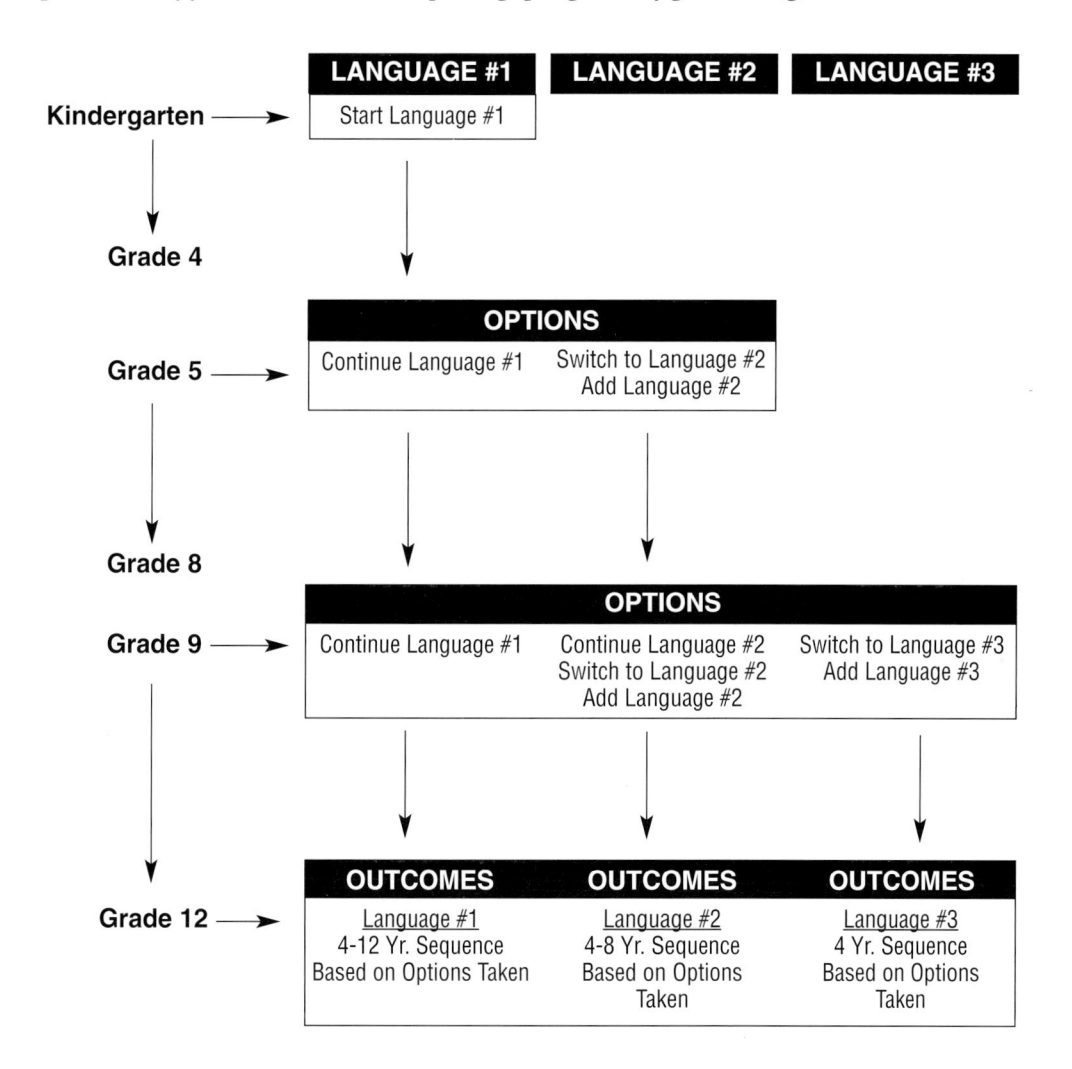

	LANGUAGE #1	**LANGUAGE #2**	**LANGUAGE #3**
Kindergarten →	Start Language #1		
Grade 4	↓		
Grade 5 →	**OPTIONS** Continue Language #1	Switch to Language #2 / Add Language #2	
Grade 8	↓	↓	
Grade 9 →	**OPTIONS** Continue Language #1	Continue Language #2 / Switch to Language #2 / Add Language #2	Switch to Language #3 / Add Language #3
Grade 12 →	**OUTCOMES** Language #1 — 4-12 Yr. Sequence Based on Options Taken	**OUTCOMES** Language #2 — 4-8 Yr. Sequence Based on Options Taken	**OUTCOMES** Language #3 — 4 Yr. Sequence Based on Options Taken

Key Concepts
- Students may elect to study a second world language once some measurable competency has been achieved in their first world language.
- Students may study the language begun at the elementary level while adding ("layering") a second and/or third language in middle and/or high school.

From *New Jersey World Languages Curriculum Framework, 1999, p. 47.*

schools, but in the middle grades or high school years, provisions for other languages can be made. Learner choice becomes an increasingly important factor as students mature and their eventual competency is linked with interests and motivation. The problems associated with the monolingualism of U.S. young people is not enriched by offering them only a single second language for study when their future work and travel will engage them with multiple languages and cultures. Students who opt to remain with the study of a world language throughout their education K-12 and beyond will develop high competencies in all the goal areas of the standards. Students who choose to study more than one world language will reach levels of competency commensurate with the sequence available; their experience with language study in general often contributes to more rapid acquisition of a third language. For educational purposes, students who choose to study two or more world languages to a functional level of competency have achieved goals equally commendable to those who have studied one language but perhaps to a higher level of performance.

The framework developed for the state of New Jersey illustrates multiple entry points and language layering in the context of curriculum. Figure 2 above may be useful to local districts as they plan for a full range of language programs.

INSTRUCTIONAL APPROACHES

Current research and classroom practices indicate that a variety of approaches can successfully lead learners to the standards. The evolving research base in second-language acquisition is identifying effective practices, but all the answers are not yet in. The best instructional approach for any group of learners ranging from gifted and talented to the challenged learner differs greatly according to factors such as the student's age, home language, learning preferences, and goals for language learning. Any language user, regardless of age, must internalize (whether consciously or unconsciously) the sound system, a basic lexicon, basic grammatical structures, communication strategies, and rules about how the language is used appropriately in interaction. Very young children who learn a second language "naturally" acquire all of these skills and abilities at a level appropriate for their age. Older learners, whether in a natural or classroom setting, bring to the process their level of cognitive development as well as their experiences and abilities as skilled users of a first language. A learner may be a beginner at any age. Cognitive development is a factor which influences their progress. For example, when one's first second-language experience occurs as a seven- rather than fifteen-year old, the instructional approach must recognize differences in motivation, cognitive and motor development, background knowledge, and self-awareness. Teachers in classrooms around the United States may utilize quite different instructional formats and still promote student achievement of the standards.

It is time to dispel the myth that children who tend to encounter difficulties with learning in general will not be successful second language learners. To the contrary, all children are primed to learn languages, and they will rise to meet expectations when goals are appropriately set and the conditions for learning are designed to foster achievement.

Context determines instructional approach as well. If one is learning in an environment where face-to-face interaction with speakers of that language is not available, technology, simulation, or pen pals by "snail mail" may be a means of providing real-world contact with speakers. In contrast, in schools and communities where the second language is actively used, teachers can draw upon immediate contexts. Latin or classical Greek may be approached in ways quite distinct from those of modern spoken languages. Languages with writing systems less related to that of the learner may be approached in different ways from those that require mastering whole new systems (e.g., a Germanic or Romance language for English-speakers versus Chinese or Arabic).

SPECIAL FEATURES OF LANGUAGE STUDY

Most teachers and educators within a given subject matter or discipline have a variety of reasons for thinking that their subject matter is "special" in one way or another, from history to art, from math to music. What is rather special about language learning, however, is that it can be learned without formal schooling at all. People "learn" their first languages all over the world without schooling, even without lessons, as might be the case in learning the piano or learning to tap dance. Moreover, this sort of learning is not dependent on talent. While we may say that Mary learned to play the piano "by ear" or José was a "natural artist" from age four, or that Tina was a "natural" swimmer at age five, we do not say that Maria had a "real talent" for learning her first language, Spanish, whereas her brother did not. All children all over the world, unless they have some sort of neurological disorder, are typically fluent in their first language by age five. They gain control of various components of language for competent use long before the emergence of the cognitive skills that will be necessary for schooled learning, and they seemingly learn it "naturally," that is, without conscious effort.

Much of this same sort of natural learning can occur when children acquire a second language. There are plentiful examples of children learning a second language through exposure and use far outside of school environments—residence in the country of the language learned being a typical case. Again, neither formal lessons nor "talent" seems to enter the picture. These unique features of language acquisition as an "unschooled" learning experience contrast sharply with math, science, social studies, art, music, dance, drama, and the like—subjects we normally think of as being learned only through instruction (schools or lessons) and/or in some cases by a combination of talent and instruction.

Even for older learners, the idea persists today that the "best" way to learn a language is just to "go to the country" and learn the language "naturally" without formal instruction. Surely, it is rarely said that the best way to learn math is to just "hang around" mathematicians, or the best way to learn studio art is exposure to professional artists, or the best way to learn social studies is to "live in the society."

Putting language learning into formal educational environments does not change the features unique to language acquisition; in fact these features offer certain challenges to treating language study as a pure, sequentially mastered subject matter such as math, science, or history. In mathematics, for example, the school curriculum moves students through a fairly well-defined sequence of steps in acquiring mathematical competencies involving computation and problem solving. Subjects such as "math," "biology," and "social studies" may be taught and learned as an unfolding of increasingly complex concepts (arithmetic to algebra to calculus) and/or as the learning of a set of facts. Foreign languages, on the other hand, are not "acquired" when students learn an ordered set of facts about the language (e.g., grammar facts, vocabulary). Ideally, students need to be able to use the target language for real communication, that is, to carry out a complex interactive process that involves speaking and understanding what others say in the target language, as well as reading

▼

THEY LEARN BY DOING, BY TRYING OUT LANGUAGE, AND BY MODIFYING IT TO SERVE COMMUNICATIVE NEEDS.

and interpreting written materials. Acquiring communicative competence also involves the acquisition of increasingly complex concepts centering around the relationship between culture and communication. For some students, this acquisition process takes place in a natural setting. They have access to another language because they interact frequently with people who speak to them in this language or because they have spent time abroad. For other students, the process takes place in the classroom. For still others, it takes place in both the classroom and a real-world setting.

The standards have been written to suggest that the goals of language study cannot be divided into a set of sequenced steps. It is not the case that young students must first deal with isolated bits and pieces of language. Real communication is possible for young students as well as for students in high schools. While the progress indicators for each grade level—4, 8, and 12—reflect differences in student cognitive development, maturity, and interests, the standards at all levels offer a vision of what students should know and be able to do in another language.

About *Standards for Foreign Language Learning*

The Standards for Foreign Language Learning *were written with a variety of audiences in mind: K-12 foreign language teachers and teacher educators, curriculum writers, administrators, policy makers at all levels of government, parents, and business and community leaders. The goal of this document is to describe for all of these audiences what students of foreign languages should know and be able to do at the end of high school; it does not prescribe how students should get there. Rather, it offers guidance to those responsible for assisting them on the journey.*

A WORD ABOUT THE USE OF "FOREIGN LANGUAGE"

The use of the word "foreign" to describe the teaching of languages other than English is becoming increasingly problematic within the U.S. context. Many of the languages taught within our schools are not "foreign" to many of our students (e.g., Italian, Chinese, or Spanish), nor are they "foreign" to the United States (e.g., Native American languages, American Sign Language, Spanish, or French). Many states have recognized this situation by referring to these languages as World Languages, Modern and Classical Languages, Languages Other Than English (LOTEs), or Second Languages, to name a few of the terms used. The members of the standards task force debated this issue many times over the three-year project period. In the end, the term "foreign language" was maintained in the title of the document because it is readily understood by all prospective audiences. Within the document, however, the decision was made to avoid the term "foreign" whenever possible. Hence, the terms "second language," "target language," and sometimes simply "language" are all used interchangeably to refer to languages other than English taught as an academic subject.

ORGANIZATION AND DEFINITIONS

The standards for foreign language learning are organized within the five *goal areas* which make up foreign language education: *communication, cultures, connections, comparisons,* and *communities.* None of these goals stands alone; all are interconnected. Each goal area contains a rationale for its inclusion as a part of foreign language education and a discussion of definitions and important pedagogical issues associated with it.

Each goal area contains two to three *content standards*. These standards describe the knowledge and abilities that all students should acquire by the end of their high school education. Each standard is followed by a brief discussion to further explicate and illustrate the standard and to define its place within the goal area.

Under each standard are *sample progress indicators* for grades four, eight, and twelve that define student progress in meeting the standards, but are not themselves standards. The sample progress indicators are neither prescriptive nor exhaustive; they are designed to be applicable to many languages but not necessarily to all languages. They can realistically be achieved at some level by all students and allow for a variety of content to demonstrate the indicator. Sample progress indicators provide for a multitude of instructional possibilities and are to be interpreted by curriculum developers and classroom teachers who will transform them into classroom practice. They are measurable and assessable in numerous ways and are designed for use by states and individual districts to establish acceptable performance levels for their students.

HOW TO USE *STANDARDS FOR FOREIGN LANGUAGE LEARNING*

This new edition of *Standards for Foreign Language Learning* is a document designed for many audiences and with many purposes. Before using this document, however, it is important to understand what it is NOT. First and foremost, the standards do not describe the current state of foreign language education in this country. While they reflect the best practice in the country, they do not describe what is being attained by the majority of foreign language students. The standards described within these pages will not be achieved overnight; rather, they provide a gauge against which to measure improvement in foreign language education in the years to come.

The standards are not a curriculum guide. While this document suggests the types of content and curricular experiences needed to enable students to achieve the standards, and supports the ideal of extended sequences of study, it does not describe specific course content, nor a recommended scope and sequence.

Finally, this is not a stand-alone document. It must be used in conjunction with state and local frameworks and standards to determine the best approaches and reasonable expectations for the students in individual districts and schools. As Figure 2 indicates, each of these documents will influence and inform the others, as administrators, teachers, parents, and others work together to ensure that tomorrow's learners are equipped to function in an ever-shrinking world.

> STANDARDS... PROVIDE A GAUGE AGAINST WHICH TO MEASURE IMPROVEMENT IN FOREIGN LANGUAGE EDUCATION IN THE YEARS TO COME.

Figure 3. The Relationships Among National, State, and Local Standards Documents

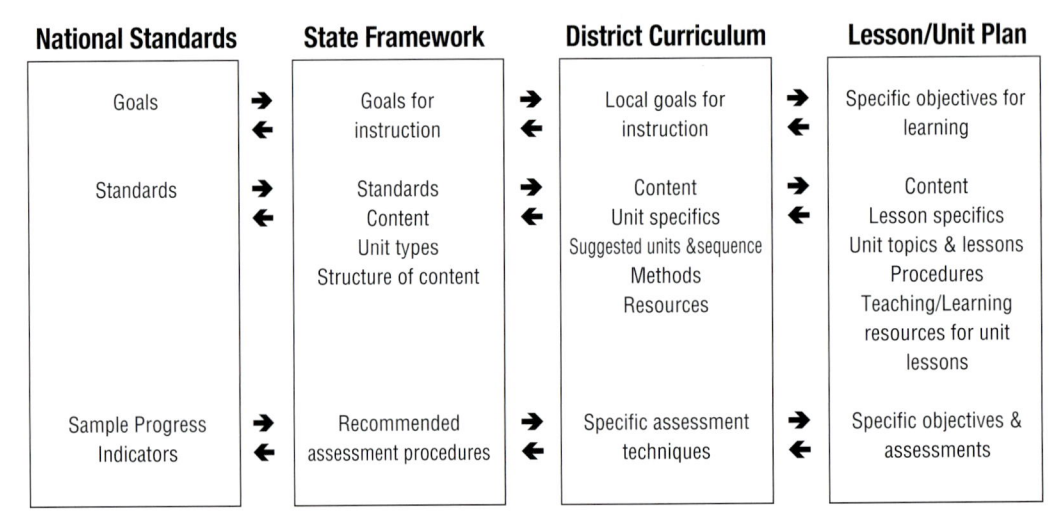

National Standards	State Framework	District Curriculum	Lesson/Unit Plan
Goals	Goals for instruction	Local goals for instruction	Specific objectives for learning
Standards	Standards Content Unit types Structure of content	Content Unit specifics Suggested units & sequence Methods Resources	Content Lesson specifics Unit topics & lessons Procedures Teaching/Learning resources for unit lessons
Sample Progress Indicators	Recommended assessment procedures	Specific assessment techniques	Specific objectives & assessments

Adapted with permission from the
Visual Arts Education Reform Handbook: Suggested Policy Perspectives on Art Content and Student Learning in Art Education
National Art Education Association, 1995

Standards and Specific Languages

Following the discussion of standards from a broad perspective that applies to all languages are sections devoted to learning Chinese, Classical Languages, French, German, Italian, Japanese, Portuguese, Russian, and Spanish. These sections do not repeat the substantive discussion in the first section that are inclusive for all languages. The language-specific standards adjust for the differences among languages: each language has distinct vocabulary, syntactic structures, sound systems, writing systems, and cultures. Each offers greater and lesser challenges to English-speaking students. In that the goals and actual standards represent the consensus of the field as to overall objectives of second-language study, they are stable.

The sample progress indicators, however, are much more fluid. Students of languages with non-Roman alphabets, for example, may need a longer time to reach some of the progress indicators for written language than do students of a language closely related to English. The original standards project provided indicators for grades 4, 8, and 12. Most of the language-specific organizations have extended those to higher education so that in this edition, sample progress indicators are also given for year "16" of study. Conversely, the cultural differences embedded in the study of non-European languages may be more readily apparent than the cultural differences in European languages. Similar challenges exist when working with visual languages (e.g., American Sign Language), languages no longer spoken (e.g., Latin and Ancient Greek), and languages with no written system (e.g., some Native American languages).

The language-specific sections discuss why students might want to learn that language in terms of its importance in literature, business, international exchange, use in the United States both historically and currently, and other compelling reasons. Most importantly, these sections provide learning scenarios to assist teachers in making the transition to standards-oriented curricula. The scenarios are based upon actual classroom activities submitted by teachers to the language-specific writing groups. Each scenario includes a list of the targeted standards, a description of the activity as it plays out in the classroom where it was used, and a reflection on how it addressed the standards. Many scenarios also suggest modifications for different age or learning levels.

Standards and Heritage Language Learners

Similar modifications will need to be made when applying the standards to students who have a home background in the language studied. As stated previously, these students may come to class able to converse in the language in home and community situations but may lack the abilities to interact comfortably in more formal settings. Further, they may be quite comfortable with oral language but possess limited skills in reading and writing. Again, the background of the learner is an important variable when developing implementation strategies for these standards.

Organizing Principles

The following pages describe the three major organizing principles used in developing the standards for foreign language learning: the broad goals of language instruction, the curricular elements necessary to the attainment of the standards, and the framework of communicative modes which provides the organizational underpinnings of the present document.

FIVE C'S OF FOREIGN LANGUAGE EDUCATION

The purposes and uses of foreign languages are as diverse as the students who study them. Some students study another language in hopes of finding a rewarding career in the international marketplace or government service. Others are interested in the intellectual challenge and cognitive benefits that accrue to those who develop competency in multiple languages. Still other students seek greater understanding of other peoples and cultures. Many learners approach foreign language study, as they do other courses, simply to fulfill a graduation requirement. Regardless of the reason for study, foreign languages have something to offer to everyone. It is with this philosophy in mind that the standards task force identified five goal areas that encompass all these reasons: Communication, Cultures, Connections, Comparisons, and Communities—five C's of foreign language education.

Communication, or communicating in languages other than English, is at the heart of second language study, whether the communication takes place face-to-face, in writing, or across centuries through the reading of literature. Through the study of other languages, students gain a knowledge and understanding of the *culture*s that use that language; in fact, students cannot truly master the language until they have also mastered the cultural contexts in which the language occurs. Learning languages provides *connections* to additional bodies of knowledge that are unavailable to monolingual English speakers. Through *comparisons* and contrasts with the language studied, students develop greater insight into their own language and culture and realize that multiple ways of viewing the world exist. Together, these elements enable the student of languages to participate in multilingual *communities* at home and around the world in a variety of contexts and in culturally appropriate ways. As is apparent, none of these goals can be separated from the other. Figure 3 below illustrates how they interconnect and suggests the richness embodied in human language.

This expanded view of language learning offers particular advantages for the teaching of foreign languages to *all* students. Regardless of educational or career aspirations, foreign language instruction committed to providing experiences in all five goal areas will be beneficial to all students. Even if students never speak the language after leaving school, they will for a lifetime retain the crosscultural skills and knowledge, the insight, and the access to a world beyond traditional borders.

COMMUNICATION

CULTURES

CONNECTIONS

COMPARISONS

COMMUNITIES

Figure 4. The Five C's of Foreign Language Study

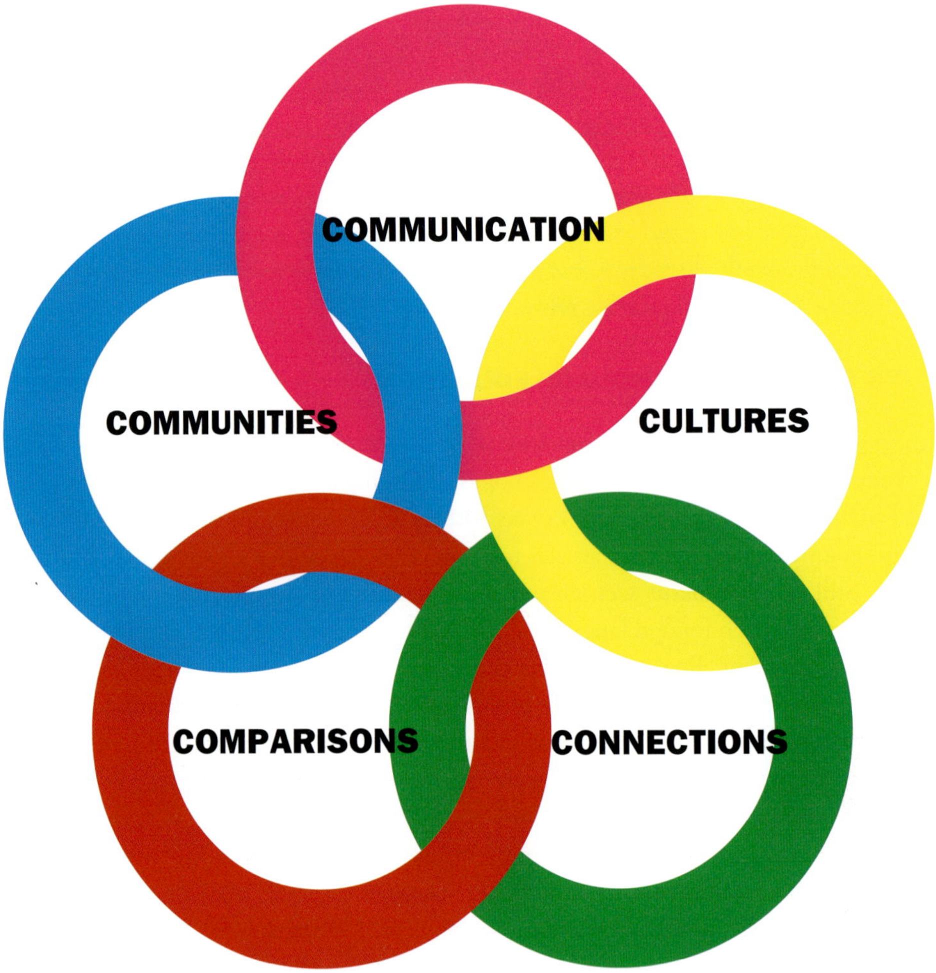

COMMUNICATION

COMMUNITIES

CULTURES

COMPARISONS

CONNECTIONS

THE "WEAVE" OF CURRICULAR ELEMENTS

The standards presented here offer a vision of what students should know and be able to do with another language. In order to attain these standards, students require a foreign language program that provides rich curricular experiences. In the past, classroom instruction was often focused on the memorization of words and grammar rules. The standards for foreign language learning require a much broader definition of the content of the foreign language classroom. Students should be given ample opportunities to explore, develop, and use communication strategies, learning strategies, critical thinking skills, and skills in technology, as well as the appropriate elements of the language system and culture. The exact form and content of each of these elements is not prescribed in the present document. Instead, the standards provide a background, a framework for the reflective teacher to use in weaving these rich curricular experiences into the fabric of language learning.

Language System

The study of language systems is what most adults typically think of when they remember their foreign language experience: memorizing words, grammar rules, and verb conjugations, learning new ways of writing, and producing new sounds. These elements are still important in the foreign language classroom, but the focus has shifted to knowing them in terms of the meanings they convey. The language system is a means for attaining the various outcomes described in this document: communicating, gaining cultural understanding, connecting with other disciplines. The language system is also much more than words and rules; it includes the sociolinguistic elements of gestures and other forms of nonverbal communication, of status and discourse style, and "learning what to say to whom and when." These elements form the bridge between language and culture and must be present if students are ever to learn to interact appropriately in the target language. The specific elements of the language system to be studied within a foreign language classroom will naturally vary by language. Some languages, for example, will require students to learn whole new alphabets, while other languages will present learners with modifications of a few letters. Some languages will have vastly different sentence structures, others will be more familiar. Those involved in the development of standards for individual languages will provide specific guidance in this domain.

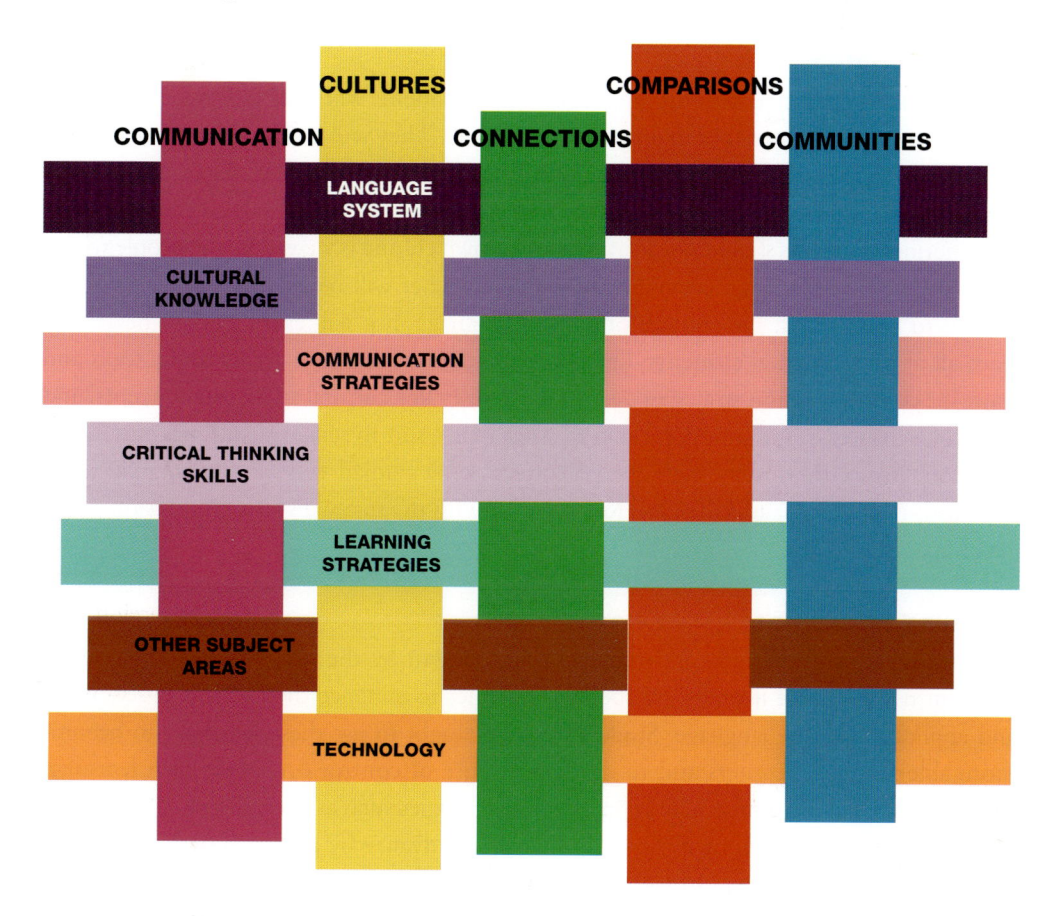

Figure 5. The "Weave" of Curricular Elements

Vertical elements: COMMUNICATION, CULTURES, CONNECTIONS, COMPARISONS, COMMUNITIES

Horizontal elements: LANGUAGE SYSTEM, CULTURAL KNOWLEDGE, COMMUNICATION STRATEGIES, CRITICAL THINKING SKILLS, LEARNING STRATEGIES, OTHER SUBJECT AREAS, TECHNOLOGY

Standards for Foreign Language Learning

Communication Strategies

Familiarity with the language system alone is not enough to enable students to engage in successful communicative activities. Learners also must acquire, through specific and focused instruction, the communication strategies that will aid them in bridging communication gaps that result from differences of language and culture. These strategies will empower students, as they learn the languages and cultures that they may encounter in the future in their personal lives and careers. These strategies include the ability to: circumlocute (say things in different ways); guess intelligently (maximize their use of what they know to achieve greater comprehension of what they hear and see); derive meaning from context; understand, interpret, and produce gestures effectively; ask for and provide clarification without fear of making errors; make and check hypotheses; make inferences, predictions, and generalizations; reflect on the nature of the interaction; draw informed conclusions; and maintain a healthy sense of humor, patience, and tenacity in the communication process.

Many of these strategies are inherent in some learners; other students will have to be taught specifically how to use strategies to interpret meaning and to deliver messages. Therefore, it is essential that teachers develop classroom activities that provide students with ample exposure and practice using those strategies as an integral part of instruction from the very earliest stages of language learning.

Cultural Content

In addition to experience with the language system, students will need to have access to the richness of the cultures of the languages being studied. They will need to learn about everyday life and social institutions, about contemporary and historical issues that are important in those cultures, about significant works of literature and art, and about cultural attitudes and priorities. Students should also learn how their own culture is viewed by the people whose language they are studying. Obviously, no single teacher will be able to know everything there is to know about the cultures of a given language, nor will every student be able to learn all of those cultural elements. Learners should, however, have access to the tools and learn the communication strategies needed to identify key cultural traits and concepts, and to select, synthesize, and interpret them in ways that result in sensitive and meaningful interaction. Again, the specific elements of culture to be studied will vary by language, and even within languages, as is the case, for example, with the many distinct cultures of speakers of Spanish or French.

Learning Strategies

Learning a language requires active mental engagement by the students. Research shows that effective language learners use specific strategies to enhance their learning, retention, and application of the language. Students can be taught to use these strategies to become more able language learners and to develop a sense of control over their own learning. Teachers can plan direct instruction on learning strategies such as: focusing students' attention on learning; teaching them how to organize in advance by previewing, skimming, or reading for the gist; helping students to reflect on what they have just learned and to summarize; teaching students specific questioning strategies to ask for clarification or explana-

> **LEARNING STRATEGIES ARE AN INTEGRAL PART OF LANGUAGE PROGRAMS, PROVIDING STUDENTS WITH THE TOOLS FOR A LIFETIME OF LEARNING.**

Standards for Foreign Language Learning

tion; and getting students to infer information from a text. Students who use learning strategies effectively begin to see themselves as language learners and take on more responsibility for their own learning. Learning strategies benefit all students since even those who use some strategies effectively can be taught additional ones. Students are also able to apply effectively these strategies to learning tasks in other disciplines. Broadening the scope of language learning strategies is an integral part of language programs. Students are able to apply the strategies that work best for them long after they leave the classroom for a lifetime of learning.

Content from Other Subjects

Students must be given interesting and challenging topics and ideas that they can read about, discuss, or analyze using their emerging skills with the new language. Many of these topics can be drawn from the wider school curriculum. Drawing upon broad curricular content has long been a part of elementary school foreign language classrooms, but is just as valuable in the upper grades. Teachers who incorporate concepts from science, social studies, math, or music not only enhance the learning of the language but also expand students' knowledge in other areas.

Critical Thinking Skills

Throughout the language learning process, starting even at the very early stages, learners engage in a wide variety of critical thinking skills ranging from the basic level of identification and recall to the higher levels of analysis and problem-solving. Instruction in the foreign language classroom, no less than in any other discipline, can be designed to promote the use of these skills, and activities can be constructed that incorporate high level thinking tasks. Students learn to identify the needs they have for specific communication tasks, select what they already know from their existing body of knowledge, and apply it to new tasks. At the same time, they develop the ability to use a variety of references to seek and incorporate entirely new knowledge in the performance of the tasks. Given a set of cultural issues or problems, they learn to identify, organize, and analyze issues or problems so as to express informed opinions, arrive at informed conclusions, and propose solutions to problems. They can also reflect upon and evaluate the quality and success of their communication so as to strengthen the nature of their interactions in the future. It is also important to remember that students can use critical thinking skills in beginning language classes by conducting some tasks in English.

Technology

Students should be given the opportunity during their school careers to take increasing advantage of new technological advances. Access to a variety of technologies ranging from computer-assisted instruction to interactive video, CD-ROM, the Internet, electronic mail, and the World Wide Web, will help students strengthen linguistic skills, establish interactions with peers, and learn about contemporary culture and everyday life in the target country. In addition, students can expand their knowledge of the target culture via edited and unedited programs available on short-wave radio, satellite broadcasts, and cassette or video recordings.

While the use of technology has become increasingly valuable in language classrooms

> **STUDENTS NEED INTERESTING TOPICS TO READ ABOUT, DISCUSS, OR ANALYZE USING THEIR NEW LANGUAGE SKILLS.**

around the country, many students continue to access target-language sources via more traditional media. Depending on a student's age, linguistic ability, interests, and classroom resources, foreign language instruction may rely heavily on communication with pen pals and the use of a variety of print sources, including children's literature and publications, magazines, newspapers, *belles lettres*, everyday authentic documents (train schedules, menus, advertisements, maps, etc.), and library reference works (encyclopedias, dictionaries). Access to authentic sources of language, through technology or other means, helps establish the necessary knowledge base for language learners.

THE FRAMEWORK OF COMMUNICATIVE MODES

Researchers from a number of disciplines have attempted to understand the nature of language proficiency and to answer the question: what does it mean to "know" a language (de Jong and Verhoeven 1992). When addressing this question, most introductory textbooks in linguistics (Fromkin and Rodman 1993) agree that knowing a language involves the ability to carry out a large variety of tasks in the language. People who know a language speak and are understood by others who know the same language. They know which sounds are in the language and which ones are not; they know that certain sound sequences make up meaningful words; and they are able to combine words to form phrases and phrases to form sentences. They can produce and understand sentences that they have never heard before. Knowing a language means controlling the linguistic system (the syntax, morphology, phonology, semantics, lexis) of a language. It also means being able to access the pragmatic, textual, and sociolinguistic aspects of language, including how to use the language to achieve communicative goals in ways that are appropriate to a particular cultural context (Bachman 1990; Savignon 1983; Canale and Swain 1980; Hymes 1985; Bialystok 1981).

Communication can be characterized in many different ways (Schiffrin 1994). The approach suggested within this document is to recognize three "communicative modes" that place primary emphasis on the context and purpose of the communication (Brecht and Walton 1994). As illustrated in Figure 5, the three modes are: (1) Interpersonal, (2) Interpretive, and (3) Presentational. Each mode involves a particular link between language and the underlying culture that is developed gradually over time.

The Interpersonal Mode. The Interpersonal Mode is characterized by active negotiation of meaning among individuals. Participants observe and monitor one another to see how their meanings and intentions are being communicated. Adjustments and clarifications can be made accordingly. As a result, there is a higher probability of ultimately achieving the goal of successful communication in this mode than in the other two modes. The Interpersonal Mode is most obvious in conversation, but both the interpersonal and negotiated dimensions can be realized through reading and writing, such as the exchange of personal letters or of electronic mail messages.

The Interpretive Mode. The Interpretive Mode is focused on the appropriate cultural interpretation of meanings that occur in written and spoken form where there is no recourse to the active negotiation of meaning with the writer or the speaker. Such instances of "one-way" reading or listening include the cultural interpretation of texts, movies, radio and television broadcasts, and speeches. Interpreting the cultural meaning of texts, oral or written, must be distinguished from the notion of reading and listening "comprehension," where the term could

> THE FRAMEWORK PLACES EMPHASIS ON THE CONTEXT AND PURPOSE OF COMMUNICATION, PROVIDING A LINK BETWEEN LANGUAGE AND ITS UNDERLYING CULTURE.

refer to understanding a text with an American mindset. Put another way, interpretation differs from comprehension in that the former implies the ability to "read (or listen) between the lines."

Figure 6. Framework of Communicative Modes

	INTERPERSONAL	INTERPRETIVE	PRESENTATIONAL
DEFINITIONS	Direct oral communication (e.g., face-to-face or telephonic) between individuals who are in personal contact Direct written communication between individuals who come into personal contact	Receptive communication of oral or written messages Mediated communication via print and non-print materials Listener, viewer, reader works with visual or recorded materials whose creator is absent	Productive communication using oral or written language Spoken or written communication for people (an audience) with whom there is no immediate personal contact or which takes place in a one-to-many mode Author or creator of visual or recorded material not known personally to listener or reader
PATHS	Productive abilities: speaking, writing Receptive abilities: listening, reading	Primarily receptive abilities: listening, reading, viewing	Primarily productive abilities: speaking, writing, showing
CULTURAL KNOWLEDGE	Knowledge of cultural perspectives governing interactions between individuals of different ages, statuses, backgrounds Ability to recognize that languages use different practices to communicate Ability to recognize that cultures use different patterns of interaction	Knowledge of how cultural perspectives are embedded in products (literary and artistic) Knowledge of how meaning is encoded in products Ability to analyze content, compare it to information available in own language and assess linguistic and cultural differences Ability to analyze and compare content in one culture to interpret U.S. culture	Knowledge of cultural perspectives governing interactions between a speaker and his/her audience and a writer and his/her reader Ability to present crosscultural information based on background of the audience Ability to recognize that cultures use different patterns of interaction

KNOWLEDGE OF THE LINGUISTIC SYSTEM
The use of grammatical, lexical, phonological, semantic, pragmatic, and discourse features necessary for participation in the Communicative Modes.

Since the Interpretive Mode does not allow for active negotiation between the reader and the writer or the listener and the speaker, it requires a much more profound knowledge of culture from the outset. The more one knows about the other language and culture, the greater the chances of creating the appropriate cultural interpretation of a written or spoken text. It must be noted, however, that cultural literacy and the ability to read or listen between the lines are developed over time and through exposure to the language and culture.

tween the lines are developed over time and through exposure to the language and culture.

The Presentational Mode. The Presentational Mode refers to the creation of messages in a manner that facilitates interpretation by members of the other culture where no direct opportunity for the active negotiation of meaning between members of the two cultures exists. Examples include the writing of reports and articles or the presentation of speeches. These examples of "one-way" writing and speaking require a substantial knowledge of language and culture from the outset, since the goal is to make sure that members of the other culture, the audience, will be successful in reading and listening between the lines.

The Communicative Framework and the Background of the Learner

This framework is useful, whether discussing the language abilities of students with home background in languages other than English or beginning language students. Heritage language learners may bring strong interpersonal communication skills in the target/home language, but they still need to develop the ability to use the language in both the interpretive and presentational modes. The varying needs of students require access to instruction that will allow them to: (1) maintain existing strengths in the language; (2) develop strengths in topical areas in which the home background has not provided support; (3) use the language for reading and writing.

The five goals of foreign language education presented here, then, are as important to home or heritage language speakers as they are to students beginning and continuing the study of language exclusively in a classroom setting. Specifically, home background students who study their first language as an academic subject at school can profit significantly from instruction that is focused on the goals and standards presented in this document: (1) expanding their communicative abilities; (2) offering them the opportunity to gain knowledge of the several cultures and national groups that speak their heritage language; (3) using their home language in an academic context to access new information and knowledge; (4) bringing to the level of awareness the views and perspectives of the two worlds with which they interact on a daily basis; and (5) expanding their ability to participate both in the U.S. and abroad as members of a language competent society.

The Communicative Framework and the Nature of the Language Being Studied

The use of a framework of communicative modes also highlights the challenge to students who study non-European languages. Cultural distance will place great demands on the interpersonal negotiated mode, because the process of negotiation requires abilities that will be unfamiliar to the typical speaker of a European language. Likewise, the amount of cultural knowledge ultimately required for the Interpretive and Presentational Modes is presumably much greater for students studying non-European languages than for students of one European language (e.g., English) studying another European language (e.g., Italian).

We expect that the Interpretive Mode would predominate in the study of classical languages such as Latin, perhaps with some attention to the Presentational Mode as a way of strengthening language knowledge and use. While some attention may be given to the oral dimension in classical languages, it is quite unlikely that such oral work is part of the Interpersonal Mode simply because there are no native speakers with whom to interact and negotiate.

Communicate in Languages Other Than English

RATIONALE

For American students, the ability to function competently in at least one language other than English will become increasingly important in the rapidly shrinking, interdependent world of the twenty-first century. Many individuals in the business and economic communities have been calling upon the educational system to prepare students with foreign language competence. At the same time, they have warned us that being able to talk about the language, to describe its grammar, and to conjugate verbs will not be enough. In the twenty-first century, students must be able to speak, to read, and to comprehend both spoken and written language. They must be able to participate appropriately in face-to-face interaction with members of other societies, and they must also be able to interpret the concepts, ideas, and opinions expressed by members of these societies through their media and their literatures.

DISCUSSION

In order to communicate successfully in another language, students must develop facility with the language, familiarity with the cultures that use these languages, and an awareness of how language and culture interact in societies. Students must apply this knowledge as they express and interpret events and ideas in a second language and reflect upon observations from other cultures. Thus, reaching the standards in the Communication Goal is central to the attainment of all the others.

To meet high communicative standards, learners must have ample opportunities to experience the second language as it is spoken and written in the target cultures. Meaningful language from real contexts becomes the basis for subsequent development of expressive skills. While language skills and cultural competencies can be developed within a wide range of content areas, it is essential that learners be surrounded with interesting and age-appropriate materials as a basis for acquisition of a new language system in its cultural contexts. People who grow up in different cultures acquire their first language in a particular cultural context; they must learn comparable cultural constructs and behaviors to communicate effectively in newly acquired languages.

In addition to the study of the language system and cultures, students must develop competencies using strategies that enhance the effectiveness of their communication and that compensate for linguistic and cultural inadequacies when they occur. Their second language classroom should provide a safe place in which to experiment with linguistic and cultural challenges. The second language learning enterprise is likewise facilitated when learners consciously develop effective strategies for reading and listening, for speaking and writing, for observing and analyzing cultures.

COMMUNICATION

COMMUNICATION

THEY LEARN BY DOING, BY TRYING OUT LANGUAGE, AND BY MODIFYING IT TO SERVE COMMUNICATIVE NEEDS.

Communicative Competence

One of the most important goals of second language study is the development of communicative competence in languages other than English. When individuals have developed *communicative competence* in a language, they are able to convey and receive messages of many different types successfully. These individuals use language to participate in everyday social interactions and to establish relationships with others. They converse, argue, criticize, request, convince, and explain effectively, taking into account the age, background, education, and familiarity of the individuals with whom they are engaged in conversation. They also use the language to obtain information from written texts and media and to interpret that information given the style, context, and purpose of the communication. In essence, a communicatively competent individual combines knowledge of the language system with knowledge of cultural conventions, norms of politeness, discourse conventions, and the like, in order to transmit and receive meaningful messages successfully.

In order to develop such competence, students must learn how interpersonal relations are conducted in the cultures in which the target language is spoken, how individuals use language effectively to achieve different purposes, how discourse conventions work, how oral and written texts are structured, and how the language system operates. They must weave this knowledge *together* in the process of transmitting and receiving meaningful messages.

Students bring the insights that they have obtained from having developed communicative competence in their first language to the study of a second one. They know how to request personal information from others, how to describe, how to argue, and how to explain. Depending on their age, they are able to obtain information from written texts and media and to interpret that information. When they do learn a second language, then, students already know how to transmit meanings effectively. They must learn how to do so by using a different language system and by following what may be very different rules of interpersonal interaction.

How Students Develop Communicative Competence in Another Language

As opposed to long-held beliefs, we now know that students do not acquire communicative competence by learning the elements of the language system first. It is not the case that learners learn best by memorizing vocabulary items in isolation and by producing limited simple sentences. We now know that even those students who learn grammar well and are able to pass tests on nouns, verb conjugations, tense usage, and the like may be quite unable to understand language when it is spoken to them outside the classroom. The study of the language system itself, while useful for some students, does not automatically result in the development of the ability to process language in real situations and in the ability to respond meaningfully in appropriate ways.

Indeed, an earlier emphasis on the learning of the language system to the exclusion of meaningful interactive activities in the classroom has led to frustration and dissatisfaction

Standards for Foreign Language Learning

COMMUNICATION

for students. Many adults complain today that although they "took" two or more years of foreign language and obtained high grades on grammar examinations, they are unable to speak the language at all. This same emphasis has led to criticism of the foreign language teaching profession by a number of individuals who have argued that languages are badly taught in this country and that language study to date has resulted in few people who can transact business in the languages studied.

The Importance of Communication Strategies in the Development of Communicative Competence

We now know that learners learn a language best when they are provided opportunities to use the target language to communicate in a wide range of activities. The more learners use the target language in meaningful situations, the more rapidly they achieve competency. Active use of language is central to the learning process; therefore, learners must be involved in generating utterances for themselves. They learn by doing, by trying out language, and by modifying it to serve communicative needs. Regardless of their stage of language acquisition, learners require strategies that allow them to compensate for language which they have not yet mastered. When breakdowns in communication occur, learners can call on these strategies in order to:

- gain access to further relevant and comprehensible communicative information;
- learn by experimenting;
- learn from mistakes and try again;
- practice and subsequently use various communication skills;
- communicate with a wide variety of audiences;
- learn how to compensate for shortcomings in communicating effectively; and
- become confident and successful in second language use.

We now know also that "good learners" adopt an immense variety of strategies concerned with seeking communicative information and experiences, with deliberate learning through practice, and with developing a conscious awareness and control. These strategies include requesting clarification, monitoring their own and others' performance, using various mnemonic techniques, using inductive and deductive reasoning, practicing sounds and structures subvocally or aloud, and using nonverbal communication strategies.

STANDARDS

The Communication Goal includes three standards based on the Framework of Communicative Modes (pp. 36-38). The first focuses on the Interpersonal Mode; the second focuses on the Interpretive Mode; the third focuses on the Presentational Mode. It should be emphasized that, while the Communication Goal is central to the achievement of

> WHILE THE COMMUNICATION GOAL IS CENTRAL... STUDENTS NEED EXPERIENCE IN THE OTHER GOAL AREAS TO HAVE CONTENT WORTH COMMUNICATING.

Standards for Foreign Language Learning

COMMUNICATION

STANDARDS: WHAT STUDENTS KNOW AND ARE ABLE TO DO AT THE END OF HIGH SCHOOL

all other goal areas, it cannot be viewed in isolation. This is clearly illustrated in the Sample Progress Indicators for each of the standards. While the focus is on the use of language and the development of communicative competence, students will need experience in the other goal areas in order to have content worth communicating. Knowledge of the linguistic system, its grammar, emerging vocabulary, phonology, pragmatic and discourse features undergirds the accuracy of communication.

STANDARD 1.1 Students engage in conversations, provide and obtain information, express feelings and emotions, and exchange opinions.

This standard focuses on interpersonal communication. In most modern languages, students can quite quickly learn a number of phrases that permit them to interact with each other. In the course of their study, they grow in their ability to converse in a culturally appropriate manner. Students who come with a home background in the language may have already acquired such abilities. Students of non-European languages may face greater challenges in this area than students of languages more closely related to English.

Sample Progress Indicators, Grade 4

- Students give and follow simple instructions in order to participate in age-appropriate classroom and/or cultural activities.

- Students ask and answer questions about topics such as family, school events, and celebrations in person or via letters, e-mail, audio, or video tapes.

- Students share likes and dislikes with each other and the class.

- Students exchange descriptions of people and tangible products of the culture such as toys, dress, types of dwellings, and foods with each other and members of the class.

- Students exchange essential information such as greetings, leave takings, and common classroom interactions using culturally appropriate gestures and oral expressions.

Sample Progress Indicators, Grade 8

- Students follow and give directions for participating in age-appropriate cultural activities and investigating the function of products of the foreign culture. They ask and respond to questions for clarification.

- Students exchange information about personal events, memorable experiences, and other school subjects with peers and/or members of the target cultures.

- Students compare, contrast, and express opinions and preferences about the information gathered regarding events, experiences and other school subjects.

Standards for Foreign Language Learning

COMMUNICATION

- Students acquire goods, services, or information orally and/or in writing.

- Students develop and propose solutions to issues and problems related to the school or community through group work.

Sample Progress Indicators, Grade 12

- Students discuss, orally or in writing, current or past events that are of significance in the target culture or that are being studied in another subject.

- Students develop and propose solutions to issues and problems that are of concern to members of their own and the target cultures through group work.

- Students share their analyses and personal reactions to expository and literary texts with peers and/or speakers of the target language.

- Students exchange, support and discuss their opinions and individual perspectives with peers and/or speakers of the target language on a variety of topics dealing with contemporary and historical issues.

STANDARD 1.2 Students understand and interpret written and spoken language on a variety of topics.

This standard focuses on the understanding and interpretation of written and spoken language. Standard 1.2, unlike Standard 1.1, involves one-way listening and reading in which the learner works with a variety of print and non-print materials. For students who come to language learning with no previous background in the language, the context in which the language is experienced and the ability to control what they hear and read may impact the development of comprehension. As a result, for some learners, the ability to read may develop before the ability to comprehend rapid spoken language. In addition, content knowledge will often affect successful comprehension, for students understand more easily materials that reflect their interests or for which they have some background. In contrast, students with exposure to the language through home life may be quite advanced in their understanding of the spoken language and less advanced in terms of their ability to read. The reading aspects of this standard make it particularly relevant to the classical languages. Reading may also develop less rapidly for languages with non-Roman writing systems.

Sample Progress Indicators, Grade 4

- Students comprehend main ideas in developmentally appropriate oral narratives such as personal anecdotes, familiar fairy tales, and other narratives based on familiar themes.

- Students identify people and objects in their environment or from other school subjects, based on oral and written description.

PROGRESS INDICATORS: DEFINE STUDENT PROGRESS IN MEETING THE STANDARDS

Standards for Foreign Language Learning

COMMUNICATION

- Students comprehend brief, written messages and short personal notes on familiar topics such as family, school events, and celebrations.

- Students comprehend the main themes and ideas and identify the principal characters of stories or children's literature.

- Students comprehend the principal message contained in various media such as illustrated texts, posters, or advertisements.

- Students interpret gestures, intonation, and other visual or auditory cues.

Sample Progress Indicators, Grade 8

- Students comprehend information and messages related to other school subjects.

- Students understand announcements and messages connected to daily activities in the target culture.

- Students understand the main themes and significant details on topics from other subjects and products of the cultures as presented on TV, radio, video, or live presentations.

- Students understand the main themes and significant details on topics from other subjects and products of the cultures as found in newspapers, magazines, e-mail, or other printed sources used by speakers of the target language.

- Students identify the principal characters and comprehend the main ideas and themes in selected literary texts.

- Students use knowledge acquired in other settings and from other subject areas to comprehend spoken and written messages in the target languages.

Sample Progress Indicators, Grade 12

- Students demonstrate an understanding of the main ideas and significant details of live and recorded discussions, lectures, and presentations on current or past events from the target culture or that are being studied in another class.

- Students demonstrate an understanding of the principal elements of non-fiction articles in newspapers, magazines and e-mail on topics of current and historical importance to members of the culture.

- Students analyze the main plot, subplot, characters, their descriptions, roles, and significance in authentic literary texts.

- Students demonstrate an increasing understanding of the cultural nuances of meaning in written and spoken language as expressed by speakers of the target language in formal and informal settings.

COMMUNICATION

- Students demonstrate an increasing understanding of the cultural nuances of meaning in expressive products of the culture, including selections from various literary genres and the visual arts.

STANDARD 1.3 Students present information, concepts, and ideas to an audience of listeners or readers on a variety of topics.

This standard focuses on the presentation of information, concepts, and ideas in spoken and written modes. This standard, in most cases, is concerned with one-way speaking and writing. Students with little or no previous experience in the language are likely to produce written and spoken language that contains a variety of learned patterns or that looks like English with words in the other language. This is a natural process. Over time, students then begin to acquire authentic patterns and to use appropriate styles. By contrast, home-background students write in ways that closely resemble the spoken language. Moreover, they control well informal oral styles. Over time, these learners develop the ability to write and speak using a variety of more formal styles.

Sample Progress Indicators, Grade 4

- Students prepare illustrated stories about activities or events in their environment and share these stories and events with an audience such as the class.

- Students dramatize songs, short anecdotes, or poetry commonly known by peers in the target culture for members of another elementary class.

- Students give short oral notes and messages, or write reports, about people and things in their school environment and exchange the information with another language class either locally or via e-mail.

- Students tell or retell stories orally or in writing.

- Students write or tell about products and/or practices of their own culture to peers in the target culture.

Sample Progress Indicators, Grade 8

- Students present short plays and skits, recite selected poems and anecdotes, and perform songs in the language for a school-related event such as a board meeting or PTA meeting.

- Students prepare tape or video recorded messages to share locally or with school peers and/or members of the target cultures on topics of personal interest.

- Students prepare stories or brief written reports about personal experiences, brief personal events, or other school subjects to share with classmates and/or members of the target cultures.

Standards for Foreign Language Learning

COMMUNICATION

- Students prepare an oral or written summary of the plot and characters in selected pieces of age-appropriate literature.

Sample Progress Indicators, Grade 12

- Students perform scenes and/or recite poems or excerpts from short stories connected to a topic from other disciplines such as world history, geography, the arts, or mathematics.

- Students perform scenes from plays and/or recite poems or excerpts from short stories commonly read by speakers of the target language.

- Students create stories and poems, short plays, or skits based on personal experiences and exposure to themes, ideas, and perspectives from the target culture.

- Students select and analyze expressive products of the culture, from literary genres or the fine arts.

- Students summarize the content of an article or documentary intended for native speakers in order to discuss the topics via e-mail with other users or speakers of the language.

- Students write a letter or an article describing and analyzing an issue for a student publication.

- Students prepare a research-based analysis of a current event from the perspective of both the U.S. and target cultures.

Gain Knowledge and Understanding of Other Cultures

RATIONALE

The study of another language enables students to understand a different culture *on its own terms*. The exquisite connections between the culture that is lived and the language that is spoken can only be realized by those who possess a knowledge of both. American students need to develop an awareness of other people's world views, of their unique way of life, and of the patterns of behavior which order their world, as well as learn about contributions of other cultures to the world at large and the solutions they offer to the common problems of humankind. Such awareness will help combat the ethnocentrism that often dominates the thinking of our young people. Oliver Wendell Holmes' contention that the human mind, once stretched to a new idea, never returns to its former dimensions (*The Autocrat of the Breakfast Table*) underscores the benefits which the study of cultures through their own language can bring.

DISCUSSION

What is Culture? The term "culture" is generally understood to include the philosophical perspectives, the behavioral practices, and the products—both tangible and intangible—of a society. The diagram below illustrates how the products and practices are derived from the philosophical perspectives that form the world view of a cultural group. It also shows how these three components of culture are closely interrelated.

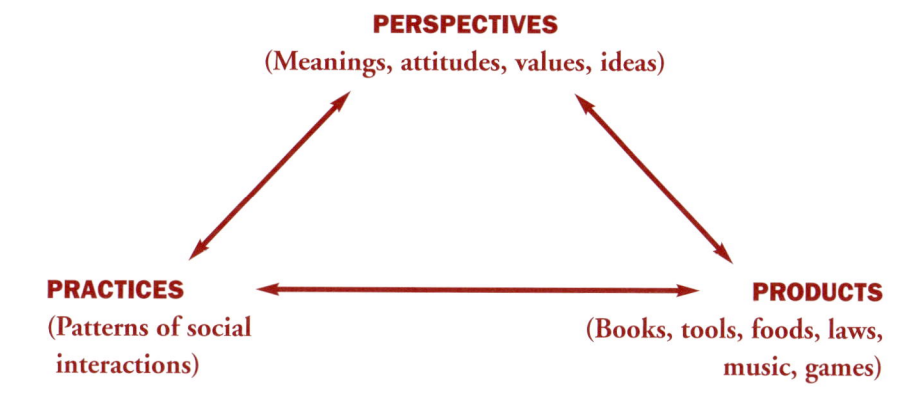

PERSPECTIVES
(Meanings, attitudes, values, ideas)

PRACTICES
(Patterns of social interactions)

PRODUCTS
(Books, tools, foods, laws, music, games)

Because language is the primary vehicle for expressing cultural perspectives and participating in social practices, the study of a language provides opportunities for students to develop insights in a culture that are available in no other way. In reality, then, the true content of the foreign language course is not the grammar and the vocabulary of the language, but the cultures

CULTURES

CULTURES

expressed through that language. It is important that students become skilled observers and analysts of other cultures.

In the last few decades, members of the foreign language profession have tended to divide culture into two bins: "Big C" (formal) and "little c" (daily life) cultures. Most teachers were comfortable with the concept of "Big C"(formal) culture, which required some knowledge of the formal institutions (social, political, and economic), the great figures of history, and those products of literature, fine arts, and the sciences that were traditionally assigned to the category of elite culture. The "little c" (daily life) culture bin included those aspects of daily living studied by the sociologist and the anthropologist: housing, clothing, food, tools, transportation, and all the patterns of behavior that members of the culture regard as necessary and appropriate. This "Big C" (formal), "little c" (daily life) division was valuable initially because it drew attention to the sociological components of culture that in the past had been virtually ignored in textbooks and classrooms. However, because both aspects of culture are inextricably woven into the language of those who live in the culture, and because understanding and involvement with both is vitally important for students at all levels of language learning, they are viewed as inseparable in this document.

Avoiding Cultural Misunderstandings. People who share the same native language share many common perspectives, practices, and products. Speakers of a single language may live in various parts of the world; consequently, they belong to different cultures, the traditions and expressions of which have been shaped by time, geographical location, and various profound and unique experiences that cause groups to differ from each other even though they share a language. To apply a single set of criteria in analyzing, teaching, and interacting with those cultures would be to ignore reality and fail to respect the dignity of disparate cultural groups. To assume, for example, that the Spanish-speaking cultures in Latin America are essentially the same as the cultures of Spain, or the cultures of immigrants from Mexico or the Caribbean living in the United States, is to deny the special identity of each group. The same can be said for the French-speaking cultures of Africa, North America, the Caribbean, the South Pacific, and France itself. Such examples of cultural diversity within commonly shared languages are numerous and significant, and their impact has been particularly poignant in the pluralistic society of the United States.

It is equally important that students recognize that members of one culture tend to make assumptions and draw corresponding conclusions about other cultures based upon their own values. Opinions and attitudes, both hidden and expressed, are often based upon a surface examination of other cultures using criteria that can be applied with validity only to one's own culture. The erroneous judgments that result from such assumptions, born of a lack of adequate information, understanding, and sensitivity, eventually lead to negative reactions to members of different cultures. To counteract this tendency, teachers can provide learning activities appropriate to grade level that explore the process of stereotyping

> **BOTH ASPECTS OF CULTURE (FORMAL AND DAILY LIFE) ARE INEXTRICABLY WOVEN INTO THE LANGUAGE OF THOSE WHO LIVE IN THE CULTURE.**

Standards for Foreign Language Learning

CULTURES

and the role stereotypes play in forming and sustaining prejudice. Finally, it is critical to provide opportunities for many different kinds of interaction with members of other cultures, so that students draw informed conclusions and develop sensitivity to the perspectives, practices, and products of others.

Teaching Similarities and Differences. While nobody doubts that both similarities and differences exist among any given cultures, the question that concerns teachers is which to present first. There is some evidence to show that a positive point of departure—underscoring ways in which members of the other culture share similar interests and behaviors with language learners in the United States—establishes a favorable mindset toward speakers of the other language. It is essential, however, that cultural differences not be swept under a pedagogical rug. It is the differences in world view and the behavior patterns based on those differing assumptions and values that give rise to misunderstandings and conflict. It is important to help students *expect* differences and learn how to *analyze* observed differences (how to put them into perspective within the cultural framework of the other language). At every stage of language learning, *both* similarities and differences among the students' own culture and the other cultures should be presented. Interactions with representatives of the other cultures and experience with a variety of cultural expressions (personal anecdotes, poetry, headlines, editorials, laws, music, museums, trains, and pets, for example) help learners shape their own awareness. This personal exploration in the language of the culture enables students to develop crosscultural understanding and respect.

The Specific Role of Second Language Study. The enduring dimension of cultural study is the actual participation in the exchange of information and ideas among members of various cultures using the foreign language. While a great deal of information about other cultures can be gained through the study of other disciplines, such as the social sciences and the arts, only second language study empowers learners to engage successfully in meaningful, direct interaction, both orally and in writing, with members of other cultures. The perspectives, practices, and products of culture—be they historical or contemporary—can be shared in a special way with members of the culture in which they originated. This new, "insider's" perspective is the true catalyst for crosscultural understanding.

STANDARDS

The Cultures Goal includes two standards. The first emphasizes the practices, the second the products associated with cultural perspectives.

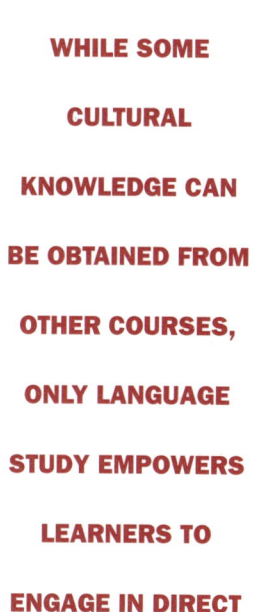

> WHILE SOME CULTURAL KNOWLEDGE CAN BE OBTAINED FROM OTHER COURSES, ONLY LANGUAGE STUDY EMPOWERS LEARNERS TO ENGAGE IN DIRECT INTERACTION WITH MEMBERS OF OTHER CULTURES.

Standards for Foreign Language Learning 49

CULTURES

CULTURAL PRACTICES: PATTERNS OF BEHAVIOR ACCEPTED BY A SOCIETY

STANDARD 2.1 Students demonstrate an understanding of the relationship between the practices and perspectives of the cultures studied.

This standard focuses on the practices that are derived from the traditional ideas, attitudes, and values (*perspectives*) of a culture. "Cultural practices" refers to patterns of behavior accepted by a society and deal with aspects of culture such as rites of passage, the use of forms of discourse, the social "pecking order," and the use of space. In short, they represent the knowledge of "what to do when and where." It is important to understand the relationship between these practices and the underlying perspectives that represent the culture's view of the world.

For example, in some Asian cultures members are positioned (a *perspective*) on a hierarchical scale based on age, social status, education, or similar variables. In those cultures, the exchange of business cards (a *product*) that provides key information is a helpful *practice*. Because these cards facilitate social interaction and are treated with respect in those cultures, one should not scribble another name or telephone number on the business card (taboo *practice*). The information on the card also directly affects the nonverbal behavior (*practice*) of those involved in the communicative interaction, as well as the choice of linguistic forms (*products*) that indicate status.

The following progress indicators relate to learning activities based on the culture studied:

Sample Progress Indicators, Grade 4

- Students observe, identify, and/or discuss simple patterns of behavior or interaction in various settings such as school, family, and the community.

- Students use appropriate gestures and oral expressions for greetings, leave takings, and common classroom interactions.

- Students participate in age-appropriate cultural activities such as games, songs, birthday celebrations, story telling, and dramatizations.

Sample Progress Indicators, Grade 8

- Students observe, analyze, and discuss patterns of behavior typical of their peer group.

- Students use appropriate verbal and nonverbal behavior for daily activities among peers and adults.

- Students learn about and participate in age-appropriate cultural practices such as games (role of leader, taking turns, etc.), sports, and entertainment (e.g., music, dance, drama).

Standards for Foreign Language Learning

CULTURES

Sample Progress Indicators, Grade 12

- Students interact in a variety of cultural contexts that reflect both peer-group and adult activities within the culture studied, using the appropriate verbal and nonverbal cues.

- Students learn about and participate in age-appropriate cultural practices, such as games, sports, and entertainment.

- Students identify, analyze, and discuss various patterns of behavior or interaction typical of the culture studied.

- Students identify, examine, and discuss connections between cultural perspectives and socially approved behavioral patterns.

STANDARD 2.2 Students demonstrate an understanding of the relationship between the products and perspectives of the cultures studied.

> CULTURAL PRODUCTS ARE REQUIRED OR JUSTIFIED BY THE UNDERLYING BELIEFS AND VALUES OF THAT CULTURE.

This standard focuses on the *products* of the culture studied and on how they reflect the *perspectives* of that culture. *Products* may be tangible (e.g., a painting, a cathedral, a piece of literature, a pair of chopsticks) or intangible (e.g., an oral tale, a dance, a sacred ritual, a system of education). Whatever the form of the product, its presence within the culture is required or justified by the underlying beliefs and values (*perspectives*) of that culture, and the cultural *practices* involve the use of that *product*.

For example, in the United States, youth has traditionally been valued more than old age (a *perspective*). As a result, *products* that purport to prolong youth and vitality (e.g., face creams, high fiber breakfast cereals, and "exercycles") have become an integral part of our culture. At the same time, *practices* that are perceived as prolonging youth and health are encouraged: school children exercise to meet the goals of the President's Physical Fitness Award; teenagers go on crash diets; whole segments of the population invest in running shoes and jogging togs (*products*).

Sample Progress Indicators, Grade 4:

- Students identify and observe tangible products of the culture such as toys, dress, types of dwellings, and foods.

- Students identify, experience, or read about expressive products of the culture such as children's songs, selections from children's literature, and types of artwork enjoyed or produced by their peer group in the cultures studied.

- Students identify, discuss, and produce types of artwork, crafts, or graphic representations enjoyed or made by their peer group within the cultures studied.

- Students recognize themes, ideas, or perspectives of the culture.

Standards for Foreign Language Learning 51

CULTURES

Sample Progress Indicators, Grade 8

- Students experience (read, listen to, observe, perform) expressive products of the culture (e.g., stories, poetry, music, paintings, dance, and drama) and then explore the effects of these products on the larger communities.

- Students search for, identify, and investigate the function of utilitarian products (e.g., sports equipment, household items, tools, foods, and clothing) of the culture studied as found within their homes and communities.

- Students identify, discuss, and analyze themes, ideas, and perspectives related to the products being studied.

Sample Progress Indicators, Grade 12

- Students identify, discuss, and analyze such intangible products of the target culture as social, economic, and political institutions, and explore relationships among these institutions and the perspectives of the culture.

- Students experience, discuss, and analyze expressive products of the culture, including selections from various literary genres and the fine arts.

- Students identify, analyze, and evaluate themes, ideas, and perspectives related to the products being studied.

- Students explore the relationships among the products, practices, and perspectives of the culture.

Connect with Other Disciplines and Acquire Information

RATIONALE

Foreign language learning expands the educational experience of all students by connecting with other disciplines in the school curriculum either formally or informally. Knowledge is power, and extending student access to information through the use of a foreign language increases student ability to "know and do." Using a foreign language to acquire information empowers students with knowledge, no matter what the topic or discipline. It also provides learners with skills and interests that look beyond the limits of their formal educational experiences.

In today's society, access to information takes on a variety of forms and occurs both in and out of school. Students may watch news releases from foreign countries, listen to interviews with foreign nationals before or during the translation, or access vast stores of information from around the world through Internet connections in their homes. Classroom instruction serves as an organizer by preparing students to access the variety of sources in the other language. They may acquire information through technology, personal interviews, newspapers, magazines, dictionaries, and encyclopedias in the school library.

The conscious effort to connect the foreign language curriculum with other parts of students' academic lives opens doors to information and experiences which enrich the students' entire school and life experience. Those connections flow from other areas to the foreign language classroom and also originate in the foreign language classroom to add unique experiences and insights to the rest of the curriculum.

DISCUSSION

Knowledge of a second language and culture combines with the study of other disciplines and shifts the focus from language acquisition to broader learning experiences for the student. Language used in this way helps students integrate the contributions from any discipline into a holistic and ever-expanding open system. For example, while learning about the origins of the German classical music tradition, students with a knowledge of the language deepen their understanding of a composer's works by reading segments of Bach's correspondence with contemporaries or excerpts from his diary describing the creative process. The same information could also be useful in other classes as students learn to forge connections across the disciplines, shifting emphasis from the learning of individual language pieces to recognition that language acquisition is a continuous process contributing to life-long learning.

Taking the shift from teacher-directed to student-directed learning one more step, students use their developing language skills to go beyond the requirements for class work and pursue

CONNECTIONS

CONCEPTS PRESENTED IN ONE CLASS ARE THE BASIS FOR CONTINUED LEARNING IN THE FOREIGN LANGUAGE CLASS.

topics further for personal interest, unrelated to the limits of academic life. In this way, students are "weaned" from language-learning and begin to nurture life-long learning skills and life-long language-using skills.

Although students entering the language classroom may have had no prior conscious experience with language learning, they are not empty vessels. They bring a wealth of experience and knowledge of the world around them (both in other areas of the curriculum and from personal experience). Furthermore, those children who know languages other than English bring additional linguistic and cultural experiences to their classrooms. With the goal of language instruction to "acquire information and connect to other disciplines," the teacher can use the classroom language learning experience to build upon what students already know. In this way, foreign language acquisition focuses on the broader education of students; it benefits their growth in non-language disciplines, encourages the transfer, enrichment, and strengthening of information; it helps students "learn how to learn."

STANDARDS

The Connections Goal includes two standards. The first focuses on target language support for content from other disciplines. The second focuses on information now available to the learner through the target language.

STANDARD 3.1 Students reinforce and further their knowledge of other disciplines through the foreign language.

Learning today is no longer restricted to a specific discipline; it has become interdisciplinary. Just as reading cannot be limited to a particular segment of the school day but is central to all aspects of the school curriculum, so, too, can foreign language build upon the knowledge that students acquire in other subject areas. In addition, students can relate the information studied in other subjects to their learning of the foreign language and culture. Students expand and deepen their understanding of and exposure to other areas of knowledge, even as they refine their communicative abilities and broaden their cultural understanding. The new information and concepts presented in one class become the basis of continued learning in the foreign language classroom. In the lower grades, for example, students in a science class are introduced to the range of vocabulary related to weather, seasons, and temperatures. At the same time, the foreign language class continues this presentation with the months of the year, seasons, and weather vocabulary in the foreign language. By comparing the weather conditions in the foreign country with those at home, students have acquired new knowledge at the same time that they have deepened their understanding of previous information.

Interdisciplinary reinforcement can occur at all levels of the school curriculum. At various stages, the foreign language teacher could teach more than the names and events pre-

Standards for Foreign Language Learning

CONNECTIONS

sented in the history class and geographical place names by introducing students to journalistic accounts of historical events or literary depictions of individuals living at that time. Furthermore, in addition to the concepts and processes introduced in science and the achievements of artists and musicians studied in art, students could read documentation in various reference materials, the descriptions of success and failure in biographical sketches of various individuals, as well as the autobiographical accounts documented in personal letters and diaries of those historical figures. Prior discussion of works of literature in the English class enables students to have a better understanding of various genres—from the detective story to the sonnet—and literary conventions when they encounter similar texts in the language classroom. Even the manipulations and story problems taught in math provide content and a basis for discussion and exploration in the foreign language classroom. Students who are grappling with a science problem are aided in their attempts to understand it by relating it to their peers in the language classroom. When integrated into the broader curriculum, foreign language learning contributes to the entire educational experience of students.

Sample Progress Indicators, Grade 4

- Students demonstrate an understanding about concepts learned in other subject areas in the target language, including weather, math facts, measurements, animals, insects, or geographical concepts.

Sample Progress Indicators, Grade 8

- Students discuss topics from other school subjects in the target language, including geographical terms and concepts, historical facts and concepts, mathematical terms and problems, and scientific information.

- Students comprehend articles or short videos in the target language on topics being studied in other classes.

- Students present reports in the target language, orally and/or in writing, on topics being studied in other classes.

Sample Progress Indicators, Grade 12

- Students discuss topics from other school subjects in the target language, including political and historical concepts, worldwide health issues, and environmental concerns.

- Students acquire information from a variety of sources written in the target language about a topic being studied in other school subjects.

Standards for Foreign Language Learning

CONNECTIONS

- Students combine information from other school subjects with information available in the foreign language in order to complete activities in the foreign language classroom.

LANGUAGE LEARNERS BROADEN THE SOURCES OF INFORMATION AVAILABLE TO THEM.

STANDARD 3.2 Students acquire information and recognize the distinctive viewpoints that are only available through the foreign language and its cultures.

As a consequence of learning another language and gaining access to its unique means of communication and ways of thinking, students acquire new information and perspectives. As learners of a foreign language, they broaden the sources of information available to them. They have a "new window on the world." In the earlier stages of language learning, they begin to examine a variety of sources intended for native speakers, and extract specific information. As they become more proficient users of the foreign language, they seek out materials of interest to them, analyze the content, compare it to information available in their own language, and assess the linguistic and cultural differences.

Sample Progress Indicators, Grade 4

- Students read, listen to, and talk about age-appropriate school content, folk tales, short stories, poems, and songs written for native speakers of the target language.

Sample Progress Indicators, Grade 8

- Students use sources intended for same-age speakers of the target language to prepare reports on topics of personal interest, or those with which they have limited previous experience.

Sample Progress Indicators, Grade 12

- Students use a variety of sources intended for same-age speakers of the target language to prepare reports on topics of personal interest, or those with which they have limited previous experience, and compare these to information obtained on the same topics written in English.

Develop Insight into the Nature of Language and Culture

RATIONALE

Students benefit from language learning by discovering different patterns among language systems and cultures. Through the study of a new language system and the way such a system expresses meanings in culturally appropriate ways, students gain insights into the nature of language, linguistic and grammatical concepts, and the communicative functions of language in society, as well as the complexity of the interaction between language and culture.

DISCUSSION

There is a generally held notion that students are better able to reflect on their first language and culture after having experienced learning a second. Evidence of this notion arises in various studies done on the effects of second language learning. Although the research remains inconclusive, anecdotal evidence supports the idea that, by engaging in comparisons between their language and the language studied, learners develop a greater understanding of their own language and culture and of language and culture in the broadest sense.

Some would argue that equivalent knowledge of language and cultural systems can be acquired in other types of courses (e.g., linguistics, anthropology). However, when students study another language and participate in communicative interactions, the actual experiential dimension makes such an understanding more real. By struggling with how to express particular meanings in a second language, how to encode them linguistically, and how to be sensitive to norms of politeness in another culture, students gain awareness of the nature of language itself.

For example, students often come to the study of another language with the assumptions that all languages are like their own. Shortly, they discover categories that exist in other languages (e.g., neuter gender) that do not exist in their own. They discover that elements to which they gave scant attention (e.g., ends of words) may be quite important in another language. Moreover, they realize that what is polite in one cultural system (e.g., when and to whom to say thank you) is not parallel in the other. These experiences direct attention to a comparison of language and cultural systems. In turn, such awareness enhances the ability not only to use the target language, but also to gain insights into the strategies their own language uses to communicate meaning. Whether or not students continue the study of that particular language, the understandings gained about the nature of language and its interaction with culture carry over into future situations where they may have to interact in other cultural settings. Students learn ways of hypothesizing and making predictions about how language is likely to work in a setting with which they are not familiar. They cease to make naive assumptions about other languages and cultures solely based upon knowledge of their own.

COMPARISONS

COMPARISONS

STRUGGLING TO EXPRESS PARTICULAR MEANINGS IN A SECOND LANGUAGE BRINGS AWARENESS OF THE NATURE OF LANGUAGE ITSELF.

The long-term experience of studying another language leads students to discover that other cultures view the world from a perspective different from their own. Students view concepts in a new light as they probe apparently similar concepts in the target culture. For example, the word "bread" evokes certain images among American students based on its role and reality in our culture. These images cannot be automatically transferred to the second language. The appearance, taste, use, and perception of bread in another culture may be entirely different. When students understand that the target culture assigns new associations to the label "bread," they are drawn to examine this concept more closely in their native language. They begin to realize that language learning is not simply a matter of learning different vocabulary words, but of acquiring an entirely new set of concepts associated with the words.

The study of a second language and the resulting intercultural exploration expand a learner's view of the world in different ways. This study creates an awareness of the existence of alternative views of other cultures while, at the same time, providing insights into the learner's native language and culture. In addition, by comparing both cultural and linguistic systems, students develop their critical thinking abilities in valuable and important ways.

STANDARDS

The Comparisons Goal includes two standards; the first standard focuses on the nature of language, the second on the concept of culture.

STANDARD 4.1 Students demonstrate understanding of the nature of language through comparisons of the language studied and their own.

This standard focuses on the impact that learning the linguistic elements in the new language has on students' ability to examine their own language, and to develop hypotheses about the structure and use of languages. From the earliest language learning experiences, students can compare and contrast the two languages as different elements are presented. Activities can be systematically integrated into instruction that will assist students in understanding how languages work.

Sample Progress Indicators, Grade 4

- Students cite and use examples of words that are borrowed in the language they are learning and their own, and they pose guesses about why languages in general might need to borrow words.

- Students realize that cognates enhance comprehension of spoken and written language and demonstrate that awareness by identifying commonly occurring cognates in the language they are learning.

COMPARISONS

- Students are aware of the existence of idiomatic expressions in both their native language and the language being learned and talk about how idiomatic expressions work in general.

- Students demonstrate an awareness of formal and informal forms of language in greetings and leave-takings and try out expressions of politeness in other languages and their own.

- Students report differences and similarities between the sound and writing systems of their own language and the language being learned.

- Students demonstrate an awareness of the various ways of expressing ideas both in their own language and the language being learned.

Sample Progress Indicators, Grade 8

- Students recognize the category of grammatical gender in languages, and their spoken and written language reflects that awareness.

- Students hypothesize about the relationship among languages based on their awareness of cognates and similarity of idioms.

- Students demonstrate an awareness of ways of expressing respect and communicating status differences in their own language and the language they are learning.

- Students demonstrate awareness that languages have critical sound distinctions that must be mastered in order to communicate meaning.

Sample Progress Indicators, Grade 12

- Students recognize that cognates have the same as well as different meanings among languages and speculate about the evolution of language.

- Students demonstrate an awareness that there are phrases and idioms that do not translate directly from one language to another.

- Students analyze elements of the target language, such as time and tense, and comparable linguistic elements in English, and conjecture about how languages use forms to express time and tense relationships.

- Students report on the relationship between word order and meaning and hypothesize on how this may or may not reflect the ways in which cultures organize information and view the world.

- Students compare the writing system of the target language and their own. They also examine other writing systems and report about the nature of those writing systems (e.g., logographic, syllabic, alphabetic).

Standards for Foreign Language Learning

COMPARISONS

LANGUAGE LEARNING IS NOT SIMPLY LEARNING NEW WORDS, BUT ALSO ACQUIRING NEW CONCEPTS ASSOCIATED WITH THE WORDS.

STANDARD 4.2 Students demonstrate understanding of the concept of culture through comparisons of the cultures studied and their own.

As students expand their knowledge of cultures through language learning, they continually discover perspectives, practices, and products that are similar to and different from those in their own culture. They develop the ability to hypothesize about cultural systems in general. Some students may make these comparisons naturally, others learn to do so. This standard helps focus this reflective process for all students by encouraging integration of this process into instruction from the earliest levels of learning.

Sample Progress Indicators, Grade 4

- Students compare simple patterns of behavior or interaction in various cultural settings.

- Students demonstrate an awareness that gestures are an important part of communication and that gestures may differ among languages.

- Students compare and contrast tangible products (e.g., toys, sports, equipment, food) of the target cultures and their own.

- Students compare and contrast intangible products (e.g., rhymes, songs, folktales) of the target cultures and their own.

Sample Progress Indicators, Grade 8

- Students contrast verbal and nonverbal behavior within particular activities in the target cultures and their own.

- Students demonstrate an awareness that they, too, have a culture, based on comparisons of sample daily activities in the target culture and their own.

- Students speculate on why certain products originate in and/or are important to particular cultures by analyzing selected products from the target cultures and their own.

- Students hypothesize about the relationship between cultural perspectives and practices (e.g., holidays, celebrations, work habits, play) by analyzing selected practices from the target cultures and their own.

- Students hypothesize about the relationship between cultural perspectives and expressive products (e.g., music, visual arts, appropriate forms of literature) by analyzing selected products from the target cultures and their own.

Standards for Foreign Language Learning

COMPARISONS

Sample Progress Indicators, Grade 12

- Students hypothesize about the origins of idioms as reflections of culture, citing examples from the language and cultures being studied and their own.

- Students compare nuances of meanings of words, idioms, and vocal inflections in the target language and their own.

- Students analyze the relationship of perspectives and practices in the target culture and compare and contrast these with their own.

- Students analyze the relationship between the products and perspectives in the cultures studied and compare and contrast these with their own.

- Students identify and analyze cultural perspectives as reflected in a variety of literary genres.

Participate in Multilingual Communities at Home and Around the World

RATIONALE

The shift from a manufacturing-based economy to one increasingly based on information, technology, and service reflects a changing America. As businesses expand domestic and international markets, American citizens need to be proficient in English and in other languages. These skills allow Americans to access directly knowledge and information generated by other countries and cultures and allow for face-to-face negotiations in political, business, and personal dealings. This proficiency is developed and sustained by the opportunity to learn and use a language over a long period of time. Moreover, students are highly motivated to excel in their study of a second language when they see immediate applications for the skills they learn. They find that their ability to communicate in other languages better prepares them for school and community service projects, enables them to expand their employment opportunities both at home and abroad, and allows them to pursue their own interests for personal benefit. Ultimately, as a result of their ability to communicate in other languages, students realize the interdependence of people throughout the world. This goal combines elements from each of the other goal areas. Once again, careful application of the components of language and culture are vital. The standards in this goal are dependent not only on careful language use, but on the ability to apply knowledge of the perspectives, products and practices of a culture, the ability to connect to other discipline areas, and the development of insight into one's own language and culture.

DISCUSSION

Recognizing the need for a productive and competitive work force, many schools are emphasizing a curriculum that better prepares students for the school-to-work or school-to-college transition. These educational efforts extend to the language classroom, preparing competent and self-confident students for work in the multilingual communities around the globe. The needs of today's society and work force are best met by weaving together the resources and expertise of vocational schools, academic institutions, businesses, governments at local, state, and national levels, and public and private organizations. A changing American society and a world of instant global communications require a strong work force that meets the needs of consumers who may not speak English. Knowledge of another language and culture puts workers in a better position to serve the needs of a global society.

Some students are fortunate to have direct access to multilingual communities through their home backgrounds; all students benefit from an awareness of the many communities in the U.S. where English and other languages are spoken—communities such as the French-

COMMUNITIES

COMMUNITIES

STUDENTS COME TO REALIZE THE ADVANTAGES INHERENT IN KNOWING OTHER LANGUAGES.

speaking Cajun areas of Louisiana, the German areas of the Texas Hill Country, the Italian communities of the Northeast, the Spanish-speaking communities of the Southeast and Southwest, and the Asian neighborhoods of the West Coast. Language students develop a keener awareness of cultures and are better equipped to function in the multilingual communities that exist in the U.S. and abroad.

In addition to the ability to communicate in more than one language as a job skill, knowledge of other languages and cultures opens the door to many types of leisure activities. From the television screen to the computer monitor, Americans have a direct link with the entire contemporary world. Through works of great literature and the arts, a deeper understanding of self is attainable. As Americans travel to other countries and interact with speakers of other languages, they realize that competence in more than one language and knowledge of other cultures empower them to experience more fully the artistic and cultural creations of those cultures.

STANDARDS

The Communities Goal includes two standards. The first standard emphasizes applied learning, while the second focuses on personal enrichment.

STANDARD 5.1 Students use the language both within and beyond the school setting.

This standard focuses on language as a tool for communication with speakers of the language throughout one's life: in schools, in the community, and abroad. In schools, students share their knowledge of language and culture with classmates and with younger students who may be learning the language. Applying what has been learned in the language program as defined by the other standards, students come to realize the advantages inherent in being able to communicate in more than one language and develop an understanding of the power of language. Well-developed language applications increase not only the marketability of the employee, but also the ability of the employer to meet the expectations of the customer. Many of the Progress Indicators for Standard 5.1 are repeated at Grade 4, 8 and 12 not only to emphasize that the activity may be similar, but also to indicate that a spiraling of tasks and competencies advances with age. As students have opportunities to use language in response to real-world needs, they seek out situations to apply their competencies beyond the school setting.

Sample Progress Indicators, Grade 4

- Students communicate on a personal level with speakers of the language via letters, e-mail, audio, and video tapes.

Standards for Foreign Language Learning

COMMUNITIES

- Students identify professions which require proficiency in another language.
- Students use the language to create imaginary situations.
- Students present information about the language and culture to others.
- Students write and illustrate stories to present to others.
- Students perform for a school or community celebration.

Sample Progress Indicators, Grade 8

- Students discuss their preferences concerning leisure activities and current events, in written form or orally, with peers who speak the language.
- Students interact with members of the local community to hear how they use the language in their various fields of work.
- Students present information about the language and culture to others.
- Students participate in club activities which benefit the school or community.
- Students write and illustrate stories to present to others.
- Students perform for a school or community celebration.

Sample Progress Indicators, Grade 12

- Students communicate orally or in writing with members of the other culture regarding topics of personal interest, community, or world concern.
- Students participate in a career exploration or school-to-work project which requires proficiency in the language and culture.
- Students use community resources to research a topic related to culture and/or language study.
- Students present information about the language and culture to others.
- Students participate in club activities which benefit the school or community.
- Students write and illustrate stories to present to others.
- Students perform for a school or community celebration.

Standards for Foreign Language Learning

COMMUNITIES

STANDARD 5.2 Students show evidence of becoming life-long learners by using the language for personal enjoyment and enrichment.

LANGUAGE STUDENTS GAIN ACCESS TO ENTERTAINMENT AND INFORMATION SOURCES AVAILABLE ONLY TO SPEAKERS OF THOSE LANGUAGES.

Language is an avenue to information and interpersonal relations. Each day millions of Americans spend leisure time reading, listening to music, viewing films and television programs, and interacting with each other. By developing a certain level of comfort with the new language, students can use these skills to access information as they continue to learn throughout their lives. Students who study a language can use their skills to further enrich their personal lives by accessing various entertainment and information sources available to speakers of the other language. Some students may have the opportunity to travel to communities and countries where the language is used extensively and, through this experience, further develop their language skills and understanding of the culture. Many of the Progress Indicators for standard 5.2 are repeated at Grade 4, 8, and 12 to emphasize that the activities may be similar. However, the sophistication and ease with which the activities are performed depend greatly on the student's age and abilities.

Sample Progress Indicators, Grade 4

- Students read materials and/or use media from the language and culture for enjoyment.
- Students play sports or games from the culture.
- Students exchange information about topics of personal interest.
- Students plan real or imaginary travel.
- Students attend or view via media cultural events and social activities.
- Students listen to music, sing songs, or play musical instruments from the target culture.

Sample Progress Indicators, Grade 8

- Students consult various sources in the language to obtain information on topics of personal interest.
- Students play sports or games from the culture.
- Students exchange information around topics of personal interest.
- Students use various media from the language and culture for entertainment.
- Students attend or view via media cultural events and social activities.
- Students listen to music, sing songs, or play musical instruments from the target culture.

COMMUNITIES

Sample Progress Indicators, Grade 12

- Students consult various sources in the language to obtain information on topics of personal interest.

- Students play sports or games from the culture.

- Students read and/or use various media from the language and culture for entertainment or personal growth.

- Students establish and/or maintain interpersonal relations with speakers of the language.

- Students attend or view via media cultural events and social activities.

- Students listen to music, sing songs, or play musical instruments from the target culture.

Conclusions

The challenge and opportunity of writing standards for K-12 learners was exciting and professionally fulfilling for all who joined the process. From the beginning of the project, the standards task force recognized the responsibility it had in attempting to represent the ideas and opinions of professionals in the field. The members of the task force, all practicing teachers, tried to envision these standards in use with all students.

Although this document reflects thousands of comments from teachers, students, researchers, and field testers, it cannot fully capture the complexities of all language learners and all language learning environments. We hope that those who use this document to modify or change fundamentally the way they look at language learning will see these standards as a starting point for more clearly defining what students should know and be able to do as a result of language study.

Standards for Foreign Language Learning in the 21st Century remains a work in progress. As the work of the standards task forces draws to a close, the goals and standards herein will continue to change and evolve as teachers at every level of instruction work toward their implementation. This new publication adds two powerful expansions by providing language-specific standards and by extending standards into higher education. The now K-16 foreign language standards, in the spirit of educational reform, set challenges for schools and teachers, for parents and communities, and certainly for learners. Furthermore, none of this is a "mission impossible," for all the components that support these standards for the twenty-first century currently exist in schools. It is simply that they do not exist in ALL schools for ALL the nation's children.

The standards have the power to act as beacons, as guidelines, for state and local districts in both short- and long-range planning.

STANDARDS FOR FOREIGN LANGUAGE LEARNING: PREPARING FOR THE 21ST CENTURY REMAINS A WORK IN PROGRESS.

Learning Scenarios

Following are a series of Sample Learning Scenarios in which classroom activities that reflect the standards are described. The scenarios have been collected from teachers throughout the country and reflect a wide variety of programs, languages, geographic locations, and school settings. Many of the scenarios originated in schools in the districts that served as pilot sites during the standard-setting process. These districts were Clovis Unified School District, Fresno, CA; Edmonds School District, Lynnwood, WA; Gwinnett County Public Schools, GA; Houston Public Schools, TX; Springfield Public Schools, MA; and Williamston Community Schools, MI. The scenarios should be considered illustrative examples of teaching and learning which incorporate the standards. Those standards applied in the scenario are highlighted prior to the description of each scenario. Following each classroom scenario is a reflection which highlights the "weave" of the scenario, including the curricular elements, such as the language system, communication strategies, culture, learning strategies, other subject areas, critical thinking skills, and technology. The reflection also contains suggestions for adapting or extending the learning activities.

ARTS AND CRAFTS

Students of Italian in upstate New York are studying the crafts of Italy with an emphasis on the products of the different geographic regions (e.g., glass in Venice, alabaster sculpture in Volterra, ceramics in Orvieto, and inlaid wood in Sorrento). Students discuss the differences between arts and crafts, the lifestyles of the people who create or use the crafts, and the information one can learn about a craftsperson from examining his/her work. As an adjunct to this unit, students participate in an Aesthetic Institute unit on the dance called "Quilts" by the Tennessee Dance Theater. This work takes its inspiration from the patterns created by traditional American quilts and from the stories of the people who created them. The students are able to approach this work as a nonverbal extension of the "message" of the craftsperson, and another way to communicate the "passing down" of skills and knowledge through the generations.

TARGETED STANDARDS

1.1 Interpersonal Communication
1.2 Interpretive Communication
1.3 Presentational Communication
2.1 Practices of Culture
2.2 Products of Culture
3.1 Making Connections
3.2 Acquiring Information
4.2 Cultural Comparisons
5.1 School and Community
5.2 Lifelong Learning

Reflection

1.1 Students discuss Italian and American crafts in the target language.
1.2 Students read and view videos on various craftspersons in Italy and interpret that information.
1.3 Students present their interpretations of perceptions on the crafts and craftspersons studied.
2.1 Students identify characteristics of Italian life that gave rise to the targeted crafts.
2.2 Students learn about the practical and aesthetic development of crafts in Italian culture by examining the products.

SAMPLE LEARNING SCENARIOS

3.1 Students reinforce content from their social studies, art, and dance classes.
3.2 Students learn about the lives of craftspersons from authentic sources.
4.2 Students are able to give historically and sociologically correct information on targeted crafts in Italy and the United States; students discuss the artistic and social dynamics of cultures.
5.1 Students work with visiting artists.
5.2 Students gain appreciation for artistry and craftsmanship.

This scenario touches upon the standards in all five goal areas. Because all cultures have unique forms of craftsmanship, this scenario can be adapted for all languages. Similarly, the focus on crafts means that the unit can be adapted for a variety of age groups and levels of language competency. By including works such as "Quilts," students gain an entry-point in the performing arts with the benefit of professional artists in the classroom.

PILOT SITE

CLOVIS UNIFIED SCHOOL DISTRICT FRESNO, CA

The students of Clovis Unified School District exemplify what most Americans think of as "typical" foreign language students. They live in a middle- to upper-middle-income, suburban community. They are highly motivated, competitive, and come from well-educated families. The majority of students are college-bound, and a large number receive credit for Advanced Placement programs. The district offers French, German, Spanish, and Chinese to students in grades 7-12.

TARGETED STANDARDS
1.1 Interpersonal Communication
2.2 Products of Culture
4.2 Cultural Comparisons

BREAD AND CHOCOLATE

Third grade students studying French in Northern California listen as the teacher describes foods typically eaten in France and typically eaten in the United States, such as *pain au chocolat* and sourdough bread with peanut butter. The students sample some food brought by the teacher. They share their impressions, describing the food in French and commenting on how it tastes. Generally, students take a piece of the *pain au chocolat*, and a couple of them like the new taste. Three students decide they don't care for the new taste. When the time comes for other students to try something new, most of them decide they won't like it and decline the offer. The teacher then asks who would like peanut butter and bread, and the whole class finds the offer irresistible. While the students are enjoying their peanut butter and bread, they learn from the teacher that most people in France would not enjoy this combination of foods. The students compare the tastes of the French and Americans and discuss the differences in food preferences. They are surprised to learn that something they consider to be tasty is not necessarily considered so by others. Some of the students then ask to try the *pain au chocolat* to experience something new.

Reflection
1.1 Students share their opinions about some foods from France and from the United States.
2.2 Students encounter a new aspect of culture that they would not otherwise know.
4.2 Students express their impressions of similarities and differences between some sampled foods from France and from the United States.

This activity addresses three goals. The students describe the foods and express their likes and dislikes in trying something new. They then compare their reactions to a new taste and to a food with which they are familiar. Finally, they discuss in English how people enjoy dif-

Standards for Foreign Language Learning

SAMPLE LEARNING SCENARIOS

ferent things, and they express their surprise that something that is generally liked in one culture is not shared by another. Similar activities can be implemented using different aspects of culture. In order to avoid stereotyping, it should be noted that customs and preferences may vary within a culture.

BUTTERFLIES

Students at Sanchez Elementary School are fascinated by the yearly migration of butterflies. Their interest is channeled into an expansive interdisciplinary learning project. The art teacher helps them make butterflies from origami and tissue paper. In language arts, students are doing research and writing a report on the

> **TARGETED STANDARDS**
> 1.1 Interpersonal Communication
> 1.3 Presentational Communication
> 3.1 Making Connections

butterfly. Social studies classes are coloring maps showing the flight path of the monarch butterfly, while math teachers are constructing butterfly shapes to study symmetry. Students in science are learning about the life cycle of a butterfly. Even in health and physical education, Coach Garcia is teaching his students how to do the butterfly stroke and how to use a butterfly band aid. Señorita Rodriguez teaches her students the names for the various parts of the butterfly in Spanish using the samples provided by the art teacher. Students point to the different colors as she calls them out in the target language. Students may also show and tell about their butterflies using familiar adjectives to describe them and identifying the six stages of their life cycle. Working in pairs, students use the cardinal numbers to trace the migration of the monarch butterfly on a map, as well as to provide information regarding shape, color, size, and symmetry. Working in cooperative groups, students are asked to compose a verse about the butterfly. The project culminates with a field trip to a local museum of natural science to observe butterflies in their natural habitat.

Reflection
1.1 Students use the language to identify parts of the butterfly and answer questions.
1.3 Students tell about their butterflies and compose a verse about them.
3.1 Students further their knowledge of butterflies in an interdisciplinary fashion.

This is an example of an integrated curriculum in which each subject seeks to provide learning opportunities for students around a common theme. The learning throughout the day is then reinforced for students, not only through different disciplines, but also through different learning modalities. This interdisciplinary aspect is particularly pertinent to language learning so that students make connections among the disciplines and see an immediate use and application for the other language. This approach is most easily accomplished now in the elementary school setting, but it can be used effectively at the middle and high schools with appropriate planning.

SAMPLE LEARNING SCENARIOS

TARGETED STANDARDS
1.2 Interpretive Communication
2.2 Products of Culture
4.2 Cultural Comparisons

CHINESE CALENDAR

In Ms. Chen-Lin's Chinese class in West Hartford, CT, eighth graders are learning about the Chinese calendar. Students listen to the folkloric tale of how the years got their names, which the teacher explains by using story cards. The students then use artistic expression to recall the details of the story by making posters that announce the race of the twelve animals in the story. They are encouraged to include on their poster the date, time, location, and prize in Chinese. On the next day, the class explores the importance of a calendar in the students' own culture and in others. The students discuss the differences found in the Chinese and American calendars. They then make a calendar using Chinese characters to be used in their homes. They include birthdays, family celebrations, school activities, and other special events.

Reflection

1.2   Students comprehend the story about the Chinese calendar.
2.2   Students read about and discuss expressive products of the culture.
4.2   Students compare and contrast calendars from the two cultures.

In this activity the students understand the calendar explanation more easily because the teacher accompanies the explanation with visuals. The use of artistic expression to check for their understanding allows students with various learning styles to be successful in showing what they understood from the story. The follow-up discussion helps students reflect on the importance of a calendar within a culture and the role that the calendar plays in American culture.

TARGETED STANDARDS
1.3 Presentational Communication
5.1 School and Community

COMMUNITY PROJECT

As a part of a larger school-wide community service project, students at Forest Park Middle School discussed the ways that foreign visitors could be made comfortable in a new community, welcomed by merchants, and encouraged to use municipal services. They concluded that making signs in various languages would demonstrate a community's invitation to visitors to use the services. An eighth grade Spanish class chose the public library as the venue for their work. Working in pairs, partners assembled a list of vocabulary words and then made a directory of places and references where certain items could be found in the library. In addition, they prepared a list of useful expressions that are applicable to library users. Partners then compared and contrasted their individual lists and reported to the whole class; after a brainstorming session, students produced a final list of relevant vocabulary and phrases. The project culminated in the creation of brochures and posters to illustrate useful expressions and designate sections of the library. Finished posters were first displayed in the school building during Foreign Language Week, before being permanently installed in the community library. Spanish brochures were made available to visitors at the reference desk.

Standards for Foreign Language Learning

SAMPLE LEARNING SCENARIOS

Reflection

1.3 Students create brochures for the library.
5.1 Students participate in an activity that benefits the community.

This activity is an example of student use of the language beyond the school setting. Assisting students in identifying and implementing community activities in which they use the language makes the learning relevant to students and helps them envision how they may be able to use the language in their personal lives in the future. Making the directory and signs for the public library would involve students' attention to the language system as any public signs should contain correct spelling and should accurately reflect how language structures are "telescoped." Students would also need to show attention to the cultures reflected in the communities so that appropriate vocabulary would be used.

COMMUNITY SERVICE PROJECT

Members of the Spanish Club at Sanchez High School undertake the clean-up of the old Spanish cemetery a few blocks from the school as their community project. On their first day at the cemetery, they are amazed at the names, birth and death dates, epitaphs, and other information inscribed on the tombstones. The history teacher becomes involved by having her students trace the historical background of some of the names inscribed on the tombstones. The art teacher has her students prepare pencil drawings of the cemetery and create "charcoal shadings/impressions" of interesting tombstones. Students from Spanish classes interview community members in the foreign language to obtain a historical perspective. They also read and study about the Day of the Dead (*El Día de los Muertos*). They follow class discussions of ancient and modern death rituals in Spanish-speaking countries with further study of the verbs "to die" and "to be born," and the numbers up to 1000.

> **TARGETED STANDARDS**
> 1.1 Interpersonal Communication
> 3.1 Making Connections
> 4.1 Language Comparisons
> 4.2 Cultural Comparisons
> 5.1 School and Community

Reflection

1.1 Students conduct interviews with members of the Hispanic community.
3.1 Students further their knowledge of another discipline.
4.1 Students make comparisons between the languages based on a discussion of the syntax.
4.2 Students compare and contrast death rituals.
5.1 Students participate in a club activity which benefits the community.

This is an example of students' use of the language beyond the school setting in an activity that expands the knowledge of the students and benefits the community. The cultural and linguistic elements of the activity ensure that students are enhancing their knowledge in both of these areas. Students may need to use dictionaries to translate some of the epitaphs

Standards for Foreign Language Learning

SAMPLE LEARNING SCENARIOS

written in the target language. Class discussion will include the most effective use of foreign language dictionaries and the linguistic issues involved in literal translations. This project may be easily expanded by comparing the information about the culture with death rituals and practices in various communities in the United States.

TARGETED STANDARDS
1.2 Interpretive Communication
4.2 Cultural Comparisons

CULTURAL COMPARISONS

Students in Ms. Gadbois' French II class at Central High School received an article, written for a teen magazine in France, about a crime that occurred in the U.S. and the unusual sentence given to the criminals. The students discuss the crime, the pros and cons of each possible legal punishment, the view of the French writer toward the event, and how the same crime was treated in the American press. As a follow-up, students write a summary of the article.

Reflection

1.2 Students comprehend the principal elements of non-fiction articles on a topic of current importance.

4.2 Students discuss the point of view of the French author and compare it to the American viewpoint.

This activity offers students the opportunity to view an event through the cultural perspective of a speaker of another language. It helps students to realize that the same event may be portrayed quite differently based on the cultural background of the reporter. By using the authentic source, students read an article that is aimed at their age group and concerns a topic with which they are all familiar. The article could also be the starting point of a discussion of idioms and vocabulary pertinent to an adolescent audience.

TARGETED STANDARDS
1.1 Interpersonal Communication
1.3 Presentational Communication
4.2 Cultural Comparisons

CULTURAL OBSERVATION

In trying to help students understand the similarities and differences between German and American cultures, students in Fresno are asked by their teacher, Ms. Koopman, to view a series of ten slides depicting cultural diversity in Germany. The students study each slide for one minute and note what they see. In groups, the students discuss their observations and each group then reveals three observations to the whole class. They view the slides a second time and their teacher relates to the class the exact nature of each picture. The students then reevaluate their original observations and talk about the varied attitudes found in their own and in German culture. Ms. Koopman then asks the students to keep a journal over the next two-week period in which they jot down various observations about cultural diversity within either the German

Standards for Foreign Language Learning

SAMPLE LEARNING SCENARIOS

or U.S. culture. The students are also asked to draw a political cartoon which illustrates the misunderstandings between two cultures.

Reflection
1.1   Students discuss their reactions to the slides in groups and write down their observations.
1.3   Students present a political cartoon representing cultural diversity.
4.2   Students demonstrate an understanding of how different cultures view diversity.

This type of activity could be used to discuss a variety of topics, such as how people live, dietary habits, dress, and expressive art forms from the culture studied. It could be done with students from elementary school, middle school, or high school with varying degrees of sophistication depending on the developmental level of the students. The final part of the activity, drawing the political cartoon, brings students' higher level thinking skills into play as they must synthesize the activity into a humorous setting.

DAILY SCHEDULES

The students in Monsieur Joseph's seventh grade French class have been learning to describe their daily routines. In their math class, they have been working with percentages, collecting and organizing data, graphing the data, and interpreting the data provided by the graphs. They have also been corresponding via e-mail with "keypals" in Dakar, Senegal. M. Joseph asks students to determine the amount of time they spend each day eating, sleeping, watching TV, and studying (in school or at home). Students determine what percentage of the school day they spend on each of these activities and display the information on a circle graph, labeling the graph in French as appropriate. Students then work in groups of four to compare data on their graphs. Students take turns interpreting the graph of the person on their right, comparing the data on their own graph to that of the other person. At the end of the activity, each student provides a statement that summarizes what the group found and dictates this information to the group recorder. On a subsequent day, students use information they have received through correspondence with "keypals" in Dakar to reflect upon how their daily schedules and allotment of time compare with those of their peers in Senegal.

TARGETED STANDARDS
1.1   Interpersonal Communication
1.2   Interpretive Communication
1.3   Presentational Communication
2.1   Practices of Culture
3.1   Making Connections
4.2   Cultural Comparisons
5.1   School and Community

Reflection
1.1   Students work collaboratively in groups.
1.2   Students comprehend their e-mail messages from Dakar.
1.3   Students present information about themselves to their group.
2.1   Students learn about the practices of the students from Dakar.

PILOT SITE

EDMONDS SCHOOL DISTRICT, LYNNWOOD, WA
Through the Edmonds 2000 initiative, this suburban district of 20,000 students has been involved in the development of world-class standards and assessments in all disciplinary areas. There is a strong commitment to site-based management. Foreign language offerings include French, German, Italian, Japanese, Russian, Spanish, and Swedish. Currently, 225 students in grades 1-6 and 3,428 in grades 7-12 are enrolled in foreign language study.

SAMPLE LEARNING SCENARIOS

3.1 Students make connections between the skills they are learning in math and their French class.
4.2 Students compare and contrast the use of time by the students in Dakar with their own.
5.1 Students use the language beyond their own community.

This activity exemplifies how skills learned in one class can be reinforced in the language class by developing meaningful activities with practical applications for students. Middle school students are focused on their lives and the lives of their peers. This activity takes that natural interest of the student and channels it into a learning activity. This might also be an opportunity for the students to focus on the language structures involved in making comparisons in French.

TARGETED STANDARDS
1.1 Interpersonal Communication
1.2 Interpretive Communication
1.3 Presentational Communication
2.1 Practices of Culture
2.2 Products of Culture
3.1 Making Connections
4.2 Cultural Comparisons

DIEGO RIVERA

The cultural focus of the fourth grade Spanish class at Perkins Elementary School is Mexico. Prior to Diego Rivera's birthday, the class begins its unit based on the book *Diego* by Jan Winters. The teacher uses props and pictures to introduce unfamiliar vocabulary. Total physical response (TPR), active listening, and question/answer activities are used to practice new vocabulary. Students use a map of Mexico to lead into the setting of the story. Students participate in a pair activity in which they instruct their partners, using a map and a toy airplane, to travel to the areas within Mexico that are important to the story and to understand the general orientation of those areas within the country. The teacher reads the story to the students several times. They illustrate and label selected scenes from the book, orally tell the story in sequence, and participate in time line and story mapping activities after the readings. The teacher shares with the students many examples of Diego Rivera's works. In small groups, they talk about what they like and do not like about the paintings, and they make lists of the topics depicted in the murals. The students create a mural with the art teacher based on the time line of Diego Rivera's life that reflects the sequence of their own lives. The foreign language teacher facilitates the writing of a language experience story about the mural.

Reflection
1.1 Students engage in conversations about the story and Diego Rivera's works.
1.2 Students comprehend the story when told by the teacher.
1.3 Students present information about the story.
2.1 Students understand the cultural practices depicted in the works of Rivera.
2.2 Students become familiar with cultural products of Mexico (Rivera's murals).
3.1 Students make connections with other disciplines (art and social studies).
4.2 Students compare the life of Rivera with their own.

SAMPLE LEARNING SCENARIOS

The basis for this activity is a work of children's literature based on the life of Diego Rivera. The techniques used by the teacher help students in an elementary FLES (Foreign Language in Elementary School) program to understand the story. Learners make a connection between the artist's life and medium (murals) with their own life. Once again, the element of culture undergirds the context for this activity.

DINOSAURS

Kindergarteners at Rockbridge Elementary School are learning about dinosaurs with the typical fascination that this subject holds for young students. To complement their study of this topic, their teacher, Señora Matos, develops an activity for their FLES Spanish class with the cooperation of the art teacher. The students use construction paper to create a "Jurassic Mountain" in the classroom. In Spanish, they learn the words for *tree*, *mountain*, and other elements of their newly created environment. However, the teacher and students realize that something is missing: the dinosaurs. Students are asked to bring dinosaurs to school, and on the next day their "Jurassic Mountain" and two other tables are covered with dinosaurs. After learning the vocabulary in Spanish, the students identify and describe the dinosaurs and classify them by size, color, and other characteristics (gentle, fierce, etc.). Students then make brightly colored papier-mâché dinosaurs as well as dioramas reflecting the appropriate habitat for their dinosaurs. At the end of the week, Señora Matos has twenty-one diverse dinosaur dioramas to be shared with the school community.

> **TARGETED STANDARDS**
> 1.2 Interpretive Communication
> 1.3 Presentational Communication
> 2.2 Products of Culture
> 3.1 Making Connections
> 5.1 School and Community

Reflection
1.2 Students understand the presentations of their classmates.
1.3 Students present information about their dinosaurs to fellow students.
2.2 Students use art media and colors that reflect Hispanic culture.
3.1 Students reinforce and further their knowledge of prehistoric life.
5.1 Students use the language within the school setting.

This scenario could occur in any language with beginners at any grade level. The content would depend on the setting. The scenario might be played out using such topics as mythical figures, medieval artisan shops, or signs of the Chinese calendar in cooperation with teachers from various disciplines. The curricular weave is highlighted in the classification aspect of the activity in which students use critical thinking skills to organize and classify the dinosaurs. By encouraging students to ask and answer questions of each other, a focus on Standard 1.1, Interpersonal Communication, could be added to this activity.

SAMPLE LEARNING SCENARIOS

PILOT SITE

GWINNETT COUNTY PUBLIC SCHOOLS LAWRENCEVILLE, GA

Gwinnett County Public Schools is a large, suburban district thirty miles northeast of Atlanta with a total student population of 75,000. The district is becoming increasingly diverse both ethnically and linguistically. Some 4,000 students speak a language other than English at home. More than 60 different languages are spoken by Gwinnett students, and the county is home to many international companies. Foreign language study is available to students beginning in the elementary grades (primarily in the form of exploratory programs) through high school. Languages offered include French, German, Japanese, Latin, Spanish, and Russian.

TARGETED STANDARDS

1.1 Interpersonal Communication
1.2 Interpretive Communication
2.1 Practices of Culture
2.2 Products of Culture
3.1 Making Connections

DOING BUSINESS IN JAPAN

Students in Mariko Jeffrey's seventh grade Japanese class have been learning Japanese for six years through a partial-immersion program. In this activity, they begin by comparing the geography of Japan with the geography of the United States and the various regional products that are available for export to other countries. Based on this information, the teacher leads the students in a discussion of products whose import and export might benefit Japanese and American businesses. From this discussion, the teacher introduces the concept of the business card in Japanese society. Using authentic business cards, students identify the types of information included. They then make their own business cards representing a product that they had suggested for export. As a final activity, students pair up and introduce themselves and their product to each other.

Reflection

1.1 Students introduce themselves and their products to each other.
1.2 Students listen to the teacher's explanations of the concept of the business card.
2.1 Students learn about the practice of exchanging business cards in Japanese society.
2.2 Students understand the role of the business card and its use.
3.1 Students learn about the various geographic features of Japan and their influence on products that are available for export.

In this scenario, the students are involved in making the transition from an elementary partial-immersion program that focused on the elementary school curriculum to the high school language program that focuses on the language. Students have a high level of listening proficiency, but need to be exposed to communicative oral activities such as introducing themselves and presenting product information. The teacher necessarily focuses on the writing system as students need to systematically increase their knowledge of Kanji. There may also be grammatical features that need to be discussed more formally than would be addressed in the elementary school program. The geographic and economic concepts maintain students' interest as they increase their knowledge of Japanese language and culture.

TARGETED STANDARDS

1.2 Interpretive Communication
1.3 Presentational Communication
5.1 School and Community

FAIRY TALES

Each student in the Spanish III class at Shiloh High School reads a fairy tale from the target language culture in order to gather information and learn the vocabulary used in this type of story. After researching the vocabulary and studying the grammatical structures, students select the information that best expresses the principal ideas and themes of the story. Students summarize this information in phrases to demonstrate an

SAMPLE LEARNING SCENARIOS

understanding of the material. Then, key verbs in the story are used in sentences. Once this activity is finished, students begin an analysis of the story in the target language. They discuss physical appearance, intellectual traits, cultural practices and perspectives, and notable characteristics of the characters. They also talk about the characters' contributions to the story, the principal and secondary themes, and the climax of the story. In pairs or small groups, students select two stories to be combined into one for the purpose of creating one new story. In order to write the new fairy tale, students discuss the characters and their function in the new story, organize the characters to fit the new theme and plot, evaluate the new situations, and provide solutions to problems and conflicts. Upon completion, each new story is then presented orally through dramatizations. Students use puppets, marionettes, or a felt board for story telling. The written story is presented in the form of a pop-up book where each page has three-dimensional illustrations and a text for narration. Each new story is videotaped for enjoyment and error correction. The written and videotaped versions of the fairy tales are kept as a part of the classroom library.

Reflection
1.2 Students read the fairy tale.
1.3 Students present their fairy tale orally or through dramatization.
5.1 Students write stories to present to others.

In this activity, students focus on the language structures and vocabulary within the authentic cultural context of a fairy tale. The process of putting the characters and themes into a new story involves the use of higher level thinking skills. The presentation aspect is a good vehicle for student expression in the target language. The students also focus as a group on error correction by pointing out common errors made on the tapes. This might be appropriately done before the final version is filmed or taped.

FILM

Viewing a film in another language is an effective way to expose students to native speakers and to provide them with an opportunity to see how people live and react to the world they inhabit. *Indochine,* a French film which takes place in Indochina in the early 1920s to 1950s, is the story of a French rubber plantation owner, her family, and how French colonialism, communism, and other social and political events completely changed their lives. Before viewing the film, Mrs. Gibson's III and IV classes at Meadowcreek High School had a short discussion of Indochina at the time period of the film. It was important to establish the history and context of France's involvement and colonial experience in Indochina. The film, 2 1/2 hours

TARGETED STANDARDS
1.2 Interpretive Communication
1.3 Presentational Communication
2.1 Practices of Culture
3.1 Making Connections
5.2 Lifelong Learning

Standards for Foreign Language Learning

SAMPLE LEARNING SCENARIOS

long, was divided into forty-minute segments, so that a discussion could occur after each segment. After the film, students wrote a "response to literature" essay, in which they summarized their personal reaction to the film, its themes, and what new information and perspectives they had gained.

Reflection

1.2   Students view the film in French.
1.3   Students write a reaction to the film.
2.1   Students gain insight into the patterns of behavior of the culture studied.
3.1   Students further their knowledge of geography and history.
5.2   Students view a French feature film.

Viewing a full-length feature film can be daunting to language learners. In this example, the teacher has effectively divided the film into smaller segments with a discussion following each part. By setting the stage with the necessary background information, the teacher prepares the students to comprehend the film effectively. Students gain a level of confidence about functioning within a culture other than their own when their classroom learning experiences include activities such as this one.

> **TARGETED STANDARDS**
>
> 1.2 Interpretive Communication
> 1.3 Presentational Communication
> 2.1 Practices of Culture
> 2.2 Products of Culture
> 3.1 Making Connections
> 4.2 Cultural Comparisons
> 5.1 School and Community

GEOGRAPHY

In many school districts, third graders study other countries and cultures in social studies. By third grade, students understand the concepts of countries and continents. They know that many cultures are represented in the United States, and they are beginning to explore the diversity of the peoples of the world. Classroom teachers may choose to study a country in Asia or Africa as a part of the third grade social studies program. The language teacher can then present information about these world regions in the language class. For example, third graders studying Spanish at Naubuc Elementary School are also studying about the country of Ghana. Even though Ghana is not a Spanish-speaking country, students use Spanish to review world geography and locate Ghana on the African continent. The language teacher, Ms. Trusz, reinforces concepts already presented in social studies by teaching the vocabulary for the products, languages, animals, weather, geography, etc., of the country. Because Ghana is a country near the equator, and many Spanish-speaking people also live in equatorial countries, the vocabulary and concepts learned about Africa reinforce information already presented about the target culture. After being asked to brainstorm the similarities and differences among a community in Ghana, a Spanish-speaking community, and their local community, the students then write several

SAMPLE LEARNING SCENARIOS

paragraphs or develop projects about Ghana in Spanish which depict these similarities and differences. The language class includes students who speak Spanish as a first language. These students are able to enrich the authenticity of the language experience by adding their insights about the local Spanish-speaking community.

Reflection

1.2   Students comprehend information about life in Ghana.
1.3   Students prepare projects and/or writing assignments for others to read.
2.1   Students learn about the cultural practices of the communities.
2.2   Students learn about the cultural products of the communities.
3.1   Students further their understanding of world geography.
4.2   Students compare and contrast life in the local community, a Spanish-speaking community, and a community in Ghana.
5.1   Students use the language in the school setting.

This scenario relates what students learn in other disciplines and what they know about the culture of the language studied to their own life experiences. The fact that native speakers of Spanish are in the class allows the teacher to vary the assignment in order to challenge students. Other topics which might be addressed in this way include schooling, professions, and political systems. The use of a Venn diagram to help students visualize the organization of the similarities and differences among the communities would encourage these young students to use high level thinking skills in organizing their writing. By including Ghana, the Spanish-speaking community, and the local community in the discussion, the students are developing a multicultural perspective that can be applied to other settings.

GUEST SPEAKER

Second year French students at Central High School listen to Monsieur Mensah, a substitute teacher in the school, describe his country, Togo, and its customs in the target language. Each student asks him two questions in French about a topic of particular interest to him/her. The visit is a success for both the visitor and

> **TARGETED STANDARDS**
> 1.1   Interpersonal Communication
> 1.2   Interpretive Communication
> 3.1   Making Connections
> 5.1   School and Community

the students. The guest is impressed by the courtesy of the class and the students' ability to comprehend his language, and the students marvel at the story of Togo, its importance in African history, and the fact that it is the second-ranked African country in attracting tourists. M. Mensah is an excellent role model as he explains the importance of French in his country, why he speaks it, the fact that his parents do not, and what opportunities it has presented to him in his lifetime. The students then prepare a resumé of what they have learned from M. Mensah in either cassette or written essay form. As a follow up, the students will research Togo via the Internet and CD-ROM.

Standards for Foreign Language Learning

SAMPLE LEARNING SCENARIOS

Reflection

1.1 Students ask questions of the visitor.
1.2 Students comprehend the main ideas and some details.
3.1 Students further their knowledge of an African country.
5.1 Students communicate with members of the other culture.

The teacher might use this opportunity to review the language system in terms of asking questions, since the students developed questions to ask the visitor. The focus on interrogatives would help students refine their language skills in this area. The follow-up using the Internet and CD-ROM would bring technology into the extension activity.

TARGETED STANDARDS

1.1 Interpersonal Communication
5.1 School and Community
5.2 Lifelong Learning

HOCKEY LESSON

Students in Long Island, New York, learn about hockey first-hand from players for the New York Islanders who were born in Canada and were raised speaking French. Teacher David Graham, from Plainview Kennedy High School, wants to give his students a French lesson in hockey so he arranges for two players from the Islanders team to address his French students. The students spend several hours asking questions in French about professional hockey and the players' personal lives. Afterwards, the students attend a specially priced hockey game with their parents in which the Islanders play opposite the Montreal Canadiens.

Reflection

1.1 Students ask questions of the players.
5.1 Students participate in a community activity.
5.2 Students show evidence of enjoyment of the language.

The teacher reports that several months after this activity the students are still excited about the experience. Having the students attend the game in addition to the assembly was important, he says, because "it takes the kids' interest in sports and ties it directly to learning a foreign language." This activity could be replicated in Spanish classes with Hispanic members of soccer teams or in German classes by interviews with German tennis players.

TARGETED STANDARDS

1.1 Interpersonal Communication
1.2 Interpretive Communication
3.1 Making Connections
3.2 Acquiring Information

INTERNATIONAL SCIENCE

Students in Ms. Welch's biology class in Jessamine County High School have been working in teams to study viruses, conducting experiments in the lab while researching a particular strain of viral infection. One team has become intrigued by the work done at the

SAMPLE LEARNING SCENARIOS

Pasteur Institute in the exploration of the virus which causes AIDS. Maria and John are both taking French and know that they could probably add significantly to the biology class if they were able to contribute information about the Institute and its work. They obtain the address of the Institute through a Minitel (national database in France) search using John's computer at home. Not finding an e-mail address, the pair decides to write the Institute and request information regarding work on the virus. The jointly composed letter becomes an entry in each of their French writing portfolios. After four long weeks, a packet of materials finally arrives. The pair is disappointed to find that the items in the packet are almost all in English. Discussion of the virus has become old news in the biology class as new topics have replaced virus study. John and Maria, however, are intrigued to find that the French perspective of the history of the discovery of the HIV virus differs subtly from what they had assumed after reading in biology class. Ms. Welch is pleased with their initiative, interested in the perspective they noticed about the research, and invites the students to share the information with classmates during a formal presentation to the rest of the class. Rather than focusing exclusively on viral infections, the ensuing discussion centers on competition in science, the scientific process, and reasons why much of the technical work in the field is written in English.

Reflection

1.1 Students compose a letter to send to the Pasteur Institute.
1.2 Students read the few materials in French that they received from the Institute.
3.1 Students further their knowledge of the virus.
3.2 Students realize that the French perspective of the discovery of the virus varies from the American.

This activity is an example of students learning to view a topic through the perspective of another culture. After realizing that the history of the HIV virus was treated slightly differently in an article written in French, students could then identify a series of current events and analyze how these topics are handled by the press in various French-speaking countries. Students would use critical thinking skills to conduct the analyses of the various treatments.

JOURNAL WRITING

Students in the German III class at Las Cruces High School write entries in a journal four times a week. The journals are written outside of class, and students are free to write on topics of their own interest. One of their weekly journal entries is the discussion of an article of the students' choice. The school has a subscription to a German newspaper and to a weekly magazine, and issues are available for the students to take home. Some of the students have access to the Internet and have found reading materials there to review in their journals.

TARGETED STANDARDS
1.2 Interpretive Communication
1.3 Presentational Communication
5.2 Lifelong Learning

PILOT SITE

HOUSTON INDEPENDENT SCHOOL DISTRICT, TX
The Houston Independent School District is a complex, urban organization that serves a dynamic, highly diversified community. The largest district in Texas, serving over 200,000 students, it now also ranks as the fifth largest in the nation. Six elementary schools, twenty-six middle schools, and twenty-six high schools provide programs in foreign languages to over 12,000 students. The most commonly taught languages are Spanish, French, and German. Other languages taught in the district include Latin, Italian, Russian, Chinese, Hindi, Hebrew, and Arabic.

Standards for Foreign Language Learning

SAMPLE LEARNING SCENARIOS

Soon the language department will have a satellite dish and access to *Deutsche Welle TV*. Their teacher plans to videotape various programs which the students can then view at home and discuss in their weekly journals.

Reflection

1.2 Students interpret articles and videos.
1.3 Students write reactions to the articles and videos.
5.2 Students use media from the culture to obtain information on topics of personal interest.

To target Standard 1.3, the students could prepare an analysis of current events, and time could be set aside each week for students to share what they have read or viewed with their classmates. The students could also use these authentic documents to identify, discuss and analyze such products of the culture as social, economic, and political institutions and thus target Standard 2.2. The teacher also helps students focus on individual difficulties with using the language system by highlighting common errors in language usage when reacting to the students' journal entries. This would not be done by correcting errors for the student, but by calling attention to areas in which students need to improve. Peer editing is another effective way to help students improve writing skills by providing an audience other than the teacher for the student writing.

TARGETED STANDARDS

1.1 Interpersonal Communication
3.1 Making Connections
3.2 Acquiring Information
5.1 School and Community
5.2 Lifelong Learning

MINITEL PROJECT

Madame Nelson's eighth graders rush into the classroom and eagerly gather at the computer to check for responses from their French penpals on the Minitel chat line. They have been able to correspond with thirteen-year-olds from a school in southern France by using the French national database (Minitel) to connect with their peers in France. Mme Nelson's students are in their second year of French, so they are able to write to their French counterparts and ask questions about a typical school day, life in French communities, and what students there like to do for fun. They are also able to share this information about themselves in French. Today in class they download the French students' responses onto their own disks. They exit Minitel and then read the responses and formulate questions and answers for their next communication. Approximately half of the class period is spent on this activity. Then their attention turns to the next assignment, in which Mme Nelson gives each group a specific amount of money and they must decide how they will spend it while dining in Paris. They return to the Minitel and access a list of restaurants in Paris and the menus of the fare offered. They are able to select menu items for a full French meal and calculate the amount spent in francs. The groups then evaluate the work of the others by ascertaining how balanced the meal was, how close the group came to spending the amount

Standards for Foreign Language Learning

SAMPLE LEARNING SCENARIOS

assigned, and whether an appropriate tip was given. The assignment for tonight is to calculate the equivalency of the amount each group spent in francs with American dollars.

Reflection

1.1   Students correspond with French "keypals."
3.1   Students discuss the nutritional value of their meal and calculate expenses.
3.2   Using technology, students access and use menus from French restaurants.
5.1   Students use the language to discuss the project with their classmates.
5.2   Students show evidence of being able to order from a French menu.

This scenario exemplifies how technology facilitates language learning and plays a role in motivating students to use the foreign language with peers. It also highlights the visionary aspect of the standards. Although some classrooms have access to Minitel, it is certainly not the norm in classrooms across the country. How soon technology will become more prevalent in language classrooms is difficult to tell. What is clear is that technology will play a critical role in bringing native speakers and current information from the culture into the classroom. The teacher can enhance the language competence of students by focusing on communication strategies from the "weave" of language learning, so that students will know how to keep the communication going with their peers even if they are not certain how to express themselves.

MYSTERY CLASS

To review material learned the previous year, students in this German II class are asked by their teacher, Sue Webber, to write a description of themselves as well as information about where they live and their interests. The students then photograph themselves holding

> **TARGETED STANDARDS**
> 1.3   Presentational Communication
> 5.1   School and Community

items that represent their hobby (e.g., fishing pole and net for salmon). Each student's picture is numbered, and the package of descriptions and pictures is mailed to the partner school. The receiving school's students read each letter and match the letter with the picture. They also guess at the location of the mystery school based on the information given by the students in their letters that might suggest region or place. Since the school is on the Internet, it is a quick process to see if the students guess correctly.

Reflections

1.3   Students write information about themselves and where they live.
5.1   Students use their language to interact beyond their own school setting.

This activity combines technology with a review of basic structures from German I and the high interest provided by communicating information with peers. This activity provides the basis for long-term communication among the students in which they may share cultur-

Standards for Foreign Language Learning   **87**

SAMPLE LEARNING SCENARIOS

al information such as use of the telephone, doors open vs. doors closed in a home, parental attention to teens' whereabouts, etc. The students are able to reflect on their own culture by reading what German students say about the differences they see between the cultures.

PILOT SITE

PUBLIC SCHOOLS OF SPRINGFIELD, MA

The second largest city in the state, Springfield is a racially and ethnically diverse community. The public school system serves a pre-K-12 student population of 24,000 with a racial and ethnic distribution that is 33% white, 29% non-white, 2% Asian, and 36% Spanish-surnamed. Sixty-two percent of the students are reported in the low-income category according to established guidelines. Eighteen schools (9 elementary, 5 middle, and 4 senior high) offer language programs to 8,500 students. Languages available include Chinese, French, German, Italian, Japanese, Latin, Russian, Spanish and Classical Greek.

TARGETED STANDARDS
- 1.1 Interpersonal Communication
- 1.2 Interpretive Communication
- 2.1 Practices of Culture
- 2.2 Products of Culture
- 3.2 Acquiring Information
- 4.1 Language Comparisons
- 4.2 Cultural Comparisons
- 5.1 School and Community

NEW YEAR'S CELEBRATION

High school students in Springfield are preparing for a Chinese New Year's Celebration in their second-year Chinese class. They read materials in Chinese and in English on the celebration, which explains several aspects of the tradition. They also view a videotape explaining the extended celebration and preparation for it. The students then discuss the perspectives, products, and practices depicted in the film and reading materials, comparing their own experiences celebrating an American New Year. Earlier in the year they had made origami "good luck wishers" and red envelopes for money. One day is spent designing cards and invitations for the New Year's celebration. Special attention is paid not only to words for the event but also to the appropriate colors. They learn how to care for the calligraphy set, grinding ink and washing brushes, and they practice the basic strokes before writing the characters on rice paper. The calligraphy work is then displayed in the school library prior to the celebration. The classes then listen and learn the words to a New Year's song and practice dance steps. After making a lion's head, they perform the lion dance for the school and in the community.

Reflection
- 1.1 Students work together to plan the celebration.
- 1.2 Students read and view materials in the language.
- 2.1 Students learn about and participate in the celebration.
- 2.2 Students experience expressive products of the culture.
- 3.2 Students learn through the language about the significance of the celebration.
- 4.1 Students analyze New Year's greetings in the two cultures.
- 4.2 Students compare celebrations.
- 5.1 Students interact with each other and perform in the community.

This scenario addresses standards in each of the five goal areas. The activities can be done within a variety of cultural contexts focusing on celebrations such as birthdays, Halloween and *El Día de los Muertos*, or Christmas. This scenario could be adapted to accommodate students in elementary and middle school programs. The focus on comparing and contrasting New Year's celebrations brings critical thinking skills into play, undergirded by cultural knowledge.

SAMPLE LEARNING SCENARIOS

NEWSCAST

In the Spanish II classes in Williamston High School, students work in groups to write, produce, and videotape a fifteen to twenty minute news show that includes current events; a live, on-the-scene report; weather; sports; and commercials. The news events include items from the Spanish-speaking world, the U.S., state, and local areas.

TARGETED STANDARDS

1.1 Interpersonal Communication
1.3 Presentational Communication
2.1 Practices of Culture
3.1 Making Connections
5.1 School and Community
5.2 Lifelong Learning

Reflection

1.1   Students work in groups to produce the newscast.
1.3   Students present the newscast.
2.1   Students reflect a perspective from the culture studied in the news stories.
3.1   Students develop news items using information from many fields.
5.1   Students create a context for using the language in the classroom.
5.2   Students develop insights necessary for media literacy.

If the students were asked to view taped newscasts and commercials from two Spanish-speaking countries and use them as models for their project, an emphasis could be placed on Standard 1.2, Interpretive Communication, and Standard 3.2, Acquiring Information. By watching foreign language broadcasts, students are acquiring information in a form that is not available to them in English. Standard 4.1 could be included by having students view newscasts and compare and contrast language styles. Students could also be asked to note cultural similarities and differences in the videotapes they viewed. This type of preparation for the project would also provide the opportunity to target Standard 2.2, with students analyzing a product of the culture studied.

NEWSPAPER

Señor Fernandez' students listened to a presentation from a professional journalist on publishing the *Mundo Hispánico* in Atlanta. The guest speaker described the process leading up to the publication of an issue in Spanish. The students take notes during this presentation, which is conducted in Spanish. Small groups of students select specific tasks listed by the guest speaker as necessary for the production of their newspaper: editorials, interviews, entertainment highlights, cartoon strips, "Querida Carmen" (similary to *Dear Abby*), sports summaries, and a horoscope. In addition, each student writes a short story. Students are not only required to prepare the information assigned to them but also to present updates on their progress to the whole class. The students produce a Spanish newspaper. They work

TARGETED STANDARDS

1.2 Interpretive Communication
1.3 Presentational Communication
3.1 Making Connections
5.1 School and Community

Standards for Foreign Language Learning

SAMPLE LEARNING SCENARIOS

collectively on editing, rewrites, and format. Three students work at the computers. The students are very proud of their finished product and share the Spanish edition with other classes.

Reflection
1.2 Students listen to the presentation of the professional journalist and take notes.
1.3 Students write an article for a student publication.
3.1 Students further their understanding of media literacy.
5.1 Students interact with members of the local community involved in a variety of professions.

This activity effectively involves students with members of the community who use the language on a daily basis in their professions. Learners also apply skills from the writing process and the technology of desktop publishing to the project. In addition, because the students share their product with their peers, there is an audience other than the teacher. This is a crucial element in motivating students to use the language correctly. The activity could be extended by publishing the newspaper on a regular basis and involving the students from other Spanish classes by having them submit letters to the editor and questions to the "Querida Carmen" column.

TARGETED STANDARDS
1.1 Interpersonal Communication

PEN PALS AND "KEY PALS"

In classrooms in Glastonbury, CT, and Palo Alto, CA, sixth graders exchange e-mail and letters with each other in Spanish. Their teachers have facilitated the communication, and once a week the students exchange information on various topics with their pals across the continent. They discuss their families, hobbies and interests, school life, and plans for the upcoming vacation. Some trade photos and brochures from their community for use in a social studies project.

Reflection
1.1 Students describe people and things in their environment and ask questions to obtain information; students write informal messages to each other.

The importance of this activity is that students are seeing a relevant and immediate application of their language learning. Although technology is used for e-mail communication, some students are also writing letters. Students are motivated to find out how their peers across the country are dealing with the same issues they are. This activity can be expanded to involve students in the target language country.

SAMPLE LEARNING SCENARIOS

PRE-ROMAN ITALY

Students in the Italian V class of T.R. Proctor Senior High School make a comparative study of the life and culture of pre-Roman Italy, concentrating on the creations and contributions of the Greek colonies of southern Italy and the Etruscan communities of central Italy. Research and discussion include daily life, towns, religion, and the arts. Students make particular note of the contributions of these cultures that are still seen and used today (i.e., Etruscan arch and funerary art, Greek architecture, city planning, and theater). Students extrapolate information on the lives of the Etruscans by studying their tomb frescoes. In small groups, students then create a series of frescoes depicting the "life-journey" of a modern person. Each group then tries to interpret the work of the other groups as if the frescoes were unearthed in the year 4000. After studying some of the Greek myths and legends that take place in Italy, students create classical theater masks for a videotaped dramatization of the legend of Ulysses and the Cyclops.

TARGETED STANDARDS	
1.1	Interpersonal Communication
1.2	Interpretive Communication
1.3	Presentational Communication
2.1	Practices of Culture
2.2	Products of Culture
3.1	Making Connections
3.2	Acquiring Information
4.1	Language Comparisons
4.2	Cultural Comparisons
5.2	Lifelong Learning

Reflection

1.1 Students use language to discuss their findings of pre-Roman life; they work in groups to produce the murals and the play.
1.2 Students read and interpret the messages of a pictorial history (mural) and the moral of a classical myth.
1.3 Students perform a dramatization.
2.1 Students learn about the development of artistic and theatrical traditions in western culture.
2.2 Students identify elements of pre-Roman architecture, sculpture, theater, city planning, etc.
3.1 Students make connections to disciplines of social studies, history, and the arts.
3.2 Students extrapolate the causes for the results of the evolution of Italian culture from its ancient roots.
4.1 Students develop the ability to express conjecture by the use of grammatical formulas peculiar to Italian, as well as revisit corresponding structures in English.
4.2 Students discuss the artistic and social dynamics of cultures.
5.2 By developing a knowledge of fundamental concepts in art, architecture, drama, and social structure, students will better understand and appreciate new encounters in those areas.

This scenario touches upon the standards in all five of the goal areas. Activities are adaptable to various levels. The unit lends itself to cooperative, aesthetic, and interdisciplinary ap-

SAMPLE LEARNING SCENARIOS

proaches. Similar scenarios could be designed on a variety of topics that are of particular interest to students or in which the teacher has a particular specialization.

> **TARGETED STANDARDS**
> 1.1 Interpersonal Communication
> 2.2 Products of Culture

PUERTO RICO HERE WE COME!

In order to acquaint students with the culture of the language they are learning, kindergarteners in Rockbridge Elementary School's FLEX (Foreign Language Experience) program learn about the culture of Puerto Rico and the traditional dishes that are eaten in this culture. A map and pictures of the island give the students a better view of its location, but original music, traditional dress, traditional food, and authentic musical instruments are still missing. In order to become familiar with these cultural aspects, the students decide to "take a trip" to the island of Puerto Rico in the form of an extended role play. The sound of an airplane departing and arriving is used to make this activity more exciting. After they "arrive" on the island, they listen to taped, authentic music. Using pictures and photographs, they take a trip around the island looking at various things, including traditional homes and dress. Students listen to the vocabulary and repeat it after the teacher. After they "travel" and have fun going from place to place, they are hungry. What better way of ending this activity than eating a traditional dish from the island: *arroz con pollo y habichuelas*.

Reflection

1.1 Students learn pertinent vocabulary and ask and answer simple questions about Puerto Rico.
2.2 Students see, hear, and sample various products of the culture studied.

This activity exemplifies the rich experiences that can be provided in a FLEX class. The students are actively involved in learning about the culture in a hands-on experience. The language is introduced as it relates to the cultural topics. A variety of modalities and senses are used so that students are able to "experience" the culture. This activity may be adapted for any grade level or language program model.

> **TARGETED STANDARDS**
> 1.2 Interpretive Communication
> 1.3 Presentational Communication
> 3.2 Acquiring Information
> 5.2 Lifelong Learning

RESEARCH PORTFOLIO

Second year students in Gwinnett County complete an in-depth study of a Spanish-speaking country in this hemisphere in a multi-step process during the semester. In the school media center, the high school students are introduced to the "Countries of the World" CD-ROM program and *DC Newsbank*, in addition to traditional resources in the form of encyclopedias, maps, etc. Some of the reference sources are available in Spanish. The students produce a portfolio with the following components: a travel brochure describing the

SAMPLE LEARNING SCENARIOS

country they select; an article in Spanish from the media resources, as well as three pictures, maps and/or drawings; a biography of a famous person from the country; the recipe of a national dish; a song (performed and recorded on an audio or video tape); and an item of the student's choice related to the environment, economics, or politics. The portfolios are kept in the classroom for later use as reference.

Reflection

1.2   Students read the information provided on the CD-ROM and in print.
1.3   Students prepare materials for inclusion in the portfolio.
3.2   Students acquire information from authentic documents.
5.2   Students consult resources to obtain information on a topic of interest.

This activity demonstrates to students how to access information from the community on a topic of interest. Technology applications are made during this process as students make selections for inclusion in the portfolio. Students are guided through the process, but are also allowed to select an item related to their own interest. The fact that the portfolio will remain in the classroom as a resource for other students makes this activity highly motivating and relevant for the students. The teacher could include peer editing in the process in order to improve the level of accuracy in the materials developed.

RITES OF PASSAGE

The students in Señora Juarez' seventh grade Spanish class in a Dade County middle school have been discussing the traditions in Spanish-speaking countries for identifying when one enters "adulthood." They have been comparing and contrasting ceremonies and rituals, such as the "*los quince años*" with "Sweet Sixteen" parties in the United States. They have also discussed first communions and other religious coming-of-age celebrations. They have made a chart of specific rights and responsibilities that are granted at certain ages in the United States, such as getting a driver's license and being able to vote. Since these students have been learning Spanish since the second grade, they have an extensive vocabulary and are able to communicate on a wide variety of topics relating to their personal interests and needs. From this background, they develop a questionnaire regarding these rites of passage and are assigned to survey at least five members of the Spanish-speaking community and five members of other ethnic backgrounds. Working in groups, they collect and analyze the responses and make summary statements regarding the traditions about one's passage to adulthood in American culture and in the Spanish-speaking world.

TARGETED STANDARDS
1.1   Interpersonal Communication
1.2   Interpretive Communication
2.1   Practices of Culture
4.2   Cultural Comparisons
5.1   School and Community

PILOT SITE

WILLIAMSTON COMMUNITY SCHOOLS WILLIAMSTON, MI
Williamston Community Schools serve a total student population of fewer than 1700, almost all of whom are involved in foreign language study. Until their elementary teacher moved away, this small, rural community supported a K-12 sequence of Spanish instruction. Currently, the district maintains its program for grades 6-12.

SAMPLE LEARNING SCENARIOS

Reflection
1.1 Students discuss the topic of coming of age.
1.2 Students comprehend significant details from their interviews.
2.1 Students learn how the other country views coming of age.
4.2 Students analyze societal rites of passage in their own culture and in the culture studied.
5.1 Students use the language in the school and in the local community.

Using geography textbooks from the culture studied, students could research how cultures in various parts of the world mark the coming of age. In some instances they might participate in celebrations which occur in these cultures or reenact some of the celebrations themselves. Participating in a celebration outside of school would add a focus on Standard 5.2, Lifelong Learning. Reenacting such a celebration would provide the opportunity to target Standard 1.3, Presentational Communication. Other topics that might be addressed in this manner include marriage and death rituals.

THE ROMAN FAMILY

> **TARGETED STANDARDS**
> 1.1 Interpersonal Communication
> 1.2 Interpretive Communication
> 2.1 Practices of Culture
> 2.2 Products of Culture
> 4.1 Language Comparisons
> 4.2 Cultural Comparisons

When Ms. Bauer presents the Roman family in her first-year Latin class in Fairfax County, the students practice simple sentences aloud and answer questions in Latin regarding the members of the family, what they are wearing, and what they are doing in the picture. This leads to a discussion of the role of each family member in ancient Rome: the father as head of the household; the mother as the primary teacher of the daughter, who marries around the age of twelve; and the son as the student who learns to conduct business as his father does. Ms. Bauer then asks the students to discuss how the family roles in American culture are different and some of the reasons for these differences. Students who have a background in other cultures are encouraged to discuss the roles of family members of their culture. Ms. Bauer then introduces the students to a passage in Latin that discusses the Roman family, which the students are easily able to comprehend because of the prior oral and visual preparation. Finally, Ms. Bauer asks students to summarize what they noticed in the story with regard to adjectives that describe, respectively, female and male members of the family. Students describe what they noticed in the passage and how this relates to noun/adjective agreement and gender in the English language.

Reflection
1.1 Students use Latin to ask and answer questions.
1.2 Students read and understand the Latin passage.
2.1 Students understand the organization and the roles of the Roman family.
2.2 Students understand the setting of the Roman house and some Roman clothing.

Standards for Foreign Language Learning

SAMPLE LEARNING SCENARIOS

4.1 Students understand the concept of noun/adjective agreement and gender and how it compares to the English language.
4.2 Students recognize the similarities and differences found in the concept of family and how this concept relates to that of American and other cultures.

The discussion of the family is relevant to all languages and could also be focused on a myriad of topics. The first-year class would be appropriate for elementary, middle school, or high school students. Relating this discussion to information from history or social studies (either from an earlier year, or currently) would help move the scenario into a focus on Standard 3.1. The language system as a curricular element plays a role in helping students understand the Latin syntax and compare it with English. If the class included students who spoke a Romance language at home, a third comparison could be made. These students already control adjective agreement in their first language and find the Latin not to be a problem. The use of Latin orally while using visuals helps students internalize language structures, which facilitates their comprehension of the Latin passage.

ROMAN MARRIAGE

In Mr. Burgess' first year Latin class, the students are planning a re-creation of an authentic Roman wedding. Each of the Brockwood High School students receives a handout from their teacher about Roman marriage. The handout includes the marriage contract, the sequence of events, and the script the participants will read during the ceremony, along with pertinent vocabulary in Latin. After discussing the handout, the students choose roles. There will be a bride and a groom, priest, augur, and many other Romans. All of the students who do not have a specific role will participate in the procession to the groom's house. After they have enacted the ceremony in Latin, they discuss information in the handout and compare Roman weddings with weddings in American culture.

> **TARGETED STANDARDS**
> 1.3 Presentational Communication
> 2.2 Practices of Culture
> 4.2 Cultural Comparisons

Reflection
1.3 Students participate in the ceremony using Latin.
2.2 Students participate in the reenactment of a ceremony from the culture studied.
4.2 Students discuss differences in the historical re-creation and practices in today's society.

An extension of this activity could include searching a CD-ROM containing literary works of Latin authors for references to Roman marriages by using the vocabulary learned to search for appropriate passages. Students could be asked to compare the marriage customs through the centuries as presented by various authors during different literary periods. To bring in the language system, the teacher might ask students to identify specific syntax that is found in the marriage ceremony and how this reflects the attitude of the Romans toward marriage and the role of bride and groom in the ceremony.

SAMPLE LEARNING SCENARIOS

TARGETED STANDARDS

1.1 Interpersonal Communication
3.1 Making Connections
5.1 School and Community

RUSSIAN SCIENCE PROJECT

Students at Captain Nathan Hale Middle School in Connecticut begin a pen pal correspondence on the Internet with a school in Moscow. Over the years, this leads to an exchange of students, teachers, and community members between the Connecticut and Russian communities. A Russian teacher reads about the exchange in the local newspaper and volunteers to teach students Russian. Since the students are involved in a science project on rocketry with their Russian counterparts, the first words they learn are Russian space terms and how to count backwards from ten for lift-off. They build model rockets and launch them in Moscow and Coventry, CT. The students use computer software to develop stacks of pictures and words in English and Russian, along with the pronunciation and Russian background music. Russian language instruction is now an integral part of the curriculum at Nathan Hale Middle School.

Reflection

1.1 Students use written language to communicate with their Russian peers via the Internet.
3.1 Students acquire information about science in the target language.
5.1 Students communicate orally and in writing with members of the other culture regarding topics of personal interest, community, or world concern.

This scenario illustrates how a purposeful learning activity with students in another country can motivate students to learn the language and influence foreign language offerings in the school. The focus of the language instruction is also driven by the science topic that the students are currently studying, providing an excellent example of making connections across disciplines.

TARGETED STANDARDS

4.2 Cultural Comparisons

STEREOTYPES

At Trickum Middle School, students in the FLEX program are learning to recognize that cultures view situations from varying perspectives. The class discusses several aspects of stereotyping, and Frau Campbell shows taped television commercials, music videos and geography films from Germany to the group. The students, in turn, make generalizations about what they viewed. The students then compare and contrast American and German television commercials and music videos and note similarities and differences. They then interview an exchange student from Germany to get her reaction to their generalizations. Following the interview the students write and perform skits in English that focus on the misunderstandings that might occur when American tourists visit Germany or when German tourists are in the U.S.

Reflection

4.2 Students compare and contrast cultural traits.

Because this is an exploratory program, the students participate in similar projects in French and Spanish. They are highly interested in the activity because it makes use of items that are very familiar to them, i.e., commercials and music. Students with more advanced language skills could conduct the interview in the foreign language.

Standards for Foreign Language Learning

Frequently Asked Questions

WHY STANDARDS FOR GRADES 4, 8, AND 12?

Many teachers ask why the standards task force drafted standards for these grades, given that most foreign language study in our schools occurs in high schools, primarily at grades 9-10. The task force developed foreign language standards within parameters that have encompassed all the disciplinary projects, be it science, history, or the arts. Our mandate was to establish content standards (what students "know and are able to do"); we chose to establish progress indicators at grades 4, 8, and 12 to align ourselves with all the other disciplines. Were we to stand alone with standards only for high school—currently the most common grade levels for foreign language study—we would lose any possibility of a stronger position in the core curriculum.

WHAT IS THE RELATIONSHIP OF STANDARDS TO STATE AND LOCAL DISTRICTS?

Standards are intended to serve as a gauge for excellence as states and local districts carry out their responsibilities for curriculum in the schools. The political context requires that national standards be voluntary and that they do not usurp the role of the states. National standards are neither curriculum nor are they substitutes for state frameworks; that is why they do not reflect a level of detail that teachers are accustomed to seeing in local documents. We do expect that the usefulness of the standards lies in their definition of the field and their reflection of the profession. They also set out the possibilities that accrue from an extended sequence of language study. We adhered to the advice to be parsimonious in the number of standards created, while maintaining rigor in depth and breadth.

HOW DO STANDARDS RELATE TO THE PROFICIENCY GUIDELINES?

Informed teachers will recognize within the standards the work that has preceded this initiative under rubrics of proficiency-oriented or communication-based instruction, as well as the broadening of the teaching of target cultures to encompass lifestyle and civilization. However, in keeping with the attempt to create broadly conceived standards, we did not carve standards into separate skill areas of listening, speaking, reading, and writing. Instead, we addressed communication in its overarching purposes of interpersonal interactions, interpretation, and presentation. Regardless of modality, communication must be culturally grounded. Teachers will note that the standards venture into new areas that become possible to achieve given earlier starts and longer sequences for our learners.

ARE THE STANDARDS MANDATORY?

The standards are voluntary. They are intended to serve as a model to state and local policy makers and curriculum developers as they reconsider the role of foreign languages in their schools. Regardless of the changing fiscal or political circumstances, the impact of the standards will undoubtedly be felt in classrooms around the country as individuals teachers modify their instruction to assist their students in making progress toward achieving the five C's of foreign language education: communication, cultures, connections, comparisons, and communities.

Standards for Foreign Language Learning

FREQUENTLY ASKED QUESTIONS

▶ **WHY DOES THIS DOCUMENT SPECIFY THAT FOREIGN LANGUAGES ARE FOR ALL STUDENTS?**

In the twenty-first century, few working situations in the United States will not involve interaction with speakers of languages other than English. Whether a student engages in a career of international affairs or is hired by a local business that serves a multilingual community, knowledge of a language other than English will increasingly be viewed by employers as an important skill. This is one of the primary reasons that all students should have the opportunity to pursue learning another language. However, since foreign language programs have not traditionally accommodated all students, this proposal may seem challenging to foreign language teachers. For this reason, an important part of this document is the inclusion of a broader sense of what constitutes learning a language (i.e., connecting with other disciplines and developing insight into one's own language and culture) and other components (i.e., communication strategies and learner strategies) that have not traditionally been integrated into a student's language experience. Including these components in the instructional program will give students an important sense of themselves as language learners responsible for their learning. By becoming responsible language learners, students will become more motivated to engage themselves actively in the language learning process. By participating in language programs that reflect the standards of all five goals, students will see a usefulness to language learning that has never before been evident to the student population at large. In the twenty-first century, citizens of the United States will increasingly witness the practical application of languages in all areas of the work force as well as the community. The implementation of these goals and standards will help prepare our students for that world.

▲▲▲

▶ **BUT WHAT ABOUT THOSE STUDENTS WHO REALLY CAN'T LEARN A FOREIGN LANGUAGE?**

Historically, foreign language instruction has been limited to college bound and high achieving students under the mistaken assumption that only those students could be successful learners. However, it has been shown in a variety of educational settings that high expectations accompanied by appropriate instructional support result in remarkable student achievement. The very same techniques that apply to learning for all students, in general, apply to this group of students, as well. For example, when Frederic Cohen, a principal of a New York State high school, did not inform teachers which of their students were non-Regents students, the overall number of students obtaining Regents' diplomas at the end of the school year increased 15% (Shanker 1995). When teachers were "underprepared," they succeeded in teaching all students more successfully. In another school district, middle school students who had been placed in special education classes were enrolled in a three-year foreign language program. As a consequence of carefully planned goals and instruction, all of those students were successful in achieving the course goals, and several continued their language study, passing the Regents' examination, and participating in student exchange programs abroad (Foreign Language Project 1985).

▲▲▲

FREQUENTLY ASKED QUESTIONS

WILL TEACHERS BE GIVEN ASSISTANCE TO HELP THEM TO WORK WITH THE STANDARDS?

Professional development for practicing teachers is crucial. Many workshops and seminars have already taken place around the country to acquaint teachers with the standards. Just as professional organizations in other disciplines have intensified their efforts to provide continuing education for their colleagues, our professional organizations recognize the need to provide opportunities to revitalize and expand the disciplinary and pedagogical expertise of language teachers. These organizations are currently exploring a variety of ways, such as technology, distance learning, sequential workshops, or mentoring networks, to assist teachers in their ongoing efforts to remain abreast of current developments in education. National, state and local professional organizations that support foreign language educators, postsecondary institutions, and some local school districts are crafting the extended sequence of professional development needed to translate the standards into curriculum and classroom practices that facilitate student success.

▲▲▲

ARE ALL THE GOALS THE SAME?

No, the five goals—communication, cultures, connections, comparisons, and communities—are not the same. They are, however, considered parts of an interconnected whole. These goals and the standards are fairly fixed in that they represent the consensus of the field as to the overall objectives of second language study.

▲▲▲

BUT WHAT IF I THINK THE COMMUNICATION GOAL IS THE MOST IMPORTANT?

The communication goal is indeed important. However, students in the twenty-first century need to be able to understand cultures, to respond in culturally appropriate ways, to access information only available within the foreign language, to gain insight into their own language and culture, and they need to be prepared to apply what they learn beyond the school setting. Focusing on a single goal will not provide adequate preparation for the future.

▲▲▲

WHAT IS THE ROLE OF GRAMMAR?

In the past, foreign language instruction focused primarily on the memorization of words and grammar rules. The standards require a much broader definition of the content of the language classroom, one in which students are given ample opportunities to explore, develop, and use communication strategies, learning strategies, and critical thinking skills, as well as the appropriate elements of the language system and culture.

Unfortunately, as generations of language students have taught us, grammar by itself does not produce individuals who can speak or understand the language that they studied. Foreign languages are not "acquired" when students learn an ordered set of facts about the language (e.g., grammar facts, vocabulary). Students need to be able to use the target language for real communication, that is, to carry out a complex interactive process that involves speaking and understanding what others say in the target language as well as reading and interpreting written materials.

Standards for Foreign Language Learning 99

FREQUENTLY ASKED QUESTIONS

Grammar is nevertheless important in the study of a language. Goal four focuses the students' attention on the nature of linguistic systems by asking them to compare their own language and the language studied along a number of key dimensions.

▲▲▲

► HOW DO I USE THE STANDARDS IF MY DISTRICT'S PROGRAM DOESN'T BEGIN UNTIL THE SEVENTH GRADE?

Although the standards document describes an ideal sequence of study and set of standards, some districts and program models are presently not able to provide these experiences for students. While working to encourage districts to extend the language sequence into the lower grades in the elementary schools, teachers and curriculum planners can examine the standards in light of the programs that are being provided locally. Knowing that the results will vary dramatically between programs that offer two years of study versus twelve, teachers can elect to cover some standards and use some of the grade 4 progress indicators adjusted for age-appropriate content to describe shorter sequences of study. At the state and local level, curriculum planners can use the standards document as a tool for planning present programs and as a powerful description of what could be accomplished if resources and time could be provided for extended sequences of language study.

▲▲▲

► WHY STUDY A LANGUAGE AT AN EARLY AGE?

The painful truth is that learning to speak, read, write, and think in another language takes a long time; and age and attitude have an effect on one's ability to become proficient in another language. Just as mathematical reasoning skills should be learned and applied in many contexts and operations according to the age and developmental level of the child, so too should the elements of another language and culture be learned and applied. Also, traditionally, subjects relegated to the fringes of the educational core are not as valued by students or parents. Students, not knowing what they are missing, avoid learning altogether, or worse, think that two years of minimal exposure to the language will result in advanced proficiency in the language. The foreign language standards show students, parents and policy makers what students should know and be able to do after a longer sequence of study. By using the progress indicators as samples of student progress along the way to greater proficiency, students and parents will gain a realistic picture of what it takes to learn another language.

▲▲▲

► HOW DO WE ARTICULATE WITH A STANDARDS-BASED PROGRAM?

A major articulation issue is the placement of students who have participated in a standards-based program before new assessment instruments have been developed to measure what they know and are able to do. States and districts are now being asked to develop the performance standards which address the question of how well the students need to do in meeting the standards. Before this can happen, the profession needs to engage in a collaborative discussion regarding the program goals across instructional levels. We need these discussions to establish not only seamless instruction, but also seamless learning.

Appendix A: References and Further Reading

REFERENCES

American Council on the Teaching of Foreign Languages. 1986. *ACTFL Proficiency Guidelines*. Hastings-on-Hudson, NY: American Council on the Teaching of Foreign Languages.

Bachman, L.F. 1990. *Fundamental Considerations in Language Testing*. Oxford: Oxford University Press.

Bialystok, E. 1981. The role of linguistic knowledge in second language use. *Studies in Second Language Learning,* 1:31-45.

Brecht, R.D., and A.R. Walton. 1994. The future shape of language learning in the new world of global communication: Consequences for higher education and beyond. In R. Donato and R.M. Terry (Eds.), *Foreign Language Learning: The Journey of a Lifetime*. Lincolnwood, IL: National Textbook Company.

Canale, M., and M. Swain. 1980. Theoretical bases of communicative approaches to second language teaching and testing. *Applied Linguistics,* 1:1-47.

Chamot, A., and J.M. O'Malley. 1994. *The CALLA Handbook: Cognitive Academic Learning Approach*. White Plains, NY: Addison-Wesley Publishing Company.

Cooper, T. 1987. Foreign language study and SAT-Verbal Scores. *The Modern Language Journal*, 71 1:381-87.

de Jong, J.H.A.L., and L. Verhoeven. 1992. Modeling and assessing language proficiency. In L. Verhoeven and J.H.A.L. de Jong (Eds.), *The Construct of Language Proficiency*. Amsterdam: John Benjamins.

Foreign Language Project. 1985. East Ramapo Teacher's Center, Spring Valley, New York.

Fromkin, V. and R. Rodman. 1993. *An Introduction to Language*. New York: Holt, Rinehart, and Winston.

Hymes, D. 1972. On communicative competence. In J.B. Pride and J. Holmes (Eds.), *Sociolinguistics,* Harmondsworth: Penguin Books.

_____. 1985. Toward linguistic competence. *Revue d l'AILA:AILA Review*, 2:9-23.

Olsen, S., and L. Brown. 1992. The relation between high school study of foreign languages and ACT English and mathematics performance. *ADFL Bulletin* (28)3:47-48.

Savignon, S.J. 1983. *Communicative Competence: Theory and Classroom Practice*. Menlo Park, CA: Addison-Wesley Publishing Company.

Schiffrin, D. 1994. *Approaches to Discourse*. Oxford: Blackwell.

Shanker, A. 1995. Raising the ceiling and the floor. *The New York Times*, June 14, 1995, p. E7.

REFERENCES AND FURTHER READING

The following documents were used extensively by the standards task force in conceptualizing the framework and format of the final standards:

Center for Civic Education. 1994. *National Standards for Civics and Government.* Calabasas, CA: Center for Civic Education.

Consortium of National Arts Education Associations. 1994. *National Standards for Arts Education.* Reston, VA: Music Educators National Conference.

National Council of Teachers of Mathematics. 1989. *Curriculum and Evaluation Standards for School Mathematics.* Reston, VA: National Council of Teachers of Mathematics.

National Task Force for Social Studies Standards. 1995. *Expectations of Excellence: Curriculum Standards for Social Studies.* Washington, DC: National Council for the Social Studies.

Scarino, A., D. Vale, P. McKay, and J. Clark. 1988. *Australian Language Levels (ALL) Guidelines.* Canberra: Curriculum Development Centre.

The University of the State of New York. 1984. *Modern Languages for Communication: The New York State Syllabus.* Albany, NY: The State Education Department.

FURTHER READING

1. General

Curtain, H.A., and C. A. Pesola. 1994. *Languages and Children—Making the Match.* 2nd edition. White Plains, NY: Longman Publishing Group.

Draper, J. 1993. National standards in foreign language education: Answering the questions. *ERIC/CLL Bulletin* (17) 1.

Genesee, F. (editor). 1994. *Educating Second Language Children: The Whole Child, the Whole Curriculum, the Whole Community.* Cambridge: Cambridge University Press.

Education Week. 1995. *Struggling for Standards: An Education Week Special Report.* Washington, DC: Education Week.

Phillips, J. 1995. Testing. In V. Galloway and C. Herrin (Eds.), *Research Within Reach II.* Valdosta, GA: Southern Conference on Language Teaching.

Phillips, J., and J. Draper. 1994. National standards and assessments. In G. Crouse (Ed.), *Meeting New Challenges in the Foreign Language Classroom.* Report of the Central States Conference on the Teaching of Foreign Languages. Lincolnwood, IL: National Textbook Company.

REFERENCES AND FURTHER READING

2. Communication Goal

Chaudron, C. 1988. *Second Language Classrooms: Research on Teaching and Learning*. Cambridge: Cambridge University Press.

Ellis, R. 1985. *Understanding Second Language Acquisition*. Oxford: Blackwell Publishers.

———. 1990. *Instructed Second Language Acquisition*. Oxford: Blackwell Publishers.

Gass, S. M., and J. Schachter, Eds. 1989. Linguistic Perspectives on Second Language Acquisition. Cambridge: Cambridge University Press.

Hadley, A. O. (Ed.) 1993. *Research in Language Learning: Principles, Processes, and Prospects*. Lincolnwood, IL: National Textbook Company.

Larsen-Freeman, D., and M. H. Long. 1991. *An Introduction to Second Language Acquisition Research*. New York: Longman.

3. Cultures Goal

Gollnick, D., and P. Chinn. 1994. *Multicultural Education in a Pluralistic Society*. Riverside, NJ: Macmillan.

Kramsch, C. 1993. *Context and Culture in Language Teaching*. New York: Oxford University Press.

Samovar, I., and R. Porter. 1994. *Intercultural Communication: A Reader*. Belmont, CA: Wadsworth Publishing Company.

Seelye, H.N. 1993. *Teaching Culture: Strategies for Intercultural Communication*. Lincolnwood, IL: National Textbook Company.

Stewart, E., and M. Bennett. 1991. *American Cultural Patterns: A Cross-Cultural Perspective*. Yarmouth, ME: Intercultural Press.

4. Heritage Languages

Benton, R.A. 1986. Schools as agents for language revival in Ireland and New Zealand. In P. Spolsky (Ed.) *Language and Education in Multilingual Settings* (pp. 53-76). San Diego: College Hill Press.

Benyon J., and K. Toohey. 1991. Heritage language education in British Columbia: Policy and programs. *Canadian Modern Language Review*, 47(4).

Churchill, S. 1986. *The Education of Linguistic and Cultural Minorities in the OECD Countries*. Clevedon, England: Multilingual Matters.

Cummins, J. 1983. *Heritage Language Education: A Literature Review*. Toronto, Ontario: Ministry of Education.

Cummins, J. (Ed.) 1984. *Heritage Languages in Canada: Research Perspectives*. Ottawa: Ontario Institute for Studies in Education.

REFERENCES AND FURTHER READING

Danesi, M. 1986. *Teaching a Heritage Language to Dialect-Speaking Student*s. Ontario: Ontario Institute for Studies in Education.

Extra, G., and L. Verhoeven (Eds.). 1993. *Immigrant Languages in Europe.* Clevedon, England: Multilingual Matters.

Fernandez, S., A. Pauwels, and M. Clyne. 1993. *Unlocking Australia's Language Potential: Profiles of 9 Key Languages in Australia, Volume 4.* German. (ED 365114). Australian National Languages and Literacy Institute.

Feuerverger, G. 1991. University students' perceptions of heritage language learning and ethnic identity maintenance. *Canadian Modern Language Review,* 47 4:660-677.

Fishman, J., and B.R. Markman. 1979. *The Ethnic Mother Tongue School in America: Assumptions, Findings and Directory.* (Final Report to the National Institute of Education, Ferkauf Graduate School, Yeshiva University).

Ingram, D.E. 1984. Language policy in Australia in the 1990's. In R.D. Lambert (Ed.), *Language Planning Around the World: Contexts and Systemic Change* (pp. 69-109). Washington, DC: National Foreign Language Center.

Merino, J.J., H.T. Trueba, and F.A. Samaniego (Eds.). 1993. *Language and Culture in Learning: Teaching Spanish to Native Speakers of Spanish.* London: The Palmer Press.

Roca, A. 1990. Teaching Spanish to the bilingual college student in Miami. In J.J. Bergen (Ed.), *Spanish in the United States: Sociolinguistic Issue*s (pp. 127-36). Washington, DC: Georgetown University Press.

Valdés, G. 1980. Teaching ethnic languages in the United States: Implications for curriculum and faculty development. *ADFL Bulletin,* 11 (3), 31-34.

_____. 1992. The role of the foreign language teaching profession in maintaining non-English languages in the United States. In H. Byrnes (Ed.), *Languages for a Multicultural World in Transition: 1993 Northeast Conference Report*s (pp. 29-71). Skokie, IL: National Textbook Company.

_____. 1995. The teaching of minority languages as "foreign" languages: Pedagogical and theoretical challenges. *Modern Language Journal,* Vol. 79 (3).

Valdés, G., A.G. Lozano, and R. Garcia-Moya (Eds.) 1981. *Teaching Spanish to the Hispanic Bilingual: Issues, Aims, and Methods.* New York: Teachers College Press.

Appendix B: Project Personnel

Project Director: *June K. Phillips, Weber State University, Ogden, UT*

K-12 Student Standards Task Force

Christine Brown (Chair)
Glastonbury Public Schools
Glastonbury, CT

Marty Abbott Fairfax County Public Schools Fairfax County, VA	Denise Mesa Sabal Palm Elementary North Miami Beach, FL	A. Ronald Walton National Foreign Language Center Washington, DC
Keith Cothrun Las Cruces High School Las Cruces, NM	Genelle Morain University of Georgia Athens, GA	John Webb Hunter College High School New York, NY
Beverly Harris-Schenz University of Pittsburgh Pittsburgh, PA	Marjorie Tussing California State University Fullerton, CA	Thomas Welch Jessamine County Public Schools Nicholasville, KY

Guadalupe Valdés
Stanford University
Palo Alto, CA

Board of Directors

Fred Jenkins AATF Champaign, IL	Robert LaBouve Texas Education Agency (Retired) Austin, TX	C. Edward Scebold ACTFL Yonkers, NY
Hiroko Kataoka University of Oregon Eugene, OR	Lynn Sandstedt AATSP Greeley, CO	Helene Zimmer-Loew AATG Cherry Hill, NJ

Advisory Council

A. Graham Down (Co-Chair)   Protase E. Woodford (Co-Chair)
Council for Basic Education (retired)   Educational Testing Service (retired)
Washington, DC   Titusville, NJ

Gordon Ambach Council of Chief State School Officers Washington, DC	Heidi Byrnes Georgetown University Washington, DC	Benjamin Canada Atlanta Public Schools Atlanta, GA
Douglas Charchenko Kidder, Peabody, & Co. San Francisco, CA	Christopher J. Dodd United States Senate (D-CT) Washington, DC	Alvino Fantini SIETAR Washington, DC
Maxine Frost Board of Education Riverside, CA	Fred Genesee TESOL Montreal, Canada	Joel Gómez National Clearinghouse for Bilingual Education Washington, DC

PROJECT PERSONNEL

Advisory Council (continued)

Fred Hechinger
The Carnegie Corporation
New York, NY

Claire Jackson
Brookline Public Schools
Brookline, MA

Robert Lafayette
Louisiana State University
Baton Rouge, LA

Myriam Met
Montgomery County Public Schools
Rockville, MD

Jeffrey Munks
AT&T Language Line
San Jose, CA

Rubén Puga
John Deere International
Moline, IL

Ramón Santiago
Lehman College
Bronx, NY

Paul Simon
United States Senate (D-IL)
Washington, DC

Henry Thomas
The Urban League
Springfield, MA

Elizabeth Welles
Modern Language Association
New York, NY

Pilot Sites

Clovis Unified School District, Fresno, CA
Peggy Blanton, Coordinator

Edmonds School District, Lynnwood, WA
Sally Harrison, Coordinator

Gwinnett County Public Schools, GA
Elizabeth Rieken, Coordinator

Houston Public Schools, TX
Ray Maldonado, Coordinator

Springfield Public Schools, MA
Kathleen Riordan, Coordinator

Williamston Community Schools, MI
Cindy Kendall, Coordinator

Project Staff

Jamie B. Draper, Project Manager
ACTFL, Yonkers, NY

June Hicks, Project Assistant
ACTFL, Yonkers, NY

Stephanie Soper, Washington Liaison
Council for Basic Education
Washington, DC

Program Officers

Anne Fickling
U.S. Department of Education
Washington, DC

Jeff Thomas
National Endowment for the Humanities
Washington, DC

Board of Reviewers

Arnhilda Badia
Florida International University
Coral Gables, FL

Virginia Ballinger
Ohio Department of Education
Columbus, OH

Harriet Barnett
Dobbs Ferry, NY

Walter Bartz
Indiana Department of Education
Indianapolis, IN

Patty Bohanan
Oklahoma Foreign Language Association
Dewey, OK

Kathleen Boykin
Slippery Rock University
Slippery Rock, PA

Deborah Brown
West Virginia Department of Education
Charleston, WV

Anita Bruce
Hawaii Department of Education
Honolulu, HI

Art Burnah
Woodland Hills, UT

Erick Byrd
University of Georgia
Athens, GA

Sachiko Cantrell
Mountain View, MO

Standards for Foreign Language Learning

PROJECT PERSONNEL

Board of Reviewers (continued)

I. Carduner
Huron High School
Ann Arbor, MI

Celeste Carr
Maryland Foreign Language
Association
Catonsville, MD

Alice Kalalian Cataldi
University of Delaware
Newark, DE

Kuan-Yi Rose Chang
International Association of
Language Laboratories
Morgantown, WV

Amie Ciemenski
Upland, CA

Paul Cirre
San Antonio, TX

Beth Clemens
Southern Regional High School
Manahawkin, NJ

Donna Clementi
Wisconsin Foreign Language
Teachers Association
Appleton, WI

Maria Collins
Kansas Department of Education
Topeka, KS

Jill Conrad
Downington Senior High School
Downington, PA

Audrey Cournia
Reed High School
Sparks, NV

Jim Currin
SW Educational Development Lab
Austin, TX

Louis D'Aquila
Sayville, NY

Desa Dawson
Oklahoma Foreign Language
Teachers Association
Midwest City, OK

Terrance DePasquale
Jeannette, PA

Joseph Dial
Seattle Central Community College
Seattle, WA

Richard Donato
University of Pittsburgh
Pittsburgh, PA

Janet Durgin
Mt. Hemon, MA

Judith Eaton
Indiana Foreign Language
Teachers Association
Edinburgh, IN

Bonnie Elliott
Confederation of Oregon Foreign
Language Teachers
Redmond, OR

Heather Emberson
World Cultures Institute
Corvallis, OR

Emelda Estelle
Illinois Foreign Language
Teachers Association
Chicago, IL

B.J. Fairbanks
Utah Foreign Language Association
Salt Lake City, UT

Thekla Fall
Pennsylvania State Modern
Language Association
Pittsburgh, PA

Carl Falsgraf
Eugene, OR

Barbara Freed
Carnegie Mellon University
Pittsburgh, PA

Kay Freire
Wyoming Foreign Language
Teachers Association
Casper, WY

Inés García
Texas Education Agency
Austin, TX

Paul A. García
School District of Kansas City
Kansas City, MO

David Graham
American Association of Teachers
of French
Northport, NY

Maria del Carmen Graham
NM Department of Education
Santa Fe, NM

Christopher Gram
Foreign Language Association of
Maine
Anson, ME

Virginia Gramer
Illinois Council on the Teaching
of Foreign Languages
Oak Brook, IL

Susan Grier
Arkansas Department of Education
Little Rock, AR

Susan Gross
Cheyenne Mountain Junior High
Colorado Springs, CO

Gail Guntermann
Arizona State University
Tempe, AZ

Julia Hanley
Stone Mountain, GA

David P. Hill
University of South Carolina
Columbia, SC

Helena Hill
Marymount School
Santa Barbara, CA

Wolfgang Hirsch
Washington Department of
Education
Olympia, WA

Paul Hoekstra
Iowa Department of Education
Des Moines, IA

Elizabeth Hoffman
American Association of Teachers
of German
Omaha, NE

Duane Jackson
Office of Public Instruction
Helena, MT

Suzanne Jebe
Minnesota Department of Education
Saint Paul, MN

Sylvia L. Jones
California Foreign Language
Teachers Association
Pasadena, CA

Jonel Jones Yunker
Maysville, KY

Standards for Foreign Language Learning 107

PROJECT PERSONNEL

Board of Reviewers (continued)

Joel Judd
Missouri Department of Education
Jefferson City, MO

Dora Kennedy
University of Maryland
College Park, MD

Joachim Korner
Morganton, NC

Claire Kramsch
University of California
Berkeley, CA

Dick Kuettner
International Association of
Language Laboratories
Lexington, VA

Katherine Kulick
Foreign Language Association of
Virginia
Williamsburg, VA

Patricia S. Kuntz
University of Wisconsin
Madison, WI

Flavia Laviosa
Wellesley College, MA

Nancy Lawrence
Albuquerque Public Schools, NM

Lucy Lee
Livingston High School
Princeton, NJ

Maria Lindia
Rhode Island Department of
Education
Providence, RI

Gladys Lipton
University of Maryland-Baltimore
County

Judith Liskin-Gasparro
University of Iowa
Iowa City, IA

Nancy Lister
Classical Association of New
England
Manchester, CT

Sherwin Little
Indian Hill High School
Cinncinnati, OH

Antonio Llazcano
University of Wisconsin, Eau Claire

Sheri Spaine Long
University of Alabama
Birmingham, AL

Yafa Malashock
Jewish Day School
Rockville, MD

Grace Mannino
American Association of Teachers
of Italian
Brentwood, NY

Alice Mannix
Brown County High School
Nashville, IN

Adele Martinez
Sacramento, CA

Norman Masuda
National Council of Secondary
Teachers of Japanese
Mountain View, CA

Philip Mataruga
Nevada Language Association
Reno, NV

Elaine McAllister
Foreign Language Association of
Georgia
Marietta, GA

David McAlpine
University of Arkansas
Little Rock, AR

Sharon McNeely
Gainesville, FL

Frank Medley
West Virginia University
Morgantown, WV

Millie Mellgren
Minnesota Council on the
Teaching of Languages and
Cultures
Plymouth, MN

Cherron Miller
Delaware Council on the
Teaching of Foreign Languages
Newark, DE

Mary Mills
Westville, NJ

Frank Mulhern
Pennsylvania State Modern
Language Association
Lansdale, PA

Jill Nelson
Dallas, TX

Bert Neumaier
Connecticut Organization of
Language Teachers
Vernon, CT

Mel Nielsen
Nebraska Department of Education
Lincoln, NE

Ruth Norton
Greenwood Laboratory School
Springfield, MO

Marie O'Donnell
Kirkland School
Houston, TX

Frina Olssen
McCullough High School
The Woodlands, TX

Diane Parmeter
Clinton Community College
Plattsburgh, NY

Joan Patterson
Utah Department of Education
Salt Lake City, UT

Alicia Ramos
Columbia University
New York, NY

Patrick T. Raven
Wisconsin Association of Foreign
Language Teachers
Milwaukee, WI

Mary Lynn Redmond
Foreign Language Association of
North Carolina
Greensboro, NC

Don Reutershan
Maine Department of Education
Augusta, ME

Alice Reynolds
Bloomington, IN

Bernadette M. Reynolds
Parker, CO

Nancy Rhodes
Center for Applied Linguistics
Washington, DC

Elizabeth Rieken
Gwinnett County Public Schools
Lawrenceville, GA

PROJECT PERSONNEL

Board of Reviewers (continued)

Bonnie Robb
Delaware Council on the
Teaching of Foreign Languages
Middletown, DE

Marty Roberts
Prescott, MI

Robert E. Robison
Columbus Public Schools
Columbus, OH

Hector Romero
Indiana University
South Bend, IN

Annie Rooney French
Littleton, CO

Marcia Rosenbusch
Iowa State University
Ames, IA

Cecile Rousseau
Nevada Language Association
Las Vegas, NV

Paul Sandrock
Wisconsin Department of Public
Instruction
Madison, WI

Renate Schulz
University of Arizona
Tucson, AZ

Catherine Scott
New York, NY

Martie Semmer
Breckenridge, CO

Richard Shelburne
Sidney Lanier High School
Montgomery, AL

Michele Shockey
American Association of Teachers
of French
Atherton, CA

Jane Shuffleton
American Council of Teachers of
Russian
Rochester, NY

Felix Siciliano
Lakewood High School
Shrewsbury, NJ

Andrew Simon
University of Vermont, Burlington

Peggy Singer
Louisiana Department of Education
Baton Rouge, LA

Marcia Spielberger
Georgia Department of Education
Atlanta, GA

Charles Stansfield
Second Language Testing, Inc.
North Bethesda, MD

Chih-Wen Su
CLASS
Amherst, MA

James Swann
Northeast Texas Community
College
Mt. Pleasant, TX

Gregory Swanson
Foreign Language Association of
Missouri
Salem, MO

Louise Terry
Bayport, NY

Ngoc-Diep Thi Nguyen
Illinois Resource Center
Des Plaines, IL

Julie Thornton
Arlington, VA

John C. Traupman
St. Joseph's University
Philadelphia, PA

Marie Trayer
Nebraska Department of
Education
Lincoln, NE

Rebecca Valette
Boston College
Chestnut Hill, MA

Diane J. Viskochil
Michigan Foreign Language
Association
Traverse City, MI

Rosa Volpe
Vanderbilt University
Nashville, TN

Arlene F. White
Salisbury State University
Salisbury, MD

Ida Wilder
American Association of Teachers
of Italian
Rochester, NY

Lisa Williams
Washington, DC

Hal Wingard
California Language Teachers
Association
San Diego, CA

Dorothy R. Winkles
Tennessee Foreign Language
Teachers Association
Knoxville, TN

Anna Wolin
Herricks High School
New Hyde Park, NY

Mary L. Young
Confederation of Oregon Foreign
Language Teachers
Lake Oswego, OR

Standards for Foreign Language Learning

Standards for Learning Arabic K–16 in the United States

This document is guided by the generic *Standards for Foreign Language Learning in the 21st Century*. It is a collaborative effort of the Arabic K–12 Materials Development Project, the National Capital Language Resource Center, the National Standards Collaborative, the American Association of Teachers of Arabic, and the National Middle East Language Resource Center. In addition, this document reflects the sound and careful advice from many others who commented on drafts and generously gave of their time to this effort.

The Task Force is also extremely grateful to the National Foreign Language Education Project for its generous financial assistance for Task Force meetings and its sustained support through the development of the *Standards for Learning Arabic K–16*.

THE TASK FORCE ON STANDARDS FOR THE LEARNING OF ARABIC K-16

Mahdi Alosh (Chair), Ohio State University, Columbus, OH
Nesreen Akhtarkhavari, private consultant, Chicago, IL
Christine Brown, Glastonbury Public Schools, Glastonbury, CT
Ferial Demy, Foreign Service Institute, U.S. Department of State, Washington, DC
Muhammad S. Eissa, Eissa & Associates, Chicago, IL
Shawn Greenstreet, National Capital Language Resource Center, Washington, DC
Iman Arabi-Katbi Hashem, Occidental College, Los Angeles, CA
Wafa Hassan, Islamic Saudi Academy, Alexandria, VA
Dora Johnson, National Capital Language Resource Center, Washington, DC
Lina Kholaki, New Horizon Schools, Los Angeles, CA
Wafaa Makki, Dearborn Public Schools, Dearborn, MI
Kathleen McBroom, Dearborn Public Schools, Dearborn, MI
Khitam Abder-Ruhman Omar, Fairfax Public Schools, Fairfax, VA

Standards for Learning Arabic

ADVISORY COMMITTEE

Azmeralda Alfi
Bureau of Islamic and Arabic Education
Los Angeles, CA

Kirk Belnap
National Middle East Language
Resource Center
Provo, UT

John C. Eisele
College of William and Mary
Williamsburg, VA
American Association of
Teachers of Arabic

REVIEWERS

Faith Andrus
Green High School
Green, OH

Kirk Belnap
National Middle East Language
Resource Center
Provo, UT

Elizabeth Bergman
Center for Advanced
Proficiency in Arabic
Georgetown University
Washington, DC

Michele Chalhoub-Deville
University of Iowa
Iowa City, IA

John C. Eisele
College of William and Mary
Williamsburg, VA
American Association of
Teachers of Arabic

Zeina El-Ayi
Granada Islamic School
Santa Clara, CA

Foazi El Barouki
Defense Language Institute
Foreign Language Center
Monterey, CA

Mohssen Esseesy
The George Washington University
Washington, DC

Salah-Dine Hammoud
U.S. Air Force Academy
Colorado Spring, CO

Lamis T. Hashem
Independent consultant
Rossmoor, CA

Gerald Lampe
National Foreign Language Center
American Association of
Teachers of Arabic
College Park, MD

David Mehall
Center for Advanced Study of Language
University of Maryland
College Park, MD

Samia Montasser
The United Nations
New York, NY

Karen Petersen
Alan Leis Instructional Center
Falls Church, VA

Karin Ryding
Georgetown University
Washington, DC

Nada Shaath
MontessoriMe
Torrance, CA

Marjorie Tussing
California State University at Fullerton
Fullerton, CA

Brandon Zaslow
Occidental College
Los Angeles, CA

Table of Contents

STANDARDS FOR LEARNING ARABIC — **114**

INTRODUCTION — **115**

CHARACTERISTICS OF THE ARABIC LANGUAGE — **116**

ABOUT THE STANDARDS FOR LEARNING ARABIC K–16 IN THE UNITED STATES — **117**
- Development Process — 117
- Statement of Philosophy — 118

COMMUNICATION Goal 1 — **120**

CULTURES Goal 2 — **128**

CONNECTIONS Goal 3 — **132**

COMPARISONS Goal 4 — **136**

COMMUNITIES Goal 5 — **140**

LEARNING SCENARIOS, GRADES K–4 — **144**
- The Food Pyramid — 144
- Marble Games in the Arab World — 145
- Arabic Restaurant for a Day — 146

LEARNING SCENARIOS, GRADES 5–8 — **147**
- My Dream Job — 147
- The Arabic Day — 148
- What Can We Learn from Fables? Making A Difference — 149

LEARNING SCENARIOS, GRADES 9–12 — **150**
- Interview Famous People — 150
- Which Tour Would You Like to Take? — 151
- The Islamic Calendar and the Origin of the English Word "Calendar" — 152

LEARNING SCENARIOS, COLLEGE — **153**
- Planning a Middle Eastern Meal — 153
- Al-Razi: An Arab Scholar — 154
- Historical Drama — 155

Standards for Learning Arabic

COMMUNICATION — GOAL ONE
Communicate in Arabic

Standard 1.1 Students engage in conversations and correspondence in Arabic to provide and obtain information, express feelings and emotions, and exchange opinions.

Standard 1.2 Students understand and interpret written and spoken Arabic on a variety of topics.

Standard 1.3 Students present information, concepts, and ideas in Arabic to an audience of listeners or readers on a variety of topics.

CULTURES — GOAL TWO
Gain Knowledge & Understanding of the Cultures of the Arab World

Standard 2.1 Students demonstrate an understanding of the relationship between the practices and perspectives of the various cultures of the Arab world.

Standard 2.2 Students demonstrate an understanding of the relationship between the products and perspectives of the various cultures of the Arab world.

CONNECTIONS — GOAL THREE
Use Arabic to Connect with Other Disciplines & Acquire Information

Standard 3.1 Students reinforce and further their knowledge of other disciplines through Arabic.

Standard 3.2 Students acquire information and recognize the viewpoints that are only available through the Arabic language and cultures.

COMPARISONS — GOAL FOUR
Develop Insight into Language & Culture

Standard 4.1 Students demonstrate understanding of the nature of language through comparisons between Arabic and their own languages.

Standard 4.2 Students demonstrate understanding of the concept of culture through comparisons between the cultures of the Arab world and their own.

COMMUNITIES — GOAL FIVE
Participate in Multilingual Communities at Home & in the World

Standard 5.1 Students use Arabic both within and beyond the school setting.

Standard 5.2 Students show evidence of becoming lifelong learners by using Arabic for personal enjoyment and enrichment.

Introduction

ARABIC TEACHING IN THE UNITED STATES

Although enrollments in Arabic language classes have been increasing steadily since the 1970s, schools have seen an unprecedented jump in these enrollments since September 11, 2001. According to a nationwide survey of K–12 schools by the National Capital Language Resource Center, at least 18 public and charter schools currently teach Arabic as part of their regular foreign language curriculum. The survey found that at least 80 private Islamic schools teach Arabic and that preparatory schools have an active interest in offering it. The American Association of Teachers of Arabic (AATA) Web site lists over 165 institutions of higher education that teach Arabic in the United States. Both the number of programs and the numbers of students enrolled in them are expected to increase.

In response to the diverse needs of students who come from a variety of sociolinguistic backgrounds and whose goals have included developing proficiency in all skills—speaking, listening, reading, and writing—the teaching of Arabic today includes introducing it as a vibrant language that is the medium of expression at all levels of society, rather than only teaching it as a medium for literary texts. However, since the language is taught for communication purposes, it has raised some issues that are still being debated in the field.

Arabic is a diglossic language; that is, two forms of it exist side by side. One form is more highly coded, while the other is used casually for everyday interaction. For this reason, teaching Arabic as a single language has been somewhat problematic. Modern Standard Arabic (MSA), the coded form or *fusHa*, is the language of newspapers, presentations, speeches, newscasts, and any other medium of expression that can be presented in writing. Dialect forms, or *'ammiya*, are used in informal settings, public square conversations, family contexts, and increasingly in the media in venues such as comedy shows and movies. In the effort to prepare their students well, teachers of Arabic disagree on whether their students should be taught only MSA or a dialect or a mixture of both. There is agreement that students' needs should determine the type of Arabic to be taught; teaching should adopt an integrative approach that allows the learner to develop control of the communication process. In addition, there is undisputed agreement by teachers and scholars that a thorough understanding of MSA is important. In this document, the term "Arabic" is used to cover both the formal and non-formal varieties of the language.

Most of the growth in Arabic language teaching has been at institutions of higher education, where Arabic has been taught primarily as a foreign language. The increasing enrollments in K–12 have created some different dynamics in the teaching of Arabic. Many of the K–12 programs were created because of significant numbers of heritage language speakers in the schools, even though the intent was to teach Arabic as a foreign language. Thus programs in the schools have had to contend with students with varying degrees of fluency, from those who are highly fluent and literate to those with what is commonly referred to as "kitchen" language to those with no language background at all. The combination of heritage language speakers and foreign language learners has created challenges for K–12 programs that will take some time to resolve. In developing the standards for Arabic, the Task Force took into consideration the needs of heritage language speakers, although teachers will need to continue to adapt their classroom teaching to accommodate these students.

CHARACTERISTICS OF THE ARABIC LANGUAGE

Spoken by over 250 million people, Arabic is the sixth most commonly used language in the world. It has a rich literary tradition. A member of the Semitic family of languages, it shares the major characteristics of those languages, such as short and long vowels, a root system composed of a set of three, or sometimes four, consonants, and a distinctive system of marking verbs.

Arabic is also distinguished by the diversity of its varieties. The *fusHa* (the "purer" language) is the formal variant that is used throughout the contemporary Arab world in print publications and as an oral medium of expression in newscasts, presentations, and other formal situations. *FusHa* is the direct descendant of the Arabic of the Qur'an and the classical literature of the Golden Age of Islam and is also referred to as Modern Standard Arabic (MSA) in the West. It is the variant that all speakers of Arabic share, though the degree to which a given individual controls it depends on education, environment, and other factors.

Each community within the Arab world also has its own dialectal or colloquial form, or *'ammiya* (the "common" language). The *'ammiyas* differ by region and also by social factors such as education and socioeconomic status. Many of the *'ammiyas* show the influence of other languages; for example, the Moroccan dialects contain words and structures from the language of Morocco's Berber population. The *'ammiyas* are used in informal situations at home, at work, and in almost all social settings.

In oral communication, contemporary speakers of Arabic do not observe a strict separation between *fusHa* and *'ammiya*, but mix them in varying degrees depending on the level of formality of the situation, the complexity of the subject matter, the identity of co-participants in the conversation, and their own levels of control of *fusHa*. An essential part of knowing Arabic is knowing both the *fusHa* and one or more *'ammiyas*, and mastering how, when, and to what extent to mix them, either by introducing colloquialisms into *fusHa* or by bringing *fusHa* structures into *'ammiya*. Being aware of this continuum of language use will serve teachers well since it applies to heritage language speakers and to those who are learning it as a foreign language.

There is a persistent question in the Arabic language field as to how teachers handle heritage language speakers and those who are encountering the language for the first time. There is also a myth that all heritage language speakers come with fairly good speaking skills, albeit a dialect. This is not necessarily true. There are at least three categories of heritage language speakers: those who come with "kitchen" language; those who come with lots of cultural knowledge but virtually no language proficiency at all; and those who are quite proficient in their dialect and have fair to (sometimes) very good command of the formal variety.

Another question that the committee members had to resolve in developing the standards has to do with the role of culture in the Arab world. The Arab world covers some 22 countries; the fact that Arabic is spoken in all of those countries does not necessarily mean that the cultures are all similar. However, there are highly recognizable societal features that make up what can generally be called "Arab culture." For example, the Arab family is distinctive in its relationships and expectations, and the role of religion is culturally definitive, no matter what the affiliation. However, there are also distinct differences between the societal features of countries such as Saudi Arabia, Morocco, and Lebanon, to name a few. The Task Force thus decided that it would approach Arab culture as a whole and that part of the work of teachers and students would be to study and analyze the features that are specific to each country.

Finally, although the standards presented in this document are based on current pedagogical theory and practice, limited space does not allow for discussion of these. Traditional Arabic language teaching has time-honored approaches that have been practiced for generations, the main approach being one that teaches literacy rather than communication. This approach has had to be modified substantially in U.S. classrooms, and these standards recognize those modifications. Thus adherence primarily to grammar and the written word is part of the five goals, rather than the overall goal of teaching Arabic. These standards are designed to guide the teaching of communication in all of its aspects.

ABOUT THE STANDARDS FOR LEARNING ARABIC K–16 IN THE UNITED STATES

Development Process

The *Standards for Learning Arabic K–16 in the United States* were developed by the Task Force on Standards for the Learning of Arabic K–16 in 2004–2005 under the sponsorship of the Arabic K–12 Materials Development Project, the National Capital Language Resource Center, the National Standards Collaborative, the American Association of Teachers of Arabic, and the National Middle East Language Resource Center. The Task Force represented teachers, administrators, researchers, and scholars. As part of the development process, the Task Force presented drafts and received comments and feedback at the American Council on the Teaching of Foreign Languages conference (November 2004); at the Council for Islamic Education in America conference (February 2005); and at the Northeast Conference on the Teaching of Foreign Languages and the National Council of Less Commonly Taught Languages (April 2005). The revised draft was also sent to reviewers who provided a great deal of comment on the content. These standards reflect the advice of the participants.

The process of developing standards raises a number of questions that demand answers. Standards describe outcomes not curriculum. They serve as a road map; they are not to be considered the final statement on what should be taught in a language class. Teachers will need to adapt their teaching to meet the demands and needs of their students. For example, very few schools have a complete K–12 Arabic language program. If an Arabic language program is being introduced in high school, the language that is to be taught at the beginning level will be close to what is listed for Grade 4, and the content will need to be adapted to an older audience. However, the standards are absolutely necessary to give the Arabic language teaching profession a process for planning curriculum and developing assessment tools in accordance with commonly accepted precepts.

The standards contain benchmarks called Sample Progress Indicators. These benchmarks are only samples; they are not intended to be followed blindly. The Task Force encourages users to build on the Sample Progress Indicators and use them to develop learning scenarios that meet the needs of their students. Scenarios have been provided at the end of the Goals that will give users practical ideas on how to build units based on standards.

As the Task Force embarked on developing the standards, members were acutely aware of the fact that there is almost a desperate need for age appropriate and culturally appropriate materials for students learning Arabic in the U.S. The Task Force was also acutely aware that the standards do not produce materials; they are guides to their development. In addition, there are no assessment instruments to test whether these standards are being met or not. The Task Force expects that the standards will serve as a base for developing curricula, materials, and assessment instruments, but is also cognizant that these will take years before they are easily available and that it is up to teachers and program directors to create curricula and materials. The Task Force is also aware that as the standards get used and feedback is provided, there will be changes in subsequent editions.

In summary, the basic approach to these standards is for teachers of Arabic to become familiar with the road map that we are calling the standards. Then they can develop curricula that will provide the specifics based on the needs and demands of their students and program, and begin the process of being able to assess how well their students are doing.

Statement of Philosophy

The Task Force on Standards for the Learning of Arabic K–16 began its work by developing the following statement of philosophy. The statement identifies the Task Force's ultimate aim: to develop standards for instruction that will enable teachers and administrators in grades K through 16 to give their students an effective working knowledge of the Arabic language and Arab culture. This statement of philosophy guided all of the Task Force's subsequent work.

Our philosophy is based on three core beliefs: all students can develop competency in the Arabic language and appreciation for Arabic culture; all students can learn; and instruction must be interactive, learner-centered, and reflect current best practices. We have relied on these beliefs to guide us in the creation of goals and standards for the teaching of Arabic. These standards will help students develop levels of proficiency that will enable them to communicate with native speakers of Arabic both at home and abroad in a culturally appropriate manner. All students will be able to enhance their understanding and knowledge of the Arabic language and culture and recognize the contributions of Arabs to Western and world civilizations.

Our content standards are aligned with those identified in the *Standards for Foreign Language Learning in the 21st Century*, and our performance standards follow the norms established in the *American Council on the Teaching of Foreign Languages Guidelines*. These standards also reflect current best practice principles of curriculum design and instructional methodology.

The Task Force further defines three main premises:
1. Competence in the Arabic language and cultural awareness enable students to:
    - communicate and express themselves in Arabic orally and in writing
    - read and understand Arabic language print materials in various contexts

- comprehend the Arabic language and develop insight into its system
- develop awareness of diverse Arabic cultures and demonstrate culturally appropriate behaviors
- appreciate and value a vast body of literary, religious, and intellectual heritage
- enrich language learning experience by making intellectual and pedagogical connections between the Arabic language and other academic subject areas

2. All learners:
   - learn in a variety of ways and settings
   - acquire proficiency at varying rates
   - achieve varying levels of proficiency
   - can maintain and increase proficiency by seeking contact with Arabic-speaking communities and through study or travel in the Arab world
   - can become lifelong learners who extend their learning beyond the school setting by seeking distance learning programs, participating in self-managed learning, and actively seeking contact with native speakers

3. Arabic language and culture education:
   - is part of the core curriculum in grades K-12
   - is interactive and learner-centered
   - focuses on communication and cultural understanding
   - develops basic communication skills as well as higher-order thinking skills
   - incorporates effective learning and teaching strategies and assessment procedures
   - encourages the use of instructional technologies, including emerging technologies

Communication
Communicate in Arabic

Goal One

STANDARD 1.1 Students engage in conversations and correspondence in Arabic to provide and obtain information, express feelings and emotions, and exchange opinions.

This standard focuses on oral and written interpersonal communication. In most modern languages, students can quickly learn a number of phrases that permit them to interact with each other. In the course of their study, they grow in their ability to converse and write in a culturally appropriate manner. Students who come with a heritage background in Arabic may have already acquired such abilities in informal registers. The ultimate goal of the Arabic language program is to develop speakers who are able to communicate effectively and appropriately in a variety of formal and informal contexts.

Sample Progress Indicators, Grade 4

- Students give and follow simple instructions in Arabic in order to participate in age-appropriate classroom and/or cultural activities.
  Examples: Playing games; preparing Arabic food or drink.

  عمل لبن عيران ، لعبة البرجيس ، خبز مناقيش.

- Students ask and answer simple questions in person or in writing about topics such as family, school events, familiar objects, possessions, daily routine and activities, and celebrations.
  Example: Exchanging simple personal information.

  كيف حالك ، ما اسمك ، أين تسكن ، ماذا تفعل.

- Students share likes and dislikes with each other regarding various common objects, topics, people, and events in their everyday lives.
  Example: Interviewing classmates about their favorite things and activities.

  مقابلة أحد أفراد الصف وسؤاله عن عدد إخوته ، ما هي النشاطات التي يحب القيام بها ، نوع الألعاب الرياضية التي يمارسها ، إلخ.

- Students exchange descriptions with peers about people, places, and products of Arab culture, such as toys, clothing, food, monuments, and types of dwellings.
  Example: Exchanging information about family members or family activities.

  هذه أسرتي ، لي أخ وأخت ، أخي أكبر مني ، أختي في الصف الأول ، إلخ .

- Students role-play everyday situations, such as shopping or eating at a restaurant.
  Example: Choosing items in a grocery store.

  أريد "عرنوص ذرة" . من فضلك أريد كوبا من عصير الفواكه ، المنجة من فضلك ياعم والفراولة والتفاح والبرتقال ولا أريد موزا معه.

Sample Progress Indicators, Grade 8

- Students exchange information in Arabic, orally or via notes and e-mail, about personal events, memorable experiences, and school subjects with classmates or peers in Arabic-speaking communities in the U.S and in the Arab world.
  Examples: Interviewing classmates; eating at an Arabic restaurant; planning an Eid party.

  كيف كانت زيارتك إلى ....؟

Standards for Learning Arabic

- Students use Arabic to acquire goods, services, or information through developmentally appropriate oral communication, writing, or technology.
  Examples: Practicing frequently asked questions about a field trip; buying a book or CD at an Arab store.

  ما هي الأشياء التي تحتاج إليها في هذه الرحلة ؟ ماذا اشتريت من هناك ؟

- Students work as a class or in small groups to propose, discuss, and develop school or community-related activities.
  Examples: Discussing a plan for an Arab cultural display for a school carnival; practicing Arabic songs to perform at different celebrations.

  ما هي معروضات المتحف الذي زرته ؟

- Students extend, accept, and decline informal and formal invitations, using expressions and behavior appropriate to a variety of situations.
  Examples: Inviting friends to a birthday party; inviting a friend's mother to meet your mother; declining an invitation to go to the swimming pool.

  أعتذر عن عدم حضور حفلتك بسبب مرضي.

- Students explore Arabic language Web sites and send and receive e-mail in Arabic.
  Examples: Exchanging information via e-mail concerning an interesting Arabic Web site; visiting Arabic language newspaper Web sites.

  وجدت موقعا جديدا عن الرياضة.

Sample Progress Indicators, Grade 12

- To manage conversation in a variety of real-life situations, students use appropriate expressions that take into consideration the speakers and their relationships and contexts, such as male, female, older, younger.
  Examples: Making introductions; expressing gratitude and regret; stating complaints; apologizing.

  يسعدني أن أقدم لكم فلانة مديرة مدرسة المتفوقين.

- Students discuss their personal feelings, orally or in writing, about significant current or past cultural events in the Arab world or discuss topics being studied in other classes.
  Examples: Exchanging personal feelings about driving regulations in different Arab countries; sharing opinions on social and political issues relevant in the Arab world.

  لماذا لا تسمح لك عائلتك بالخروج معي ؟

- Students work in groups to propose, develop, and defend solutions to issues and problems that are of concern to members of their own cultures as well to the Arab culture.
  Example: Discussing topics related to health, the environment, and employment.

  مناقشة فوائد الرياضة واتباع نظام غذائي نباتي على الصحة.

- Students gather and obtain information through a variety of sources on topics of interest and exchange opinions in a culturally appropriate manner.
  Examples: Conducting surveys and interviews; creating charts, videos, and reports.

  عمل استبيان حول حدث من أحداث الساعة ذي أهمية للجالية العربية.

- Students discuss their understanding of Arab practices and perspectives about topics such as family life, free time, school, and jobs, or give their opinions about Arab products such as clothes, food, and technology.

Examples: Discussing the role of women in the workforce, segregated schools, or cell phones and satellite dishes.

هل أدى استعمال الهاتف الجوال إلى تحسين التواصل أم إلى مشاكل جديدة؟

Sample Progress Indicators, Grade 16

- Students share their reactions to literary texts and analyze them, such as poems, plays, short stories, and novels, or discuss other topics of interest, such as lifestyles, sports, films, and popular music.
  Examples: Talking about their favorite character in a story; explaining why they like or dislike a film.

  مماذا تمثل شخصية اللص في قصة اللص والكلاب لنجيب محفوظ.؟

- Students work in groups to develop and propose solutions to social issues and problems (housing, street violence) related to the school or the community.
  Examples: Developing plans for reducing overcrowding in the immediate community; proposing solutions to personal safety.

  إيجاد حل لتخفيف الكثافة السكانية.

- Students exchange and support their opinions and individual perspectives with peers and other Arabic speakers on a variety of contemporary and historical issues.
  Examples: Debating the relative qualifications of two candidates for political office or two systems of government; building a Power Point presentation to argue for public transportation.

  ما صفات المرشح السياسي الذي تؤيده ؟

- Students prepare and share personal information appropriate for professional contexts.
  Example: Preparing résumés and biographical information related to education and work experience.

  كتابة السيرة الذاتية وإرفاق رسالة معها تبين مواطن القوة في خبرته.

STANDARD 1.2 Students understand and interpret written and spoken Arabic on a variety of topics.

This standard focuses on the understanding and interpretation of written and spoken Arabic. Standard 1.2, unlike Standard 1.1, involves one-way listening and reading in which the learner works with a variety of print and non-print materials. For students who come to Arabic language learning with no previous background in Arabic, the context in which the language is experienced and the ability to control what they hear and read may affect the development of comprehension. As a result, for some learners, the ability to read may develop before the ability to comprehend rapid spoken language. In addition, content knowledge will often affect successful comprehension, for students understand more easily materials that reflect their interests or for which they have some background. In contrast, students with exposure to Arabic through home life may be quite advanced in their understanding of the spoken language and less advanced in terms of their ability to read. The ultimate goal of Arabic instruction is to produce students who are able to understand the full range of informal and formal styles that may be used in written and especially spoken Arabic.

Sample Progress Indicators, Grade 4

- Students understand and follow oral and written directions in Arabic related to daily classroom activities.
  Example: Responding to daily or classroom routines.

  افتحوا الكتب، اغلقوا الكتب، لونوا الصورة، امسك القلم.

- Students identify people and objects in their natural surroundings, based on oral and written descriptions in Arabic.
  Examples: Identifying familiar people when listening to descriptions; pointing out objects in the classroom as the teacher reads descriptions of them.

  ما هذا / ما هذه ؟ من ؟ أين ؟

- Students comprehend main ideas in developmentally appropriate oral narratives such as personal anecdotes, well-known fairy tales, and other narratives based on familiar themes.
  Examples: Retelling the main points of a fairy tale; identifying and making a list of the main characters and events of a narrative.

  ما شخصيات هذه القصة ؟

- Students comprehend brief written messages and short personal notes on familiar topics such as family, school events, and celebrations.
  Examples: Re-telling the content of a greeting card; identifying the subject of a note from a parent.

  عيد سعيد

- Students interpret gestures, intonation, and other visual or auditory cues in Arabic-language media such as videos, films, and TV programs.
  Example: Using simple descriptions such as "happy," "sad," "angry" to describe characters in a video.

  أنا سعيدة ، أشعر بالحر .

Sample Progress Indicators, Grade 8

- Based on Arabic oral and/or written descriptions, students identify concepts and objects from other school subjects, such as historical and contemporary figures.
  Example: Demonstrating their comprehension of three or four important points about Ibn Sina, Ibn Battuta, or Ahmad Zewail.

  اعطوا ثلاثة أو أربعة أمثلة عن رحلات ابن بطوطة . تحدثوا عن الأعمال الطبية التي أنتجها ابن سينا.
  تكلموا عن المقالات التي كتبها أحمد زويل.

- Students comprehend information, announcements, and messages in Arabic related to daily activities and other school subjects.
  Examples: Understanding daily bulletins in Arabic; recognizing Arabic names and phrases in science, geography, or mathematics.

  فهم الاعلانات التي تنشر في اليوميات. التعرف عن الأسماء والجمل في الميادين الجغرافية والعلمية والرياضية.

- Students understand the main ideas or themes from visual Arabic media or live Arabic presentations on topics of personal interest.
  Examples: Understanding media programs about hobbies; understanding main ideas and some details in Arabic television programs such as interviews and talk shows.

  مع من هذه المقابلة ؟ ما موضوع المقابلة ؟

Standards for Learning Arabic

- Students identify the principal characters and comprehend the main ideas and themes in age-appropriate Arabic literary texts such as folk tales and poems.
  Example: Goha (Juha) stories.

  قصص جحا مع لقمة.

- Students use knowledge acquired in other settings and from other subject areas to comprehend spoken and written messages in Arabic.
  Example: Using knowledge of the Middle East gained in social studies class to help interpret an article in Arabic; listening to a guest speaker discuss his or her Arab heritage.

  ضيف يتكلم عن نشأته في الوطن العربي .

Sample Progress Indicators, Grade 12

- Students demonstrate an understanding of the main ideas and some details of live or recorded Arabic discussions concerning current events, Arab culture, or subjects being studied in other classes.
  Examples: Understanding the gist and the specific examples in a presentation on cultural stereotypes; comparing main points in two Arabic TV programs on the Middle East.

  تحديد أوجه الاختلاف والتشابه بين البرنامجين ، أي البرنامجين أعجبك ولماذا ؟

- Students demonstrate an understanding of the principal elements of non-fiction articles in Arabic print sources on topics of current and historical importance.
  Example: Understanding the main points expressed in an online opinion piece on voting rights for women in Saudi Arabia.

  مقارنة آراء المشاركين في مناقشة على الشبكة العالمية .

- Students demonstrate the ability to recognize levels of formality/informality in written and spoken Arabic and to understand their significance.
  Example: Comparing the speaking styles of two television personalities and understanding how the informality of their language corresponds to topic or attitude.

  مقارنة مراسلات تلفزيونية في محطتي إل بي بي سي والجزيرة .

- Students demonstrate an increasing understanding of linguistic and cultural nuances of meaning in written and spoken language as expressed by speakers of Arabic in informal settings.
  Example: Understanding the ways in which Yusuf Idris uses formal and informal Arabic in a selected play or novel.

  في أي مجال يستعمل يوسف إدريس العامية والفصحى ؟

- Students demonstrate an increasing understanding of cultural nuances of meaning in expressive products of the culture, including literary works and the visual arts.
  Example: Understanding the Egypt-specific elements in the work of Naguib Mahfouz.

  ما العناصر التي تشير إلى مصر خصوصا في كتابات نجيب محفوظ ؟

Sample Progress Indicators, Grade 16

- Students demonstrate an understanding of the main ideas and most supporting details of live or recorded Arabic discussions concerning current events or interesting topics pertinent to Arab culture or subjects being studied in other classes.
  Example: Understanding the main ideas and significant details of a discussion on the situation of Palestinians in Jordan.

  فهم الأفكار المطروحة حول وضع الفلسطينيين في الأردن من خلال مشاهدة مناقشة حول الموضوع .

- Students analyze, discuss, and debate the main plot, subplots, and roles and significance of characters in authentic Arabic literary texts.
  Example: Naguib Mahfouz's trilogy.

  حبكة ثلاثية نجيب محفوظ وشخصياتها الرئيسية .

- Students demonstrate the ability to demonstrate levels of formality/informality in written and spoken Arabic and to understand their significance.
  Example: Comparing the writing styles of two Arabic newspaper editorial writers and understanding how the formality or informality of their language corresponds to topic or attitude.

  مقالات عوني بشير (فيها بعض العامي) ومقالات غيره من الكتاب. كتابة رسائل قصيرة غير رسمية ورسائل رسمية.

- Students understand and analyze linguistic and cultural nuances of meaning in written and spoken language as expressed by speakers of Arabic in informal settings.
  Example: Analyzing the ways in which Ghassan Kanafany uses formal and informal Arabic in his plays and novels.

  تحليل كتابة غسان كنفاني .

- Students understand and analyze cultural nuances of meaning in expressive products of the culture, including selections from various literary genres and the visual arts in Arabic.
  Example: Understanding the ways in which Sa'adallah Wannous goes beyond traditional Arabic literary forms in his writings.

  عناصر التجديد اللغوي في كتابة سعد الله ونوس .

STANDARD 1.3 Students present information, concepts, and ideas to an audience of listeners or readers on a variety of topics.

This standard focuses on the presentation of information, concepts, and ideas in spoken and written modes. This standard, in most cases, is concerned with one-way speaking and writing. Writing in Arabic involves several challenges, including the ability to recognize and produce the symbols of the Arabic alphabet, letter/sound correspondence, phonemic recognition, right to left orientation, and word order. Students with little or no previous experience in Arabic are likely to produce written and spoken language that contains a variety of learned patterns that cast Arabic phrases into English syntactical patterns or phrases that look like English with words in Arabic. This is a natural process. Over time, students begin to acquire authentic patterns and to use appropriate styles. By contrast, students with a heritage background in Arabic write in ways that closely resemble the spoken language and incorporate informal oral styles. Over time, learners develop the ability to write and speak using a variety of more formal registers. Advanced learners develop the ability to write about and give presentations on topics of personal and professional interest in domains such as art, history, economics, and politics.

Sample Progress Indicators, Grade 4
- Students prepare illustrated stories in Arabic about activities or events in their environment and present them to the class.

Examples: Creating big books, posters, and dioramas about daily activities with families or classmates.

صنع معروضات تحوي صورا وكلمات .

- Students dramatize familiar Arabic songs, short folktales, or poems.
  Example: Singing and acting out *zaraʻana jazara jazara*, "We have planted a carrot."

تمثيل و غناء قصة زرعنا الجزرة: أغنية الجزرة .

- Students prepare short oral or written Arabic messages about people and things in the school environment and exchange the information with other Arabic language classes either in person or via technology.
  Example: Sharing field trip experiences with students in another class.

الحديث عن تجارب رحلة مدرسية .

- Students tell or retell Arabic stories orally or in writing.
  Example: Reading *Ali Baba and the Forty Thieves* and then retelling it orally.

يسرد التلاميذ قصة علي بابا والأربعين حرامي .

- Students use Arabic to write or tell peers in or out of school about their own cultures or cultural products and practices.
  Examples: Listing activities or basic information about holiday celebrations, family events, and food.

يتكلم التلميذ عن نفسه من خلال احتفاله بالأعياد .

Sample Progress Indicators, Grade 8

- Students present short plays and skits, recite selected poems and anecdotes, and perform songs in Arabic for a school or community related event such as a board of education or parent-teacher meeting.
  Example: Creating skits and practice songs for an Arabic theatrical performance.

إعداد تمثيليات وقصائد عربية وعرضها للزوار .

- Students prepare audio, video, or digitally recorded messages in Arabic to share with school peers and/or members of the Arab community on topics of personal interest.
  Examples: Creating a videotape about the steps needed to perform the *dabkeh*; creating a commercial about a product.

إعداد تسجيل مرئي أو صوتي لتعليم الآخرين خطوات الدبكة .

- Students prepare brief written reports about personal experiences and events or other school subjects in Arabic to share with classmates and/or members of the Arab community.
  Examples: Creating a travel brochure; creating a poster describing students in the class.

إعداد نشرة حول السفر إلى بلد عربي .

- Students express preferences and feelings about information they have gathered about events, experiences, everyday activities and other school subjects.
  Example: Creating lists of favorite musicians, foods, classes, sports, and hobbies and explaining the reasons for their preferences.

إعداد قوائم بأمور ذات أهمية للتلاميذ وتعليل سبب اختيارهم لها .

- Students prepare short oral and written descriptions in Arabic about the plot and characters in selected pieces of age-appropriate literature.
  Examples: Describing the plot and the characters of one of the Sinbad tales.

وصف حبكة إحدى قصص السندباد وشخصياتها .

Sample Progress Indicators, Grade 12

- Students write extended descriptions in Arabic about the people and objects present in their everyday environment in and out of school.
  Examples: Describing your best friend; writing about your favorite television show.
  وصف دقيق للصديق المفضل وللبرنامج التلفزيوني المحبب .
- Students describe in paragraph style in Arabic how to perform a task.
  Examples: Describing how to set a table, make tabbouleh, or play a game.
  وصف كيفية تحضير طاولة الطعام ، تحضير تبولة أو المشاركة في لعبة .
- Students use Arabic to perform scenes and/or create simple poems or short stories connected to a topic from another discipline such as world history, geography, or art.
  Examples: Impersonating a famous author or personality; acting out a historic scene.
  تقليد شخصية سياسية .
- Students use Arabic to perform scenes from plays and to recite poems or excerpts from stories familiar to Arabs.
  Example: Performing a well-known play such as *Al-Ṣafqa* by Tawfiq Al-Hakim.
  يمثل التلاميذ مشاهد من قصص أو مسرحيات عربية مثلا مسرحية "الصفقة" لتوفيق الحكيم.
- Students prepare research-based reports in Arabic on current events from the perspectives of both U.S. and Arab cultures.
  Example: Comparing the role of women in the United States and Saudi Arabia.
  يقوم التلاميذ ببحث عن سياسة الولايات المتحدة تجاه معاملة المرأة في السعودية .

Sample Progress Indicators, Grade 16

- Students select and analyze expressive products of Arab cultures presented in various literary genres or the fine arts.
  Example: Analyzing the elements of the travel literature of Ibn Battuta and Marco Polo.
  تحليل عناصر رحلات ابن بطوطة وماركو بولو .
- Students summarize in writing the content of an article or documentary intended for native speakers of Arabic in order to discuss the topics electronically with other learners of Arabic.
  Example: Summarizing an article found on the Internet.
  تلخيص مقالة تختار من الشبكة العالمية .
- Students give presentations in Arabic on research-based analyses of current events from the perspectives of both U.S. and Arab cultures.
  Example: Presenting findings on research conducted about globalization.
  تقديم بحث عن مفهوم العولمة ومدى قبوله في المجتمع العربي .
- Students use the Internet, library resources, and technology in Arabic to build support for their opinions and present them.
  Example: Creating Power Point presentations in Arabic to support perspectives on a topic.
  تناسب العمارة الإسلامية مع التركيب الاجتماعي .

Cultures *Goal Two*
Gain knowledge and understanding of the cultures of the Arab world

STANDARD 2.1 Students demonstrate an understanding of the relationship between the practices and perspectives of the various cultures of the Arab world.

This standard emphasizes social interactions. Students interpret cultural patterns demonstrated by social interactions of native speakers of Arabic to identify cultural attitudes and values. Students will use this knowledge to develop the cultural awareness to interact in Arabic with native Arabic speakers in a culturally appropriate manner. Standard 2.1 focuses on the cultural practices that reflect the traditions, norms, beliefs, and structures of the Arab world.

Sample Progress Indicators, Grade 4
- Students use appropriate body language, gestures, and Arabic expressions for greetings, leave taking, and common classroom interactions, such as shaking hands and standing when an adult enters the room.
- Students demonstrate familiarity with social customs and practices of Arabs that are of interest to children. Topics may include appropriate interactions with family members, traditional foods, and typical holidays in various Arab countries.
- Students learn about and participate in age-appropriate cultural activities such as games, songs, dances, celebrations, storytelling, drama, computer games, and children's programs.

Sample Progress Indicators, Grade 8
- Students identify and use appropriate Arabic verbal and non-verbal greetings and expressions in formal and casual communication, such as the custom of the "greeting kiss."
- Students analyze patterns of Arabic language use and language expressions such as titles, greetings, and pleasantries, and interpret the ideas, perspectives, and beliefs expressed by Arabs through these expressions, such as the use of titles, "uncle" and "aunt" to address distant relatives and family friends.
- Students learn about and participate in activities enjoyed by Arab youth such as games, sports, music, dance, drama, and celebrations.
- Students recognize and develop awareness of the diversity of social customs in Arab countries based on history, geographical regions, and religious beliefs. Topics may include family life, dress code, food, and typical holidays such as Ramadan, Christmas, and independence days in different Arab countries.

Sample Progress Indicators, Grade 12

- Students discuss and participate in activities enjoyed by Arab teenagers, such as sports, music, dance, games, and entertainment, and examine the social norms that underlie these activities.
  Examples: Soccer (football); celebration dances, such as at weddings.
- Students discuss family ties and relationships in the Arab world and examine the role of intergenerational connections in Arab communities.
  Example: The effect of extended family ties and loyalties on behavioral patterns.
- Students analyze the political, legal, and economic systems and practices in various Arab countries and discuss the factors that influenced the development of these systems.
  Examples: The role of newspapers and freedom of expression; the role of labor unions.
- Students discuss social issues in different Arab communities and examine their impact on the behavioral patterns of individuals, families, and communities.
  Examples: Gender roles; education; family tradition; political freedom.
- Students use acquired knowledge of Arab culture in interacting in a culturally appropriate manner with Arabs in a variety of contexts.
  Examples: Introducing a speaker in a formal setting; expected behavior on a field trip; visiting in a home for the first time; expectations in informal settings, such as developing relationships with Arabs.

Sample Progress Indicators, Grade 16

- Students analyze cultural, social, and business practices in different Arab countries and determine the influence of religious, economic, social, and political factors on the development of these practices.
  Examples: The role of family relationships and personal contacts in conducting business in the Arab world; living arrangements of single adult children.
- Students analyze changes in Arab communities and the impact of technology and telecommunication on the practices of the young generation of Arabs, and their influence on young Arabs' perceptions and beliefs.
  Example: Discussing ways in which information is accessed and exchanged among younger Arabs.
- Students analyze contemporary issues in the Arab world, such as gender relations, political conflicts, education, family traditions, environmental concerns, employment, and politics, and examine their impact on current world affairs.
  Examples: Exploring the role of women in the work force; discussing the issues of access to water in different Arab countries.
- Students examine major elements of Arab cultures such as family connections and concepts of time and space, and analyze how they are perceived by people from other cultures.
  Examples: Examining the role of physical proximity between individuals; examining the role of authority when conducting business in the Arab world.
- Students interact in a culturally appropriate manner with Arabic-speaking individuals in a variety of contexts, such as hosting Arabic discussion circles with topics relevant to the Arab world, introducing speakers, and visiting Arabic-speaking countries.

STANDARD 2.2 Students demonstrate an understanding of the relationship between the products and perspectives of the various cultures of the Arab world.

This standard emphasizes cultural appreciation. It focuses on the cultural products of the Arab world and how they relate to the traditions, beliefs, and structures of Arab cultures and societies. Students learn to interpret and analyze the many cultural products of Arab civilization, such as music, film, literary texts, poems, calligraphy, textiles, and architecture, and to identify the underlying cultural values and norms reflected in these products.

Sample Progress Indicators, Grade 4

- Students examine tangible products of various Arab cultures, such as food, clothing, types of dwellings, modes of transportation, flags, famous monuments, pottery, and carvings.
  Example: Students study and compare different dwellings in Arab countries, urban and rural, such as nomadic dwellings in the Western Sahara and in Jordan.
- Students become familiar with children's Arabic literature, video games, and television programs, and learn children's songs and games from different Arab regions.
  Examples: Children's TV shows: افتح ياسمسم *Iftaḥ ya Simsim* or عالم سمسم *'Aalam Simsim*.
- Students become familiar with simple elements of Arabic art and calligraphy and, when appropriate, produce similar products.
  Example: Using calligraphy to make cards that celebrate different occasions and holidays.
- Students study the different geographical environments in which Arabs live, and examine the impact of these environments on the lifestyles of various Arab communities.
  Examples: Life in the desert as it affects food preservation; the use of animals.

Sample Progress Indicators, Grade 8

- Students identify and explore the function of utilitarian products from Arab countries and discuss how these products reflect the lifestyles and norms of Arabs and Arab communities.
  Examples: Household items; clothing; musical instruments.
- Students examine expressive products of Arab culture and identify the lifestyles and social practices reflected through these products.
  Examples: Music; films; storytelling; puppet theaters; television series.
- Students study and produce simple forms of various products of Arab cultures from different countries, such as music, dance, fashion, tapestry, art, and cuisine, and develop an appreciation of these cultural aspects.
  Example: Create a fashion show depicting traditional and modern dress.
- Students recognize the contributions of Arab scientists and scholars to science, medicine, astronomy, mathematics, chemistry, agriculture, economics, and social sciences.
  Examples: The contribution of Al-Razi to medicine, literature, and science; Ibn Sina to medicine; Mohamad bin Musa al-Khawarizmi to mathematics/algebra.
- Students examine the co-existence of major religions in early Arab society and their influences on each other.
  Example: Architecture as an example of the co-existence of Arab Muslims and Jews in early Spain.

Sample Progress Indicators, Grade 12

- Students analyze and discuss the images and perceptions presented in classical and modern products of the Arab media and in different literary genres, including drama.
  Examples: *Qais wa Layla, 'Antar wa 'Abla,* and the works of Al-Mamluk al-Sharid and satire, such as Goha's (Juha) adventures and the Gahwar soap opera.
- Students examine, analyze, and appreciate major artistic products of Arabic cultures such as calligraphy works by major Arab artists and famous architectural structures, and examine their impact on the development and advancement of these fields.
  Examples: The impact and contributions to all aspects of Spanish culture, such as architecture, food, and music.
- Students examine the impact of Arab scientists and scholars on the advancement of science, agriculture, economics, medicine, astronomy, mathematics, chemistry, and social sciences in ancient and modern civilizations.
  Example: Mohammad bin Musa Al-Khawarizmi's contribution to logarithm through the introduction of the zero digit.
- Students attend and organize Arabic discussion forums, concerts, plays, musical performances, and poetry recitations.
  Example: A poetry recitation based on the style of Souk Okaz.
- Students identify various Arabic Internet sites and utilize them to learn more about Arab cultures and issues related to the Arab world.
  Example: Comparing an Internet site on Arabic poems with one on culture and folklore literature.

Sample Progress Indicators, Grade 16

- Students analyze patterns of Arabic language use and linguistic expressions used by the media and analyze the context and historical usage of some of these expressions to identify Arabs' thoughts and perspectives.
  Examples: Examining similar news articles in *Al-Watan al-'Arabi,* published in London, and *Al-'Aalam al-'Arabi,* published in Cairo.
- Students analyze the products of Arab media such as news, commercials, documentaries, newspaper articles, television programs, and Web sites to identify beliefs, cultural patterns, and social behaviors of Arabs.
  Example: Working in teams to present a news broadcast in Arabic.
- Students read, analyze, and appreciate Arabic literature and poetry and discuss its role in expressing the beliefs and political views of their authors and the society or ideology they represent.
  Example: Examine the concept of "mother" in Arabic literature and poetry and its influence on Arab culture and society.
- Students analyze the impact of technology and modernization on the changes in social norms and practices of Arabs and their cultures and societies.
  Example: Analyze the influence of chat rooms and the development and change in relationships among youth.
- Students become familiar with social, political, and cultural issues discussed at various Arabic forums, Internet sites, chat rooms, and blogs.

Connections   Goal Three
Use Arabic to connect with other disciplines and acquire information

STANDARD 3.1 Students reinforce and further their knowledge of other disciplines through Arabic.

This standard stresses the interdisciplinary nature of learning and the use of Arabic to broaden and deepen all of a student's learning experiences. Students relate the information studied in other subjects to their learning of the Arabic language and culture, expanding and deepening their understanding of other areas of knowledge as they refine their communication abilities and broaden their cultural understanding. The information and concepts presented in content classes form the basis for continued learning in the Arabic language classroom. Advanced learners are able to use Arabic to learn and communicate with others about domain-specific content areas such as art, history, economics, and politics.

Sample Progress Indicators, Grade 4

- Students use Arabic vocabulary to refer to items and concepts learned in other subject areas.
  Examples: Naming animals in Arabic; identifying transportation, the weather, and foods.
  تسمية حيوانات - أماكن مثل الصحراء - الغابة - الحديقة - وسائل النقل - حالة الجو - أنواع الطعام .

- Students use numbers, recognize quantities, and use measurements, and recognize those concepts as also fundamental to the Arab intellectual tradition.
  Examples: Counting numbers on a graph; measuring the length of objects around the classroom.
  حساب أشياء حسب الطول والحجم .

- Students identify family members, family relationships, and broader family social relationships in the community.
  Examples: Creating a family tree and identifying one's relationship to the names.
  الأسرة والعلاقات الأسرية: هذا أبي - أخي - أختي - عمي - خالي - جدي - جدتي.

Sample Progress Indicators, Grade 8

- Students discuss topics of other school subjects, including language arts, geographical terms and concepts, historical facts and famous people, mathematical concepts, and scientific concepts.
  Examples: Solving word problems in mathematics; recognizing historical people and important dates.
  حل مسائل حسابية متنوعة. تحديد بلاد عربية أو الموقع على خريطة العالم.

- Students comprehend through illustrated story books and short videos topics that have been studied in other classes.
  Example: Watching a video on human vital organs and identifying the importance of these organs.
  مشاهدة فيديو عن جسم الإنسان وتحديد أهمية كل عضو من هذه الأعضاء.

Standards for Learning Arabic

- Students elaborate on their study of classroom geography by studying the countries, cities, and major geographical features of the Arab world.
  Examples: Topography; climates; urban and rural areas.
  تحديد العناصر المؤثرة على مناخ البلاد العربية.
- Students elaborate on their study of world history by studying the history of the Arab world.
  Examples: Exploring the Web site of the Arab American National Museum in Michigan.
  البحث في الشبكة العالمية عن مشاهير العرب الأمريكيين ومساهمتهم في المجتمع الأمريكي.
- Students recognize the contributions of Arab historical and contemporary figures, such as Ibn Batuta or Zaman al Wasl to the arts, sciences, mathematics, and literature and Helen Thomas to news reporting.
  Examples: Exploring famous Arab Americans and their contributions to American society.

Sample Progress Indicators, Grade 12

- Students discuss topics in Arabic such as music, art, history, science, and literature.
  Example: Discussing environmental issues such as pollution and recycling.
  مناقشة العوامل المؤثرة على البيئة .
- Students exchange views in Arabic on topics learned about in other content classes.
  Example: Choosing a nutritional plan and writing about its efficacy.
  اختيار نوع من أنواع الحمية الغذائية والكتابة عن جدواه .
- Students broaden their understanding of world art, music, and literature through their study of Arabic language and cultures.
  Examples: Research the influence of the Arabic art, music, and Islamic architecture in Spain.
  بحث عن تأثير الأدب والفن العربي في الحضارة الإسبانية .
- Students elaborate in Arabic on their study of world history, politics, and economics by studying relevant events and factors in the countries of the Arab world.
  Example: Discussing current events in the Arab world and its effects on life in the U.S.
  مناقشة الأحداث الراهنة وتأثيرها على العيش في أمريكا .

Sample Progress Indicators, Grade 16

- Students obtain and use information available in Arabic related to their field of study and topics of interest.
  Example: History majors read articles in Arabic on Arabic history and present summaries in class.
- Students use Arabic language resources to gather information in Arabic on the work and knowledge of professionals in their fields of study.
  Example: Examining and reporting about the information of subjects studied from original resources.
  الحصول على معلومات من المراجع الأصلية .
- Students combine information acquired in Arabic, English, and other languages to meet the needs of their fields of study.
  Example: Preparing an economic study using data gathered from Internet sites and print sources from around the world as part of an international relations project.

STANDARD 3.2 Students acquire information and recognize viewpoints that are only available through the Arabic language and culture.

This standard emphasizes the unique nature of the perspective that students gain when they study Arabic language and culture. As students gain access to styles of Arabic, they broaden the sources of information available to them and develop a new "window on the world." In the earlier stages of language learning, they begin to examine a variety of sources intended for native speakers and extract specific information. As they become more proficient users of the Arabic language, they seek out materials of interest to them, analyze the content, compare it to information available in their own language, and assess the linguistic and cultural differences.

Sample Progress Indicators, Grade 4

- Students are able to listen to folktales, stories, and poems in Arabic that describe various cultural historical figures.
  Examples: Listening to stories about Aladdin and Sinbad.

  الاستماع إلى قصص علاء الدين .

- Students broaden their understanding of children's literature through learning traditional Arabic songs/lyrics and poetry.
  Examples: Learning birthday songs, Mother's Day songs, and Ramadan songs.

  أناشيد دينية للأطفال - عيد الأم - وأعياد الميلاد .

- Students broaden their understanding of history and culture through exposure to pictures of famous Arab historical monuments.
  Examples: Identifying pictures, such as the Nile, the Red Sea, Petra, and the Omayyad Mosque.

  التعرف على صور للنيل والبحر الأحمر وبطرة ومسجد أمية.

- Students broaden their understanding of world cultures through exposure to traditional and contemporary Arab clothing and accessories of various regions, games and pastimes, and different kinds of Middle Eastern cuisine and cooking utensils.
  Example: Examining different kind of clothing in the Arab world and how it reflects perspectives about local environments.

  أنواع الملابس المختلفة في العالم العربي .

Sample Progress Indicators, Grade 8

- Students are able to read Arabic language folktales.
  Examples: Read the story Two Ducks and the Talkative Turtle.

  البطتان والسلحفاة الثرثارة .

- Students broaden their understanding of world cultures through the study of Arabic cultural and religious events.
  Examples: Studying Ramadan, Mother's Day, the New Year, and Lent; the weekly calendar.

  التعرف على رمضان وعيد الام والسنة الجديدة والصوم الكبير والتقويم الأسبوعي.

- Students broaden their understanding of the contributions of Arab civilization to the development of present day mathematical and scientific discoveries.
  Examples: Studying the contributions Al Khawarizmy and Ibn Sina.

  مساهمات الخوارزمي وابن سينا .

Sample Progress Indicators, Grade 12

- Students use a variety of Arabic-language sources to understand the unique viewpoints and perspectives of the Arab world.
  Examples: Reading and distinguishing the viewpoints in print and online newspapers, magazines, and e-mail; watching videos related to history, social issues, science and technology.
- Students read, observe and listen to a variety of sources intended for Arabic speakers of their age on topics of interest.
- Examples: Music, the Internet, films, literature, and other media types that provide information in Arabic.
- Students obtain information and viewpoints available through Arabic-language media and compare them with information and viewpoints written in the United States for an English-speaking audience.
  Example: Compare an article on the same subject in *An-Nahar* and *The Washington Post*.

  مقارنة جريدتي النهار وواشنطون بوست في مقال يعالج نفس الموضوع .

Sample Progress Indicators, Grade 16

- Students compare information available in Arabic-language media, compare it with information on the same topics available in English, and analyze the different perspectives and/or biases shown in the sources.
  Examples: Comparing the viewpoints of reporting on the same events by CNN and Al-Jazeera.

  المقارنة بين وجهتي نظر في التقارير المقدمة على قناتي الجزيرة وسي إن إن في معالجة نفس الحدث.

- Students regularly use information from Arabic-language sources to communicate in oral and written formats with Arabic speakers and other learners about topics relevant to their fields of study.
  Examples: Discussing the political issues of increasing oil production by OPEC; analyzing and evaluating the effect of cheap imports on the U.S. economy.

  تحليل وتقييم تأثير المستوردات الرخيصة على الإقتصاد الأمريكي .

Comparisons   Goal Four
Develop insight into language and culture

STANDARD 4.1 Students demonstrate understanding of the nature of language through comparisons between Arabic and their own language.

This standard focuses on the impact that learning the linguistic elements of Arabic has on students' ability to examine their own language, and to develop hypotheses about the structure and use of languages in general. From the beginning of their Arabic language learning experience, students can compare and contrast it with other languages they know as different elements are presented. Activities that will assist students in understanding how languages work can be systematically integrated into instruction.

Sample Progress Indicators, Grade 4

- Students cite and use examples of borrowed words in Arabic and their own language, and they make the connection between Arabic and other languages.
  Example: Algebra الجبر; sugar سكر; chemise قميص
- Students are aware of the existence of idiomatic expressions in both Arabic and English and talk about the use of idiomatic expressions.
  Example: Haste makes waste, في التأني السلامة وفي العجلة الندامة
- Students demonstrate an awareness of formal and informal forms of language in greetings and leave-takings and use expressions of politeness in Arabic and in English.
  Examples: How are you? (informal and formal); goodbye (informal and formal).
  كيفك ، كيف الحال ، مع السلامة ، رافقتكم السلامة.
- Students demonstrate an awareness of the differences and similarities between the sound and writing systems of English and Arabic.
  Example: Making a diagram to compare and contrast Arabic letters and Roman letters a, b, c, d, alif (a), ba (b), ta (t), tha (th).

	a b c d	ا ب ت ث
	د س ب ا	th t b a

- Students recognize the category of grammatical gender and number in Arabic.
  Example: Comparing the Arabic dual and plural forms to the English plural. *bint, bintaan, banaat* (girl, girls); *talib, taliba* (male student, female student); *talib, talibaan, tullaab* (male student, students); *kataba, katabaa, katabu* (he wrote, they wrote).

a girl, two girls, girls	بنت - بنتان - بنات
male student, female student	طالب - طالبة
a student, two students, students	طالب - طالبان - طلاب
he wrote, they wrote (two), they wrote	كتب - كتبا - كتبوا

Sample Progress Indicators, Grade 8

- Students examine the way languages borrow vocabulary from each other.
  Examples: تلفاز television; بنك bank; أمير البحر Admiral; مخزن magazine; شراب syrup
- Students demonstrate an awareness of ways of expressing respect and communicating status differences in English and in Arabic.

Example: Describing the differences between a conversation with children and a conversation with an adult; you أنت، أنتم. "at your service." حضرتك، حضرتكم

- Students demonstrate an ability to recognize and correctly use the sounds that are distinctive to Arabic.
  Examples: ha and ḥ, t and ṭ, th and ḍ, a and 'a.
  ع   ا   ظ   ط   ذ   ت   ح   هـ

- Students recognize differences and similarities in word order between Arabic and English.
  Examples: The adjective and noun الصفة والموصوف: Short Sentence (lit. sentence short) باب كبير big door ; جملة قصيرة

- Students compare the organizing principle in the Arabic language from "general to specific" with the organizing principles of English.
  Example: Compare and contrast dates/time written in Arabic and English
  15/ 9 /2004 ?(Arabic) vs. 9/15/2004 (English).

Sample Progress Indicators, Grade 12

- Students demonstrate awareness that some phrases and idioms do not translate directly from one language to another.
  Examples: I play the piano أنا ألعب، أعزف بيانو، ألعب بالبيانو
  wear perfume أتعطر، ألبس عطر

- Students analyze elements of Arabic, such as time and tense, and comparable linguistic elements in English, and conjecture about how languages use forms to express time, number, and gender relationships.
  كتب - كتبت؛ كتبوا - كتبن؛ يكتبون - سيكتبون

Sample Progress Indicators, Grade 16

- Students demonstrate an awareness of the differences between the English and Arabic paragraph.
  Example: The use of topic sentence in the English paragraph versus the process of developing and expanding a single idea to develop an Arabic paragraph.

- Students compare the use of collocations in English and Arabic.
  Examples: شرب سيجارة (lit.: drank a cigarette) smoked a cigarette; شن حربا to wage a war.

- Students compare how poetry and musical lyrics reflect social issues and conflict.
  Examples: The poetry of Nizar Gabani and Mahmoud Darwish are often set to popular music, a practice not common in modern western culture.

STANDARD 4.2 Students demonstrate understanding of the concept of culture through comparisons between the cultures of the Arab world and their own.

This standard stresses development of a broad understanding of culture through examination and comparison of specific examples. As students expand their knowledge of cultures through language learning, they continually discover perspectives, practices, and products that are similar to and different from those in their own culture and others that they know, and they develop the ability to hypothesize about cultural systems in general. This standard helps focus this reflective process for all students by encouraging integration of this process into instruction from the earliest levels of learning.

Sample Progress Indicators, Grade 4

- Students compare simple patterns of behavior and verbal interaction in various cultural settings.
  Examples: Comparing proper greetings and leave-takings; comparing customs and expectations about hand shaking.
- Students demonstrate awareness that gestures are an important part of communication and that gestures may differ among languages and cultures.
  Example: Arabs use a clockwise rotation gesture of one hand to indicate a question, whereas Americans use open palms to do the same.
- Students compare and contrast tangible products and practices of various cultures.
  Examples: The use of bread in picking up food and the use of a spoon to eat rice in the Arab world versus western customs.
- Students compare and contrast intangible products of different cultures.
  Examples: Comparing rhymes, songs, and folk tales and games, such as *Taq Taq Taqiyah* طاق طاق طاقية and musical chairs.
- Students recognize the interests and practices that they have in common with their Arab peers and peers in various other cultures.
  Examples: Video games, sports, fast food, and clothing.

Sample Progress Indicators, Grade 8

- Students identify the similarities and differences between school and family life in their own region and in various regions of the Arabic-speaking world.
  Example: Comparing the length of the school year, classes and homework in the U.S. versus Arab countries.
- Students contrast verbal and nonverbal behavior within particular activities among friends, classmates, family members, and teachers in Arab cultures and in the U.S.
  Examples: Table manners and saying *Du'a*; behavior for private parties, such as time of arrival and expectations about gift giving and receiving.
- Students demonstrate awareness that they, too, have a culture, by comparing sample daily activities in Arab cultures and their own.
  Examples: Study time, personal hygiene routines, work ethics, family and meal times.
- Students examine the relationship between cultural perspectives and practices, such as holidays, celebrations, work habits, and play, by analyzing selected practices from Arab and U.S. cultures.

Examples: The appropriate dress expected to be worn on holidays; the gifts of money contrasted with other kinds of gifts.
- Students examine the relationship between cultural perspectives and expressive products by analyzing selected products from the target cultures and their own.
Examples: Aesop's Fables versus *Kalilah wa Dumma*; creating a quilt or collage that represents Arab cultures as well as American culture.

Sample Progress Indicators, Grade 12
- Students identify variations in musical rhythm and instrumentation as reflections of local sources and history.
Example: The use of *rabada* by Bedouins and the piano by westerners.
- Students compare and analyze nuances of meanings of words, expressions, and idioms in Arabic and English.
Examples: The tone of a written text or speech; nonverbal behavior, such as smiling, body language (sitting/crossing the legs), and hand gestures (scratching one's head).
- Students analyze the relationship between perspectives and practices in Arab cultures and compare these with those evident in U.S. culture.
Examples: Students' lifestyles, such as living at home while attending college as opposed to leaving home at age 18; the status of the elderly in Arab and U.S. society.
- Students analyze the relationship between perspectives and products in Arab cultures and compare these with those evident in U.S. culture.
Examples: The role of religious institutions; architecture; meal times.
- Students identify and analyze cultural perspectives as reflected in a variety of literary genres.
Examples: The use of *zajal* used mainly in wedding and celebratory festivities; the theatre as a forum for political satire and debate; poetry used to express nationalistic, romantic and political sentiments.

Sample Progress Indicators, Grade 16
- Students compare thematically similar Arabic and American films, focusing on specific cultural practices.
Example: Comparing *The Extras* (Syria) with *Fahrenheit 911*.
- Students compare the ways in which current events are covered in the U.S. and in the Arab press.
Example: Comparing the Arabic and English versions of *An-Nahar* with the *Des Moines Register* and *The Washington Times*.
- Students compare TV programs broadcast in Arabic and in English.
Examples: Comparing البيت مش بيتك with Survivor; Star Academy with American Idol.
- Students develop a model Arabic League and compare it to a model U.N.
- Students analyze and compare legal, social, and economic systems between Arab and U.S. society.
Example: Examine the development of the concept of "*shura*" in Arab society and compare it to legal arbitration in Western societies.

Communities *Goal Five*
Participate in multilingual communities at home and in the world

STANDARD 5.1 Students use Arabic both within and beyond the school setting.

This standard focuses on Arabic as a tool for communication with other Arabic speakers throughout one's life in schools, in the community, and abroad. Applying what has been learned in the Arabic language program, students come to recognize the advantages inherent in being able to communicate in more than one language and develop an understanding of the power of language. As students have opportunities to use Arabic in response to real-world needs, they seek out situations beyond the school in which they can apply their competencies. Advanced learners of Arabic are able to use Arabic as a life-long tool for communication in their professional as well as in their personal lives.

Sample Progress Indicators, Grade 4

- Students participate in conversations with native Arabic speakers about everyday matters and daily experiences.
  Example: Sharing feelings about lunches served at school; sharing information about after school activities.
- Students communicate orally and write simple messages to Arabic speakers in the community and abroad concerning everyday matters and daily experiences.
- Students participate in special performances that demonstrate an understanding of Arab cultures.
  Examples: Dance, song, music, drama, drumming.
- Students invite community members to participate in Arabic language or culture-related school events.
  Example: Inviting a member of the community to talk about experiences growing up in an Arabic-speaking country.
- Students participate in before-and-after-school activities related to Arabic language and cultures.
  Example: Interviewing adults about where Arabic can be used, e.g., in the professions or in business.

Sample Progress Indicators, Grade 8

- Students use Arabic to talk to or write to peers and other members of the local or international Arabic-speaking community about daily life, various experiences, and special events.
  Example: Exchange letters and e-mails about school and life with Arabic speaking students in Arab countries.
- Students interact with Arabic-speaking members of the community to learn about community relations and possible future career options.
  Example: Interview a person who uses Arabic in their work and report to the class.

- Students use Arabic to plan activities that benefit the school or community.
  Examples: Organizing a school fundraising event with an Arabic theme, where students play Arabic music, serve Arabic food, and display artifacts and items that represent Arab culture.
- Students invite community members to participate in Arabic language or culture-related school events.
  Examples: Career exploration, speakers, demonstrations, tutoring, clubs.
- Students participate in communication activities and projects with Arabic-speaking peers outside of school.
  Example: Volunteering at a local community center and discussing the experience.

Sample Progress Indicators, Grade 12
- Students use Arabic to communicate orally or in writing with members of the local or international community about personal interests or community and world events.
  Example: Joining Arabic language listservs and contributing to Internet chat rooms that address topics of interests.
- Students use Arabic to interact with or help newcomers to the school and community.
  Example: Serving as mentor to an Arab newcomer to the school, assisting him/her in learning about the school culture and making new friends.
- Students participate in school-to-work projects or career-exploration activities in areas that require proficiency in the Arabic language.
  Example: Exploring a summer volunteer project at an Arabic-speaking cultural center.
- Students communicate in Arabic with community members and visitors from abroad about specific issues related to the local community.
  Example: Interviewing visitors about their impressions of American fast food establishments.
- Students participate actively in community activities, such as tutoring, helping acclimate newcomers to the community, or acting as role models for younger members of the Arabic-speaking community.

Sample Progress Indicators, Grade 16
- Students job-shadow members of the Arabic-speaking community to learn occupation-specific vocabulary, expressions, and protocol.
- Students participate in internships in Arabic-speaking countries or with local companies and organizations in positions that require Arabic language skills.
- Students actively participate in community activities.
  Examples: Tutoring, helping newcomers to the community, or acting as role models for younger members of the Arabic-speaking community.
- Students use Arabic language resources in the community or local universities to research topics of vocational interest.
- Students provide Arabic language services to the community.
  Example: Translating and interpreting for social agencies or schools.

STANDARD 5.2 Students show evidence of becoming lifelong learners by using Arabic for personal enjoyment and enrichment.

This standard stresses the ways in which students may use Arabic as an avenue to information and interpersonal relations. When students develop a level of comfort with Arabic, they can gain access to entertainment and information sources available to native Arabic speakers. If they have the opportunity to travel to countries where Arabic is used extensively, they then can further develop their language skills and understanding of the culture. Advanced learners can use Arabic to enhance knowledge in their professions as well as for personal enjoyment and enrichment.

Many of the progress indicators for standard 5.2 are repeated at the different grade levels to emphasize that the activities may be similar. However, the sophistication and ease with which the activities are performed depend greatly on the student's age and language proficiency.

Sample Progress Indicators, Grade 4

- Students use various media (books, CDs, films) in Arabic for personal enjoyment.
- Students participate in recreational activities that reflect Arab cultures.
- Students attend cultural events or social activities that reflect Arabic culture.
- Students listen to music, sing songs, play instruments or perform dances that reflect Arab culture.
  Example: Learning and performing the stick dance and playing the drum طبلة.

Sample Progress Indicators, Grade 8

- Students use various media in Arabic for personal enjoyment.
  Examples: Reading books, listening to CDs, surfing Arabic Web sites.
- Students attend cultural events or social activities that reflect Arabic cultures.
  Examples: Plays, concerts, social events.
- Students listen to music, sing songs, play instruments or perform dances that reflect different Arab countries.
- Students gather information on personal interests related to Arabic language and culture.
  Example: Researching the contribution of Ibn Sina to modern science; examining the Arabs' views regarding dating.
- Students create a community of Arabic learners at their grade level in school.
  Example: Forming an after-school Arab club and organizing events, such as watching Arabic movies and taking field trips to places that have Arab culture resources, such as the Arab American National Museum in Dearborn, Michigan.

Sample Progress Indicators, Grade 12
- Students access various media in Arabic for personal enjoyment.
  Examples: Reading books, listening to CDs, reading online newspapers and magazines.
- Students attend cultural events or social activities that reflect Arabic culture.
  Examples: Puppet shows, storytelling, plays, concerts, museums.
- Students gather information on personal interests related to Arabic language and culture topics.
  Examples: Gathering information on and analyzing the life and work of Gibran Khalil Gibran and his contributions to English literature and culture; examining the concept of democracy in Arab societies.
- Students act as volunteers or mentors to younger Arabic language learners.
- Students create a community of Arabic learners at their grade level in school.
  Examples: Helping organize events and presentations that explore Arabic-related topics; organizing and participating in field trips to Arabic libraries, restaurant, and museums.

Sample Progress Indicators, Grade 16
- Students continue to develop their worldview through participating in Arabic cultural conferences at local colleges and universities or attending Arabic institutes.
- Students continue to read and review major works of Arabic literature and culture.
- Students maintain a collection of books in Arabic on topics of interest.
- Students create Web sites and blogs in Arabic that facilitate dialogue about Arab language and culture.
- Students travel to the Arab world for leisure and education.

Learning Scenarios, Grades K–4

THE FOOD PYRAMID

The kindergarten class at New Horizon School listens to a story about good food "alta'aam aljayed الجيد الطعام. The story is about different animals that visit a newly opened restaurant and their adventure in learning about the food pyramid and eating healthy food. Students recycle previously learned Arabic words for the fruits and vegetables and learn how to express

TARGETED STANDARDS	
1.1	Interpersonal Communication
1.2	Interpretive Communication
1.3	Presentational Communication
2.2	Products of Culture
3.1	Making Connections
4.2	Cultural Comparisons

their likes and dislikes. Students become familiar with the names of the food groups and the items in each through various games and activities. They examine a variety of Arabic foods, such as falafel, and determine in which food group each belongs. As a final activity, students interview their parents about what they eat and draw the results on a provided copy of the food pyramid. Then they share the information with their class. Also, students bring an example of healthy food and a picture of unhealthy food to show their classmates. Finally, students enjoy eating the healthy food.

Reflections

1.1 Students ask and answer questions regarding the food. Also they express likes and dislikes and identify the "healthy" and "non healthy" food they eat.
1.2 Students understand and interpret the story.
1.3 Students present the results of their interviews about their parents' eating habits to their groups.
2.2 Students identify Arabic foods and discuss how they fit into the food pyramid.
3.1 Students reinforce and further their knowledge of food, nutrition, and the food pyramid.
4.2 Students compare and contrast similarities and differences between American and Arabic food items.

This activity could be used at a higher grade level, especially where the food pyramid is part of the health curriculum. Students can then analyze the food they eat for a week and assess their personal eating habits. Also, students can compare and contrast diets in various Arabic countries and in the United States. Finally, students can design a healthy Arabic food menu for a day and propose it to the cafeteria. In this case the fifth goal, school and community, would be addressed.

Submitted by Lina Kholaki

(LU'UB EL GIL): MARBLE GAMES IN THE ARAB WORLD

Students of Arabic in the third grade learn to play games common in the Arabic speaking world using *gil* (marbles). In groups, students generate a list of words that describe the *gil*, including their material, color, size, shape, and texture. They also guess about the uses of the *gil*. Students then view several video clips in which they watch Arabic-speaking children playing a variety of games with the *gil*. Using the language experience approach, students list the steps viewed in the game that most interested them, then they order scrambled strips that contain the sequence of activities in the game. Volunteers demonstrate activities in the sequence through Total Physical Response. In groups, students take turns telling other members to perform the activities necessary to play the game. In addition, students compare the children's uses of marbles in the United States and in the Arab world. As a culminating project, students create their own games and write instructions so other members of the class know how to play them.

TARGETED STANDARDS	
1.1	Interpersonal Communication
1.2	Interpretive Communication
1.3	Presentational Communication
2.1	Practices of Culture
3.1	Making Connections
4.2	Cultural Comparisons
5.2	Lifelong Learning

Reflection

1.1 Students work in groups to generate a list to describe the *gil* and playing games.
1.2 Students view a video and describe how to play the *gil* games.
1.3 Students create and present orally and in writing a game using the *gil*.
2.1 Students identify the way children from the Arabic culture interact while playing games.
3.1 Students make connections with math.
4.2 Students note cultural similarities and differences in the way children play with the *gil* in the U.S. and in the Arab world.
5.2 Students play new games for personal enjoyment.

This scenario helps young children relate to the children in the Arab world since both groups enjoy playing games. Students from Arabic heritage backgrounds can ask their parents how, when, and with whom they played this game when they were young. Additionally, students can compare their findings from the interview with those of their classmates.

Submitted by Nada Shaath

ARABIC RESTAURANT FOR A DAY

Fourth grade students invite the school principal and their parents to attend the grand opening of their mock Arabic restaurant. In order to create this restaurant, students learn new vocabulary through pictures, store fliers, drawings, and actual food. They read menus in Arabic and learn about dishes that come from different Arab countries. Students then practice using Arabic to order a meal and pay the bill. They use acquired vocabulary to create a menu and invitations for the final project, and role-play restaurant skits in order to practice what they will say and how they will act during their final presentation. Additionally, students compare the kinds of food served in Arabic countries with those found in the U.S. They reinforce their math skills by calculating the prices of food and by comparing food prices in Arabic countries and in the U.S. At the end of the unit, each student prepares a favorite dish and brings it to class. They rearrange the classroom to make it a restaurant setting. The parents and the school principal join the students in the classroom, and the students serve the food using appropriate Arabic language. Then they enjoy the food themselves.

TARGETED STANDARDS
1.1 Interpersonal Communication
1.2 Interpretive Communication
1.3 Presentational Communication
2.1 Practices of Culture
2.2 Products of Culture
3.1 Making Connections
4.2 Cultural Comparisons
5.1 School and Community
5.2 Lifelong Learning

Reflection

1.1 Students ask and answer simple questions in Arabic about what they prefer to eat and share likes and dislikes regarding food. Students use Arabic to role play.
1.2 Students read authentic Arabic menus and store fliers.
1.3 Students write the menus and invitations, and they host the grand opening of their restaurant. They present the scenario of a meal at an Arabic restaurant to the principal and their parents.
2.1 Students learn how to use polite words while asking what type of food the guests will order.
2.2 Students choose, prepare, and taste different kinds of authentic food from Arab countries.
3.1 Students make connections with math.
4.2 Students compare tangible cultural products (food). Students collect menus from restaurants in the community and compare them with Arabic ones.
5.1 Students serve Arabic food to members of the community.
5.2 Students enjoy the Arabic food and feel proud of their ability to host their parents.

This scenario gives students an opportunity to learn vocabulary associated with ordering a meal. In addition to the language skills learned, students are able to prepare and enjoy authentic Arabic recipes.

Submitted by Amal Saker

Learning Scenarios, Grades 5–8

MY DREAM JOB

Students in a fifth grade Arabic heritage language class are learning about professions in America and the Arab world while exploring which professions are highly regarded and why. Students start with brainstorming activities about the professions in today's society and in their community, the clothes professionals wear, where these professions are performed, and the types of activities and qualifications that are necessary in each profession. As a whole class, students develop a chart that identifies the pieces of information they need to know about each profession. Students then listen to a guest speaker who is a doctor describing his or her work, telling what it took to become a doctor, and explaining why he or she chose this career. While listening, students take notes by filling in the chart and asking follow-up questions. As homework, students interview their parents about their profession, the needed qualifications, and the reason for their choice of that profession. The next day, students share the collected information. Students read some excerpts, famous sayings, and poems that highlight the importance and the status of certain jobs. As a whole class, students compare and contrast the reasons that motivate choice of profession in the U.S. and in the Arab world. As a culminating project, each student writes or creates a board about his/her dream career, including what he or she needs to do to achieve that goal and the reason for his/her choice. They then present the project to the class. Students come to the presentation day dressed in attire appropriate to their chosen profession and carrying props that are used in that profession. Students answer questions regarding their presentation.

> **TARGETED STANDARDS**
> 1.1 Interpersonal Communication
> 1.2 Interpretive Communication
> 1.3 Presentational Communication
> 2.1 Practices of Culture
> 3.1 Making Connections
> 3.2 Acquiring New Information
> 4.2 Cultural Comparisons
> 5.2 Lifelong Learning

Reflections

1.1 Students exchange information that they gathered through interviewing their parents. Later they answer questions about why they chose this job and other details.
1.2 Students listen to a guest speaker.
1.3 Students present their dream job.
2.1 Students explore the daily practices and schedules for several jobs in the Arab world.
3.1 Students make connections with social studies by talking about jobs in the community.
3.2 Students collect information about the status of different jobs by reading proverbs, sayings, and poems.
4.2 Students explore the cultural similarities and differences in the status of different jobs in the Arab world and the United States.
5.2 Students obtain information about jobs of personal interest.

This scenario can be adapted to fit different types of programs, different age groups, and students at different language proficiency levels.

Submitted by Hanan Essa

THE ARABIC DAY

Students in 5th through 8th grade host a one-day exhibition that simulates an Arab community. The exhibit includes Arabic calligraphy, traditional clothes, games, musical instruments, an Arabic seating area, a coffee shop, food stands, and, of course, cart vendors of corn (*ballout*) and lima beans (*foul*). Students are divided into two groups, "exhibitors" and "visitors." The more proficient students are the exhibitors. To prepare for "Arabic Day," these students decide what they want to exhibit, read authentic materials, interview parents and community members, and collect artifacts. The visitors are provided with foreign currency (such as the *dinar*) in order to buy in the "market" and be part of a simulated real-world situation. Students who are exhibitors explain how to make certain foods and how to play cultural games. They decide when and where Arab people wear certain clothes. They show the different types of musical instruments and when they are used. Exhibitors also sell food and serve their customers. Students who are visitors listen to exhibitors, take notes, buy food, visit the coffee shop, order drinks, and try to bargain for better prices.

TARGETED STANDARDS
1.1 Interpersonal Communication
1.2 Interpretive Communication
1.3 Presentational Communication
2.1 Practices of Culture
2.2 Products of Culture
3.1 Making Connections
3.2 Acquiring New Information
5.1 School and Community
5.2 Lifelong Learning

Reflections

1.1 Students discuss and plan the project, explain exhibits, buy and sell, and ask questions.
1.2 Students read written materials about their part of the exhibit.
1.3 Students write about and present the information they have collected.
2.1 Students learn cultural practices such as bargaining and playing games.
2.2 Students learn about Arabic food, musical instruments, cafés, shops, calligraphy, and clothes.
3.1 Students make connections with art, music, the computer, and other topics.
3.2 Students collect relevant information about Arab culture and life from Arabic resources.
5.1 Students use Arabic beyond the classroom.
5.2 Students seek out information of personal interest about Arab culture.

It is important for students of Arabic to understand the complexity of the cultural reality in which Arabs live. This scenario gives students at all levels of proficiency the opportunity to practice and participate in real world and culturally appropriate situations.

Submitted by Iman Arabi-Katbi Hashem

WHAT CAN WE LEARN FROM FABLES? MAKING A DIFFERENCE

As a part of a unit on fables, students of Arabic in the sixth grade learn to identify moral lessons that can be derived from a story. With support from pictures from the story "The Lion and the Mouse," students identify the characters, guess at the story line, and then read the story in order to confirm their hypotheses. Selected students read portions of the text followed by various questions/prompts to determine student comprehension. Students sort components of the story into the categories who, what, where, when, and why. They learn the structure of a fable, the reasons for personifying animals, and the reasons for embedding a moral in the plot. In a whole-group format, students identify the moral of the story, which presents the idea that everyone can help no matter how small he or she is. As a connection to their community service class, students identify situations in which they can help to make a difference in their community. As a culminating project, students participate in community service and describe orally and in writing how they applied the lessons learned in the fable to their own lives.

> **TARGETED STANDARDS**
> 1.1 Interpersonal Communication
> 1.2 Interpretive Communication
> 1.3 Presentational Communication
> 2.2 Products of Culture
> 3.1 Making Connections
> 4.2 Cultural Comparisons

Reflection

1.1 Students identify characters and predict the story line before reading.
1.2 Students read a story and interpret its meaning.
1.3 Students present their findings orally and in writing.
2.2 Students demonstrate knowledge about fables and how they reflect Arabic culture.
3.1 Students identify community situations in which they can provide help and services.
4.2 Students compare and contrast the use of fables in other cultures.

The use of fables provides an excellent connection to the culture and how it reflects universal morals. Identifying this moral link allows students to appreciate and respect the lives and thinking of people in different parts of the world. At New Horizon School, students also connected this story to two other content areas. In science, they connected the story to their study of insects because one of the characters in the story is a butterfly. Students went to the school garden to catch butterflies while conversing in Arabic. During this activity, photos of the students were taken. Then each group used its picture to describe the butterfly orally and in writing. As a culminating activity, students compiled their photos and their descriptions into a class book about insects. In religious studies, students connected the story to their learning of verses from the Qur'an about the importance of helping and making a difference. By doing this activity, students acquired new information from an authentic Arabic source.

Submitted by Ilham Zayat

Learning Scenarios, Grades 9–12

INTERVIEW FAMOUS PEOPLE

Students at a high school videotape a mock interview with a famous person. As a start, they work in groups to predict what kind of information they will gather from the interview. They watch a taped interview with a famous person to find out if their predictions were correct. Then students examine the interview and identify all of its elements, including the basic questions asked, the nature of the questions asked, the way the interviewer conducted the interview, and the way the interviewee responded. Students practice interviewing each other through an activity called "Tea Party." Then they work in groups to decide on a person they would like to pretend to interview. They use the Internet and the library to gather information about their famous person, decide on each student's role in the interview, create the interview skit, and videotape it. Each group presents its videotaped interview to the class while the rest of the class takes notes. Then the presenting group asks the class questions about the interview.

TARGETED STANDARDS	
1.1	Interpersonal Communication
1.2	Interpretive Communication
1.3	Presentational Communication
2.1	Practices of Culture
2.2	Products of Culture
3.1	Making Connections
3.2	Acquiring New Information
4.1	Language Comparisons
4.2	Cultural Comparisons
5.2	Lifelong Learning

Reflections:

1.1 Students exchange opinions when deciding on what they know. Later they answer questions about their video.
1.2 Students view a video and read, Web-based Arabic materials about a famous person.
1.3 Students present their video.
2.1 Students identify daily practices.
2.2 Students learn about films, songs, and what is produced by the famous person.
3.1 Students make connections with technology, history, art, and other areas appropriate to the person they are pretending to interview.
3.2 Students collect information about the famous person via Arabic Web sites and written materials.
4.1 Students analyze the language varieties (dialects) used in the interview.
4.2 Students explore the cultural similarities and differences between the Arab world and the U.S. by comparing the ways in which interviews are conducted.
5.2 Students use Web sites to obtain information of personal interest about famous persons.

This activity can be adjusted to fit different levels of language proficiency, since it can have a range of format and content, from a simple interview that elicits basic information about the interviewee to a sophisticated interview format such as *Shahedun `ala al-`Asr*. This activity can be used to encourage heritage language learners to conduct a real interview with a prominent leader in the heritage community.

Submitted by Wafaa Makki

WHICH TOUR WOULD YOU LIKE TO TAKE?

High school students pretend to be travel agency tour planners. They work in groups to design tours to Arab countries. Each group plans a tour to two Arab countries that are enjoyable and educational. Students begin the project by examining Web sites that show various travel agencies in the Arab world and identify the elements that need to be included in their project. The teacher then guides students through scaffolded activities to gather information about Arab countries from Web sites, books, brochures, videos, and interviews with parents of heritage students and community members from the specific countries. Students write a detailed itinerary for the trip, including airlines, hotels, restaurants, places to visit, and leisure activities. They develop a written document to promote their trip, including the itinerary. The groups can choose to create a Power Point presentation, a brochure, or a Web site. Students engage in peer editing prior to submitting their drafts for teacher feedback. Students then give a class presentation about the tour supported by their written document. The student groups listen to each other's presentations, read each other's materials, ask questions, and give feedback to each other. Parents may attend a session in which each group presents and promotes its tour plan. At the end, students complete a project evaluation form, contributing insights into what they have learned and what they wish they had known to better complete the project.

TARGETED STANDARDS	
1.1	Interpersonal Communication
1.2	Interpretive Communication
1.3	Presentational Communication
2.2	Products of Culture
3.1	Making Connections
3.2	Acquiring New Information
5.1	School and Community
5.2	Lifelong Learning

Reflections:

1.1 Students discuss and plan the projects in groups, conduct interviews, and ask and answer questions.
1.2 Students view videos, read books, and consult brochures and Web sites about Arab countries.
1.3 Students present their tour trip in both oral and written forms.
2.2 Students learn about monuments, artifacts, and Arabic food.
3.1 Students make connections with geography, history, the computer, and other topics.
3.2 Students learn what aspects of Arab countries Arab travel agents promote to Arabs.
5.1 Students interview community members and present their tours to their parents.
5.2 Students learn information about traveling to Arab countries.

This scenario can be adapted to students of varying ages and levels of ability. It gives them much knowledge of Arabic culture, history, and monuments. It also develops their understanding of how to prepare for travel in Arab countries.

Submitted by Iman Arabi-Katbi Hashem

THE ISLAMIC CALENDAR AND THE ORIGIN OF THE ENGLISH WORD "CALENDAR"

Students studying Arabic in high school learn about the Islamic calendar. The teacher explains that the English word "calendar" originated from the Middle Eastern name for tax collectors, which was "calendar." The calendar/tax collector used to keep a close eye on time; therefore, when a way was created to record time, it took its name from the name for tax collectors.

TARGETED STANDARDS
1.2 Interpretive Communication
2.2 Products of Culture
4.2 Cultural Comparisons

Following this discussion, the students listen as the teacher explains the history of the Islamic calendar and the meaning of the name of each month. The teacher shows the students an index card for each of the twelve Arabic months (figure 1), then asks each of the students to draw a picture for one month on a piece of paper. The students put their illustrations together in the order of the Islamic year to create a calendar. Students and teacher then compare the Islamic months/year with the month/year system used in the U.S.

محرم	صفر	ربيع الأول	ربيع الثاني
جمادى الأول	جمادى الثاني	رجب	شعبان
رمضان	شوال	ذو القعدة	ذو الحجة

Figure 1. The Islamic months of the lunar year.

Reflections:
1.1 Students listen to and discuss the teacher's explanation of the origin of the English word "calendar" and the meanings of the names of the months in the Islamic year.
2.2 Students create an Islamic (lunar) calendar of their own.
4.2 Students compare the Islamic (lunar) calendar with the Western (solar) calendar.

Submitted by Khitam Abdur-Rahman Omar

Learning Scenarios, College

PLANNING A MIDDLE EASTERN MEAL

College students in second-year Arabic share their final project with the entire class: a meal that they have collaboratively created, featuring traditional Middle Eastern cuisine. The class starts by learning vocabulary through pictures and authentic materials such as store fliers, flash cards, and restaurant menus. Students watch a video on traditional Middle Eastern cooking. The teacher introduces verbs, adjectives, and colloquial expressions that relate to eating and drinking habits from that part of the world. Additionally, students explore the concept of Middle Eastern hospitality. Students also learn about the nutritional value of a vegetarian diet, as well as other dietary observances such as avoiding pork. Additionally, the class explores the difference between daily fare and foods reserved for special occasions, such as Christmas, Ramadan, weddings, and so on. Students identify eating habits and family relationships while honing their conversational skills and increasing their knowledge of Middle Eastern culture. At the end of the project, students plan their menus for a special occasion of their choice, write its recipes, prepare sample dishes, and present the food to the class.

TARGETED STANDARDS	
1.1	Interpersonal communication
1.2	Interpretive communication
1.3	Presentational communication
2.1	Practices of culture
2.2	Products of culture
4.2	Cultural comparisons

Reflection

1.1 Students discuss with their classmates their menu choices, and role-play a traditional social conversation at the dining table.
1.2 Students interpret advertisements, menus and video material.
1.3 Students present their prepared dishes and menus to the class.
2.1 Students learn about Middle Eastern conventions regarding dining, hospitality and entertaining.
2.2 The students' menu choices reflect an understanding of dietary restrictions regarding pork and prevalence of vegetarian dishes in Middle Eastern cuisine. They also experience foods distinctive to this region as well as cooking techniques unique to this culture.
4.2 Students compare home dining experiences with Middle Eastern practices.

This activity gives students the chance to gain an understanding of the cultural experience of a typical Arabic family eating a meal together. Students learn the importance of everyone gathering around the table, how guests are made to feel at home, how it is customary to provide an overabundance of food and a wide variety of dishes, and how the host will urge guests to eat more in the spirit of boundless generosity.

Submitted by Ferial Demy

AL-RAZI: AN ARAB SCHOLAR

College students studying Arabic learn about the famous Arab scholar Abu Bakr Mohammad Ibn Zakariya Al-Razi and his many contributions to culture and science. At a young age, Al-Razi was a musician and singer. His attention turned to medicine as he watched the sick finding comfort in music. Through friendship with a nearby pharmacist he then became interested in chemistry. He wrote many books on medicine, made alcohol and used it in the formulation of drugs, and established procedures for conducting and recording research in medicine and chemistry. One well known story about Al-Razi is the method he devised for choosing the location of a hospital in Baghdad. This same procedure was used by a U.S. president to select the site of the University of Virginia.

TARGETED STANDARDS
1.1 Interpersonal Communication
1.2 Interpretive Communication
1.3 Presentational Communication
2.2 Products of Culture
3.1 Making Connections
3.2 Acquiring Information
4.2 Cultural Comparisons

Following this discussion, students divide into two groups to cover two homework assignments:
1. The first group reports on the story of the choice of site for the University of Virginia.
2. The second group reports on *al-'ud*, the most famous instrument in Arabic music and Al-Razi's favorite and compares it with the guitar, the corresponding instrument in the U.S.
3. Students report on and discuss the results of their research in the next class period.

Reflections:
1.1 Students discuss the life and accomplishments of Al-Razi
1.2 Students conduct research on topics related to Al-Razi's work.
1.3 Students present the results of their research to one another.
2.2 Students learn about products that were developed by or of interest to Al-Razi and how they spread from Arab culture to society at large.
3.1 Students make connections with music, science, medicine, and history.
3.2 Students discover the contributions to medicine and science made by this Arab scholar.
4.2 Students compare a musical instrument from Arab culture with one familiar to Western audiences.

Submitted by Khitam Abdur-Rahman Omar

HISTORICAL DRAMA

As a term project, second-year university students enrolled in an Arabic language course receive from their instructor video CDs, each containing one episode from a historical drama produced in Standard Arabic (for example, al-Ziir Salem, abu Zayd al-Hilali, Sayf bin dhi Yazan, al-Suquur, Salahuddiin). No two VCDs are identical, and each has the episode number deleted. In aggregate, they form a connected series, beginning with episode number 1. Through a variety of individual and group tasks, the students provide a background for the drama series, put the episodes in a logical order, present each episode in 15 minutes individually, compare the story to a relevant saga from Western civilization, and collectively provide a conclusion to the story.

TARGETED STANDARDS	
1.1	Interpersonal Communication
1.2	Interpretive Communication
1.3	Presentational Communication
2.1	Practices of Culture
2.2	Products of Culture
3.1	Making Connections
4.2	Cultural Comparisons

Reflections:

1.1 Students discuss the content among themselves in pairs or groups of three in order to determine the relevance of the plot in each episode to the other episodes.

1.2 Students make lists of unfamiliar and low frequency vocabulary items. They also create a glossary of key words for each episode. They identify the structures familiar to them and explain how their understanding of the meaning was facilitated (or hampered) by these structures. On a scale of 3, they rate the level of the language in comparison to texts they have dealt with before.

1.3 Each student presents his or her episode, beginning with a descriptive background of the events. They summarize the events of the episode in the order in which they occur and provide their own expectations of what event might follow.

2.1 Students learn how Arabs in the past exchanged niceties. They make a list of all or most the expressions used and compare them to what people use today.

2.2 Students try to identify in each episode samples of Arab cultural products be they in the form of poetry, handicraft, fashion, or some other format.

3.1 Students make connections with historical facts, determine the amount of deviation from facts, and provide a timeline for each episode. They also situate the action in a geographical area and provide a map showing it.

4.2 Students compare and contrast the drama series at hand with similar American movies, shows, and documentaries. They point out areas of similarities and differences.

This scenario provides the students with an opportunity to learn low frequency vocabulary items and structures used in literary and Classical Arabic. They become able to recognize characteristics of the text that make it at a higher or lower level stylistically and hence get a handle on register in Arabic. In addition, they can compile lists of quotable sayings, proverbs, and lines of poetry used and the contexts in which they are employed. This scenario is intended for advanced students in order to develop higher level proficiency.

Submitted by Mahdi Alosh

全美中小學中文學習目標
Standards for Chinese Language Learning

A Project of the Chinese Language Association of Secondary-Elementary Schools (CLASS)

TASK FORCE MEMBERS

Chih-Wen Su (Co-Chair)
Amherst Regional Middle/ High School, Amherst, MA

Lucy Lee (Co-Chair)
Livingston High School, Livingston, NJ

Carol Shao-Yuan Chen-Lin
Choate Rosemary Hall, Wallingford, CT

Yu-Lan Lin
Boston Public Schools, Boston, MA

Claire Kotenbeutel
James Madison Memorial High School, Madison, WI

Hal Nicolas
Cape Elementary/ Dunbar Middle/ Fort Myers High School, Ft. Myers, FL

Catherine Yen
Abraham Lincoln High School, San Francisco, CA

REGIONAL COMMITTEE

Tom Buckingham, Cape Elementary/Trafalgar Middle/Cape Coral High School, Ft. Myers, FL
Floyd Chamberlin, Southport High School, Indianapolis, IN
Xiaoling Chang, Abraham Lincoln High School, San Francisco, CA
Vicky Chin, Lowell High School, San Francisco, CA
Lina Hsieh, Sidwell Friends School, Washington, DC
Caroline Huang, Venice High Schoo, Los Angeles, CA
Dorothy Ong, Lowell High School, San Francisco, CA

Special thanks to the following K-12 teachers for their valuable contributions to the project: Katherine Chang, Su-Chuan Chung, Jerald Clayton, Rebecca He, Barbara Hudpet, Susan Olson, Margaret Wong, Shu-Han Chou Wang, and Kristine Wogstad; and to many CLASS members for their great input and continuing support.

全美中小學中文學習目標
Standards for Chinese Language Learning

ADVISORY COUNCIL

Richard Chi, University of Utah, Salt Lake City, UT
Madeline Chu, Kalamazoo College, Kalamazoo, MI
Cornelius C. Kubler, Williams College, Williamstown, MA
Scott McGinnis, University of Maryland, College Park, MD
Sarah J. Moore, National Foreign Language Center, Washington, DC (Retired)
June K. Phillips, Weber State University, Ogden, UT
Larry Shyn, National Council Associations of Chinese Language Schools, Yorktown, NY
Shou-Hsin Teng, National Taiwan Normal University, Graduate Institute of TCSL, Taipei, Taiwan
Wei-ling Wu, Secondary School Chinese Language Center, Princeton, NJ
Tao-chung Yao, University of Hawaii-Manoa, Honolulu, HI
Xueying Wang, Johns Hopkins University, Baltimore, MD

BOARD OF REVIEWERS

Christine Brown, Glastonbury Public Schools, CT
Maylani L. Chang, Punahou Jr. School, Honolulu, HI
Phyllis Trautman Chen, Great Neck South High School, Great Neck, NY
Martha Gallagher, U.S. Military Academy, West Point, NY
Gary Hart, J.A. Rogers Middle School, Kansas City, MO
Baozhang He, Harvard University, Cambridge, MA
Mei-Ju Hwang, School of Science and Technology, Springfield, MA
Theresa Jen, Bryn Mawr College, Bryn Mawr, PA
Chuanren Ke, University of Iowa, Iowa City, IA
Welton Kwong, Homestead High School, Cupertino, CA
Shou-ping Li, McDowell Intermediate High School, Erie, PA
Jennifer Liu, Indiana University, Bloomington, IN
Jeng-heng Ma, Wellesley College, Wellesley, MA
Mimi Met, Montgomery County Public Schools, Rockville, MD
Joyce Ranieri, Hong Kong International School, Tai Tam, Hong Kong
Kathleen Riordan, Springfield Public Schools, MA
Chaofen Sun, Stanford University, Stanford, CA
Dali Tan, St. Catherine School, Richmond, VA
Galal Walker, Ohio State University, Columbus, OH
Suzy Shen Zien, Bethesda-Chevy Chase High School, Bethesda, MD

Table of Contents

STANDARDS FOR CHINESE LANGUAGE LEARNING		**160**
INTRODUCTION		**161**
ABOUT THE CHINESE STANDARDS PROJECT		**161**
NATURE OF THE DOCUMENT		**162**
IMPORTANCE OF CHINESE		**163**
CHINESE LANGUAGE EDUCATION IN THE UNITED STATES		**163**
CHARACTERISTICS OF THE CHINESE LANGUAGE		**165**
COMMUNICATION	**Goal 1**	**167**
CULTURES	**Goal 2**	**174**
CONNECTIONS	**Goal 3**	**178**
COMPARISONS	**Goal 4**	**181**
COMMUNITIES	**Goal 5**	**185**
SAMPLE LEARNING SCENARIOS		**190**
Sìhéyuàn – Chinese Family Residence		190
Evolution of Chinese Characters		191
Chinese Kites		192
Peking Opera		192
Neighborhoods		194
A Chinese Folk Tale Play		194
Sun, Moon, and Planets in the Solar System		195
Romance in Literature		196
Ti Jianzi – Chinese Shuttlecock		197
Dragon Wings		198

全美中小學中文學習目標
Standards for Chinese Language Learning

COMMUNICATION 溝通 GOAL ONE
運用中文溝通
Communicate in Chinese

Standard 1.1 語言溝通
Students engage in conversations, provide and obtain information, express feelings and emotions, and exchange opinions in Chinese.

Standard 1.2 理解詮釋
Students understand and interpret written and spoken language on a variety of topics in Chinese.

Standard 1.3 表達演示
Students present information, concepts, and ideas to an audience of listeners or readers on a variety of topics.

CULTURES 文化 GOAL TWO
體認中國多元文化
Gain Knowledge and Understanding of the Cultures of the Chinese-Speaking World

Standard 2.1 文化習俗
Students demonstrate an understanding of the relationship between the practices and perspectives of the cultures of the Chinese-speaking world.

Standard 2.2 文化產物
Students demonstrate an understanding of the relationship between the products and perspectives of the cultures of the Chinese-speaking world.

CONNECTIONS 貫連 GOAL THREE
貫連其他學科
Connect with Other Disciplines and Acquire Information

Standard 3.1 觸類旁通
Students reinforce and further their knowledge of other disciplines through the study of Chinese.

Standard 3.2 博聞廣見
Students acquire information and recognize the distinctive viewpoints that are only available through the Chinese language and culture.

COMPARISONS 比較 GOAL FOUR
比較語言文化之特性
Develop Insight into the Nature of Language and Culture

Standard 4.1 比較語文
Students demonstrate understanding of the nature of language through comparisons of the Chinese language with their own.

Standard 4.2 比較文化
Students demonstrate understanding of the concept of culture through comparisons of Chinese culture with their own.

COMMUNITIES 社區 GOAL FIVE
應用於國內與國際多元社區
Participate in Multilingual Communities at Home and Around the World

Standard 5.1 學以致用
Students use the Chinese language both within and beyond the school setting.

Standard 5.2 學無止境
Students show evidence of becoming life-long learners by using Chinese for personal enjoyment and enrichment.

Introduction

Standards for Chinese Language Learning is part of a series of nine language-specific standards documents that complement the *Standards for Foreign Language Learning: Preparing for the 21st Century.* The goals and standards in the generic document describe a K-12 foeign language program in a core curriculum for all students. The Chinese-specific standards are intended to be used only in conjunction with the generic document and do not, therefore, reiterate major sections of the generic document, such as the Statement of Philosophy, Implication of Standards, Weave of Curricular Elements, Diverse Learners, Instructional Approaches, Multiple Entry Points, Learning Strategies, Critical Thinking Skills, and Technology. Within the content of the generic standards, these Chinese-specific standards are intended to provide an attainable vision for the future of Chinese language education in the United States. This vision is for a long, well-articulated sequence of Chinese language instruction that leads to high levels of competency in Chinese and enables students to know how, when, and what should be said to whom and the reason why. This set of content standards will serve as a guide for locally developed Chinese language curricula to support the needs of particular states and districts. It is anticipated that these content standards will create a compact connection among learners, school, and society; enhance students' problem-solving and creative skills; provide opportunities for native speakers of Chinese to maintain and enhance their proficiency; and develop a firm foundation for lifelong learning. These standards will also improve the continuity and cumulative effect of language learning and provide a seamless linkage to connect K-12 Chinese programs with post-secondary programs as well as to the programs offered at Chinese community language schools.

ABOUT THE CHINESE STANDARDS PROJECT

Standards for Chinese Language Learning is the result of a cooperative effort of the National Standards in Foreign Language Collaborative Project and the Chinese Language Association of Secondary-Elementary Schools (CLASS). In the fall of 1995, with the inspiration and encouragement of the late Dr. Ronald Walton, CLASS launched an important Chinese Standards Project to develop the Chinese-specific standards. A Task Force organized under this project produced the current document based on valuable input sought and received from CLASS members across the country and from other sources, including the Chinese Language Teachers Association (CLTA), professors of various post-secondary institutions, teachers at Chinese heritage schools, and an array of foreign language specialists. The members of the Task Force came from three regional CLASS committees (Western, Eastern, and Southern/Midwestern regions), and all committee members were practicing K-12 teachers representing both public and private schools and both urban and suburban settings. They also represented (a) native speakers with various backgrounds in the Chinese-speaking world

THIS VISION IS FOR A LONG, WELL-ARTICULATED SEQUENCE OF CHINESE

and (b) non-native speakers who received their Chinese education primarily in American colleges and who had spent various amounts of time in China.

The Chinese standards document took about three years to complete. The feedback solicited through presentations at various state and national conventions, from K-12 Chinese teachers, college Chinese instructors, as well as specialists in the foreign language field, has been invaluable in honing and refining various sections of the document. The Advisory Council members—consisting of representatives from the Chinese Language Teachers Association (CLTA), the National Foreign Language Center (NFLC), and the National Council of Associations of Chinese Language Schools (NCACLS), and of various foreign language teaching professionals—also offered diverse input and advice at various stages during development of the project. Every effort was made to ensure that this document is the product of the Chinese language teaching profession.

NATURE OF THE DOCUMENT

The standards are not a stand-alone document, nor do they constitute a curriculum or syllabus. Rather, they are intended to assist educators—whether at the level of the individual classroom, school, or district—in developing standards-based Chinese curricula. The document is divided into five goals taken directly from the generic document for foreign language learning. Each goal is supported by two or more content standards that elaborate what students should know to achieve the goals. They are followed by sample progress indicators that describe what students need to be able to do to meet the standards at different developmental stages – represented by grade levels four, eight, and twelve. These sample progress indicators are cumulative, but not intended to be prescriptive or exhaustive. Any classroom teacher will immediately note that some progress indicators do not directly reflect current practice in the profession; rather, they set forth a vision of what might be possible if a long-sequence Chinese language program were implemented without interruption from kindergarten through the twelfth grade. One intention of the standards is to enable school districts to recognize the desirability, even necessity, of this vision and to implement such programs accordingly.

Nonetheless, the standards are also adaptable to current classroom reality. The sample progress indicators for any grade level can easily be spiraled up or down in level of sophistication in order to accommodate learners of different language backgrounds and levels. The standards are also applicable to heritage learners who are often already familiar with various aspects of Chinese culture. In recent years, a growing number of heritage learners have been entering the K-12 Chinese programs with prior background in Mandarin Chinese or another Chinese dialect. These standards, therefore, contain some sample progress indicators, *marked by asterisks under the Grade 12 sections*, to keep advanced level students and Chinese heritage learners challenged and performing at their maximum level of ability. The Chinese-specific examples under each sample progress indicator serve as a starting point for teachers to conceptualize how the standards might be applied in the classroom. In addition, field-tested sample learning scenarios, submitted by practicing K-12 teachers, demonstrate how the standards and progress indicators might be used as the foundation for a unit or a daily lesson. Most of the sample learning scenarios can be expanded or modified for different classroom situations at various levels.

SAMPLE PROGRESS INDICATORS, MARKED BY ASTERISKS, KEEP ADVANCED LEVEL STUDENTS AND CHINESE HERITAGE LEARNERS CHALLENGED

The Chinese standards were developed with an integrated approach in mind, encouraging the use of speaking, listening, reading, and writing, to be transacted through a spiraling and recursive process at all levels to lead toward developmentally appropriate communicative proficiency and literacy in Chinese. The regular inclusion of the latest instructional technologies brings the Chinese language and culture into the classroom in an immediate and authentic way, and it provides an additional means for achievement of the standards. The accessibility to information and opportunities for interaction with others through the interactive technologies will enhance the ability of students in their learning to become self-sufficient, life-long learners.

IMPORTANCE OF CHINESE

The teaching and learning of Chinese language hold an increasingly vital place in American education. The Chinese language has considerable importance to Americans on personal, community, and national levels. The emergence of China as a major player in the world scene has created a need for greater understanding of what is the world's most populous nation. The United States government has designated America's relations with China to be one of the most important foreign policy issues now and in the foreseeable future. Clearly, successful communication in Chinese is the key for promoting a better understanding of China; yet, many American schools do not offer basic instruction in Chinese. The promotion and development of Chinese language education is of critical importance to the United States in terms of both economic advantages and the national interest in the dynamic global community of the 21st century. In addition to these national and international concerns, ever-broadening U.S.-China relations are continuing to increase the Chinese presence in American communities. Chinese visitors, immigrants, and Chinese-Americans are all becoming more involved in all facets of the American society, including business, education, the arts, and various services in the community. Being able to communicate with and better understand these community members can only be of benefit to our multicultural society.

Abundant opportunities for government and business careers as well as for scientific, scholarly, and cultural exchanges await the student of Chinese. In addition, the Chinese language is the key to the accumulated knowledge and experience of one of the world's oldest civilizations, as well as the path to communication with over one billion people. Thus, the opportunities for personal growth and enjoyment through reading, conversing, traveling, and making friends are almost limitless.

CHINESE LANGUAGE EDUCATION IN THE UNITED STATES

Chinese language instruction in the United States dates back to the latter part of the nineteenth century. Until after World War II, instruction was pointed towards college and graduate school students desiring to become scholars of the Chinese language and culture, children whose parents were ethnic Chinese and who wanted their children to learn the language and culture of their ancestors, and adults who had a special need to learn the Chinese language, such as missionaries. Each of them developed its own traditions in pedagogy, teaching materials, and goals. Scholars were more pointed towards mastering the written word; ethnic Chinese were more interested in transferring their cultural identi-

Standards for Chinese Language Learning

fication to the next generation. The interests of the diffuse group of adult learners ranged from mastering any one of the spoken Chinese languages or dialects to mastery of the written language, or both.

The state of Chinese language instruction changed in the late 1950s, particularly after the passage of the National Defense Education Act of 1958. For the first time, under Title VI of that Act, the federal government encouraged students to study the less commonly taught languages, including Chinese. The number of colleges and universities offering instruction in Chinese expanded. At the same time, the reason to study Chinese began to change slowly from focusing mostly on mastery of the written language towards mastery of both the spoken and written languages. However, as China became less accessible to Americans during this period, reasons for adults to learn the language narrowed, and adult instruction withered. There was little change in instructional patterns among ethnic Chinese, as the desire to transfer their Chinese heritage to the next generation remained strong. The first efforts to introduce Chinese language instruction into pre-collegiate education emerged in the early 1960s when the Carnegie Corporation encouraged several colleges to cooperate with nearby school districts in the introduction of Chinese. Most of these first pre-collegiate programs were short-lived. Major expansion and development of pre-collegiate Chinese language instruction didn't take place until the 1980s, a period of time in which schools were generally trying to expand their offerings and introduce new areas of study. Chinese language programs were given a substantial boost when the Geraldine R. Dodge Foundation, in its Chinese Initiative, provided funds to sixty secondary schools to introduce or expand their Chinese language programs. Most of the programs funded by the Dodge Foundation still exist in 1998.

There has also been a tremendous increase in enrollments in Chinese at both the pre-collegiate and collegiate levels in this period of time. High school enrollments have grown from 309 students in 6 states in 1962 to 7,354 students in 32 states in 1990[1] and 9,456 in 1994.[2] At the same time, post-secondary enrollments have expanded from 10,259 students in 174 programs in 1974 to 19,268 students in 407 programs in 1990 and 26,330 students in 384 programs in 1995.[3] Chinese has moved up in rank from the eighth to the sixth most commonly taught language in post-secondary institutions according to the Modern Language Association Report.[4] There are no comparable data over time for enrollments in heritage Chinese language programs. A 1995 report by the National Council of Associations of Chinese Language Schools indicates that there were 82,675 pre-collegiate students studying Chinese in a heritage school setting.[5]

---

[1] Moore, Walton, and Lambert. Introducing Chinese into High Schools: The Dodge Initiative. The National Foreign Language Center, 1992. p. 5.

[2] American Council on the Teaching of Foreign Languages 1994 Survey.

[3] "Variations in Foreign Language Enrollments through Time: Update Incorporating Data from Fall 1995." Modern Language Association, n.d. Table.

[4] "MLA Releases Preliminary Findings of Fall 1995 Registrations in Foreign Languages." Fall, 1996. p. 12.

[5] Xueying Wang. "Forging a Link: Tapping the National Heritage Language Resources in the U.S." The National Foreign Language Center, 1998.

The 1980s were a fertile period not only for expansion in the number of students learning Chinese, but also for the developments in the field of Chinese language instruction. Prior to the 1980s there was little need for colleges to pay attention to pre-collegiate language instruction because so few students, other than ethnic Chinese, entered college with any prior exposure to the Chinese language. That has changed. Now professors of Chinese are regularly faced with the need to place entering students from a wide variety of backgrounds and exposure to Chinese into classes appropriate to their level of skills. The growing need to articulate long-sequence Chinese instruction from pre-collegiate and Chinese heritage school programs to those offered by colleges and universities has led to efforts by representatives of these groups to try to come to some agreements about what the nature of instruction should be at various levels of learning. These efforts include the *Guildelines for Chinese Language Instruction in Secondary Schools* developed by CLASS as part of the Mellon Fellows program at the National Foreign Language Center in 1989 and *NFLC Guide for Basic Chinese Language Programs* funded by the National Endowment for the Humanities and published in 1997. *Standards for Chinese Language Learning* provides specificity and concreteness to these earlier efforts. It also offers a point of departure for program articulation as all teaching levels in the Chinese language profession – elementary, secondary, and postsecondary – come to consensus on a vision for the field through the process of the Chinese-specific standards development.

CHARACTERISTICS OF THE CHINESE LANGUAGE

Mandarin Chinese is spoken by more people than any other language in the world. It is one of the daily languages of the people who live in mainland China, Taiwan, Singapore, and the overseas Chinese communities. As a member of the Sino-Tibetan language family, Chinese is distantly related to languages such as Burmese and Tibetan. However, it is unrelated to the Indo-European language family, to which English and most other European languages belong. Nor is it genetically related to Japanese or Korean, even though its writing system and a portion of its vocabulary were borrowed and adapted by speakers of those languages.

China is a land of many languages, dialects, and cultures. In the borderlands, non-Chinese languages such as Mongolian, Uighur, and Tibetan are spoken. In much of northern and western China, various varieties of Mandarin are the native language. In southeastern China, a number of widely divergent, mutually unintelligible "dialects"—such as Cantonese, Hakka, and Taiwanese—are the daily language of the people. Mandarin, spoken by more than two-thirds of the Chinese population, is the official medium of school and all other governmental organs for the purposes of cross-dialect communication. Although there are many different spoken dialects of the Chinese language, only one common written language (Chinese characters) is used to communicate effectively between speakers of different dialects in China.

Compared to other languages, the sound system of Mandarin Chinese is relatively simple. There are only 405 basic syllables—far fewer than in English, which has several thousand. Chinese syllables are traditionally divided into twenty-two initial sounds and thirty-seven final sounds. One of the special characteristics of Chinese is that most Chinese

▼

GERALDINE R. DODGE FOUNDATION PROVIDED FUNDS TO SIXTY SECONDARY SCHOOLS TO INTRODUCE OR EXPAND THEIR CHINESE LANGUAGE PROGRAMS

syllables are pronounced with one of four tones. The same basic syllable pronounced with different tones is likely to have completely different meanings. Because almost all Chinese syllables have distinct meanings of their own, Chinese is often referred to as being "monosyllabic." But this does not mean that every Chinese word has only one syllable.

Chinese has a considerable number of grammatical rules, although many of them differ substantially from those of Western languages. The endings of Chinese words don't change depending on gender, case, number, person, or tense, as in many Western languages. For this reason, Chinese is often termed an "isolating" or "analytic" language. In general, Chinese grammar depends heavily on word order, function words, and context. As in English, the normal sentence order is Subject-Verb-Object, with adjectives preceding nouns. Verbs have aspect rather than tense; classifiers are used before nouns when preceded by a number or specifier; and reduplication (repeating the same syllable twice) is often used to alter the meanings of words.

While the single syllable (morpheme) is the basic building block of modern Chinese, two-syllable words predominate. Words are easily broken down into their constituent parts because each syllable has its own character, which usually makes its meaning immediately apparent. Because of the long and largely independent development of Chinese culture, there are few cognates shared between Chinese and English. During the last century, the number of borrowings from English and other Western languages into Chinese has steadily increased. While sounds are sometimes borrowed, usually it is the meaning of the foreign term that is translated into Chinese. Due to increased contact and a greater amount of shared knowledge, Chinese and English—as well as Chinese and American culture in general—seem slowly to be moving closer together, which has made learning Chinese considerably easier than it once was.

Chinese characters, each formed by a combination of strokes written in a prescribed order, communicate ideas and word meanings but give only limited information about pronunciation. There is an alternative way of representing Chinese speech through the use of phonetic transcription systems. The transcriptions are not meant to be substitutes for characters; rather, they are intended to serve as useful tools in the learning of Chinese sounds and for special purposes such as computer entry. Chinese characters, in either traditional or simplified form, are the authentic writing system used in the Chinese-speaking world. The largest dictionaries include over 50,000 characters, but only about 3,000 characters are in common use. Often one character will have more than one pronunciation or meaning, or several different characters may sound alike but have different meanings. In reading Chinese, recognizing characters is only a part of the process; at least as important is recognizing words written with combinations of words, comprehending written Chinese grammar, gaining reading fluency, and so forth.

In view of the large number of characters, the huge differences between spoken and written Chinese, and the fact that there are two different sets of characters (traditional and simplified), learning to read and write Chinese takes a long time. It is important, therefore, that Chinese instruction be offered for at least as many, if not more, years as the European languages, and that those involved with Chinese programs not expect students' skills to advance as rapidly as those of students studying other languages.

MANDARIN IS THE OFFICIAL MEDIUM OF SCHOOL AND ALL GOVERNMENTAL ORGANS

Communication   Goal One
運用中文溝通

Across thousands of miles in China, through thousands of years of its history, Chinese people have been connected by the Chinese language, which is one of the oldest continuous languages in the world. Understanding written and spoken Chinese enables students to gain access to the historical civilization and the distinctive viewpoints of the Chinese-speaking world, as well as to develop communicative skills essential for the 21st century.

Since language is a product of human behavior, the interactions among the speakers of the language bring about many complexities in communication patterns. In a society as old and enormous as China, this phenomenon is especially true. Students need to learn proper language usage in order to interact with Chinese speakers of different ages and social status, and they need to understand cultural and linguistic nuances. In comprehending spoken Chinese, students need to be aware not only of the difference between formal and informal speech patterns in verbal and nonverbal modes, but also of the style of subtlety—an "unspoken" aspect of the language. In comprehending written Chinese, students need to experience all sorts of written materials, ranging from literary texts to writings in the spoken form. Finally, in the presentational dimension, students need to demonstrate command of everyday spoken Chinese (Kǒutóu yǔ) and formal written Chinese (Shūmiàn yǔ). All three of these communicational modes must therefore be introduced and explained in cultural context in order for students to develop true understanding of and proficiency in the Chinese language.

> **CHINESE GRAMMAR DEPENDS HEAVILY ON WORD ORDER, FUNCTION WORDS, AND CONTEXT**

Standard 1.1   Students engage in conversations, provide and obtain information, express feelings and emotions, and exchange opinions.

Interpersonal Communication 語言溝通

Interpersonal communication is the primary means of entering the Chinese-speaking world and often is the standard by which people are judged. Accordingly, abundant opportunities for such communication must be integrated into the classroom. In order to build interpersonal relationships and to establish effective lines of communication, students must be able to master contextually and culturally appropriate utterances.

Sample Progress Indicators for K-4

- Students give and follow simple instructions to participate in age-appropriate classroom and/or Chinese cultural activities.

    Example: Follow classroom routines and commands.
    大家站起來，小朋友坐下。

- Students ask and answer simple questions about topics such as family, school, daily routine, and activities.

Standards for Chinese Language Learning

Example: Exchange simple personal information.
你叫什麼名字？你今年幾歲？你住在哪？

- Students share likes and dislikes regarding various common objects and everyday activities.

    Example: Interview classmates about their favorite things and activities.
    你喜歡吃什麼？你喜不喜歡看電視？

- Students exchange descriptions of people and common objects with each other.

    Example: Exchange information on family members while sharing family albums.
    這是我媽媽，那是我妹妹。

- Students exchange essential information such as greetings and leave-takings with each other.

    Example: Practice greeting teachers and classmates.
    老師好，小朋友好，謝謝您，老師再見。

- Students understand common classroom interactions using culturally appropriate gestures and oral expressions.

    Example: Students in China traditionally stand up when a teacher enters the room.
    學生瞭解在中國老師走進教室時，學生起立敬禮。

Sample Progress Indicators for K-8

- Students follow and give directions for participating in age-appropriate Chinese cultural activities. They ask and respond to questions for clarification.

    Example: Use directional complements to ask and clarify direction.
    東西南北，前後左右上下。

- Students exchange information about personal events, memorable experiences, and school subjects with peers and/or Chinese speakers.

    Example: Interview classmates.
    你喜歡什麼課？昨天你到哪兒去了？

  - Students express opinions and preferences about people, events, and everyday activities.

    Example: Exchange lists of favorites and compare them with those of peers.
    交換最喜歡的活動項目。

- Students use Chinese to acquire goods, services, or information through developmentally appropriate oral communication, writing, or the Internet.

    Example: Practice frequently asked questions for a field trip to Chinatown.
    小美飯館在哪？

- Students make reference to Chinese characters to clarify meanings in conversation.

    Example: Write characters on the palms to indicate the character used in a spoken context.
    用手在手掌或空中寫字，以辯明適當的字。

Sample Progress Indicators for K-12

- Students initiate, sustain, and close a conversation in a variety of real-life situations that reflect social amenities such as making introductions, expressing gratitude and regret, stating complaints, apologizing, and communicating preferences.

    Example: Engage in a simulated situation to initiate a conversation.
    對不起，我來晚了。

- Students discuss and support their personal feelings and ideas with peers and/or speakers of the Chinese language.

    Example: Exchange personal feelings on college education.
    學生表達對升大學的看法。

- Students share their personal reactions to selected literary texts such as poems, plays, short stories, and novels.

    Example: Exchange personal views on a selected literary text.
    學生交換讀書心得。

- Students exchange their opinions and discuss individual perspectives on a variety of topics including school or community related issues, or current and past events in Chinese culture.

    Example: Compare and contrast points of view on dating.
    交換對青少年交男女朋友的看法。

* Students develop and propose solutions to issues and problems that are of concern to Chinese communities in group activities.

    Example: In small groups, exchange solutions on how to protect pandas.
    中文高班的學生分小組討論如何保護熊貓。

* Students exchange, support, and discuss their opinions and individual perspectives with peers and/or Chinese speakers on a variety of topics dealing with contemporary and historical topics.

    Example: Research and discuss the evolution of Chinese characters.
    中文程度較高的學生談中國文字的演變。

Standard 1.2 Students understand and interpret written and spoken language on a variety of topics in Chinese.

Interpretive Communication 理解詮釋

The unique nature and certain characteristics of the Chinese language in both its spoken and written forms place great demands on students as they work to develop both listening and reading comprehension. In listening, the abundance of homophones requires attentiveness to both tones and context. Phonetic transcription systems, such as Pinyin romanization, the Chinese Phonetic Alphabet, and the Wade-Giles system, are aural guides in verbal acquisition as well as valuable transitional tools in the introduction of spoken and written Chinese. In reading, both traditional and simplified Chinese characters are widely used in the Chinese-speaking world; thus, a developmentally appropriate competency in reading both forms is recommended.

Sample Progress Indicators for K-4

- Students listen and respond to directions and commands related to classroom tasks.
    Example: Respond to simple classroom commands.
    請把門關上，大家跟我說。

- Students comprehend the main ideas and identify main characters in illustrated children's stories.
    Example: Dramatize a children's story. 小兔乖乖。

- Students comprehend simple characters used in brief messages and notes on familiar topics.
    Example: Signs 出口，入口；dates 三月二日；
    greeting cards 生日快樂！

- Students interpret gestures, intonation, and other visual or auditory cues.
    Example: Match pictures with various hand gestures.
    搖手，擺手，拱手。

Sample Progress Indicators for K-8

- Students comprehend the principle information contained in conversations on familiar topics.
    Example: Listen to a short sample dialogue. 聽一段對話。

- Students understand and interpret the main ideas and significant details from selected authentic audiovisual and multimedia sources.
    Example: Listen to songs and view video clips. 聽歌曲，看電視。

- Students understand announcements and messages connected to daily activities in Chinese culture.
    Example: Find out the schedule of a sports event. 看球賽時間表。

- Students identify the principle characters and comprehend the main ideas and themes in selected literary texts.
    Example: Identify the main characters in a literary text.
    閱讀簡短的小故事。

- Students understand verbal and nonverbal Chinese signals used in communication.
    Example: Finger gestures indicating numbers. 用手表達數字。

- Students recognize the multiple ways in which an idea may be expressed in Chinese.
    Example: Express different ways of greeting and apologizing.
    不好意思，對不起；沒事兒，沒關係，不要緊。

> **PHONETIC TRANSCRIPTION SYSTEMS ARE AURAL GUIDES IN VERBAL ACQUISITION AS WELL AS VALUABLE TRANSITIONAL TOOLS IN THE INTRODUCTION OF SPOKEN AND WRITTEN CHINESE**

Sample Progress Indicators for K-12

- Students comprehend the main themes and some details on topics of interest as found in sources printed in Chinese such as newspaper announcements, magazine advertisements, and cartoon strips.

    Example: Compare the content of two movie advertisements and select a favorite one.
    看電影廣告。

- Students demonstrate an increasing understanding of cultural nuances in written and spoken Chinese in both formal and informal settings.

    Example: Comprehend Chinese cultural nuances in spoken Chinese.
    哎喲小王， 哪陣風把你給吹來了？
    （學生瞭解言外之意。）

- Students comprehend, analyze, and interpret the basic content of selected literary texts.

    Example: Analyze the use of words in a selected essay.
    閱讀朱自清的 【春】 然後討論。

- Students demonstrate an understanding of the principle elements of nonfiction articles in newspapers and magazines on topics of current and historical importance to Chinese speakers.

    Example: Engage in a simulated news interview.
    學生模擬報導一段新聞。

- Students demonstrate an understanding of the main ideas of lectures or presentations on topics associated with Chinese current and historical events.

    Example: Organize a panel discussion after a current events workshop.
    中文高班的學生交換對時事討論會的心得。

- Students analyze the main plot, subplot, characters, their descriptions, roles, and significance in authentic literary texts.

    Example: Discuss and analyze a selected Chinese authentic literary text.
    中文程度較高的學生選讀一段或一篇小說。

- Students demonstrate an increasing understanding of the cultural nuances of meaning in expressive products of the Chinese culture, such as various literary genres and the visual and performing arts.

    Example: Learn about the Chinese performing arts.
    增進中文高班的學生對中國地方戲劇以及各類文藝民俗作品的認識。

Standards for Chinese Language Learning

Standard 1.3 Students present information, concepts, and ideas to an audience of listeners or readers on a variety of topics in Chinese.

Presentational Communication 表達演示

This communicational mode requires various learning strategies to master both formal and informal presentations in both spoken and written Chinese. Students must also master tones and contextual clues to meaning, as described in Standards 1.1 and 1.2. The challenge of learning characters in order to produce intelligible essays or articles makes the attainment of competency in this area particularly time-consuming for students of Chinese, yet worthwhile. At the beginning stages, students may use phonetic transcription to facilitate their written communication of ideas. It is important that students' ability in writing Chinese characters should be developmentally enhanced through all learning stages. Students at all levels should be able to use phonetic transcriptions to produce computer-generated text.

▼

STUDENT'S WRITING ABILITY IN WRITING CHINESE CHARACTERS SHOULD BE DEVELOPMENTALLY ENHANCED THROUGH ALL LEARNING STAGES

Sample Progress Indicators for K-4

- Students give brief oral messages and presentations about home and family, school activities, and common objects.

    Example: Talk about pictures of the 12 animals represented in the Chinese calendar.
    用動物圖片介紹十二生肖。

- Students recite or dramatize songs, short anecdotes, or poems familiar to their Chinese peers.

    Example: Recite nursery rhymes or riddles.
    唱兒歌，表演帶動唱，猜謎，說繞口令。

- Students tell or retell children's stories orally or in writing.

    Example: Retell a familiar folk tale.
    讓學生講一遍剛聽過的故事。

- Students learn how to write simple Chinese characters with correct stroke orders.

    Example: Learn the basic strokes in writing.
    山，水，上，下，大，中，小。

- Students restate and rephrase simple information from materials presented orally and visually in class.

    Example: Point out the major cities on a Chinese map.
    這是北京。這是上海。這是廣州。

Sample Progress Indicators for K-8

- Students present skits, recite selected poems, tell anecdotes, and perform songs in Chinese for school events.

    Example: Perform a short skit at a China Night in school.
    表演短劇，背誦詩歌。

Standards for Chinese Language Learning

- Students write simple notes and reports about people and things at school.
    Example: Prepare captions for a class album.
    為課堂照片寫簡短說明。
- Students prepare stories or brief written reports about personal experiences, events, or other school subjects to share with peers and/or Chinese speakers.
    Example: Make a list of daily routines. 列一張日常作息表。
- Students summarize the plot and describe characters in literature such as poems, short stories, folk tales, and anecdotes.
    Example: Share famous Chinese stories with classmates.
    講故事給同學聽。
- Students learn how to identify radicals and components of Chinese characters.
    Example: Make a poster to show radicals and components of characters.
    制作部首偏旁的海報。

Sample Progress Indicators for K-12

- Students write descriptions of the people and objects present in their everyday environment and in school.
    Example: Describe one's best friend.
    寫以我的好朋友為題的短文。
- Students prepare written and oral reports with the use of a Chinese dictionary or thesaurus.
    Example: Use Chinese radicals to find words in a dictionary.
    學用筆劃部首查字典或詞典。
- Students create stories or skits in both spoken Chinese (Kǒutóu yǔ) and written Chinese (Shūmiàn yǔ).
    Example: Create a dialogue for a play. 用口頭語寫短劇。Write an invitational letter to a teacher. 用書面語寫請帖給老師。
- Students write various types of texts such as letters or essays.
    Example: Write various types of compositions. 寫便箋或短文。
- Students analyze and express their opinions about stories, plays, poems, radio/ TV programs, songs, films, or visual arts.
    Example: Learn a popular Chinese song and analyze its lyrics.
    學習唱【茉莉花】，並討論歌詞。
- Students perform and/or recite poems or excerpts from stories connected to topics from other disciplines such as world history, geography, the arts, science, or mathematics; or from material commonly read by speakers of Chinese.
    Example: Summarize the voyage of Zheng He and make a visual presentation to tell the story about this Chinese historical figure.
    中文程度較高的學生介紹鄭和航海的經過。

- Students prepare a research-based analysis of a current event from the perspectives of both the United States and Chinese cultures.

    Example: Write an essay about issues related to environmental protection.
    中文高班的學生報導環保問題。

- Students write a letter or an article describing and analyzing an issue for a student publication.

    Example: Write an article about personal views on school uniforms.
    中文程度較高的學生對學生應否穿制服發表意見。

▼

"CHINESE CULTURE" PRESENTED IN THIS DOCUMENT IS UNDERSTOOD TO INCLUDE THE DIVERSE CULTURAL PERSPECTIVES, THE SOCIAL PRACTICES, AND THE PRODUCTS OF CHINESE SPEAKING SOCIETIES.

Cultures — *Goal Two*
體認多元文化

Developing cultural understanding is as important a goal as developing language proficiency. Indeed, it is much easier to make sense out of the Chinese language when students come to a true understanding of the important linguistic and cultural variations of the Chinese-speaking world. Recognizing China's ethnic and linguistic diversity, the term "Chinese culture" presented in this document is understood to include the diverse cultural perspectives, the social practices, and the products of Chinese-speaking societies. In studying the culture, students need to be taught not only the history and geography of China, but also the Chinese people's philosophical perspectives, their way of life, and contributions to world civilization. With clearer insights into the diverse perspectives of Chinese culture, students begin to understand why and how Chinese people may behave and interact in certain ways that differ from their own. They will then be able to make cultural comparisons with an open mind. Studying Chinese language provides students with the key that opens the door to understanding Chinese traditional values, attitudes, and ideas.

Given the thousands of years of Chinese civilization, plus the ethnic and regional diversity within China's borders, students are abundantly furnished with magnificent examples of cultural products, ranging from fine arts, literature, architecture, medicine, and scientific inventions to vastly different regional foods, music, clothing, customs, and dialects. Studying aspects of these traditional and contemporary cultural products leads to clearer glimpses into the Chinese way of life. Students should be afforded as much exposure as possible to a range of learning experiences that reflect the richness of the diverse cultures encompassed in the Chinese-speaking communities. Through a thoughtful integration of culture and language studies, students will gain clearer insights and a better understanding of one of the oldest human civilizations.

Standard 2.1 Students demonstrate an understanding of the relationship between the practices and perspectives of the cultures of the Chinese-speaking world.

Practices of Culture 文化習俗

Chinese cultural practices are derived from a long period of history and reflect the social structures, traditional ideas, attitudes, and values of the Chinese people. In the understanding of social patterns and the practice of conventions, students must be aware that Chinese views of society, government, family roles, and interpersonal relationships have similarities and differences from their own. Therefore, it is important for the students to experience numerous examples of Chinese customs and cultural practices, so that they can learn to interact appropriately in Chinese cultural settings.

Sample Progress Indicators for K-4

- Students observe and identify simple patterns of behavior or interaction in various settings.
    Example: Watch video clips on Chinese New Year celebrations.
    看中國新年的圖片或電視節目剪輯。

- Students use appropriate gestures and oral expressions for greetings and leave-takings in family and social settings.
    Example: Role-play greetings with the elder members of the family.
    奶奶您好。

- Students participate in age-appropriate cultural activities such as games, songs, festival celebrations, story telling, and dramatizations.
    Example: Simulate a Dragon Boat Race. 摹擬端午節划龍舟。

Sample Progress Indicators for K-8

- Students observe and describe culturally based behavior patterns of Chinese youth.
    Example: Conduct proper behaviors and manners toward teacher.
    練習中國學校情境，學生遇見老師要行禮。

- Students use appropriate verbal and nonverbal communication for the practice of 禮 Lǐ (etiquette) for daily activities among peers and adults.
    Example: Practice Chinese family etiquette.
    長輩走進來時，坐著的小輩應該站起來。

- Students learn about and participate in age-appropriate cultural practices such as Chinese cooking, martial arts, and games.
    Example: Play a tangram 玩七巧板，watch shadow puppets 看皮影戲，make dumplings 包餃子。

Sample Progress Indicators for K-12

- Students use appropriate verbal and nonverbal cues in a variety of cultural contexts that reflect both peer group and adult activities such as receiving gifts, accepting compliments, and using "kè tào huà."

    Example: The person receiving tea says 不敢當, the person offering it says 不客氣 or 沒關係。 Both should hold the cup with both hands.

- Students learn about and participate in age-appropriate cultural practices.

    Example: Engage in Chinese cultural activities, such as Chinese chess 下象棋, Tài Jí Quán 打太極拳, and Peking opera 欣賞京劇。

- Students identify, examine, and discuss connections between cultural perspectives and socially approved behavior patterns as well as Chinese taboos. 忌諱 (Jì Huì)

    Example: Discuss Chinese customs.
    各地過年習俗, 送禮不送鐘, 忌諱四。

* Students identify, analyze, and discuss patterns of behavior and/or interaction in the context of Chinese culture.

    Example: Students discuss and analyze patterns of behavior as observed in segments of movies, videos, news broadcasts, and articles of newspapers or magazines of Chinese culture.
    中文程度較高的學生用電視電影的剪輯或報章雜誌的文章分析中國文化。

> CHINESE ALSO DEVELOPED A RICH BODY OF PHILOSOPHY, LITERATURE, AND LANGUAGE THAT OPENS THE DOOR TO A BROADER UNDERSTANDING OF CHINA.

Standard 2.2 Students demonstrate an understanding of the relationship between the products and perspectives of the cultures of the Chinese-speaking world.

Products of Culture 文化產物

For thousands of years, China has continuously generated a wealth of cultural products that have profoundly influenced the world. Silk, compasses, paper, gunpowder, rockets, rudders, movable type, decimal mathematics, oil derricks, paper currency, astrolabes, and seismographs are just some of the significant inventions and innovations created by the Chinese. In addition to these inventions, the Chinese have also developed a rich body of philosophy, literature, and language that opens the door to a broader understanding of China as well as its neighboring countries. Therefore, a deep knowledge of Chinese contributions in science, technology, and the humanities will not only enable students to better appreciate Chinese culture but also help them function intellectually in the Chinese-speaking world.

Standards for Chinese Language Learning

Sample Progress Indicators for K-4

- Students identify and observe tangible products of Chinese culture.
    - *Example:* Hands-on experience with food (餃子), children's games (毽子, 陀螺), decoration (燈籠), and Chinese dress (旗袍).
- Students participate in and learn about age-appropriate cultural activities such as children's nursery rhymes, songs, and selections of children's literature.
    - *Example:* Recite poems and nursery rhymes.
        兒童詩歌，童話，兒童文學讀物。
- Students identify, discuss, and produce artwork, crafts, and games enjoyed or produced by Chinese children.
    - *Example:* Practice calligraphy (書法), paper folding (摺紙), or Peking opera masks (京劇臉譜).
- Students learn about Chinese symbolism of colors, animals, numbers, and other items.
    - *Example:* Make red envelopes for the Chinese New Year celebration.
        紅色代表喜慶。

Sample Progress Indicators for K-8

- Students identify and learn about expressive products of Chinese culture (e.g., stories, poetry, music, painting, dance, and drama) and explore the way in which these products reflect the lifestyles in the Chinese-speaking communities.
    - *Example:* Make a video to illustrate the use of Chinese calligraphy scrolls as decoration in a Chinese home.
        中國家庭常用中國畫或字畫裝飾室內。
- Students explore and identify the function of utilitarian products (e.g., sports equipment, household items, tools, foods, and clothing) of Chinese culture as found within their homes and communities.
    - *Example:* List Chinese kitchenwares.
        筷子，碗，湯匙，蒸籠，炒菜鍋。
- Students identify and study major Chinese cultural and scientific contributions to the world.
    - *Example:* Make a list of important Chinese discoveries or inventions.
        列出數項中國科學發明，以及文房四寶紙墨筆硯的來源及重要性。

Sample Progress Indicators for K-12

- Students identify, discuss and analyze themes, ideas, and perspectives as revealed in the products of the Chinese-speaking world.
    - *Example:* Compare and contrast the themes of different festivals and their foods.
        中秋節吃月餅，端午節吃粽子。

Standards for Chinese Language Learning

- Students experience (read, listen to, observe, perform), discuss, and analyze expressive products of Chinese culture, including selections from various literary genres and the fine arts.

    Example: Explore the perspectives of Chinese culture presented in Chinese paintings.
    歲寒三友 松，竹，梅 的含義。

- Students identify, discuss, and analyze intangible products of Chinese culture, such as social, economic, and political institutions, and explore relationships among these institutions and the perspectives of Chinese culture.

    Example: Discuss the examination system in China.
    中文高班學生討論中國的考試制度。

- Students explore the relationships among the products, practices, and perspectives of Chinese culture.

    Example: Examine and find examples of red couplets used for the Chinese New Year.
    中文程度較高的學生分析春聯的用途及所表達的意義。

BY USING CONTENT FROM OTHER SUBJECTS TO EXPAND CHINESE LANGUAGE, VOCABULARY, AND CONCEPTS AS THE TOPICAL BASES FOR COMMUNICATION IN THE CHINESE LANGUAGE

Connections — *Goal Three*
貫連其他學科

Learning Chinese creates numerous opportunities for students to expand their knowledge. Various topics and concepts learned in other subjects can all be integrated with and further reinforced through the study of Chinese. As students progress in their knowledge of the language, the possibility of gaining access to information and materials only available through Chinese becomes apparent. This firsthand information can take many forms, ranging from ancient texts to satellite broadcasts from such places as Beijing, Hong Kong, or Taipei. The accessibility to this abundance of authentic sources adds another dimension to language learning beyond the classroom.

With multimedia and computer technologies, the capacity to make connections to other subjects as well as to acquire more direct access to Chinese sources has been greatly enhanced. Students can now navigate through the information highway to access materials about China and Chinese-speaking communities around the world. Students can use Internet sites in Chinese, as well as multimedia materials, to gain knowledge and research information about topics of interest to them. The use of technology is not only an important tool by which to strengthen their language skills, but also guides them in becoming self-directed learners. Connecting with other disciplines, acquiring information, and using technology all are means that enable students to broaden their knowledge, cultivate their interest, and support a life-long learning process.

Standard 3.1 Students reinforce and further their knowledge of other disciplines through the Chinese language.

Making Connections 觸類旁通

Since the content of Chinese language instruction frequently overlaps with that of other subject areas, many opportunities exist for interdisciplinary reinforcement. Students can accomplish this standard by acquiring knowledge through Chinese sources to be applied to other disciplines, and by using content from other subjects to expand Chinese language, vocabulary, and concepts as the topical bases for communication in the Chinese language. School, grade, or team-based interdisciplinary units especially serve to empower students to make these connections as well as to teach them that Chinese can be an integral part of their growing knowledge base.

Sample Progress Indicators for K-4

- Students demonstrate an ability to use Chinese to name concepts learned in other subject areas.

    Example: Name the animals in Chinese or identify different types of transportation common in China.
    說出動物昆蟲的中文名字，列出常用的交通工具。

Sample Progress Indicators for K-8

- Students discuss topics of other school subjects, including geographical terms and concepts, historical facts and concepts, mathematical terms and problems, and scientific information.

    Example: Identify famous Chinese and American historical figures and their contributions.
    列舉孫中山，華盛頓 或其他歷史人物。

- Students comprehend illustrated story books or short videos on topics being studied in other classes.

    Example: Use Chinese folk art design and symbols to make mobiles.
    用中國美術圖案做手工。

- Students present reports in Chinese, orally and/or in writing, on topics being studied in other classes.

    Example: Create a map depicting the major cities and products in China.
    用地圖解說中國各大城市及各地物產。

Sample Progress Indicators for K-12

- Students acquire information from a variety of Chinese sources written about a topic being studied in other school subjects.

    Example: Gather information from Chinese newspapers on sports.
    剪貼有關運動的新聞報導。

Standards for Chinese Language Learning

- Students combine information from other school subjects with information available in Chinese to complete activities in the Chinese class.

    Example: Make a poster of the solar system in Chinese. 畫太陽系的海報。

- Students use Chinese to discuss topics from other school subjects, including political and historical concepts, health issues, and social concerns.

    Example: Conduct a class discussion on the issue of Chinese population. 中文高班的學生表達對中國人口問題的看法和意見。

Standard 3.2 Students acquire information and recognize the distinctive viewpoints that are only available through the Chinese language and culture.

Acquiring New Information 博聞廣見

The Chinese language is most often the only pathway to gain information about China. The vast majority of modern publications as well as the accumulative scholarship of thousands of years are only accessible through the Chinese language. Students can use this pathway to obtain a wealth of knowledge that will enable them to reach a genuine understanding of many important facets of both traditional and contemporary Chinese culture.

Sample Progress Indicators for K-4

- Students read and/or listen to age-appropriate folk tales, short stories, poems, and songs written for Chinese speakers.

    Example: Read aloud popular Chinese nursery rhymes. 朗讀童謠詩詞，聆聽兒童故事。

Sample Progress Indicators for K-8

- Students use age-appropriate Chinese sources to prepare reports in Chinese and/or English on topics of personal interest.

    Example: Make a collage of Chinese clothing from different time periods. 剪貼不同時代中國服飾的圖片。

Sample Progress Indicators for K-12

- Students use a variety of Chinese sources to prepare reports in Chinese and/or English on topics of personal interest, or on those with which they have had limited previous experience. They compare Chinese language information to information obtained on the same topics written in English.

    Example: Use the Internet to search for information on Chinese food recipes, and compare their nutritional values based on the USDA Food Pyramid. 用中英文資料研究中國食物的營養價值。

Comparisons   Goal Four
比較語言文化之特性

Students of any foreign language begin a process of alternating comparisons, constantly reflecting on their own language and culture through the perspective of the new language they learn. Through this process they emerge from a state of cultural-linguistic naivete to the realization that there are multiple world views and forms of expression. Students of Chinese discover many aspects of the language that differ from their own, such as the logographic writing system, lack of cognates shared with English, and the tonal system. In addition they find words and concepts in Chinese that have no counterpart in their own language, and vice versa. In the realm of culture, students also find marked differences, as they learn, for example, why in the Chinese culture respecting elders and honoring the family name are at the core of Chinese social norms, how the Chinese people retained their cultural continuity through so many tumultuous years of history, and what principle schools of thought gave rise to Chinese art, music, and literature. Through these linguistic and cultural comparisons, students benefit in three important ways: (1) they gain a better understanding of Chinese people and culture; (2) they understand their own culture and language better; and (3) they significantly develop their critical thinking skills.

Standard 4.1 Students demonstrate understanding of the nature of language through comparisons of the Chinese language with their own.

Language Comparisons 比較語文
Students of Chinese will notice major contrasts between Chinese and their own language. The tonal nature of the spoken language and the logographic written system are two salient features of the Chinese language. The lack of cognates demonstrates the different linguistic nature of Chinese to some students. However, many basic grammatical structures also provide a basis for comparisons. Of particular importance is the emphasis on Chinese word order to convey appropriate structure and common meaning.

Sample Progress Indicators for K-4
- Students cite and use examples of borrowed words in the language they are learning and their own, and they pose guesses as to why languages in general might need to borrow words from other languages.

    Example: List "borrowed" words: 漢堡 (hamburger), 七喜 (Seven-up), 可口可樂 (Coca-Cola).

- Students use Chinese measure words and compare them with similar elements in their own language.

    Example: Compare and contrast measure words: 一張紙 = a piece of paper 一杯茶 = a cup of tea.

> **STUDENTS EMERGE FROM A STATE OF CULTURAL-LINGUISTIC NAIVETE TO THE REALIZATION THAT THERE ARE MULTIPLE WORLD VIEWS AND FORMS OF EXPRESSIONS.**

Standards for Chinese Language Learning

- Students talk about differences and similarities between the sound system of their own language and the Chinese language.

    Example: Talk about and practice the four tones.
    四聲：媽，麻，馬，罵 (mā, má, mǎ, mà).

- Students demonstrate an awareness of formal and informal speech in greetings and leave-takings, compare expressions of politeness in other languages, and use courteous language in Chinese.

    Example: Practice daily formal and informal expressions.
    禮貌用語和日常用語的區別：請進 / 進來。

- Students demonstrate an awareness of the differences and similarities between the Chinese writing system and their own.

    Example: Make a diagram to compare and contrast Chinese characters and Roman letters. 分辨中國方塊文字和英文字母的異同。

Sample Progress Indicators for K-8

- Students recognize the unique function of Chinese time indicators—time words, aspects, particles, and patterns—and use them properly.

    Example: Identify the use of time indicators: 昨天我沒上學, (Yesterday I didn't go to school), 下雨了 (It's raining!), 我們學了三年中文了 (I have been learning Chinese for three years).

- Students express respect and are aware of usage to reflect status differences in both Chinese and in their own language.

    Example: Make a list of different ways to ask a person's name and age.
    您貴姓？ / 你姓什麼？ / 你叫什麼名字？

- Students demonstrate awareness that the Chinese language has distinctive sounds and/or tones that must be mastered in order to communicate correctly.

    Example: Compare and contrast the meanings of words that are the same sound but have different tones. 飽了 / 爆了 (bǎole / bàole), 水餃 / 睡覺 (shuǐjiǎo / shuìjiào), 重要 / 中藥 (zhòngyào / zhōngyào).

- Students recognize the relative lack of parsing in the Chinese written language and its effect on reading comprehension.

    Example: Compare and contrast sentences that could be misread due to lack of experience in determining word breaks. 他<u>晚上</u>下班<u>以後</u>來看你 may be misread as 他晚<u>上下班</u>以<u>後來</u>看你。

- Students compare the organizational principle in the Chinese language of "general to specific" with that of their own language.

    Example: Compare and contrast dates/time written in Chinese and English.
    一九九八年二月二十八號上午九點十分 (The sequence presented in Chinese is read as – 1998 year, February 28, morning 9 o'clock, 10 minutes.)

Sample Progress Indicators for K-12

- Students demonstrate an awareness of the style of formal written Chinese and conversational Chinese, and compare them with formal as well as informal usage in their own language.

    Example: Compare the use of 閑人免進 and 不可以進去。

- Students demonstrate an awareness that Chinese principles of word order may differ from their own language.

    Example: In general, time and place precede action.
    他今天下午三點在學校等你。

Standard 4.2 Students demonstrate understanding of the concept of culture through comparisons of Chinese culture with their own.

Cultural Comparisons 比較文化

Students discover cultural differences ranging from everyday customs and habits, such as eating utensils and table manners, to belief systems and traditions, such as ancestor worships and holiday celebrations. Through thoughtful comparisons, students arrive at a better understanding of their own culture and a deeper appreciation of the cultures of the Chinese-speaking world.

Sample Progress Indicators for K-4

- Students compare simple patterns of behavior and interactions in various cultural settings.

    Example: Compare different use of eating utensils, such as chopsticks (筷子), knives, and forks (刀叉).

- Students demonstrate an awareness that gestures are an important part of communication.

    Example: Identify Chinese gestures revealed in pictures or video clips.
    敬禮，鞠躬，握手，及手勢和臉部表情。

- Students compare and contrast tangible products such as toys, sports equipment, and Chinese food with such products in their own culture.

    Example: Compare and contrast toys and food items with these products of their own culture.
    比較玩具：陀螺，扯鈴 vs 玩具熊，芭比娃娃
    比較食品：包子，餃子 vs 漢堡飽，熱狗

- Students compare and contrast intangible products of Chinese culture such as rhymes, songs, and folktales with similar products of their own culture.

    Example: Compare and contrast children's nursery rhymes such as "Hickory Dickory Dock" with 小老鼠上燈台。

Sample Progress Indicators for K-8

- Students contrast verbal and nonverbal behavior in activities common in Chinese culture and their own.

    Example: Make a diagram to illustrate different expressions and gestures.
    比較不同的手勢。

- Students demonstrate an awareness of differences in daily activities in Chinese culture and their own.

    Example: Talk about table etiquette and manners in different cultural settings.
    比較各地吃飯習俗，以及主客坐位的安排和上菜順序。

- Students analyze why certain products are significant in Chinese culture while different products have gained prominence in other cultures.

    Example: Compare and contrast the significance of historical monuments such as the Pyramids (金字塔) and the Great Wall (長城).

- Students compare the relationship between cultural perspectives and traditional practices (e.g., holidays, celebrations, work habits) within Chinese culture and their own.

    Example: Make a Venn diagram showing the similarities and differences between Thanksgiving and the Moon Festival.
    比較中秋節和感恩節。

Sample Progress Indicators for K-12

- Students compare proverbs as reflections of culture, citing examples from both Chinese culture and their own.

    Example: Compare and contrast proverbs. "Kill two birds with one stone" with 一箭雙鵰。

- Students compare nuances of meanings of words, idioms, and phrases in the Chinese language and their own.

    Example: Compare and contrast idioms.
    請，請上坐；不敢當，那裡那裡；
    沒事兒，沒事兒。

- Students analyze the relationship between perspectives and practices in Chinese culture and compare and contrast these with their own.

    Example: Compare and contrast family relationships in China and their own culture.
    比較家庭親屬關係。

- Students identify and analyze cultural perspectives as reflected in a variety of literary genres.

  Example: Identify the cultural perspectives represented in poems and selected excerpts from literature. 中文高班的學生瞭解 a poem 靜夜思（思鄉）, a proverb 磨杵成針（恆心）, and a familiar story 管仲和鮑叔牙的故事（友誼）。

- Students analyze the relationship between the perspectives and expressive products (e.g., music, visual arts, and various forms of literature) in Chinese culture and compare and contrast these with their own.

  Example: Analyze the concept of ideology presented in books of *Utopia and The Great Harmony.* 中文程度較高的學生分析理想國與禮運大同篇。

Communities   Goal Five
應用於國內與國際多元社區

This goal combines elements from each of the other goal areas. As students use Chinese to communicate in authentic real-life contexts, come to understand Chinese culture through its products and practices, and use Chinese beyond the classroom setting, they will inevitably access resources from Chinese community organizations, business or government agencies; they will also utilize electronic resources, broadcast media, and print media. Chinese language learners will become more proficient in Chinese through developmentally appropriate exposure to programs and activities in the schools and community.

The first standard of this goal emphasizes the use of Chinese to communicate at school, in the community, at the workplace, and abroad. The second focuses on personal enjoyment and enrichment through exposure to Chinese history, literature, art, music, opera, dance, and other cultural activities. As students progress in the Chinese language, they will ideally not only seek out every possible opportunity to apply their competencies in the real world, but will also continue to pursue their life-long studies out of an intrinsic interest in Chinese culture.

Standard 5.1 Students use the Chinese language both within and beyond the school setting.

School and Community 學以致用

Students of Chinese must have opportunities within the school setting as well as outside to practice and hone their communicative and cultural competencies in a progressive fashion. They will use the Chinese language to access information and resources, and transfer knowledge acquired outside the Chinese classroom to their language learning process. The proximity of Chinese communities and their affiliated institutions (cultural centers, heritage language schools, community organizations, etc.) facilitates the practical application of the Chinese language. Students should be encouraged to make use of such local resources to learn the language and culture of the Chinese-speaking world.

> STUDENTS WILL NOT ONLY SEEK OUT EVERY POSSIBLE OPPORTUNITY TO APPLY THEIR COMPETENCIES... BUT ALSO CONTINUE TO PURSUE THEIR LIFELONG STUDIES OUT OF AN INTRINSIC INTEREST IN CHINESE CULTURE

Sample Progress Indicators for K-4

- Students communicate on a personal level with Chinese speakers via dialogues, notes, and cards.

    Example: Make a birthday card for a Chinese friend.
    送自己做的生日卡給中國小朋友。

- Students identify professions that require proficiency in the Chinese language.

    Example: Identify jobs that require the use of Chinese language such as Chinese bilingual or language teacher (雙語老師或中文老師), diplomat (外交人員), or translator (翻譯員).

- Students present information about the Chinese language and culture to others in Chinese, English, or both.

    Example: Use play dough or sticks show the formation of Chinese numbers from one to ten.
    用小木棒或玩具麵做成中國數字一到十的形狀，或教同學寫中國數字。

- Students illustrate Chinese stories to present to others.

    Example: Make an illustrated storybook on a familiar Chinese folk tale.
    畫嫦娥奔月的故事。

- Students perform for a school or community celebration.

    Example: Sing songs and perform dances at a school assembly.
    唱中國兒歌，跳中國舞。

Sample Progress Indicators for K-8

- Students discuss their preferences concerning leisure activities and current events, in written and oral form, with Chinese speakers.

    Example: Read a headline on sports in a Chinese newspaper.
    閱讀中文報紙體育新聞版的大標題。

- Students interact with members of the local community to hear how they use Chinese in their work.

    Example: Interview local people who use Chinese at work.
    訪問中國城的商店及餐館。

- Students present information about the Chinese language and culture to others.

    Example: Give a calligraphy demonstration to other classes.
    中文班的學生到別班示範用毛筆寫中國字。

- Students participate in Chinese culture-related activities that benefit the school or community.

    Example: Participate in a Chinese New Year celebration.
    參加中國新年公演或才藝表演。

- Students write and illustrate Chinese stories to present to others.
    - *Example:* Create an illustrated storybook.
    分小組編寫有插圖的故事書。
- Students perform for a school or community celebration.
    - *Example:* Participate in a community event.
    表演唱歌，舞蹈，或畫畫。

Sample Progress Indicators for K-12

- Students present information about the Chinese language and culture to others.
    - *Example:* Teach elementary students about the Chinese sound system and Chinese character writing.
    高中學生到小學或其他班級介紹中文，或用海報介紹中文。
- Students write and illustrate Chinese stories to present to others.
    - *Example:* Make a calendar, with each month depicting an aspect of a Chinese immigration history.
    用早期移民歷史大事設計月曆。
- Students participate in a career exploration or school-to-work project that requires proficiency in the Chinese language and culture.
    - *Example:* Research job opportunities in Chinese-American communities.
    中文程度較高的學生用中文網路及中文報章雜誌調查職業資料以瞭解中國社區的就業情形和需要。
- Students use community resources to research a topic related to the Chinese language and culture.
    - *Example:* Utilize a Chinese community library to do research.
    中文高班的華裔子弟使用社區圖書館的資料，瞭解中國移民在美國的生活情形。

Standard 5.2 Students show evidence of becoming life-long learners by using the Chinese language for personal enjoyment and enrichment.

Life-long Learning 學無止境

Personal interest in the language and culture ensures that the students will become self-motivated, life-long learners of Chinese. Many students of long-sequenced K-12 Chinese programs will continue to pursue their studies of Chinese in college, attend study abroad programs, or take trips to China to enhance their language competency and cultural understanding. Therefore, personal appreciation of and experience with the language and culture make life-long learning of Chinese attainable.

Sample Progress Indicators for K-4

- Students read materials and/or use various media from the Chinese language and culture for enjoyment.

    Example:　Watch Chinese cartoons.
    看童話圖片及欣賞中文卡通片。

- Students play Chinese sports or games.

    Example:　Play jump ropes or games.
    玩跳繩和老鷹捉小雞的遊戲。

- Students interact with Chinese speakers in activities of personal interest.

    Example:　Participate in a children's singing or dance performance.
    參加兒童合唱團的演唱或舞蹈表演。

- Students plan a real or imaginary trip to a Chinese-speaking community.

    Example:　Gather pamphlets and use pictures to make a collage of an imaginary trip to China.
    向旅行社索取資料剪貼中國旅遊圖片。

- Students attend cultural events and social activities or view them through various media.

    Example:　Watch selected Chinese children's TV or video programs.
    看兒童電視節目的節錄。

- Students listen to Chinese music, sing Chinese songs, or learn about traditional Chinese musical instruments.

    Example:　Learn to sing Chinese children's songs.
    唱兒歌，聆聽中國樂器演奏。

Sample Progress Indicators for K-8

- Students consult various sources in Chinese to obtain information on topics of personal interest.

    Example:　Gather information on the excavation of terra cotta figures.
    利用圖書館或網路查詢對個人有興趣的資料
    （例如秦俑的發現）。

- Students play Chinese sports or games.

    Example:　Make a Chinese chess set and play the game with peers.
    學生學習做象棋和下象棋。

- Students exchange information with Chinese speakers about topics of personal interest.

    Example:　Participate in a summer camp organized by Chinese-American communities.
    參加華人組織舉辦的夏令營活動。

- Students use various Chinese media for entertainment or personal growth.

    Example:　Watch a Chinese movie or video clips with or without English subtitles.
    觀賞中國電影或電視綜藝節目的剪輯。

- Students attend Chinese cultural events or social activities.

    Example: Participate in a parade assoicated with an Asian event.
    參加華人代表隊。

- Students listen to Chinese music, sing Chinese songs, or learn about Chinese musical instruments for enrichment.

    Example: Listen to a Chinese music concert.
    學生聆聽國樂團的演奏，入二胡，琵琶，鼓，古箏。

Sample Progress Indicators for K-12

- Students consult various sources in Chinese to obtain information on topics of personal interest.

    Example: Gather information via various authentic sources.
    學生閱讀報章雜誌，搜集網路資料。

- Students play sports or games that reflect Chinese culture.

    Example: Learn how to play popular Chinese games.
    學習扯鈴，下跳棋或下圍棋。

- Students read and/or use Chinese media for entertainment and personal growth.

    Example: Read books or watch video on Chinese cooking.
    閱讀有關中國烹飪的書籍。

- Students listen to Chinese music, sing Chinese songs, and/or learn about Chinese musical instruments.

    Example: Listen or learn how to play a Chinese musical instrument.
    學生聆聽或學習中國樂器及中國歌曲。

- Students attend Chinese cultural events and social activities or view them through various media.

    Example: Organize a cultural event to raise funds to benefit a Chinese institution or individuals in China.
    中文程度高的學生為領養中國鄉村圖書室募捐籌款，並與負責人聯繫辦理領養手續。

- Students establish and/or maintain interpersonal relations with Chinese speakers.

    Example: Participate in a Chinese performing arts organization and become actively involved in its activities.
    中文程度較高的學生參加中國社團活動，邀請中國學者專題演講及舉辦討論會。

Sample Learning Scenarios

TARGETED STANDARDS
1.1 Interpersonal Communication
1.2 Interpretive Communication
1.3 Presentational Communication
2.1 Practices of Culture
2.2 Products of Culture
3.1 Making Connections
3.2 Acquiring Information
4.2 Cultural Comparisons

SÌHÉYUÀN - CHINESE FAMILY RESIDENCE

In Boston, Ms. Lin's second year Chinese class at Snowden International School learns about the Sìhéyuàn, a traditional dwelling with four-sided enclosed courtyards. Students view pictures presented by the teacher and discuss the physical structure of the Sìhéyuàn. Students identify common features of traditional Chinese architecture and make a Venn diagram to compare the Sìhéyuàn to homes in their own neighborhoods. At the end of the unit, each student makes a floor plan of his/her own dream home. Students make visual presentations of their dream homes. They talk about the way in which the family hierarchy and family values were reflected in the layout of the Sìhéyuàn, the application of "fengshui" (geomancy) for selecting home sites that are harmonious with nature, and the changing role and responsibilities of each member within the family in China today.

Reflection

1.1 Students discuss the traditional family residence in China.
1.2 Students comprehend information presented by the teacher.
1.3 Students present their dream homes.
2.1 Students learn how the arrangement of Chinese houses reflected the family hierarchy and family values.
2.2 Students identify the physical structure of a Sìhéyuàn.
3.1 Students make connections to social studies, history, and architecture.
3.2 Students acquire cultural information.
4.2 Students compare the Sìhéyuàn with their own homes.

The Sìhéyuàn lends itself to many related topics which can be incorporated either at this second year level or a later year. For example, expanding the Sìhéyuàn unit can include examining other Chinese architectural structures such as the Forbidden City, ancient Chinese palaces, and temples that were built basically on the pattern of the Sìhéyuàn. These courtyard houses were common throughout different regions of China but the Sìhéyuàn now accommodates several unrelated families instead of one big family with multiple generations. Studying the Sìhéyuàn enables students to discuss the pros and cons of both traditional and modern family living quarters.

EVOLUTION OF CHINESE CHARACTERS

TARGETED STANDARDS	
1.1	Interpersonal Communication
1.2	Interpretive Communication
1.3	Presentational Communication
2.1	Practices of Culture
4.1	Language Comparisons

Ms. Chung's third graders at Rebecca Johnson School at Springfield, Massachusetts learn how Chinese characters evolved by playing a game. The teacher prepares five sets of cards (Figure 1). Each set is comprised of the same ten characters written in a particular style. In addition to the first set of the picture cards (red), the second set (yellow) contains 10 pictographs : Xiàngxíng (象形) used in the Neolithic Age; the third set (blue) uses Zhuànzì (篆字) developed in 221 B.C.; the fourth set (orange) uses Lìshū (隸書) style; and the fifth set (green) uses Kǎishū (楷書) which is the style used today. Students choose one card from each stack at random and try to group the cards themselves by finding the matching characters written in different styles. They then show how the characters evolved by putting the cards in the correct order of development.

Reflection
1.1 Students exchange responses during the character game.
1.2 Students understand different styles of characters.
1.3 Students form groups to present the same characters in different styles.
2.1 Students understand the evolution of characters.
4.1 Students compare the evolution of the Chinese language to that of their own.

For advanced students, this learning activity requires students to discuss, compare and negotiate without using color-coded cards as a cue.

Figure 1.

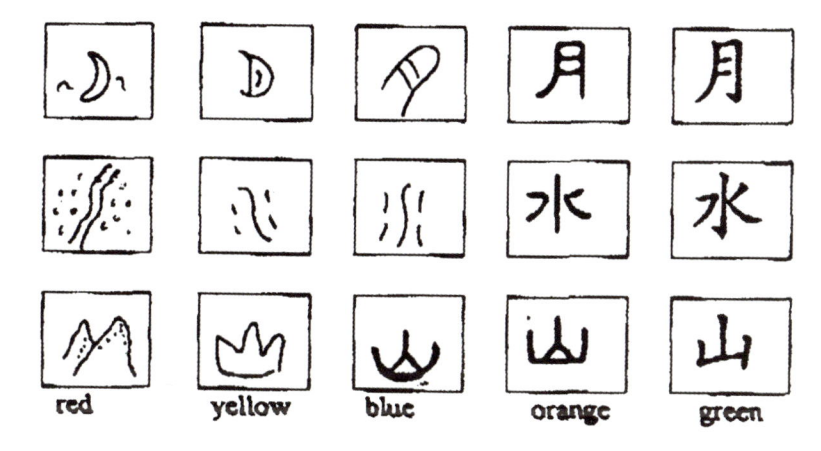

TARGETED STANDARDS	
1.1	Interpersonal Communication
1.2	Interpretive Communication
1.3	Presentational Communication
2.1	Practices of Culture
2.2	Products of Culture
3.1	Making Connections
4.2	Cultural Comparisons
5.1	School and Community
5.2	Life Long Learning

CHINESE KITES

Mrs. Kotenbeutel's Chinese class at James Madison High School in Wisconsin learns the history of kites in China and concepts in making kites. The students read a short story in Chinese about kite flying and popular "insect" kites. They review vocabulary on weather, colors, seasons, and learn new vocabulary related to kites. After viewing video clips and diagrams on kite making, students work in groups to design and build their own kites. Later, they describe orally their completed kites to the class. After school, they fly the kites on the football field.

Reflection

1.1 Students work together to build kites and discuss the finished products.
1.2 Students read and listen to information about kites.
1.3 Students describe their kites orally in class.
2.1 Students learn the history of Chinese kites.
2.2 Students participate in making kites.
3.1 Students connect arts, shapes and weight, winds, and altitude to kite making and flying.
4.2 Students compare Chinese and American concepts of kites and styles.
5.1 Students fly kites on the school football field and the community playground.
5.2 Students fly kites for personal enjoyment.

Students can further use their kite-making skills to build more kites of different designs and establish a kite-flying club. Community members can be invited to the class to share their experiences. Advanced students can be required to compare and contrast the concepts of Chinese kite-making with the Wright Brothers' theory of flying.

TARGETED STANDARDS	
1.1	Interpersonal Communication
1.2	Interpretive Communication
1.3	Presentational Communication
2.1	Practices of Culture
2.2	Products of Culture
3.2	Acquiring Information
4.2	Cultural Comparisons

PEKING OPERA

Second year Chinese students at Lincoln High School in San Francisco learn about Peking Opera. The teacher, Ms. Chang, first shows the class slides taken in Beijing, giving background information on the opera and describing well-known Peking Opera stories. Students compare and contrast the makeup, colors, and costumes worn by various characters. Students examine the language spoken in Peking Opera and compare it to the spoken language used today. Students have a chance to watch a Peking Opera performed by a local opera club. They compare and contrast Peking Opera to Western operas in terms of theme, plot, costumes, makeup, music, and stage design. At the end of this unit, students make Peking Opera masks and give a presentation about the masks and their significance.

Reflection

1.1 Students discuss Peking Opera.
1.2 Students comprehend the information presented by the teacher.
1.3 Students give a presentation on masks.
2.1 Students understand the symbolism reflected in the makeup and costumes of Peking Opera.
2.2 Students view a Peking Opera performance.
3.2 Students acquire information about Peking Opera.
4.2 Students compare and contrast Peking Opera and Western operas.

This learning scenario offers the students the opportunity to learn about Peking Opera, a Chinese performing arts treasure. Visual and audio demonstrations help students to comprehend the plot, characters, and themes found in Peking Opera. Students also deepen their knowledge of Chinese traditions and values through their study of Peking Opera. Advanced students may compare and contrast the opera with other regional performing arts such as the Shadow Puppet Show 皮影戲, and the Puppet Show 布袋戲.

NEIGHBORHOODS

Ms. Hsieh's students at Sidwell Friends School in Washington, D.C., learn about the city of Beijing. In pairs, they interview each other to learn about their classmates' neighborhoods and what they like to do in their neighborhoods. They present to the class what their partners like/dislike about their neighborhoods. As a reinforcement, students bring in pictures, maps, or photographs to illustrate the living environment of their hometowns. They talk about why they like their neighborhoods. Finally, students research one area in Beijing and compare its neighborhoods with their own.

TARGETED STANDARDS	
1.1	Interpersonal Communication
1.2	Interpretive Communication
1.3	Presentational Communication
3.2	Acquiring Information
4.2	Cultural Comparisons

Reflection

1.1 Students interview each other on their neighborhoods.
1.2 Students comprehend information about Beijing.
1.3 Students make presentations on their partner's neighborhoods.
3.2 Students use authentic resources to collect information about Beijing.
4.2 Students compare one area of Beijing with that of their own neighborhood..

This unit gives students an opportunity to observe and describe the physical features of their locality, the seasons, the weather, and the flora and fauna, to learn environmental characteristics, the human impact on the environment, and ecology. They can discuss the things they would like to do to make their environment a better place in which to live. Students may also prepare a story or write a letter to a penpal or an imaginary Chinese friend in Beijing describing their living environment.

TARGETED STANDARDS	
1.1	Interpersonal Communication
1.2	Interpretive Communication
1.3	Presentational Communication
2.1	Practices of Culture
2.2	Products of Culture
3.1	Making Connections
4.2	Cultural Comparisons
5.1	School and Community

A CHINESE FOLK TALE PLAY

Third to fifth grade students in Mr. Nicholas' class in the Lee County Chinese Program at Ft. Myers in Florida prepare a presentation of a dramatic adaptation of *"The Foolish Old Man Moves the Mountain"* (yúgōngyí shān). Students learn about the story and talk about the main characters. Then, they choose roles and are given Chinese scripts to learn. With the cooperation of the music teacher, Chinese instruments and music are incorporated into the production. Students borrow costumes from the local Chinese community or ask their parents to make them. The play is then performed in conjunction with a school-wide function or a "China Night" open to the general public. One or more student "interpreters" provide English translations for the parents and other members of the audience.

Reflection
1.1 Students work together on the play and interact in simple Chinese.
1.2 Students comprehend the story.
1.3 Students present the story in the form of a play.
2.1 Students learn about a popular Chinese folk tale and speculate on what it may reflect about the Chinese view of the world.
2.2 Students use Chinese costumes and musical instruments as props.
3.1 Students acquire knowledge in art and music through the use of Chinese costumes and music.
4.2 Students compare ideas about perseverance and delayed gratification in the folk tale and in their own culture.
5.1 Students present information about the Chinese folk tale to others.

In this activity, parents and community members, as well as the students themselves, become familiar with a famous Chinese folk tale, as well as with Chinese music and costumes. Students also learn Chinese language associated with the story. Other Chinese folk tales can be studied and presented in a similar manner, for example, "Wǔsōng dǎ hǔ." For middle and high school students, this activity can be expanded to include reading authentic texts of various Chinese folk tales, writing a summary of the plot and describing main characters. They can then create skits and perform for a school event.

SUN, MOON, AND PLANETS IN THE SOLAR SYSTEM

Mrs. Su's students at Amherst Middle School in Amherst, Massachusetts, learn seven basic characters that represent the sun, moon, and planets in the solar system. Those seven characters are radicals commonly used to form other characters. Students learn the concept of Yīn Yáng and the five essential elements (Wŭxíng) in Chinese culture. They are asked to match the characters with the names of the sun, moon and the planets of Mars, Mercury, Jupiter, Venus, and Saturn. Each student produces a poster of the solar system in Chinese and displays it in the school. As a follow-up activity, students look for characters from various authentic sources such as signs, newspapers, and books that contain one of these seven radicals, and they show how these characters relate to one another. Students make comparisons with the use of these seven characters (月，火，水，木，金，土，日) as days of the week in Japanese. Students learn that other languages, such as Spanish, French, and Latin, also use the sun, moon, and five planets in their calendrical terms.

TARGETED STANDARDS	
1.1	Interpersonal Communication
1.2	Interpretive Communication
1.3	Presentational Communication
2.1	Practices of Culture
2.2	Products of Culture
3.1	Making Connections
3.2	Acquiring Information
4.1	Language Comparisons
4.2	Cultural Comparisons
5.1	School and Community

Reflection

1.1 Students discuss the use of a radical as part of other characters.
1.2 Students match radicals with names of the sun, moon, and five planets.
1.3 Students present their posters of the solar system to peers.
2.1 Students learn about the concept of Yīn Yáng Wŭxíng.
2.2 Students examine the Yīn Yáng sign and its cultural significance.
3.1 Students reinforce information learned in science class.
3.2 Students acquire knowledge of the five essential elements in Chinese culture.
4.1 Students compare days of the week represented in Chinese, Japanese, French, and Spanish calendars.
4.2 Students compare Chinese and Western astrology.
5.1 Students search for characters from authentic sources outside the classroom setting.

This scenario can be expanded for more sophisticated activities. Advanced students can research the Yīn Yáng Wŭxíng in *The Book of Change* (I-Ching) and study *fengshui* and its application to the daily life of the Chinese people. These seven characters illustrate the Chinese concept of the universe and the positions of the planets, which are believed to affect an individual's personality and health. Students can also examine how the Chinese people use the Yīn Yáng Wŭxíng to select the location of houses or business buildings, decide interior decorations, conduct match-making, and other activities.

Figure 2.

Pinyin	Character	Meaning	Wǔxíng	Solar System	Chinese characters used in Japanese Calendar	
yuè	月	moon	Yīn	Moon	月曜日	Monday
huǒ	火	fire	Temperament	Mars	火曜日	Tuesday
shuǐ	水	water	Intelligence	Mercury	水曜日	Wednesday
mù	木	wood	Integrity	Jupiter	木曜日	Thursday
jīn	金	metal	Talkative	Venus	金曜日	Friday
tǔ	土	earth	Generosity	Saturn	土曜日	Saturday
rì	日	sun	Yáng	Sun	日曜日	Sunday

TARGETED STANDARDS

1.1 Interpersonal Communication
1.2 Interpretive Communication
1.3 Presentational Communication
2.1 Practices of Culture
3.1 Making Connections
4.2 Cultural Comparisons
5.1 School and Community

ROMANCE IN LITERATURE

Fourth year students at Lowell High School in San Francisco read an adaptation of "Liáng Shānbó" and "Zhù Yīngtái," a famous story about two student lovers in the Tang Dynasty. Students write a script based on this classical story, prepare a stage play, and videotape the performance for the school. As a follow-up activity, students compare the story of Liáng and Zhù with that of Romeo and Juliet. Students examine similarities and differences in the social and cultural settings for the two stories. They also discuss how people can come into confrontation with the norms of a society and culture, and the consequences, both intended and unintended. To add another dimension to the discussion, students may also debate whether a similar tragedy could occur today.

Reflection

1.1 Students discuss and debate issues presented in the story.
1.2 Students comprehend the story of Liáng Shānbó and Zhù Yīngtái.
1.3 Students present their interpretations of the story in the form of a play.
2.1 Students discuss the confrontations with cultural norms presented in the story.
3.1 Students make connections with other disciplines such as English literature, social studies and history.
4.2 Students compare and contrast the social and cultural norms of today with those of the past.
5.1 Students perform a stage play for the school.

This activity offers students an opportunity to view human emotions and to explore complexity through comparative literature. In the discussions, students analyze topics such as social systems, family values, traditions and customs, and religious beliefs. Students may explore other classical novels such as *Dream of the Red Chamber* (紅樓夢) and *The West Chamber* (西廂記). This activity is also applicable to advanced-level heritage learners. Such an activity may help students develop a deeper understanding and genuine appreciation of Chinese literature, which is a powerful and integral aspect of Chinese culture.

TI JIÀNZI – CHINESE SHUTTLECOCK

Mrs. Lee's third grade students in Livingston, New Jersey, use three pieces of colored tissue paper, a quarter or two metal washers, scissors, and a piece of string to make a Jiànzi (Chinese shuttlecock). Students first review colors and the name of materials used in this activity. They use the math concept of fractions to fold papers. Students follow the procedures step by step and repeat simple instructions after the teacher. Students count the numbers when their teacher shows them how to play. Students learn to recite a children's rhythm that gives commands to use different parts of the body to play Jiànzi. (jiǎo bǎn xīn, shǒu bǎn xīn, dào guǎizi, luódǐ xīn, zuǒ shǒu dǎ lái yi tiáo xīn.) In pairs, students give and respond to the commands, such as yòng zuǒ jiǎo tī sān xià (use the left foot to kick three times). Students compete in small groups and choose a winner from each group to perform at the school talent show.

TARGETED STANDARDS	
1.1	Interpersonal Communication
1.3	Presentational Communication
2.2	Products of Culture
3.1	Making Connections
4.2	Cultural Comparisons
5.2	Life Long Learning

Reflection
1.1 Students learn to follow instructions and respond to simple commands.
1.3 Students perform and make presentations at a school talent show.
2.2 Students participate in making and playing authentic children's games.
3.1 Students use math concepts, and reinforce their skills for arts and physical education.
4.2 Students compare the differences and similarities of Jiànzi with "hacky sack."
5.2 Students play Jiànzi for personal enjoyment.

This activity can be extended to middle and high school students. Middle students can watch a video and learn different authentic ways of playing Jiànzi. High school students can make a report on the history of Jiànzi and write down detailed instructions for making them. This activity is fun for students, their friends, and their family members as a physical fitness exercise. Playing Jiànzi provides good training for eye, hand, and leg movements.

TARGETED STANDARDS	
1.1	Interpersonal Communication
1.2	Interpretive Communication
1.3	Presentational Communication
2.1	Practices of Culture
2.2	Products of Culture
3.1	Making Connections
3.2	Acquiring Information
4.2	Cultural Comparisons
5.1	School and Community

DRAGON WINGS

Mrs. Yen's Chinese for Native Speakers class at Lincoln High School in California read Lawrence Yep's *Dragon Wings*. Students are divided into four groups to write a script for a four-act play in Chinese based on the *Dragon Wings* story. The first act focuses on the boy prior to his departure from his family in China; the second act shows him being reunited with his father in San Francisco; the third act depicts the survival of the boy and his father after the 1905 earthquake; and, the last act shows the fulfillment of the father's dream in which building and flying a glider become reality. Students divide up the roles and responsibilities, produce props, make their own costumes, and present the entire play to an audience of Chinese language learners in school. In order to support their views and exchange reflections about this book, students may research past and current immigration laws, analyze social and economic issues during different periods in the history of Chinese immigration to the United States, and compare the background of early immigrants in the book with those newly arrived. Students will interview local community people and compare their life styles with the characters in the book.

Reflection
1.1 Students produce a play and interview community people.
1.2 Students infer cultural facts and values based on *Dragon Wings*.
1.3 Students write and present their play.
2.1 Students learn about family values and traditions.
2.2 Students learn the Chinese art of kite-making.
3.1 Students make connections to other subjects such as arts, science, and social studies on issues in early twentieth century America.
3.2 Students research information on immigration and other topics through authentic materials.
4.2 Students compare the life styles of the Chinese immigrants with those of other immigrants in America.
5.1 Students interview community people.

This is a semester-length project. Before engaging students in this project, the teacher will present background information relating to the history of Chinese immigration. Students who have recently immigrated may contribute information about their experiences to their peers. This project will help native Chinese students to understand the text better through analyzing the story, selecting crucial elements, and interpreting them into Chinese.

Standards for Chinese Language Learning

Standards for Classical Language Learning

*A Collaborative Project of
The American Classical League and
The Americal Philological Assocation and
Regional Classical Associations*

TASK FORCE ON STANDARDS FOR CLASSICAL LANGUAGE LEARNING
Richard C. Gascoyne, University at Albany, SUNY, Albany, NY (Chair)
Martha Abbott, Fairfax County Public Schools, Fairfax, VA
Philip Ambrose, The University of Vermont, Burlington, VT
Cathy Daugherty, The Electronic Classroom, Richmond, VA
Sally Davis, Arlington County Public Schools, Arlington, VA
Terry Klein, North Allegheny School District, Pittsburgh, PA
Glenn Knudsvig, University of Michigan, Ann Arbor, MI
Robert LaBouve, Southwest Educational Development Laboratory, Austin, TX
Nancy Lister, Vernon Public Schools, Vernon, CT
Karen Lee Singh, Florida State University School, Tallahassee, FL
Kathryn A. Thomas, Creighton University, Omaha, NE
Richard F. Thomas, Harvard University, Cambridge, MA

CLASSICAL LANGUAGES

Standards for Classical Language Learning

is a collaborative project of

The American Classical League
and **The American Philological Association**

and regional classical associations, including
the Classical Association of the Atlantic States,
the Classical Association of New England,
and the Classical Association of the Middle West and South.

Cover: Coin (upper): head of the goddess Roma, denarius, about 268-240 B.C., Boston Museum of Fine Arts; Coin (lower): Athena's owl, olive leaves, and the first three letters of the Athenian people's name, Bibliothèque Nationale

Title page: Logo (left): American Classical League (ACL); Logo (right): American Philological Association (APA)

Standards for Classical Language Learning is aligned with and is a companion document for *Standards for Foreign Language Learning: Preparing for the 21st Century* (National Standards in Foreign Language Education Project, 1996).

© Copyright 1997 American Classical League. All rights reserved

Permission to copy or reprint this document or portions of it should be sought from the American Classical League; Miami University; Oxford, Ohio 45056; (513) 529-7741; fax: 513-529-7742; email: AmericanClassicalLeague@MUOhio.edu

Permission is routinely granted for educational and classroom use contingent upon appropriate credit being given to the American Classical League.

Table of Contents

STANDARDS FOR CLASSICAL LANGUAGE LEARNING AND SCHOOL REFORM	**203**
THE STATUS OF CLASSICAL LANGUAGE LEARNING IN THE UNITED STATES TODAY	**204**
NATIONAL STANDARDS, STATE FRAMEWORKS, AND LOCAL CURRICULA	**205**
STANDARDS FOR CLASSICAL LANGUAGE LEARNING	**206**
COMMUNICATION — Goal 1	**207**
CULTURES — Goal 2	**208**
CONNECTIONS — Goal 3	**210**
COMPARISONS — Goal 4	**211**
COMMUNITIES — Goal 5	**212**
WEAVING THE STRANDS TOGETHER: THE FIRST STEP IN CURRICULUM DEVELOPMENT	**214**
LEARNING SCENARIOS	**216**
The *Aeneid*: Words and Pictures	216
C is for *Canis*	217
A Geography Lesson	219
The Greek and Latin Connection	220
Greek Medicine in Athens and Epidauros	221
In Principio Erat Verbum: The Verb as Key to Syntax	222
Is Vergil's Dido "Miss Saigon"?	223
Language Connections	225
Market Day in a Roman Province	226
Pronoun Poems	227
Quis Caesarem Interfecit?	228
Quis Es Tu?	229
Roman Drama	230
A Roman Election	231
The Voyage of St. Brendan	232
GLOSSARY	**234**
FREQUENTLY ASKED QUESTIONS	**236**
BIBLIOGRAPHY AND RESOURCES	**240**

STANDARDS FOR CLASSICAL LANGUAGE LEARNING AND SCHOOL REFORM

Educational reform in the United States took off in a new direction in 1989 when state and national leaders reached consensus on six national education goals for public schools. In 1994 Congress passed *Goals 2000: Educate America Act,* endorsing those goals and expanding Goal Three to include foreign languages in the core curriculum. Goals 2000 and the complementary federal legislation, *Improving America's Schools Act,* encourage the development of voluntary high standards in the core disciplines.

The publication in January 1996 of *Standards for Foreign Language Learning: Preparing for the 21st Century* was the culmination of three years' work by the language profession in developing foreign language standards. The standards include suggestions from the volunteer reviewers and language educators in the field. While four national modern language groups wrote the proposal and the Federal government funded it, the project was very much a product of the entire language profession.

From the beginning those who formed the policy for the project and those who crafted the standards considered classical languages to be part of the effort. The following statement comes from the "Statement of Philosophy" of *Standards for Foreign Language Learning*: "The United States must educate students who are equipped linguistically and culturally to communicate successfully in a pluralistic American society and abroad. This imperative envisions a future in which ALL students will develop and maintain proficiency in English and at least one other language, modern or classical." Classicists held positions on the board of directors and the task force of the project.

The goals and standards in *Standards for Foreign Language Learning* are visionary and describe a K-12 foreign language program in a core curriculum for all students and languages. While broad goals establish the framework for the language program, content standards describe what students need to know and do in a language. The language profession believes the standards are world class, yet realistic and attainable by most students. Language educators realize that the generic standards will have to be made language specific. The ACL/APA Task Force on *Standards for Classical Language Learning* has in this document adapted the standards to the learning of classical languages.

With this publication in hand, curriculum specialists and school classicists can begin the process of translating the standards into curriculum. These voluntary standards for classical language learning provide the impetus for the development of state foreign language frameworks and local curriculum guides. The task force believes the standards for classical language learning will become an especially valuable resource for states and local schools that do not have specialists in classics or funds to devote to Latin and Greek for curriculum development. It is clear that *Standards for Classical Language Learning* will have an impact upon curriculum development and instruction in those schools that choose to use the standards. Finally, the standards should promote articulation in classical language programs from school to school and school to college.

Standards for Classical Language Learning begins a process and positions classicists to play a role in standards-based school reform. The task force has proposed standards; now we trust that classicists will review and revise them, and then promote, implement, and assess them, fully realizing that the standards will never be set in concrete.

▼

...PROFICIENCY IN ENGLISH AND AT LEAST ONE OTHER LANGUAGE, MODERN OR CLASSICAL...

THE STATUS OF CLASSICAL LANGUAGE LEARNING IN THE UNITED STATES TODAY

At the turn of the century—and the millennium—the teaching of classical languages continues to hold a vital place in American education. We are traditional, the inheritors of Periclean Athens of the 5th century B.C. and of Augustan Rome at the beginning of the first millennium of this era; but we are innovative, timely and practical, prepared to enter a new millennium. Our appeal does not depend on political or economic interests, but rather on educational beliefs that do not go out of style.

There are an estimated half million students in Latin classes in the United States today. Ancient Greek is standard in leading colleges and universities in the country; the more recent addition of courses in classical civilization, etymology, and mythology has increased the vitality of Greek and Latin as staples in the college curriculum. Continuing interest in Greco-Roman culture is paralleled by the continued vigor of Latin language study, in part, from the recognition that the study of Latin can be a very effective aid in improving language skills in English and in the subsequent learning of other foreign languages. As a corollary of Latin's resurgence, there is a growing need for a new generation of Latin teachers.

> **LATIN, IN FACT, IS FOR ALL STUDENTS**

The persistent popularity of Latin in the last two decades has also brought forth a spirited array of creative, exciting, and more effective teaching materials. Latin classrooms are increasingly lively and engaging. Students learn to read with an emphasis on authentic materials from the ancient world: its literature, graffiti, coins, and inscriptions. Students make connections from their reading to the other subjects they are studying in school and to the communities that surround them. They examine the products and practices of ancient peoples in the light of their own experiences and are challenged to make comparisons.

Latin has come to the elementary and middle schools. Latin is, in fact, for all students. Thousands of young people from inner-city schools, often in impoverished areas, have boosted their chances for academic success through model Latin programs, such as those begun in the 1960s and 1970s in Washington, D.C., Detroit, Los Angeles, and Philadelphia. The continuing development of innovative programs, materials, and methods ensures the survival of classical language programs in the next century—and millennium.

ABOUT STANDARDS FOR CLASSICAL LANGUAGE LEARNING

The words, ideas, and culture of the ancient world are communicated to us in the writing and the archaeological remains of the people and their institutions. The ancient Greeks and Romans, breaking barriers of time and place, have communicated their message through the ages and continue to communicate to the modern world; we, in turn, communicate more clearly to each other in word, in practice, and in product as a result of that contact.

Standards for Classical Language Learning applies five goals of communication to a context appropriate for Latin and Greek.

The standards for classical language learning are organized within the five goal areas which make up classical language education: communication, culture, connections, comparisons, and communities. Each goal is one strand in a fabric that must be woven into curriculum development at the state, district, and local levels.

Each goal area contains two content standards. These standards describe the knowledge and abilities students should acquire.

Under each standard are sample progress indicators for beginning, intermediate, and advanced students. The sample progress indicators are neither prescriptive nor exhaustive. Intermediate and advanced students are expected to exhibit the progress indicators of the lower levels as well as the progress indicators of their own level.

What is a beginning, intermediate, or advanced student? If Latin or Greek is taught continuously from the early grades, it would be reasonable to assume that a beginning student might demonstrate progress indicated by the beginning sample progress indicators by grade 6 or 8. Students who study Latin or Greek every day in grades 7 and 8 should be able to demonstrate the beginning progress indicators by the end of grade 8. Level I high school students may demonstrate beginning status by the end of their Level I course. Intermediate students may demonstrate their progress at the end of a Level III course. Advanced students may demonstrate their progress at the end of an Advanced Placement Course. Such designations as Level I, II, and III place learning in a time frame and organize it into courses that standards of excellence seek to avoid. Course and curricula are products of the district and school. In the scheme presented here, the progress of students in terms of standards of excellence, or proficiency, is the factor to be measured, not time.

NATIONAL STANDARDS, STATE FRAMEWORKS, AND LOCAL CURRICULA

Standards for Classical Language Learning is intended for many audiences and for many purposes. It describes on a national level what we expect our students to know and be able to do; it is our message to legislators, educators, boards of education, communities, parents, and students; it is a guide for state curriculum frameworks; at the district level it is a guide for curriculum development.

It is important to understand that this document is not meant to be a classroom tool. It is not a curriculum for a Latin or Greek course; it is not a guide for daily lesson planning. *Standards for Classical Language Learning* does not mandate methodology; it is not textbook bound. It does not tell how to teach. It provides a destination, not a road map.

Standards for Classical Language Learning is a statement of what students should know and be able to do. State frameworks provide a curricular and programmatic context. District curriculum guides further define course content in a coordinated sequence. Lesson plans translate curriculum into meaningful and creative activities for the individual classroom.

> ... STANDARDS FOR CLASSICAL LANGUAGE LEARNING PROVIDE THE IMPETUS FOR THE DEVELOPMENT OF STATE FOREIGN LANGUAGE FRAMEWORKS AND LOCAL CURRICULUM GUIDES ...

Standards for Classical Language Learning

COMMUNICATION
Communicate in a Classical Language

Standard 1.1: Students read, understand, and interpret Latin or Greek.

Standard 1.2: Students use orally, listen to, and write Latin or Greek as part of the language learning process.

CULTURES
Gain Knowledge and Understanding of Greco-Roman Culture

Standard 2.1: Students demonstrate an understanding of the perspectives of Greek or Roman culture as revealed in the practices of the Greeks or Romans.

Standard 2.2: Students demonstrate an understanding of the perspectives of Greek or Roman culture as revealed in the products of the Greeks or Romans.

CONNECTIONS
Connect with Other Disciplines and Expand Knowledge

Standard 3.1: Students reinforce and further their knowledge of other disciplines through their study of classical languages

Standard 3.2: Students expand their knowledge through the reading of Latin or Greek and the study of ancient culture.

COMPARISONS
Develop Insight into Own Language and Culture

Standard 4.1: Students recognize and use elements of the Latin or Greek language to increase knowledge of their own language.

Standard 4.2: Students compare and contrast their own culture with that of the Greco-Roman world.

COMMUNITIES
Participate in Wider Communities of Language and Culture

Standard 5.1: Students use their knowledge of Latin or Greek in a multilingual world.

Standard 5.2: Students use their knowledge of Greco-Roman culture in a world of diverse cultures.

Communication — *Goal One*
Communicate in a Classical Language

Goal 1 defines "communication" as it applies to the learning of a classical language. The written messages from the ancient world, from epic poetry to Pompeian graffiti, are the major source of knowledge and our major line of communication to the Greeks and Romans. ***Reading, then, is the first standard and the key to communicating with the ancient world.*** But the Forum and the Agora were alive with the sounds of commerce, the speeches of politicians, the noise of gossip. The recitation of poetry published the sounds of an active literature. To hear these sounds, to imitate those cadences in the classroom, to practice writing words and ideas in the ancient language enhance the ability to read. The second standard of the communication goal emphasizes the importance of oral skills, listening, and writing as tools to improve reading.

STANDARD 1.1 Students read, understand, and interpret Latin or Greek.

Sample Progress Indicators, Beginning
- Students read words, phrases, and simple sentences and associate them with pictures, and/or other words, phrases and simple sentences.
- Students demonstrate reading comprehension by answering simple questions in Latin, Greek, or English about short passages of Latin or Greek.
- Students demonstrate a knowledge of vocabulary, basic inflectional systems, and syntax appropriate to their reading level.

Sample Progress Indicators, Intermediate
- Students read and understand passages of Latin or Greek composed for acquisition of content and language skills.
- Students read and understand, with appropriate assistance, passages of Latin or Greek adapted from the original authors.
- Students read and understand short unadapted passages of Latin or Greek when provided with appropriate assistance.
- Students demonstrate reading comprehension by interpreting the meaning of passages they read.
- Students recognize some figures of speech and features of style of the authors they read.
- Students demonstrate a knowledge of vocabulary, inflectional systems, and syntax appropriate to their reading level.

Sample Progress Indicators, Advanced
- Students read and understand prose and poetry of selected authors with appropriate assistance.
- Students interpret the meaning of the passages they read.

READING IS THE FIRST STANDARD AND THE KEY TO COMMUNICATING WITH THE ANCIENT WORLD

Standards for Classical Language Learning

- Students recognize, explain, and interpret content and features of style and meter of the authors they read.
- Students demonstrate a knowledge of vocabulary, inflectional systems, and syntax appropriate to the authors they read.

STANDARD 1.2 Students use orally, listen to, and write Latin or Greek as part of the language learning process.

Sample Progress Indicators, Beginning
- Students recognize and reproduce the sounds of Latin or Greek.
- Students respond appropriately to simple questions, statements, commands, or non-verbal stimuli.
- Students sing songs in Latin or Greek.
- Students write simple phrases and sentences in Latin or Greek.

Sample Progress Indicators, Intermediate
- Students read Latin or Greek aloud with accurate pronunciation, meaningful phrase grouping, and appropriate voice inflection, by imitating the models they have heard.
- Students respond appropriately to questions, statements, commands, or other stimuli.
- Students write phrases and sentences in Latin or Greek.

Sample Progress Indicators, Advanced
- Students read Latin or Greek prose and poetry aloud with attention to such features as metrical structure, meaningful phrase grouping, and appropriate voice inflection.
- Students respond appropriately to more complex spoken and written Latin or Greek.
- Students write passages of connected sentences in Latin or Greek.

> ... THE FORUM AND THE AGORA WERE ALIVE WITH THE SOUNDS OF COMMERCE, THE SPEECHES OF POLITICIANS, THE NOISE OF GOSSIP ...

Culture — *Goal Two*
Gain Knowledge and Understanding of Greco-Roman Culture

Formulating an understanding of the perspectives of the Greeks or Romans through their practices and through their products is key to an understanding of their culture. The focus in Goal 2 is on the ability of students to hear (i.e., read) and see (in physical remains) the message of the Greeks or Romans. Their daily life, education, politics, history, philosophy, and religious practices tell students about their perspectives, revealed both in their literary products and in remaining artifacts. Literature, as well as non-literary writing, is key to an understanding of culture; it is a product of the culture and a primary source for understanding ancient practices.

Standards for Classical Language Learning

STANDARD 2.1 Students demonstrate an understanding of the perspectives of Greek or Roman culture as revealed in the practices of the Greeks or Romans.

Sample Progress Indicators, Beginning
- Students demonstrate a basic knowledge of the daily life of the ancient Greeks or Romans.
- Students demonstrate knowledge of some famous Greeks or Romans and of selected facts of history and geography of the ancient world.

Sample Progress Indicators, Intermediate
- Students demonstrate a knowledge of the daily life and thought of the ancient Greeks or Romans, gained in part from the Latin or Greek texts they read, and apply that knowledge to an understanding of Greek or Roman culture.
- Students demonstrate a knowledge of the people and facts of Greek or Roman history and political life, gained in part from the Latin or Greek texts they read, and relate that knowledge to an understanding of Greek or Roman perspectives.

Sample Progress Indicators, Advanced
- Students demonstrate a broad knowledge of Greek or Roman history, customs, and private and political life, gained from their reading of Latin or Greek authors, and use that knowledge in analyzing Greek or Roman culture.
- Students demonstrate knowledge of philosophy, religion, and the arts of the ancient Greeks or Romans, gained from their reading of Latin or Greek authors, and relate that knowledge to an understanding of Greek or Roman perspectives.

Perspectives (Meanings, attitudes, values, ideas)

Practices (Patterns of social interactions)

Products (Books, tools, food, laws, music, games)

STANDARD 2.2 Students demonstrate an understanding of the perspectives of Greek or Roman culture as revealed in the products of the Greeks or Romans.

Sample Progress Indicators, Beginning
- Students identify the principal Greek or Roman deities and heroes by their names, deeds, and spheres of influence.
- Students recognize basic architectural features and art forms of the Greeks or Romans.

Sample Progress Indicators, Intermediate
- Students relate their reading of selected texts, literary and non-literary, adapted and unadapted, to an understanding of Greek or Roman culture.
- Students demonstrate a knowledge of architectural styles, art forms, and artifacts of the Greeks or Romans and use them in analyzing Greek or Roman culture.

Sample Progress Indicators, Advanced
- Students demonstrate knowledge of an author, a genre, and/or a literary period gained from authentic materials and unadapted texts in Latin or Greek and apply it to an understanding of Greek or Roman culture.
- Students demonstrate a knowledge of archaeological evidence, art forms, and artifacts of the Greeks or Romans and use it in analyzing Greek or Roman culture.

Connections Goal Three

Connect with Other Disciplines and Expand Knowledge

Goal 3 focuses on connecting the knowledge and understanding gained under Goal 1 (Communication) and Goal 2 (Culture) to the core subject areas: English, mathematics, science, social studies and foreign languages. It also provides opportunities for interdisciplinary experiences in all areas of the curriculum. In addition, students use their knowledge of Greek or Latin to acquire new information as they read authentic works which may also relate to other subject areas.

STUDENTS USE THEIR KNOWLEDGE OF GREEK AND LATIN TO ACQUIRE NEW INFORMATION

STANDARD 3.1 Students reinforce and further their knowledge of other disciplines through their study of classical languages.

Sample Progress Indicators, Beginning
- Students use their knowledge of Latin or Greek in understanding a specialized vocabulary in such fields as government and politics.
- Students recognize and use Roman numerals and the vocabulary associated with counting.

Sample Progress Indicators, Intermediate
- Students recognize and make connections with Latin or Greek terminology in the sciences and technology.
- Students recognize and make connections with Latin or Greek terminology in the social sciences and history.

Sample Progress Indicators, Advanced
- Students demonstrate in their written and spoken vocabulary a knowledge of philosophical, legal, artistic, and musical terms associated with Latin or Greek.
- Students demonstrate their knowledge of Latin or Greek terminology in the social sciences and history.

STANDARD 3.2 Students expand their knowledge through the reading of Latin or Greek and the study of ancient culture.

Sample Progress Indicators, Beginning
- Students acquire information about the Greco-Roman world by reading passages of Latin or Greek with a culturally authentic setting.
- Students recognize plots and themes of Greco-Roman myths in the literature of other cultures.
- Students demonstrate a knowledge of the geography of the ancient world and connect it to the modern world.

Sample Progress Indicators, Intermediate
- Students acquire information about the Greco-Roman world by reading adapted or selected Latin or Greek sources.

- Students connect their knowledge of ancient history and social and political systems to events and systems in the modern world.

- Students connect their knowledge of the Latin or Greek language to their knowledge of literature and artistic achievement.

Sample Progress Indicators, Advanced
- Students acquire information about the Greco-Roman world by reading Latin or Greek literary and non-literary sources.

- Students transfer their knowledge of Latin or Greek literature to their understanding of world literature.

- Students demonstrate their knowledge of the influence of Greco-Roman mythology, history, social and political systems, and artistic achievements on world cultures.

Comparisons
Goal Four
Develop Insight into Own Language and Culture

Goal 4 focuses on the comparisons that students make between the ancient and modern worlds. Through their study of the Latin or Greek language, students develop a greater understanding of the structure and vocabulary of English. By examining and analyzing the public and private lives of the ancient Greeks and Romans, students acquire a perspective from which to examine and analyze their own culture more objectively.

> **STANDARD 4.1** Students recognize and use elements of the Latin or Greek language to increase knowledge of their own language.

Sample Progress Indicators, Beginning
- Students demonstrate a basic knowledge of Latin and Greek roots, prefixes, and suffixes by recognizing them in English words of Latin or Greek origin.

- Students understand some Latin or Greek phrases, mottoes, and abbreviations used in English.

- Students demonstrate an understanding of basic language patterns of English as they relate to the structure of Latin or Greek.

Sample Progress Indicators, Intermediate
- Students demonstrate the relationship of Latin or Greek words to their derivatives and cognates in English.

- Students demonstrate an increased use of English words from or related to Latin or Greek.

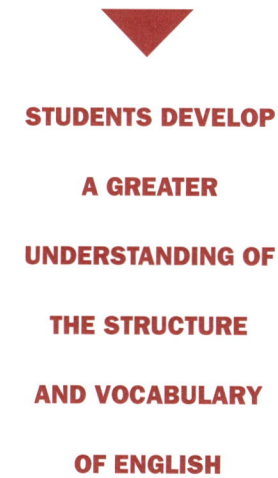

> STUDENTS DEVELOP A GREATER UNDERSTANDING OF THE STRUCTURE AND VOCABULARY OF ENGLISH

- Students compare and contrast the language patterns and grammar of Latin or Greek to the structure and grammar of English.

Sample Progress Indicators, Advanced
- Students demonstrate the relationship of Latin or Greek words to their derivatives and cognates in English and apply some principles of word building and word transfer.

- Students demonstrate an enhanced ability to read, write, understand, and speak English based on the vocabulary and grammar of Latin or Greek.

STANDARD 4.2 Students compare and contrast their own culture with that of the Greco-Roman world.

STUDENTS ACQUIRE A PERSPECTIVE FROM WHICH TO EXAMINE AND ANALYZE THEIR OWN CULTURE MORE OBJECTIVELY

Sample Progress Indicators, Beginning
- Students look at the architectural features of the buildings around them and recognize the Greco-Roman elements in them.

- Students compare and contrast aspects of their own public and private lives to those of the Greeks or Romans.

- Students compare the themes and heroes of classical mythology to the themes and heroes of their own folklore and culture.

Sample Progress Indicators, Intermediate
- Students identify elements in their own art and literature that have their basis in the Greco-Roman world.

- Students reflect on classical influence on the political institutions, law, and history of their own culture.

- Students recognize in their reading of modern stories and literature the influence of the myths and literature of the ancient world.

Sample Progress Indicators, Advanced
- Students recognize the influence of Greco-Roman history, private and public life, art, and architecture on their own world and make comparisons and draw conclusions based on that knowledge.

- Students compare and contrast elements of the literature, mythology, and philosophy of their own world with those of the ancient world.

Communities *Goal Five*
Participate in Wider Communities of Language and Culture

Goal 5 focuses on the application of the knowledge of Latin or Greek to wider linguistic and cultural communities extending from school to later life. Knowledge of Latin or Greek enables students to develop a full understanding and appreciation of classical influences in today's world as they encounter new language-learning situations and other cultures. Students understand the link between classical languages and certain professional fields through their specialized terminology. Understanding Greco-Roman culture provides students with a basis for interpreting events of the modern world. The tools of technology and telecommunication provide links to the resources of the worldwide classical community.

STANDARD 5.1 Students use their knowledge of Latin or Greek in a multilingual world.

Sample Progress Indicators, Beginning
- Students present and exchange information about their language experience to others in the school and in the community.
- Students recognize the influence of Latin or Greek on the specialized language of various professional fields and recognize its use in the media.

Sample Progress Indicators, Intermediate
- Students combine the tools of technology with their classical language skills to communicate with other students in a global community.
- Students interact with community members who are involved in a variety of careers to understand how they have used their study of classical languages.

Sample Progress Indicators, Advanced
- Students use their knowledge of Latin or Greek in communicating within the student and adult community of classical language learners.
- Students use their knowledge of Latin or Greek in learning other languages.

STANDARD 5.2 Students use their knowledge of Greco-Roman culture in a world of diverse cultures.

Sample Progress Indicators, Beginning
- Students recognize from their study of Greco-Roman culture that cultural diversity has been an integral feature of society from antiquity.
- Students share with others in schools and communities their understanding of cultural differences in the Greco-Roman world.

Sample Progress Indicators, Intermediate
- Students compare the issues that reveal cultural differences in the ancient world with similar issues in modern cultures.
- Students combine the tools of technology with their knowledge of Greco-Roman culture to share cultural experiences.

Sample Progress Indicators, Advanced
- Students participate in the community of classical scholars in cultural events, contests, lectures, and scholarship.
- Students show evidence of connecting the past to the present by applying their knowledge of ancient cultures to their own thoughts and actions.

> ... A BASIS FOR INTERPRETING EVENTS IN THE MODERN WORLD...

Weaving the Strands Together: The First Step in Curriculum Development

Stanndards for Classical Language Learning seeks to separate the threads of the discipline in order that they may be seen independently. This separation, however, is nearly impossible, and, in fact, Goal 1–Communication (i.e., the language strand) and Goal 2–Culture (i.e., the cultural strand) are woven through Goals 3, 4, and 5. In each case the language strand is the first standard (i.e., Standard 3.1, 4.1, and 5.1), and the cultural strand is the second standard (i.e., Standard 3.2, 4.2, and 5.2).

This document leads naturally to the next step: curriculum development, which weaves together discrete elements, such as vocabulary, grammar, and derivation, as well as literature, mythology, and daily life, into a fabric of creative design that fosters learning and works in the classroom.

The scenarios that follow are snapshots of classroom lessons and activities that integrate the separate strands of communication, culture, connections, comparisons, and communities. They are the final product in the process of translating standards to the classroom. They give life to the standards.

STUDENTS COMBINE THE TOOLS OF TECHNOLOGY WITH THEIR CLASSICAL LANGUAGE SKILLS

	GOAL 3 *connections* Connect with Other Disciplines and Expand Knowledge	GOAL 4 *comparisons* Develop Insight into Own Language and Culture	GOAL 5 *communities* Participate in Wider Communities of Language and Culture
GOAL 1 — *communication* — **Communicate in a Classical Language** **Standard 1.1** Students read, understand, and interpret Latin or Greek **Standard 1.2** Students use orally, listen to, and write Latin or Greek as part of the language learning process.	**Standard 3.1** Students reinforce and further their knowledge of other disciplines through their study of classical languages.	**Standard 4.1** Students recognize and use elements of the Latin or Greek language to increase knowledge of their own language.	**Standard 5.1** Students use their knowledge of Latin or Greek in a multilingual world.
GOAL 2 — *culture* — **Gain Knowledge and Understanding of Greco-Roman Culture** **Standard 2.1** Students demonstrate an understanding of the perspectives of Greek or Roman culture as revealed in the practices of the Greeks or Romans **Standard 2.2** Students demonstrate an understanding of the perspectives of Greek or Roman culture as revealed in the products of the Greeks or Romans.	**Standard 3.2** Students expand their knowledge through the reading of Latin or Greek and the study of ancient culture.	**Standard 4.2** Students compare and contrast their own culture with that of the Greco-Roman world.	**Standard 5.2** Students use their knowledge of Greco-Roman culture in a world of diverse cultures.

Standards for Classical Language Learning

Learning Scenarios

It is a bold leap from national standards to classroom scenarios. There is an important piece of material missing; between national standards and classroom scenarios a firm fabric of curriculum development needs to be woven. The standards are basic; the scenarios present a product in full dress. The fact that the product exists in exemplary classrooms attests to the fact that the philosophy of *Standards for Classical Language Learning* is already a part of current practice.

The following collection of fifteen scenarios represents a selected sample of scenes from today's Latin and Greek classrooms throughout the nation. Limited space and a desire to represent the diversity of exemplary programs has prevented the inclusion of all of the many samples received from teaching colleagues. The scenarios are based in real classrooms; the descriptions have been edited and reworked to illustrate the document.

TARGETED STANDARDS

1.1 Students read, understand, and interpret Latin or Greek.
2.2 Students demonstrate an understanding of the perspectives of Greek or Roman culture as revealed in the products of the Greeks or Romans.
3.1 Students reinforce and further their knowledge of other disciplines through their study of classical languages.
5.1 Students use their knowledge of Latin or Greek in a multilingual world.

The *Aeneid*: Words and Pictures

Two students from Ms. Gushman's Advanced Placement Vergil class at Yorktown High School, a suburban public school, are making a presentation to their classmates, in a 90-minute block-scheduled class. One, using a laser pointer, highlights details in a slide of a Greek vase, which depicts a scene of Aeneas escaping from Troy with his father and his small son. He tells what is known of the artist and identifies the figures in the painting, pointing out the attributes of the divinities and the hero. His partner gives some background on the technique of Athenian black figure vases. Next, both recall with the class the details of the story and ask how this episode relates to the major themes of the epic. Then they give the class a handout they have prepared with the Latin text and translation of the relevant passages in the *Aeneid,* and the class reads these with special attention to the Greek vase. They invite the class to make a close comparison between the words of Vergil's text and the artistic depiction on the slide, asking which is more detailed and what significant differences there are.

After their ten-minute presentation, the next team explains its slide until all nine have been presented. At the next class meeting, Ms. Gushman invites discussion comparing the different media, the different approaches to the conceptualization of the scenes, and their relative effectiveness. Students are encouraged to choose their favorites and justify their preferences.

The class assignment was to research nine works of art based on themes from the *Aeneid*. The nine slides include: *The Judgment of Paris,* Attic black-figure amphora, Antimenes Painter; *Zeus Carrying Off Ganymede,* painted terracotta from Olympia; *The Wedding of Peleus and Thetis,* The Françoise Vase; *Zeus,* bronze statue from Cape Artemision; *Laocoön,* marble statue, Rome; *Varvakeion Athene,* marble cult statue; *King and Warriors / Ajax and Achilles Gaming, with Athena,* Attic black-figure amphora; *Achilles dragging the body of Hector around the tomb of Patroclus,* Attic black-figure hydria; *Escape of Aeneas with Ascanius and Anchises,* Attic black-figure amphora.

Each team was responsible for one slide, which they researched by using the following tools in their media center: slides (provided by the teacher) and slide viewers; The Paratext Vergil Reference CD-ROM, containing the Latin text, notes and translation; a manual of mythology; quotations; word lists; search capabilities; Web sites for Greek and Roman art (especially *Perseus*); resource books from the media center, e.g., the sixteen-volume *World Encyclopedia of Art.*

The students spend one 90-minute block period in the media center, a week to meet on their own with their teams and prepare the presentation on their assigned slide, another block period in the presentations, and about twenty minutes in a wrap-up discussion.

Reflection

1.1 Students read passages from the *Aeneid* depicted in the art works.
2.2 Students examine products of ancient artists and note how these artists interpreted the scenes from the *Aeneid* that they are currently reading .
3.1 Students use knowledge of the *Aeneid* to understand the works of art, and vice versa.
5.1 Students use the tools of technology to participate in the community of classical scholars to gain and share knowledge.

This assignment proves especially valuable for its interdisciplinary nature, allowing students to research art techniques and topics in the history of art. Besides introducing students to a new way of seeing characters and events in the *Aeneid,* a very attentive examination of Vergil's words is required for their correlations.

Using CD-ROM and Internet technology provides a valuable tool for future academic and personal projects. Further use of this sort of technology is applicable to archaeological, geographical, historical or political topics related to many Latin texts. Classical literature has inspired countless art works. A natural follow-up to this activity would be a visit to an art gallery to view ancient (and/or modern) sculpture or painting on ancient themes.

Ms. Kevin Gushman, Yorktown High School, Arlington, Virginia

C IS FOR *CANIS*

The third-grade students at Thomas O'Brien Academy of Science and Technology, an inner city public elementary magnet school, are studying *Living Things — Plants, Animals, and Homo Sapiens* as part of a whole school curricular theme. Students look at a picture of a dog and hear Mrs. Gascoyne, their Latin teacher, pronounce the Latin word *canis*. Students repeat the Latin word *canis*. They think of how it might be spelled (someone suggests a "k")

TARGETED STANDARDS

1.1 Students read, understand, and interpret Latin or Greek.
1.2 Students use orally, listen to, and write Latin or Greek as part of the language learning process.
2.2 Students demonstrate an understanding of the perspectives of Greek or Roman culture as revealed in the products of the Greeks or Romans.
3.1 Students reinforce and further their knowledge of other disciplines through their study of classical languages.
4.1 Students recognize and use elements of the Latin or Greek language to increase knowledge of their own language.
4.2 Students compare and contrast their own culture with that of the Greco-Roman world.

and watch as the Latin word is written on the board. Then the students try to think of an English word that starts out like *canis* and means "of or like a dog." They suggest and then discuss the words *canine, canine teeth,* and the genus *canis* used in scientific names. All of a sudden "K-9" has new meaning.

Next students look at a picture of the dog *Cerberus* and answer simple Latin questions about the number of heads, eyes, noses, mouths, ears, legs, and feet that *Cerberus* has: *Quot capita habet Cerberus? - oculos? nasos? ora? crura? pedes?* They know numbers and body parts from previous games they have played. Students share what they already know about the mythology of *Cerberus,* often from Saturday morning cartoons. Students listen as the teacher fills in further information about this unusual dog. Students then look at a constellation chart and search for the word *canis* among the stars. They find *Canis Major* and *Canis Minor* and discover what these Latin expressions mean. Finally, students look at a photograph of the *Cave Canem* mosaic from ancient Pompeii. The class learns the location of the mosaic, its purpose, and the meaning of the Latin phrase in the design. In the course of discussing the phrase, students will notice the difference in the spelling of *canis* and *canem*. A developmentally-appropriate grammar explanation follows. "He's *canis* when he does something and *canem* when somebody does something to him," according to Mrs. Gascoyne. "But that doesn't make sense," says Sara. Mrs. Gascoyne asks Sara to tell the class that she sees the dog. Sara says, "I see the dog." Then Mrs. Gascoyne asks her to tell the class that the dog sees her. "The dog sees me," says Sara. "Sara, why did you call yourself *"I"* in one sentence and *"me"* in the second sentence?" This concept takes a while to grasp, but some students get it.

Students talk about how people today would call public attention to the presence of a watchdog by putting a sign in the window. The next day the class reviews the lesson by listing on chart paper the various ways in which the Latin word *canis* was used and is still used today. Working in small groups, students fashion mobiles that illustrate the vocabulary and phrases learned in the lesson. They end the lesson by singing a bilingual song about their dog named B-I-N-G-O. But, *mirabile dictu,* his name has changed to C-A-N-I-S.

Reflection

1.1 Students read and understand Latin words and phrases that include canis, the Latin word for dog.

1.2 Students hear, pronounce, sing, and write the Latin words and phrases that include canis and words for numbers and body parts.

2.2 Students expand their knowledge of mythology through the story of Cerberus and understand how Roman houses might be guarded by watchdogs and how people were warned of their presence; they see the *Cave canem* mosaic from Pompeii.

3.1 Students learn about the use of the Latin word *canis* in scientific names and constellations.

4.1 Students recognize and use English words that are related by derivation to the Latin word *canis*.

4.2 Students compare and contrast the use of watchdogs and how attention is directed to their presence today even as it was in ancient Roman times.

Third graders are eager to learn and share what they know. The theme that they are studying runs through all their subject areas. In this class Latin is the medium for learning about animals, a part of the current interdisciplinary theme for the whole school. The content of the Latin class merges into the regular third grade classroom lessons in science and language arts.

The lesson builds on previously learned vocabulary and language structures and from the content of the world that inner city children bring to school. Students are encouraged to talk and share and to discover things on their own—to search for the stars, to make sense out of a language that uses two forms of the word for the same thing, to meet a dog with three heads, to make a mobile and feel the Latin words in their fingers, to sing an old song with new words.

Joanne Gascoyne, Thomas O'Brien Academy of Science and Technology, Albany, New York

A GEOGRAPHY LESSON

Students at Lincoln High School, a large public school in Tallahassee, Florida, are learning classical geography in the early weeks of their Latin I class. Mrs. Bower first points out the major cities, provinces, rivers, lakes, seas, and other geographical features on a wall map of the Roman world at the time of Trajan. She identifies each one in complete Latin sentences, which the students repeat after her. Students earn points by giving answers in Latin to a series of questions such as *"Quae insula est haec?"* or by responding to commands such as *"Demonstra duas Romas in charta mundi novi."* (A map of the Western hemisphere is also available.)

> **TARGETED STANDARDS**
> 1.1 Students read, understand, and interpret Latin or Greek.
> 1.2 Students use orally, listen to, and write Latin or Greek as part of the language learning process.
> 2.2 Students demonstrate an understanding of the perspectives of Greek or Roman culture as revealed in the products of the Greeks or Romans.
> 3.2 Students expand their knowledge through the reading of Latin or Greek and the study of ancient culture.
> 4.1 Students recognize and use elements of the Latin or Greek language to increase knowledge of their own language.
> 4.2 Students compare and contrast their own culture with that of the Greco-Roman world.
> 5.2 Students use their knowledge of Greco-Roman culture in a world of diverse cultures.

After this oral exercise the teacher leads a discussion in English on Carthage and the effect which its location had on Rome. This leads to a review of the students' prior knowledge of Hannibal and his trek across the Alps, which the students located earlier in the lesson. The teacher adds a mythological dimension to this discussion by narrating briefly the story of Dido and Aeneas.

Students then receive blank maps and a list of the locations just discussed in class. They proceed to locate and write a short sentence in Latin about each item. The students then read each other's work.

Reflection

1.1 Students read each other's short Latin sentences about geographical locations.
1.2 Students listen to Latin questions on geographical locations and respond to them in Latin.
2.2 Students learn classical geography and relate that knowledge to history and myth.
3.2 Students connect their knowledge of classical geography to that of the modern world.
4.1 Students understand noun/adjective and subject/verb agreement in both Latin and English.

4.2 Students compare the nomenclature of classical geography to that of North America.

5.2 Students compare the geographical interdependence of the ancient world to modern examples.

This activity could be used throughout the year and in successive courses at increasing levels of complexity. It may be especially suitable for introducing new units or new authors. Students learn correct pronunciation and noun/adjective and subject/verb agreement as well as geography and reinforce their knowledge through speaking and writing Latin. They also point out obvious similarities in the nomenclature of classical and modern geography and thus build a storehouse of geographical and linguistic information. In addition to assessing the students' work in the Latin discussion session, a written or oral test on the entire map lesson might be given the following day.

Lois Ann Bower, Lincoln High School, Tallahassee, Florida

TARGETED STANDARDS

1.1 Students read, understand, and interpret Latin or Greek.
1.2 Students use orally, listen to, and write Latin or Greek as part of the language learning process.
3.1 Students reinforce and further their knowledge of other disciplines through their study of classical languages.
4.1 Students recognize and use elements of the Latin or Greek language to increase knowledge of their own language.

THE GREEK AND LATIN CONNECTION

In Mr. Higgins' Latin IV class in The Gilbert School, a public high school in Winsted, a small rural town in Connecticut, students learn the Greek alphabet. They are learning the words for the letters by chanting them after the teacher who has grouped the alphabet into six groups of four letters: alpha, beta, gamma, delta ... epsilon, zeta, eta, theta ... iota, kappa, lambda, mu ... etc.). The students learn the chant quickly and echo back and forth in the fashion of a football cheer. The teacher turns to the board and writes each letter, first upper case, then lower case, as the students slowly prompt him with their chant, to accommodate the teacher's writing on the board. Students then see, in Greek, some words that have been taken from the Greek into Latin and then English. They see words in Greek and discover that the English transliteration is *Parthenon, Socrates, drama, panther, crisis, phenomenon, hymn, and ocean.* They use a good English dictionary to determine more of the etymology of the words, and they use a Greek/English dictionary to discover meanings and changes that occur in the transformation from Greek to English. They keep a notebook to record what they have found. Then they practice their own skill by writing sample Greek alphabets as they quietly chant to themselves and check the letters with the sample on the board. In subsequent classes the students see some short quotations in Greek, e.g., *gnothi se auton* and *en arche en ho logos* (in the beginning), which they practice saying aloud, translate into English, and discuss. In a subsequent class, the students review and practice counting in Latin from one through ten. They write the words and Roman numerals, write the corresponding numbers in Greek, and compare them. The teacher explains that in antiquity, and to some extent in modern times, the Greeks used the letters of the alphabet as numbers. The students discover and discuss other ways in which Greek and Latin number words and symbols are used today in mathematics and sciences.

Reflection

1.1 Students begin to read words and sentences of ancient Greek.
1.2 Students learn the Greek writing system.
3.1 Students learn that some languages use different alphabets, and they observe the use of Greek and Latin in mathematics and science.
4.1 Students practice the Greek alphabet with English derivatives, and they observe interconnections of Greek, Latin, and English.

This lesson, with variations, can be carried out in one class period or several as a filler and a break from the regular routine. The lesson uses an oral technique as an introduction to writing and provides a quick way to learn the alphabet with a rousing drill. The lesson opens the door to reading short phrases of authentic ancient Greek. At more advanced levels the students could be given Greek phrases and sentences which parallel passages from the Latin authors they are reading (e.g., Homer's *Odyssey* and Vergil's *Aeneid*, Aristotle's *Nichomachean Ethics* and Cicero's *De Amicitia*). The lesson sparks Latin students with a curiosity for Greek to push for more (perhaps a separate class next year).

Based on an idea contributed by John Higgins, The Gilbert School, Winsted, Connecticut

GREEK MEDICINE IN ATHENS AND EPIDAUROS

Students in Dr. Caswell's Level I ancient Greek class at Boston Latin Academy have been studying the chapter in *Athenaze* on Greek medicine and healing sanctuaries.

Half the class forms pairs, one being the patient and one being the physician. Each pair has been allotted an ailment. The patients must be able to explain and write what their ailments are in very simple Greek. The physicians must then, having prepared ahead of time, go through the proper motions of healing, using simple phrases in Greek. At the end of each three-minute scenario, the doctor must either pronounce the patient cured or recommend a visit to Asklepios at Epidauros, again in Greek. Both patient and doctor will also give a list of Greek words they have used which have English derivatives.

> **TARGETED STANDARDS**
> 1.1 Students read, understand, and interpret Latin or Greek.
> 1.2 Students use orally, listen to, and write Latin or Greek as part of the language learning process.
> 2.1 Students demonstrate an understanding of the perspectives of Greek or Roman culture as revealed in the practices of the Greeks or Romans.
> 2.2 Students demonstrate an understanding of the perspectives of Greek or Roman culture as revealed in the products of the Greeks or Romans.
> 4.1 Students recognize and use elements of the Latin or Greek language to increase knowledge of their own language.

While half of the class is engaged in this activity, the other half of the class is preparing to re-enact the scene from Aristophanes' *Plutus* Act II, in which Plutus' healing at Epidauros is described. A simplified dialogue based on the original has been provided by the teacher. Students who do not have the dialogue of a character will form the chorus and recite the unadapted original.

This activity requires two class periods as well as some homework. Students are provided with a translation of the play, which they read in preparation, along with scenarios from a surgery from Guido Majno's book *The Healing Hand.* The two groups present their dialogues to the class. As a follow-up, slides of Epidauros, Cos, and Pergamum, and artifacts relating to Greek medical practice, are shown. In addition, students discuss the topic of comedy and its role in Greek society, along with the questions that this activity inevitably raises: Why was healing considered an appropriate topic for comedy, and how do you, living in the world of modern medical technology, relate to being an ancient Greek patient or physician, or visiting a healing sanctuary?

Reflection

1.1   Students read and interpret modified texts on Greek medicine.
1.2   Students recite and comprehend medical findings.
2.1   Students investigate the details of Greek medicine.
2.2   Students discuss the attitude of the Greeks to medical science.
4.1   Students relate Greek medical terminology to such terminolgy in English.

Cooperative learning and presenting its results in a culturally "authentic" format involve students in the feel of Greek medicine and comedy. A similar dialogue activity could be used in a discussion among Athenian generals to decide how to pursue the war with the Persians, or to create a conversation between Pericles and other generals about the relative strengths of Athens and Sparta.

Caroline Caswell, Boston Latin Academy, Boston, Massachusetts

---

TARGETED STANDARDS

1.1 Students read, understand, and interpret Latin or Greek.
1.2 Students use orally, listen to, and write Latin or Greek as part of the language learning process.
2.1 Students demonstrate an understanding of the perspectives of Greek or Roman culture as revealed in the practices of the Greeks or Romans.
4.1 Students recognize and use elements of the Latin or Greek language to increase knowledge of their own language.

IN PRINCIPIO ERAT VERBUM: THE VERB AS KEY TO SYNTAX

Toward the end of their first year, Mr. Wooley's students at Phillips Exeter Academy read aloud the *Iudicium Paridis* (The Beauty Contest) in 230 words of Latin prose. In addition to translating the passage, they write about fifteen sentences from Latin into English and ten sentences from English into Latin with vocabulary previously learned but with syntax based in part on the Latin narrative. This lesson is part of a carefully coordinated progression to the reading of Caesar in the fourth term. Quantity of vocabulary is considered less important than its being well understood, not only semantically but syntactically. Each of the few new vocabulary items allows a review of basic paradigms: e.g., *amor, amoris* is declined with an *-us, -a, -um* adjective in order to review both third and second declensions simultaneously. The relative pronoun *qui, quae, quod* presents the students with a new option in syntax, the relative adjective clause, which they compare with adverbial subordinate clauses (already learned) introduced by *cum, ubi, quod,* and *dum.* Students consult their teacher's own handbook on the World Wide Web as a resource for constructing their sentences: Some Rules of the Road for the Art of Translating Latin (http://academy.exeter.edu:80/~awooley).

Reflection

1.1 Students read and understand an adapted passage of Latin, demonstrating a knowledge of vocabulary, basic inflectional systems, and syntax.

1.2 Students read a passage of Latin aloud with accurate pronunciation and phrase grouping, and they write sentences in Latin reflecting the syntax learned from their reading.

2.1 Students read and analyze a passage of Latin that narrates a famous Greek myth.

4.1 Students compare the Latin and English use of the verb and the construction of complex sentences in both languages.

This is a comprehensive presentation of Latin verb syntax. Students learn how the verb's primacy binds it to all the other words in the sentence or clause. The sentences for translation (in both directions) give practice in the linking verb, intransitive action verbs, transitive verbs, verbs complemented with dative, genitive, or ablative, and verbs with accusative direct object and objective complement.

The lesson has six steps: 1) Reading aloud a Latin text; 2) translating Latin sentences; 3) writing Latin sentences; 4) reviewing previous vocabulary, grammar and syntax; 5) analyzing new syntax; 6) reviewing the initial text. This general approach could be applied to many lessons at any level.

Allan Wooley, Phillips Exeter Academy, Exeter, New Hampshire

IS VERGIL'S DIDO "MISS SAIGON"?

Mrs. Haukeland's Advanced Placement Vergil students at Schreiber High School, a large suburban public school near New York City, are involved in a lively discussion about whether Dido could have acted differently and avoided the tragedy that ended her life. On the previous day, Mrs. Haukeland took her class to see the musical "Miss Saigon," whose plot is very similar to Book IV of the *Aeneid*. In both, a foreign soldier on his way home from war falls in love with a proud but vulnerable woman; a pseudo-wedding is held; ghosts visit and warn in both stories; and both end in abandonment, curses, and suicide. Both heroes, Aeneas and the young American soldier, Chris, unwittingly bring death to the women they love.

> **TARGETED STANDARDS**
> 1.1 Students read, understand, and interpret Latin or Greek.
> 2.1 Students demonstrate an understanding of the perspectives of Greek or Roman culture as revealed in the products of the Greeks or Romans.
> 3.2 Students expand their knowledge through the reading of Latin or Greek and the study of ancient culture.
> 4.2 Students compare and contrast their own culture with that of the Greco-Roman world.
> 5.2 Students use their knowledge of Latin or Greek in a multilingual world.

One student suggests that it is the war that is to blame: war always disrupts; rules of civilization no longer apply. Another suggests that Dido and her counterpart, the beautiful young Vietnamese Kim, had to be sacrificed for "the greater good." Mrs. Haukeland asks how the greater good which Vergil envisions differs from America's in the chaotic aftermath of the Vietnam war.

The discussion moves on to "culture clash." Is it possible that neither of these couples had even the smallest chance of a lasting relationship because of the wide divergence in the perspectives and values of their different cultures? The students, in general, reject this suggestion, but one points out that Aeneas' Roman concept of honor *(pietas)* is very ethnocentric. The conflicts in both stories result from viewpoints that are inflexible and insulated. Another student suggests that these first encounters with "the other" often result in tragedy, but sometimes pave the way for subsequent understanding. The discussion passes quickly on to questions of conscience, honor, a woman's role in a relationship, and Fate—was the outcome inevitable from the beginning?

Before seeing the play, Mrs. Haukeland's class reviewed the plot, characters, and conflicts in Book IV of the *Aeneid*, which they have just finished reading and translating over the previous five weeks. Knowing the details from Vergil's story so well has enabled them to draw these numerous comparisons with the Broadway play and to produce such a spirited discussion. Mrs. Haukeland concludes their colloquium with a comment about timelessness and the reason that the classics are called classics.

Reflection

1.1 Students read Book IV of Vergil's *Aeneid* in Latin.
2.1 Students demonstrate an understanding of Roman perspectives through the reading of Book IV of the Aeneid.
3.2 Students recognize the influence of Latin literature on the artistic achievements of the modern world.
4.2 Students compare the themes and heroes of the Aeneid with those of their own culture.
5.2 Students recognize from their study of the Aeneid that cultural diversity has been an integral feature of society from antiquity.

Linking their reading of Vergil's *Aeneid* with attending a Broadway show caused many students to see the *Aeneid* in a completely new light. For instance, the experience capitalizes on the importance of music in the students' lives by considering Vergil's poetry in the light of its musical elements. The comparison of the two works enables students to view problems created by war and the ensuing collision of cultural values in a personal context. The students' emotional response to the living characters on stage affects their reactions to Dido and Aeneas' anguished parting.

The central questions of life—love vs. duty, self vs. society, destiny vs. action—are asked by both works. Each one provokes illuminations and responses in its own way. This kind of lesson goes far beyond the classroom and is very successful in creating a deeper personal involvement in the Latin literature that students read in class. The insights into Roman perspectives that provide the substance for this kind of discussion can only be gleaned from a careful reading of Vergil's text.

This type of comparative activity can be implemented with reinterpretations of ancient themes in various media, such as film, opera, live theater, and videotapes, e.g., *A Funny Thing Happened on the Way to the Forum* (Plautus); G.B. Shaw's *Pygmalion* and *My Fair Lady* (Pygmalion); and *Romeo and Juliet* (Pyramus and Thisbe).

Ruth Adams Haukeland, Schreiber High School, Port Jefferson, New York

LANGUAGE CONNECTIONS

Most of the students in Ms. Marston's elementary Latin class speak Spanish as their first language; they are from an inner city background; English is their second language. They eagerly look forward to the Latin lessons each week that assist them in building connections between their native language and English through the study of Latin. As Ms. Marston circulates throughout the class, the students watch her hold up picture cards depicting

> **TARGETED STANDARDS**
> 1.1 Students read, understand, and interpret Latin or Greek.
> 1.2 Students use orally, listen to, and write Latin or Greek as part of the language learning process.
> 2.1 Students demonstrate an understanding of the perspectives of Greek or Roman culture as revealed in the practices of the Greeks or Romans.
> 4.1 Students recognize and use elements of the Latin or Greek language to increase knowledge of their own language.
> 4.2 Students compare and contrast their own culture with that of the Greco-Roman world.
> 5.1 Students use their knowledge of Latin or Greek in a multilingual world.

members of a Roman family involved in various activities. They listen to her describe what is happening in the picture cards, e.g., *Marcus edit* or *Marcus sedet* and the students repeat in unison. When she asks the students, *Quid agit Marcus,* as she holds up a card, the students' hands shoot up in eager anticipation of reciting.

After students have demonstrated their understanding of the action verbs, they see an overhead transparency with three headings written across the top: Latin, Spanish, and English. Students discuss the word meanings under each heading and suggest additional derivatives in both Spanish and English. They see the connections that join their native language, their second language, and Latin. Students use sentence strips to compose their own descriptive statements in Latin and come, in turn, to the front of the class and hold up their sentences. As students are called upon to read the sentences aloud in Latin, another student holds up the corresponding picture. Ms. Marsten explains the role of each family member depicted on the picture cards, and the students spend a few minutes comparing these roles to those in their own families. At the end of the lesson, students record their vocabulary notes onto a replica of the overhead transparency and work in small groups to expand their list of derivatives. Since this lesson is part of a unit of lessons on food and dining habits of the ancient Romans, students then work on a "playlet" centering on a Roman family at a dinner, which they are preparing to present to their parents during a school assembly.

Reflection
1.1 Students read and understand simple Latin sentences.
1.2 Students repeat simple Latin phrases and respond to simple questions in Latin.
2.1 Students learn about the role of specific family members in a Roman family.
4.1 Students recognize words in Spanish and English that are derived from Latin.
4.2 Students compare the role of the members of their own families with those of the Roman family.
5.1 Students present their "playlet" at a school assembly for parents.

The activities included in this lesson involve student use of all four modalities: listening, speaking, reading, and writing. Because comparisons are made to English and Spanish, Latin becomes a vehicle for students to strengthen both their native and second language skills. The main focus of the program, however, is on learning the Latin language and Roman culture. Here this happens in a broad context that can enrich a student's entire academic program and sharpen life's skills.

Eilene Marston, Washington Elementary School, Burbank Unified School District, Los Angeles, CA

> **TARGETED STANDARDS**
>
> 1.1 Students read, understand, and interpret Latin or Greek.
> 1.2 Students use orally, listen to, and write Latin or Greek as part of the language learning process.
> 2.1 Students demonstrate an understanding of the perspectives of Greek or Roman culture as revealed in the practices of the Greeks or Romans.
> 4.1 Students recognize and use elements of the Latin or Greek language to increase knowledge of their own language.
> 4.2 Students compare and contrast their own culture with that of the Greco-Roman world.

MARKET DAY IN A ROMAN PROVINCE

Mrs. Pope's 700 Latin I students are learning Latin in a two-way video, one-way audio distance learning classroom encompassing twenty-four states in the continental United States. Early in the school year the Latin class reads a passage in Latin from their textbook depicting a typical Roman family's visit to the market. They read the dialogue between the father, mother, and shop keeper and practice reading the Latin out loud, trying to comprehend the Latin. They are then presented with a video dramatization produced by the distance learning teaching staff in which elaborate costuming, sets, and props to simulate a market experience have been incorporated. Students then work with a partner on the Latin conversation given in their book. The teacher calls on students at different schools to read the conversation on the air while the other students listen. The discussion broadens to include trade, goods, money, clothing, roles of family members, numbers, derivatives, a comparison of cultures, and shopping practices. Over a two-day period students write a Latin conversation that a family visiting the market might use to buy goods. A handout is provided with formulaic conversation and guidelines for the project. The students are required to write a conversation in Latin using the language skills and vocabulary they are working on at the time. They also research and design a background for their set and gather props. The students perform their skit and record it on a videotape that they send to the teacher. The teacher evaluates the tapes and then plays the skits for the other students to view during class. Students continue to practice their aural comprehension while they watch classmates enact these Roman scenes.

Reflection

1.1 Students read a simple Latin passage from their text.
1.2 Students read a dialogue out loud and comprehend the oral Latin. Students write a simple Latin skit.
2.1 Students learn and role-play a Roman market day.
4.1 Students recognize English words derived from the vocabulary being used.
4.2 Students compare and contrast their own shopping experiences with ancient marketing practices.

The basic activity of developing a dialogue and producing a skit can be used in a variety of cultural studies at all levels of Latin instruction, in both regular classroom and distance learning situations. It can be set at a variety of sites throughout the Roman world, thereby giving access to other cultures of the region. At upper levels peer editing can be incorporated into the final evaluation of the project. At all levels students become more efficient at integrating language, vocabulary, and cultural content through this type of activity. Most students thrive when given creative license within a structure of language and culture, rather than relying on predetermined, non-integrated textbook exercises.

Cindy Pope, TI-IN Network, San Antonio, Texas

PRONOUN POEMS

Ms. Luongo's eighth graders are finishing their first semester of Latin at St. Andrew's Middle School, an urban private school in Austin, Texas. They have learned nouns in five cases and have met the personal pronouns in the first and second persons. This week's

> **TARGETED STANDARDS**
>
> 1.1 Students read, understand, and interpret Latin or Greek.
> 1.2 Students use orally, listen to, and write Latin or Greek as part of the language learning process.
> 4.1 Students recognize and use elements of the Latin or Greek language to increase knowledge of their own language.
> 5.1 Students use their knowledge of Latin or Greek in a multilingual world.

lesson focuses on the third person pronoun, *is, ea, id*. Ms. Luongo introduces the pronoun forms orally in sentences. The students determine their meaning from the context. The teacher then presents the full declension of the pronoun for students to learn. Students chant the paradigm together and practice reading Latin sentences containing the pronoun forms. They discuss why the Romans often do not use this pronoun as the subject of the sentence, and they determine when they might want to use it. They compare the Latin with the English use of the subject pronoun. Then the students are instructed to write a poem in Latin entitled "The Ten Best Things About . . . (their dog, their best friend, a family member . . .)" using forms of *is, ea, id* wherever possible. Students are required to use two or more case forms of the pronoun in their poems. Students supplement the vocabulary that they know by consulting English-Latin dictionaries. Students submit rough copies for their teacher's comments and then spend time in the computer lab, typing their poems onto a disk. Students read each other's poems in the lab and help to proofread for errors. Final copies of the poems are illustrated and submitted for publication in the school's literary magazine, which features works in English, Spanish, and Latin.

Reflection

1.1 Students read simple Latin sentences containing *is, ea, id*.
1.2 Students recite and comprehend oral Latin. Students write simple Latin poems.
4.1 Students compare the forms and use of pronouns in Latin and English.
5.1 Students share their Latin poems with their school community.

This activity could be used at any level. Other pronouns or grammar points could be emphasized as well. The activity could be modified for different themes or holidays, such as "Things for which I am thankful" at Thanksgiving. A peer editing component could be added before the teacher gives feedback. Students could look for correct case forms and other required elements based on a peer-review guide supplied by the teacher. If a school does not have a literary magazine, students could create their own magazine or make posters with illustrations to hang in the school's halls. If the school sends home a parent newsletter, sample poems and translations could be included there. This activity is a good skill-builder since, in addition to providing a variety of ways to learn *is, ea, id,* it also promotes use of the other personal pronouns and practice in subject/verb and noun/adjective agreement.

Jennie Luongo, St. Andrew's Middle School, Austin, Texas

TARGETED STANDARDS
1.1 Students read, understand, and interpret Latin or Greek.
1.2 Students use orally, listen to, and write Latin or Greek as part of the language learning process.
2.2 Students demonstrate an understanding of the perspectives of Greek or Roman culture as revealed in the products of the Greeks or Romans.
4.2 Students compare and contrast their own culture with that of the Greco-Roman world.

QUIS CAESAREM INTERFECIT?

When Latin II students in Dr. Beaton's class at Griffin High School, a suburban public school in Georgia, are introduced to the concept of indirect statement, they use the traditional *Clue* game. The activity stimulates responses in Latin to who killed Caesar, where, with what, and when. They explore a variety of other situations that result from the initial question. Students also read an adapted passage of Suetonius' "Death of Caesar" in the *Divus Iulius*. They then review the plan for a Roman house and record the Latin names of the rooms on flash cards, which they arrange properly within a model of the Roman house. Next, students review the use of the *ablative of place where* with the names of the Roman rooms. They then review the use of the *ablative of means* and finally, the formation and use of the five Latin infinitives. The teacher distributes a sample Roman house plan to each student. Students are divided into four equal groups. Students shuffle and distribute the person cards, place cards, and weapon cards to the four groups, reserving one from each as the solution cards. Upon entry into a particular room, a team makes its accusation by stating in Latin who killed Caesar in that room and with what weapon. After questioning another team for possible solution cards, the team may begin moving to another room or make a final accusation and recommend a course of action.

A discussion following the activity focuses on the differences that exist between ancient and modern houses. Discussion can also center on the character of Caesar and the reasons that he was targeted for destruction.

Reflection

1.1 Students use Latin to determine who is Caesar's killer.
1.2 Students formulate and understand a traditional Latin grammatical construction.
2.2 Students develop an understanding of the traditional Roman *domus*.
4.2 Students see and recognize the similarities and differences between modern and ancient homes. Students compare historical events of the ancient and modern worlds.

This activity integrates historical content with language use; it integrates communication and culture; it centers on a major historical character. The formulaic structure of the game allows the student to review the grammatical concepts of *ablative of place where* and *ablative of means,* in addition to proper formation and use of Latin infinitives with subject in the accusative case; and it requires the student to exercise judgment in supplying the appropriate infinitive. The activity stimulates the student to respond in Latin and to listen to oral responses from team members and to connect their language learning to a meaningful cultural activity centering on the *domus*.

This activity is also appropriate for a first year class where the teacher may change the indirect statement formula to a simple direct question. The cultural dimension of this activity can be changed by using a different setting, e.g., the ancient architectural wonders of the city *Roma*. The students may also explore another character from Roman history or mythology who would stimulate questions and discussion on the character and associated history. Other readings to support these changes would then be incorporated into the lesson.

Richard Beaton, Griffin High School, Griffin, Georgia

QUIS ES TU?

At Marshall Middle School, a suburban public school in Pittsburgh, Pennsylvania, eighth grade students in Mrs. Hannegan's Introduction to Latin A course are beginning the second nine weeks' term. They have learned the third person forms of present tense verbs from all four conjugations and the verb *sum*. In this lesson, students learn the pronouns *ego* and *tu* and the corresponding verb endings by asking and answering questions, writing dialogues and sentences, and reading stories.

> **TARGETED STANDARDS**
> 1.1 Students read, understand, and interpret Latin or Greek.
> 1.2 Students use orally, listen to, and write Latin or Greek as part of the language learning process.
> 2.2 Students demonstrate an understanding of the perspectives of Greek or Roman culture as revealed in the products of the Greeks or Romans.
> 3.1 Students reinforce and further their knowledge of other disciplines through their study of classical languages.
> 4.2 Students compare and contrast their own culture with that of the Greco-Roman world.

In the classroom is a box of props, each of which represents a person and his or her occupation (e.g., a spoon for the *coquus,* a money bag for the *argentarius,* a serving jug for the *ancilla,* a scroll for the *poeta)*. As each item is pulled from the box, students identify the member of Roman society associated with the prop and how and why he or she would use it (e.g., the *poeta* and his scroll). Students listen while the teacher holds each item and says, *"Ego sum coquus. Ego cenam coquo,"* or *"Ego sum ancilla. Ego vinum porto."* After a few repetitions, the teacher hands the items to students at random and asks, *"Quis es tu?"* The students respond to this question and to follow-up questions such as *"Quid tu coquis"* or *"Quid tu portas?"* Next, the students hand their props to other students and the questions are repeated with students questioning students.

After all students have responded to questions, the teacher gives out an exercise that requires them to ask and answer questions in writing. On the worksheet are pictures of characters with empty dialogue balloons. The students write appropriate questions and answers in the balloons. Later the students listen to and read a story containing dialogues that reinforce the new pronouns and verb endings. Finally, students use the new pronoun and verb forms in Latin sentences of their own.

Reflection

1.1 Students read simple sentences and stories containing first and second person pronouns as subjects.
1.2 Students make "I" and "you" statements and ask "you" questions orally. Students write Latin sentences containing first and second person pronouns and verb forms.
2.2 Students employ props representative of everyday items used by the Romans and discuss their cultural significance.

This is a high interest activity because of the use of props and the level of student involvement. Students hear and speak Latin and become accustomed to patterns before they see words in writing. After written exercises, students are able to draw conclusions about pronoun and verb forms and to apply their knowledge to further readings and to their own Latin composition. Culture is embedded in the lesson by the use of culturally authentic props and by reference to common Roman occupations.

Melody Hannegan, Marshall Middle School, Pittsburgh, Pennsylvania

> **TARGETED STANDARDS**
> 1.1 Students read, understand, and interpret Latin or Greek.
> 1.2 Students use orally, listen to, and write Latin or Greek as part of the language learning process.
> 2.1 Students demonstrate an understanding of the perspectives of Greek or Roman culture as revealed in the practices of the Greeks or Romans.
> 4.2 Students compare and contrast their own culture with that of the Greco-Roman world.

ROMAN DRAMA

Students in Ms. Jog's seventh grade Latin class at Westridge School for Girls in Pasadena, California, are working on the fifth stage (chapter) of the *Cambridge Latin Course*. The Westridge School is an independent day school of 430 students; Latin is required in the seventh and eighth grades. The seventh grade class meets three days a week; this learning scenario encompasses four days of class time. The students first read aloud in Latin and then translate the Latin passages in the stage, not only for reading comprehension and accurate translation but also for the background they provide in understanding Roman drama. They discuss various types of dramatic performances focusing on pantomime, farce, and comedy. They make comparisons between these and other forms of entertainment they enjoy, such as slapstick (the Three Stooges) and sitcoms. Previously they have read in English selected scenes from Roman comedies (the *Aulularia, Rudens,* and *Mostellaria),* and scenes from Shakespeare *(Comedy of Errors)* for comparison.

The students group themselves into groups of three or four students to write their own dramas in English and Latin. Different types of drama are represented by the several groups. Each group must write five sentences in Latin, which become part of their drama. The students identify all grammatical aspects of the sentences they write. They spend a day writing and correcting their Latin sentences for accurate vocabulary, grammar and syntax. The teacher checks the content and mechanics of all the Latin sentences before the performance.

Each group rehearses and then presents its miniature drama to the entire class. Students prepare costumes and props for their performances. They even provide cushions for their audience and spray scented water into the air of their "theater." They gloss on the blackboard Latin words not known to the entire class.

Reflection
1.1 Students read Latin passages on Roman drama.
1.2 Students write Latin sentences to incorporate into their drama.
2.2 Students experience Roman culture by performing comedy.
3.1 Students compare Roman comedy to Shakespearean comedy.
4.2 Students compare modern entertainment to Roman comedy.

The goal of the lesson is to immerse seventh graders in reading Latin, to have them use the language actively in a culturally authentic situation, to help them experience an understanding of Roman drama and its influence, and to make comparisons of Roman drama to Elizabethan and modern comedy.

The teacher assesses the students in terms of the content of the written script, the accuracy of their Latin, oral and written, their use of the dramatic form, and their performance.

Anita Jog, Westridge School for Girls, Pasadena, California

A ROMAN ELECTION

Mrs. Robinson's eighth grade Latin students at Harbor Day School in Corona del Mar stage an election while they are studying the Roman Republican Period. Students read a variety of original and adapted texts on the topic, including passages from Cicero, Catullus, and Pompeian campaign graffiti.

> **TARGETED STANDARDS**
> 1.1 Students read, understand, and interpret Latin or Greek.
> 1.2 Students use orally, listen to, and write Latin or Greek as part of the language learning process.
> 2.2 Students demonstrate an understanding of the perspectives of Greek or Roman culture as revealed in the products of the Greeks or Romans.

Students discuss thoroughly the Roman political system, how elections were held, and what political campaigns were like. Students then prepare to reenact the election of 63 B.C. Cicero presided over this election, and one of the two consular seats was hotly contested by the lawyer Sulpicius and the general Murena. Students discuss the different personalities and qualifications of these two men and the general state of affairs in the Roman world, and they compare them to modern American elections, campaigns, and candidates.

Students receive instruction on Latin commands, greetings, questions, and responses. Simple sentence constructions are reviewed. Then every student receives a personal "voter profile" with name, occupation, family background, ties to candidates, and other pertinent information. Two students, chosen by the teacher to portray the candidates, write campaign speeches and learn how to respond in character to questions from the voters. The remaining students work in groups to produce Latin campaign posters to decorate the room and hall on election day. Latin slogans are checked for historical and linguistic accuracy. Election events can last one to three hours (longer versions include Roman lunch and victory games sponsored by the winner). Students dress in Roman attire. "Cicero" conducts the opening ceremonies.

After the candidates are introduced, they give their speeches, answer questions from the voters, give rebuttals, and mill among voters for a little handshaking. Finally, after all voters file past the voting boxes and cast their tokens, Cicero congratulates the winner who is acclaimed by the "voters."

Reflection

1.1 Students read and understand Latin slogans on campaign posters. More advanced students read background materials in Latin, such as Cicero's *Ep. ad Fam.* 4.1, 4.2, 4.5, 4.6, 4.12, *Att.* 1.1, *Pro Murena*, *9th Philippic*, *De pet. cons.*; Catullus' poems 49, 52, and 93.
1.2 Students and teachers use Latin commands, greetings and simple sentences and write Latin campaign slogans on posters.
2.1 Students demonstrate knowledge of the political life of the Romans.

4.2 Students read information on Roman campaigning and compare those practices with modern campaigns.

Staging a mock Roman election can be an exciting learning experience, complete with historical characters, priests, centurions, and forum campaigning. It also allows students with different talents to shine. Students discuss and write essays comparing modern and ancient campaigning. They write essays discussing their "Roman" family background and political ties and why they chose to vote for or against a candidate. Did they follow or break with family traditions? By introducing unadapted text and activities that use more Latin and less English, this scenario, originally created for beginning students, becomes appropriate for intermediate or advanced students.

Kathleen Robinson, Harbor Day School, Corona del Mar, California

> **TARGETED STANDARDS**
> 1.1 Students read, understand, and interpret Latin or Greek.
> 2.1 Students demonstrate an understanding of the perspectives of Greek or Roman culture as revealed in the practices of the Greeks or Romans.
> 3.2 Students expand their knowledge through the reading of Latin or Greek and the study of ancient culture.
> 4.2 Students compare and contrast their own culture with that of the Greco-Roman world.
> 5.1 Students use their knowledge of Latin or Greek in a multilingual world.
> 5.2 Students use their knowledge of Greco-Roman culture in a world of diverse cultures.

THE VOYAGE OF ST. BRENDAN

When reading a section from the *Voyage of St. Brendan,* a medieval Latin text, Mr. Hayes' Latin II and III students in William Hall High School, in a suburban Connecticut town, discuss the use of Latin in the Middle Ages, how it developed through the years, and to what extent it reflected both common and formal speech. Students draw on their studies in a course in World Civilization to contribute to the discussion of the culture of the medieval period, especially as it continues, amplifies, or challenges the structures put in place in the late Roman empire.

Students, in pairs, read the Latin text which describes a group of sea-faring monks unwittingly camping out on the back of a whale, and the unexpected consequences that follow. They first read out loud in Latin, skim silently looking for the main idea, generate a list of cognates, as well as a list of problem words which will be needed to render the passage into good English.

Students translate the first half of the text into English as accurately as possible and try to guess how the story will end. Then they read the second half and compare it to their guesses, and finally they relate the subject matter of this chapter to the previous chapters they have read.

Students then compare the story with other epic tales and long journeys in the literature with which they are familiar, making connections between the *Voyage of St. Brendan* and the *Odyssey,* the *Aeneid,* the *Bible,* and other texts. Finally, students mine the chapter for traces of linguistic change, both in terms of word formation and choice as compared to "classical" Latin, and also in the developing vocabulary of the nascent Romance languages.

As a culminating exercise, each student draws a simple black and white picture of the major action or a major feature of the text. The most cogent are reproduced on transparencies and used as guides in review and further discussion.

Reflection

1.1 Students read and understand an unadapted passage of medieval Latin.
1.2 Students observe the culture of some sea-faring monks at sea.
3.2 Students recognize the continuity of cultures as exemplified in the literatures of the ancient and medieval worlds.
4.2 Students learn how a basic theme, sea narrative, is changed and reshaped to reflect the age and culture that is retelling it.
5.1 Students learn about and reflect upon the development of the Romance languages from Latin.
5.2 Students read an exciting story by a first-rate story teller, whose authentic Latin is accessible to second year students.

Medieval texts provide a variety of material accessible and exciting for the intermediate Latin student. Here students learn that Latin is a communicative vehicle that survived the classical period and that good Latin literature continued to be produced well into the Renaissance. Cooperative learning is a good strategy for extensive reading and for engaging students in the acquisition of content as well as language skills. The lesson may be expanded to a short sequence of lessons or a unit as long as three weeks.

Thomas Hayes, William Hall High School, West Hartford, Connecticut

Glossary

- **Authentic materials** For students and teachers of classical languages, authentic materials are the products of the ancient world. For students of Latin and Greek, unadapted literature is the most important authentic material. All the remains of the classical world contribute to our knowledge of their practices, their perspectives, their culture: literature, non-literary records, artifacts, art, architecture, and all the things that archaeologists unearth.

- **Beginning / Intermediate / Advanced** Elementary students, if Latin or Greek is taught continuously from the early grades, may be expected to demonstrate progress indicated by the beginning sample progress indicators by grade 6 or 8 (perhaps even by grade 4 if they begin a well coordinated program in kindergarten). Middle school students who study Latin or Greek every day in grades 7 and 8 should demonstrate beginning progress indicators by the end of grade 8. High school students should demonstrate beginning status by the end of their Level I course, intermediate status by the end of a Level III course, and advanced status by the end of a Level V or Advanced Placement Course. Such designations as Level I, II, and III place learning in a time frame that standards of excellence seek to avoid. In the scheme presented here, the progress of students in terms of standards of excellence or proficiency is the factor to be measured, not time. *(see Frequently asked Question 8, p. 191)*

- **Culturally authentic** The most culturally authentic materials are those the Romans used, read, saw, and touched. Because these materials are rare or inaccessible to most students, it is necessary to create materials that approximate what was known in the ancient world, e.g., a story in Latin about a Roman child's day in school. Although comprehension of an unadapted text is the ultimate goal, that is not often attainable by a beginning 7th grader. If the emphasis in created materials is culturally authentic, students learn culture at the same time that they are learning language.

- **Curriculum** State frameworks provide a curricular and programmatic context. District curriculum further defines course content in a coordinated sequence. Course curriculum is a teacher's outline for a specific course of study (e.g., Latin I, Latin in grade 7, exploratory Latin for 10 weeks). Lesson plans translate curriculum into meaningful and creative activities for the individual classroom. The standards are meant as a guide to curriculum development, not a substitute for it. Curricula vary according to teaching style, learning style, the teacher's philosophy of teaching and learning, students' ability, textbooks used, and available resources. Curricula designed to achieve the standards should vary in many ways: in specific lesson plans, in types of drill, and in choice of authors and literary works.

- **Framework** Many states have chosen the word "framework" to title their documents guiding curriculum development at the district and local level.

- **Goal** The standards are organized within five goal areas that make up classical language education: communication, culture, connections, comparisons, and communities. These are the goals established in *Standards for Foreign Language Learning: Preparing* *for the 21st Century.* Each goal is one strand that must be woven into the fabric of curriculum development at the state, district, and local levels.

- **Guidelines** For Latin, a set of "national guidelines for Latin I and II" can be found in Davis, Sally, *Latin in American Schools,* Atlanta GA: Scholars Press, 1991. Some states are producing curriculum guides with more detailed models as supplements to their frameworks for curriculum development. These guides usually have models of classroom activity similar to the scenarios that appear in *Standards for Classical Language Learning.*

- **Level** See "Beginning / Intermediate / Advanced," p. 188 and "Frequently Asked Questions 8," p. 191.

- **Literature** Greek and Latin literature ranges at least from the 8th century B.C. through the classical periods of Greece and Rome, the Byzantine and Middle Ages, the Renaissance, and even into the present age. Epic, lyric, tragic and comic drama, satire, history, biography, oratory, philosophy, scientific, agricultural, and medical treatises, even the novel are among the genres read by students of Latin and Greek. This wealth of literature provides a broad base for choosing authors or genre. In addition, non-literary Latin and Greek provide a storehouse of authentic material to read: graffiti, inscriptions, coins, curse tablets. Caesar, Cicero, and Vergil have long been standard fare for high school students; they continue to be important models. However, the wealth of non-traditional authors and non-literary sources should not be ignored. *Standards for Classical Language Learning* does not mandate the study of any particular set of authors but is intended to guide students toward a mastery of the language that will enable them, at the most advanced level, to read any author of Latin or Greek.

- **Oral Latin or Greek** The oral use of Latin or Greek includes reading or reciting Latin or Greek texts aloud (with proper attention to metrical structure, if the passage is poetry), asking and responding to questions, making statements, issuing and responding to commands. The word "speak," a more natural substitute for "use orally," has been avoided in order not to imply that "conversation" is an important part of the standard.

- **Progress Indicator** A progress indicator gives a quick picture of what a student who has mastered a standard knows and can do in a specific situation. Under each standard are sample progress indicators for beginning, intermediate, and advanced students. The sample progress indicators are neither prescriptive nor exhaustive. Intermediate and advanced students are expected to exhibit the progress indicators of the lower levels as well as the progress indicators of their own level.

- **Reading** Reading includes all of the following: reading aloud, paraphrasing content, analyzing grammar and syntax, interpreting meaning, and translating. All of these skills cannot be demonstrated simultaneously, and good pedagogy would elicit practice and assessment of the separate skills for different and specific purposes. Reading that employs all methods needed for an accurate interpretation of the original text is, in the broadest sense, philology.

- **Scenario** A scenario is a picture in words of student performance in a classroom situation. It is a fully developed segment of curriculum, is articulated in a lesson plan, has activities, and uses specific linguistic and pedagogical strategies. The scenarios in *Standards for Classical Language Learning* list the standards addressed and the reflections of the teacher on the lesson.

- **Standard** A standard describes what students should know and be able to do. Each goal area in *Standards for Classical Language Learning* contains two content standards.

- **Translation** Translations are versions of a text in another language. They can range from close adherence to the original syntax to a free interpretation of content. Translations can be a teaching device to measure comprehension; they can also be high art, demanding an expert command of English and Latin. (See "Frequently Asked Questions," 6, p. 191.)

- **Writing** *Standards for Classical Language Learning* uses "writing" to mean any of the following: taking dictation, translating from English into Latin or Greek, transforming Latin or Greek into different patterns of Latin or Greek while maintaining the meaning, or creating free composition in Latin or Greek. The primary aim of such written work is to enhance the ability of students to read the languages.

Frequently Asked Questions

1. **Why have national standards for classical language learning been developed when national standards for all foreign languages already exist?**

   Language specific documents aligned with *Standards for Foreign Language Learning: Preparing for the 21st Century* have been commissioned by the National Standards in Foreign Language Education Collaborative Project. The joint effort of the American Classical League, the American Philological Association, and regional classical organizations has been endorsed and commended by our modern language colleagues. They are engaged in a similar activity within their professional organizations. The language specific standards documents are meant to be companion documents to the national foreign language standards.

2. **Are the standards mandatory?**

   No; the standards as published here are voluntary. They are intended to serve as a model for state and local policy makers and curriculum developers as they consider the role of classical languages in their schools. The standards propose a model to implement students' progress in reading classical languages and in achieving the five goals: communication, culture, connections, comparisons, and communities.

3. **Which goal is most important?**

   These standards have been developed with each goal relying heavily on the basic goal of reading the classical language. Reading Latin or Greek (Goal 1, Standard 1) permeates the other four goals. By reading the classical language students become immersed in the culture (Goal 2), make connections (Goal 3) and comparisons (Goal 4), and understand and move more comfortably in the communities (Goal 5) of the world. Unlike the national standards for foreign language learning, the classical language standards stress the prime importance and value of reading.

4. **Where is the list of classical authors, the usual canon?**

   As school districts develop curriculum from the standards, they select the appropriate authors to be studied in their own schools. (See "Literature" in the "Glossary," p. 189.)

5. **Where is the grammar?**

   Grammar (morphology and syntax) is an important tool for understanding meaning. Students need tools and strategies to read with comprehension. Because each state, county, district, and teacher will choose the tools of instruction appropriate for its own students, curriculum guides and course outlines that are written as a subsequent step in the process of curriculum development will determine what items of grammar should be included to meet specific instructional needs. Grammar is addressed directly in Standard 1.1 and is implied throughout the standards. Each learning scenario needs to include the tools of grammar necessary to accomplish it.

6. **Where and how does translation fit into the classical language learning standards?**

   Reading and understanding Latin or Greek is Standard 1.1. There are many ways of determining what a student reads and understands. Translation into English is one of them. The standards for classical language learning do not mandate method; they are not textbook bound. Individual districts, textbook selection, an individual teacher's creativity, students' learning styles, and specific situations will determine where and how much translation into English is appropriate. Translating is an artful skill; sometimes what passes as a "literal translation" from Latin or Greek into English is not English at all.

7. **Why does this set of standards not use grades 4, 8 and 12 as benchmarks for indicating progress as the national document does?**

   Current Latin and Greek programs start at many places in grades K-12 and in the college and university curriculum. We do not anticipate that most programs will begin in kindergarten and extend through high school and beyond. Sample progress indicators are described for beginning, intermediate, and advanced classical language students regardless of their age or grade level. Activities, of course, must be age-appropriate and developmentally appropriate to the student.

8. **What happened to Level I, Level II, and Level III?**

   Many innovative Latin programs have been developed since the 1960s that start Latin instruction in the early grades. New textbooks have been created for schemes more diverse than high school Latin I and II. Some states have mandated that foreign language instruction begin below the high school level. An increasingly more common program scheme is Latin in grades 7 and 8 that includes all the skills for entering Latin II in grade 9. This scheme allows for Latin V in grade 12 and an opportunity to use both of the separate Advanced Placement syllabi. In this scheme the progress indicators would be appropriate as follows: Beginning—grades 7 and 8 (Latin I); Intermediate—grades 9 and 10 (Latin II and III); Advanced—grades 11 and 12 (Latin IV and V, Advanced Placement). Students' progress in terms of standards of excellence or proficiency is the factor to be measured, not time. (See "Glossary, Beginning / Intermediate / Advanced," p. 188.)

9. **What is the relationship of these standards to state frameworks, district curriculum, local curricular guidelines and lesson plans?**

    Standards for Classical Language Learning is a national statement of what students should know and be able to do at three points in their development. State frameworks provide a curricular and programmatic context. District curriculum further defines course content in a coordinated sequence. Lesson plans translate curriculum into meaningful and creative activities for the individual classroom.

10. **Where does assessment fit into the standards for classical language learning?**

    Curriculum, instruction, and assessment are all parts of a fabric so tightly woven that the seams are barely detectable. Assessment is a part of instruction; a good teacher is constantly evaluating and assessing the student and the instruction. On the basis of the assessment, curriculum is adjusted. An assessment may be as informal as noting a student's smile of recognition or as formal as an Advanced Placement examination. The standards can serve as the basic blueprint for a final exam, as the plan for a textbook, or as the foundation of curriculum. They can also be the basis for state or national examinations.

11. **How do the standards relate and connect to the Advanced Placement Tests in Latin, the Latin Achievement Test, the National Latin Exam, the National Greek Exam, and various regional and state examinations?**

    Standards for Classical Language Learning should be a standardizing force in the development of local, state, and national assessment tools. Each local, state, or national examination measures achievement of specific curriculum. Since *Standards for Classical Language Learning* already describes what is best in current classical language teaching and learning, some current assessment tools may adequately assess what the standards for classical language learning outline. All assessment tools, local, state, and national, need to be reviewed in light of the standards.

12. **Will classical language teachers be given training to implement these standards?**

    The ACL and APA hope to establish a team which will meet with various classical associations across the country to assist and train teachers and curriculum writers in the implementation of the standards.

13. **What are the implications of these standards for college and university Classics programs and teaching?**

    Standards of excellence are appropriate to students of all ages. Progress indicators may be different for beginners of different ages, but the standards will be the same. It may take four years for a middle school student to demonstrate the progress indicators of a beginning student. It may take one semester for a college student to demonstrate the same beginning progress. It may take a high school student three years to demonstrate intermediate progress. A university student may do it in two semesters. Standards are not measured by time nor by a student's age; they are measured by progress, i.e., what a student knows or can do at a specified point.

14. **What are the implications of these standards for teacher training programs in Classics?**

    Teachers new and experienced will need to know what their colleagues deem to be the learning standards for their discipline. Standards can guide curriculum development, as well as national, state, and local testing. Teachers need to be aware of the latest developments in their field; and teacher training programs in the Classics will need to reflect what is happening, guide prospective teachers, and lead the field in developing new teaching and learning strategies.

15. **Are national standards an instrument intended to be used for teacher evaluation?**

    No. Standards describe what students should know and be able to do. If anything, they provide a base for student assessment. What a student knows and can do is, in part, the result of a teacher's instruction. Good teachers are aware of current pedagogical thinking and create an atmosphere that fosters learning as described in the sample progress indicators.

16. **Why does *Standards for Classical Language Learning* specify that classical languages are for ALL sudents?**

    When language instruction is appropriate to the ages, abilities, and learning styles of students, ALL students can learn classical languages. Model Latin programs in Philadelphia, Los Angeles, New York, Washington, Detroit, and Kansas City, among others, led the way in experiments to show that young students, students of many cultural backgrounds, and students of differing abilities can make progress toward learning a classical language and can demonstrate progress on the scale outlined in *Standards for Classical Language Learning*. Successful programs in classical languages currently exist in pre-kindergarten through graduate school; successful programs in classical languages currently exist for the academically talented and for the physically and/or academically challenged. Students study Latin and Greek whose native languages are not English and whose cultural heritages are widely diverse. Classical languages are for ALL students.

Bibliography and Resources

CLASSICAL LANGUAGE LEARNING AND TEACHING RESOURCES

Bender, H. V. 1996. "Audio-visual materials in the classics 1996 survey," *Classical World* 89.4.
This resource, which includes a complete list of providers, is updated and published by *Classical World* on an annual basis. See corresponding entry under *Sebesta* below.

Burns, M.A. and J.F. O'Connor. 1987. *The Classics in American Schools: Teaching the Ancient World.* Scholars Press.

Davis, S. 1991. *Latin in American Schools: Teaching the Ancient World.* Scholars Press.
This work is the most recently published work on the state of the profession. Davis describes the current situation of Latin and Greek programs in the United States, Canada, and Britain at each level from elementary school through university and provides curricular guidelines for high school Latin I and II. She appends a brief bibliography and list of useful addresses.

Davis, S., G. Daugherty, D. Larick, J. Mikalson, and J. Miller. 1991. "Preparation and training for teachers of Latin," *Classical Journal* 86.3 (February-March 1991) 262-267.

Jenkins, F.W. 1996. *Classical Studies. A Guide to the Reference Literature.* Libraries Unlimited.
This resource should be made available to every teacher and student of Classics at each level. The book is divided into seventeen chapters in three sections: Bibliographical Resources, Information Resources, and Organizations. See especially ch. 4: Topical Bibliographies; ch. 5: Bibliographies of Individuals (i.e., individual Greek and Latin authors); ch. 8: Specialized Dictionaries, Encyclopedias, and Handbooks (e.g., Art and Archaeology, History, Literature, and Mythology); ch. 15: Internet Resources; and ch. 17: Professional Associations and Societies. This resource also includes an Author/Title Index and Subject Index.

Jenkins, F.W. and N. Courtney. 1997. "Internet resources for classical studies," *College and Research Libraries News* 255-259.
This article provides some additional information supplemental to ch. 15 in the previous entry.

LaFleur, R. A. (ed.) 1987. *The Teaching of Latin in American Schools.* Scholars Press.

LaFleur, R. A. (ed.) 1998. *Latin for the 21st Century: From Concept to Classroom.* Glenview, IL: Scott Foresman-Addison Wesley.
This is the first Latin methods and resource text to appear since the 1960s.

Lawall, G. 1988. *ACTFL Selected Listing of Instructional Materials for Elementary and Secondary School Programs: Latin and Greek.* Yonkers, NY: ACTFL.

Santirocco, M. S. (ed.) 1987. *Latinitas.* The tradition and teaching of Latin. Special issue of *Helios* (14) 2.

Saraceni, J. E. 1997. "What's on line? Digging into the World Wide Web, Part II," *Archaeology* 50. March/April 71-77.
 The editors of *Archaeology* include an informative section on multimedia in each issue. Other recent topics: Creative offerings from *Time-Life* (January/February 1996); Surfing ancient lands. A Guide to CD ROMS (May/June 1996).

Sebesta, J. L. 1996. "Textbooks in Greek and Latin, 1996 Survey." *Classical World,* 89.4.
 This resource is updated on an annual basis by the publishers of *Classical World.* In addition to providing a meticulously up-to-date and complete listing of available texts, Sebesta provides a full directory of textbook publishers.

Solomon, J. (ed.). 1993. *Accessing Antiquity. The Computerization of Classical Studies.* University of Arizona.

NATIONAL STANDARDS IN FOREIGN LANGUAGE EDUCATION

National Standards in Foreign Language Education Project. 1996. *Standards for Foreign Language Learning: Preparing for the 21st Century.* Lawrence, KS: Allen Press.
 This work presents the current national standards for foreign language education in the United States. The following works provide additional information:

Draper, J. 1993. "National standards in foreign language education: Answering the questions." *ERIC/CLL Bulletin* (17) 1.

Education Week. 1995. *Struggling for Standards: An Education Week Special Report.* Washington, DC: Education Week.

Phillips, J. and J. Draper. 1994. "National standards and assessments," in G. Crouse (ed.), *Meeting New Challenges in the Foreign Language Classroom.* Report of the Central States Conference on the Teaching of Foreign Languages. Lincolnwood, IL: National Textbook Company.

SOME USEFUL ADDRESSES

ACL/NJCL National Latin Exam. c/o Jane Hall, Director, P.O. Box 95, Mt. Vernon, VA 22121.

American Classical League and Teaching Materials Resource Center. Miami University, Oxford, OH 45056. c/o John A. Dutra, Director. Tel: 513-529-7741. Fax: 513-529-7742. *Access:* http://www.umich.edu/~acleague/.

American Philological Association. John Marincola, Executive Director, 19 University Place, Room 328, New York University, New York, NY 10003-4556. Tel: 212-998-3575, Fax: 212-995-4814. e-mail: american.philological@nyu.edu
Access: http://scholar.cc.emory.edu/APA/APA-MENU.html.

Archaeological Institute of America. 675 Commonwealth Ave., Boston, MA 02215. Tel: 617-353-9361. Fax: 617-353-6550.
Access: http://csaws.brynmawr.edu:443/aia.html.

Classical Association of the Atlantic States. c/o Jerry Clack, Executive Director, Department of Classics, Duquesne University, Pittsburgh, PA 15282-1704. Tel: 412-396-6450. Fax: 412-396-5197.
Access: http//wings.buffalo.edu/academic/department/AandL/classics/caas/.

Classical Association of New England. c/o Allan Wooley, Executive-Secretary, Dept. of Classical Languages, Phillips Exeter Academy, Exeter, NH 03833. Tel: 603-772-4311. Fax: 603-778-4384. E-mail: awooley@exeter.edu.
Access: http://www.hnet.uci.edu/classics/cane/cane.html.

Classical Association of the Middle West and South. c/o Prof. Gregory N. Daugherty, Department of Classics, Randolph-Macon College, P.O. Box 5005, Ashland, VA 23005. Tel: 804-752-3732. Fax: 804-752-7231.
Access: http://www.rmc.edu:80/~gdaugher/oca.html.

Classical Association of the Pacific Northwest. c/o Prof. Catherine M. Connors, Department of Classics, Box 351110, University of Washington, Seattle, WA 98195.
Tel: 206-543-2267. Fax: 206-543-2266.
Access: http://weber.u.washington.edu/~alain/CAPN/CAPN_Homepage.html.

Committee for the Promotion of Greek. c/o Prof. Kenneth F. Kitchell, Jr., Department of Foreign Languages, Prescott 222, Louisiana State University, Baton Rouge, LA 70808-5306.
Tel: 504-388-6616. Fax: 504-343-5623.

National Committee for Latin and Greek. c/o Virginia Barrett, Chair, 11371 Matinicius Ct, Cypress, CA 90630.
Tel: 714-373-0588. Fax: 714-897-6681.

National Junior Classical League. Miami University, Oxford, OH 45056. Tel: 513-529-7741. Fax: 513-529-7741.

Vergilian Society of America. c/o John Dutra, Executive Secretary, P.O. Box 817, Oxford, OH 45056. Tel: 513-529-1482. Fax: 513-529-1516.
Access: dutra_jack@msmail.muohio.edu.

Standards for the Learning of French, K-16

AATF Task Force on Standards for the Learning of French

AATF TASK FORCE ON STANDARDS FOR THE LEARNING OF FRENCH

Rebecca M. Valette, Boston College, Chestnut Hill, MA, Co-chair
Margot M. Steinhart, Northwestern University, Evanston, IL, Co-chair
Barbara C. Anderson, Normandale French Immersion School, Edina, MN
Pat Barr-Harrison, Prince George's County Schools, Capitol Heights, MD
Assia Bérubé, Good Counsel High School, Chicago, IL
N. Patricia R. Duggar, Paul Breaux Middle School, Lafayette, LA
Eveline Leisner, Los Angeles Valley College, Van Nuys, CA
Joyce P. Lentz, Las Cruces High School, Las Cruces, NM
Janel Lafond Paquin, Rogers High School, Newport, RI
Alain Ranwez, Metropolitan State College, Denver, CO
Flore Zéphir, University of Missouri, Columbia, MO

FRENCH

Standards for the Learning of French

AATF COMMISSION FOR STUDENT STANDARDS

Barbara C. Anderson (MN), Co-chair
Robert C. Lafayette (LA), Co-chair
Pat Barr-Harrison (MD)
Assia Bérubé (IL)
Judy Dharini Charudattan (FL)
Michel Couet (SC)
Patricia Duggar (LA)
Barbara Freed (PA)
Kathy Freeman (TX)
David Graham (NY)
Virginia Gramer (IL)
Andrea Javel (MA)
Nancy Milner Kelly (MA)
Eveline Leisner (CA)
Joyce Pierro Lentz (NM)
Gladys Lipton (MD)
Barbara Maitland (IA)

Frances Novak (PA)
Janel Lafond Paquin (MA)
Alain Ranwez (CO)
Mimi Reed (NJ)
Lydia Ruiz (IA)
Christine Salmon (IN)
Michèle Shockey (CA)
Marcia Spielberger (GA)
Margot M. Steinhart (IL)
Toni Theisen (CO)
Flore Zéphir (MO)
Jayne Abrate (IL)
Constance F. Alexandre (TX)
Wendy W. Allen (MN)
Susan Arandjelovic (AZ)
Joyce Beckwith (MA)
Janet Kosonen-Biscan (IL)

The AATF Task Force on Standards for the Learning of French
wishes to thank the following colleagues for submitting learning scenarios
and/or for reviewing the document:

Michèle Bissière (NC)
Leah Bolek (IL)
Lisette Brisebois (IL)
Deborah Brown (WV)
Jane Castle (IL)
Alice Charles (VT)
Judy Dharini Charudattan (FL)
Marcia Colliat (AZ)
Michel Couet (SC)
Joanna Breedlove Crane (AL)
Brenda Crosby (IL)
Karen V. de Waal (NY)
S. Pascale Dewey (PA)
Maureen Curran-Dorsani (MN)
Lou Ann Erikson (IL)
David W. Flaccus (NY)
Nancy J. Gadbois (MA)
David Graham (NY)
Virginia Gramer (IL)
Ann Hajicek (IL)
Annahi Hart (IL)
A. Anne Hebert (IL)
Elise Helland (IL)
Mary Ann Hockman (IL)
Louise Ann Hunley (FL)

Elaine Jastrem (MA)
Nancy Milner Kelly (MA)
Cathy Kendrigan (IL)
Carol A. Kidd (MD)
Linda King (IL)
Francine M. V. Klein (MN)
Ann Koller (IL)
Eveline Leisner (CA)
Colette G. Levin (PA)
Gladys Lipton (MD)
Helen M. Lorenz (TX)
Lena L. Lucietto (LA)
Robert J. Ludwig (NY)
Ann Elkin McBride (KY)
Joan McCloskey (LA)
Mary Ellen McGoey (IL)
Isabelle Main (AZ)
Joan F. Militscher (NY)
Nancy Mirsky (NY)
Tricia Engelhardt-Nagel (IL)
Susan W. Norvich (IL)
Geraldine O'Neill (NY)
Mary Brackman Perrot (IL)
Bernard Petit (NY)
Jo Ann L. Piotrowski (PA)

Jayne Prater (IL)
Karen Kus Provan (IL)
Maija Racevskis (OH)
Cherre Rogers (AZ)
Jo Ellen Sandburg (IL)
Kay Saxvik (IL)
Laura M. Scanlan (NJ)
Phaedra R. Shively (NM)
Michèle Shockey (CA)
Jane W. Shuffelton (NY)
Marian St. Onge (MA)
Margot M. Steinhart (IL)
Judy Sugarman (IL)
Louise P. Terry (NY)
Toni Theisen (CO)
Maria G. Traub (PA)
Rebecca M. Valette (MA)
Fernande Wagman (NJ)
Alan Wax (IL)
Marie-Christine Weidmann Koop (TX)
Sheryl Wiitala (NE)
Claudia Windfuhr (CA)
Robin Wolf (IL)
Marie Yonkers (AZ)

Table of Contents

STANDARDS FOR THE LEARNING OF FRENCH		**246**
INTRODUCTION: THE STATUS OF FRENCH LANGUAGE LEARNING IN THE UNITED STATES TODAY		**247**
ABOUT STANDARDS FOR THE LEARNING OF FRENCH		**249**
COMMUNICATION	**Goal 1**	**251**
CULTURES	**Goal 2**	**257**
CONNECTIONS	**Goal 3**	**262**
COMPARISONS	**Goal 4**	**265**
COMMUNITIES	**Goal 5**	**270**
FRENCH LEARNING SCENARIOS		**274**
Les Actions: French Investments		275
Les Actualités: A French Newscast		275
L'Art haïtien: Naïf Art In Haiti		276
Le Concert: A Live Concert		277
La Dernière Classe: A Short Story		278
Les Entrevues ethnographiques: Ethnographic Interviews		278
Une Fable de la Fontaine: Dramatization of a Fable		279
La Famille: Genealogy		279
L'Impressionnisme: An Impressionist Gallery		280
Le Maroc: Moroccan Showcase		281
Paris en métro: Paris by Subway		282
Le Petit Prince: The Little Prince		283
Les Stages: Summer Internships in Strasbourg		284
Les Vêtements: Mail Order Catalogue		284
Les Voyageurs: The French *Voyageurs*		285

Standards for the Learning of French

COMMUNICATION — GOAL ONE
Communicate in French

Standard 1.1 Interpersonal Communication
Students engage in conversations or correspondence in French to provide and obtain information, express feelings and emotions, and exchange opinions.

Standard 1.2 Interpretive Communication
Students understand and interpret spoken and written French on a variety of topics.

Standard 1.3 Presentational Communication
Students present information, concepts, and ideas in French to an audience of listeners or readers.

CULTURES — GOAL TWO
Gain Knowledge and Understanding of the Cultures of the Francophone World

Standard 2.1 Practices of Culture
Students demonstrate an understanding of the relationship between the practices and perspectives of the cultures of the francophone world.

Standard 2.2 Products of Culture
Students demonstrate an understanding of the relationship between the products and perspectives of the cultures of the francophone world.

CONNECTIONS — GOAL THREE
Use French to Connect with Other Disciplines and Expand Knowledge

Standard 3.1 Making Connections
Students reinforce and further their knowledge of other disciplines through French.

Standard 3.2 Acquiring Information
Students acquire information and recognize the distinctive viewpoints that are only available through francophone cultures.

COMPARISONS — GOAL FOUR
Develop Insight through French into the Nature of Language and Culture

Standard 4.1 Language Comparisons
Students demonstrate understanding of the nature of language through comparisons of French and their native language.

Standard 4.2 Cultural Comparisons
Students demonstrate understanding of the concept of culture through comparisons of francophone cultures and their own.

COMMUNITIES — GOAL FIVE
Use French to Participate in Communities at Home and Around the World

Standard 5.1 School and Community
Students use French both within and beyond the school setting.

Standard 5.2 Lifelong Learning Students show evidence of becoming lifelong learners by using French for personal enjoyment and enrichment.

Introduction

THE STATUS OF FRENCH LANGUAGE LEARNING IN THE UNITED STATES TODAY

French in the World

French is spoken in all regions of the world, including over thirty-five countries in Europe and Africa and many areas in North America, as well as in Haiti, French Guyana, and numerous islands in the Indian Ocean and the South Pacific. In Canada, our neighbor to the north and our primary trading partner, all imported goods must be labeled in French and English, and all user manuals for manufactured products must be printed in both languages. French is also a working language of the United Nations and the European Union, as well as an official language of the Olympic Games. French is the second most spoken language in Europe. Moreover, French is a second language in many non-English speaking areas of the globe. Over 100 million people living in non-francophone areas are learning or have learned French. French is the fourth language in the world for most books in print. Proficiency in French allows Americans direct access to knowledge and information generated in these countries and cultures and allows face-to-face negotiations in political, business, and personal dealings. Students will find that their ability in French prepares them for school and community service projects, increases their employment options both at home and abroad, and expands their opportunities for leisure activities.

To respond to changes created by instant global communication, American society requires an effective work force able to meet the needs of consumers who may not speak English. Knowledge of the French language and francophone cultures increases the ability of our citizens to interact effectively with people around the world. French is also an important language of scientific and technological research. Not surprisingly, it is the second language of the Internet.

French and our American Heritage

In their study of French, students grow to appreciate the multi-faceted role that France and French-speakers have played in the history of the North American continent. Beginning with the explorations of Jacques Cartier, followed by Champlain, LaSalle, Joliet, and Marquette, the French continued to have an influence in the New World through their participation in the fur trade in New England, New York, Pennsylvania, Ohio, the Great Plains, and the Rocky Mountains. As a result, many place names in these areas reflect the presence of the French, who also explored the Great Lakes and the Mississippi River down to the Gulf of Mexico and established settlements in places like Baton Rouge, Mobile, Louisville, St. Louis, Duluth, Chicago, Detroit, and Laramie.

> FRENCH IS AN INTERNATIONAL LANGUAGE, SPOKEN IN ALL REGIONS OF THE WORLD.

FRANCE AND THE UNITED STATES HAVE BEEN ALLIES FOR OVER TWO CENTURIES.

Writers of the Declaration of Independence and the United States Constitution spent time in France and found inspiration in the writings of the French *philosophes*, such as Rousseau and Montesquieu. During the American Revolution, young Lafayette offered his assistance to General Washington, while France contributed to the decisive battle of Yorktown by sending significant military reinforcements under General Rochambeau and a naval fleet commanded by Admiral de Grasse. In the twentieth century, the United States was able to reciprocate by sending military forces to assist its French allies in World War I and World War II, and by contributing in a philanthropic way to the renovation of such sites as Versailles and Monet's gardens in Giverny.

Over the centuries, groups of immigrants have settled in the United States. In the seventeenth century, French Huguenots came to New England, and one of the best known descendants, Paul Revere, is part of American history and folklore. When the Acadians or Cajuns were expelled from Canada in the eighteenth century, many found a safe haven in Louisiana and were soon joined by Creoles from Saint Domingue, now Haiti. In the nineteenth and twentieth centuries, French speakers from Quebec came to work in the mill towns of New England. More recently, groups of Haitian immigrants have made their home in the United States, as have Africans from countries like Senegal and the Ivory Coast and refugees from the countries which were once part of French Indochina: Vietnam, Cambodia, and Laos. The United States is home to 1.7 million people who consider French their first language. As a result, French is the second most frequently spoken foreign language in the United States. There are now over ten million Americans with French or francophone ancestry.

French Teaching in the United States

As a result of the American entry into World War I in 1917 and the ensuing anti-German sentiments, French emerged as the most popular modern foreign language. This privileged position was maintained for almost fifty years. With the focus of foreign language instruction at that time on the receptive skills of reading, and to a lesser extent on listening, knowledge of French was seen as opening the door to a rich and varied world of literature, philosophy, art, music, dance, and film. In the 1920s and 1930s, American writers, intellectuals, and artists of all backgrounds and races found inspiration and acceptance in France. After World War II, large numbers of students, including many returning GIs, considered a trip to Paris or a year in France as one of the most rewarding experiences of their university career.

By the mid-1960s, Americans were becoming more aware of their Latin American neighbors, and Spanish began to catch up with French in popularity. As the percentage of Hispanic Americans in this country increased, Spanish was seen to be a practical language and, in some areas, a major language of communication. By the 1990s, the ratio of Spanish students to French students reached three to one at the secondary level.

This shift in language popularity has been accompanied by an infusion of new energy into French instruction at all levels and a reconsideration of the goals of foreign language programs in general and of French in particular. French teachers around the United States are revitalizing their classes by aligning their curricula with the five "C's" of the foreign language standards.

- The current emphasis on building oral proficiency is being expanded to include a broader range of **Communication** skills, which include international e-mail and links to schools, as well as expanded access to French-language sites on the Internet, films, videos, books, magazines, and music.

- In meeting the **Culture** goal, students learn to appreciate the products, practices, and beliefs of multi-ethnic communities both in the United States and abroad.

- Interdisciplinary **Connections** range from sports (hockey, cycling, skiing, and baseball) and athletics (Olympic games), to music, dance, film, drama and theater, visual arts, architecture, fashion, cuisine, restaurant and hotel management, international business, philosophy and history, *négritude* and women's studies, and science and medicine (high-speed transportation, space technology, and AIDS research).

- Through cultural and linguistic **Comparisons** students increase their understanding of how society works and expand their command of English. Since the Norman Invasion of England in 1066 when French was the language of the ruling class, twenty percent of the words in the French language have been assimilated into English. About forty to fifty percent of the words in English are of French origin or from Latin via French.

- In reaching out to **Communities,** students join hands with peoples around the world and develop interests that will stimulate them to become lifelong learners of French.

ABOUT STANDARDS FOR THE LEARNING OF FRENCH

The generic *Standards for Foreign Language Learning: Preparing for the 21st Century* is a visionary document based on the premise that every American student should have the opportunity to develop proficiency in a second language in an articulated sequence of instruction. Consequently, the Sample Progress Indicators contained in the generic document reflect this ideal learning situation and describe in broad terms the expected outcomes of such an extended curriculum. It is important to note that the generic standards document, which grew out of the ACTFL Proficiency Guidelines, reflects a progression in our understanding of how language is used. We have moved beyond the traditional framework of the four skills of listening, speaking, reading, and writing plus culture. These elements are certainly present but they are more fully integrated into the outcomes for foreign language study in the generic standards document. Like the latter document, the French-specific document is based on the five C's, but the French standards extend the K-12 sequence described in the generic standard to K-16 and include the post-secondary level.

At the present time, however, there is only a modest number of school systems, private or public, which offer a K-12 articulated curriculum in foreign languages. However, there are schools that offer longer sequences in French, including some very successful immersion programs. It is important to recognize that the great majority of French students in the United States begin their studies at the middle school or secondary school level, and some do not begin until college or university. For those students who speak Spanish natively or who have had prior experience learning Spanish, French may be a third language.

Although the wording of the Goals and Standards for the learning of French parallels that of the generic document, the Sample Progress Indicators have been written to reflect the current status of French instruction in this country with its multiple entry points and wide variety of curricular sequences.

Applying the Sample Progress Indicators to the French Curriculum

The purpose of Sample Progress Indicators is to serve as a general checklist to help teachers define the progress their students are making in meeting the standards. The Sample Progress Indicators found under each standard in this document are not exhaustive or prescriptive, but rather reflect a variety of student activities that can be readily incorporated at the classroom level. Where appropriate, sample materials, themes, and topics are suggested. These Sample Progress Indicators are designed to inspire French teachers to think of other types of activities that can also be developed to achieve a given standard. In designing classroom practice activities, teachers should be guided by the premise that the Sample Progress Indicators they select should define what realistically can be achieved at some level by all students.

SAMPLE PROGRESS INDICATORS MAY SERVE AS GUIDELINES FOR THE FRENCH CURRICULUM.

Adapting the Sample Progress Indicators to Reflect Multiple Entry Points

Under each level heading (Grades 4, 8, 12, and Post-secondary), the Sample Progress Indicators are sequenced from those which can be reached by students who have recently begun learning French to those which are designed for students in a longer articulated sequence or students with significant prior experience with another language, particularly with another Romance language. At times, Sample Progress Indicators for subsequent levels may also be attainable by students at an earlier stage; for example, some high school students may be able to reach some Sample Progress Indicators designated for Post-secondary students. While not the only factor, the length of an articulated program does significantly affect the level of competency and proficiency that students can be expected to attain.

Using the Sample Progress Indicators with Immersion Programs

Students in immersion programs may be able to attain some Sample Progress Indicators at an earlier age. This is especially true for the Communication standards (Goal 1) where, for example, Grade 4 students may be able to meet some of the Sample Progress Indicators suggested for Grade 8. Indicators for other goals that are more related to cognitive development than length of exposure to the language may be reached later.

Extending the Sample Progress Indicators to the Post-secondary Level

Whereas the generic document addresses only the K-12 curriculum, the Sample Progress Indicators for French have been extended to include students at the post-secondary level. Of these, some students are beginning their study of French in college or university while others are improving the skills they developed at the secondary level by enrolling in more advanced classes. It is during their post-secondary years that many students have the opportunity to use their French in the workplace or to spend an academic semester or a year in a francophone region.

Communication
Communicate in French

Goal One

For American students, the ability to communicate in French will become an increasingly important asset in the rapidly shrinking, interdependent world of the 21st century. In the course of their work or their leisure activities, students who have studied French may be called upon to interact with speakers from areas around the globe in face-to-face conversation, as well as by telephone, in writing or via electronic mail. They must be able to interpret the concepts, ideas, and opinions expressed by French speakers through their media and their literatures. They may be asked to present information for an audience orally or in writing.

Goal 1 focuses on **language use** and **communicative competence**. It is clearly evident that schools and universities across the country employ a great variety of approaches, methods, and techniques in teaching French, depending on the level of the students, the make-up of the class, and the aims of the curriculum. The key consideration, however, is the quality of the results. Consequently, Goal 1 does not refer to specific course content, but rather to the outcome of instruction, that is, how students are able to use French to communicate with others, and how effectively they can use communication strategies to cope in linguistically unfamiliar or challenging situations. These linguistic outcomes can be broken down into three communicative modes: the interpersonal mode, the interpretive mode, and the presentational mode.

- **Interpersonal mode:** *Two-way communication via conversation or written exchanges*

  In the interpersonal mode, two or more individuals interact with one another. As they take turns expressing themselves in speech and through body language or in writing, they have the opportunity to negotiate meaning, that is, to check whether their intentions are accurately understood and, if not, to make necessary adjustments or clarifications. Most commonly, the interpersonal mode is employed in face-to-face conversation and telephone calls, but it is also used in the exchange of notes and e-mail messages.

- **Interpretive mode:** *Understanding what one hears or reads*

  In the interpretive mode, one or more individuals try to understand what others, with whom they have no direct personal contact, have said or written. The stronger the individuals' command of the language and the greater their understanding of cultural referents, the more precise this interpretation will be. The interpretive mode is used when one listens to the radio, lectures, and recordings, when one goes to a concert or to the theater, when one watches television or a movie, and when one reads a book or a magazine.

- **Presentational mode:** *Expressing one's ideas in speech or writing*

  In the presentational mode, one or more individuals communicate their thoughts to listeners or speakers with whom they may have no immediate personal contact. These activities may take the form of an oral presentation, a phone message, an audio or video recording or a written text.

These communicative modes are reflected in the three standards under Goal 1. To meet these communicative standards, students must have ample opportunities to experience

> **GOOD COMMUNICATION REQUIRES EFFECTIVE STRATEGIES AND SKILLS IN LISTENING, SPEAKING, READING, AND WRITING, AS WELL AS OBSERVING, AND INTERPRETING CULTURAL REFERENCES.**

Standards for the Learning of French

French as it is spoken and written in France and in other francophone countries and communities. They need to develop effective strategies for expressing themselves and for understanding authentic, spoken and written materials in French.

STANDARD 1.1 INTERPERSONAL COMMUNICATION
Students engage in conversations or correspondence in French to provide and obtain information, express feelings and emotions, and exchange opinions.

This standard focuses on interpersonal communication. In beginning French classes, students can quickly learn a number of phrases that permit them to interact with each other. In the course of their study, they grow in their ability to communicate with others in French in a culturally appropriate manner on a variety of topics.

Sample Progress Indicators, Grade 4

- Students use appropriate French expressions and gestures to greet and take leave of teachers and classmates.

- Students give and follow simple instructions in French in order to participate in classroom activities.

- Students share their likes and dislikes in French with each other or with students in other schools via notes, letters or e-mail.

- Students role play in French everyday situations, such as buying ice cream or ordering a beverage in a *café*.

- Students talk about and describe aspects of the francophone world, such as food, clothing, types of dwellings, modes of transportation, buildings, and monuments.

- Students ask and answer questions in French about topics, such as family, school, animals, familiar objects, and possessions. These exchanges may be done in person or via notes, e-mail, or audio and video recordings.

Sample Progress Indicators, Grade 8

- Students use French with culturally appropriate gestures in everyday social situations, such as greeting, leave-taking or introductions.

- Students give and follow instructions in French related to daily classroom activities.

- Students engage in French role-play situations where they request and receive information, goods, and services, such as going to a restaurant and ordering food.

- Students share opinions, preferences, and feelings in French with their classmates.

- Students exchange information in French via notes, letters or e-mail on familiar topics, such as personal interests, memorable experiences, school activities, and family life.

- Students use French to discuss reading selections, songs, and videos from francophone cultures.

> **STUDENTS LEARN BY DOING, BY TRYING OUT LANGUAGE, AND BY MODIFYING IT TO SERVE COMMUNICATIVE NEEDS.**

Sample Progress Indicators, Grade 12

- Students use French to greet one another and engage in conversation about everyday topics, such as weather, friends, leisure activities, school, and family.

- Students use French to talk with classmates about past activities and future plans.

- Students use French to correspond with other teenagers via letter, e-mail, audio or video recordings on topics of mutual interest.

- Students exchange information in French via notes, letters or e-mail on familiar topics, such as personal interests, memorable experiences, school activities, and family life.

- Students share their opinions, via discussion or written exchanges in French, on what they have recently read or seen, such as articles, short stories, books, comics, movies or film clips, videos, music, and art, for example: Camara Laye's *L'enfant noir* (*The Black Child*) and the French-language films *Kirikou et la sorcière (Kirikou and the Sorceress)* and *La Grande Séduction (Seducing Dr. Lewis)*.

- Students engage in French role-play or participate in authentic situations where they clarify information, such as comparing transportation schedules with a clerk, or solve problems, such as exchanging an inappropriate item in a store.

- Students use French to discuss current issues or historical events, for example, presidential visits to francophone areas.

Sample Progress Indicators, Post-Secondary

- Students use French to greet one another and engage in conversation about everyday topics, such as weather, friends and family, studies, and university activities.

- Students use French to talk with classmates about past and future activities, such as weekend plans, vacation, jobs, and travel.

- Students use French to discuss topics pertinent to their personal and professional lives, such as career choices, goals, and aspirations.

- Students engage in French role-play or participate in real-life situations where they clarify information, such as reporting an incident to authorities, or solve problems, such as negotiating conditions for a part-time job.

- Students compare, contrast, and analyze in French their opinions on topical issues, such as recent films and current events.

- Students conduct interviews in French with individuals on personal, social, and professional topics, for example, Franco-African students' views of the American system of education.

- Students use French to discuss in groups social issues and problems, such as immigration, homelessness or unemployment.

- Students use French to analyze the social and philosophical ideas expressed in literature they are reading.

STANDARD 1.2 INTERPRETIVE COMMUNICATION
Students understand and interpret spoken and written French on a variety of topics.

This standard focuses on the understanding and interpretation of spoken and written French, that is, listening and reading comprehension. In the area of listening, students have a variety of opportunities to develop their comprehension ability, including following classroom instructions, listening to audio and video recordings, watching movies in French, attending concerts of francophone artists, and hearing guest speakers or lecturers. In addition, students of French have access to a wealth of authentic reading materials, including comic books, stories, poems, magazine and newspaper articles, novels, and plays, as well as electronic documents from the Internet.

Sample Progress Indicators, Grade 4

- Students follow oral instructions in French related to daily classroom activities.

- Students understand oral and/or written statements in French on familiar topics, such as numbers, time of day, and weather.

- Students read and/or listen in French to descriptions and identify the corresponding pictures or illustrations, such as people, animals, objects, places, common activities, weather, and time of day.

- Students understand familiar songs, poems, videos, stories and fairy tales in French, such as *Le Petit Chaperon Rouge* (*Little Red Riding Hood*).

- Students understand brief spoken or written French messages on familiar topics, such as personal preferences, family, school, and celebrations.

- Students understand the content of simple French-language realia, such as picture books, menus, posters or advertisements.

Sample Progress Indicators, Grade 8

- Students understand and follow oral and written directions in French related to daily classroom activities.

- Students understand spoken and written messages in French on topics of personal interest, such as family life, leisure and school activities, and everyday occurrences.

- Students understand and identify main ideas and principal characters in brief reading selections from francophone cultures.

- Students understand information from simple and accessible French-language materials, such as television programs, youth magazines, the Internet, and videos.

Sample Progress Indicators, Grade 12

- Students understand the main ideas and significant details of materials in French, which are accessible to teenage readers, such as magazine articles, short stories, poetry and short novels, for example, Bernard Dadié's short story *Le Pagne Noir* (*The Black Pagne*).

- Students understand the main ideas and significant details of level-appropriate spoken and recorded materials in French, such as songs, videos, commercials, interviews, and live presentations, for example, music by Youssou N'Dour, MC Solaar, King Daddy Yod, Isabelle Boulay, and Bénabar.

- Students understand information from French Internet sources on a variety of topics, for example, weather, current events, and sports.

- Students analyze the plots, characters, and themes in francophone literary works.

Sample Progress Indicators, Post-Secondary

- Students understand in French the main ideas and significant details of level-appropriate spoken and recorded materials, such as songs, videos, commercials, films, interviews, and live presentations.

- Students understand the important concepts presented in French in formal lectures or group discussions.

- Students understand in French the principal elements and main ideas of newspaper and magazine articles, as well as Internet pages, on current events and topics of general interest.

- Students read and analyze French-language literary works, such as poems, short stories, and novels.

- Students understand some French-language humor, such as jokes and plays on words.

STANDARD 1.3 PRESENTATIONAL COMMUNICATION
Students present information, concepts, and ideas in French on a variety of topics to an audience of listeners or readers.

This standard focuses on the presentation of information, concepts, and ideas in spoken and written French. This standard includes oral presentations, whether live or on video, and the writing of a variety of texts, ranging from captions, slogans, letters, and poems to longer stories and skits, articles, and essays.

Sample Progress Indicators, Grade 4

- Students dramatize French-language songs and poems, such as Amadou Sambé's poem *Tam Tam*.

- Students prepare and present in French short illustrated personal descriptions of topics, like their home or their family.

- Students prepare and present and/or record in French puppet shows, short skits, and simple plays based on familiar folktales and stories, such as *Les Trois Petits Cochons* (*The Three Little Pigs*).

- Students retell stories in oral or written French.

- Students prepare and contribute information in French for an audio or video exchange or for a Web page on topics, such as school and hobbies.

Sample Progress Indicators, Grade 8

- Students prepare and present short announcements in French, such as the current date, time, and weather information.

- Students prepare and present brief reports in French about personal experiences, school happenings, and current events.

- Students prepare, illustrate, and present materials in French, such as advertisements, posters, and menus.

- Students dramatize poems, stories, songs, skits or short plays in French, for example, a Franco-African folk tale.

- Students prepare and record original materials in French, such as puppet shows, fashion shows, Mardi Gras parades, and video or audio newscasts.

Sample Progress Indicators, Grade 12

- Students create and present skits or short plays in French on a variety of topics.

- Students prepare and present oral reports in French on topics of their choice.

- Students demonstrate and explain in French how to accomplish a task, such as making *crêpes* (thin pancakes) or traditional *couscous*, (semolina), decorating hands or feet with henna patterns, or playing *boules* (like bocci ball).

- Students give dramatic recitations in French of poems or prose excerpts, for example, René Philombe's poem *L'Homme qui te ressemble* (*The Man Who Looks Like You*).

- Students perform scenes from French-language plays, live or on video.

- Students summarize in French orally and/or in writing the content of materials they have read or seen, such as Mansour Sora Wade's film *Three Tales from Senegal* (from California Newsreel, San Francisco), Molière's plays, such as *Le Médecin malgré lui* (*The Doctor in Spite of Himself*), or the text, film or musical version of *Le Fantôme de l'Opéra* (*The Phantom of the Opera*).

- Students write original compositions and/or journal entries in French on topics of personal interest.

- Students create and disseminate a French newsletter or Web page.

- Students write and produce an original French-language video recording, such as a newscast, a talk show or a game show.

- Students analyze French-language literary works orally and/or in writing, such as selections from Lilyan Kesteloot's *Anthologie Négro-Africaine* (*Black African*

Anthology) or integral texts, such as Gide's *La Symphonie Pastorale* (*The Pastoral Symphony*).

Sample Progress Indicators, Post-Secondary

- Students participate in and perform scenes in French from plays and/or recite poems or excerpts from short stories.

- Students write original poems, song lyrics, stories, and/or pastiches of works by French authors.

- Students prepare a personal résumé in French and write a sample job application or other business letters.

- Students write and produce an original French-language video recording, such as a newscast, a talk show, or a game show.

- Students participate in a panel discussion where they review and critique a French movie, such as *L'Auberge espagnole* (*The Spanish Apartment*), *La Haine (Hate)*, *Les Glaneurs et la glaneuse* (*The Gleaners and I*), or *Keïta, L'Héritage du Griot (Keita, the Heritage of the Griot)*.

- Students evaluate, analyze, and critique in writing the content of an article or documentary intended for native French speakers, such as from the magazines *L'Express*, *Le Figaro Magazine*, *Jeune Afrique* or the newspaper *Le Journal de Québec*.

- Students prepare a written analysis of a French-language literary work.

Cultures   *Goal Two*
Gain Knowledge and Understanding of the Cultures of the Francophone World

The study of the French language enables students to understand diverse cultures of the world. It also prepares them to interact successfully with members of communities with a minimum of misunderstanding. As global proximity increases, American students need to develop a greater awareness of other peoples' worldviews, their way of life, and their patterns of behavior. They also need to recognize the significant contributions that French and other francophone cultures have made to world civilization. These include the early explorations of the North American continent, the philosophical writings which inspired the framers of the U.S. Constitution, the French literary tradition, which reached out to embrace writers from Africa, Asia, and the Americas, and the vision in all areas of endeavor that led to the development of products as varied as pasteurization, haute couture, French cuisine, supersonic jet planes, and high-speed trains.

Goal Two focuses on **cultural competence**, that is, the ability to understand francophone cultures, and, eventually, the ability to function in a culturally appropriate manner in a French-speaking milieu. In addition, Goal Two includes **humanistic aims**, which constitute one of the traditional objectives of French instruction. As part of their French curriculum,

> CULTURAL COMPETENCE IS THE ABILITY TO FUNCTION IN A MANNER CONSISTENT WITH THE PHILOSOPHICAL PERSPECTIVES AND THE SOCIAL PRACTICES OF A SOCIETY.

students arrive at a greater understanding of *la condition humaine* as reflected across the centuries and around the globe in francophone literature, art and philosophy, including such seminal themes as *liberté* and *négritude*.

The acquisition of knowledge and understanding of cultures depends on several key factors, including the ability to observe and analyze culture, and supports the development of empathy toward other peoples. The AATF Commission on Cultural Competence has created a framework for organizing and teaching culture entitled *Acquiring Cross-Cultural Competence: Four Stages for Students of French* (ISBN 0-8442-1784-0:NTC/Contemporary Publishing) (out of print), which further examines these issues and offers a system for organizing cultural information.

Within this standards document, the term "culture" is understood to include the philosophical perspectives, the social practices, and the products of a society.

> **PERSPECTIVES SPRING FROM THE VALUES, BELIEFS ATTITUDES, AND IDEAS OF A SOCIETY. THEY SUGGEST "WHY" AND ANTICIPATE "HOW" A SOCIETY ACTS.**

- The **perspectives** of a culture are derived from its values, beliefs, attitudes, and ideas. There is not a single "francophone culture" but rather many cultures, which embrace the French language as their means of expression and communication. In fact, each country, region or sub-group has its own philosophical perspectives and worldview. The interrelationship of ideas and values helps to explain "why" and to anticipate "how" a particular culture will respond to events, problems, and questions. Since a given curriculum cannot include all of the francophone cultures, most programs focus on France plus several representative regions, such as Quebec, Cajun Louisiana, Haiti, and Senegal.

- The **practices** of a culture are seen in its patterns of social interaction and reflect the traditional ideas, beliefs, attitudes, and values (perspectives) of its people. Each country, region or sub-group has developed its own system of interpersonal interaction, which is reflected in conversational conventions, gestures, social etiquette, business and legal procedures, leisure activities, religious customs, and the like. In short, these forms of social behavior embody the knowledge of "what to do when and where." Some of these may be similar to American practices, while others may be quite different, giving rise to possible misunderstandings by those who do not know how to interpret them within their own cultural context.

- The **products** of a culture include concrete aspects of daily life, such as foods, clothing, types of housing, utensils, and inventions, as well as the concrete and abstract elements of social organization, found in educational, health, scientific, business, entertainment, recreational, and judicial institutions. Francophone cultures have provided the stimulus to produce many important scientific, technological, literary, and artistic achievements.

The above three aspects of culture are interwoven within the standards under this goal.

STANDARD 2.1 PRACTICES OF CULTURE
Students demonstrate an understanding of the relationship between the practices and perspectives of the cultures of the francophone world.

The first standard emphasizes *Social Interaction*. Students interpret francophone social patterns in terms of corresponding cultural values and attitudes and interact with speakers of

French in a culturally appropriate manner. It focuses on cultural practices that reflect the traditions, beliefs, and structures of societies.

Sample Progress Indicators, Grade 4

- Students use appropriate gestures and French expressions for greetings, leave-takings, and common classroom interactions.

- Students participate in age-appropriate cultural activities such as games, songs, dances, celebrations, story telling, dramatizations, or computer games.

- Students identify social customs that are of interest to children; topics may include traditional foods, aspects of family life, and typical holidays in various francophone regions.

Sample Progress Indicators, Grade 8

- Students observe and use age-appropriate French verbal and nonverbal greetings in conversational exchanges.

- Students learn about and participate in activities enjoyed by young French-speaking people, such as games, sports, music, dance, drama, and celebrations.

- Students identify the similarities and differences between school life in their own region and in one or more francophone regions.

- Students recognize and develop an awareness of the diversity of social customs in the French-speaking world; topics may include family life, folklore, and typical holidays, such as Christmas, New Year's or Ramadan.

- Students discuss generalizations that Americans may make about the people and customs of francophone cultures, such as "All French people wear berets," "French-Canadians all play hockey," "and "Africans all dress in colorful native robes."

Sample Progress Indicators, Grade 12

- Students learn about and participate in activities enjoyed by French-speaking teenagers, such as sports (World Cup Soccer and the *Tour de France*), music, games, and entertainment.

- Students interact in a culturally appropriate manner with French-speaking people of various backgrounds in a variety of contexts, such as welcoming guest speakers or exchange students, participating in field trips or studying abroad.

- Students watch movies, commercials or documentaries from the francophone world and identify typical cultural patterns and social behaviors that they see on the screen.

- Students analyze social, economic, geographic, and historical factors that affect cultural practices in various francophone cultures, such as weddings, family celebrations, gender roles, education, social and governmental institutions, and religious observances, e.g., dress codes for adolescent girls and women in Muslim countries.

Sample Progress Indicators, Post-Secondary

- Students interact in a culturally appropriate manner with people of various francophone backgrounds in a variety of contexts, such as interacting with exchange students, hosting guest speakers or participating in work and study abroad programs.

AWARENESS OF CULTURAL PRACTICES HELPS US KNOW "WHAT TO DO WHEN AND WHERE."

- Students learn about and participate in cultural practices characteristic of various regions of the francophone world, such as preparing typical foods, attending musical and theatrical performances, and participating in sports events.

- Students examine and discuss connections between cultural perspectives and behavioral patterns typical of various cultures as seen in French-language films and videos, for example, *La Promesse* (*The Promise*) (Belgium), *Les Choristes* (*The Chorus*) (France), *Le Fabuleux Destin d'Amélie Poulain* (*Amélie*) (France), and *Les Invasions barbares* (*The Barbarian Invasions*) (Quebec).

STANDARD 2.2 PRODUCTS OF CULTURE
Students demonstrate an understanding of the relationship between the products and perspectives of the cultures of the francophone world.

PRODUCTS OF CULTURE MAY BE THE OBJECTS FOUND IN DAILY LIFE. THEY MAY ALSO BE THE CONCRETE AND ABSTRACT ELEMENTS IMBEDDED IN A SOCIETY'S ACHIEVEMENTS AND ITS ORGANIZATION OF GOODS AND SERVICES.

The second standard focuses on *Cultural Appreciation*. Students learn to interpret the many varied products of francophone civilizations, such as music, films, literary texts, architecture, and inventions, in terms of underlying cultural values and attitudes. This standard focuses on the cultural products of francophone areas of the world and how they relate to the traditions, beliefs, and structures of the society.

Sample Progress Indicators, Grade 4

- Students identify and recognize products and symbols of the francophone world, such as foods, clothing, types of dwellings, modes of transportation, flags, and famous monuments.

- Students recognize and experience or interact with the products of francophone cultures, such as children's songs (*Frère Jacques*), children's videos, and selections from children's literature (*Babar*) and comic strips (Titeuf).

- Students identify age-appropriate folk art and crafts typical of francophone cultures, and, where appropriate, produce similar pieces, such as Mardi Gras or African masks.

Sample Progress Indicators, Grade 8

- Students identify and learn about products reflecting the lifestyle of people in various francophone communities, such as household items, clothing, and foods.

- Students identify the general characters and themes of French-language comic books, for example, Spirou, Tintin, and Lucky Luke, and youth magazines, such as *Okapi*.

- Students listen to music and watch French-language films or television programs that are popular with young people in various parts of the world.

- Students learn about and recognize artistic contributions from francophone cultures in areas such as art, music, dance, drama, theater, film, fashion, and cuisine.

- Students learn about and identify major scientific contributions from France and other francophone areas of the world, such as the development of pasteurization.

Sample Progress Indicators, Grade 12

- Students identify and explore the function of everyday products from the francophone world, such as food, clothing, household items, tools, sports equipment, and musical instruments.

- Students identify the general themes of music and recognize performers, such as Patricia Kaas, Corneille, Lara Fabian, Baaba Maal, Boubacar Traoré, and Renaud, films, and television programs that are popular among teenagers in various parts of the francophone world.

- Students identify the characters, themes, and perspectives in French-language comic books, for example, Astérix and Tintin, and teen magazines, such as *Pilote* and *Phosphore*.

- Students view films from and about parts of the francophone world and pick out representative cultural products, for example, chocolate, lace, textiles, masks, jewelry, timepieces, perfume, dolls, and musical instruments.

- Students discuss and analyze various artistic products of francophone regions, such as theater and dance performances, novels and poetry, sculpture and painting, cinema, and crafts.

- Students explore social, economic, political, scientific, and religious institutions of francophone cultures and learn how they reflect the values of the people.

- Students identify major French historical, political, and scientific contributions to world civilization, such as the plan for the unification of Europe, the Napoleonic Code, Braille, high speed trains, and telephone cards with computer chips.

Sample Progress Indicators, Post-Secondary

- Students discuss and analyze concrete products that reflect daily life in various regions of the francophone world, such as foods, dwellings, transportation, and leisure activities.

- Students listen to music and view films from France and other parts of the francophone world and identify cultural values and perspectives, for example, Ousmane Sembene's *Faat Kine* (from California Newsreel).

- Students view current French-language television programs, such as newscasts or morning variety shows (available via SCOLA or TV5) and note the types of topics that are emphasized and the cultural perspectives they reveal.

- Students identify, discuss and analyze the contributions of the francophone world in the domains of literature, the arts, technology, and science.

- Students discuss and analyze the social, political, and educational institutions in francophone areas of the world.

- Students identify, analyze, evaluate, and compare themes, ideas, and perspectives related to the products of francophone cultures in light of the student's own culture, leisure time, after school or work activities, and family and personal responsibilities.

- Students read and discuss current articles found through the Internet or in print from leading periodicals or newspapers of francophone countries and analyze the perspectives suggested by the author or the publication.

Connections *Goal Three*
Use French to Connect with Other Disciplines and Expand Knowledge

Goal Three encourages students to use their French communication skills, developed under Goal One, and their cultural understanding of the world, developed under Goal Two, as a way of broadening knowledge. This goal recognizes that "knowledge is power" and that people who can use a second language to acquire information will be better equipped to function in the world of the twenty-first century. When the study of French is connected to other disciplines, students' learning expands beyond a limited focus on language acquisition to encompass a broader and more enriching educational sphere.

The interdisciplinary activities related to this goal help students identify and use information available to them in French. In addition to getting information from human resources, students consult print resources, such as encyclopedias, books, magazines, and newspapers, as well as other media, radio, television, film, CD-ROMs, and the Internet.

The Connections Goal includes two standards. The first encourages the building of connections between French and other disciplines. The second focuses on using French to acquire information.

KNOWLEDGE OF FRENCH CAN BUILD TWO-WAY CONNECTIONS WITH OTHER DISCIPLINES.

STANDARD 3.1 MAKING CONNECTIONS
Students reinforce and further their knowledge of other disciplines through French.

In this standard, students use French to learn more about other subject areas, either within the French language class or in French immersion courses. Students are also encouraged to use French as a tool to access additional resources linked to other courses they are taking and to integrate the information acquired in French into these other courses.

As schools and colleges become increasingly committed to an interdisciplinary approach to education, French teachers are well placed to integrate a broad range of disciplines into their programs. Within the French classroom it is natural to introduce topics such as geography, history, art, music or science. In immersion programs, French is the medium of instruction for all disciplines in the curriculum.

Sample Progress Indicators, Grade 4

- Students demonstrate in French an understanding of basic concepts they are learning in other classes, such as weather, math facts, simple measurements, and plant and animal life.

- Students expand their understanding of topics studied in other classes by making comparisons in French, such as comparing climate in their own area and in francophone parts of the world.

- Students expand their knowledge, through French, of other subject areas, such as social studies, by learning the names and locations of major countries.

Sample Progress Indicators, Grade 8

- Students discuss topics from other school subjects in French, such as geographical information, math facts and measurements (conversions to and from the metric system), weather and other scientific phenomena, and historical facts and highlights.

- Students understand simple articles or video segments in French on topics from other school subjects, such as social studies (French exploration, World War II), fine arts (Monet, Debussy, Le Corbusier, and African masks), and science (Madame Curie).

- Students present reports in French, either orally and/or in writing, on topics being studied in other classes.

- Students expand their information in other subject areas, such as geography, by studying the geographical features of France and other francophone countries.

Sample Progress Indicators, Grade 12

- Students broaden their awareness of other disciplines by expanding topics presented in their French classes: a reading of Saint-Exupéry's *Le Petit Prince* (*The Little Prince*), can lead to a study of early airmail routes between France, Africa, and South America.

- Students discuss in French topics from other school subjects, such as fine arts (impressionism), history (French Revolution, colonialism, and post-colonialism), worldwide health issues (AIDS), and environmental concerns (pollution).

- Students present reports in French, orally and/or in writing, on topics being studied in other classes.

Sample Progress Indicators, Postsecondary

- Students broaden their awareness of other disciplines by expanding on topics presented in their French classes: a reading of Camus' *L'Etranger* (*The Stranger*) can lead to a study of the French colonial presence in North Africa.

- Students discuss in French topics from other college courses such as history, political science, sociology, philosophy, art, and music.

- Students, as part of their French coursework, expand their knowledge about the countries and communities of the francophone world (Belgium, Switzerland, Quebec, Indochina, North Africa, West Africa, and the Caribbean).

STANDARD 3.2 ACQUIRING INFORMATION
Students acquire information and recognize the distinctive viewpoints that are only available through the French language and francophone cultures.

In this standard, students use their French-language skills to acquire new information and discover new cultural perspectives. This may occur within the school setting or in conjunction with work and leisure activities.

As students develop their French skills, they acquire new perspectives on language and culture. By knowing French, they significantly expand the sources of information available to them. They can talk with French speakers. They can discover the contributions of French writers, philosophers, and scientists to world civilization. Moreover, they can take advantage of the extensive French-language resources available on the Internet.

Sample Progress Indicators, Grade 4

- Students look at illustrations in French-language children's books that show views of people and places in the world.

- Students listen to and sing French-language folksongs that introduce them to aspects of the world, for example, *Sur le pont d'Avignon*.

- Students read, listen to, and talk about works of children's literature created by native speakers of French, such as folktales, poems, picture books, and videos.

Sample Progress Indicators, Grade 8

- Students read, listen to, and talk about French-language folk tales, short stories, and poems that have been written for young people.

- Students visit a local museum or consult art books to see how artists from francophone areas portray their country and fellow citizens, for example, Haitian landscapes, masks from the Ivory Coast, portraits by Gauguin, and scenes by Watteau.

- Students gather information from authentic French materials, such as books, newspapers, magazines or the Internet, to create short reports on topics of interest, such as the *Tour de France*, a cycling competition.

- Students interview French speakers in their community about their childhood on topics such as family life, school, hobbies, and leisure activities.

Sample Progress Indicators, Grade 12

- Students search for answers from French sources to questions encountered in school subjects or through their favorite leisure activities on the Internet and through the print and visual media.

- Students read a variety of French-language sources, such as magazines, encyclopedias, and Internet sites, to prepare reports on topics of personal interest.

- Students acquire information from French-language sources about topics being studied in other classes, such as French exploration in the New World, the American Revolution, American Impressionists in France, the French views of visitors to the United States, such as de Tocqueville, and post-colonialism in francophone Africa or Indochina.

- Students interact in a culturally appropriate manner with French-speaking people of various backgrounds in a variety of contexts, such as welcoming guest speakers or exchange students, participating in field trips or studying abroad.

- Students understand the distinctive viewpoints expressed in French-language literary works that they are reading, such as Voltaire's *Candide*, Duras' *Moderato Cantabile*, Corneille's *Le Cid*, Sartre's *Les Jeux sont faits* (*The Die is Cast*), Chraïbi's *La Civilisation, ma mère* (*Civilization, My Mother*).

THROUGH FRENCH, STUDENTS GAIN ACCESS TO NEW INFORMATION.

Sample Progress Indicators, Post-Secondary

- Students find information on research topics assigned in other college classes from a variety of French-language sources, such as newscasts from SCOLA or TV5, encyclopedias and other print resources, and documentary films.

- Students carry out research on francophone cultures using contemporary French-language sources, such as newspapers, journal articles, books, films, documentaries, and/or Internet sites.

- Students understand the distinctive viewpoints expressed in French-language literary works, such as Flaubert's *Madame Bovary* or Bâ's *Une si longue lettre* (*Such a Long Letter*).

- Students interview French speakers in the community to gain insights into sociological and cultural issues, such as life in France during World War II, the Quebec separatist movement, and problems faced by Haitian immigrants.

Comparisons Goal Four
Develop Insight into the Nature of Language and Culture

As American students learn how the French language works, they come to understand new linguistic and grammatical concepts. While striving to express themselves in French, they gain greater awareness of the nature of language itself. For example, students often begin their study of French with the assumption that all languages are like their own. Soon they encounter linguistic elements, such as gender and subject-verb agreement, that play a critical role in French but a much smaller role in English. They discover that spoken French and English use very different sound systems. They learn that a concept that is rendered by one word in one language, such as "window," might be rendered by several words in the other, such as *fenêtre*: window of a house; *vitrine*: shop window; and *guichet*: ticket window. One especially welcome outcome of the study of French is that students increase their English vocabulary since almost all the English words of Latin origin entered the language via French.

As students are introduced to francophone cultures and observe how they function, they begin to realize, for example, that what defines polite manners in one cultural system may be considered inappropriate in another. They discover the complexity of the interaction between language and culture. As a result of their French study, students develop a more open mind and make naive assumptions less often about other cultures, based solely upon their experience with American culture.

Goal 4 encourages students to expand their worldview, that is, their awareness of the multi-lingual and multi-ethnic nature of contemporary world society. These experiences invite a comparison of language and cultural systems. In turn, such comparisons enhance the students' ability to use French and allow them to gain insights into strategies used to communicate meaning in English. Linguistic observations and cultural comparisons are most effective when drawn from authentic texts and realia, such as, French-language magazines, newspapers, Internet sites, commercials, songs, television programs, and movies. Students whose first language is not English or who have studied another language and culture have additional resources for making comparisons among languages.

The Comparisons Goal includes two standards. The first standard focuses on linguistic diversity and the nature of language. The second emphasizes cultural diversity and the comparisons of cultures.

STANDARD 4.1 LANGUAGE COMPARISONS
Students demonstrate understanding of the nature of language through comparisons of French and their native language.

From their earliest classroom experiences, students find themselves comparing and contrasting French and English or another language as they learn to mimic new sounds and encounter a new spelling system. The teacher can build on this natural curiosity by encouraging classroom activities that help students understand how languages work. Students with knowledge of other languages and cultures besides French and English have an additional opportunity to consider linguistic and cultural similarities and differences.

BY COMPARING FRENCH AND ENGLISH, STUDENTS BEGIN TO APPRECIATE HOW LANGUAGES WORK.

Sample Progress Indicators, Grade 4

- Students demonstrate an awareness of formal and informal forms of greetings, leave-takings and expressions of politeness in French, such as *Bonjour!* vs. *Salut!* (Hello! vs. Hi!); *s'il vous plaît* vs. *s'il te plaît* (formal and informal *please*).

- Students cite examples of French words used in English, such as *croissant, boulevard,* and *garage,* and English words that are used in French, such as *le week-end, un test,* and *un hamburger.*

- Students show awareness of cognates by pairing similar French and English words, such as *la musique* vs. music, *horrible* vs. horrible, *la photo* vs. photo.

- Students identify differences and similarities between the sound and writing systems of English and French, such as the pronunciation of orange vs. *orange*; train vs. *train*; petit vs. *petit*, and telephone vs. le *téléphone*.

Sample Progress Indicators, Grade 8

- Students demonstrate an awareness of the use of *tu* and *vous* (you) in conversations with children vs. conversations with adults.

- Students recognize the existence of grammatical gender in French, and their spoken and written language reflects that awareness, such as *Il est français. Elle est française* (He/she is French).

- Students recognize cognates in French as well as idiomatic expressions that may or may not have exact English equivalents, such as *regarder* vs. look at, watch, regard.

- Students discover that English and French have their own critical sound distinctions that must be mastered to communicate meaning, such as *ship* vs. *sheep*; *rue* vs. *roue,* and that these are not the same in both languages.

- Students recognize differences in word order between French and English, for example *une maison rouge* vs. a red house.

Standards for the Learning of French

- Students demonstrate an awareness that linguistic expressions may differ in French and English, such as *J'ai une faim de loup.* vs. I'm as hungry as a bear.
- Students compare French grammatical structures to those of English, such as *la maison d'Anne* vs. Anne's house.

Sample Progress Indicators, Grade 12

- Students can recognize cognates and false cognates in French, such as *lecture* = reading, and not "lecture," *rester* = to remain and not "to rest."
- Students demonstrate an awareness of idiomatic phrases and linguistic expressions and realize that there is not a word-for-word correspondence between French and English, such as *Il m'a manqué.* = I missed him (He was lacking to me).
- Students recognize and compare nuances of meaning of words and idioms, in French and in English, such as *avoir froid, être froid, faire froid.*
- Students compare French and English linguistic elements, such as time, tense, and mood, and analyze how each language often uses different grammatical structures to express time and tense relationships, for example, "when" + present vs. *quand* + future, as in "When he arrives, he will come to see me." = *Quand il arrivera, il viendra me voir.*
- Students recognize that words in French and English may have different ranges of meaning, such as ball = *balle, ballon*; *ballon* = ball, balloon, or reflect distinctions that are not made in both languages, such as "the day" = *le jour* vs. *la journée.*
- Students recognize the relationship between word order in French and meaning, for example, *un pauvre homme* = a poor, unfortunate man vs. *un homme pauvre* = a poor man, without money.
- Students recognize and identify differences in pronunciation of French throughout the francophone world, for example, the Provençal accent in the film *Jean de Florette* and the West African accent in the film *Tableau Ferraille (Scrap Heap).*

Sample Progress Indicators, Post-Secondary

- Students are familiar with common French-English cognate patterns, and recognize false cognates, as well as words in the two languages that have different ranges of meaning, such as *grisé*, which corresponds not only to "tinted with gray" but also literally to "intoxicated," and figuratively, as in *grisé par le succès* (intoxicated by success).
- Students compare grammatical elements of French, such as tense, mode, and word order, with corresponding structures in English, such as *Ils venaient de finir.* = They had just finished.
- Students recognize that French and English have different ways of expressing feelings and emotional intensity, for example use of disjunctive pronouns in French vs. stressing pronouns in English by saying them more loudly: *Je l'ai vu, lui, mais il ne m'a pas vu.* = I saw HIM, but he didn't see me.
- Students are aware of how French and English use various verbal and written expressions in different social contexts to indicate levels of formality, such as informal

and formal ways of asking people to leave you a little room: *Pousse-toi!* vs. *Pourriez-vous me laisser un peu plus de place?* (Move over! vs. Would you kindly leave me a little more room?).

- Students recognize that just as there are differences between English as spoken in Great Britain and the United States, so are there differences between French as spoken in France and in other parts of the world, for example, *une boisson gazeuse* (soft drink) in France vs. *une liqueur douce* in Quebec.

STANDARD 4.2 CULTURAL COMPARISONS
Students demonstrate understanding of the nature of culture through comparisons of francophone cultures with their own.

As students expand their knowledge of francophone cultures, they discover that certain perspectives, practices, and products differ from those of American culture. With guidance, they develop the ability to hypothesize about cultural systems in general. At first, students will make these comparisons in English, and then, as they progress in their language study, they can express their cultural observations in French.

Sample Progress Indicators, Grade 4

- Students compare common American patterns of interaction with those of francophone societies, such as the French use of handshakes and *bises* (kisses) for greetings and leave-takings.

- Students realize that gestures are an important part of communication and that gestures may differ in French and English, such as when counting on one's fingers, French people begin with the thumb whereas Americans begin with the index finger.

- Students compare and contrast American children's products, such as toys, games, and clothing, with those of francophone cultures.

- Students compare and contrast English folk tales with their counterparts in francophone cultures, for example, Kipling's *How the Leopard Got its Spots,* and animal legends from Niger, such as *Pourquoi l'araignée tisse sa toile* (*Why the Spider Spins Her Web*).

Sample Progress Indicators, Grade 8

- Students compare aspects of French and American daily life, such as school schedules, weekend activities, and vacations.

- Students watch videos of young Francophones and contrast their verbal and nonverbal behavior patterns with the way American young people would act and react in similar situations.

- Students learn about holidays in France and other francophone countries and compare them to American holidays in terms of how they are celebrated and the underlying beliefs.

- Students compare and contrast French-language and American proverbs.

Sample Progress Indicators, Grade 12

- Students research topics of personal interest using a variety of French-language sources, such as sports and teen magazines, radio, video, the Internet, and catalogs, and compare the information they find to that which is available to them on the same topics in English.

- Students hypothesize about the origins of idioms as reflections of culture, citing examples from French language and francophone cultures and their own, such as *un tien pour toi* (Democratic Republic of the Congo: your own for you) = *un pourboire* (a tip); *Elle a mis papier dans sa tête* (Ivory Coast: She put paper in her head.) = *Elle a reçu de l'instruction.* (She was educated.); and *bon comme du pain* (France: good as bread) = good as gold;

- Students identify products of francophone areas, such as Moroccan leather goods, North African rugs, and mineral water or wine from France, and learn what cultural roles these products play.

- Students compare and contrast francophone and American cultural practices in areas such as popular sports (soccer and American football) or national holidays, for example, *le premier mai* (May Day) vs. Labor Day.

- Students compare and contrast the American view of some aspect of daily life, such as meals or the importance of education, with the view of a francophone area. For example, in North and West Africa, sharing a communal meal from one bowl is customary, whereas this practice is infrequent in the United States.

- Students identify and analyze the cultural perspectives reflected in a literary selection, film or work of art from a francophone country and compare these to the perspectives found in a corresponding American work, for example, *Le Petit Prince* (*The Little Prince*) and *ET*.

Sample Progress Indicators, Post-Secondary

- Students compare and contrast familiar products of American culture with their counterparts from French-speaking societies, for example, menus from an American fast-food chain and its French counterpart, or American and French rap.

- Students compare American cultural manifestations in a variety of artistic domains with those of a francophone region, such as the arts section of a major American newspaper with its equivalent in Casablanca, Dakar, Geneva, Paris or Quebec.

- Students compare their own body language and gestures with what they observe in contemporary films from francophone countries.

- Students study contemporary magazines and films to compare and contrast lifestyles of the various francophone peoples with their own lifestyle.

- Students compare and contrast the cultural components of popular French films and their American remakes, for example, *Trois Hommes et un Couffin* (*Three Men and a Cradle*) vs. *Three Men and a Baby*, *Le Retour de Martin Guerre* (*The Return of Martin Guerre*) vs. *Sommersby*, *La Cage aux folles* (*Birds of a Feather*) vs. *The Birdcage*, and *Nikita* vs. *Point of No Return*.

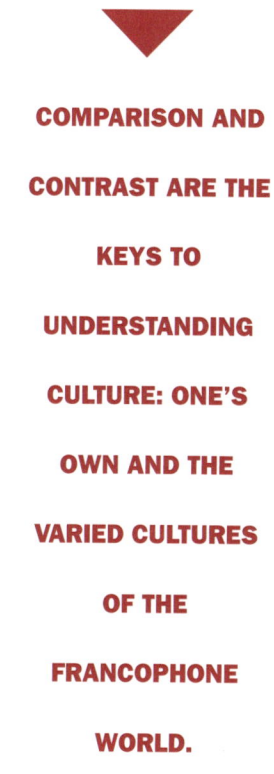

COMPARISON AND CONTRAST ARE THE KEYS TO UNDERSTANDING CULTURE: ONE'S OWN AND THE VARIED CULTURES OF THE FRANCOPHONE WORLD.

Communities
Goal Five
Use French to Participate in Communities at Home and Around the World

The acquisition of French becomes meaningful if students are motivated to seek other opportunities to use their language skills and cultural knowledge once they leave the classroom.

Goal Five focuses on **practical applications** of the students' French communication skills outside the classroom, in the world of work and politics, as well as in travel and leisure activities. Through their ability to use the French language and their knowledge of cultures, students are better able to appreciate and communicate with visitors or immigrant groups in the United States. Furthermore, they can interact with communities around the world: in North America and Europe, as well as in Africa, the Caribbean, Asia, and the South Pacific. Even those students who have little opportunity to travel can broaden their leisure-time activities by watching French-language movies, following the *Tour de France* on television or eating at French, Cajun, Haitian, and Vietnamese restaurants.

The Communities Goal includes two standards. The first standard emphasizes using one's French skills beyond the classroom, while the second focuses on ways in which French language and culture can enrich one's personal life.

STANDARD 5.1 SCHOOL AND COMMUNITY
Students use French both within and beyond the school setting.

Whereas Goal One focuses on the acquisition of French communication skills, this standard goes a giant step farther and asks students to use the language they have learned in the world around them: at school, in the workplace, in the community, and in their travels.

This standard encourages students to share their knowledge of French and the cultures of the world with classmates and with younger students who may be learning the language. By applying what they have learned in their French classes, students realize the advantages inherent in being able to communicate in more than one language, and they develop an understanding of the power of language. This standard becomes particularly meaningful when students have the opportunity to visit French-speaking communities and travel to francophone regions.

Through career exploration projects and internships at home or abroad, students come to recognize how ability to communicate in French and sensitivity to cultures can enhance future employment opportunities. As students have occasion to use French in response to real-world needs, they seek out situations in which they may apply their competencies beyond the school setting.

Sample Progress Indicators, Grade 4

- Students perform songs, poetry, stories, skits or plays in French for a classroom, school or community event.

- Students retell familiar stories or create and illustrate stories in French to present to others.

BY KNOWING FRENCH, STUDENTS CAN INTERACT WITH COMMUNITIES AROUND THE WORLD — IN NORTH AMERICA, THE CARIBBEAN, EUROPE, AFRICA, ASIA, AND THE SOUTH PACIFIC.

- Students communicate in French through letters, e-mail, and audio and video recordings with elementary school students in other French classes or in schools in francophone regions of the world.

Sample Progress Indicators, Grade 8

- Students perform in French for a school or community cultural event.
- Students teach French-language songs and simple conversational expressions to students at a local elementary school.
- Students participate in French Club activities which benefit the school or community.
- Students talk about topics of mutual interest with exchange students from French-speaking regions.
- Students use French in a setting in the community, such as ordering food in a French restaurant.
- Students communicate in French through letters, e-mail, and audio and video recordings with students around the world.
- Students participate in an extended French immersion experience, such as an immersion weekend or a French-language camp.
- Students travel with their family or class to a francophone region and use French to communicate and obtain services.

Sample Progress Indicators, Grade 12

- Students discuss in French topics of mutual interest with exchange students.
- Students participate in a career exploration or school-to-work project that requires proficiency in the French language and knowledge of francophone cultures.
- Students, either individually or as a class, exchange information in French by letter or e-mail, by video or audio recording with peers in French-speaking areas on topics of personal interest, community or world concern.
- Students stage a French-language play or create a comedy routine in French as part of a school/community event or for a local TV station.
- Students interview French-speaking members of the community or use other French resources to research topics of interest, such as World War II experiences and the Haitian immigrant experience.
- Students participate in an extended French immersion experience, such as an immersion weekend or a French-language camp.
- Students travel with their family or class to a francophone country and use French to communicate with others and to obtain services.

Sample Progress Indicators, Post-Secondary

- Students interview French-speaking members of the university or the local community regarding cross-cultural differences and/or topics of mutual interest.
- Students use French-language resources in the university or community to research topics of personal interest.

Standards for the Learning of French

- Students use French to tutor other students or to assist students from abroad to integrate into the college or university.
- Students provide French language services in the community, such as translating at a hospital or airport.
- Students spend a semester or year in a French-speaking university.
- Students participate in a career exploration and/or talk with members of the community who have jobs where French proficiency is an asset.
- Students do an internship in a francophone country or in an American company which employs people with French-language skills.

FRENCH CAN TRANSPORT THE LEARNER BEYOND THE CLASSROOM AND INTO THE WORKPLACE AND THE GLOBAL COMMUNITY.

STANDARD 5.2 LIFELONG LEARNING
Students show evidence of becoming lifelong learners by using French for personal enjoyment and enrichment.

Through French, students discover the richness of the francophone world and expand their recreational and entertainment options. As lifelong learners, students can use French to access information about topics of personal interest. Some students may travel to French-speaking communities or countries and, through this experience, further develop their language skills and their understanding of francophone cultures. Others may be encouraged to meet and interact with French speakers who live in their own geographic area.

Sample Progress Indicators, Grade 4

- Students play sports or games or other social activities typical of the francophone world, such as soccer or *la marelle* (hopscotch).
- Students listen to music from the francophone world, sing songs in French or play musical instruments from various francophone cultures.
- Students watch French-language videos or cartoons for enjoyment.
- Students help prepare and sample typical foods from the francophone world, such as *mousse au chocolat* (chocolate mousse), *couscous*, and *fondue*.
- Students attend a children's play or puppet show, performed in French.
- Students participate in francophone celebrations, such as a *Mardi Gras* costume party at the local *Alliance Française*, an international French organization that sponsors educational and cultural programs.

Sample Progress Indicators, Grade 8

- Students participate in sports, games or other French social and cultural activities.
- Students listen to music, sing songs, and become familiar with musical instruments representative of francophone cultures.
- Students attend a French play, movie or concert.
- Students plan a real or imaginary trip to a francophone area and share their experience with others.

Standards for the Learning of French

- Students read French comics or magazines for personal enjoyment.
- Students go to a local restaurant and order from a French-English menu, sampling the cuisine from francophone areas of the world, such as Quebec, France, Haiti, and Vietnam.
- Students visit exhibits at local museums that present aspects of the francophone world.
- Students explore French Internet sites for personal entertainment and enjoyment.

Sample Progress Indicators, Grade 12

- Students enjoy sports or games typical of francophone countries, either as participants or as spectators.
- Students listen to music, sing songs or play musical instruments from areas of the francophone world.
- Students establish contacts with other French speakers, such as members of the community, exchange students, and Internet users.
- Students participate in French cultural events and social activities, such as films, plays, concerts or activities at the local *Alliance Française*.
- Students read French-language magazines or watch French-language films and videos for entertainment and personal growth.
- Students visit exhibits at local museums that present aspects of the francophone world.
- Students explore French Internet sites for personal entertainment and enjoyment.
- Students with their class or with their families go to restaurants featuring the cuisine of francophone areas of the world.
- Students spend vacation time in a francophone area of the world.

Sample Progress Indicators, Post-Secondary

- Students read books, magazines, and newspapers, watch films or videos, and listen to music from the francophone world for personal entertainment.
- Students attend French-language cultural events and social activities sponsored by student groups or local communities.
- Students invite their friends to restaurants featuring the cuisine of francophone areas of the world.
- Students establish interpersonal relations with speakers of French, such as others in the community, foreign students, and contacts made through the Internet.
- Students explore French Internet sites for personal entertainment and enjoyment.
- Students spend vacation time in a francophone area of the world, doing volunteer work, participating in a business internship, traveling, studying or relaxing.

▼

KNOWING FRENCH INCREASES THE OPTIONS FOR RECREATION, ENRICHMENT, AND ENTERTAINMENT.

French Learning Scenarios

The following learning scenarios are activities designed for the elementary, middle school, high school, and post-secondary French classroom, which describe how particular standards might be met. They are examples which teachers can use as models or as inspiration for learning scenarios that they will create for their own students. They provide a window whereby teachers and administrators can see how the *Standards for the Learning of French* have already been put into practice in schools and universities across the country. These scenarios do not specify a particular methodology or indicate how the students have been learning the French language, although language learning is clearly the basis on which the standards are founded. Rather, they show how students at various ages and at various stages in their language instruction are able to use French to meet one or more of the standards under the five goals of Communication, Cultures, Connections, Comparisons, and Communities.

By design, the order for the presentation of the French learning scenarios is alphabetical and not by level of instruction. While each scenario identifies students by class level, practitioners will want to consider how they might apply or modify any scenario for their own students, whatever the level of the original scenario. No reader should assume that the level identified is the only level at which the learning scenario can effectively be used. Some scenarios that describe what post-secondary students do may also accurately reflect what some high school programs already include in their curriculum. By reading the "Reflection" following each scenario, teachers will consider ideas for expansion of the original scenarios and be encouraged to create their own applications. Whenever a scenario specifies a particular city, region, holiday or event, readers can also substitute other options. These learning scenarios are examples of activities that are already being done in French classes to meet standards. Given the uniqueness of each student learning situation, one cannot expect that each scenario will be replicated exactly in every classroom or on every campus. Indeed, that is the nature of a sample; a sample provides a potential model, which can be recast by each teacher to meet other standards and to match the level of the learners. The function of the learning scenarios is to serve not as the absolute model but as an illustration that will engender reflection, creativity, planning, and implementation of new learning scenarios.

Because of space limitations, this document can present only a limited number of learning scenarios selected from among the many samples received by the Task Force from French teachers in response to the requests made in the *AATF National Bulletin* and at the AATF web site. Those included here are all based on real classroom situations. The descriptions have been edited and reworked to fit the style and format of this handbook. In some instances, similar scenarios received from two or more teachers have been merged into a single text. The names of all those who contributed to these scenarios are listed in this document.

It is the intention of the AATF National Commission on Student Standards to make additional learning scenarios available to French teachers via the Internet, as well as in future publications of the AATF Materials Center. Information as to their availability will be published in the *AATF National Bulletin* and posted on the AATF web site: http://frenchteachers.org.

LEARNING SCENARIOS DESCRIBE HOW TEACHERS ARE DESIGNING ACTIVITES TO MEET PARTICULAR STANDARDS.

LES ACTIONS: FRENCH INVESTMENTS (high school)

As part of their second semester Business French curriculum, students in a combined fourth/fifth year high school class become investors in a simulated stock market. Students are divided into pairs, and each team is given an imaginary $100,000 to invest in stocks of one or more of the ten French companies regularly listed in *The New York Times*. First, the students convert their dollars to euros, at the official rate, and then they constitute their portfolios. Next, every two weeks, the teams spend twenty minutes discussing how their holdings are doing and buying and selling a portion of their stocks. In the course of the term, each team researches one of the companies and reports to the rest of the class. On a given date at the end of the term, the teams all sell their holdings and reconvert the euros into dollars to determine who has made the best investments.

TARGETED STANDARDS
1.1 Interpersonal Communication
1.2 Interpretive Communication
2.2 Products of Culture
3.1 Making Connections
3.2 Acquiring Information

Reflection
1.1 Students use French with their partners as they discuss investments and prepare reports.
1.2 Students read French newspapers, financial statements, and Internet sources on the various companies.
2.2 Students identify and become acquainted with leading French companies.
3.1 Students expand their knowledge of international business and currency exchange rates.
3.2 Students use French sources, such as those found on the Internet or in French newspapers, to acquire information on French companies.

This scenario generates great enthusiasm as teams of students compete to see who will realize the most "profits" by the end of the term. It could also be readily adapted to a post-secondary language course. French nationals from local businesses with a French connection or business people from multinational corporations with a French interest could serve as guest speakers on business or business culture topics. To expand the topic, students could research and compare French and American business practices and ethics by reading Polly Platt's *French or Foe: Getting the Most out of Living and Working in France* (Cultural Crossing) or the French version, *Ils sont fous les Français* (The French Are Crazy) (Bayard Press).

LES ACTUALITÉS: A FRENCH NEWSCAST (post-secondary)

Students in a college intermediate French class prepare and film their own news broadcast, *Les actualités*. First, they view televised news broadcasts from France or Quebec and compare and contrast American and French or Canadian news broadcasts. As preparation for their own project, students are assigned to play roles and/or participate in the preparation of various segments of the program, for example, news anchor, sportscaster, weather person, traffic reporter, film critic, restaurant reviewer, traffic reporter, "celebrity" interviewer, and advertising spots. The first assignment is the preparation of the scripts. These are corrected and returned, and students are encouraged to rehearse by recording their texts in the laboratory. One class day is then devoted to

TARGETED STANDARDS
1.1 Interpersonal Communication
1.2 Interpretive Communication
1.3 Presentational Communication
4.2 Cultural Comparisons
5.1 School and Community

Standards for the Learning of French

a "dry run" of the program, and a subsequent day is devoted to the filming. Students are evaluated on their first assignment, their rewrite of the errors noted, their production of French in the assigned role, and the group's final product, their video. If several sections of intermediate French each prepare their own programs, these can be performed for an evening of entertainment with the French Club.

Reflection

1.1 Students discuss with one another in French how to put together the program.
1.2 Students listen to authentic news broadcasts in French and to one another's presentations during the filming, and then view the final video.
1.3 Students present a news segment in French.
4.2 Students compare American news broadcasts with French or French-Canadian news broadcasts.
5.1 The newscast video is shown to friends, parents, and other students at the university.

Students bring tremendous creativity and enthusiasm to this project. The journalism students help frame the filming, the art students produce marvelous backdrops and graphics, and the theater students show creativity in developing the "advertisements" and public service announcements. The ultimate reward, of course, is the final product: all students bring their own blank videotapes or DVDs to have the audio-visual department copy the class result.

TARGETED STANDARDS
1.2 Interpretative Communication
1.3 Presentational Communication
2.2 Products of Culture
3.1 Making Connections
4.2 Cultural Comparisons
5.2 Lifelong Learning

L'ART HAÏTIEN: NAÏF ART IN HAITI (middle school)

Haitian art, in its *naïf* style, depicts daily life in the Caribbean. The teacher of a middle school French class frequently uses scenes from Haitian paintings to teach common vocabulary, such as city and country, transportation, parts of the body, colors, sizes, and daily activities. Using books found in the library, students in pairs take turns looking at the illustrations and selecting a favorite painting. They then present their painting to the class, describing the scene in simple terms in French. Using the paintings the students have selected in juxtaposition with American scenes by Grandma Moses, the teacher asks the students to compare and to contrast life in the two countries as seen through the eyes of the artists. Using contemporary photos of Haiti, students compare the scenes with the art representations. Finally the students, with the help of the art teacher, make their own *naïf* paintings, in the Haitian style, to show scenes of their own daily activities. The students then present their paintings to the class.

Reflection

1.2 Students listen to and understand descriptions of Haitian art in French.
1.3 Students make oral presentations in French about a Haitian painting of their choice and about their own paintings.
2.2 Students learn about Haitian art and how it reflects the perspectives of the culture.
3.1 Students find out information about Haiti and its people.

4.2 Students compare and contrast *naïf* art and painting created by Haitian artists to the paintings done by an American *naïf* artist. They also compare and contrast scenes created by artists with contemporary scenes of Haiti in photographs.

5.2 Students develop an interest in *naïf* art and painting.

Haitian art can be introduced into French classes at all levels. The colorful scenes combine culture with the learning of daily life vocabulary and basic structures.

LE CONCERT: A LIVE CONCERT (middle school)

Seventh grade students had the opportunity to experience French outside of the school setting when they went on an evening field trip to a neighboring university to attend a concert given by two folk-singers, Gifrantz from Haiti and Eric Vincent from France. The students were delighted to be able to understand familiar words and to sing along with the audience (*Au revoir, mon ami, au revoir!* (Goodbye, my friend, goodbye!) and *Oui, j'aime ça!* (Yes, I like that!)). After the concert they had their programs autographed and exchanged greetings in French with the artists. They were all delighted with their ability to speak with "real live" French speakers. As a follow-up the students marked on world maps all of the countries mentioned in the songs: Haiti, Brazil, Mexico, Madagascar, Reunion, and the Ivory Coast. The teacher was able to purchase an Eric Vincent videocassette of songs with captions that enabled the students to learn many of the lyrics.

> **TARGETED STANDARDS**
> 1.1 Interpersonal Communication
> 1.2 Interpretive Communication
> 2.2 Products of Culture
> 3.1 Making Connections
> 5.1 School and Community

Reflection

1.1 Students communicate with the French singers, and they talk about the songs in class.
1.2 Students listen to authentic French-language songs and find they can understand familiar words and phrases.
2.2 Students become acquainted with music from Haiti and France.
3.1 Students expand their knowledge of world geography in French.
5.1 Students communicate with French speakers outside the school setting.

This scenario shows how a field trip, which was originally organized to build enthusiasm by giving students the opportunity to experience French as real language, became a springboard for additional classroom activities during which they could strengthen their language skills by practicing French-language songs and learn some geography. Because the students were able to thank the singers in person and ask for autographs, they also had the opportunity to communicate with French speakers.

Once students have learned the lyrics to a recorded song, they could perform a "lip-synch" while dramatizing the composition on video. Either a live version or a music video of "Putting on the Hits" could be performed for classmates, parents or a community audience. Students could also be asked to write a brief critique of the concert, to compare the themes used by each singer or to prepare a French "news release" about the concert.

> **TARGETED STANDARDS**
> 1.1 Interpersonal Communication
> 1.2 Interpretive Communication
> 2.1 Practices of Culture
> 3.2 Acquiring Information
> 4.2 Cultural Comparisons

LA DERNIÈRE CLASSE: A SHORT STORY
(post-secondary)

As a preparation for reading Daudet's *La Dernière Classe* (*The Last Class*), students in an intermediate college French class are given a brief presentation on the historical and geographical background of Alsace. After reading and discussing the short story, students are asked to suggest related discussion questions. These topics often include school and studies, language and culture, war and its consequences, and the nature of patriotism. Students in groups talk about a selected topic and write a short résumé of their discussion. The next day, the students share their résumés with one another. In conclusion, the instructor leads a full-class discussion on the key role that language plays as an affirmation of culture. Comparisons are made to the problems of identity faced by minorities and to those who live in occupied areas of the world today.

Reflection

1.1 Students use French to discuss meaningful topics of interest.
1.2 Students develop strategies and skills to read and to listen in French.
2.1 Students become aware of educational practices in France (and especially in Alsace) in the second half of the nineteenth century.
3.2 Students acquire information about French history.
4.2 Students compare and contrast the role of language in France and the United States.

This scenario allows students to compare their own experiences to those of people living in another country in a different period. They also realize that there are areas of France where more than one language is spoken. The relationship of language and culture in terms of identity and maintenance can be expanded to include the United States and francophone countries, such as Switzerland, Belgium, Canada, and Senegal.

> **TARGETED STANDARDS**
> 1.1 Interpersonal Communication
> 2.1 Practices of Culture
> 4.2 Cultural Comparisons
> 5.1 School and Community

LES ENTREVUES ETHNOGRAPHIQUES: ETHNOGRAPHIC INTERVIEWS
(post-secondary)

As a spring semester project, college students in all four sections of the third-year French course conduct ethnographic interviews with French speakers from various parts of the world. In preparation for the project, the course coordinator identifies and contacts willing participants: foreign students, university employees, and other members of the community. First, the students view a video and are taught to conduct interviews on perceived cultural differences and learn to tailor their questions to the responses of the person interviewed. (For example, if a Belgian exchange student says that he is surprised at how small classes are in the United States, the students will then ask about the size of classes in Belgium.) Next, the students are divided into groups, assigned an interviewee, and instructed to record their interview in audio or video format. In class, the groups each give oral reports and replay what they consider to be one of the most interesting segments of their interview. This is followed by a discussion in which students compare and contrast the cultural practices in various francophone areas.

Reflection

1.1 Students interview native speakers of French.
2.1 Students learn about the cultural practices of the region represented by the French-language speaker they interview.
4.2 Students compare the culture of the interviewees with their own.
5.1 Students use French to interact with members of the community.

Student evaluations at the end of the term indicate that this is one of the most stimulating projects of the course. The students are pleased to use their conversational skills in real-life contexts on a subject of interest to them. They also comment on how their view of other cultures has been broadened. As an extension of the project, students could prepare written summaries of the interview and transcribe certain portions of the recorded interview. Students could also draw cultural comparisons between American and various francophone perspectives on specific topics, and after listening to or viewing the recordings, they could make linguistic comparisons between French and English usage.

UNE FABLE DE LA FONTAINE: DRAMATIZATION OF A FABLE (elementary)

The teacher presents La Fontaine's fable *La cigale et la fourmi* (*The Grasshopper and the Ant*) to a class of fourth-grade students using pictures, gestures and TPR activities to ensure comprehension. Students are then divided into pairs: "*la cigale*" (the cicada or the locust, "the grasshopper") and "*la fourmi*" (the ant). Students in each pair act out their part as the teacher narrates. Eventually every student will have the opportunity to play both parts. Songs, dances, supplementary roles, and supplementary dialogue are added to create a short play, which then is performed or video recorded for parents and/or other French classes.

> **TARGETED STANDARDS**
> 1.2 Interpretive Communication
> 1.3 Presentational Communication
> 2.2 Products of Culture
> 5.1 School and Community

Reflection

1.2 Students understand the fable and the teacher's instructions for the dramatization.
1.3 Students present the fable to an audience of students and/or parents.
2.2 Students learn a traditional French fable.
5.1 Students use French within the school setting as they present the fable to others.

Prior to this activity, students need to learn the seasons in French, some action verbs such as *chanter* and *danser*, and expressions such as *j'ai faim* and *j'ai froid*. Students with more French experience can narrate the play. Students may also prepare simple scenery depicting the seasons. As a substitute for a live presentation, the play may be filmed and viewed by other classes or at a PTA meeting.

> **TARGETED STANDARDS**
> 1.1 Interpersonal Communication
> 1.2 Interpretive Communication
> 1.3 Presentational Communication
> 3.1 Making Connections
> 5.1 School and Community

LA FAMILLE: GENEALOGY (high school)

Students in a New England high school French II class learn family vocabulary and terms related to the creation of a family tree. With this vocabulary, they ask each other questions about the birth, marriage, and death of their family members and note the information on a simple family tree chart. A field trip is taken to a local genealogical society specializing in French-Canadian ancestry where students learn the correct techniques for researching their ancestors and where they are able to view several more detailed forms for recording family history. Students then research and complete their own family tree and make a simple oral presentation to the class. The "trees" are displayed in a prominent location in the school and/or in the public library.

Reflection

1.1 Students exchange information in French about their ancestors.
1.2 Students listen to family tree presentations in French.
1.3 Students present orally in French their family trees to their classmates.
3.1 Students further their knowledge of history through ancestral research.
5.1 Students display their family trees in a prominent location either in school or in a public building, such as the library.

This scenario could be adapted for French III and IV students by using the more complex forms for recording family history, which provide more detailed information about family members. For classes in which students might not have French ancestors or might be uncomfortable discussing their family, students could select famous people from France or other francophone regions and research their family tree. They might also interview a French speaker in their community and trace that person's ancestry. If there is a local genealogical society, they might research the ancestry of a historical figure in their community who has French or francophone ancestry.

> **TARGETED STANDARDS**
> 1.2 Interpretive Communication
> 1.3 Presentational Communication
> 2.2 Products of Culture
> 3.1 Making Connections
> 3.2 Acquiring Information
> 5.2 Lifelong Learning

L'IMPRESSIONNISME: AN IMPRESSIONIST GALLERY (high school)

High school students in French III are introduced to the French Impressionists through an illustrated lecture presented in English by a docent from a local art museum or by an art teacher. Each student then researches an individual artist (biography, major works, composition and technique) through books, videos, and French museum sites on the Internet. Students share their findings in one of the following ways:

1. The creation of *Une Galerie des Impressionnistes* (a Gallery of Impressionist Art): Students hang prints of their artists' works on the wall and lead their classmates on a tour of their gallery. The prints may be prints found in the art museum, the school art department, the library or through the Internet.
2. Each student creates a poster about the artist and his/her work and then uses the poster to

present the artist to the class.
3. Teams of students create a video or a multimedia presentation about one or two artists and their works, thus giving their classmates an idea of the Impressionist movement within its social, political, and artistic context.

Reflections

1.2 Students read and view materials in their research on an Impressionist artist.

1.3 Students make oral presentations in French about an artist of their choice.

2.2 Students learn about French artists and the Impressionist movement.

3.1 Students learn about the social and political climate of France and about the history of Impressionism in the latter part of the nineteenth century.

3.2 Students use French-language Internet sites to gain information about their chosen artists and their works.

5.2 Students develop an interest in art and art history.

In addition to making presentations in French for their own classmates or those in other French classes, students can expand their presentations in English for community groups or groups planning to travel to France. If possible, students may arrange a field trip to view the Impressionist holdings at a nearby museum. The "gallery" may also be used to showcase artists from other periods. To expand the topic of Impressionism, students could identify American Impressionists, such as Prendergast, and discuss the influences of the movement in France on American painting.

LE MAROC: MOROCCAN SHOWCASE (high school)

Students in a French IV high school class work together to prepare a Moroccan showcase. First students are introduced to the Moroccan lifestyle through a documentary video from Flying Monk Films. The teacher prepares a list of individual topics, which students draw from a hat. Possible topics include history, geography, cuisine, fashion, culture, and religion. The students may use the

TARGETED STANDARDS
1.3 Presentational Communication
2.2 Products of Culture
3.2 Acquiring Information
4.1 Language Comparisons
5.1 School and Community

Internet and other available French-language sources, such as travel pamphlets, *Le Matin* (Moroccan daily newspaper), *La Citadine* or *Femmes* (Moroccan monthly magazines) or library materials. Students then each write three paragraphs summarizing information on the topic they are studying. At the same time, each student is encouraged to find ten new vocabulary words of Moroccan origin, such as *la djellabah* (long robe with long sleeves and hood), *le turban* (headdress of long cloth wound around the head), *le fez* (man's red brimless hat), *le couscous* (dish with steamed semolina), *les babouches* (slippers: leather for men and leather or hand-embroidered velvet for women), *le beldi* (general term for traditional clothing), *le khôl* (black eye liner), *le henné* (coloring from a plant, which turns red after application, used for temporary tattooing on the body for special occasions), *la bastilla* (dish similar to pigeon pie, made with filo dough and filled with almonds, served for special occasions). Students use their reports and their vocabulary lists to make an illustrated poster on their topic, which will serve as a visual aid for an oral presentation. As a final project, all the posters are then assembled on a ten to fifteen foot foam-like board, which can be displayed at an open house or in the media center.

Standards for the Learning of French

Reflection

1.3 Students present information in French on Moroccan culture and life style.

2.2 Students learn about and identify products of Moroccan culture.

3.2 Students read authentic sources to get information on Morocco.

4.1 Students learn about and identify Moroccan expressions found in French and compare these in spelling and pronunciation to their English equivalents.

5.1 Students exhibit their posters for the school and community.

A teacher of Moroccan background, who shared her love for her country with her students, created this scenario. Teachers with differing backgrounds or interests might select other regions of the world for a similar project.

TARGETED STANDARDS
1.1 Interpersonal Communication
2.2 Products of Culture
3.1 Making Connections
3.2 Acquiring Information

PARIS EN MÉTRO: PARIS BY SUBWAY (middle school)

Students in seventh and eighth grade French learn about Paris through the city's monuments and subway system. Through visuals and video materials, students become familiar with the major monuments in the city. Students are then divided into groups and given a copy of a Paris map that shows the major monuments and the metro lines. Each group decides which major monuments to visit during an imaginary two-day trip to Paris. They plot their itinerary around Paris, beginning at a class-determined hotel site, and arranging to visit three major sites per day. They use the Internet and the *Guide Michelin: Paris* to find information about the monuments they want to visit and also to consult a more detailed map of Paris. The groups write out their itinerary and then create a personal *carte orange* (I.D. card permitting purchase of a discount ticket to ride the metro or the bus) using their photos and orange construction paper. As a follow-up project, the major metro lines are marked on the floor. Each group demonstrates its itinerary by walking the metro lines, making the necessary *correspondances* (transfers). As they emerge from the metro, the students see the desired monument in poster or picture form, provided by the teacher or created by the students, and participate in a short dialog in which they talk about the monument, take photos, and share their reactions.

Reflection

1.1 Students talk about the sites they see in Paris.

2.2 Students read and interpret the Paris maps.

3.1 Students create an itinerary for visiting Paris and using its transportation system.

3.2 Students acquire information about Paris from Internet sites as well as from print and visual materials.

This scenario introduces the students, especially those who do not live in or near large cities, to the use of the metro to travel around a large city. They learn about Paris and its wonderful monuments, choose which to visit, and plan a short two-day tour. This involves group work, mapping skills, a possible use of the Internet to illustrate how to use the metro, and an explanation and use of the *carte orange*. If it is impossible to lay out a map of Paris on the classroom floor, students can demonstrate their routes on an overhead transparency of the Paris metro map, or with PowerPoint slides. Where available, a large metro map of Paris could be displayed and a student guide could trace the route. Other cities with subways, such as Montreal, or with city bus routes could become the focal point for this activity. Researching the names of the metro stations could provide another activity to connect Paris with its historical, cultural, and linguistic roots.

LE PETIT PRINCE: THE LITTLE PRINCE (high school)

Students in French III spend six to eight weeks reading *Le Petit Prince*. As a preliminary activity, the teacher gives a short introduction to St. Exupéry's life and his role in airmail routes from Paris to Dakar and South America. Before beginning to read the story, students are shown reproductions of illustrations from the text in order to establish a base vocabulary and are invited to express their own interpretations. As they finish each chapter, students give oral summaries of what they have read and express their personal reactions to events and characters in the story. The unit also includes a variety of creative assignments, such as writing an illustrated postcard to the rose describing one of the planets visited, composing a new ending for the story or inventing a female companion for the Little Prince. Students also create three-dimensional models of the Little Prince's planet and give a brief oral presentation to their peers, describing the artistic medium used and the elements represented on the planet. At the completion of the story, students view the French version of *ET* and compile a list of the similarities and differences between both main characters. If facilities are available, students work in groups of two or three students to create scenes for their own rendition of *Le Petit Prince*, which is videotaped and shown to French classes at all levels in order to encourage the continued study of French. Finally, the students submit a completed packet of assignments in scrapbook form and share with their peers the most rewarding aspect of their experience with *Le Petit Prince*. The teacher then places student planets and packets in glass display cases at different locations in the school.

> **TARGETED STANDARDS**
> 1.1 Interpersonal Communication
> 1.2 Interpretive Communication
> 1.3 Presentational Communication
> 2.2 Products of Culture
> 4.2 Cultural Comparisons

Reflection

1.1 Students discuss in French their readings of *Le Petit Prince* and share their personal reactions to the characters and events depicted in the text.
1.2 Students read *Le Petit Prince*.
1.3 Students prepare and produce in French short skits or videos based on *Le Petit Prince*.
2.2 Students become familiar with a French author.
4.2 Students compare the American film *ET* with the French story of *Le Petit Prince* and note cultural similarities and differences.

Le Petit Prince is a very popular book at all levels of instruction. Activities can be varied according to the ages and interests of the students. As possible pre-reading activities, students can examine the old French 50-franc note showing St. Exupéry and scenes from *Le Petit Prince* and the 1999 series of French commemorative stamps with scenes from *Le Petit Prince* and compare French and American currency and postage stamps. Using music composed and performed by Gilbert Bécaud, which recalls some of the characters and events of St. Exupéry's story, students can also discuss a number of the themes evoked in the story. In addition, Bécaud's rendition of *L'Important c'est la Rose* (CD: *40 Ans en chansons*) could be compared and contrasted to the English-French version of *L'important c'est la Rose* by Jane Olivor (CD: *First Night*). Another musical resource is the operatic version in English of *The Little Prince* by Rachel Portman and Nicholas Wright.

TARGETED STANDARDS
1.1 Interpersonal Communication
2.1 Practices of Culture
2.2 Products of Culture
3.2 Acquiring Information
4.2 Cultural Comparisons
5.1 School and Community

LES STAGES: SUMMER INTERNSHIPS IN STRASBOURG (post-secondary)

Under the aegis of the Boston/Strasbourg Sister City Association, Boston College and the IECS (Institut d'Etudes Commerciales Supérieures) in Strasbourg have established a summer exchange internship program. The initiative places American university students in a variety of Alsatian companies, while an equal number of businesses in Boston welcome students from France. Each host city provides its interns with housing, meals, local transportation, and pocket money, and also finds and coordinates the business placements. Because of the nature of the exchange, special visas or work permits are not required. Each city also organizes cultural visits and tours so that the students get to know the area they are visiting. As a result of their six-week total immersion in a French business atmosphere, the American students consolidate their language skills and broaden their appreciation of French culture. They may earn academic credit for their internship by completing a research paper on a topic related to their placement.

Reflection

1.1 Students use French as their daily means of interpersonal interaction.
2.1 Students acquire first-hand experience with French cultural practices: interpersonal relations, meal etiquette, and daily schedules.
2.2 Students acquire first-hand experience with French cultural products: newspapers, television shows, transportation, and leisure activities.
3.2 Students use French to learn about their internship and its requirements.
4.2 Students compare French and American business practices.
5.1 Students communicate with French speakers in the Strasbourg business community.

This summer internship exchange program, which has been in existence for fifteen years, is particularly effective in helping university students recognize that knowledge of French can be a strong asset in the business world. Students who participate strengthen their communication skills as well as their awareness and appreciation of cultural differences. The Boston/Strasbourg Sister City Association has also established a summer exchange program with home stays for secondary school students of the two cities, as well as their teachers. Internships can provide opportunities for students to use French along with knowledge and skills acquired through other disciplines to explore the world of work.

TARGETED STANDARDS
1.1 Interpersonal Communication
1.2 Interpretive Communication
1.3 Presentational Communication
2.2 Products of Culture
3.1 Making Connections
4.1 Language Comparisons

LES VÊTEMENTS: MAIL-ORDER CATALOGUE (high school)

High school students in a French IV class develop their own mail-order fashion and clothing catalogues and order forms. They begin by browsing the *Trois Suisses* catalogue, in print or online at http://www.3suisses.fr, studying color photographs of clothing and accessories, checking prices, and reading the brief item descriptions. The students can make either a general clothing catalogue or one directed to a specific age or interest group. The students are shown sample pages from the catalogue on a transparency or by other visual projection, to discover what French words are used to describe nuances of color and how much the items cost in euros. They are asked to determine whether clothing is for women, men, boys, girls or infants, for what occasions the articles might be worn, in which colors the items are available, and what sizes are appropriate. They note the presence of English in the descriptions and compare these words with French terms they have seen in American catalogues or advertisements. In addition, students learn how to order from a French catalogue by mail, e-mail, telephone or fax. As a final project, they produce their own catalogue complete with order forms. Students use one another's catalogue pages to create conversations in which they discuss items they like and/or role-play the placing of phone orders.

Reflection

1.1 Students express their preferences on catalogue options from a French catalogue and the ones they create.
1.2 Students understand the information and choices presented in French catalogues.
1.3 Students design and create in French their own catalogue pages.
2.2 Students identify the styles and prices of clothing typically worn in France and analyze how these items relate to French cultural perspectives.
3.1 Students relate prices in euros and dollars and sizing in metric and American standards.
4.1 Students compare French and American presentations of mail-order catalogues, noting differences and similarities in vocabulary.

This project may be adapted to other grade levels, including middle school. It may also be adapted to other catalogue themes, such as furniture and home furnishings, fishing and boating, skiing, food items, and cosmetics. Another catalogue to consult is *La Redoute*, in print or on-line at http://www.redoute.fr.

LES VOYAGEURS: THE FRENCH VOYAGEURS (elementary)

A study of the colorful and demanding life of the French *voyageurs* and their role in the fur trade provides an excellent complement to the elementary school social studies curriculum. The teacher can introduce the topic in French via video (for example, *Les Voyageurs,* VHS, from the Canadian Film Distribution Center, SUNY Plattsburg), by reading the French coloring book about the *voyageurs* from the Minnesota Historical Society or by playing the role of a *voyageur* himself/herself. Students then learn to describe the clothing worn by the *voyageurs*, discovering as

TARGETED STANDARDS
1.1 Interpersonal Communication
1.2 Interpretive Communication
1.3 Presentational Communication
2.1 Practices of Culture
2.2 Products of Culture
3.1 Making Connections
3.2 Acquiring Information
4.2 Cultural Comparisons
5.1 School and Sommunity

they do which items are European in origin and which are adapted from Native American dress. They make red *tuques*, the woolen caps so readily identified with the *voyageurs*. The students dramatize each facet of the life of the *voyageurs*, including loading the canoe, paddling and singing, portaging, resting, eating pea soup, trading with Native Americans, and dancing at a *rendez-vous*. They also learn to identify and describe the animals hunted for their fur, and they make a map showing the itinerary of the *voyageurs'* travels. Students may also perform a re-enactment of the life of the *voyageurs*, including songs and dances, in a presentation for students in other classes and/or for parents.

Reflection

1.1 Students describe the clothing, activities, and daily life of the *voyageurs*. They describe the fur trade animals, and they learn to bargain in French.

1.2 Students comprehend information presented about the *voyageurs*. They respond to commands given in French in order to dramatize the *voyageurs'* lives and to make *tuques*.

1.3 They re-enact the life of the *voyageurs* for an audience.

2.1 Students comprehend the life and culture of Franco-Canadians in New France at the time of the fur trade.

2.2 Students learn how French Canadians of that era dressed, they learn some of their songs and dances, and they may eat some typical food (pea soup).

3.1 Students will reinforce their knowledge of North American geography and mapping in French.

3.2 They acquire new information in the field of social studies.

4.2 They compare Native American and French Canadian food, customs, and clothing.

5.1 Students, wearing their hand-made *tuques*, re-enact the lives of the *voyageurs* for other classes and/or for their parents.

This topic is most appropriate for fourth grade students who have had prior experience with French. The richness of the subject makes it also appropriate for elementary students in an immersion setting, as well as for French students of all ages. There are innumerable extensions possible for students with a more advanced level of French, such as reading about the *voyageurs*, writing research reports about animals important to the fur trade, preparing a diary of a *voyageur's* life or solving related math number problems.

Standards for Learning German

A Project of the American Association of Teachers of German

K-16 STUDENT STANDARDS TASK FORCE

Marjorie Tussing (Co-Chair), California State University-Fullerton, CA
Susan Webber (Co-Chair), Meadowdale Sr. High School, Lynnwood, WA
Liette Bohler, Tidewater Community College, Virginia Beach, VA
Thomas Keith Cothrun, Las Cruces High School, Las Cruces, NM
Carol Ann Pesola Dahlberg, Concordia College, Moorhead, MN
Paul A. García, School District of Kansas City, MO (Retired)
Margaret Hampton, Earlham College, Richmond, IN
Carl H. Johnson, Texas Education Agency, Austin, TX
Zoe E. Louton, Educational Service Unit #5, Beatrice, NE
Karl F. Otto, Jr., University of Pennsylvania, Philadelphia, PA
Jim Sheppard, Screven County High School, Sylvania, GA
Helene Zimmer-Loew, American Association of Teachers of German, Cherry Hill, NJ

Standards for Learning German

BOARD OF REVIEWERS

Rosemarie Bahmani
Poway High School
Poway, CA

Richard E. Hartzell
Goshen, NY (retired)

Gerd Bräuer
Emory University
Atlanta, GA

Charles Teubner,
East Windsor, NJ

Wendy W. Allen
St. Olaf College
Northfield, MN

Catherine C. Fraser
Indiana University
Bloomington, IN

Christa N. Garcia
D.A.N.K. National School
Glen Ellyn, IL

Carol Gratton
Valley Springs Public Schools
Valley Springs, AR

Dora F. Kennedy
University of Maryland
College Park, MD

Maureen Helinski
North County High School
Glen Burnie, MD

Gretchen LaTurner
Enumclaw High School
Enumclaw, WA

Keith Mason
New Providence High School
New Providence, NJ

Charlotte Melin
University of Minnesota
Minneapolis, MN

Hildegard Merkle
Holy Childhood Elementary School
St. Paul, MN

Robert A. Morrey
Cupertino High School
Cupertino, CA

Teresa Reber
University of Arizona
Tucson

Jim Rorke
Methodist College
Fayetteville, NC

Sigrid Rother
Aquinas College
Grand Rapids, MI

Robert M. Terry
University of Richmond, VA

Donna Van Handle
Mount Holyoke College
Mount Holyoke, MA

Table of Contents

STANDARDS FOR LEARNING GERMAN — **290**

INTRODUCTION — **291**

ORGANIZING PRINCIPLES — **292**

THE GERMAN AMERICAN CONTEXT: YESTERDAY AND TODAY — **295**

GERMAN IN THE UNITED STATES: TOMORROW — **295**

GERMAN PROGRAMS, K-16 — **296**

COMMUNICATION — Goal 1 — **297**

CULTURES — Goal 2 — **302**

CONNECTIONS — Goal 3 — **305**

COMPARISONS — Goal 4 — **307**

COMMUNITIES — Goal 5 — **311**

SAMPLE LEARNING SCENARIOS — **314**
- Models for K-4 and K-8 Programs — 314
  - *Die drei Bären* — 314
  - *Mein Haus, mein Zimmer* — 315
  - *Gute Besserung* — 316
- Models for 6-12 Programs — 317
  - *Einwanderer* — 317
  - Goethe's *Erlkönig* — 318
  - *Damals war es Friedrich* — 319
  - *Karneval, die 5. Jahreszeit* — 320
- Models for 9-16 Programs — 321
  - *Umweltprobleme in Deutschland* — 321
  - Business Practices — 321
  - Connecting with Germany's Past — 322
  - Heinrich Kleist's Comedy, *Der zerbrochene Krug* — 323

FREQUENTLY ASKED QUESTIONS — **324**

SELECTIVE BIBLIOGRAPHY — **327**

Standards for Learning German

COMMUNICATION — GOAL ONE
Communicate in German

Standard 1.1 Students engage in conversations, provide and obtain information, express feelings and emotions, and exchange opinions.

Standard 1.2 Students understand and interpret spoken and written language on a variety of topics.

Standard 1.3 Students present information, concepts, and ideas to an audience of listeners or readers on a variety of topics.

CULTURES — GOAL TWO
Gain Knowledge and Understanding of the German-Speaking World

Standard 2.1 Students demonstrate an understanding of the relationship between the practices and perspectives of the cultures studied.

Standard 2.2 Students demonstrate an understanding of the relationship between the products and perspectives of the cultures studied.

CONNECTIONS — GOAL THREE
Connect with Other Disciplines and Acquire Information

Standard 3.1 Students reinforce and further their knowledge of other disciplines through German.

Standard 3.2 Students acquire information and recognize the distinctive viewpoints that are only available through German and the German-speaking world.

COMPARISONS — GOAL FOUR
Develop Insight into the Nature of Language and Culture

Standard 4.1 Students demonstrate understanding of the nature of language through comparisons between German and their own languages.

Standard 4.2 Students demonstrate understanding of the concept of culture through comparisons between the cultures in German-speaking countries and their own.

COMMUNITIES — GOAL FIVE
Participate in Multilingual Communities at Home and Around the World

Standard 5.1 Students use German both within and beyond the school setting.

Standard 5.2 Students show evidence of becoming life-long learners by using German for personal enjoyment and enrichment.

Introduction

This document is complementary to the generic *Standards for Foreign Language Learning* and is part of a collaborative effort of the American Associations of Teachers of French, German, Italian, and Spanish and Portuguese, the American Classical League, the American Council of Teachers of Russian, the American Council on the Teaching of Foreign Languages, the National Council of Secondary Teachers of Japanese/Association of Teachers of Japanese and the Chinese Language Association of Seconday-Elementary Schools/Chinese Language Teachers Association.

Our intention is to expand the generic *Standards* into a language- and culture-specific version for German. It is not intended as a curriculum or a syllabus. It is a guide for the preparation of programs, curricula, or courses. It will be used together with state frameworks, district curriculum guides and local lesson plans.

The philosophy statement from the generic document envisions a future in which the diverse American student population demonstrates proficiency in English and at least one other language. The study of another language offers all students an opportunity to communicate and to learn to respond appropriately in a variety of cultures. It encourages them to make comparisons and connections and to interact with communities at home and abroad in an increasingly competent manner. The standards encourage schools to consider the advantages of long sequences of study in order to develop a range of competencies needed in the twenty-first century. The standards provide for a long-term framework of study for students in a variety of programs as they pursue their interests in German together with other core subjects such as the language arts, math, science and the arts.

Foreign languages are a core subject

These Standards specify the knowledge and competencies that all learners of a second language need to acquire. They are content standards designed for a core subject. The programs that accompany this model are designed to begin in early childhood at the kindergarten level and continue uninterrupted through the high school and college years—in urban, suburban, and rural settings. The document provides sample progress indicators for Grades Four, Eight, Twelve, and Sixteen with examples to illustrate possibilities for teachers in different kinds of programs. The culminating section of sample learning scenarios illustrates the standards in representative settings around the United States.

ORGANIZING PRINCIPLES

A major tenet of our documents holds that although students have varying reasons for learning languages, the organizing principles apply to all students and to all languages. The Standards offer a new way to view language learning and language teaching focusing on what students need to know and be able to do.

The Standards provide three major organizing principles:

- The five goals: communication, cultures, connections, comparisons, and communities;

- The weave of curricular elements: language system, cultural knowledge, communication strategies, critical thinking skills, learning strategies, other subject areas, and technology.

- The framework of communicative modes including cultural knowledge and knowledge of the linguistic system.

The Five Goals

Each goal focuses on a different aspect of learning German and together they provide interrelated preparation for the student who anticipates using German in the real world in a variety of cultural settings.

Goal	Key Concepts for Teaching and Learning
Communication	Understanding of the difference between negotiated and non-negotiated use of the German language
Cultures	Understanding of the relationship among the perspectives, practices, and products of German-speaking cultures
Connections	Acquisition of information available only through German language and cultural sources
Comparisons	Understanding of the relations between communication in German and the cultures of German-speaking countries and the language and cultures the learner brings
Communities	Ability to use German outside the formal program and to link the language and culture experience to life-long learning goals

The Weave of Curricular Elements

Specific to teaching and learning the German language and cultures of the German-speaking areas are language system, cultural knowledge, communication strategies, critical thinking skills and learning strategies in addition to other subject areas and technology.

Communication Strategies. These are important for producing meaningful written and spoken German and for understanding German. Students must also be familiar with structural and semantic building blocks and with strategies for putting them together. Here are several examples of how communication strategies support the five goals:

Communication:
- using context to interpret meaning
- circumlocution (using different ways of expressing the same ideas)
- using cognates and loan words

Cultures:
- using and interpreting culturally appropriate gestures
- using formulas for politeness and conventions for different interpersonal relationships
- using information about products of culture as starting points for communication

Connections:	• recognizing that prior knowledge provides access to new information
	• recognizing that something new can be learned only through the German language
Comparisons:	• recognizing that important information is at the beginning or at the end of messages in German
	• recognizing that principles of compounding allow for interpretation of complex ideas
	• recognizing that loan words in German and English allow for "educated guessing"
Communities:	• using a variety of resources as opportunities for initiating and sustaining communication (magazines, local speakers of German, Internet)

Learning Strategies. Learners come to German classes with a variety of learning strategies developed in many different contexts. It is important to support the strategies students bring to the experience and to assist them in applying these strategies to the language learning context. It is also important that learners develop specific strategies that will help them as they work toward the five goals of life-long language learning.

Communication:	• negotiating interpersonal communication through questioning and restatement
	• being alert to elements of highly repetitive language and using them as a building block for developing messages
	• understanding the importance of focusing on the message in order to maintain communication
	• using rehearsal and other strategies such as mnemonics, color coding, tactile or spatial systems, in order to help retain and use vocabulary or grammatical patterns meaningfully
Cultures:	• observing behaviors and practices carefully before drawing conclusions about new cultures
	• using forms of address and body language to interpret relationships and guide behaviors
Connections:	• transferring learning strategies from other school subjects to German
	• using an integrated content approach that brings the general curriculum into the language classroom or takes the language into another content area
	• seeking German resources beyond the classroom for enriching content learned in other classes
Comparisons:	• seeking links between one's first or second language and German to enhance learning of the new language
	• looking for similar and contrasting patterns of behavior as a new step toward functioning successfully in a new culture
Communities:	• using available media in the German language such as magazines, newspapers, libraries, and the Web to extend opportunities for communication and learning beyond the classroom
	• initiating conversations in German with local contacts
	• using the understanding of the language and culture in the immediate environment

The Framework of Communicative Modes

The ability to use the language in culturally appropriate communicative tasks is the basic goal of most learners, yet communication is understood in many different ways. Communication encompasses all five goals and appears in all three modes that link language and underlying culture: interpersonal, interpretive and presentational. The primary distinction between the interpersonal mode on the one hand, and the interpretive and presentational on the other is the element of negotiated language. Interpersonal language is language in which the individuals have the opportunity to interact directly and to use a process of repetition, clarification, questions and answers, gestures and cues to understand each other's message–to "negotiate" meaning. Interpersonal communication can be oral or written. E-mail is such an example of spoken language written down.

In the interpretive and presentational modes, communication is primarily non-negotiated, or one-way. Printed text, movies, radio and television broadcasts and speeches are examples of interpretive communication. The reader, listener, or viewer must take what he or she sees, reads, or hears and fit it into a cultural message being conveyed. There is no opportunity to "talk back". Presentational communication is exemplified by the writing of articles or reports or of making speeches. The person creating the speech or article must understand the culture of the audience in order to communicate effectively, but the delivered text is a non-negotiable product. The interpretive and presentational aspect of communication thus must rely to a large extent on underlying cultural elements to carry meaning.

Cultural knowledge and knowledge of the linguistic system are essential components of the framework. Cultural knowledge is described in the section on the sample progress indicators later in this document. Below is a list of basic components included in the knowledge of the linguistic system. The sample progress indicators listed under Standard 4.1 contain several appropriate examples for German.

KNOWLEDGE OF THE LINGUISTIC SYSTEM

Grammatical:	To be competent in another language, grammar is essential. The learner must know the grammar and be able to apply this system effectively to communicate in German.
Lexical:	An age and grade appropriate working vocabulary is necessary. Appropriate content is selected depending on the needs and the cultural elements of the German program.
Phonological:	The ability to use the phonological features of the German language is a primary component of communication.
Semantic:	knowledge of the underlying meaning of oral and written communication is essential to adequate communication.
Pragmatic:	Pragmatic features involve understanding and the capacity to comprehend and produce messages in culturally appropriate ways.
Discourse:	Discourse features provide the means for effective oral and written communication.

THE GERMAN-AMERICAN CONTEXT: YESTERDAY AND TODAY

According to the 1990 census, almost fifty-eight million Americans or 23.3% claim German "ancestry or ethnic origin," more than any other nationality to immigrate to the United States thus far.

Indeed, more than seven million German-speakers arrived over three centuries. There were German-speakers in the Colonies from the earliest times, beginning with Fort Royal and Jamestown in the early seventeenth century, and the first all-German group consisting of thirteen families arrived in Philadelphia in 1683. From that time on, immigrants from German-speaking countries continued to leave Europe because of religious, political, and racial persecution, crop failures, overpopulation, failed revolutions, and two disastrous wars. The most recent and largest influx of German speakers into the United States occurred in the 1950s and 60s. This was the third "brain drain" (the first having occurred after the Revolution of 1848 and the second during the 1930s), consisting of about 800,000 highly qualified workers and professionals who sought new opportunities and the possibility of an international exchange of ideas in the United States.

The German-Americans supported their own churches where services were entirely in German, published newspapers and eventually broadcast radio programs in German, established and joined a variety of German social and athletic clubs, and held large public events such as parades, holiday celebrations, and festivals. They contributed greatly to the cultural, civic, and social life of the towns and cities where they settled by supporting German restaurants, theaters, concert halls, museums and art galleries, orchestras, opera companies, singing societies, and other such activities.

Throughout the nineteenth and early twentieth century, many activist German-speaking parents insisted that public schools teach their children in German. Their purpose was to preserve a fragment of ethnic identity in their children for whom American culture appeared irresistible. They also supported many private schools throughout the United States where the content curriculum was taught entirely or partially in German. At the beginning of the First World War, German was studied by 24% of the students attending public schools. Today, although the percentage is lower, German is the third most taught language in schools, colleges and universities in the United States.

In terms of individual contributions, one could name hundreds of prominent German-Americans who have influenced American business, industry, technology, politics, medicine, art, letters, film, music, education, science, and religion. One need only look at a map of the United States to locate thousands of names that are also German place names. Contributions to the American culinary scene are also numerous. Dozens of German words have found their way into American daily usage.

GERMAN IN THE UNITED STATES: TOMORROW

Whether learning the German language or learning about German-speaking cultures for professional or personal reasons, the primary goal is communication with others in the language. Some make the decision because they eventually want to work or study abroad, while others decide to pursue German because they know of German, Austrian, or Swiss companies and businesses operating in their region. Some students choose German because they have an interest in the history, civilization, art, music, business, philosophy and literature of German-speaking cultures. Others may be drawn to German because of an instructor's reputation at their institution. Still others may be interested in pursuing the language of their immigrant forebears or to conduct research into German-American studies or German heritage in the U.S.A.

As preparation for the twenty-first century, knowledge of another language and culture is essential for all citizens. Germany, Austria, and Switzerland are poised to play a major role in central and eastern Europe and beyond. Today, all nations and peoples are brought ever closer through rapid advancements in communications. It is a world in which mutual cooperation and understanding are paramount. Therefore, it is important to go beyond the "how to say" stage when learning German. There is a diverse population of men and women around the world who speak German, and thus one must recognize and affirm the culturally sensitive and appropriate aspects of what and how to communicate. German is not simply a language to be spoken and studied by heritage speakers; it is a language that one hears on every continent.

The designers and proponents of German programs must meet the challenges that face the language-teaching profession. There must be articulation among various levels of German instruction, and the benefits of such collaboration needs to be recognized. German instructors can help all students meet the challenges ahead by understanding the dynamics of diversity. Successful German programs will help students become life-long learners, as well as encourage them to make connections that go beyond the classroom experience. Such programs must show students that, through learning German, they will enrich their lives.

GERMAN PROGRAMS, K-16

The German profession is committed to a variety of programs. These programs currently range from the "Kinder lernen Deutsch" in K-8 settings to the many possibilities existing in high schools, community colleges, and universities. Among the advantages of an extended sequence which begins in the primary grades and extends through high school and then continues in a college or university setting is the attainment of the standards in ways not currently possible in the predominant model of two to three years of high school experience. Programs such as Advanced Placement and the International Baccalaureate can be expected to grow since the number of students with extensive prior experience will increase. Programs for students who do not plan to continue their studies beyond high school can also be expected to increase.

Postsecondary programs in German will expand in culture, literature, politics, history, and economics in order to be commensurate with students' abilities and proficiency in the language as they continue their studies. Opportunities will need to be developed and provided that allow students to pursue careers demanding German language and cultural competencies in such fields as international business and trade, environmental studies, philosophy, politics, international studies and diplomacy, medicine and other professions.

Teacher education candidates will enter professional programs with a higher level of proficiency than is now generally the case. Teacher preparation programs will need to adjust their course work and to provide experiences that meet the range of competence that reflects the students' K-16 experience.

AATG is committed to the implementation of the standards and to supporting programs in bringing about the changes necessary for students to reach the goals set out in this document. A description of possible K-16 models and program types can be found in the generic section of this document on pages 20-22. For further information on professional development programs, contact your local AATG chapter or the Executive Director, Helene Zimmer-Loew, at the national office.

Communication   *Goal One*
Communicate in German

The focus of the communication goal is on the relationship between the individual who creates the language and the individuals who receive the language. There are three forms of communication which offer a new view of language learning. They are based on cultural appropriateness for a specific audience or range of audiences, and a consideration of the speaker or writer who creates the text.

Interpersonal …may include any combination of the modalities of speaking, writing, listening, reading or viewing

…is negotiable since it is two-way communication during which either party may ask for clarification or can provide additional input

Interpretive and Presentational …distinguished from the interpersonal in that they are non-negotiable since the language is provided in a static format (such as a pre-recorded telecast) and cannot be modified by the person receiving the message

…is either written language presented as a reading text or an oral format in a situation where audience interaction is restricted or is nonexistent

…involve listening, viewing, or reading on the part of the receiver and speaking or writing on the part of the person creating the language

STANDARD 1.1 Students engage in conversations, provide and obtain information, express feelings and emotions, and exchange opinions.

Sample Progress Indicators, Grade 4:

- Students give and follow simple instructions in order to play German games (*Brettspiele, Kartenspiele, Fangen*), make a German dish or meal (*Käsebrot, Brezel*), or participate in age-appropriate classroom and/or cultural activities.

- Students ask and answer questions about topics such as family, school events, and celebrations in person or via letters, e-mail, audio, or prepare videotapes or a family photo album depicting and narrating celebrations (summertime activities, Christmas, birthday party).

- Students share likes and dislikes (foods, movies, clothes) with the class (list favorites and interview a classmate to compare preferences, prepare a questionnaire on favorites and chart the results, role-play an interview between an American and German student discussing likes and dislikes in each culture).

- Students exchange descriptions of people and tangible products of German-speaking cultures such as toys (*Pluschtiere*), dress (everyday and *Trachten*), types of dwellings (pictures of German cities and homes), and foods (*Nutella*) with one another.

- Students exchange essential information such as greetings, leave-takings, (*Grüß Gott, Tschüs*) and common classroom interactions using culturally appropriate gestures and oral expressions on a daily basis (*Darf ich zur Toilette, bitte?*).

Sample Progress Indicators, Grade 8:

- Students follow and give directions for participating in age-appropriate cultural activities (organize a *Faschingsparty* or Advent celebration with costumes, music, food, decorations) and for investigating the function of products of German-speaking cultures. They ask and respond to questions for clarification.

- Students exchange information about personal events, memorable experiences, and other school subjects with peers (exchange a diary entry) and/or members of German-speaking cultures (via e-mail).

- Students compare, contrast, and express opinions and preferences about the information gathered regarding events (athletic or arts programs), experiences, and other school subjects.

- Students acquire goods, services, or information orally and/or in writing (local German deli/bakery/restaurant).

- Students develop and propose solutions to issues and problems (ecology, homelessness, violence) related to the school or community through group work.

Sample Progress Indicators, Grade 12

- Students discuss, orally or in writing, current or past events that are of significance in the German-speaking cultures (European Union, employment, scientific and technological advances), or that are being studied in another subject.

- Students develop and propose solutions to issues and problems (education, global warming) that are of concern to members of their own and the German-speaking cultures.

- Students exchange, support, and discuss their opinions and individual perspectives with peers and/or speakers of German (via e-mail, chat rooms) on a variety of topics dealing with contemporary and historical issues (democracy, feudalism, totalitarianism, colonialism).

- Students share their analyses and personal reactions to expository and literary texts (news articles, poems, and plays) with peers and/or speakers of German.

Sample Progress Indicators, Grade 16

- Students discuss in detail, orally or in writing, past, current or projected events that are of significance in German-speaking cultures (Euro vs. U.S. dollar) or that are being studied in other areas (political trends).

- Students develop detailed, well-substantiated solutions to issues and problems (environmental solutions, infrastructure) that are of concern to members of their own and to German-speaking cultures.

- Students exchange, support and discuss their opinions and individual perspectives with peers and/or speakers of German on a variety of topics dealing with contemporary, historical and projected issues of importance (*Zeppelin, Die Grünen,* East/West Germany, minority cultures in German-speaking countries) both to their own culture and to German-speaking cultures.

- Students share their substantiated analyses and personal reactions to expository and literary texts (magazine articles, discipline-based reading, East German authors) with both peers and speakers of German.

STANDARD 1.2 Students understand and interpret written and spoken language on a variety of topics.

Sample Progress Indicators, Grade 4

- Students comprehend main ideas in developmentally appropriate oral narratives such as personal anecdotes, familiar fairy tales (*Schneewittchen, Rotkäppchen, Dornröschen*), and other narratives (nature programs for children, *InterNationes* materials, National Park Service videos) based on familiar themes.

- Students identify well known people and objects in their environment or from other school subjects (German settlers in America), based on oral and written descriptions.

- Students comprehend brief, written messages and short personal notes (letters from pen/key pals, messages from students in upper grades, and/or other schools) on familiar topics such as family, school events, and celebrations (*Geburtstag, Namenstag, Weihnachten*).

- Students comprehend the main themes and ideas and identify the principal characters of stories or children's literature (*Struwwelpeter, Oh wie schön ist Panama*).

- Students comprehend the principal message contained in various media such as illustrated texts, posters, or advertisements (*Bilderbücher, Kindermagazin*).

- Students interpret gestures (match pictures with various body language), intonation, and other visual or auditory cues (*Darf ich mal durch, bitte*).

Sample Progress Indicators, Grade 8

- Students comprehend information and messages related to other school subjects (daily bulletin read in German, information from print and Internet sources for interdisciplinary projects).

- Students understand announcements and messages (programming from *Deutsche Welle*, weather maps for various German cities from Internet) connected to daily activities in the target culture.

- Students understand the main themes and significant details on topics from other subjects and products of the cultures as presented on TV, radio (short-wave or SWF, NDR broadcasts via Internet or *Deutsche Welle*), video, or live presentations (local lecture series, theater, or festivals).

- Students understand the main themes and significant details on topics from other subjects and products of the cultures as found in newspapers, magazines, e-mail, or other text sources used by speakers of German (*JUMA*).

- Students identify the principal characters and comprehend the main ideas and themes in selected literary texts (biographies of well-known Germans, *DTV Jugendbücher*).

- Students use knowledge acquired in other settings (travel, television) and from other subject areas to comprehend spoken and written messages in German (art and science).

Sample Progress Indicators, Grade 12

- Students demonstrate an understanding of the main ideas and significant details of live and recorded discussions (visit to a German heritage organization, e.g., Germans from Russia, German-American Club), lectures, and presentations (television program or German church service).

- Students demonstrate an understanding of the principal elements of non-fiction articles in newspapers, magazines, and e-mail (bulletin board discussion in German) on topics of current and historical importance to members of German-speaking cultures.

- Students analyze the main plot, subplot, characters, their descriptions, roles, and significance in authentic texts (Borchert, Dürrenmatt, Aichinger, von Trotta, Seghers, Grass).

- Students demonstrate an increasing understanding of the cultural nuances of meaning in written (letters to German, Swiss, and Austrian agencies vs. e-mail messages) and spoken language (interaction with exchange students or teachers) as expressed by speakers of the target language in formal and informal settings.

- Students demonstrate an increasing understanding (describe and compare setting, ambience, audience) of the cultural nuances of meaning in expressive products of the culture (classical or rock musical performances, *JUMA, Stern/Spiegel*, poetry of Mey, Opitz).

Sample Progress Indicators, Grade 16

- Students demonstrate an understanding of the main ideas, significant details, and the implications of live and recorded discussions, lectures, and presentations on current or past events from German-speaking cultures or that they encounter in their own environment (role play discussion from *Deutsche Welle*).

- Students demonstrate an understanding of the theoretical/political slant of the principal elements of non-fiction articles in various newspapers, magazines, and the electronic media on topics of current and historical importance to members of German-speaking cultures (cost of rebuilding the East, move of capital to Berlin, immigration in Switzerland and U.S.).

- Students analyze in detail the main plot, sub-plot, characters, their descriptions, roles and significance in authentic text (production of a Brecht play).

- Students interpret and evaluate the cultural nuances in formal and informal written, spoken, and expressive products (*Jugendstil*, graffiti, computer art, *Expressionismus*) of German-speaking cultures, including selections from visual (organize a departmental art show featuring slides or prints from a range of periods) and performing arts.

STANDARD 1.3 Students present information, concepts, and ideas to an audience of listeners or readers on a variety of topics.

Sample Progress Indicators, Grade 4

- Students prepare illustrated stories (big books, posters, dioramas, cartoons) about activities or events in their environment and share these stories and events with an audience such as the class.

- Students dramatize songs (*Ein Mann, der sich Kolumbus nannte*), short anecdotes (*Nikolauslegende*), or poetry commonly known by peers in German-speaking cultures for members of another elementary class.

- Students give short oral notes and messages or write reports about people (local heroes) and things in their school environment (field trip or habitat of local fauna/flora) and exchange the information with another language class either locally or via e-mail.

- Students tell or retell stories (fairy tales, fables, or stories from family lore) orally or in writing.

- Students write or tell about products and/or practices (holiday celebrations) of their own culture to peers in German-speaking cultures.

Sample Progress Indicators, Grade 8

- Students present short plays and skits, recite selected poems and anecdotes, and perform songs (*O Tannenbaum, Stille Nacht*) in German for a school-related event such as a board meeting or PTA meeting.

- Students prepare tape- or video-recorded messages representing home or school life to share locally or with school peers and/or members of German-speaking cultures on topics of personal interest.

- Students prepare stories or brief written reports about personal experiences or subjects from other disciplines (how rain clouds form, an aspect of local history) to share with classmates and/or members of German-speaking cultures.

- Students prepare an oral or written summary of the plot and characters in selected pieces of age-appropriate literature (*Ben liebt Anna, Paul und Paula, Die Ilse ist weg*).

Sample Progress Indicators, Grade 12

- Students perform excerpts from short stories, recite poems, or perform scenes from dramas (*Biedermann und die Brandstifter*) connected to a topic from other disciplines such as world history, geography, the arts, or mathematics.

- Students perform scenes from plays (Friedrich Dürrenmatt's *Der Besuch der alten Dame*) and/or recite poems or excerpts from short stories (perform Kafka's *Gib's auf!*) commonly read by speakers of German.

- Students create stories and poems, short plays, or skits based on personal experiences and exposure to themes, ideas, and perspectives from the German-speaking cultures (*Fasching*, *Ausländer*, multicultural Germany).

- Students select and analyze expressive products of German-speaking cultures, from literary genres (*Novelle* vs. *Kurzgeschichte*) or the fine arts (musical products of Wagner, Mozart, Beethoven, Stockhausen, or artistic groups *Blaue Reiter*, *Bauhaus*).

- Students summarize the content of an article (*Focus*, *Bild*) or documentary (*Deutsche Welle*, *ARD/DZF*) intended for native speakers in order to discuss the topics via e-mail with other users of German.

- Students write a letter for a German newspaper or an article describing and analyzing an issue for a student publication.

- Students prepare a research-based (electronic and print media) analysis of a current event from the perspective of both the U.S. and German-speaking cultures using sources in both languages.

Sample Progress Indicators, Grade 16

- Students perform original scenes or skits based on personal experiences (college or job/internship experience) and exposure to themes, ideas, and perspectives (Greek system vs. *Burschenschaften*) from German-speaking cultures.

- Students select, analyze, and interpret either orally or in writing expressive products of German-speaking cultures from literary genres, the dramatic arts or the fine arts (Wolf, Bachmann, Goethe/Schiller, *die Weimarer Klassik/die Romantik*, von Droste-Hülshoff) for presentation to peer or community groups.

- Students synthesize and interpret the content of an article (*der Spiegel/Frankfurter Allgemeine*) or documentary (*ARD/ZDF*) intended for German-speaking cultures and present it to an audience.

- Students write an article for publication in which they provide a detailed theoretical basis that supports their thesis (*die Unterrichtspraxis*, *The German Quarterly*).

Cultures   Goal Two
Gain Knowledge and Understanding of the German-Speaking World

The standards present a new framework for learning about culture in which the student is asked to demonstrate understanding of the interaction among the ***perspectives of a culture*** and their relationship to the ***products and the practices*** of the culture. When considering the implementation of the standards under the culture goal, the focus is on illustrating that the student can demonstrate an understanding of the interdependent and interactive relationship of the perspectives, practices, and products.

STANDARD 2.1 Students demonstrate an understanding of the relationship between the practices and perspectives of the culture studied.

Sample Progress Indicators, Grade 4

- Students observe, identify, and/or discuss simple patterns of behavior or interaction in various settings such as school (*Schultüte*, home for lunch), family (multi-generational family living arrangement), and the community (*Nikolaustag, Weihnachten* celebrations).

- Students use appropriate gestures (hand-shaking) and oral expression for greetings (greeting the teacher vs. greeting other students), leave-takings, and common classroom interactions.

- Students participate in age-appropriate cultural activities such as games (*Himmel und Erde*), songs (*Mein Hut, der hat drei Ecken*), birthday celebrations (presents, cakes), storytelling, and dramatizations.

Sample Progress Indicators, Grade 8

- Students observe, analyze, and discuss patterns of behavior typical of their peer group (*Jugendgruppen*, sports clubs) and discuss differences in school life (*Klassensprecher*, running errands).

- Students use appropriate verbal (use of *du/Sie*) and nonverbal behavior (body language/gestures) for daily activities among peers and adults.

- Students learn about and participate in age-appropriate cultural practices, such as field trips and overnight trips, games, sports, and entertainment.

Sample Progress Indicators, Grade 12

- Students interact in a variety of cultural contexts that reflect both peer-group and adult activities within German-speaking cultures, using the appropriate verbal and nonverbal cues.

- Students learn about and participate in age-appropriate cultural practices, such as games, sports, and entertainment (going to discos, attending a concert or play).

- Students identify, analyze, and discuss various patterns of behavior or interaction typical of German-speaking cultures (rites of passage including driving, *Schulabschluß, Heiraten*).

- Students identify, examine, and discuss connections between cultural perspectives (environmental issues, results of and reactions to the *Wiedervereinigung*).

Sample Progress Indicators, Grade 16

- Students interact appropriately and comfortably in groups across all age levels, both formally and informally (living or studying abroad), using appropriate verbal and nonverbal cues.

- Students identify and analyze cultural perspectives reflected in historical, political, and religious events and practices (the rise of the *Gewerkschaft*, the concept of *Mitbestimmung*).

- Students identify, analyze, and discuss connections among cultural perspectives, customs, and behavioral patterns in various levels of society and various areas of the German-speaking world (personal ads, *der grüne Punkt*).

STANDARD 2.2 **Students demonstrate an understanding of the relationship between the products and perspectives of the culture studied.**

Sample Progress Indicators, Grade 4

- Students recognize themes, ideas, or perspectives of German-speaking cultures (the concept of *Gesundheit*) and recognize how they are reflected in specific products.

- Students identify and observe tangible products of German-speaking cultures, e.g., toys, dress, types of dwellings, and foods.

- Students identify, experience, or read about expressive products of the culture such as children's songs, selections from children's literature, and types of artwork enjoyed or produced by their peer group in German-speaking cultures (exchange art with partner school, compare children's television programming), and identify, discuss, and produce types of artwork, crafts, or graphic representations enjoyed or made by their peer group within German-speaking cultures (Easter eggs, *Papierlaternen, Schultüten*, flower boxes).

Sample Progress Indicators, Grade 8

- Students learn about perspectives of German-speaking cultures and then explore the effects these perspectives have had on the larger communities (discuss the contributions of WilhelmTell, Hans and Sophie Scholl, Pastor Martin Niemoeller; compare museums in a German city and an American city).

- Students search for, identify, and investigate the function of utilitarian products (BMW, Mercedes, VW), sports equipment, household items, tools, foods (*Spätzle, Knödel, Schnitzel*), and clothing of German-speaking cultures as found within their homes and communities.

- Students identify, discuss, and analyze themes, ideas, and perspectives related to the products being studied (the influence of religion in Germany, holidays in Switzerland and Austria).

Sample Progress Indicators, Grade 12

- Students identify, discuss, and analyze intangible products of German-speaking cultures (school system, DAX and stocks in Germany), and political institutions (parties and the 5% rule), and explore relationships among these institutions and the perspectives of the culture.

- Students experience, discuss, and analyze expressive products of German-speaking cultures (radio, TV, newspapers, film, advertising), including selections from various literary genres and the fine arts (music, opera, theater in Austria).

- Students identify, analyze and evaluate themes, ideas, and perspectives related to the products being studied (the tradition in the arts, openness to new forms of art).

- Students explore the relationships among the products, practices, and perspectives of the culture (the role of music and performance art).

Sample Progress Indicators, Grade 16

- Students analyze, interpret, and evaluate such intangible products of the German culture as social (the education system), economic (*GmbH, AG*), political (the federalist political structure), and religious institutions (the relationship of church and state including church tax, leaving the church), exploring historical and contemporary relationships among them.

- Students analyze, interpret, and evaluate their experiences with expressive products of the various German-speaking cultures and historical periods (literary genres, music, dance, propaganda, national anthem, articles about minorities in German media).

- Students analyze, interpret, and evaluate themes, ideas, perspectives and philosophies related to tangible and intangible products of the culture (patriotism and national identity through German history, feudal system, Holocaust, role of minorities, National Socialism).

- Students analyze, interpret, and evaluate the relationships among products, practices, and perspectives of various German-speaking cultures (compare political/economic systems of Austria, Germany, Switzerland and the cultural traditions of each country).

Connections *Goal Three*
Connect with Other Disciplines and Acquire Information

Another key element in the Standards is the focus on a variety of content areas that are accessible to the student through the medium of a new language and a new culture. An essential link to these contact areas is technology and its ability to take the student into a new learning experience beyond the walls of the classroom. The scenarios that emphasize this goal contain examples of content areas and learning experiences that make connections to other disciplines. These content areas have not traditionally been part of the curriculum for students learning German.

STANDARD 3.1 Students reinforce and further their knowledge of other disciplines through German.

Sample Progress Indicators, Grade 4

- Students demonstrate in German an understanding about concepts learned in other subject areas typically taught at the elementary school level (using maps, drawing shadows on sidewalk and comparing measurements from morning to afternoon).

- Students demonstrate an understanding about concepts learned in other subject areas in the target language, including weather (drawing weather maps), math facts, measurements, animals, insects, holiday celebrations (compare with American traditions), or geographical concepts.

Sample Progress Indicators, Grade 8

- Students discuss in German topics, terms, and concepts from other subject areas, such as geography, history (German materials on Native Americans), math, science (weather maps and Fahrenheit vs. Celsius, metric unit in science, the rainforest).

- Students comprehend articles or short videos in German on topics being studied in other subject areas (social studies materials and *Transparente Landeskunde*).

- Students present in German oral or written reports on topics being studied in other subject areas (the Romans in Germany, media literacy and censorship, German mercenaries in early American history).

Sample Progress Indicators, Grade 12

- Students discuss in German topics from other school subjects (economics through stock market games) including those about German-speaking in the European Union, and historical and social concepts and concerns.

- Students acquire information from a variety of sources (Internet, *InterNationes*, German newspapers and magazines) about a topic being studied in other school subjects.

- Students use information from other school subjects (science–Koch, Meitner, Röntgen; Math–Einstein, Gauß; Music--Schumann, Beethoven, Orff; Art–Barlach, Marc, Klee, Kollwitz; Literature–Seghers, Kafka, Grass; further examine history of the former GDR, the politics and government of the FRG) in order to complete activities in the German classroom.

Sample Progress Indicators, Grade 16

- Students synthesize and evaluate information gathered in German language and culture study to enhance their understanding of another discipline (Holocaust, art in the *Weimarer Republik*, history of German-speaking countries, and their contributions to other cultures, GDR Literature).

- Students synthesize and evaluate information gathered in other disciplines (*Wirtschaftswunder*, Luther's impact on Western Civilization, the influence of Freud and Jung on psychology, Marx and the socialist theory) to enhance their understanding of German language and culture.

STANDARD 3.2 Students acquire information and recognize the distinctive viewpoints that are only available through German and the German-speaking world.

Sample Progress Indicator, Grade 4

- Students read, listen to, and talk about age-appropriate subject content such as folk tales (*Hänsel und Gretl, Der Riese Glombatsch, Regenbogenfisch*), short stories, poems, and songs written for native German speakers.

Sample Progress Indicator, Grade 8

- Students use sources (catalogs, keypals, Web sites, magazines) intended for same-age speakers of German to prepare reports on topics of personal interest (gathering information on favorite sports, hobbies, environmental issues, health; creating an ad for *Quelle*).

Sample Progresses Indicator, Grade 12

- Students use a variety of sources in German intended for same-age speakers to prepare reports on topics of personal interest, or on topics with which they have had limited previous experience (*Rosinenbomber* in Berlin), and then compare this information to information obtained on the same topics in English.

Sample Progress Indicator, Grade 16

- Students synthesize and evaluate a variety of sources intended for adult speakers of German to prepare reports on topics of personal interest (geological formations in various parts of the world, engines from various cars, past and present architectural styles), or on topics with which they have had limited previous experience.

- Students develop and support a point of view (pros and cons of a particular product, the European Union and the role of the U.S.) based on the synthesis and evaluation of information acquired from a variety of sources in German and in other languages.

Comparisons   *Goal Four*
Develop Insight into the Nature of Language and Culture

Within this focus, students are able to compare what they know with what they are learning. This helps them make more meaningful comparisons among the systems and the patterns of both language and culture. This goes well beyond what has traditionally been part of a rationale for second language study in the schools.

STANDARD 4.1 Students demonstrate understanding of the nature of language through comparisons of German and their own languages.

Sample Progress Indicators, Grade 4

- Students cite and use examples of loan words in German and their own language, and they make the connection between German and English (Kindergarten, park, bus, computer, auto).

- Students realize that cognates (*Milch*/milk; *Haus*/house; *Maus*/mouse; *Knie*/knee; *Kinn*/chin; *Fuss*/foot; *tanzen*/dance) enhance comprehension of spoken and written language and demonstrate that awareness by identifying them.

- Students demonstrate an awareness of the existence of idiomatic expressions in both the native language and German (Chip off the old block/*Der Apfel fällt nicht weit vom Baum*; When the cat's away, the mice will play/*Wenn die Katze schläft, dann tanzen die Mäuse*).

- Students demonstrate an awareness of formal and informal language (*Tag*/*Guten Tag*; *Wie geht's?*/*Wie geht es Ihnen?*; *Tschüs!*/*auf Wiedersehen*) and use expressions of politeness in German.

- Students recognize differences and similarities between the sound and writing systems of English and German (capitalizing nouns in German, spelling and pronouncing *ei/ie* in German, comparing sounds of "sch" and "sh" in English, singing alphabet song for letter recognition).

- Students demonstrate an awareness of the various ways of expressing ideas in their own language and in German (compare greetings/leave-takings of Southern and Northern Germany with those of regions of the United States).

Sample Progress Indicators, Grade 8

- Students recognize that there are three genders in German that are different from gender use in American English or other languages they know.

- Students demonstrate an awareness that German has critical sound distinctions (*Kirche*/*Kirsche*; *schön*/*schon*; *Uhr*/*Ohr*) that must be learned in order to communicate meaning.

- Students hypothesize about the relationship among languages based on their awareness of cognates (*Markt*/Market), compare past tense in English and German (*singen, sang, gesungen*; *trinken, trank, getrunken*), and similarity of idioms (*Es geht mir so auf die Nerven!*/It really gets on my nerves).

- Students demonstrate an awareness of ways of expressing respect and communicating status differences in German and in English (language register).

Sample Progress Indicators, Grade 12

- Students recognize that cognates (*Vater*/Father; *Mutter*/mother; *Tochter*/daughter; *Salz*/salt and different animals sounds in both languages) have the same as well as

Standards for Learning German

different meanings among languages and recognize the historical connection between German and English.

- Students demonstrate an awareness that there are phrases and idioms that do not translate directly from one language to another (*es gibt*/there are, *gefallen*/pleases, *Gemütlichkeit*/[no translation]).

- Students analyze elements of German such as time and tense, and comparable linguistic elements in English, and conjecture about how languages use forms to express time (use of present tense to indicate future) and tense relationships (use of past tense forms).

- Students report on the relationship between word order and meaning (location of important elements at the end or beginning of a sentence in German) and hypothesize on how this may or may not reflect the ways cultures organize information.

- Students compare the German writing system and their own. They also examine other writing systems and report about the nature of those writing systems (*Auslaut und Verhärtung*; logographic, syllabic, alphabetic).

Sample Progress Indicator, Grade 16

- Students report on the relationship between word order and meaning (location of subordinate clauses, use of relative pronouns, word order in relation to time, place, matter) and hypothesize on how this may or may not reflect the ways in which cultures organize information (research a topic using a variety of newspapers to examine the feeling, tone, and information communicated through style of language and analyze and synthesize stylistic effects on language) and view the world (analyze how to communicate an idea/topic/theme to a variety of audiences).

STANDARD 4.2 Students demonstrate understanding of the concept of culture through comparisons of the German-speaking cultures studied and their own.

Sample Progress Indicators, Grade 4

- Students compare simple patterns of behavior or interaction in various cultural settings (proper greetings and leave-takings, use of eating utensils in Germany and in the United States).

- Students demonstrate an awareness that gestures are an important part of communication and that they may differ among languages (thumb indicates the number one; pointing to the forehead can be an insult; rapping on the desk vs. clapping).

- Students compare and contrast tangible products (toys), sports (kicking balls vs. throwing balls), food (*Kinderschokolade, Gummibären*) of the German-speaking cultures and their own.

- Students compare and contrast intangible products (rhymes, songs, Grimm's fairy tales and Disney versions) of the German-speaking cultures and their own.

Sample Progress Indicators, Grade 8

- Students contrast verbal and nonverbal behavior within particular activities in the German-speaking cultures and their own (German/American classrooms, ideas of personal space and comfort zones, sports opportunities in each culture).

- Students demonstrate an awareness that they, too, have a culture, based on comparisons of sample daily activities (work ethic, *Feierabend*, family meal time) in the German-speaking culture and their own.

- Students speculate on why certain products originate in and/or are important to particular cultures by analyzing selected products from the German-speaking cultures and their own (Birkenstocks, exercycles, clubs/gyms).

- Students hypothesize about the relationship between cultural perspectives and practices (German vs. American holidays–3 October, 11 November, 4 July), celebrations, work habits, and play by analyzing selected practices from the German-speaking cultures and their own.

- Students hypothesize about the relationship between cultural perspectives and expressive products (popular music in Germany and America), visual arts, appropriate forms of literature (Anne Frank) by analyzing selected products from the German-speaking cultures and their own.

Sample Progress Indicators, Grade 12

- Students hypothesize about the origins of idioms (*Kind und Kegel*) as reflections of culture, citing examples from German and American language and culture.

- Students compare and analyze nuances of meanings of words, idioms, and vocal inflections in German and English (the tone of a written text or of speech, nonverbal behavior, smiling, body language, hand gestures).

- Students analyze and evaluate the relationship of perspectives and practices in the German-speaking culture and compare and contrast these with their own (the importance of family gatherings).

- Students analyze the relationship between the products and perspectives in the German-speaking cultures and compare and contrast these with their own (shop hours and eating times).

Sample Progress Indicator, Grade 16

- Students identify and analyze cultural perspectives as reflected in a variety of literary genres (*Gedicht/Epik, Märchen/Kunstmärchen*).

Communities   Goal Five
Participate in Multilingual Communities at Home and Around the World

The real world focus of the standards directs the student's attention to the applications and uses of language in a variety of settings. These settings extend beyond the classroom and into a local as well as a global community that may be in the immediate area or accessible, either interpersonally or though print or electronic media.

STANDARD 5.1 Students use German within and beyond the school setting.

Sample Progress Indicators, Grade 4

- Students communicate on a personal level with German-speaking visitors and/or via letters or electronic media (exchange e-mail or audiotape messages with partner schools, middle school/high school students, or senior citizens who speak German visit class).

- Students identify professions (engineers, teachers) which require proficiency in another language (list international businesses in the area, people they know who speak German on the job).

- Students present information about German-speaking cultures through story telling (retell Grimm's fairy tales to other classes) and reports (talk about visitor from Switzerland or a visit to Switzerland, report on holiday celebrations in Austria).

- Students perform a short play, or sing *Frühlingslieder* for a school or community celebration, or present a dance performance for heritage month or foreign language week activities.

Sample Progress Indicators, Grade 8

- Students discuss leisure activities and current events, orally or in writing, with peers who speak German or are learning German (visit other schools on a class trip, participate in immersion days/camps).

- Students interact with members of the local community (visit museums, businesses, consulate where German is used or invite representatives of various institutions to visit the school) to learn how German is used in various fields of work.

- Students present information (bake or cook a meal, do a "show and tell" in other classes, write and perform a simple play on cultural misunderstandings) about German-speaking cultures to others.

- Students participate in club and classroom activities that serve and enrich the school (assist teachers and/or tutor younger students in German) or community members through performances and presentations (perform a short play).

- Students write and illustrate stories to present to others through a variety of media (present German skit written by the students, write simple presentation on German-American day to present on local radio).

- Students perform for a school or community celebration (participate in German-American Day parade, perform simple play for PTA, explain *Fasching* to another class).

Sample Progress Indicators, Grade 12

- Students communicate orally (via distance learning, audio-bridges, or with employees from international companies) with representatives of German-speaking cultures regarding topics of personal interest, community or world concern.

- Students participate in a career exploration or a school-to-work project that requires proficiency in German (visit German-based companies in the USA, obtain mini-apprenticeships with German-based companies, attend a career day in German with Euro-based company representatives, work-study programs).

- Students use community and electronic resources to research a topic related to culture (local German history) and/or the study of German.

- Students present information (a virtual trip to Austria, information on a product or company) about German-speaking cultures to others, based on personal experiences, such as those achieved by travel to a German-speaking country (GAPP, Congress-Bundestag Exchange), or through electronic correspondence .

- Students write, illustrate, and present stories, plays, news reports and films to others through a variety of media (a news broadcast for radio and/or TV, a play for videotaping, an illustrated storyboard).

- Students organize and participate in club and classroom activities that serve and enrich the school or community members (perform a play for a peer group from another school, volunteer to teach a portion of class, participate in competitions during German Day at a local college).

Sample Progress Indicators, Grade 16

- Students communicate orally with representatives of German-speaking cultures (guest professors in various fields) regarding topics of personal interest, community or world concern (law, business, medicine, literature).

- Students use their communication skills in internships or community service projects (teach German Saturday school, participate in internships with German companies).

- Students present information or design and present a culturally authentic program based on personal experience (multi-media presentation of internship or travel study in German-speaking country) and research for the benefit and enrichment of the community.

- Students present reports and provide information on stories, plays, films, and current events to others through a variety of media (introduce a performance, write a critique or review of a film or play).

- Students provide volunteer services to community agencies (tutoring, teaching German classes or assisting in genealogical research).

- Students produce and present a major research project (senior thesis or program portfolio).

STANDARD 5.2 Students show evidence of becoming life-long learners by using German for personal enjoyment and enrichment.

Sample Progress Indicators, Grade 4

- Students read German print materials and use media for enjoyment (read cartoons, jokes, short tales, fairy tales, or read and listen to German books on tape).

- Students play culturally authentic games (at home, with neighbors or children at other schools) and perform in programs for others (in musical programs at social functions).

- Students present information about German-speaking cultures that are of interest to them (share information on teddy bears with other groups), and exchange information about topics of personal interest.

- Students plan real or imaginary travel (a trip to the local German restaurant or social club).

- Students experience cultural events or performances (attend a play or performance of a German children's program or reader's theater).

- Students experience and participate in the performing and visual arts (perform a play for PTA or social club, produce culturally authentic art for an art competition).

Sample Progress Indicators, Grade 8

- Students utilize a variety of resources to investigate areas or topics of personal interest (use the Internet to plan a trip to a German-speaking area with their parents or to gather information on sports, fashion, music).

- Students participate in leisure-time activities related to German culture, including the use of various media, for entertainment (gather and share information on rock groups beyond those introduced in class and share the information with the class or collect information from maps, posters and brochures on areas they would like to visit).

- Students exchange information on topics of personal interest (use German in personal conversations on the phone with classmates).

- Students experience and participate in the performing and visual arts (visit a children's exhibit, plan a visit to a museum).

Sample Progress Indicators, Grade 12

- Students initiate oral or written exchanges of information with representatives of German-speaking cultures (contacts with new keypals) as they investigate topics of personal interest.

- Students participate in a career exploration or school-to-work project which requires proficiency in German (contact regional German-American Chamber of Commerce for information on possible career choices or internships).

- Students continue to expand and enhance their knowledge of topics of interest for personal enjoyment and growth (develop a scrapbook on topics of interest or list of Internet bookmarks).

- Students participate in leisure activities related to German cultures (collect classical or rock CDs, posters from German-speaking areas, attend a concert or tennis match featuring a prominent player).

- Students enhance their knowledge of German-speaking culture through various means, including preparation of a presentation or program attendance (gather information on performer or sports figure prior to a concert or event and share it with the German Club).

- Students establish and maintain interpersonal relations with speakers of German (maintain a long-term relationship with a penpal, former exchange student, GAPP or exchange partners, participate as an exchange student to German-speaking country).

Sample Progress Indicators, Grade 16

- Students establish and maintain interpersonal relationships with speakers of German (provide promotional presentations for GAPP or exchange programs by going back to high school to talk about personal interests/experiences).

- Students use their background in German language and cultures to pursue a topic of personal or professional interest (attend German film series, contact agencies for information on work-study programs or internships).

- Students design and present a culturally-authentic program (background information and introduction to a play or film presented by the drama department or for a local film series) based on experience and research for personal enrichment.

- Students present reports and provide information on the narrative and performing arts, travel and current events to others through a variety of media (research a German-speaking area for travel groups, organize a *Theaterabend* and introduce playwright and the play).

- Students analyze and evaluate the relationship between the products and perspectives in cultures studied and compare and contrast these with their own (students returning from exchange or intern programs make presentations comparing German business practices with American business practices, speak at the Rotary Club).

- Students analyze and evaluate cultural perspectives as reflected in a variety of literary genres (research a Turkish author who writes in German, present interpretation to *Lesekreis* or annual AATG or MLA meeting, refine thesis project for publication).

Learning Scenarios
Models for K-4 and K-8 Programs

TARGETED STANDARDS
1.1 Interpersonal Communication
1.2 Interpretive Communication
3.1 Making Connections

DIE DREI BÄREN

While reading and interpreting the story of *Die drei Bären* in German, pupils are able to experience some of the scenes from the story and to relate this to life in another place as they also learn the process of cooking porridge (*Grütze*). Working in groups, they learn to measure the quantities of the ingredients in the format they use at home with tablespoons and measuring cups. Then they compare the same ingredients using metric measurements that weigh what they want to cook. In the cooking process, utensils and ingredients are provided for a number of cooking stations so that each pupil participates in adding ingredients and/or stirring until the food is cooked. Some groups cook using cups and tablespoons, and other groups use grams and liters. The teacher asks the students to describe what each one is doing. They first compare the quantity of the *Grütze* to see who has more. While some are stirring the food, other children do a "bear walk", a version of follow the leader, around the room and out the door. After they return, they are ready to taste what they have prepared and to further experience the story. They check to see how hot the *Grütze* is using Celsius and then check again using Fahrenheit to compare which temperature is too hot and which is too cold, and which is just right.

They share comments on their likes and dislikes, and they relate this to each of the figures in the story. They want to experience other elements of the story and set out to measure chairs that could be used by each of the different characters. Using a yard stick and a metric measuring tape, they designate which chairs could be big enough for each character. The pupils compare what they have measured to be sure that the chairs measured using a yard stick are the same those measured metrically. They discover that the information is different. Finally, they draw their own version of the story and compare what they have understood.

Reflection

1.1 Students exchange comments in German on other foods they like or dislike, and they could also exchange information on the foods they cook in their homes.

1.2 Students illustrate in non-verbal ways by acting out the story or drawing another version of the story to show that they understood.

3.1 Students expand the drawings from German illustrations and compare them to similar situations in their own community.

The next time the teacher reads this story with a class, more time will be spent working with other differences using the metric system as well as in measuring using inches and yards. The students will also write their own version of the story as an English language arts assignment using process writing. They will write about foods they like and about new foods and how different these foods taste to different people. They may also write about their experience using different means to measure things. The pupils will develop a portfolio of illustrations from stories they have written and later share this with another class. The story is expanded to include German illustrations, which they compare with their own community.

MEIN HAUS, MEIN ZIMMER

Students in a middle school program are asked to draw layouts of their homes and give particular emphasis to their own rooms. Then they learn about design and layout of model houses in German-speaking areas. Students describe the various models including

> **TARGETED STANDARDS**
> 2.1 Practices of Culture
> 2.2 Products of Culture
> 3.1 Making Connections

apartments, farm houses, and single family houses. Students compare these with models from a variety of German-speaking areas representing rural and urban as well as north and south locations. Some students connect with their social studies class and bring in models designed in other cultures such as Native Americans and early U.S. settlers (hogans, log cabins, and sod houses). Students compare various aspects of the dwellings and relate these elements to particular lifestyles in various settings. Students then draw their own example of an exemplary house, their dream house or a house from another period of time. They share these models with the class and discuss how the designs reflect the various perspectives of the cultures.

Reflection

2.1, 2.2 Students make the models part of their social studies class and explain to their peers how certain cultural perspectives are reflected in the homes (products) of different German-speaking areas.

5.1 At a special function for family and members of the community, the students report on how people are changing the ways they live in order to be more responsive to the environment.

Students compare renditions and find other models on the Internet which represent different regions. Then they discuss why houses are built differently in various countries and areas and show how these plans reflect different cultural perspectives. Students demonstrate their understanding of how different layouts in living quarters reflect different lifestyles in various cultures. If the class has keypals in Germany or other schools in the US, this is a good topic for e-mail discussion or presentation on the home page. Pictures of homes can be posted on the respective home pages and then discussed by e-mail.

TARGETED STANDARDS
1.2 Interpretive Communication
2.1 Practices of Culture
2.2 Products of Culture
4.2 Cultural Comparisons

GUTE BESSERUNG

Middle school students in a German class have been working on a unit on wellness. They have learned to ask for and give advice about various aspects of health. In class, they receive packaging for various medications and health care products. They are instructed to ascertain the name of the medication, symptoms it is meant to alleviate, how to take the medication, dosage, cautions, possible side effects, and storage instructions. After each student has found the required information, the class makes observations about the types of medication and health care products they examined. They compare these products and their usage to those commonly used in their own homes. The students notice the number of homeopathic and natural remedies and discuss the attitudes toward health such products might reflect.

Reflection

1.2 Students use German to obtain practical information about product content and use.
2.1 Students expand their understanding of health care practices in the target language culture and explore the cultural perspectives, which lead to these practices.
2.2 Students demonstrate understanding of how products available in Germany reflect cultural perspectives about wellness and health care.
4.2 Students compare and contrast health care products and practices of the US with those in German-speaking countries.

Students may then use German to present information and ideas to an audience on the topic of health care. This could be done in another German class, or in English in a social studies or health class at the same school. This context provides the opportunity to make comparisons on the ways health care is made available to people in German-speaking countries and for students to compare this with their own community. Students could also take their findings to make presentations to other German classes beyond their own school or at a weekend immersion camp to community groups.

Models for 6-12 Programs

EINWANDERER

While reading and discussing the story, *Einwanderer*, the true story of a contingent of Germans who fled Gau-Algesheim, Hesse-Darmstadt in the year 1847 and immigrated to Wisconsin, students (junior high school/high school) also analyze and interpret information from primary historical sources including: a picture, a ship manifest, U.S. census documents, a map, an 1850's German ledger, a German letter from 1849, and excerpts from local German language newspapers.

> **TARGETED STANDARDS**
> 1.2 Interpretive Communication
> 1.3 Presentational Communication
> 3.1 Making Connections
> 3.2 Acquiring Information
> 4.2 Cultural Comparisons

Students read a letter written in 1849 to a Gau-Algesheim resident to discern some reasons why the Algesheimers fled their homeland. They also read and interpret both a population and an agricultural census. The agricultural census helps them determine what kinds of animals and crops were raised on an immigrant farm, while the population census provides information on families, place of birth, occupations and degree of wealth. Students develop an even better understanding of the daily life of the immigrants as they fill in sections of an early map, extract information from an 1850's ledger, and read the letter for more detail. They compare the accounts of the newcomers to the experiences of the people currently living in the area. They learn about the legacy of the German immigrants through a German newspaper advertisement announcing the 25th anniversary of the *Sängerbund*, an organization still active today, 150 years later. They gather information on a local nineteenth-century German-American, write a report in German, and then present the report to the class. They use at least two primary historical sources in their research and produce an overhead transparency, highlighting one of these sources, as part of the report. In small groups, the students then design brochures to attract new residents to their city, just as was done by the early Germans living in Wisconsin.

Reflection

1.2 Students read the *Lesestücke* as well as excerpts from authentic texts.
1.3 Students present a report on a local German-American from the last century.
3.1 Students make connections to social studies, history, and the German-American heritage of America.
3.2 Students acquire information from authentic documents.
4.2 Students make comparisons between the German-speaking world and the U.S. of the Nineteenth century.

Students expand their knowledge of the German heritage of the U.S. Students also understand the importance of having language-proficient scholars to help interpret German ethnic history, much of which lies unread in archives across this country. A follow-up trip to a German cemetery, an 1850's German farmhouse, and a German-American restaurant further remind students of the wealth of German history in their community. Students also explore their own family backgrounds, be they German-American or other. In so doing, most students will need some of the same types of historical sources that were used in the *Einwanderer* unit.

TARGETED STANDARDS
1.1 Interpersonal Communication
1.2 Interpretive Communication
1.3 Presentational Communication
3.1 Making Connections

GOETHE'S *ERLKÖNIG*

Students in a third year class in Pennsylvania have read Goethe's *Erlkönig*. The students are also learning about *Lieder*. They listen to three different interpretations of Franz Schubert's *Der Erlkönig*, discuss various nuances and decide which version they think best captures the essence of Goethe's poem. The students divide up into groups. Each group is asked to interpret the poem and to present their interpretation to the class. Some of the artistically inclined students draw, sculpt or paint the story of the *Erlkönig*, others write their own version of the poem, some as a poem, others as a play; still others compose their own music and perform for the class. Upon completion of the presentations, each is discussed by the whole class. Some of the students' work is exhibited in a display case in the school lobby.

Reflection

1.1 Students express their ideas and feelings, exchange opinions and are aware of the viewpoints of their peers.
1.2 Students seek to uncover the deeper meaning of the poem.
1.3 Students present their interpretations to the class and learn different ways of looking at the same thing.
3.1 Students make connections between literature, music and the visual arts.

Students discuss sociolinguistic and culturally "loaded" terms in the poem (e.g., the differences between the German *reiten* and English "to ride") to make a comparison between the languages and cultures represented in the poem and in their own experiences. This discussion could then lead to an awareness of culturally rooted interpretations of a literary idea. The students could also read Sir Walter Scott's *The Erl-King*, comparing it to Goethe's *Erlkönig*. A member or the music department could be invited to give a lecture and demonstration on *Lieder*. Students could also listen to Louis Spohr's musical interpretations of *Erlkönig* and compare it to Schubert's song.

DAMALS WAR ES FRIEDRICH

The students in the fourth year German course at Las Cruces High school have spent the past three weeks reading *Damals war es Friedrich*, a novel by Hans Peter Richter that focuses on the relationship of a Jewish and non-Jewish boy growing up during the 1930's. While reading, the students discuss various literary aspects of the novel, including its structure and relationship to other literary works that they have read, the relationships of the characters to each other, and the historical setting of the novel. The nine students decide in a brainstorming session to produce a "documentary" film based on the historical period depicted in the novel and focused on the period's impact on families. Students plan to contact history teachers in the school, professors in the German and history departments at the local university, the Jewish community leaders, and the leadership of *Freude der deutschen Sprache*, a community organization for German speakers. Some students videotape interviews with members of the community who had lived in Germany during that time period. Other students write scripts for scenes from the book emphasizing the Jewish boy's perspective. With members of the class taking on the various roles, these scenes are also taped by the group. Still other students do historical research. One student's inquiries lead to the discovery of a holocaust museum in a neighboring city, which the class visits. The students interview the museum's founder and director and capture many of the displays on video tape. The group also views several films including *Europa, Europa, Die Weisse Rose, Schindler's List*, and parts of a documentary films on *Entartete Kunst* (Degenerate Art) and film maker Leni Riefenstahl. Using two VCRs, they edit the scenes that they filmed, including relevant parts of the interviews, and footage from the museum visit. Finally they add introductory and closing comments and voice-over narration by some of the students. The finished film is about twenty-five minutes long and is augmented by a written synopsis of the project.

TARGETED STANDARDS
1.1 Interpersonal Communication
1.2 Interpretive Communication
1.3 Presentational Communication
2.1 Practices of Culture
2.2 Products of Culture
3.1 Making Connections
3.2 Acquiring Information
4.1 Language Comparisons
5.1 School and Community
5.2 Lifelong Learning

Reflection

1.1 Students brainstorm and plan their project using the language. Students interview community leaders.
1.2 Students read a novel, view a film, and research a project using secondary sources. Students produce a film and a synopsis.
2.1 Students discover through their reading, viewing, and research how the historical period was presented in the culture.
2.2 Students view films produced by the culture studied.
3.1 Students further their knowledge of the period.
3.2 Students find perspectives that differ from those presented in their history textbooks.
4.1 In viewing a film, students comment on the difference in the spoken dialogue and subtitles.
5.1 Students use the community as a resource.
5.2 Students research a topic using resources other than print material. A copy of the film is sent to the museum for their archives.

This scenario illustrates how a literary work can serve as the basis for an interdisciplinary project. Even though this community does not have a large number of native speakers, the students were able to locate speakers of the language who could contribute to their project. A logical extension of the project would be to broadcast the video on a local cable channel or university channel for the community to see, or to host a screening attended by all those interviewed. The final product in this scenario could also have been a print publication of some variety

KARNEVAL, DIE 5. JAHRESZEIT

> **TARGETED STANDARDS**
> 2.1 Practices of Culture
> 2.2 Products of Culture

Goethe identified the *Karneval* season as the fifth season of the year in Cologne. Students collect products and practices of individual German-speaking communities to confirm Goethe's statement. After first researching origins of the celebration through Roman civilization, pagan practices, and the Christian calendar, students will identify cities of German-speaking countries, which have major public carnival season celebrations. The various terms for those celebrations (*Fassnacht, Fasteloovend, Fasching,* and *Karneval*) will be used to identify groupings for further research.

Thus the class will divide into groups to research the events and traditions of each of those communities, compiling unique vocabulary, information, ads, announcements that might be found on the Internet, as well as descriptions of masks and costumes, organizations, events, foods, and music for these celebrations. Each group will report to the class by creating its own simulation of the local tradition through pictures and self-created products or mock-ups. This may be scheduled to coincide with the actual dates of *Karneval*, so that pictures and reports from the Internet (or *Deutsche Welle*) can be used. Students might well plan a *Karneval* party to take place during the actual *Karneval* season.

Reflection

2.1, 2.2 Students demonstrate an understanding of the relationship between the practices and perspectives concerning *Karneval*, as well as an understanding of the relationship between the products and perspectives of *Karneval*.

Contrasts should be made between the many traditions practiced regionally. These may also be compared and contrasted with festivities in other countries, including the United States (New Orleans, for example). Several classes could be involved by having each class investigate the traditions of a different major community and explain their traditions for the other classes. As an alternative, videotapes of the speeches and presentations could be presented to other classes.

Models for 9-16 Programs

UMWELTPROBLEME IN DEUTSCHLAND

As part of a unit on the environment, students in Ohio explore specific problems of water pollution, its effect on wildlife, and the difficulties of water clean-up (e.g., the Rhine, the Elbe). Through brainstorming and webbing, pertinent vocabulary is introduced and

> **TARGETED STANDARDS**
> 1.2 Interpretive Communication
> 1.3 Presentational Communication
> 3.1 Making Connections

compiled in a computer data base. The persistence of pollutants in a body of water is demonstrated by a simple experiment. Drops of food coloring representing the pollutants continue to color the water after repeated dilutions. The students then conduct additional experiments, which demonstrate the effects of oil spills on bird feathers and eggs. A third experiment asks the students to hypothesize successful ways of removing oil from water by testing water filters of their own design. The final experiment has the students construct a sand/gravel water filter and test its effectiveness. Terms for scientific equipment are presented in a poster display, and pertinent vocabulary is added to the data base.

Tables or charts representing facts and figures regarding famous oil spills such as the *Exxon Valdez* are analyzed and discussed. Oil spill occurrences are researched by the students on the Internet and presented to the class with posters, collages, or oral presentations. Students then write their own reports or newspaper articles about the effects of pollution on the water in their geographic area.

Reflection

1.2 Students interpret experimental results and draw conclusions.
1.3 Students share factual information, results and opinions through discussion, presentation, and research.
3.1 Students expand their knowledge and understanding of ecology through German.

Students can be instructed about the design and function of water treatment plants with videos and/or diagrams. Instruction on this topic can include a field trip to the local water treatment plant or making and labeling a model of a water treatment facility.

BUSINESS PRACTICES

In a business German course at a community college in Virginia, students learn and discuss the structure of the corporate world in both Germany and the U.S. Then students, in small groups, proceed to create a profile of a local German company (Siemens, Stihl, etc.). After reading the informational and promotional materials supplied by the company, students interview workers, administrative assistants,

> **TARGETED STANDARDS**
> 1.1 Interpersonal Communication
> 1.2 Interpretive Communication
> 1.3 Presentational Communication
> 2.1 Practices of Culture
> 2.2 Products of Culture
> 4.2 Cultural Comparisons

managers, CEOs, etc., in order to learn more about it. Students put together a portfolio of the company, including information about the products of the company, and present, in German, their findings to the class, as well as to non-school groups, e.g., AIESEC, Chamber of Commerce or similar groups.

Reflections

1.1, 1.2 Inside the classroom, students read and interpret texts on the business world in Germany. Outside the classroom, they learn about German companies through interviews with people in the work force.

1.3 Students present their findings to their fellow students, and furthermore, they make their newly acquired information available to a broader audience by having their portfolios available for viewing/reading at their school library.

2.1 Students show how the German work ethic, team-working, priorities, holidays, etc., reflect the perspectives of German culture.

2.2 Students compare ads for various German-made products in relation to the quality of the products offered for sale. Students learn about the products that the respective companies manufacture.

4.2 Through interviewing German employees in German, students recognize that there are different viewpoints in different cultures. Students compare the German company that they researched with a similar American company.

Students make presentations at local school-to-work, school-to-career conferences or career days at such local schools. With the introduction of a number of career possibilities, students can find companies that are interested in employees who have competence in German. They can use the Internet to find a internship or a position where they can apply what they have learned.

TARGETED STANDARDS
1.1 Interpersonal Communication
1.2 Interpretive Communication
3.1 Making Connections
3.2 Acquiring Information

CONNECTING WITH GERMANY'S PAST

While reading Paul Celan's *Todesfuge*, students will make numerous connections to the fields of history, ethics, and psychology. Pre-reading activities and post-reading activities will enable the student to learn about daily life in a concentration camp for both Jewish inmates and for the SS guards overseeing their captivity. The connections the students will make to the disciplines of history, ethics and psychology are numerous. The imagery is accurate and the poem dynamically makes the connections to historical events with which students are familiar, yet which may have never been presented to them before in German.

During discussion, students have the opportunity to engage in conversations, provide and obtain information, express feelings and emotions, and exchange opinions about the poem. Students will read historical, ethical, and psychological reports and treatises on the concentration camps and the period of the Third Reich. Talking with survivors would provide personal information. Finally, they would themselves write a report in which they assume the role of either victim or guard.

Reflections

1.1 Students discuss what they have read with their classmates.
1.2 Students read and interpret a poem.
3.1 Students make connections with history, ethics, and psychology.
3.2 Students acquire information about the Third Reich from a German perspective.

Students write interpretive essays about being a victim or guard. They may present these to a variety of audiences outside the program, e.g., a conference on diversity in or outside the school.

HEINRICH KLEIST'S COMEDY, *DER ZERBROCHENE KRUG*

Students in a third year course at a university in Pennsylvania have discussed portions of *Der zerbrochene Krug* by Heinrich von Kleist. In discussing the comedy, they decide to adopt roles of the specific characters and to present their interpretation of

> **TARGETED STANDARDS**
> 1.2 Interpretive Communication
> 1.3 Presentational Communication
> 4.1 Language Comparison

these characters to the class. The process includes conducting interviews with other students to elicit information about the specific characters they are representing. After the students have had the opportunity to present the characters to the class, they want to present them to a wider audience; they decide to use the interviews as a basis for articles in a newspaper they will share with other third and fourth year students in the program. The process of conducting interviews and then writing the articles occurs several times during the discussion of the play; hence the articles serve as a serial in the newspaper to show the progress of the "investigation." Students will write for different types of papers, so that they learn to accommodate register in a variety of written formats (e.g., *Bild-Zeitung, Die Welt, Neue Züricher Zeitung, Frankfurter Allgemeine Zeitung*).

Many of the problems surrounding the play are resolved within the play as well as by the students. After the articles have dealt with all aspects of the case, some students begin to interview other students as to their reactions to the resolution of the problem and to the meaning of the play in general.

Reflection

1.2 Students interpret the themes of the play and act them out to a variety of audiences.
1.3 Students present their viewpoints through the medium of print.
4.1 Students in a more advanced course learn how to accommodate register in a variety of written formats.

The next time the instructor works with students on this play, the class expands the interview process and functions as an editorial team to mesh the collection of articles into the background information needed for a talk show on the responsibility of the individual in society. The talk show is videotaped for viewing in other classes with new groups of students in the program. Students demonstrate an understanding of the concept of culture through comparisons of the culture studied and their own. Here, students would work on learning about the period in which Kleist wrote (c. 1806) and the culture prevalent in Prussia at that time (a rather deteriorating patriarchal court system, repression of peasants, blackmail, bribery) and compare this period with their own culture (either historical or present).

Standards for Learning German

Frequently Asked Questions

Why are there German Standards at all? Aren't the generic standards sufficient?
The German Standards, like those for Chinese, French, Italian, Japanese, Russian, Spanish, Portuguese, and the Classical languages, have been developed as companion documents to the national standards (*Standards for Foreign Language Learning: Preparing for the 21st Century*). Commissioned by the National Standards in Foreign Language Education Collaborative Project, the language-specific standards are intended to provide descriptions of the unique aspects of German, its history and culture, and its current utility in today's world.

As a companion document to the national standards and flowing from them, the German Standards provide German-specific examples within the standards themselves, for the learning scenarios, for the progress indicators, and for classroom and bibliographic resources educators may use to translate the standards into the local German curriculum. While current reality may be that most German programs occur in Grades 7-12, the standards and progress indicators are written to allow for multiple entry points, with the understanding that specific classroom activities will always need to be age-appropriate and developmentally appropriate for the student.

Do we really mean that German is for all students?
Yes, given the opportunity, all students are capable of and can benefit from the study of German. German should not be perceived as better reserved for college-bound students. The practicality of an early start and an extended sequence for students of German and the interconnectedness of German Standards with other aspects of the curriculum and student learning ensure that each student can learn and make reasonable progress in developing proficiency in German.

Why does the German document include Grade 16 as a benchmark while the generic document does not?
The mandate and funding for the development of the national standards document was specifically limited to K-12 programs. The German language-specific document, as determined by the National Standards in Foreign Language Education Collaborative Project, saw the need and took the opportunity to describe an extended and articulated sequence for German that would include college and university programs in the language.

Why do the Standards for German use Grades 4, 8, 12 and 16 as benchmarks for progress when most programs begin at the high school or the middle school level?
The vision of the German Standards is to describe the early start and extended sequence of language study that has as its goal the development of proficiency in German by students, and, practically, to be in alignment with the other core curriculum areas.

Are there models of articulated K-12 or K-16, or extended sequence programs in existence to lead the way in implementing these Standards for German?
There are such programs, and AATG will endeavor to identify and keep track of them, so that their experience can be shared.

How can the Standards for German be useful to those of us who have Grade 9-12 programs when they describe a K-16 sequence? Where are the old Level I and Level II concepts?
The K-16 Standards provide the vision for an extended sequence of instruction for students. Those German programs that begin at various points along the continuum will still be able to use the standards themselves as they plan local curriculum, and can use the progress indicators at the four checkpoints to guide them as they adapt them to be age- and developmentally-appropriate for their students.

What sources, resources, bibliographical references are available to teachers that would detail and flesh out some of the names, titles, words, idioms, and concepts cited in the Standards for German?
The AATG has a large collection of materials that already provide the support for teachers who are integrating the standards into their daily lessons. The association continually seeks out materials from other sources and encourages its members to share their best ideas. Future plans include developing a database of resources that specifically support the concepts mentioned in the German Standards document.

Where are the specific literature references and lists at the advanced levels of German study?
The German Standards do not describe or offer specific literary references for recommendation or by prescription. As the schools themselves develop curricula from the standards, they will select the appropriate authors/works/readings to be studied in their own programs. Examples of specific sources and literature in German are provided, however, within some of the Sample Progress Indicators and Scenarios.

How do the Standards for German mesh with the goals and realities of Advanced Placement and International Baccalaureate courses and tests in German?
The Standards should serve as a foundation on which to base all assessment instruments, whether be they local, state, or national examinations. Current assessments should be reviewed and revised, where appropriate, in light of the German Standards.

What professional development plans will be available for German teachers to implement the Standards for German?
Through its professional development program and the meetings of its 61 chapters, the AATG offers teachers of German at all levels of instruction the opportunity to work with colleagues in developing standards-based programs.

What are the necessary steps to be taken to translate the generic Standards and the Standards for German into implementation of effective classroom programs?
The *Standards for Learning German* represent a national perspective and description of contents for Grades 4, 8, 12, and 16 that outline what students should know and be able to do. Performance standards to be developed nationally will outline stages of proficiency. Local districts will then need to develop appropriate assessment rubrics that reflect the performance standards. States will most often provide the curricular context and further definition in their own framework documents, and then school districts will detail course content and an articulated sequence for their programs based on the standards and state documents.

From the local district documents, teachers will be able to design lesson plans that will translate curriculum into appropriate and meaningful activities for the German classroom.

What changes might be expected and necessary for college and university German programs as a result of these Standards?
For students of German coming to colleges and universities from an extended sequence of German in grades K-12, studies in German, German culture, and German literature will need to be provided that are commensurate with the students' abilities and proficiencies in the language. In addition, opportunities will need to be developed and provided that will allow students to pursue careers demanding German language and cultural competencies, whether it be for international business, engineering, medicine, or another life profession.

What changes might be expected and necessary for teacher training institutions that prepare German teachers as a result of these Standards for German?
Teacher preparation institutions will need to provide course work and experiences specifically tailored to the needs of teachers of German. The programs will ensure that the prospective teachers have an opportunity to acquire and learn to apply the linguistic and cultural competencies and professional and pedagogical skills they need to implement the standards and become effective teachers. The program will include and require: a specific language proficiency level, knowledge of German culture, interdisciplinary learning experience, language and cultures comparisons, communities at home and abroad and their role in language teaching and learning, language acquisition and instruction theories, technological opportunities available and appropriate for German teachers, and German language assessments.

If communication is the primary goal of the program described in the Standards for German, how can teachers ensure that there is an appropriate balance and contribution from the other four program goals?
When program developers and teachers keep all five goals and eleven standards in mind, they will be able to create a balanced program of instruction. Not all five will be evident in every single lesson, but in the course of a week, a unit, a quarter, or other time period, students should work within all five areas. The five goals are not intended to be addressed, taught, or practiced in isolation, but rather content or activities may come from cultures, connections, comparisons, and/or communities, with communication being a constant part of German instruction.

How can Connections and Communities be added to an existing German program?
Connections and Communities should not be considered "add-ons" to the current German program. They should already be a part of the language learning process. When students study numbers, art, geography, and culture, for example, in the context of a thematic unit that talks about the weather, these represent true connections to the existing curriculum. Likewise, the use of e-mail, the Internet, pen pals, local celebrations, newspaper and magazine articles collected by students and teachers can make the Communities goal an integral part of the classroom.

Where is the word or concept of grammar within the German Standards? What role does grammar play in proficiency-oriented German instruction?

Although knowledge of German grammar was once viewed as a primary or isolated goal of language study, grammar is now understood as a tool to support the broader goal of learning to communicate by viewing, listening, speaking, reading, and writing. It remains a valuable source for understanding meaning. Grammar is both directly and indirectly addressed in the standard for Communication and implied throughout the other standards.

Is there a link between the student standards for German and any assessments that would follow?

Since good assessment closely parallels instruction and curriculum, the German Standards should be used at least as a general basis or blueprint for any classroom, program, or larger state or national assessments.

Can we or should we be able to use these Standards for German as a means of evaluating students and also teachers?

The standards specifically describe what students should know and be able to do, and so they do provide a basis on which to formulate and plan assessments for students. The standards, however, are not intended as a specific accountability measure for teachers or instruction.

Selective Bibliography

1. General

Bausch, K.-R., H. Christ, and H.-J. Krumm (Eds.). 1995. *Handbuch Fremdsprachenünterricht.* Tubingen: Francke-Verlag.

Häussermann, U., and H.E. Piepho. 1996. *Aufgaben-Handbuch Deutsch als Fremdsprache- Abriß einer Aufgaben- und Übungstypologie.* Munich: Iudicium-Verlag.

Huth, M. 1997. *Hits für den Unterricht - Lehren und Lernen interkulturell/antirassistisch.* Baltmannsweiler: Schneider-Verlag.

Kuhn, B. 1993. *Gedächtniskunst im Unterricht.* Munich: Iudicium-Verlag.

Mueller, B.-D. 1987. *Anders lernen im Fremdsprachenunterricht - Experimente aus der Praxis.* Munich: Langenscheidt.

Neuner, G., and H. Hunfeld. 1993. *Methoden des fremdsprachlichen Unterrichts.* Munich: Langenscheidt.

Neuner, G, M. Krueger, and U. Grewer. 1981. *Übungstypologie zum kommunikativen Deutschunterricht.* Munich: Langenscheidt.

Sperber, H.G. 1989. *Mnemotechniken im Fremdsprachenerwerb mit Schwerpunkt "Deutsch als Fremdsprache."* Munich: Iudicium-Verlag.

Weigmann, J. 1993. Unterrichtsmodelle für Deutsch als Fremdsprache. Ismaning: Max Hueber Verlag.

2. **German-American**

Adams, W.P. 1993. *The German-Americans, An Ethnic Experience.* Trans. & adapted by LaVern J. Rippley and Eberhard Reichmann. Indianapolis: Max Kade German-American Center. Indiana University-Purdue University.

Galicich, A. 1989. The German-Americans. New York: Chelsea House.

Haller, C. R. 1995. *Distinguished German-Americans.* Bowie, MD: Heritage Books.

O'Connor, R. 1968. *The German-Americans: An Informal History.* Boston: Little, Brown & Co.

Rippley, L. J. 1984. *The German-Americans.* Lanham, MD: University Press of American.

Rippley, L. J. 1970. *Of German Ways.* Minneapolis: Dillon.

Tolzmann, D. H. (Ed.) 1995. *German Achievements in America: Rudolf Cronau's Survey History.* Bowie, MD: Heritage Books.

3. **Links to Web Sites of Interest to Teachers of German**

http://www.aatg.org   (AATG's homepage, with numerous links)

http://www.germany-info.org   (German Information Center/German Embassy)

http://www.austriaculture.net (Austrian Cultural Institute)

http://www.swissemb.org   (Embassy of Switzerland)

http://www.goethe.de   (Goethe-Institut)

http://inform.ospi.wednet.edu/languages/Consultants/
                               (homepage of German language consultants)

http://www.dwelle.de   (Deutsche Welle)

http://www.spiegel.de   (Der Spiegel)

http://www.collegeboard.org/ap/ (Advanced Placement information)

http://www.inter-nationes.de   (Inter Nationes homepage)

Standards for Learning Italian

National Standards Task Force of the American Association of Teachers of Italian

ITALIAN

TASK FORCE MEMBERS

Dr. Grace Mannino (Co-Chair), Brentwood High School, Brentwood, NY; SUNY at Stonybrook; and Suffolk Community College, Selden, NY

Ida Giampietro Wilder (Co-Chair), Greece Athena High School and Nazareth College, Rochester, NY

Writers

Rosa Bellino-Giordano, Lyons Township High School, LaGrange, IL
Mario Donatelli, Ramapo High School, Spring Valley, NY
Bruna Furgiuele, East Rochester Middle School, East Rochester, NY
Lucrezia Lindia, Eastchester Middle/High School, Eastchester, NY and Westchester Community College, NY
Alfred J. Valentini, T. R. Proctor High School, Utica, NY

Standards for Learning Italian

Prepared by
The American Association of Teachers of Italian
National Standards Task Force

Contributor
Salvatore Bruno, Dos Pueblos High School, Goleta, CA

Board of Reviewers
Mark Epstein, College of New Jersey
Paolo Giordano, Loyola University Chicago
Christopher Kleinhenz, University of Wisconsin
Susan Mancini, Ohio State University
Lois Pontillo Mignone, SUNY at Farmingdale
Dolores Mita, New York State Education Department (Retired)
Joseph A. Tursi, SUNY at Stony Brook

Table of Contents

STANDARDS FOR LEARNING ITALIAN		**332**
INTRODUCTION		**333**
WHY STUDY ITALIAN?		**333**
COMMUNICATION	Goal 1	**334**
CULTURES	Goal 2	**339**
CONNECTIONS	Goal 3	**342**
COMPARISONS	Goal 4	**345**
COMMUNITIES	Goal 5	**348**
SAMPLE LEARNING SCENARIOS		**350**

All in the Family	351
Il Barbiere di Siviglia	351
Bocce	352
Buildings Tell a Story	353
Carnevale	354
Columbus	354
Fairy Tales	355
Family Ties	356
Food and Meals	356
House Hunting	357
Immigration and Family Heritage	358
Italy by Train	358
Let's Stay Healthy	359
A Love Story	360
Made in Italy	360
Il Mercante di Venezia	361
La Moda	361
Numbers Around the Classroom	362
Our Neighborhood	363
People and their Environments	363
Photographs Have a Voice	364
A Picture is Worth a Thousand Words	365
Sports	366
Tasteful Family Secrets	366
Trovarsi un Lavoro	367
Weather	368

Standards for Learning Italian

COMMUNICATION — GOAL ONE

Communicate in Italian

Standard 1.1 Students engage in conversations, provide and obtain information, express feelings and emotions, and exchange opinions.

Standard 1.2 Students understand and interpret spoken and written Italian on a variety of topics.

Standard 1.3 Students present information, concepts, and ideas in Italian to an audience of listeners or readers on a variety of topics.

CULTURES — GOAL TWO

Gain Knowledge and Understanding of Italian Culture

Standard 2.1 Students demonstrate an understanding of the relationship between the practices and perspectives of Italian culture.

Standard 2.2 Students demonstrate an understanding of the relationship between the products and perspectives of Italian culture.

CONNECTIONS — GOAL THREE

Connect with Other Disciplines, Acquire Information, and Expand Knowledge

Standard 3.1 Students reinforce and further their knowledge of other disciplines through the study of Italian language and culture.

Standard 3.2 Students acquire information and recognize the distinctive viewpoints provided through the knowledge of Italian language and culture.

COMPARISONS — GOAL FOUR

Develop Insight into the Nature of Language and Culture

Standard 4.1 Students demonstrate understanding of the nature of language through comparisons of the Italian language and their own.

Standard 4.2 Students demonstrate understanding of the concept of culture through comparisons of Italian culture and their own.

COMMUNITIES — GOAL FIVE

Participate in Communities at Home and Around the World

Standard 5.1 Students use Italian both within and beyond the school setting.

Standard 5.2 Students show evidence of becoming life-long learners by using Italian for personal enjoyment and enrichment.

Introduction

In 1989, state and national leaders met in Virginia to establish criteria for higher educational goals: "By the year 2000, all American students will demonstrate competency in challenging subject matter." This initiative led to the formation of the National Standards in Foreign Language Education Project whose task force prepared generic language standards published as *Standards for Foreign Language Learning: Preparing for the 21st Century*. A collaborative project with national language organizations such as the American Association of Teachers of Italian resulted in the preparation of language-specific standards.

Standards for Learning Italian, prepared by the AATI Task Force, identifies the essential skills and knowledge all students, from grade K–16, need to acquire in learning the Italian language and culture. It provides various learning scenarios and sample progress indicators for grades 4, 8, 12, and 16. Progress indicators may be repeated at successive grade levels incorporating a spiraling effect where tasks performed will advance according to the age, competence, and interests of the student. This document outlines the dynamic interaction between language and culture, and the progress indicators reflect the content stated within it. The interweaving of the five goals–Communication, Cultures, Connections, Comparisons, and Communities–provides an opportunity to expand language learning beyond the classroom walls into the real world. The implementation of these goals predicates an interdisciplinary approach in which all students, regardless of socioeconomic background, are exposed to a common core of learning experiences. The standards are not a curriculum, but a guide to be used by individual states and school districts to establish their own educational frameworks.

When applying the standards to Italian heritage learners (i.e., those students who are exposed to Italian or a dialect at home), some modifications may be needed. Some students may be proficient in spoken "Standard Italian" but possess limited skills in reading and writing. Furthermore, some students may be able to understand and converse in dialect but may lack the ability to interact in Italian. Teachers need to acknowledge the fact that learning "Standard Italian" does not minimize the cultural importance of dialects.

It is the mission of the AATI Task Force to outline strategies in the teaching of Italian that are congruent with the *Standards for Foreign Language Learning: Preparing for the 21st Century* (National Standards in Foreign Language Education Project, 1996).

WHY STUDY ITALIAN?

There are sixty million inhabitants in Italy. More than five million Italians live outside of the country. About half live in other European countries, the rest mainly in the United States, Canada, South America, and Australia. Over twenty million Americans are of Italian descent and many speak standard Italian or an Italian dialect. According to ACTFL re-

> **THE INTERWEAVING OF THE FIVE GOALS … PROVIDES AN OPPORTUNITY TO EXPAND LANGUAGE LEARNING … INTO THE REAL WORLD**

search, over 50,000 students, grades K-12, study Italian in the United States. Over the past thirty-seven years, college registration in the study of Italian has risen 300%. Not only are students taking advantage of "on campus" classes, enrollments are strong in university programs situated all over Italy. In addition to traditional programs, Italian is studied in diverse contexts: distance learning programs, extension classes, heritage language schools, and immersion programs for children and adults (e.g., Aurora programs and IACE programs in New York, New Jersey, and Connecticut; *La Scuola Italiana*). Today, Italy ranks among the top five economic giants of the world. It exports close to thirteen billion dollars worth of goods and services to the United States. The groups Fiat, Luxottica, ENI, and IRI have cumulative sales of nearly seven billion dollars and employ approximately 28,000 people in the United States. Other employment opportunities are available in the fields of teaching, finance, commerce, tourism, airline, and fashion industries. Therefore, knowledge of the Italian language and culture allows students to secure excellent positions and to compete successfully in the global economy of America's future.

> **KNOWLEDGE OF THE ITALIAN LANGUAGE AND CULTURE ALLOWS STUDENTS ... TO COMPETE SUCCESSFULLY IN THE GLOBAL ECONOMY OF AMERICA'S FUTURE**

Throughout history, Italy's unique geographical position in the Mediterranean Sea has kept her in the midst of important events. As the center of the Roman Empire, as the springboard for Christianity, then, through its commerce and wealth, as the birthplace of the Renaissance, Italy ushered in a new humanistic outlook with the rise of universities and the arts. From the age of exploration, with the voyages of Columbus, Vespucci, Verrazano, Strozzi, and Father Chino, to the lean years of the nineteenth century, when multitudes of Italian immigrants brought their civilization with them to their new homes, a bond between the Old and New Worlds was forged.

Italy has contributed outstanding and well known innovations in the visual arts spanning the genius of Giotto, Botticelli, Michelangelo to De Chirico and Manzù. Bellini, Donizetti, Rossini, Verdi, and Puccini are giants of the performing arts. The Italian cinema includes the great neorealists, Rossellini and De Sica, and the more contemporary Fellini, Antonioni, Wertmüller, Zeffirelli and Bertolucci. Italian designers who have influenced our concept of fashion include: Versace, Armani, Valentino, Krizia, Missoni and others. The epitome of automotive style takes form in the Alfa Romeo, Ferrari, and Lamborghini. Italian science has given us the work of Da Vinci, Galileo, Volta, Marconi, Fermi, and Levi-Montalcini. In addition, many prominent American businesses rely on the technology of such companies as Olivetti and Iveco.

When Thomas Jefferson coined the phrase "...all men are created equal", he was echoing ideologies he had discussed with his friend, the political thinker, Filippo Mazzei. Maria Montessori's methodology has made an important contribution to education in the United States. There are many more concrete examples of Italian influence throughout the United States: in buildings that adorn our cities, in the renewal of interest in opera and even in the recognition of the Mediterranean diet as one of the most salutary for a long and healthy life.

As one of the five Romance Languages, Italian has many cognates that are not only found in Latin but in English as well. Up to sixty percent of English words have Latin or Italian roots. Students who have studied Italian have demonstrated great success by achieving commendable scores on standardized tests. In fields such as art, music, architecture, and cuisine, Italian "loan words" are international reference points. Literary standards still recognized today were set by early Italian writers (e.g., Petrarcan sonnet, Boccaccio's short stories). Dante's *Divina Commedia* is still considered one of the masterpieces of western literature.

The study of any foreign language can improve critical and creative thinking skills. By studying Italian, the student is provided with the communicative tools to facilitate success in a variety of fields.

In June 2003, the Trustees of the College Board approved a plan for four new AP courses and exams in world languages: Italian, Chinese, Japanese and Russian. The AP Italian Language and Culture, the first new language offering to be added to the AP Program since its inception in 1955, represents a commitment by the College Board to enhance secondary school curricula by furthering multilingualism and multiculturalism. AP Italian has been designed to provide instruction and assessment not only in language proficiency but also in cultural understanding, all within the framework articulated in the *Standards for Foreign Language Learning*. The culture component of the exam assesses the student's knowledge of Italian geography, contemporary life in Italy, arts and sciences, social customs and traditions, and contributions of Italians and Italian Americans, through a composition on one of these topics.

Communication — Goal One
Communicate in Italian

By implementing the standards presented here, students will be able to communicate effectively in a global setting. The progress indicators establish observable behaviors at different stages of linguistic and sociocultural development. Our task is attainable as long as we keep pace with communications technology. Teachers and students must take advantage of opportunities for communicative exchange between Italian students in Italy and students of Italian in the United States. This is made possible by student exchange trips, correspondence via e-mail, the use of the Internet, etc.

To meet high communicative standards, learners must have ample opportunities to practice and use the language. We must reach out into the community to maintain those rich pockets of dialect, while continuing to train our students in the use of contemporary standard Italian and seize the many and ever expanding opportunities to experience Italian as it is spoken and written in Italy.

In order to communicate successfully in Italian, students must develop facility with the language, and an awareness of how the language and culture interact in the modern world. Reaching the standards in the Communication Goal is essential to the attainment of all the other goals.

The Communication Goal includes three standards based on the Framework of Communicative Modes. The first focuses on the Interpersonal Mode; the second focuses on the Interpretive Mode; the third focuses on the Presentational Mode.

STANDARD 1.1 Students engage in conversations, provide and obtain information, express feelings and emotions, and exchange opinions.

This standard focuses on interpersonal communication (e.g., face to face, telephonic, written).

> STUDENTS MUST DEVELOP FACILITY WITH THE LANGUAGE AND AN AWARENESS OF HOW THE LANGUAGE AND CULTURE INTERACT

Sample Progress Indicators, Grade 4

- Students give and follow simple instructions in order to participate in playing games (e.g., *Tombola, 7 e mezzo, Scopa, Bocce, Uno*).

- Students exchange information about themselves, family and friends, in person, or via short notes or e-mail.

- Students discuss likes and dislikes concerning games, sports, school subjects, daily chores, etc.

- Students greet each other and issue and follow commands used in everyday classroom interactions (e.g., *Ciao!, Siediti!, Apri il libro! Girati!, Ad alta voce!*).

- Students express themselves using body language, facial and hand gestures (e.g., *Vieni qua!, Cosa fai?, Che buono!, Cosa vuoi?*).

Sample Progress Indicators, Grade 8

- Students give and follow directions for arriving at various places in their community.

- Students ask for clarification about programs, schedules, fees, crowd conditions, and exhibits (e.g., museum, bus, train).

- Students role play the purchasing of clothes, food, and souvenirs (e.g., *al mercato, ai grandi magazzini, al negozio*).

- Students correspond with Italian students via mail and e-mail concerning school routine, hobbies and other interests.

- Students write letters to inquire about rates and services in Italian hotels, to obtain travel brochures, to order catalogues from Italian department stores, (e.g., *Standa, Upim, Rinascente, Postal Market*).

- Students fill out simple forms (e.g., hotel registration, ID cards, contest entries, passport applications, order forms).

Sample Progress Indicators, Grade 12

- Students compare, contrast and express lifestyles and career choices.

- Students compare, contrast, and express opinions and preferences about various Italian artists, musicians, movie directors and their films.

- Students exchange information and opinions about Italian designers and their respective styles found in magazines, films, and television programs.

- Students discuss and write about politics, sports, and the environment (e.g., the Euro, World Cup, *deforestazione*).

- Students stage a fashion and/or craft show, narrating, exchanging information, and expressing preferences.

Sample Progress Indicators, Grade 16

- Students share their analyses and personal reactions to Italian literary texts both orally and in written form.

- Students compare and contrast formal and thematic developments in Italian and American and/or English literature.

- Students discuss and propose solutions to political, social, and environmental issues (e.g., pollution, career opportunities, immigration).

STANDARD 1.2 Students understand and interpret written and spoken Italian on a variety of topics.

This standard focuses on the understanding and interpretation of written and spoken language.

Sample Progress Indicators, Grade 4

- Students comprehend main ideas in children's stories and familiar fairy tales (e.g., *Pinocchio, Cappuccetto Rosso, Cenerentola*) and identify key characters and words.

- Students identify classmates and famous personalities from photographs, based on oral and/or written descriptions.

- Students read greeting cards, short notes, and invitations.

- Students interpret hand and facial gestures by identifying the phrase which accompanies each.

- Students identify the principal message contained in public safety posters, advertisements, and other illustrated texts.

Sample Progress Indicators, Grade 8

- Students read and compare Italian report cards, television schedules, telephone cards, advertisements, public safety announcements, museum floor plans, city maps, restaurant menus, etc.

- Students demonstrate an understanding of the main themes of age-appropriate selections from Italian children's stories, riddles, television, radio, magazines, and newspapers, by discussing them in class and/or writing comments/opinions about them.

- Students read and discuss short biographical sketches of Italian and Italian-American historical and contemporary personages (e.g., Columbus, Vespucci, Joe DiMaggio, Geraldine Ferraro).

Sample Progress Indicators, Grade 12

- Students read and discuss poems, plays, and short stories from Italian literature and write comments and opinions about them.

- Students view Italian television programs and films, listen to recorded literature, read articles from Italian magazines and newspapers, and write critical reviews.

- Students visit Italian language web sites and correspond via e-mail.

Sample Progress Indicators, Grade 16

- Students demonstrate an understanding of the principal elements of non-fiction articles in newspapers and magazines on topics of current and historical importance by engaging in discussion and/or writing commentaries.

- Students analyze the main plot, subplot, characters, their descriptions, roles, and significance in Italian poems, plays, and short stories.

- Students attend an Italian language play, opera, or movie for enjoyment and discussion.

STANDARD 1.3 Students present information, concepts, and ideas to an audience of listeners or readers on a variety of topics.

This standard focuses on the presentation of information, concepts, and ideas in spoken and written modes. In most cases, it is concerned with one-way speaking or writing.

Sample Progress Indicators, Grade 4

- Students prepare illustrated story boards about Italian fairy tales and folk tales they have heard or read, and talk about them.

- Students dramatize songs (e.g., *Giro, giro tondo, Alla fiera dell'est, Al mio bel castello!*), short anecdotes, and poems, using gestures and pantomime.

- Students compose shopping lists and simple messages involving meeting times and places.

- Students write birthday cards, party invitations, thank you cards, etc.

- Students design ads and posters for Italian products found in their neighborhood.

Sample Progress Indicators, Grade 8

- Students present short plays and skits, recite selected poems, and talk about personal habits and anecdotes.

- Students prepare tape or video-recorded messages to share with school peers and/or Italian students on topics such as clubs, teams, hobbies, etc.

- Students design posters illustrating Italian proverbs and idioms, and discuss them (e.g., *Dimmi con chi vai e ti dirò chi sei; Le bugie hanno le gambe corte; avere le mani bucate; avere la testa fra le nuvole*).

- Students prepare oral and/or written reports on historical figures from Italian and Italian American culture.

Sample Progress Indicators, Grade 12

- Students recite poems and perform scenes or excerpts from short stories connected to a topic from other disciplines such as social studies, the sciences, or the arts.

- Students create stories and poems, short plays, or skits based on personal experiences (e.g., autobiography, journal).

- Students engage in debates on targeted issues (e.g., progress vs. pollution, preservation vs. progress, women's rights, stereotypes).

- Students present an "interview" with an historical figure.

- Students present "demonstration" speeches (e.g., how to set a table, how to play a sport).

Sample Progress Indicators, Grade 16

- Students write a business letter to promote their community to an Italian speaking audience.

- Students write an article for a class newspaper based on an interview with foreign exchange students via e-mail, mail, phone, etc.

- Students write an essay describing and analyzing one aspect of a political, social, or economic issue (e.g., environmentalism, restoration, immigration and discrimination), comparing and contrasting American and Italian responses to it.

- Students present critical reviews of films, concerts, or performances with comparisons to contemporary artists and/or the author's/performer's larger body of work.

- Students present a critique of a literary text they have read.

Cultures   *Goal Two*
Gain Knowledge and Understanding of Italian Culture

PRODUCTS OF ITALIAN CULTURE INCLUDE LITERATURE, ART, MUSIC, ARCHITECTURE, FASHION, CUISINE

Goal Two focuses on students' understanding of the perspectives, practices, and products of Italian culture by reading, viewing, and listening to cultural material in Italian and/or English. In understanding perspectives of the Italian people, students come to know what Italians value. Students learn why Italians act as they do by the study of their practices, such as patterns of behavior or modes of interaction in their daily lives. Products of Italian culture include literature, art, music, architecture, fashion, cuisine, and others. Studying a culture as rich as the Italian provides students with a knowledge of the nature of culture itself.

The Cultures Goal includes two standards. The first emphasizes the practices or patterns of social interactions, the second the products associated with cultural perspectives such as language, literature, art, music, architecture, fashion, cuisine, educational system, games, and sports.

STANDARD 2.1   **Students demonstrate an understanding of the relationship between the practices and perspectives of Italian culture.**

This standard focuses on patterns of social interactions that reflect the attitudes, values, and traditions of Italians.

Sample Progress Indicators, Grade 4

- Students observe, identify, and/or discuss simple patterns of behavior in various settings such as school, family, and community.

- Students use appropriate gestures and oral expressions for greetings, leave takings, and common interactions (e.g., handshaking, kissing on both cheeks, *tu* vs. *Lei*, *salute*, *scusi*, *permesso*).

- Students participate in games, songs, celebrations, storytelling, and skits (e.g., *Gioco dell'oca, Palla pallina, Paroliere, La Befana*).

Sample Progress Indicators, Grade 8

- Students observe, analyze, and discuss patterns of behavior of Italian students (e.g., school life, after-school activities).

- Students learn about and participate in games, sports, music, and dance enjoyed by Italian students their age.

- Students compare and contrast the celebration of traditional and folkloric festivals, dances, and special events (e.g., *onomastico, scacchi viventi, la quadriglia*).

Sample Progress Indicators, Grade 12

- Students learn about and/or participate in cultural practices enjoyed by Italians, such as games, sports, and entertainment (e.g., *Briscola, Scala 40, Giro d'Italia, Carnevale, Palio, calcio, calcetto*).

- Students identify, analyze and discuss various patterns of behavior (e.g., *la passeggiata*, walking arm in arm, café life).

- Students identify, examine, and discuss connections between Italian cultural perspectives and socially approved behavioral patterns (e.g., dating practices, driving, drinking age, living at home, military service, *mammismo*).

Sample Progress Indicators, Grade 16

- Students research social changes in modern day Italy (e.g., size of the family, education, gender roles).

- Students initiate and sustain discussion on various topics (e.g., women in the workplace, immigration, dual citizenship, political issues such as "*mani pulite,*" *il Mezzogiorno*).

- Students trace social practices through targeted literary works (e.g., Levi's *malocchio*, Verga's *padronismo*).

STANDARD 2.2 Students demonstrate an understanding of the relationship between the products and the perspectives of Italian culture.

This standard focuses on the cultural products of Italy (language, literature, art, music, architecture, fashion, cuisine, sports, educational system) and how they relate to the perspectives (attitudes, values, ideas) of Italians.

Sample Progress Indicators, Grade 4

- Students identify and observe the types of toys Italian children play with, as well as the type of food they eat (e.g., *Pinocchio, Topo Gigio, Nutella, biscotti, uovo di Pasqua, colomba pasquale*).

- Students listen to and sing songs Italian children sing and read selections of Italian children's literature (e.g., *La pecora nel bosco, Biancaneve e i sette nani*).

- Students identify, discuss and produce artwork and crafts enjoyed or made by Italian children of the same age group (e.g., puppets, models, Venetian masks, *carretto siciliano*).
- Students identify Italian products found in their homes and community, and explore why they are so popular in Italy (e.g., tile, marble, olive oil).

Sample Progress Indicators, Grade 8

- Students read, listen to, and perform Italian stories, poetry, music, and folkloric dance.
- Students identify and research Italian cuisine and fashion (e.g., regional cuisine, fashion designers).
- Students identify and discuss the major contributions in art and music accomplished by Italians (e.g., listen to or attend an opera, view an art collection at a local museum).
- Students learn about and identify major scientific and historical contributions made by Italians (e.g., Galileo, Volta, Marconi, Meucci, Mazzei).

Sample Progress Indicators, Grade 12

- Students expand their knowledge of private and public life of Italians as they read and interpret authentic texts (e.g., magazines, newspapers, menus, travel brochures, Internet).
- Students demonstrate a knowledge of the various contributions in architecture, art, music, and literature accomplished by Italians (e.g., read plays/short stories, attend an opera).
- Students identify, analyze, and evaluate an author, a genre, and/or a literary period through readings in Italian literature (e.g., Dante, Goldoni, Ginzburg, Logorio).
- Students research and give multimedia presentations of an Italian artist and his work (e.g., Michelangelo, Da Vinci, etc.).
- Students research regional *artigianato* products and crafts (e.g., Murano glass, alabaster, Florentine gold and leather, ceramics, cameos, porcelain, lace).

Sample Progress indicators, Grade 16

- Students experience, discuss, and analyze Italian contributions to world civilization, in the domain of literature, fine arts, philosophy, and science.
- Students discuss and analyze societal products such as social and political institutions and educational systems.

Connections
Goal Three
Connect with Other Disciplines, Acquire Information, and Expand Knowledge

Goal Three focuses on students' ability to communicate (Communication Goal) and on their knowledge of Italian culture (Cultures Goal) to work with content from other disciplines. It provides interdisciplinary experiences for the learner in the areas of language arts, social studies, arts, and sciences. In addition, students use their knowledge of Italian to acquire new information as they read, listen to, and see authentic realia and literature which relates to other disciplines.

The conscious effort to connect the foreign language curriculum with other parts of students' academic lives opens doors to information and experiences which enrich the students' entire school and life experience. Those connections flow from other areas to the foreign language classroom and also originate in the foreign language classroom to add unique experiences and insights to the rest of the curriculum.

The Connections Goal includes two standards. The first focuses on support for content from other disciplines through the study of Italian. The second focuses on information now available to the learner through the knowledge of Italian.

... STUDENTS CAN RELATE THE INFORMATION STUDIED IN OTHER SUBJECTS TO THEIR LEARNING OF ITALIAN LANGUAGE AND CULTURE

STANDARD 3.1 Students reinforce and further their knowledge of other disciplines through the study of Italian language and culture.

Learning today is no longer restricted to a specific discipline; it has become interdisciplinary at all levels of instruction. Just as reading cannot be limited to a particular segment of the school day, but is central to all aspects of the school curriculum, Italian can build upon the knowledge that students acquire in other subject areas. In addition, students can relate the information studied in other subjects to their learning of Italian language and culture. Students expand and deepen their understanding of, and exposure to, other areas of knowledge, even as they refine their communicative abilities and broaden their cultural understanding. The new information and concepts presented in one class become the basis of continued learning in the Italian classroom. When integrated into the broader curriculum, the learning of Italian contributes to the entire educational experience of students.

Sample Progress Indicators, Grade 4

- Students demonstrate an understanding about concepts learned in other subject areas (e.g., geography - physical features; social studies - families, communities, and recreation; science - weather).

- Students use systems common in Italy (e.g., science - weights and measures in cooking projects; social studies - social practices dealing with time, meal schedules; mathematics - metric system).

- Students demonstrate a general knowledge of significant contributions of Italians and the Italian language in the arts and sciences as well as to the culture of their own country (et.al, Da Vinci - science and mathematics; Columbus - age of encounters; Michelangelo - art; music - *alto, basso, forte*, et al).

Sample Progress Indicators, Grade 8

- Students recognize and use Italian terminology in the sciences and technology (e.g., electronics - volts; physical science - galvanize; model building - pilaster).

- Students recognize and make connections with Italian influence and terminology in the social sciences, history, and the arts (e.g., Rome - history, architecture, sculpture; opera - musical terminology and styles; Machiavelli; Montessori).

- Students comprehend and discuss ads, short articles, tapes, and videos on topics being studied in class (e.g., publicity - daily life; music videos - pop culture).

- Students present short, oral or written reports in Italian on topics being studied in class (e.g., cities, monuments, personalities, historical figures).

- Students initiate and sustain simple conversations in Italian about daily activities in appropriate cultural contexts.

Sample Progress Indicators, Grade 12

- Students combine information from other disciplines with information available in Italian in order to complete activities (e.g., use Italian resources in reports for other disciplines, and conversely, the resources of other disciplines in reports intended for Italian).

- Students comprehend and discuss topics from other subjects in Italian, including political and historical concepts, worldwide health issues, and environmental concerns.

- Students initiate and sustain conversation, discussion, and debate on appropriate topics for grade level (e.g., "Columbus: discovery or encounter?", "Plastics: environmental hazard or salvation?").

Sample Progress Indicators, Grade 16

- Students research topics and write commentaries on a variety of subjects found in publications intended for native speakers of Italian.

- Students view, listen to, and discuss media presentations on topics intended for native speakers (e.g., *telegiornale*, Internet).

- Students initiate and sustain discussion on various topics. They propose theses and defend them with a broad knowledge of the topic drawn from native sources, as well as those the student may have already encountered in other areas of study.

Standard 3.2 Students acquire information and recognize the distinctive viewpoints that are provided through the knowledge of Italian language and culture.

As a result of learning Italian and gaining access to its unique means of communication and ways of thinking, students acquire new information and perspectives. As learners of Italian, they broaden the sources of information available to them. They have a "new window on the world." In the earlier stages of language learning, they begin to examine a variety of sources intended for native speakers and extract specific information. As they become more proficient users of the foreign language, they seek out materials of interest to them, analyze the content, compare it to information available in their own language, and assess the linguistic and cultural differences.

Sample Progress Indicators, Grade 4

- Students gather information about Italy and Italian culture by reading and listening to short presentations in English (e.g., travel videos, brochures, magazines).

- Students listen to, discuss, and learn short dialogues, passages, poems, and songs in Italian (e.g., counting and nursery rhymes, *Trenta giorni ha novembre, Funiculì funiculà, Quel mazzolin di fiori*).

- Students recognize and identify major geographical features, cities, and monuments of Italy (e.g., create maps, puzzles, word searches, collages of cities).

Sample Progress Indicators, Grade 8

- Students use sources intended for same-age speakers of Italian to prepare reports and presentations on topics of personal interest or those with which they have limited previous experience (e.g., sports - *La Gazzetta dello Sport*; school life - Internet and school home pages).

- Students recognize and identify Italian contributions toward the development of world culture in the sciences, arts, and society in general (e.g., Marconi, Bernini, Gucci, Da Vinci).

Sample Progress Indicators, Grade 12

- Students demonstrate in their written and spoken vocabulary a knowledge of the impact of Italian language and culture on the development of western ideas on the arts, letters, and sciences (e.g., Machiavelli, Dante, Montessori, Cabrini).

- Students use sources intended for same-age speakers of Italian to prepare reports and presentations on topics of personal interest or enrichment, comparing and contrasting the information they find with what they know about their own culture (e.g., sports - *Corriere dello Sport*; current events - newspapers, Internet; the arts - magazines, virtual museums on-line).

- Students have informed discussions based on knowledge gained through the use of resources available to them in the Italian language (e.g., comparisons of life styles, current events, immigration).

Sample Progress Indicators, Grade 16

- Students recognize and are able to explain the viewpoint of the Italian speaker as presented in literature and media, and discuss these characteristics in Italian (e.g., Moravia's short stories, neorealistic films, magazines).

- Students recognize the basis of particular points of view of an Italian speaker grounded in his/her culture and subsequently define and explain it (e.g., social issues, preservation of antiquities).

- Students use resources intended for native speakers to obtain information in particular areas of interest to pursue career goals.

- Students take a position on a topic and defend it from the perspective of an Italian native speaker (e.g., attitudes toward immigrants, inhabiting a "living museum," consumerism and quality).

Comparisons
Develop Insight Into the Nature of Language and Culture

Goal Four

Students benefit from learning Italian by discovering similarities that exist between English and Italian (such as cognates, borrowings, prefixes, and suffixes). By analyzing linguistic forms, students not only gain insight into the way the Italian language works but take a critical look at their own. Students gain an understanding of the concept of Italian culture through a comparison of their own culture and that of Italy.

Goal Four includes two standards. The first standard focuses on the nature of language, the second on the concept of culture.

STANDARD 4.1 Students demonstrate understanding of the nature of language through comparisons of the Italian language and their own.

Learning the linguistic elements in Italian provides the students with the ability to examine their own language and develop hypotheses about the structure and use of languages. From the earliest language learning experiences, students can compare and contrast the two languages as different elements are presented. Activities can be systematically integrated into instruction that will assist students in understanding how languages work.

Sample Progress Indicators, Grade 4

- Students cite and use examples of English words that are borrowed from Italian (e.g., pasta, opera, piano).

- Students identify cognates (e.g., *università, ombrello, presidente*).

- Students demonstrate an awareness of idiomatic expressions in Italian by contrasting them with their English counterparts (e.g., *Come ti chiami? Quanti anni hai?*).

- Students demonstrate an awareness of formal and informal form of address in language patterns and in greetings and leavetaking (e.g., *Come sta?/Come stai?, Buon giorno/Ciao*).

Sample Progress Indicators, Grade 8

- Students recognize the existence of grammatical gender in Italian.

- Students hypothesize about the relationship between English and Italian based on their awareness of cognates and similarity of idioms and proverbs (e.g., "The early bird catches the worm." vs. "*Chi dorme non prende pesci.*").

- Students demonstrate an awareness of ways of expressing respect and acknowledging status in English and Italian (e.g., *tu/Lei*; titles - *dottore, ingegnere*).

> STUDENTS BENEFIT FROM LEARNING ITALIAN BY DISCOVERING SIMILARITIES THAT EXIST BETWEEN ENGLISH AND ITALIAN

- Students demonstrate awareness that Italian has critical sound distinctions that must be mastered in order to communicate meaning (e.g., Italian - *casa/cassa, gli/li*; English - red/read/read [past tense], "ough" [as in through/tough]).

Sample Progress Indicators, Grade 12

- Students recognize that cognates have the same as well as different meanings and speculate about the evolution of language (e.g., *università*/university, *probabile*/probable, vs. false friends: *restare* ≠ to rest, *assistere* ≠ to assist, *collegio* ≠ college).

- Students use phrases and idioms that do not translate directly from English to Italian and vice versa in their proper contexts (e.g., Have a good time!/*Divertiti!*; to pack/*fare le valigie*).

- Students analyze aspects of the Italian language, such as tense and mood, and compare them to their linguistic counterparts in English (e.g., *passato prossimo/imperfetto, indicativo/congiuntivo*).

- Students recognize the importance of word order in certain expressions in Italian and their connotation in English (e.g., *un uomo povero/un povero uomo, Io ci penso/Ci penso io*).

- Students compare nuances of meanings of words, idioms and vocal inflections in Italian and in English (Statements vs. questions via voice inflection) (e.g., *è partito!*: he is drunk/he left; *è cotto!*: he is in love/it is cooked).

Sample Progress Indicators, Grade 16

- Students gain knowledge and skills in analyzing the linguistic features of Italian and English regional differences (e.g., *passato prossimo* vs. *passato remoto*, use of *Lei* vs. *voi* for formal address, you vs. y'all, pop vs. soda).

- Students analyze and synthesize stylistic effects on language (e.g., Italian vs. American journalistic styles in the various media).

- Students compare, contrast, and use language of the business and professional world (*linguaggio settoriale*) (e.g., language of commerce, language of finance, professional correspondence).

STANDARD 4.2 Students demonstrate understanding of the concept of culture through comparisons of Italian culture and their own.

As students of Italian expand their knowledge of cultures through the study of language, they continually discover perspectives, practices, and products that are similar to and yet different from those in their own culture. They develop the ability to hypothesize about cultural systems in general.

Sample Progress Indicators, Grade 4

- Students compare simple patterns of behavior or interaction in various cultural settings (e.g., family gatherings, familiar/formal relationships).

- Students demonstrate an awareness that gestures are an important part of communication and that gestures in Italian differ from English (e.g., waving goodbye, counting with your fingers).

- Students compare and contrast tangible products of the Italian culture and of their own (e.g., toys, sports, money, food).

- Students compare and contrast rhymes, songs, and folktales of the Italian culture and of their own.

Sample Progress Indicators, Grade 8

- Students contrast verbal and nonverbal behavior within particular activities in the Italian culture and their own (e.g., differences in body language).

- Students speculate on why certain products are important to the Italian culture and make comparisons with their own (e.g., building materials, agricultural products).

- Students hypothesize about the relationship between cultural perspectives and practices by analyzing selected practices from Italian culture and their own (e.g., holidays, celebrations, work habits, recreation).

Sample Progress Indicators, Grade 12

- Students analyze the relationship of perspectives and practices in Italian culture and compare/contrast these with their own culture (e.g., teenage employment opportunities, extra-curricular activities).

- Students hypothesize about the origins of idioms as reflections of culture, citing examples from Italian language and culture and their own (e.g., *parlare a quattr'occhi, fare una bella figura, essere al verde*).

- Students hypothesize about the relationship between cultural perspectives and aesthetic products by analyzing selected examples from Italian culture and their own (e.g., music, visual arts, literature).

Sample Progress Indicators, Grade 16

- Students identify and analyze cultural perspectives as reflected in a variety of literary genres.

- Students compare and contrast political, social, and educational issues in Italy and in their own country.

- Students compare socioeconomic conditions as viewed on film. (*Ladri di biciclette, Roma città aperta, Ladro di bambini, La famiglia*).

Communities
Participate in Italian Communities at Home and Around the World

Goal Five

Increasing foreign competition in commerce and technology, and the growing need for international understanding between governments, have made the knowledge of Italian advantageous for Americans. It is important in this era of instant mass communication for students to be able to comprehend and communicate in Italian. This knowledge will enrich the life of the learner and contribute to his/her future achievements. In addition to the benefits derived in the workplace, the knowledge of Italian language and culture provides the student with a greater appreciation of the arts, fashion, literature, cuisine, entertainment, music, science, etc. Italy has been and remains a center of innovation and inventions. As Americans travel to Italy, their competence in Italian will empower them to experience more fully the artistic and cultural beauty of the country.

Goal Five includes two standards. The first standard emphasizes applied learning, while the second focuses on personal enrichment.

STANDARD 5.1 Students use Italian both within and beyond the school setting.

> ... COMPETENCE IN ITALIAN WILL EMPOWER THEM TO EXPERIENCE MORE FULLY THE ARTISTIC AND CULTURAL BEAUTY OF THE COUNTRY

This standard focuses on using the Italian language as a tool for communication throughout one's life. Within the school setting, students share their knowledge with teachers, classmates, younger and older students at varied degree of language proficiency. When the opportunity arises, students apply what they have learned in their Italian class to communicate with the community at large.

Sample Progress Indicators, Grade 4

- Students participate in a pen/key pal project via letter, e-mail, audio/video tapes.

- Students present fables in Italian to other students (e.g., *Pinocchio, La volpe e il lupo, La cicala e la formica, I tre orsi*).

- Students perform songs in Italian at school assemblies.

- Students make Halloween masks incorporating characters from the *Commedia dell'arte* (e.g., *Pantalone, Arlecchino, Pulcinella*).

Sample Progress Indicators, Grade 8

- Students interview members of the local community to learn how Italian is used in their various fields of work.

- Students discuss how the knowledge of Italian has enhanced the careers of various community members.

- Students create an Italian mini-yearbook and share it with their families.

- Students write get well cards, holiday cards, and birthday cards in Italian and deliver them to various nursing homes in their community.

Sample Progress Indicators, Grade 12

- Students prepare an Italian language school newspaper.
- Students perform for a school or community celebration (e.g., international day, foreign language week, Columbus Day).
- Students present mini-lessons during or after school to younger students.
- Students present a made-up or real travelogue on Italy to various organizations (e.g., Rotary Club, PTA, Senior Citizens Club, Board of Education).

Sample Progress Indicators, Grade 16

- Students organize and direct activities for a children's Italian immersion day.
- Students serve internships with local companies that have direct or indirect ties to Italy (where possible).
- Students prepare and share their resumé in Italian (where possible).
- Students interview employees of local Italian companies (where possible).

STANDARD 5.2 Students show evidence of becoming life-long learners by using Italian for personal enjoyment and enrichment.

Students who study Italian use their knowledge to enrich their personal lives by accessing information which is available to native speakers. Some students may have the opportunity to travel to Italy and through this experience further develop their language skills and understanding of the culture. In their daily lives, students develop a greater appreciation for Italian products available in their community.

Sample Progress Indicators, Grade 4

- Students play games or sports popular in Italy (e.g., soccer, *Bocce*, *Giro giro tondo*).
- Students sing Italian songs (e.g., *Fra Martino campanaro*, *Nella vecchia fattoria*, *La pecora nel bosco*, "*Cucù, cucù*", *Alla fiera del mastro André*).
- Students view and comment on cartoon videos in Italian (e.g., *Pinocchio*, *Il re leone*, Peter Pan, *La bella e la bestia*).
- Students perform Italian dances (e.g., *la tarantella, il ballo del qua qua, il liscio, la furlana, il ballo sardo*).

Sample Progress Indicators, Grade 8

- Students go to Italian restaurants and order in Italian.
- Students prepare Italian recipes at home and share with the class.
- Students plan a real or imaginary trip to Italy using the Internet and/or other resources (e.g., weather, accommodations, transportation).
- Students plan and carry out activities for a cultural event (e.g., *Carnevale* - organize *un ballo in maschera*; *La Befana* - students dress up as *la Befana* and pass out small tokens; *Il Palio di Siena* - students represent the seventeen *contrade* and make *i barberi*; *Festa di San Giuseppe* - students prepare various foods and share them).

- Students perform in a talent show impersonating Italian or Italian-American celebrities (e.g., Columbus, Andrea Bocelli, Sofia Loren, Liza Minnelli, Frank Sinatra, Al Pacino, Eros Ramazzoti, Jovanotti).

Sample Progress Indicators, Grade 12

- Students view Italian films, engage in discussions, and write critiques (e.g., *Il Postino*, *Cinema Paradiso*).

- Students read Italian books (e.g., *Ti ho sposato per allegria*, *Don Camillo*, *I bianchini non hanno ricordi*, *Andreuccio da Perugia*), magazines (*Panorama*, *La Gazzetta dello Sport*, *Grazia*, *Topolino*) during their leisure time, and make reports.

- Students explore Italian language Internet sites and use them as a basis for writing reports on Italian culture.

- Students attend Italian cultural events and activities (e.g., opera, museum, feasts, concerts).

Sample Progress Indicators, Grade 16

- Students participate in Italian cultural conferences at local colleges and Italian institutes, where available.

- Students read an Italian book, write a review and/or discuss it (e.g., *Novelle per un anno*, *Cristo si è fermato ad Eboli*, *Agostino*).

- Students communicate in Italian with other students via Internet in the "chat room."

- Students research, plan, and travel to Italy, if possible, for personal enjoyment or study opportunities

Learning Scenarios

Following is a series of Learning Scenarios depicting classroom activities that reflect the standards described. These scenarios, contributed by the Standards for Learning Italian Task Force, are examples of activities and approaches that have been actually used and proven in the classroom. They should be considered illustrative examples of teaching and learning, and may be used in part or in their entirety to produce positive learning experiences. The particular standards addressed in the scenarios are listed with the description of each scenario. Following each is a reflection which highlights the "weave" of the curricular elements, such as the language system, communication strategies, culture, learning strategies, other subject areas, critical thinking skills, and technology. The reflection also contains suggestions for adapting or extending the learning activities. In addition to the scenarios provided here, there are two other scenarios for the Italian classroom included in the generic standards: "Arts and Crafts" and "Pre-Roman Italy." The teacher is encouraged to consult learning scenarios from all the languages for valuable ideas and activities that can be used with some changes.

Most scenarios, although targeted for a particular level, can be adapted for students of diverse ability levels. In addition, the use of English or Italian must be determined by the teacher, based on the competence of the learners. The scenarios provide opportunities to make interdisciplinary connections as the teacher introduces new material and concepts that bridge academic areas. Teachers may consult colleagues in these areas, plan collaborative units, or have students do independent work in those areas.

ALL IN THE FAMILY

Students in a level IV Italian class at Greece Athena High School in Rochester, NY, learn about Italian families of today. After reviewing and/or learning the vocabulary for family members (including blended family), students reflect on their own family relationships by writing poems about family members, discussing their roles and responsibilities in their families, and role playing interesting family situations. By reading current events articles, they learn about the changes in the family of modern Italy (size, habits, divorce, etc.). Also, students read about the differences and similarities in the families of the north, center, and south. Then they make a comparison of family dynamics between Italy and the United States. Finally, students view pertinent films such as *Stanno tutti bene*, *La famiglia*, *Tre fratelli*, etc.

TARGETED STANDARDS
1.1 Interpersonal Communication
1.2 Interpretive Communication
1.3 Presentational Communication
2.1 Practices of Culture
3.2 Acquiring Information
4.1 Language Comparisons
4.2 Cultural Comparisons

Reflection
1.1 Students role play family situations.
1.2 Students read articles about modern families and view films.
1.3 Students perform situations for class and write poems as creative expression.
2.1 Students understand changes in today's Italian families.
3.2 Students research current information on Italian families and identify regional differences.
4.1 Students learn and discuss new vocabulary that deals with blended families.
4.2 Students compare Italian and American families.

This scenario reinforces the notion that the family is still the stronghold and basis of Italian society in spite of some changes. Students engage in critical thinking skills as the family dynamics are then compared in American and Italian societies. The films illustrate the changes in Italian society and the family values and relationships. Students discuss aspects of family life such as pros and cons of working mothers, differences between Italian and American families, and how changes in current society have affected and continue to affect both Italian and American families.

IL BARBIERE DI SIVIGLIA

This scenario was designed for an advanced/college level course in Utica, NY. Students learn about the components of opera and do an in-depth study of the libretto of a work. They learn about the theatrical traditions of comedy in Italian opera, as well as learn, and use, musical terminology required of musicians in the opera. They explore the visual arts required in the production of opera scenery and costumes. Students study the history of the period in which the opera was written. Comparisons are made between the life styles of the characters and those of today. Students begin with a study of stock characters and their development in the

TARGETED STANDARDS
1.1 Interpersonal Communication
1.2 Interpretive Communication
1.3 Presentational Communication
2.1 Practices of Culture
2.2 Products of Culture
3.1 Making Connections
3.2 Acquiring Information
4.1 Language Comparisons
4.2 Cultural Comparisons
5.1 School and Community
5.2 Lifelong Learning

▼

... MAY BE USED IN PART OR IN THEIR ENTIRETY TO PRODUCE POSITIVE LEARNING EXPERIENCES

Commedia dell'arte. Students learn the personality traits of each "mask" and experiment in role play activities of those characters. These activities are followed by a study of the history of opera and of the time period in which *Il Barbiere* is set. Such points as social caste, mores, and customs of the time are explored. Students now read the libretto. Discussion of developing relationships, comical scenes, shifts in character status, and motivation are explored. A study of the development of opera and musical notation and style are added to the unit as students see and hear how the composer added his particular interpretation of the text. Students are now ready to see a performance/video.

Reflection

1.1 Students discuss developing relationships, comical scenes, shifts in character status and motivation in the opera.
1.2 Students learn the personality traits of each "mask" and experiment in role play activities of those characters.
1.3 Students do oral readings and interpretations of the libretto in preparation for the performance. They create distinct character types in written, spoken, and visual form.
2.1 Students make comparisons between the life styles of the characters and life today.
2.2 Students learn about the development of opera and theatrical traditions of Italy.
3.1 Students make connections to drama, music, literature, and visual arts.
3.2 Students learn the origins of an established artistic institution.
4.1 Students discover how much Italian still remains a part of the international vocabulary of musical, theatrical, and visual arts.
4.2 Students make comparisons to and draw conclusions about life today by studying the social castes, mores, and customs of the period of the opera.
5.1 Students receive necessary background on the opera from practicing artists who visit the classroom, where possible.
5.2 Students become life-long learners by developing an appreciation for opera.

This scenario touches upon the standards in all five goal areas. Its interdisciplinary approach opens opportunities for ample exploration in many directions. The adaptability of the scenario is quite broad, as activities may be chosen for age appropriate audiences. There are also multiple opportunities for evaluation in the four skill areas.

TARGETED STANDARDS

1.3 Presentational Communication
3.1 Making Connections
5.1 School and Community
5.2 Lifelong Learning

BOCCE

Students studying leisure time activities in an eighth grade class at a junior high school in Pomona, NY, learn the roles and strategies of the game of *bocce*. They learn to measure comparative distances in centimeters and announce the results of each throw in Italian ("the red ball is closer," "the green ball is closer," etc.). The actual "playing" occurs during specific immersion sessions scheduled outdoors throughout the school year, depending upon weather conditions. The scoring of points is also awarded for the number of phrases spoken in Italian (subtracted for those in English). The students can further have challenge matches against *bocce* players in the community or against students in other language classes.

Reflection

1.3 Students give directions for playing a game, supply a running commentary as it unfolds, and record the results, in Italian.
3.1 Students measure distances using the metric system.
5.1 Students have the opportunity to make intergenerational connections.
5.2 Students enjoy a new game.

BUILDINGS TELL A STORY

In an advanced/college-level Italian class in Utica, NY, students learn about the contributions to the world of architecture that have roots in Italy. Four periods of architecture are explored: Greco-Roman, Romanesque, Gothic, Renaissance and their direct lines of descent to common American types such as: Greek Revival, Romanesque Revival, Gothic Revival, Renaissance Revival, Victorian Italianate, Richardson Romanesque, Beaux Arts Style, Georgian Style, Palladian Style, and Neo-Classical Revival. Students not only study the architectural components of each style, they also learn about the history and the people who produced them. Through gained knowledge about the architectural styles, students conjecture the message that selected buildings in Italy and in their own community give to the viewer. Students create biographical sketches of the people who may have originally lived or worked in those buildings. Students create multimedia presentations on particular buildings in their community.

TARGETED STANDARDS	
1.1	Interpersonal Communication
1.2	Interpretive Communication
1.3	Presentational Communication
2.1	Practices of Culture
2.2	Products of Culture
3.1	Making Connections
3.2	Acquiring Information
4.1	Language Comparisons
4.2	Cultural Comparisons
5.2	Lifelong Learning

Reflection

1.1 Students discuss identifiable characteristics of selected buildings.
1.2 Students draw conclusions on the intent of the architect.
1.3 Students present their research and imaginative speculations on selected buildings.
2.1 Students learn the reasons for the evolution of certain architectural motifs.
2.2 Students learn about important buildings and monuments in Italian culture as well as in their own.
3.1 Students learn what historical events shaped the architecture of the past and the influence it had on later styles.
3.2 Students use architecture as an entry point into the study of the history of Italy, as well as develop new understandings about the origins of familiar places in their own communities.
4.1 Students learn vocabulary and see the influence of Italian language in architecture.
4.2 Students examine the forces that determine our lives and how those forces find expression in architecture.
5.2 Students acquire aesthetic tools to appreciate the architectural splendor of Italy as well as that of their own communities. This sensibility may help them to participate in the preservation of architectural treasures for generations to come.

This scenario connects Italian studies to the student's environment and gives ample opportunities for student evaluation.

TARGETED STANDARDS
1.1 Interpersonal Communication
1.2 Interpretive Communication
2.1 Practices of Culture
2.2 Products of Culture
3.1 Making Connections
3.2 Acquiring Information
4.2 Cultural Comparisons
5.1 School and Community

CARNEVALE

On Long Island, NY, Brentwood High School students are preparing for the celebration of *Carnevale* in their third-year Italian class. They begin by reading material that explains the celebration. They view a video on the festivities and the costumes worn by Venetians as they stroll through the piazzas of Venice which holds one of the greatest celebrations in all of Italy. After the viewing and the reading, students discuss the perspectives, products, and practices depicted, and compare them to their experiences and knowledge of Halloween and/or Mardi Gras. As a class project, they make and decorate masks in conjunction with the Art Department. The teacher introduces them to the characters of the *Commedia dell'arte*. The Home and Careers teacher helps them sew costumes and prepare foods. Students design invitations to the *ballo in maschera* for parents and the community. Special attention is paid not only to words for the event, but also to the appropriate colors of *Carnevale* such as purple and gold. The proverb "*A Carnevale ogni scherzo vale*" is discussed and displayed in the classroom. Masks and costumes are displayed in a showcase in the school library. The Music Department teaches about Vivaldi as students listen to his music and particularly to his "*Ring of Mystery--a Tale of Venice and Violins*" which takes place amid the *Carnevale* celebration in Venice.

Reflection

1.1 Students work together to plan the celebration.
1.2 Students read and view materials in Italian.
2.1 Students learn about and participate in the celebration.
2.2 Students make typical masks and costumes and prepare foods.
3.1 Students make connections to the disciplines of Art, Music, and Home and Careers.
3.2 Students acquire information about the significance of the celebration.
4.2 Students compare celebrations.
5.1 Students bring the language and culture to the rest of the school and the community.

TARGETED STANDARDS
1.1 Interpersonal Communication
1.2 Interpretive Communication
1.3 Presentational Communication
2.2 Products of Culture
3.1 Making Connections

COLUMBUS

Eighth grade students at Eastchester Middle School, Eastchester, NY, learn about Columbus and the "Encounter" in English. All the activities that follow this introduction are done in Italian. Students engage in activities such as drawing a picture of Columbus according to the 1504 description of Angelo Trivigiano (Columbus' portrait was never painted in his lifetime), and writing a brief story to explain "a day in the life" of one of Columbus' crewmen. Students rearrange paper strips containing biographical information about Columbus in chronological order. In collaboration with a social studies teacher, students learn about the historical significance of Columbus and participate in a mock trial in which they defend or prosecute Columbus and other explorers. In Home and Careers class, students learn about the foods available in 1492, and they prepare Columbus' farewell meal, consisting of mint and spinach ravioli and cherry cheesecake. In Art, students draw products and livestock that went from the Old World to the New and vice versa. Once the students complete their drawings, they cut them out and create a food mobile. In the Italian classroom, the teacher makes a *tombola* board transparency with pictures of these products. In groups, students take turns matching the words with the pictures. Another transparency game which gets all students involved at once is *Il paroliere* (Boggle).

Reflection

1.1 Students ask and respond to questions.
1.2 Students listen to presentations.
1.3 Students write stories and draw pictures to share with classmates.
2.2 Students identify and observe tangible products of the culture.
3.1 Students reinforce content from their Art, Home and Careers, and Social Studies classes.

FAIRY TALES

Students in a third-year Italian class in La Grange, IL, first read a familiar fairy tale in Italian such as *Pinocchio* or *Cappuccetto Rosso*. They discuss how these stories were changed to appeal to an American audience. The students continue this unit of study by reading other fairy tales which are unfamiliar to them (e.g., Italo Calvino's *Modern Italian Folktales*). They demonstrate an understanding of the relationship between practices and perspectives of Italian

TARGETED STANDARDS

1.2 Interpretive Communication
1.3 Presentational Communication
2.1 Practices of Culture
2.2 Products of Culture
3.1 Making Connections
3.2 Acquiring Information
4.2 Cultural Comparisons
5.2 Lifelong Learning

culture, for the folktales embody the attitudes and the creativity of the Italian people. Students dramatize the stories through skits in the classroom or perform for a wider student body, complete with costumes and stage designs. Lastly, students create original fairy tales complete with text, drawings, and/or videos.

Reflection

1.2 Students listen to fairy tales.
1.3 Students retell a fairy tale by using pictures and/or by presenting skits.
2.1 Students demonstrate an understanding of the relationship between practices and perspectives of Italian culture by participating in story telling and skits.
2.2 Students identify, experience, and read Italian children's literature.
3.1 Students see the connection between Italian and American fairy tales.
3.2 Students read authentic stories.
4.2 Students compare and contrast original Italian fairy tales with subsequent versions.
5.2 Students develop an appreciation of storytelling.

The format of this scenario can be modified to be used at any level. In a beginning class the teacher can tell a story using pictures, story strips, and very simple sentences. Based on this example, the students take pictures from story books which they mount on poster board, and they begin to summarize the stories with simple sentences in Italian. More advanced students create their own fairy tale complete with study guides, as well as drawings to accompany the story. Students take turns presenting and teaching these original stories to their classmates.

TARGETED STANDARDS
1.1 Interpersonal Communication
1.2 Interpretive Communication
1.3 Presentational Communication
3.2 Acquiring Information
4.2 Cultural Comparisons
5.1 School and Community

FAMILY TIES

In this scenario students in a second year Italian class in Pomona, NY read a poem by Aldo Palazzeschi, *Dramma Intimo in Cinque Atti*, a poem about intergenerational conflicts. They then formulate a series of questions to conduct an interview with a member of their own family or an Italian-American immigrant in their community. Through the interview students gather information about regions of origins, dates of emigration, foods and customs of the region, personal preferences, and habits. They take the information collected during the interview and compose an original poem using Palazzeschi's as a rhetorical model.

Reflection

1.1 Students conduct interviews with Italian speakers in the community.

1.2 Students read a poem.

1.3 Students write a poem and present it to the class.

3.2 Students acquire information about various Italian regions, their dialects, foods, traditions, etc.

4.2 Students compare traditions brought over by Italian immigrants with those of Americans.

5.1 Students interview someone in their own family or an Italian-American immigrant in their community.

TARGETED STANDARDS
1.1 Interpersonal Communication
1.2 Interpretive Communication
2.1 Practices of Culture
2.2 Products of Culture
3.1 Making Connections
4.2 Cultural Comparisons
5.1 School and Community
5.2 Lifelong Learning

FOOD AND MEALS

In a fifth-grade Italian class in East Rochester, NY, students learn about foods and meals. The vocabulary is introduced with pictures, store fliers, drawings or actual food. Verbs, adjectives, expressions dealing with eating and drinking, the culture of the family eating together, the time of the meals, and the types of food are also introduced. Other disciplines such as Health can collaborate in this unit by having students learn the nutritional value of various foods. In Home and Careers, students prepare meals. In Math, students learn about the metric system to convert recipes. The students use acquired vocabulary to create menus and invitations for the final project. They are encouraged to bring in their family's favorite recipe to connect, compare, and gain knowledge of their own culture's eating habits. At the end of the unit, the students share a meal together, within or beyond the school setting. Some options are to serve the food to their families and/or to senior citizens.

Reflection

1.1 Students work together to plan a meal.

1.2 Students read Italian menus.

2.1 Students identify the foods associated with certain meals and the time of meals.

2.2 Students prepare and taste authentic cuisine.

3.1 Students make connections with Health, Home and Careers, and Math.
4.2 Students compare Italian foods and meals with their own.
5.1 Students serve Italian foods to members of the community.
5.2 Students show evidence of being able to order and appreciate Italian foods.

HOUSE HUNTING

In a level II Italian class in Utica, NY, students make use of authentic materials to find an appropriate dwelling. Students discuss characteristics of their ideal dwelling and, looking through classified ads for Italian real estate, discover what Italians consider to be positive selling points for particular dwellings. Students are divided into teams of four. Two play the role of clients and two of real estate agents. While clients formulate a "wish list" of desirable attributes of a prospective dwelling, agents comb several pages of Italian classified ads on the Internet, where available, or from printed matter, and choose three different kinds of dwellings to be their listings for the day. Students role play interaction between clients and agents to determine which of the three available properties comes closest to the clients' requirements. Working together, the team creates a written summary of how things evolved. The written work contains what the clients were looking for, what the agents were offering, and which dwelling was chosen and why.

TARGETED STANDARDS
1.1 Interpersonal Communication
1.2 Interpretive Communication
1.3 Presentational Communication
2.2 Products of Culture
3.1 Making Connections
3.2 Acquiring New Information
4.2 Cultural Comparisons

Reflection

1.1 Students discuss differences and similarities in American and Italian dwellings.
1.2 Students create visuals of the features and layout of Italian dwellings.
1.3 Students present their information to each other and then negotiate based on the information provided.
2.2 Students learn about Italian preferences in dwellings.
3.1 Students make connections to the way people live around the world.
3.2 Students learn about Italian dwellings.
4.2 Students make comparisons between what they have discovered and the way they live in their own country.

Using Italian resources induces students to use their interpretive skills. Bringing preconceived notions to the bargaining table forces students to evaluate what is really important to them and consider what would work for them in another cultural environment. The activity is adaptable to various levels of language instruction.

Standards for Learning Italian

TARGETED STANDARDS
1.2 Interpretive Communication
1.3 Presentational Communication
2.1 Practices of Culture
2.2 Products of Culture
3.1 Making Connections
3.2 Acquiring Information
4.2 Cultural Comparisons
5.1 School and Community
5.2 Lifelong Learning

IMMIGRATION AND FAMILY HERITAGE

Students in a third-year Italian class in La Grange, IL, learn about immigration patterns of the Italian community from 1890 to the present. The economical, philosophical, political, social, and educational differences within the Italian culture are covered. Students acquire knowledge and understanding of Italian-Americans represented in the classroom and in their immediate community. Through videos and lectures students learn about the various problems Italian immigrants faced when they entered the United States. They trace the steps taken by the immigrants to begin the Americanization process and the efforts of second or third generation Italians to retain or return to their roots. Students research their own family immigration history and present their findings in a multimedia report in Italian. Students make a personal connection to the Italian-American immigration experience.

Reflection

1.2 Students view videos and read original materials dealing with immigration.
1.3 Students give oral presentations of their families' heritage through pictures, posters, passports, maps, etc.
2.1 Students analyze and discuss their ancestors' patterns of behavior, attitudes, and values which were key factors in their emigration.
2.2 Students analyze and discuss their ancestors' traditions in the form of holiday celebrations, language, cuisine, etc. that are still present in their lives.
3.1 Students make connections to their social studies curriculum through investigation of immigration patterns throughout history.
3.2 Students learn about this period in history through the use of available resources.
4.2 Students make comparisons between their family customs today and those of their ancestors.
5.1 Students gather information about their heritage by interviewing family members.
5.2 Students gain the tools to become life-long learners by discovering appropriate resources during their investigation.

This scenario is recommended for intermediate and advanced level students. The content depends on the setting and the targeted outcomes. The material presented in the form of lectures, videos, and readings can be in English as well as in Italian, depending on the students' abilities. The students' presentations can also be in either language. Researching the history of Italian immigration, students discover universal experiences of immigrants of all national origins, particularly those of their own families.

TARGETED STANDARDS
1.1 Interpersonal Communication
1.2 Interpretive Communication
1.3 Presentational Communication
2.1 Practices of Culture
3.1 Making Connections
4.2 Cultural Comparisons

ITALY BY TRAIN

In this scenario a third-year Italian class in Spring Valley, NY, plans an itinerary for train travel in Italy. They research train schedules, travel distances and time of travel between cities, converting kilometers

Standards for Learning Italian

to miles. Students create travel brochures with information gathered from various sources and present them to the class.

Reflection

1.1 Students provide and exchange travel information.

1.2 Students read Italian train schedules, maps, and travel brochures.

1.3 Students design and discuss the tours they have developed, and write letters requesting accommodations in Italian hotels.

2.1 Students research Italian travel practices via the Internet.

3.1 Students use math to calculate distances and convert kilometers into miles. They further calculate times of travel between cities by various means of transportation.

4.2 Students demonstrate knowledge of preferences in national transportation modes in Italy and the United States.

LET'S STAY HEALTHY

As the Drug Awareness Campaign approaches in East Rochester Middle School, NY, sixth-graders in an Italian class are introduced to the vocabulary dealing with body parts, symptoms of illness and remedies for various diseases. Students discuss cultural similarities and differences, such as products available in pharmacies, the predominance of male nurses in hospitals, death announcements in newspapers as well as on posters affixed on doors and walls of Italian towns. By playing Simon Says using flash cards, writing and reciting poems, doing board drawings, and making collages, students reinforce their acquired knowledge. To connect with the cultural aspect of Italy and the Drug Awareness Campaign in the United States, students create a death announcement poster about themselves, a family member who has died, an imaginary person, or a famous Italian. They incorporate the date of birth and death, the date and location of the funeral, along with the drawings of the person's interests. Students also present reasons why they should remain drug free. The slogans in Italian will be generated by the students with the help of the teacher (e.g., Say no to drugs; Kids need hugs, not drugs). The students' presentations are videotaped and if possible, shared with the other classes through the school-wide media system.

> **TARGETED STANDARDS**
> 1.1 Interpersonal Communication
> 1.2 Interpretive Communication
> 1.3 Presentational Communication
> 2.1 Products of Culture
> 3.1 Making Connections
> 4.2 Cultural Comparisons
> 5.1 School and Community
> 5.2 Lifelong Learning

Reflection

1.1 Students use Italian to identify body parts.

1.2 Students understand the cause and effect of drugs and create posters.

1.3 Students prepare a project for the Drug Awareness Campaign through a skit and/or a poster.

2.1 Students gain insight in viewing different stages of one's life.

3.1 Students make connections to other disciplines: health, art, and science.

4.2 Students compare how death is viewed in different cultures.

5.1 Students bring the language and culture of Italy to the rest of the school via media.

5.2 Students gain knowledge to make wise choices as they grow up.

This scenario adapts itself well to young students, as the reality of choices will be present in their lives.

TARGETED STANDARDS
1.1 Interpersonal Communication
1.2 Interpretive Communication
1.3 Presentational Communication
2.1 Practices of Culture
2.2 Products of Culture
5.2 Lifelong Learning

A LOVE STORY

Students in an Italian III class in La Grange, IL, receive a list of vocabulary words before they read the play, *Ti Ho Sposato per Allegria*. Based on this information, the students write a love story. They create a title, they list the characters, they give background information about each, and they give a summary of the plot. The students share their stories with their peers in cooperative groups or they present their stories orally to the class. By using the vocabulary given and creating plausible plots, students familiarize themselves with the words and similar plot of the actual play to be read in class. Thus, this exercise facilitates their comprehension of the play in Italian.

Reflection

1.1 Students exchange stories with peers in their group.
1.2 Students read and discuss an Italian play and write comments and opinions.
1.3 Students give oral or written presentations of their stories.
2.1 Students read newspaper articles discussing connections between Italian cultural perspectives and socially approved behavioral patterns (e.g., *mammismo*).
2.2 Students identify, analyze and evaluate the works of an Italian writer like Natalia Ginzburg.
5.2 Students develop an appreciation for Italian literature by reading original works.

TARGETED STANDARDS
1.1 Interpersonal Communication
1.2 Interpretive Communication
1.3 Presentational Communication
2.2 Products of Culture
4.2 Cultural Comparisons
5.1 School and Community
5.2 Lifelong Learning

MADE IN ITALY

In a level II Italian class in California, students discover the products in this country that are manufactured in Italy. Students make comparisons of certain American products with those made in Italy. Topics such as cars, food, clothing, giftware, jewelry and leather are divided among cooperative groups. Students create advertising and marketing strategies based on Italian promotional literature. Suggested end products for this unit are: posters, videos, dialogues, ads, brochures, short reports, consumer reports, show and tell with Italian products, etc.

Reflection

1.1 Students role-play buying and selling of products.
1.2 Students read ads, view videos, and research products via the Internet.
1.3 Students create and present commercials of targeted products.
2.2 Students become familiar with Italian craftsmanship.
4.2 Students compare products as well as notions of style.
5.1 Students become aware of many Italian products in their community.
5.2 Students become informed consumers.

Standards for Learning Italian

This scenario can be adapted to any level. The context will depend on the setting and the targeted outcome. Assessment is based on the ability of the students to interpret, deconstruct, and recreate models. Students make informed choices.

IL MERCANTE DI VENEZIA

In the Italian IV classes at Eastchester High School, NY, students are reading *The Merchant of Venice*. This is an interdisciplinary project in which students are exposed to the themes in English, foreign language, and business law classes to demonstrate the persuasiveness of language in affecting people's attitudes and prejudices. In the Italian class they learn about Venice, the commercial center of Europe, through slides and print materials. Students read the story in Italian (facilitated) and participate in story-mapping activities after the readings. Shakespeare's work on racial, ethnic, and religious discrimination is then discussed in small groups. At the end of the story, students watch the movie, *The Merchant of Venice*, a video adapted and directed by John Sichel (1973, ITC Distributor). Class discussions on discrimination and prejudice ensue. Next, everyone shares their personal experiences with prejudice, first in written form, then orally. Finally on the night of the *Festa Italiana*, students perform for the community a play written by them.

TARGETED STANDARDS
1.1 Interpersonal Communication
1.2 Interpretive Communication
1.3 Presentational Communication
2.1 Practices of Culture
2.2 Products of Culture
3.1 Making Connections
4.2 Cultural Comparisons
5.1 School and Community

Reflection
1.1 Students engage in conversation about the story.
1.2 Students comprehend the story through videos, slides, and other materials.
1.3 Students present information about the story and produce a play.
2.1 Students learn about the cultural practices of Venice during that era.
2.2 Students learn about the cultural products of Venice: clothing, spices, etc.
3.1 Students make connections with other disciplines such as business and English.
4.2 Students compare their own experiences with discrimination.
5.1 Students present their play to the community.

LA MODA

Students in a first year class of Italian in Western Springs, IL, stage a style show of Italian fashion. Students explore Italian-language Internet sites as well as fashion magazines to use them as a basis for their report. They work in groups to learn about designers and their styles, and history of the fashion industry in Italy. Students present a style show to clubs or to the community.

TARGETED STANDARDS
1.1 Interpersonal Communication
1.3 Presentational Communication
2.2 Products of Culture
3.2 Acquiring Information
4.2 Cultural Comparisons
5.1 School and Community
5.2 Lifelong Learning

Reflection

1.1 Students exchange information and opinions about designers and their styles.

1.3 Students stage a fashion show, describing items of clothing.

2.2 Students learn about the Italian fashion industry.

3.2 Students use the Internet and magazine sources to prepare reports and presentations on fashion.

4.2 Students observe and compare Italian designs and styles to American styles.

5.1 Students present a style show to clubs or to the community.

5.2 Students develop necessary skills to choose fashion.

TARGETED STANDARDS
1.1 Interpersonal Communication
1.2 Interpretive Communication
2.1 Practices of Culture
2.2 Products of Culture
3.1 Making Connections
4.2 Cultural Comparisons
5.2 Lifelong Learning

NUMBERS AROUND THE CLASSROOM

In Italian II classes in Utica, NY, several learning stations are set up around the classroom in order to learn how Italians use numbers in various circumstances. At station one, students find a meter stick and are given instructions to measure different objects and their own height in meters. At the second station, students find a meteorological report from a newspaper with necessary formulas to transfer the Fahrenheit to Celsius scale and vice versa. Here they prepare weather data for selected cities around the world. At the third station, students find formulas for the conversion of pounds to kilos. Here, they are instructed to give equivalent weights for various items and for their own body weight. At the fourth station, students find piles of Italian play money (color coded to keep piles separate) and the international currency exchange rates from *The New York Times*. Students must first determine how many *lire* are in each pile and then calculate their worth in United States dollars. The fifth station has sketches of an Italian apartment building and typical floor plans for Italian apartments. Family names are indicated at each floor of the building sketch, and in the sketch of the floor plan, appropriate furniture is drawn in each room. At this same station, students also find classified ads about apartments taken from *La Pulce*, a publication from Florence. Students are instructed to determine on which floor certain families live, how many rooms, baths, etc. various apartments have, and they are asked to select an apartment from the classified ad and explain the layout of their choice. Students are arranged in teams of four or five and assigned stations. After a predetermined length of time, the teams are periodically instructed to rotate to other stations in the room. Each student keeps a record of the collected. At the conclusion of the rotation of all of the stations, data is compared and discussed.

Reflection

1.1 Students discuss their data within their groups and later with the class.

1.2 Students interpret authentic materials from Italy (*La Pulce*, floorplans).

2.1 Students learn how Italians share numerical data in various circumstances.

2.2 Students learn about Italian housing, as well as measuring instruments.

3.1 Students make connections to science and mathematics.

4.2 Students observe and compare various practices of Italian culture.

5.2 Students develop necessary skills to deal with their future needs in travel and living in a "metric" world.

This scenario provides ample interaction. Students get the opportunity to unshackle themselves from their desks and participate in a voyage of discovery.

OUR NEIGHBORHOOD

In an elementary level Italian class in Western Springs, IL, students learn about the people and the business facilities in their community. Students identify stores, services, buildings, and the people who work there. Each student chooses a store and makes a collage of the products sold there. In a cooperative group, they create and label an imaginary city on a large piece of poster board and describe it

TARGETED STANDARDS
1.1 Interpersonal Communication
1.2 Interpretive Communication
1.3 Presentational Communication
2.1 Practices of Culture
2.2 Products of Culture
4.2 Cultural Comparisons
5.1 School and Community

to the class. Students label and place cut-out figures representing people in their town. Students set up an imaginary city in the classroom, bringing typical products found in each establishment. As a culminating activity, students come dressed as professionals, describe themselves and what they do. The imaginary city serves as a setting for situational dialogues. Given a situation to role-play, students are able to give and obtain directions, arrive at a destination, and request services. Comparisons can be made to those of other cultures in the community. They also learn about the differences in business hours and they compare and contrast the products sold in certain stores in Italy and in their own neighborhoods.

Reflection

1.1 Students work together to create and label the imaginary city.
1.2 Students understand the presentations of their classmates.
1.3 Students tell about their city and the people who work there.
2.1 Students understand the cultural practices of Italian establishments.
2.2 Students learn about the variety of Italian products.
4.2 Students compare schedules and the type of products sold in particular stores.
5.1 Students use the language in Italian neighborhoods or stores if available.

PEOPLE AND THEIR ENVIRONMENTS

Students in an Italian I class at Greece Athena High School in Rochester, NY, work in cooperative learning groups to describe various places around the world. After learning vocabulary and expressions to describe physical environment, groups choose places to research (e.g., Italy and its regions, U.S. states, or countries they studied in their social studies classes). Students describe the weather, land features, and

TARGETED STANDARDS
1.1 Interpersonal Communication
1.3 Presentational Communication
3.1 Making Connections
3.2 Acquiring Information
4.1 Language Comparisons
4.2 Cultural Comparisons

cities. They discuss the type of clothing worn and the possible activities for people in particular places. After creating visuals such as a map, weather map, posters, etc., students are videotaped making presentations to their classmates.

Standards for Learning Italian

Reflection

1.1 Students discuss geographical areas, climate, and activities.

1.3 Students give weather reports and present geographical information.

3.1 Students create labeled maps and overheads of other countries.

3.2 Students research the climate, geography, and habits of the people of other lands.

4.1 Students learn geographical cognates.

4.2 Students discover lifestyles in various areas.

Students practice newly acquired vocabulary of physical environment to talk about a country or state. Simultaneously they review the geographic features, general weather patterns, and the name in Italian of the people of that particular place. The country's environmental practices can also be discussed. This unit lends itself to an interdisciplinary approach with social studies.

PHOTOGRAPHS HAVE A VOICE

TARGETED STANDARDS

1.1 Interpersonal Communication
1.2 Interpretive Communication
1.3 Presentational Communication
2.1 Practices of Culture
2.2 Products of Culture
3.1 Making Connections
4.2 Cultural Comparisons
5.2 Lifelong Learning

Students in upper levels of Italian studies in Utica, NY use the following scenario to develop writing skills while learning about Italian culture. Students are given the necessary vocabulary to facilitate three different writing activities about selected photographic collections from the George Eastman House in Rochester, NY (on loan to the school through collaboration with the local Arts in Education Institute). The writing activities require students to first create an analytical composition that addresses the photographer's intentions (e.g., Is this photograph an example of journalism, a commercial promotion, historical recording, propaganda, persuasive evidence) and techniques in creating a selected work (e.g., perspective, lighting, shading, chiaroscuro, framing, composition, juxtaposition). The second activity involves the students in creating a narrative, real or imagined, from the photographer's point of view explaining how he/she came about creating the work. The third writing activity is a monologue spoken by the photograph itself to the viewer. In this activity the person in the photo expresses his/her feelings at the time the photograph was taken and reveals biographical information. As a follow-up to the above activities, students select a photograph from the book, *A Day in the Life of Italy* (Erwit, Rowan et al, Editors, San Francisco, Collins Publishers, 1990) and create short compositions of the three types previously studied. Work is presented orally and discussed with the rest of the class. All student work is evaluated for appropriateness, form, presentation, and development.

Reflection

1.1 Students discuss their interpretations of photographic works.

1.2 Students interpret visual clues found in photographic works.

1.3 Students share their work with peers.

2.1 Students interpret practices depicted in photographic works.

2.2 Students discuss products depicted in photographic works.

3.1 Students make connections to visual arts and photography

4.2 Students make comparisons between scenes depicted in photographs with similar or different situations in their own experience.

5.2 Students develop an appreciation for the art of photography and its messages.

This scenario is easily duplicated using any variety of photographic resources. It is adaptable for students of various ability levels.

A PICTURE IS WORTH A THOUSAND WORDS

In a level V Italian class in Utica, NY, students examine representative examples of Italian painters from various periods of history using slides, art books, or reproductions. Through their studies, students distinguish characteristics of major periods and schools of art. Students also determine focal points and ancillary details within specific works of art that contribute to the overall impact on the observer. In this activity, students use both basic and more advanced vocabulary and structures in verbal and written analysis of the works of art. After the teacher has introduced samples of art that cover the periods under study, students work in pairs to do a complete analysis of another work of art not yet discussed. Partners look for characteristics of the period and the artist, as well as determine the manner in which the artist intended the viewer to "read" the work. Finally, the pair describes the impact the work has on the viewer and its relative success at achieving that goal. Pairs produce a written commentary, as well as an oral presentation for the rest of the class.

TARGETED STANDARDS
1.1 Interpersonal Communication
1.2 Interpretive Communication
1.3 Presentational Communication
2.1 Practices of Culture
2.2 Products of Culture
3.1 Making Connections
3.2 Acquiring New Information
4.2 Cultural Comparisons
5.2 Lifelong Learning

Reflection
1.1 Students exchange information working with partners and classmates.
1.2 Students interpret visual images and iconography in selected works of art.
1.3 Students share their work with the rest of the class.
2.1 Students examine works of art to better understand the relationship between the visual imagery and the mores of the time.
2.2 Students examine the artwork as a product of a particular era.
3.1 Students make connections about Italian history learned in social studies classes and its figurative representation in targeted works of art.
3.2 Students learn details about individual artists' lives and works.
4.2 Students make comparisons between aesthetic choices appropriate to the time of works of art under study and what choices might be made today if an artist were to try to deliver a similar message.
5.2 Students develop the skills for critical analysis and appreciation of works of art that they will encounter later in life.

This has been successfully performed by students in advanced high school and college classes using Italian as the means of communication but can be adapted for younger students with the integration of more English into their presentations. The unit lends itself to a collaborative approach with art and social studies specialists.

TARGETED STANDARDS
1.1 Interpersonal Communication
1.2 Interpretive Communication
1.3 Presentational Communication
2.1 Practices of Culture
3.1 Making Connections
4.2 Cultural Comparisons

SPORTS

Eighth-graders learning Italian at Eastchester Middle School, Eastchester, NY, are talking about sports and sports personalities from Italy and from the United States. Vocabulary is introduced via TPR method. Famous people in sports are associated with their activities, so students can guess which sport is being described. Open-ended questions are asked by the teacher on sports and personalities (e.g., clothing, nationality, age, etc.). A Venn diagram is then drawn on the board to show the differences and commonalities. Students write the shared characteristics in the central, overlapping area, and those that differ, in the two side areas. Discussion about cultural similarities and differences takes place in English or Italian depending on the entry level of the students. Students make connections to the health curriculum when the teacher talks about the importance of a proper diet. In a cooperative learning setting, students categorize athletic activities by season, list what sports they practice, and write down what items they can buy in a sporting goods store. In pairs, some students write stories about a sport using the "shape stories" method, others write cinquain poems or silly rhymes, as modeled after examples studied in English class. Students select a picture of their favorite sport and use it for the basis of an oral and written presentation, which is then displayed. Graphs are made to illustrate students' sports preferences, and player/team statistics.

Reflection

1.1 Students exchange information about sports.
1.2 Students associate players with their sport.
1.3 Students present projects to their classmates on their favorite sports.
2.1 Students learn about Italian sports.
3.1 Students make connections in English, Health, and Math.
4.2 Students compare sports in the United States with sports in Italy.

TARGETED STANDARDS
1.2 Interpretive Communication
1.3 Presentational Communication
2.1 Practices of Culture
3.1 Making Connections
5.1 School and Community
5.2 Lifelong Learning

TASTEFUL FAMILY SECRETS

A tenth grade, third-year Italian class in Spring Valley, NY, studying foods and recipes invites a chef of a local Italian restaurant to give a demonstration lesson in the Home and Careers classroom. Students record the recipe. They read recipes from Italian cookbooks. They then obtain a family recipe (where possible) and present it to the class in Italian. They supply any background information (personal and/or regional) associated with the dish. They write out the collected recipes which are then "published" in book form with each student responsible for a double-page spread. Some of the students work on computer stations in the classroom with desktop publishing software, others compose theirs by hand. This publication is auctioned off to raise money for the Italian Club at the annual Italian dinner.

Reflection

1.2 Students read recipes in Italian.
1.3 Students demonstrate and write their own recipes.
2.1 Students begin to identify regional Italian cooking.
3.1 Students make connections to Home and Careers.
5.1 Students interact with a chef from a local restaurant and eat a delicious dish.
5.2 Students learn cooking skills.

TROVARSI UN LAVORO

Students in an Italian 4/5 class prepare necessary tools for job hunting. Over the years of their instruction, students study the names of various professions in Italian. In the upper level course, this list is expanded not only with the names of additional careers, but the activities and in many cases equipment involved in the day-to-day practices of these careers. Through research on the Internet, examples of actual resumes of Italians looking for jobs are retrieved as models for students. Additionally, examples of applications for specific jobs, employment services and state-controlled exams are found. Students create their own curriculum vitae after the Italian models. Students fill out reproductions of applications. Students create self-promotional compositions and letters of intent to be attached to the job portfolio. In cases where students lack the actual experience and education for a desired job, they are encouraged to use their imaginations in pretending that they have their college years behind them and enter what they consider to be appropriate data where necessary.

TARGETED STANDARDS

1.1 Interpersonal Communication
1.2 Interpretive Communication
2.1 Practices of Culture
2.2 Products of Culture
3.1 Making Connections
3.2 Acquiring Information
5.2 Lifelong Learning

Reflection

1.1 Students create material to promote their capabilities on the job market.
1.2 Students read and decipher career-oriented publications from Italy.
2.1 Students observe and interpret protocol in the Italian job market.
2.2 Students retrieve authentic documents through the Internet.
3.1 Students make connections to the particular fields pursued in their research.
3.2 Students acquire new information by further research into a field of interest.
5.2 Students acquire skills necessary for employment in a global economy.

A most practical activity, students get first-hand knowledge of the importance of knowing another language. By investigating career opportunities in this fashion, doors open for those students who may have only considered employment at home.

TARGETED STANDARDS
1.1 Interpersonal Communication
1.2 Interpretive Communication
1.3 Presentational Communication
2.1 Practices of Culture
3.1 Making Connections
4.2 Cultural Comparisons

WEATHER

Seventh-graders at Eastchester Middle School, Eastchester, NY, are studying weather expressions. They recognize common statements about the weather and become familiar with the climate in various Italian regions. Students review weather terms, seasons, and months using visuals. They present weather reports to the class in Italian, incorporating the date, present weather conditions, high and low temperatures of the day, sunrise, sunset, sky conditions, etc. Students then ask each other what they like to do during various seasons, using names of sports and their favorite activities, as well as the items of clothing useful in different weather conditions. Food and drinks that students prefer in different types of weather are also discussed while they work in a cooperative setting. Students look at the weather section from a local Italian newspaper, listen to an Italian weather forecast, and consult the Internet to collect data. They make a chart to show the warmest cities, in that particular month, and the meteorological differences between geographical areas. They construct a bar graph, illustrating the temperature in various parts of Italy and comparing it to the United States. Interdisciplinary connections are made to the math/science curricula as students learn about evaporation, winds, water cycle, the water droplets that form clouds, and temperature conversion from Celsius to Fahrenheit. Students are assigned a weather "scavenger hunt" for homework, in which they match the weather item with the descriptions. As part of a creative writing activity, students write "shape stories" (e.g., drawing an umbrella, cloud, or raindrop) with words in or around the shape.

Reflection

1.1 Students discuss weather and related activities.
1.2 Students interpret Italian weather reports.
1.3 Students present weather reports in class.
2.1 Students learn about Italian habits influenced by weather.
3.1 Students make connections with other disciplines: Science, English, and Math.
4.2 Students compare the weather in the United States with that in Italy.

Standards for Japanese Language Learning

*A collaborative project of the
National Council of Japanese Language Teachers
and the Association of Teachers of Japanese*

JAPANESE

Prepared by the Japanese National Standards Task Force

Pamela Delfosse, Madison West High School, Madison, WI
Yumiko Guajardo, U. S. Air Force Academy, Colorado Springs, CO
Kimberly Jones, University of Arizona, Tempe, AZ
Yoko Kano, University of North Carolina at Wilmington, Wilmington, NC
Hiroko Kataoka (Chair), California State University, Long Beach/Japan Foundation and Language Center, Santa Monica, CA
Waunita Kinoshita, Urbana High School, Urbana, IL
Norman Masuda, Palo Alto High School, Palo Alto, CA
Toyoko Okawa, Punahou School, Honolulu, HI
Carrie Penning, East Hartford Glastonbury Magnet School, East Hartford, CT
Jessica Thurrott, Maloney Magnet School, Waterbury, CT
Yasu-Hiko Tohsaku, University of California, San Diego, CA
Yasuko Ito Watt, Indiana University, Bloomington, IN

Standards for Japanese Language Learning

Board of Reviewers

Not all comments from reviewers could be incorporated into the final document, and serving as a reviewer does not constitute agreement with the entire standards document.

Marty Abbott
Fairfax County Public Schools
Falls Church, VA

Leslie Birkland
Lake Washington High School
Kirkland, WA

Yoshiko Brotherton
Clements High School
Fort Bend, TX

Anita Bruce
World Languages
Honolulu, HI

Yoshiko Elmer
Burges High School
El Paso, TX

Kyle Ennis
Aloha High School
Beaverton, OR

Fumiko Foard
Arizona State University, AZ

Lynette Fujimori
School Renewal Group
Honolulu, HI

Hiroko Furuyama,
The Japan Foundation
Santa Monica, CA

Kyoko Hijirida
University of Hawaii, Honolulu

Sonomi Ishida
Great Falls Elementary School
Fairfax, VA

Eleanor H. Jorden
Teacher Training Institute,
Exchange: Japan
Ann Arbor, MI

Takuo Kinoshita
M.L. King Elementary School
Urbana, IL

Hiroyuki Kuno
Spencer Elementary School
Savannah, GA

Kimi Matsumoto
Los Alamitos High School, CA

Atsuko Morse
The College Preparatory School
Oakland, CA

Marci Muench
John F. Kennedy Middle School
Palm Beach, FL

Mari Noda
Ohio State University, Columbus

Yoko Pusavat
California State University,
Long Beach

Charles Quinn
Ohio State University, Columbus

Nobuyuki Sassa
Great Falls Elementary School
Fairfax, VA

Ann Sherif
Oberlin College, OH

Donald L. Spence
East Carolina University
Greenville, NC

Christopher St. Clair
Dr. Hornedo Middle School
Lincoln Middle School
El Paso, TX

Chihiro K. Thomson
University of New South Wales
Australia

Mamiya Sahara Worland
Great Falls Elementary School
Fairfax, VA

Contributors to the Learning Scenarios

In addition to the Task Force members, the following people contributed to the writing of the learning scenarios:

Fumiko Foard, Arizona State University, Tempe
Lee Link, Madison-Oneida BOCES, Hamilton, NY
Sandra Lopez-Richter, Crestwood Middle School, FL
Kimi Matsumoto, Los Alamitos High School, CA
Teachers of Richmond School Japanese Magnet Program, Portland, OR

Special Thanks to:

Judy Brisbois, USAFA, Colorado Springs, CO
Hiroko Furuyama, The Japan Foundation and Language Center in Los Angeles
Mufi & Gail Hannemann, Honolulu, HI
Arturo Guajardo, Colorado springs, CO
Noriko Hara, Indiana University, IN
Kyoko Hijirida, University of Hawaii, Honolulu, HI
Akiko Kakutani, Earlham College, Richmond, IN
Earl K. Okawa, The Japan-America Society of Hawaii
Laurel Rasplica Rodd, University of Colorado, CO
Susan Schmidt, ATJ, c/o University of Colorado, CO
Rebecca Still, Richmond Community High School, VA
Isao Tsujimoto and others, The Japan Foundation and Language Center in Los Angeles

Table of Contents

STANDARDS FOR JAPANESE LANGUAGE LEARNING		**372**
INTRODUCTION		**373**
JAPANESE LANGUAGE EDUCATION IN THE UNITED STATES		**374**
HOW TO USE THIS DOCUMENT		**376**
COMMUNICATION	Goal 1	**378**
CULTURES	Goal 2	**384**
CONNECTIONS	Goal 3	**387**
COMPARISONS	Goal 4	**389**
COMMUNITIES	Goal 5	**392**
LEARNING SCENARIOS		**396**
Akai Tori Kotori		396
The Food Pyramid		396
Japanese Home		397
Hanami (Flower Viewing)		398
Taifuu (Typhoon)		399
Children's Book Project		399
Manzanar		400
Hosting Japanese Guests		401
"Street Corner" Interview		402
Tea		403
Gift-Giving/Telephone Shopping		403
REFERENCES		**404**

Standards for Japanese Language Learning

COMMUNICATION — Goal 1

Communicate in Japanese

Standard 1.1: Students engage in conversation, provide and obtain information, express feelings and emotions, and exchange opinions.

Standard 1.2: Students understand and interpret written and spoken Japanese on a variety of topics.

Standard 1.3: Students present information, concepts, and ideas to an audience of listeners or readers on a variety of topics.

CULTURES — Goal 2

Gain Knowledge and Understanding of Japanese Culture

Standard 2.1: Students demonstrate an understanding of the relationship between the practices and perspectives of Japanese culture.

Standard 2.2: Students demonstrate an understanding of the relationship between the products and perspectives of Japanese culture.

CONNECTIONS — Goal 3

Connect with Other Disciplines and Acquire Information

Standard 3.1: Students reinforce and further their knowledge of other disciplines through the Japanese language.

Standard 3.2: Students acquire information and recognize the distinctive viewpoints that are only available through Japanese language and culture.

COMPARISONS — Goal 4

Develop Insight into the Nature of Language and Culture

Standard 4.1: Students demonstrate understanding of the nature of language through comparisons of the Japanese language and their own.

Standard 4.2: Students demonstrate understanding of the concept of culture through comparisons of Japanese culture and their own.

COMMUNITIES — Goal 5

Participate in Multilingual Communities at Home and Around the World

Standard 5.1: Students use Japanese both within and beyond the school setting.

Standard 5.2: Students show evidence of becoming life-long learners by using Japanese for personal enjoyment and enrichment.

Introduction

The Standards for Japanese Language Learning document is the result of an effort by K-16 level Japanese language educators to link the publication *Standards for Foreign Language Learning: Preparing for the 21st Century*, developed by The National Standards in Foreign Language Education Project, directly to Japanese language classrooms in the United States.

Close examination of the Foreign Language Education Project standards allowed the task force to determine modifications appropriate to meet the unique needs of Japanese teaching and learning environments. The resulting Japanese-specific standards adopt the strengths of the standards document while incorporating changes that address issues specific to the field of Japanese language education.

As these standards are based upon the *Standards for Foreign Language Learning*, their interpretation and effective application is dependent upon familiarity with the original document. It is assumed throughout this publication that individuals are acquainted with the philosophy and content of the original standards. The organizing principles are those of the *Standards for Foreign Language Learning*. The five goals of language instruction—communication, cultures, connections, comparisons, and communities—remain the pillars of this vision. Each goal is accompanied by standards, statements of what students are familiar with and are able to do at a given educational level. Each standard is followed by several sample progress indicators that serve to describe student progress in meeting the standard. The final segment of the document offers learning scenarios, illustrative examples for teaching and learning, which incorporate the standards.

The document, *Standards for Japanese Language Learning*, was developed by a diverse team of educators. Task force members representing elementary, middle, high school, and post-secondary teachers of Japanese from diverse geographic locations and teaching contexts worked together to develop this vision for K-16 level language programs. Native and non-native speakers of Japanese shared their respective insights and expertise. The collaboration of this group of professionals resulted in a document intended to serve the needs of the diverse Japanese education field.

In developing the *Standards for Japanese Language Learning* each goal, standard, and progress indicator of the *Standards for Foreign Language Learning* was carefully assessed and modified as necessary. A draft of the Japanese standards was disseminated throughout the profession for feedback. Comments from the field informed the revision of the final document. Learning scenarios based on classroom instructional experience were elicited from practicing educators to exemplify how the standards function within the Japanese classroom context. The strength of these standards stems from invaluable contributions from educators nationwide.

The standards are designed to aid teachers and learners of Japanese, yet their benefit extends beyond the walls of the classroom. They present a vision of Japanese language education within the American educational context to administrators engaged in language planning, parents, educational advisors, teachers of other disciplines, and supporting organizations and agencies.

The philosophy and premises that underlie the *Standards for Foreign Language Learning* are the foundation upon which the Japanese standards were developed:

"Language and communication are at the heart of the human experience. The United States must educate students who are equipped linguistically and culturally to communicate successfully in a pluralistic American society and abroad. This imperative envisions a future in which ALL students will develop and maintain proficiency in English and at least one other language..." (p. 7, *Standards for Foreign Language Learning: Preparing for the 21st Century*)

Japanese language education at the K-16 level should support this vision. All learners can benefit from the study of Japanese when language programs are developed and adapted to fulfill the needs and interests of students of varying abilities and backgrounds. Individual teachers are encouraged not to limit themselves to a single approach to teaching in accomplishing program goals. Methodology and approaches to language learning will vary depending upon the composition of a class, on the educational needs of one's students, and on the individual instructor's background and style. While the standards help in setting goals and objectives, it must be recognized that there are many ways in which these can be achieved.

JAPANESE LANGUAGE EDUCATION IN THE UNITED STATES

Standards for Foreign Language Learning points out that a variety of benefits are gained by the study of a foreign language. These include learning more about one's native language and about language as a general phenomenon, gaining an appreciation of both one's own and other languages and cultures, improving general cognitive and communication skills, and gaining access to other cultures and bodies of knowledge. Studying a linguistically and culturally distant language like Japanese is especially likely to awaken in learners an understanding of the degree to which languages and cultures can vary and of what is distinctive about their own culture.

In addition to the benefits of language learning to individual learners, an increase in the number of Americans who are proficient in foreign languages benefits the United States by improving the level of knowledge of and ability to communicate with other countries in the world. With the increasing global importance of Asia and the Pacific Rim, and the economic and strategic significance of the U.S.-Japan relationship, it is important that more Americans become proficient in Japanese in order to gain access to information available only in Japanese, to increase our national level of understanding of Japan, and to better communicate a deeper knowledge of the United States to Japan.

While traditionally the study of Japanese in the United States was limited to a small number of academic and diplomatic specialists, the importance of Japan in the global and Asian contexts means that a knowledge of Japanese language and culture benefits not only those learners who will eventually become "Japan experts" but also those in a variety of different fields, such as business, tourism, journalism, science and technology, and the humanities and social sciences. A growing awareness of this fact has led to a great increase in the numbers and backgrounds of students of Japanese and a broadening of their goals during the last fifteen to twenty years.

Today, students learn Japanese in increasingly diverse contexts. In addition to traditional programs at the college and graduate level, students now study Japanese in K-12 classes, at community colleges, in heritage language schools, in immersion programs for children, in extension classes, in distance-learning programs, and on their own with the aid of computerized learning programs. Between 1986 and 1991, for example, the number of high schools offering Japanese language rose from about 200 to over 770 (Jorden, with Lambert, p. 17). Not only are students learning Japanese in more contexts, but within specific learning environments a growing variety of students take Japanese. No longer is it a language studied only by the elite.

In the near future, not only will we see an increasing number of students of Japanese; we will see a wider variety of backgrounds among students choosing to study Japanese. Students may enter Japanese classes with no, little, or considerable background in Japanese. Some may have a Japanese heritage background. Some students may come from having studied another language or languages. Some may choose to begin language at the middle school or high school level. Some may study Japanese, then another language, and later return to Japanese. Schools must provide programs with multiple entry points.

Students will benefit from the study of Japanese even when sequential Japanese may not be available for them throughout their school years from kindergarten through college: in addition to what they learn of the language and culture, they will also acquire basic language learning strategies, higher level thinking skills, and broader perspectives from their Japanese studies.

Given this situation, it is critical that those involved in Japanese language education hold high standards for the achievement of Japanese learners. Only by having high expectations can we continue improving the quality of Japanese language education in order to benefit both individual learners and the country as a whole. Teachers will find the goals, standards, and progress indicators in this document helpful as they plan a curriculum that best meets the diverse needs and abilities of their students. Teachers will be guided by looking at the sample progress indicators at various levels and will adapt them for the particular needs and abilities of their students.

Features of Japanese

The unique features of the Japanese language and culture make it highly appealing, yet sometimes challenging, for students in the United States. While studying Japanese, students develop the skills necessary to exist within a linguistic and cultural structure very different from their own. They gain access to the writing system, cultural practices, and expressive arts, as well as career opportunities available only to those who speak Japanese.

For American students who have never been exposed to non-Western cultures, the study of Japanese opens the door to Asia. For Japanese-American students, it is a venue in which to understand their cultural heritage. When planning, creating, or implementing a Japanese language program at any level, it is important to emphasize the unique and exciting, as well as the challenging, features of Japanese for American students.

One of the most important things to keep in mind when considering Japanese language learning and teaching in the United States is the length of time it takes native speakers of English to achieve a high level of proficiency. The Foreign Service Institute of the State Department, for example, has set the normal training time for a Category 4 language like Japanese at eighty-eight weeks of full time study, as compared with only 24 weeks for Category 1 languages such as Spanish and French (Ehrman, p. 87). Because of this, it is critical that those involved with Japanese programs not expect that students' skills will advance at the same rate as those of students of many of the other languages taught in the United States.

There are a variety of reasons that Japanese takes so much time for native speakers of English to learn. Both linguistically and culturally, it is very distant from English. One consequence of the linguistic distance is that there are no cognate words in English and Japanese. The grammar of Japanese is also extremely different from that of English. For example, students must get used to putting the main verb at the end of the sentence, using postpositions instead of prepositions, and putting relative clauses before instead of after the nouns that they modify. On the other hand, these difficulties are somewhat mitigated by the fact that Japanese has a relatively simple sound system and by the existence of large numbers of loanwords from English that may be easy to learn for students who already know English.

In addition to the linguistic distance, the cultural distance between the United States and Japan leads to other challenges. Basic communicative functions such as requesting, disagreeing, and inviting are performed very differently in Japanese culture. Merely translating American English interactional patterns into Japanese vocabulary and grammar does not result in acceptable Japanese communication. Learners must also grapple with new concepts such as the necessity of expressing social relationships in language. For example, the same basic content takes very different linguistic forms (or is not expressed at all) depending on social factors such as the gender, age, status, and closeness of the people speaking to each other.

Not only does the distance between English and Japanese grammar and American and Japanese cultures increase the time needed to acquire the language, the nature of the Japanese written language leads to its own set of challenges. In order to be able to read Japanese materials written for adult native speakers, students must learn two different syllabic writing systems and approximately 2000 Chinese characters (*kanji*), most of which have multiple meanings and readings. While it is true that being able to speak a given language does not imply ability to read and write, the gap between written and spoken language is particularly wide in Japanese.

HOW TO USE THIS DOCUMENT

These standards were compiled in the hope that the opportunity for Japanese language learning will become available to students across the United States beginning as early as the kindergarten years. At present, this opportunity does not exist in most communities. Therefore, it will be necessary for teachers and administrators to adapt these standards to existing programs while they explore possibilities for achieving the standards more fully in the future. In programs in which Japanese language education does not begin in kindergarten, teachers and administrators need to adapt the standards to the levels of instruction currently offered.

Learning progress indicators in the five goal areas are listed for grades 4, 8, 12, and 16. Teachers can use the grade indicators to measure their students' progress in any existing program. For example, progress indicators for grade 4 can be applied at the 8th grade level in programs in which Japanese language study begins at the 5th grade. However, when adjusting indicators, teachers must take into consideration appropriateness to the age of their students.

Experience suggests that the ideal situation for optimum language learning is daily exposure to the language. In cases where classes meet on a block or modular schedule (i.e., two or three times a week), in so-called "pull-out" programs (in which students are taken out of the regular classes for short periods of time each week), or in half-year programs (in which for staffing or economic reasons the language cannot be offered throughout the academic year), the students may not acquire language at the same pace as those who are exposed to it daily or as those students who are in immersion or partial immersion programs. Therefore, the standards must be adjusted, or adapted, to meet the circumstances of the individual program.

Other factors that may influence student progress include the percentage of time the instructor uses Japanese in class, the pedagogical methods used, and the language proficiency of the instructor. These standards encourage using Japanese in class as much as possible, including its use in giving classroom instructions and in daily expressions. However, the instructor may find it necessary to use English when explaining a topic that is beyond the current linguistic capability of the students. The occasions when use of English may be necessary have been noted in this document.

These standards do not dictate a specific course content or curriculum, although they suggest the adoption of certain activities which will help students attain the goals set forth in the standards. We have included scenarios which highlight unique aspects of the Japanese language. These scenarios are provided as examples and can be adapted to meet the needs of individual students or instructional settings.

Technology

In implementing these guidelines, instructors should remain aware of advances in technology which may accelerate or enhance the achievement of these goals and standards within the classroom. We live in an age when rapidly changing technology is a fact of life. For example, e-mail in Japanese makes direct written communication with native speakers easier than ever before. Today's students readily accept such change and are often eager to apply the latest technology to their studies. While teachers should not blindly accept every new gadget that enters the market, they need to keep abreast of changes in technology.

Communication
Communicate in Japanese
Goal One

Due to syntactic, lexical, and orthographic differences between English and Japanese, learners of Japanese may need more time and face more challenges than learners of Western European languages in achieving the same goals. This difficulty has many implications for Japanese language teaching and learning, and progress indicators in this section were developed with this point in mind. For instance, students may occasionally have to depend upon English sources due to the difficulty of authentic Japanese materials. In addition, due to the large number of *kanji* and the complexity of their usage, Japanese students need to use non-authentic as well as authentic materials during the course of their studies in order to develop their reading skills. It is also necessary for students to be exposed to handwritten materials and a variety of printing fonts to become proficient in reading Japanese.

Japanese is well known for its complexity of formality levels and styles. When deciding what style and formality level of speech students should use, teachers need to consider age-appropriateness. For example, it is not authentic for kindergarten teachers to use *desu-masu* forms all the time. As their Japanese language study progresses, students will need to gradually recognize that there are distinct differences between spoken and written Japanese, and to become familiar with a variety of styles for both.

The Standards address three modes of communication: interpersonal, interpretive, and presentational. Some characteristics of the Japanese language that require particular attention when learning interpersonal communication skills are the elaborate system of honorifics (*keigo*), the wide range of speech registers, and the sharp distinctions between formal and informal language.

The fact that Japanese can be written using only syllabic symbols (*hiragana* and *katakana*) means that, at the early stages of learning, students can very quickly attain basic literacy. However, written communication does present challenges related to the special characteristics of the Japanese writing system. Both the development of productive skills and of receptive skills related to written communication are slowed by the challenges of *kanji* and the complexity of their use in Japanese.

Presentational communication requires attention to the special formulaic language used in formal speeches, to the special discourse structures of written presentation (*ki-shoo-ten-ketsu*). And, of course, *kanji* and other facets of Japanese orthography must be mastered.

All of these special challenges must be addressed for the learner to develop interpretive communication skills; listeners and readers must recognize and understand the implications of use of a given register or level of formality, or of the choice of *katakana* for emphasis to write a particular word, for example.

STANDARD 1.1 Students engage in conversations, provide and obtain information, express feelings and emotions, and exchange opinions.

Sample Progress Indicators, Grade 4

- Students give and follow simple instructions in order to participate in age-appropriate classroom and/or cultural activities (class opening routines such as *kiritsu rei, mite/kiite/suwatte kudasai, jan-ken-pon,* making origami).

- Students ask and answer questions (*itsu, doko, dare, nanji, nannin*) about topics such as daily routine, family, school events, and celebrations in person or via simple letters, e-mail, audiotapes, or videotapes.

- Students share their likes and dislikes regarding various objects, topics, people, and events in their everyday environment (*Nihongo ga suki, yasai ga kirai*).

- Students exchange descriptions of people and tangible products of the Japanese culture (sumo wrestlers, kimono, game software, traditional and contemporary foods) with each other.

- Students use and respond to greetings, leave takings, and common classroom expressions in culturally appropriate ways (*ohayoo gozaimasu* accompanied by *ojigi*, saying *sayonara* with a wave).

- Students introduce themselves by giving information such as name, birthday, address, year in school, and nationality.

- Students ask for clarification and/or express confusion (*nan desu ka, wakaranai, e?*).

Sample Progress Indicators, Grade 8

- Students follow and give directions for participating in age-appropriate classroom and/or cultural activities (*undookai, gakugeikai*). They ask and respond to questions for clarification.

- Students exchange information about personal events, memorable experiences (language camp, eating at a Japanese restaurant), and school subjects with peers and/or members of Japanese language communities.

- Students compare, contrast, and express opinions and preferences about the information gathered regarding events, experiences, and other school subjects (*tenpura no hoo ga oishikatta, ...to omou*).

- Students acquire goods, services, or information orally and/or in writing (*sore onegaishimasu, misete kudasai*).

- Students work as a class or in small groups to discuss, propose, and develop school- or community-related activities (planning a Japanese booth for a school carnival, singing Japanese songs at nursing homes).

Standards for Japanese Language Learning

- Students use communication strategies (paraphrasing, gestures) when they cannot express their intended message adequately.

Sample Progress Indicators, Grade 12

- Students exchange information, orally and/or in writing, regarding topics of interest in Japanese language communities (Niigata Daijishin, *purikura*, *manga*), or topics that are being studied in another subject.

- Through group work students develop and propose solutions to issues and problems related to the school and community (school dress code, recycling).

- Students share their understanding of and personal reactions to simple Japanese or translated Japanese materials presented in a written, audio, or audio-visual form.

- Students gather and obtain information through a variety of sources (surveys, interviews, Internet, charts, videos, written documents) on topics of interest (*juku*, *arubaito*, Japanese pop stars).

- Students exchange opinions in an appropriate manner with peers and/or members of Japanese language communities about the information they have gathered (... *to omou/... to omoimasu kedo* ...).

Sample Progress Indicators, Grade 16

- Students discuss, orally or in writing, events and issues that are of significance in Japanese society or that are being studied in another subject (*kooreika shakai*, World War II).

- Through group work students develop and propose solutions to issues and problems that are of concern to members of their own and the Japanese culture (immigrant labor, *kankyoo mondai*).

- Students share their understanding of and personal reactions to expository and literary texts with peers and/or speakers of Japanese.

- Students exchange, support and discuss their opinions and individual perspectives with peers and/or speakers of Japanese on a variety of topics dealing with contemporary and historical issues (*ijime, Koyoo kikai kintoohoo, Meiji ishin*).

- Students demonstrate an understanding of the appropriateness and timing of introducing and pursuing various topics of conversation (when to get down to specifics in a business negotiation, topics to avoid discussing at a wedding).

STANDARD 1.2 Students understand and interpret written and spoken Japanese on a variety of topics.

Sample Progress Indicators, Grade 4

- Students comprehend the main ideas in developmentally appropriate oral narratives such as personal anecdotes, familiar stories, and other narratives accompanied by visual aids (*kamishibai, ehon,* videos).

- Students comprehend the main ideas and identify the principal characters (*Kaguyahime, Momotaroo, Anpanman, Doraemon*) of orally presented stories (children's literature) accompanied by visual aids.

- Students identify people and objects in their environment from oral and/or simple written descriptions (*Watashi wa dare deshoo?* game, *Nijuu no tobira*).

- Students comprehend brief, formulaic oral announcements, written messages, or lists connected to classroom or school activities (the day's class agenda, morning announcements over the PA system in Japanese).

- Students comprehend the principal message contained in various developmentally appropriate media such as illustrated texts (*ehon*, *manga*), posters, advertisements, or computer games (Japanese Gameboy software).

- Students interpret gestures, intonation, and other visual or auditory cues when trying to understand spoken language (*oide* accompanied by a gesture).

Sample Progress Indicators, Grade 8

- Students identify people and objects (historical and contemporary figures such as Hirohito, Hideo Nomo; means of transportation such as *Shinkansen*) in their environment or from other school subjects based on oral and/or written descriptions.

- Students comprehend brief written messages and short personal notes on familiar topics such as family, school events, and celebrations (*gyooji annai, tanjoobi no shootaijoo*).

- Students understand the main ideas and/or themes from visual media or live presentations (show-and-tell) on topics of personal interest (hobbies, friends, TV programs).

- Students use knowledge acquired in other settings and from other subject areas (science, social studies) to comprehend spoken and written messages (*tenki yohoo*, trash pick-up schedules).

- Students comprehend the principal messages in written materials on familiar topics and materials adapted for their use (*Hiragana Times*).

- Students demonstrate an emerging ability to identify the meaning of unfamiliar vocabulary, including loan words and some *kanji*, through context.

Sample Progress Indicators, Grade 12

- Students understand the main ideas/themes and some details from various media sources (movies, television and radio programs, CD-ROMS) or live presentations on topics of personal interest pertaining to Japanese language communities (current events, popular culture).

- Students understand the main themes of selected and/or adapted materials from newspapers (*Asahi Shinbun, New York Yomiuri*), magazines (*Nihongo Journal*), e-mail, or other printed sources.

- Students identify the principal characters and comprehend the main ideas and themes in selected and/or adapted texts from various literary genres (*shooto shooto, haiku, rakugo,* plays).

- Students demonstrate an emerging understanding of differences in style between and within written (personal vs. business letters) and spoken (to family vs. to strangers) language as expressed by speakers of Japanese in formal and informal settings.

- Students demonstrate an increasing ability to identify the meaning of vocabulary, unfamiliar *kanji*, and *kanji* compounds through context.

Sample Progress Indicators, Grade 16

- Students demonstrate an understanding of the main ideas and significant details of live and recorded discussions, lectures, and presentations on current or past events from Japanese culture (*baburu hookai, josei mondai,* youth violence) or that are being studied in another class.

- Students demonstrate an understanding of the principal elements of non-fiction articles from conventional and electronic media (newspapers, magazines, web pages) on topics of current and historical importance to members of Japanese culture (*shoonen hanzai, zooki ishoku, jokoo aishi*).

- Students analyze the main plot, subplot, characters, their descriptions, roles, and significance in selected authentic literary texts (*Taketori monogatari, Wagahai wa neko de aru, Kitchin, Sarada kinenbi*).

- Students demonstrate an increasing understanding of the nuances of meaning in written and spoken language as expressed by speakers of Japanese in formal and informal settings (roundabout ways of refusing or complaining, choosing between synonymous *kango* and *wago* expressions).

- Students demonstrate an increasing understanding of the cultural nuances of meaning in expressive products of Japanese culture, including selections from literary genres (*shintaishi, shoosetsu*) and the visual arts (*haiga, kabuki*).

Standard 1.3 Students present information, concepts, and ideas to an audience of listeners or readers on a variety of topics.

Sample Progress Indicators, Grade 4

- Students prepare illustrations and descriptions of people, activities, or events in their environment and share these stories with an audience such as the class.

- Students give brief oral presentations about people, activities, or events (field trips, vacations) in their everyday environment.

- Students perform with visual or verbal cues songs (*musunde hiraite, genkotsuyama no tanukisan, saita saita*), short anecdotes (*Nihon mukashibanashi*), or poetry commonly known by peers in Japanese language communities.

- Students make greeting cards (*nengajoo*), short informal messages, or audio/videotapes following a prescribed format to present to pen pals or others (classmates, family members, principal, PTA, Board of Education members).

Sample Progress Indicators, Grade 8

- Students write or tell about products and/or practices of their own culture (pop music, Thanksgiving, Independence Day) to peers in Japanese language communities.

- Students present short plays and skits, recite selected poems and anecdotes, and perform songs for school and community events.

- Students prepare tape- or video-recorded messages (*gakkoo shookai*, school news) on topics of personal interest to share locally, with school peers, or with members of Japanese language communities.

- Students prepare stories or simple written reports about personal experiences (*kazoku ryokoo*, field trip) or selected topics from other school subjects (*rika no jikken repooto*) to share with classmates and/or members of Japanese language communities.

- Students prepare an oral statement or write sentences in Japanese identifying the main ideas/themes and characters in selected pieces of appropriate/adapted literature (*Madogiwa no Tottochan* [in Japanese], *Rising Sons and Daughters*, *Botchan* [in translation]).

- Students prepare in oral or written form an "exchange diary (*kookan nikki*)" of their daily activities and those of their family and friends .

Sample Progress Indicators, Grade 12

- Students prepare stories and simple written reports about personal experiences, current events, or other course subjects to share with classmates and/or members of Japanese language communities (summer vacation, local news story, results of science experiment).

- Students prepare an oral or written summary of the plot and characters in selected pieces of original or adapted literature (short stories by Akutagawa Ryuunosuke or Hoshi Shin'ichi, Konjaku monogatari).

- Students create stories and poems, short plays, or skits based on personal experiences and exposure to themes, ideas, and perspectives from Japanese language communities (*konjoo, hon'ne to tatemae, amae, on*).

- Students recite poems or perform scenes adapted from plays or short stories commonly read by people in Japanese language communities. (*Ame nimo makezu*, "*Tomodachi*" by Abe Kooboo, *Akoorooshi*).

- Students summarize the content of products of popular culture (*manga*, TV dramas, animated movies) to present to others who speak Japanese.

- Students write letters or an article on topics of personal interest for a student publication.

- Students present the results of a survey conducted on topics of personal interest or pertaining to Japanese language communities (*kikoku shijo, ken'enken, shoonen hanzai*).

Sample Progress Indicators, Grade 16

- Students perform scenes from plays and/or recite poems or excerpts from short stories connected to a topic from other disciplines such as world history, geography, the arts, or mathematics.

- Students perform scenes from plays and/or recite poems or excerpts from short stories commonly read by speakers in Japanese language communities ("*Rokumeikan*" by Mishima Yukio, short stories by Murakami Haruki, *kabuki, kyoogen, waka*).

- Students select and analyze expressive products of Japanese culture, from literary genres, fine arts (*ukiyoe, toogei, shodoo*), or popular culture (*anime*, pop music, movies).

- Students summarize the content of an article or documentary intended for native speakers in order to discuss the topics via e-mail with others in Japanese language communities.

- Students prepare a research-based analysis of a current event from the perspective of both the U.S. and Japanese language communities (Iraq War, actions of religious cults, *chikyuu no ondanka, Kitachoosen mondai*)

Cultures — *Goal Two*
Gain Knowledge and Understanding of Japanese Culture

There are many unique and interesting aspects of Japanese culture. Learners of Japanese language need to learn about both traditional and contemporary culture.

Standards view culture through the lenses of the practices, products, and perspectives of a people. Take the giving of end-of-the-year gifts, *oseibo*, which often consist of items of practical use such as *nori*, salad oil, and soap. The practice of giving *oseibo* (the product) to clients, *jooshi*, professors, doctors, relatives, *nakoodo*, etc., reflects a typically Japanese perspective: that one should repay favors and kindnesses done for you prior to year's end in order to maintain a continuing good relationship with these people.

STANDARD 2.1 Students demonstrate an understanding of the relationship between the practices and perspectives of Japanese culture.

Sample Progress Indicators, Grade 4

- Students observe, identify, and/or discuss simple patterns of behavior or interaction in various settings such as school, family, and the community (*kyuushoku*, students cleaning the school, extended families, neighborhood *kodomokai*). (English may be necessary.)

- Students use appropriate gestures and oral expressions for greetings, leave taking, and common classroom interactions (asking permission to get a drink or go to the bathroom, gestures for waving goodbye and *oide*, bowing).

- Students participate in age-appropriate cultural activities such as games (*jan-ken-pon*), *undookai*, songs, holiday celebrations (*Kodomo no hi*, *Tanabata*), storytelling (*kamishibai* --listening in Japanese or performing in English) and plays.

- Students demonstrate an emerging awareness of age-appropriate formality levels and usages of the Japanese language (*ohayoo* vs. *ohayoo gozaimasu*).

- Students observe typical daily routines of their Japanese peer group through media, pictures, and accounts in translation.

Sample Progress Indicators, Grade 8

- Students observe and discuss patterns of behavior typical of their Japanese peer group (fashion consciousness, hand-holding). (English may be necessary.)

- Students observe and practice using appropriate verbal and nonverbal behavior for daily activities among friends, classmates, family members, teachers, and other adults (using appropriate levels of formality and variations of gestures and bows).

- Students learn about, observe when possible, and participate in age-appropriate cultural practices in games, sports (*undookai*), after-school activities (clubs, *juku*) entertainment (computer games), and study (classroom behaviors, home study habits).

Sample Progress Indicators, Grade 12

- Students observe and practice appropriate verbal and nonverbal behavior used by their peer group or by adults in a variety of cultural contexts (within peer group, within family, with different age groups, and with superiors).

- Students deepen knowledge of and, when possible, participate in age-appropriate cultural practices in games, sports, after-school activities (hanging out at *Makudo*), clubs, entertainment (movies, pop music, *karaoke bokkusu*), study, etc.

- Students identify, analyze, and discuss various patterns of behavior or interaction that commonly occur in Japanese culture (exchanging *meishi*, giving gifts, dating practices, bathing, travel).

- Students identify, examine, and discuss connections between cultural perspectives and socially approved behavioral patterns within Japanese cultural contexts (tendency to ask personal questions, attitudes about personal space, and matter-of-factness about body and bodily functions).

Sample Progress Indicators, Grade 16

- Students use appropriate verbal and nonverbal behavior (appropriate use of body language, verbal distinction between in-group and out-group members) in a variety of social and cultural contexts.

- Students analyze, discuss, and demonstrate an understanding of connections between cultural perspectives and socially approved behavioral patterns within Japanese cultural contexts (showing *enryo*, building consensus, giving gifts).

- Students analyze and evaluate the relationship between Japanese perspectives and cultural practices in games, sports, clubs, entertainment, study, etc. (*arubaito*, *senpai-koohai* relations in clubs, mahjong, *kissaten*).

STANDARD 2.2 Students demonstrate an understanding of the relationship between the products and perspectives of Japanese culture.

Sample Progress Indicators, Grade 4

- Students observe and identify tangible products of Japanese culture such as toys, clothing, housing, and foods (kites, Transformers, school uniforms, *yukata, tatami, tamagoyaki*).

- Students experience, identify, or read (in English) about expressive products of the Japanese culture such as selections from children's literature, dances (*bon odori*), and types of artwork (*shuuji*) enjoyed or produced by their peer group in Japanese language communities.

- Students identify, discuss, and produce artwork, crafts, or graphic representations enjoyed or made by their peer group in Japanese language communities (origami, *teruteruboozu*, Mother's Day picture). (English may be necessary).

- Students observe or experience making and using products used in daily life, seasonal activities, and celebrations (using chopsticks, making *mochi*, making *koinobori*).

Sample Progress Indicators, Grade 8

- Students read, listen to, observe, and perform expressive products of Japanese culture (crafts [*puramoderu, shishuu*]; literary, visual, and performing arts [writing *haiku, shuuji, Nihon buyoo*], both traditional and contemporary).

- Students search for, identify, and investigate the function of utilitarian products (sports equipment, household items, tools, foods, and clothing) of Japanese culture as found in their own homes, communities, and in the media.

- Students identify and discuss themes, ideas, and perspectives related to the products being studied (*toshikoshi soba, koinobori*).

Sample Progress Indicators, Grade 12

- Students discuss, and analyze expressive products of Japanese culture, including crafts, selections (in Japanese or English translation) from various literary genres, and the visual and performing arts (*katana, shuuji, sumie, kabuki, noo*).

- Students identify and engage in a simple analysis of themes, ideas, and perspectives related to the products being studied (origin and significance of origami, popularity of *manga/anime*, themes of popular songs).

- Students demonstrate an emerging understanding of the relationships among the products, practices, and perspectives of Japanese culture (*omiyage, meishi* exchange, Christmas cake, *kadomatsu*).

Sample Progress Indicators, Grade 16

- Students identify, discuss, and analyze such intangible products of Japanese culture as social, religious, economic, and political institutions (*doosoo kai; choonai kai*; temples, shrines, and new religions; Tokyo stock exchange; political parties and the

Diet; department stores), and explore relationships among these institutions and the perspectives of Japanese culture.

- Students experience, discuss, and analyze expressive products of Japanese culture, including selections from various arts (architecture, garden design, fashion design, fabric design, paper making) and literary genres (*utamonogatari, zuihitsu, shishoosetsu, hon'yaku shoosetsu*).

- Students identify and analyze themes, ideas, and perspectives (the role of religion in everyday life, links between traditional arts and popular culture, the role of kimono on formal occasions) related to the increasingly complex products being studied.

- Students explore the relationships among the products, practices, and perspectives of Japanese culture (*shimenawa, ema, uranai, sake, keitai denwa, girichoko*)

Connections   *Goal Three*
Connect with Other Disciplines and Acquire Information

New perspectives and approaches make it possible to incorporate other subject matters into Japanese. There are many benefits in connecting Japanese language instruction with other disciplines. In light of age-appropriateness and linguistic levels, teachers may need to use some English materials as information sources and/or carefully coordinate lessons with teachers in other subject areas.

STANDARD 3.1 Students reinforce and further their knowledge of other disciplines through the Japanese language.

Sample Progress Indicator, Grade 4

- Students demonstrate an understanding of vocabulary and some basic concepts learned in other subject areas, such as math facts, measurement (metric system), weather, plants, or geographical features.

Sample Progress Indicators, Grade 8

- Students talk about topics from school subjects in Japanese including geographic features, historical facts, mathematical problems, or scientific information.

- Students comprehend short video materials in Japanese on topics being studied in other classes (health, environment, war and peace).

- Students present oral or simple written reports in Japanese on topics being studied in other classes (nutrition, communities, transportation).

Sample Progress Indicators, Grade 12

- Students carry out simple discussions in Japanese on topics from other school subjects, including political and historical events and facts, worldwide health issues, or environmental concerns.

- Students acquire information from selected sources written in Japanese about a topic being studied in other school subjects (climate change, government structure, public health).

- Students combine information from other school subjects with information available in Japanese in order to complete activities in the Japanese language classroom (designing an ideal community, developing advice for healthy living).

- Students exchange information, orally and/or in writing, regarding topics that are being studied in other school subjects (world history, biology, music appreciation, art history).

Sample Progress Indicators, Grade 16

- Students discuss topics in Japanese from other courses, including concepts and issues in the humanities, sciences, or technology (impact of technological advances, environmental issues, comparative literature).

- Students acquire information from a variety of sources written in Japanese about a topic (treatment of the elderly, varieties of theatrical performance, political philosophy) being studied in other disciplines.

- Students exchange, support, and discuss their opinions and individual perspectives in a formal setting on a variety of topics (how society should treat the disabled or mentally ill, equal rights for women, child rearing, aesthetic evaluation) that are being studied in other courses.

STANDARD 3.2 Students acquire information and recognize the distinctive viewpoints that are only available through Japanese language and culture.

Sample Progress Indicator, Grade 4

- Students read, watch, listen to, and ask or answer questions about age- and developmentally-appropriate short stories, poems, songs, and/or content-related materials (community maps, words to songs written in *kana*, cartoons).

Sample Progress Indicator, Grade 8

- Students read, listen to, watch, and talk about age-appropriate materials intended for native speakers of Japanese, and recognize distinctive viewpoints and practices (Japanese sense of seasons, way of counting change, *aizuchi*).

Sample Progress Indicator, Grade 12

- Students use selected sources, both teacher-adapted and those intended for same-age speakers of Japanese, to prepare reports on topics of personal interest, or those with which they have limited previous experience.

Sample Progress Indicator, Grade 16

- Students use a variety of authentic sources to prepare reports on topics of personal interest, or those with which they have limited previous experience, and compare these to information obtained on the same topics written in English.

Comparisons *Goal Four*
Develop Insight into the Nature of Language and Culture

All cultures have unique features. Likewise, the languages that grow out of those cultures have distinctive characteristics. Comparison of different cultures and languages raises students' linguistic awareness and cultural understanding.

In Japan, the use of loan words, the popularity of certain American practices and products, and the perseverance of certain very traditional language and customs offer a unique and intriguing venue for comparisons and discussions. Students are able to view the great similarities between Japan and other countries while identifying the intriguing differences which make Japanese study exciting.

STANDARD 4.1 Students demonstrate understanding of the nature of language through comparison of the Japanese language and their own.

Sample Progress Indicators, Grade 4

- Students realize that there are loan words in most languages and identify examples of words used in Japanese borrowed from English (*aisukuriimu, hanbaagaa, basu, jiinzu*) and other languages (*pan, zubon, kasutera, kurowassan, karuta*). (Some English discussion may be necessary).

- Students demonstrate an emerging awareness that word order in Japanese and English are often different (*aisukuriimu o taberu* vs. I will eat ice cream).

- Students demonstrate awareness of formal and informal forms of language in greetings and leave taking and try out expressions of politeness in Japanese and in their own language (*arigatoo* vs. *arigatoo gozaimasu* and thanks vs. thank you).

- Student recognize the existence and the various usages of the three Japanese orthographies and of romanization.

Sample Progress Indicators, Grade 8

- Students are aware of the existence of idiomatic expressions in both their own (raining cats and dogs) and the Japanese language (*kao ga hiroi*).

- Students demonstrate awareness about the historical and present-day interaction between Japanese and other languages in loanwords such as *pan, karaoke,* tsunami and the Japanese use of *kanji* borrowed from Chinese.

- Students demonstrate awareness of ways of expressing respect and communicating status differences in their own language and in Japanese (*keigo*, choice of vocabulary).

- Students demonstrate awareness that languages have critical sound distinctions that must be mastered in order to communicate meaning (*byooin* vs. *biyooin*, *obaasan* vs. *obasan*).

- Students demonstrate awareness of the role of dialect, slang, and age-, status-, and gender-differentiated speech, and explore the cultural significance attributed to their use (verbs of giving and receiving, sentence-ending particles, contraction, *boku* vs. *watashi*).

Sample Progress Indicators, Grade 12

- Students recognize that loan words undergo changes in meaning and form in Japanese and other languages (*konsento, toreenaa, rimokon, pasokon,* typhoon, hibachi).

- Students demonstrate awareness that there are words, phrases, and idioms that do not translate directly from one language to another (*shakai-jin, natsukashii, hara ga tatsu, otsukaresama*).

- Students analyze elements of the Japanese language, such as time, tense, and aspect, and comparable linguistic elements in English, and conjecture about how languages use various forms to express particular meanings.

- Students report on the relationship between word order and meaning in Japanese and other languages (*daigaku no doko* vs. *doko no daigaku*).

- Students compare and contrast the writing system of the Japanese language and their own. They also examine other writing systems and report about the nature of those writing systems (logographic, syllabic, alphabetic).

Sample Progress Indicators, Grade 16

- Students gain skill in analyzing the linguistic features of Japanese and other languages.

- Students demonstrate awareness of language change and the historical development of Japanese and other languages.

- Students demonstrate their understanding/awareness of different communication styles based on variations such as regional, socioeconomic, gender, and age differences to communicate messages in Japanese and other languages.

- Students analyze the differences between spoken and written language in Japanese and other languages (selection of vocabulary, contraction, length of sentences).

- Students analyze the various styles such as private vs. public, formal vs. informal, narrative vs. expository in Japanese and other languages.

STANDARD 4.2 Students demonstrate understanding of the concept of culture through comparisons of Japanese culture and their own.

Sample Progress Indicators, Grade 4

- Students recognize the interests and practices that they have in common with their Japanese peers (video games, fast foods, clothing).

- Students point out similarities and differences between the American and Japanese cultures in simple patterns of behavior or interaction in various settings--social (school, family, community) and cultural (dining, bathing, toilet etiquette). (English may be necessary.)

- Students demonstrate awareness that gestures are important methods of communication and that gestures used in Japanese language communities and America are often different (waving goodbye, indicating oneself, handshaking vs. bowing).

- Students compare and contrast tangible products (toys, clothes, housing, food) of the Japanese culture and their own.

- Students compare intangible products (children's songs, selections from children's literature, games, and holiday celebrations) of the Japanese culture and those of their own.

Sample Progress Indicators, Grade 8

- Students contrast verbal and nonverbal behavior in activities among friends, classmates, family members, and teachers, in the Japanese culture and their own (hugging, kissing, holding hands, bowing, endearments, levels of formality, *aizuchi*).

- Students demonstrate awareness that they, too, have a culture, based on comparison of sample daily activities (study time, amusements, personal hygiene routines) in Japanese culture and their own.

- Students speculate on why certain products (sports equipment, household items, tools, foods, and clothing) originate in and/or are important to particular cultures by analyzing selected products (carpenter's tools, cooking utensils, umbrellas, snack items) from the Japanese culture and their own.

Sample Progress Indicators, Grade 12

- Students explore the relationships of practices and perspectives in Japanese culture and compare and contrast these with their own (school rules, entrance examinations, role of *juku, miyamairi, hakamairi*).

- Students explore the relationships of products and perspectives in Japanese and compare and contrast these with their own (*pokeberu, purikura*).

- Students reflect on how they feel using or thinking in Japanese compared to their first language and articulate cultural differences they perceive (awareness of status, consciousness of in-group and out-group communication).

- Students hypothesize about the relationship between cultural perspectives and practices (games, sports, entertainment, holiday celebrations, and study habits) by analyzing selected practices from the Japanese culture and their own (*ooendan* vs. cheerleaders, New Year's Day, tutoring).

- Students hypothesize about the relationship between cultural perspectives and expressive products (visual and performing arts, both traditional and contemporary; appropriate forms of literature; architecture) by analyzing selected products (*bunraku, renga, junia shoosetsu, rogu hausu*) from the Japanese culture and their own. (English may be necessary).

Sample Progress Indicators, Grade 16

- Students explore how sayings and idiomatic expressions reflect culture, citing examples from the Japanese language and culture and their own (*ishi no ue nimo sannen, deru kugi wa utareru*).

- Students compare nuances of meanings of words and expressions (*buta no yoo ni taberu* vs. eat like a horse) and vocal inflections (*soo desu ka! soo desu ka?*) in Japanese and in their own language.

- Students analyze the relationship of practices and perspectives in Japanese culture and compare and contrast these with their own (*omiai, shin'nyuu shain kyooiku*, student life style, political campaigning).

- Students analyze and discuss the relationships between products (education systems, religious institutions, department stores, types of housing) and perspectives in Japanese culture and contrast these with their own.

Communities *Goal Five*
Participate in Multilingual Communities at Home and Around the World

Japanese is no longer a language spoken only by native speakers of Japanese. The number of people outside of Japan who speak Japanese increases every year, and a large number of Japanese visit abroad. Thus, one does not have to go to Japan to communicate with others in Japanese. Japanese learners should take advantage of this trend during the course of their language studies. They also should recognize that a major goal of Japanese language learning is to contribute to community-building by making use of their language abilities. Students can reach out to parents, day care centers, senior citizen homes, etc., and share their excitement about learning Japanese through performances and presentations.

STANDARD 5.1 Students use Japanese both within and beyond the school setting.

Sample Progress Indicators, Grade 4

- Students communicate with speakers of Japanese in person or via letters, e-mail, or exchanges of audio and videotapes.

- Students identify professions that require proficiency in Japanese (travel guide, translator, Japanese teacher).

- Students participate in imaginary play (*omiseyasan gokko*, *mamagoto*).

- Students present information about the Japanese language and culture to their peers, parents, or community groups in English or Japanese.

- Students prepare illustrations or posters to present to their peers, parents, or community groups.

- Students perform for a school or community celebration (sing songs, perform a skit, dance).

- Students use Japanese outside the classroom to complete assigned tasks and to interact with peers.

Sample Progress Indicators, Grade 8

- Students use Japanese to talk or write to peers about various activities and events (family vacation, school holidays, daily activities).

- Students interact with members of the local community to learn how they use Japanese in their professional and personal lives.

- Students present information about Japanese language and culture to others (through school assemblies, exhibits at a local library or shopping mall, visit to a nursing home).

- Students participate in activities that benefit the school or community (receiving Japanese visitors, preparing bulletin boards).

- Students write and illustrate stories and reports to present to others.

- Students perform for a school and community celebration (skits, songs, dances, martial arts).

Sample Progress Indicators, Grade 12

- Students communicate orally or in writing with members of Japanese language community regarding personal interests and community or world concerns (*haikibutsu*, transportation, global warming, population increase).

- Students participate in a school-to-work project or an exploration of a career in which they might use proficiency in Japanese language and culture (travel agent, translator, business consultant, lawyer, flight attendant).

- Students use community resources (libraries, web pages, interviews) to research a topic related to Japanese culture and/or language study.

- Students present information about Japanese language and culture to others.

- Students participate in activities that benefit the school or community (gathering information about how Japanese communities deal with social problems, receiving Japanese visitors to the community, helping prepare tourist information in Japanese).

- Students write and illustrate stories and reports to present to others.

- Students perform for a school or community celebration or event (skits, songs, dances, plays, martial arts).

- Students participate in study abroad programs and share their experiences with others.

Sample Progress Indicators, Grade 16

- Students communicate orally or in writing with members of Japanese language communities regarding personal and professional interests and community or world concerns (chemical weapons, environmental issues, international trade).

- Students explore careers (e.g., through internships) that require proficiency in Japanese language and culture.

- Students present information to others in writing as well as orally.

- Students do research using Japanese language resources (books, World Wide Web, journals, native speakers, documentaries, newspapers).

- Students participate in an outreach program that helps others studying Japanese language and culture (tutoring Japanese at a local elementary school, giving presentations on Japanese culture at local service organizations and businesses).

- Students participate in study abroad programs in Japan and/or help international students from Japan at their institution.

STANDARD 5.2 Students show evidence of becoming life-long learners by using Japanese for personal enjoyment and enrichment.

Sample Progress Indicators, Grade 4

- Students use Japanese audio and visual materials for enjoyment (TV programs, children's videos, picture books).

- Students play sports (martial arts) or games (*karuta*, *sugoroku*) from Japanese culture.

- Students plan real or imaginary travel to Japan (locations to visit, mode of transportation, sights to see).

- Students attend or view via media Japanese cultural events and social activities (*bon odori*, *tanabata*, *shichi-go-san*).

- Students listen to music, sing songs, play musical instruments, or learn dances from Japan.

- Students pursue activities learned about in Japanese class on their own time (*origami*, eating Japanese foods, playing games, playing house).

- Students make friends with speakers of Japanese.

Sample Progress Indicators, Grade 8

- Students read materials (children's books, illustrated books) and/or use media (videos, computer programs) in Japanese for enjoyment or personal growth.

- Students consult various sources (children's books, illustrated articles, videos, acquaintances) in Japanese to obtain information on topics of personal interest.

- Students play sports (martial arts) or games (computer games) from Japanese culture.

- Students exchange information about topics of personal interest.

- Students attend or view via media Japanese cultural events and social activities (*mochitsuki, hanami, yukimatsuri*).

- Students listen to music, sing songs, play musical instruments or learn dances from Japan.

- Students engage in activities related to their personal interests (cooking and/or eating Japanese food, building models, calligraphy, origami).

- Students plan real or imaginary travel (locations, lodging, schedule, interactions with homestay families).

- Students establish and/or maintain interpersonal relations with speakers of Japanese.

Sample Progress Indicators, Grade 12

- Students consult various sources (books, magazines, World Wide Web, films, experts) in Japanese to obtain information on topics of personal interest.

- Students play sports (martial arts) or games (*shoogi, go*) from Japanese culture.

- Students read materials (books, magazines, *manga*) and/or use media (videos, CDs, World Wide Web) in Japanese for enjoyment or personal growth.

- Students establish and/or maintain interpersonal relations with speakers of Japanese.

- Students attend or view via media Japanese cultural events and social activities (*kabuki, matsuri,* school functions).

- Students listen to music, sing songs, play musical instruments or learn dances from Japan.

- Students plan real or imaginary travel (locations, budgets, itinerary, interactions with travel agents).

- Students engage in activities related to their personal interests (cooking and/or eating Japanese food, crafts, *sumie*, calligraphy, martial arts).

Sample Progress Indicators, Grade 16

- Students consult various sources (books, magazines, newspapers, encyclopedias and other reference works, documentaries, films, Internet, experts) in Japanese to obtain information on topics of personal interest.

- Students read and/or use various media in Japanese for entertainment or personal growth.

- Students establish and/or maintain interpersonal relations using both written and spoken Japanese.
- Students attend or view via media Japanese cultural events and social activities (*noo*, *rakugo*, concerts, plays, receptions, *konpa*, *gookon*).

Learning Scenarios

TARGETED STANDARD
1.1 Interpersonal Communication
1.2 Interpretive Communication
1.3 Presentational Communication
2.2 Products of Culture
3.1 Making Connections
3.2 Acquiring Information
5.1 School and Community
5.2 Lifelong Learning

AKAI TORI KOTORI

Kindergarten students at Waterbury Elementary School are celebrating springtime in their regular classes. As a related topic, they begin a unit on birds in their Japanese FLES classes. Students create and identify different colored birds and learn the names in Japanese of a few very common birds found in their area. Students practice the songs, "*Akai Tori Kotori*" and "*Hato Poppo*," creating pictures to go with each. As a culminating activity, students perform the songs and display their art work at a school assembly.

Reflections

1.1 Students follow instructions while coloring birds and making origami birds.
1.2 Students identify various birds native to Japan or America based on the teacher's oral description of the color markings on the birds.
1.3 Students prepare and display posters and perform songs related to birds for the school.
2.2 Students produce origami birds.
3.1 Students reinforce and expand their knowledge of the concept of springtime and the variety of bird life introduced in their regular classes.
3.2 Students read some of the words to the *"Akai Tori Kotori"* song by completing a matching/coloring activity in which they color certain words on a song sheet. Students ask and answer questions in English about the meaning of the Japanese songs learned, after learning them through gestures and pictures.
5.1 Students prepare illustrations of the Japanese songs and perform them at a school assembly.
5.2 Students are given extra origami paper and directions to reproduce the bird origami at home and to teach their families.

TARGETED STANDARD
1.1 Interpersonal Communication
1.2 Interpretive Communication
1.3 Presentational Communication
2.2 Products of Culture
3.1 Making Connections
4.2 Cultural Comparisons

THE FOOD PYRAMID

Part of the school curriculum for third grades at Mt. Washington Magnet School includes a study of nutrition. As a related unit in the FLES Japanese class, students study the American Food Pyramid. They have previously learned Japanese words for the fruits and vegetables and how to express their likes and dislikes. To introduce the unit, the teacher goes "shopping" to different food groups arranged around the room (plastic food and empty containers), telling the students which item he/she likes from each group. Students become familiar with the food group names and items in each though various games, pair interviews, and activities. Students then focus on the food pyramid itself, learning the recommended servings and assessing their personal eating habits. They examine a variety of Japanese foods such as tofu and *kon'nyaku*, and determine in which food group they belong. Students also compare the Japanese diet to the American Food Pyramid and discuss the similarities and differences in English. As a final activity, students interview a family member and present that person's one day menu to the class, assessing its "healthfulness."

Reflections

1.1 Students provide and obtain information about food in the American Food Pyramid. Also they express likes and dislikes and exchange their opinions about the "healthfulness" of their eating habits.

1.2 Students understand and interpret written words for food groups in the pyramid and food items.

1.3 Students report on their interview about one person's eating habits.

2.2 Students observe and identify Japanese foods and discuss how they fit into the food pyramid.

3.1 Students reinforce and further their knowledge of food, nutrition, and the food pyramid.

4.2 Students compare and contrast similarities and differences between American and Japanese food pyramids.

JAPANESE HOME

Fourth-grade students at Santa Teresa Elementary School learn about some typical features of Japanese homes and proper manners when visiting a Japanese home. Photo panels are used to introduce basic vocabulary such as *genkan*, *kodomobeya*, *daidokoro/kitchin*, *toire*, *tatami*, *futon*, and *beddo*. Students discuss in English about similarities and differences between American and Japanese homes and the existence of Western and Japanese styles in the same home in Japan. Students then review set phrases for greetings, leave taking, before/after eating, and thanking. After viewing some video clips depicting children visiting friends at their home, the teacher arranges for a Japanese guest to come to class and act as the Japanese host/hostess for a make-believe visit.

TARGETED STANDARD
1.1 Interpersonal Communication
2.1 Practices of Culture
2.2 Products of Culture
4.1 Language Comparisons
4.2 Cultural Comparisons
5.1 School and Community

Reflections

1.1 Students use phrases for greetings, leave taking, before/after eating, and thanking.

2.1 Students use proper gestures and oral expressions for greetings, leave taking, before/after eating, and thanking.

2.2 Students look at photo panels and video clips to observe and identify authentic rooms and objects in a Japanese home. Students experience taking off shoes and wearing slippers appropriately during the make-believe visit.

4.1 Students realize that commonly used Japanese words (such as *beddo* and *toire*) are loanwords from English, and learn that English has borrowed some words from Japanese as well (such as futon).

4.2 By looking at objects in the Japanese home that are commonly found in American homes, students recognize that there are commonalities in Japanese and American lifestyles.

5.1 Students interact with a Japanese guest.

HANAMI (FLOWER VIEWING)

TARGETED STANDARD

1.1 Interpersonal Communication
1.2 Interpretive Communication
1.3 Presentational Communication
2.1 Practices of Culture
2.2 Products of Culture
5.1 School and Community
5.2 Lifelong Learning

Students in an Indiana middle school Japanese class read a short article on *hanami* written by the teacher. Students then decide to have a *hanami* party. They divide into small groups to form committees, such as the scout committee, *karaoke* committee, games committee, invitation committee, record committee, and food committee, and discuss the various details of the party. Before the *hanami* party, the scout committee finds the best spot for flower viewing and writes an announcement of the location. The invitation committee writes an invitation letter to Japanese people in the local community. The scout committee goes to the location prior to the party and spreads a large blanket (preferably red) to secure the site. At the *hanami* party, the invitation committee greets the Japanese guests; the food committee serves food; the games committee leads the class in games; the record-keeping committee takes pictures; and the *karaoke* committee leads the group in singing Japanese songs. After the *hanami* party, representatives from each committee get together and make a poster (including photos) about the party.

Reflections

1.1 Students discuss their plans for the party; students plan in groups the details of the party; students write an invitation letter; and students talk with Japanese guests.

1.2 Students read about *hanami*.

1.3 Students write an announcement and make a poster about the *hanami* party.

2.1 Students participate in Japanese games and songs.

2.2 Students eat Japanese food.

5.1 Students invite Japanese people in their community to the party.

5.2 Students sing *karaoke*.

Students may read English articles on *hanami* if their reading proficiency in Japanese is limited. If there are no cherry blossoms in the vicinity of the campus, you can view other blossoms such as dogwood, peach, apple, magnolia, etc. If a karaoke machine is not available, you can use a tape recorder.

TAIFUU (TYPHOON)

Students at Edison Middle School learned about world meteorological phenomena in their geography class, including tornadoes, blizzards, auroras, squalls and so forth. Students decide to learn about natural disasters and phenomena in Japan such as typhoons, tsunami, earthquakes, and volcanic eruptions. In this specific unit, students investigate typhoons. They divide into groups, and use a variety of resources (web pages, books and maps, interviews with Japanese people) to do research on when typhoons come to Japan; what path they take; what Japanese people do in preparation for them; and what damage they cause. Also, students compare typhoons with natural disasters that take place in the United States. Each group presents their research results to the class orally and using visuals.

TARGETED STANDARD	
1.1	Interpersonal Communication
1.2	Interpretive Communication
1.3	Presentational Communication
2.1	Practices of Culture
3.1	Making Connections
3.2	Acquiring Information
4.2	Cultural Comparisons
5.1	School and Community

Reflections

1.1 Students discuss typhoons and other natural disasters, and students may interview Japanese people on their experience of typhoons.

1.2 Students read web pages, weather forecasts in newspapers, Japanese atlases, and so forth; students view or listen to TV/radio weather forecasts.

1.3 Students present their research results.

2.1 Students learn how Japanese people cope with typhoons.

3.1 Students further their knowledge acquired in their geography class through the Japanese class.

3.2 Students acquire information through web pages, newspapers, and other sources.

4.2 Students compare people's reactions to natural disasters.

5.1 Students interview Japanese people in the local community or use e-mail.

This could be part of a larger unit that includes earthquakes, tsunami, and volcanic eruptions, or each of the small groups could pick a different type of natural disaster to research and present to the class.

CHILDREN'S BOOK PROJECT

Students at West High School work in groups to author children's books in Japanese. Students begin the project by examining Japanese children's books, viewing several model books from past years' classes, and discussing how their work will be assessed. Students plan their stories together, integrating themes studied during the quarter (professions, community, homes, family, etc.). Students co-author the text of their books. Students engage in peer editing prior to submitting their drafts for teacher feedback. Students complete their illustrated books and read them aloud to the class. Following the reading, listeners answer comprehension questions designed by each book group. Then students visit

TARGETED STANDARD	
1.1	Interpersonal Communication
1.2	Interpretive Communication
1.3	Presentational Communication
2.1	Practices of Culture
2.2	Products of Culture
3.2	Acquiring Information
4.1	Language Comparisons
4.2	Cultural Comparisons
5.1	School and Communities

local elementary school Japanese programs to read their stories to students there. Photocopied books are made for each student to keep. Students complete a project evaluation form, contributing insights into what they learned and what they wish they had known to better complete the project.

Reflections

1.1 Students exchange opinions about Japanese children's books and previous years' books. Later they ask and answer questions about the contents of the books they wrote and presented to each other.

1.2 Students read Japanese children's books and books from previous years and listen to their classmates' presentations.

1.3 Students present their work to each other and to elementary school students.

2.1 & 2.2 Students may choose to write about Japanese topics or about a non-Japanese character negotiating life in Japan. Cultural insights are demonstrated in the books' layouts, character behavior, settings, and language choice.

3.2 Students learn about Japanese children's books, including their layouts, what type of language is used in them, and what characters and themes are common.

4.1 Students learn about how books written for children differ from standard Japanese writing and about how Japanese and American children's books are both different from and similar to each other.

4.2 Depending on the topic they choose for their stories, students may explore the concept of culture by comparing Japanese culture and their own.

5.1 Students visit local elementary school Japanese programs to present their stories.

Standard 3.1 may also be addressed if students write about topics connected to other subject areas. This activity, used toward the end of a grading period, serves as an opportunity for students to review concepts learned throughout the term. The students enjoy the opportunity to personalize their language learning by focusing on topics of interest to them. Sharing their books with elementary school students gives the class a sense of tangible success and helps to publicize the Japanese program. Even if the elementary school students have not studied any Japanese, students can help them enjoy the readings and understand the stories by acting out and showing the pictures.

MANZANAR

TARGETED STANDARD
1.1 Interpersonal Communication
1.3 Presentational Communication
2.1 Practices of Culture
2.2 Products of Culture
5.1 School and Community
5.2 Lifelong Learning

Students at Washington High School have a discussion about what they know about Japanese Americans and the WWII relocation camps. After this they read the book *Farewell to Manzanar* about the Manzanar relocation camp in California. They divide into small groups to discuss in Japanese what they found most interesting about the book. Each group picks a topic that relates to the book, to their own interests, and to one of their other subjects (U.S. history, government, world history, etc.). They then research this topic using the Internet, books, and other resources. If there are Japanese Americans or other people who are knowledgeable about their topic living in the community, students can invite them to come talk with the class or go to interview them. After their research, the groups prepare presentations about what they have learned for the rest of the class and submit a written compilation of their research to a local or regional organization (Japan-America society, Japanese teachers' association, teachers' resource centers, etc.) for dissemination.

Reflections

1.1 Students use Japanese in small group discussions.

1.3 Students use spoken and written Japanese to present information to each other and to others in the community.

3.1 Students research a topic that relates both to Japanese Americans and to one of their other school subjects.

4.2 Students compare the Japanese and American cultures and consider how they are intertwined in Japanese American culture during WWII.

5.1 Students communicate with individuals in the community present their research findings in writing to a community group.

HOSTING JAPANESE GUESTS

Students at South High School make a plan for some Japanese guests who will be visiting their school. Students read a fax message containing introductory information about the guests and questions related to their visit. The students discuss the questions and write appropriate responses. In their responses, they welcome the guests, answer their questions, and inquire about their interests and food preferences so they can

TARGETED STANDARD	
1.1	Interpersonal Communication
1.2	Interpretive Communication
1.3	Presentational Communication
2.1	Practices of Culture
2.2	Products of Culture
5.1	School and Community
5.2	Lifelong Learning

plan activities for the visit. After the guests' responses are received, the students create a plan for the visit using their knowledge about Japanese customs and cultures to make the guests feel welcome. For example, the students may plan to give the guests a *yosegaki* or a special memento of their school. The students consider what type of food they should provide for the guests. Some students may try to cook Japanese dishes they have learned about in class or find American dishes they think Japanese may like for a picnic, barbecue, or dinner party. When the guests come, students give them an initial briefing in Japanese. Their briefing uses some visual aids and includes general information about the school as well as specific details about the schedule planned for the guests. After the briefing, the students host the guests in the planned activities.

Reflections

1.1 Small groups of students discuss their plans and how to respond to the initial fax. Students interact in Japanese with the guests.

1.2 Students interpret faxes in Japanese.

1.3 Students give briefings in Japanese.

2.1 Students consider Japanese cultural practices, such as writing a *yosegaki*, in planning for their guests.

2.2 Students may learn about certain Japanese cultural products, such as specific foods or *shikishi*.

5.1 Students interact with Japanese from outside of their school.

5.2 Students may cook Japanese food for the guests.

Standard 4.1 could also be addressed by including study of Japanese conventions for writing letters and faxes. If there is no way to arrange for actual guests to visit the school, this activity can be adapted by having the teacher write the fax for imaginary guests and role-play a guest visiting the school. If only a single guest can come, the small groups could each answer one of the guest's questions and each group could propose a visit plan to be voted on by the class.

"STREET CORNER" INTERVIEW

TARGETED STANDARD
- 1.1 Interpersonal Communication
- 1.2 Interpretive Communication
- 1.3 Presentational Communication
- 2.1 Practices of Culture
- 3.2 Acquiring Information
- 4.1 Language Comparisons
- 4.2 Cultural Comparisons
- 5.1 School and Community

University students read a Japanese article on the Japanese education system and then have a discussion comparing the education systems in Japan and their home countries. Following the discussion, students form groups to identify an aspect of education in Japan in which they are interested and make a list of interview questions. The students learn appropriate ways, using *keigo*, to approach a previously unknown Japanese person, start a conversation, and then ask him or her to participate in an interview project. After practicing the interview procedure, students approach Japanese people on campus and in the community and conduct interviews with those who agree to participate. Following the interviews, students learn how to summarize the interview results. They then present the results to an audience of classmates, interviewees and/or other invited guests from the community, allowing time for questions and discussions after the presentations. Student groups are responsible for writing an article summarizing the results of their research and their reactions to the information learned. A newsletter or pamphlet is generated from these articles and distributed around campus to relevant locations (e.g., student union, study abroad office, and Asian student associations).

Reflections

1.1 Students discuss the Japanese and other education systems and interview Japanese on Japanese education.

1.2 Students read an article on the education system in Japan.

1.3 Students present their findings from interviews, write a summary article, and create a newsletter or a pamphlet.

2.1 Students learn about the educational system in Japan.

3.2 Students acquire information from Japanese people.

4.1 Students analyze the use of *keigo* when they address an unknown person.

4.2 Students compare the Japanese educational system with their own.

5.1 Students interview Japanese people and distribute their newsletter or pamphlet to the local community.

Similar activities can be implemented using topics other than education, such as environmental, social, and political issues. How the interviews are conducted (in person, by phone, via written correspondence including e-mail) is dependent upon the availability of native speakers in a given community.

TEA

Students in a Japanese class at Arizona College do a unit on tea. The students do group research projects to study topics such as how and when tea was introduced into Japan; the relationship *chanoyu* has had with Japanese art, architecture, philosophy, and religion; what roles tea played in the history of Japan; and what function tea drinking has in contemporary Japanese society. The students use a variety of resources to research their topics, including reading Japanese and English materials, viewing videos borrowed from the Japanese Consulate, searching for information on the Internet, interviewing local Japanese residents, and obtaining information from Japanese pen pals through letters or e-mail. They present their findings in Japanese, answer questions from classmates, and lead discussions related to what types of tea people in the world drink, what roles tea and other beverages have in countries other than Japan, and the health benefits of drinking tea. Students compile their written reports into a booklet about tea.

TARGETED STANDARD	
1.1	Interpersonal Communication
1.2	Interpretive Communication
1.3	Presentational Communication
2.1	Practices of Culture
2.2	Products of Culture
3.1	Making Connections
3.2	Acquiring Information
4.2	Cultural Comparisons
5.1	School and Community

Reflections

1.1 Students use Japanese to interview and write e-mail to Japanese people. They work in groups to prepare their presentation, and they discuss their findings.
1.2 Students read materials and watch videos related to tea.
1.3 Students present their findings orally and in writing.
2.1 Students learn about the custom of tea drinking in Japan.
2.2 Students learn about tea and its relationship to Japanese perspectives.
3.1 Students make connections to the disciplines of architecture, art, history, philosophy, and religion.
3.2 Students use various sources of information available in Japanese to prepare their presentations.
4.2 Students compare the custom of tea drinking in various regions of the world.
5.1 Students communicate orally and in writing with Japanese people outside school regarding tea.

This scenario can serve as a basis for content-related language learning. Research and discussion topics, ranging from traditional customs to contemporary society, are intellectually challenging to university students and stimulate their interest in learning about Japan. Similar scenarios could be designed around other products associated with Japanese culture, such as rice or paper.

GIFT-GIVING/TELEPHONE SHOPPING

Japanese language students at California State University read materials in Japanese and in English on gift-giving customs in Japan. They learn about several aspects of this tradition, including *ochuugen, oseibo,* wrapping, *noshigami,* and *okaeshi.* They examine several Japanese

TARGETED STANDARD	
1.1	Interpersonal Communication
1.2	Interpretive Communication
2.1	Practices of Culture
2.2	Products of Culture
4.2	Cultural Comparisons

department store catalogues that feature *ochuugen* and *oseibo* gift items. They discuss issues such as the functions of *ochuugen* and *oseibo* in Japanese society and what items Japanese people give as *ochuugen* and *oseibo* depending on the hierarchical relationship between giver and recipient. They also compare their own gift-giving customs with those of Japanese, including the price of gift items and occasions on which gift-giving occurs (weddings, *nyuugakushiki*, etc.). Then, students decide what items they would send to their friends, colleagues, superiors, and teachers based on their relationship to the recipients, the recipients' taste, and other factors. They fill out an order form for gifts and/or do a role-play in which they order the gifts by telephone. As a final activity, they practice writing thank-you notes for gifts.

Reflections

1.1 Students talk about Japanese and their own gift-giving customs, order gifts by phone, and write a thank-you note.
1.2 Students read about gift-giving practices in Japan and examine gift catalogues of Japanese department stores.
2.1 Students read and discuss gift-giving practices in Japan.
2.2 Students learn about common gift items used in Japan.
4.2 Students compare Japanese gift-giving customs and their own.

Using gift-giving customs in Japan as a central theme, students can learn about many different aspects of Japanese culture as well as practice a basic daily activity--shopping and ordering. Authentic materials serve as a springboard for discussions on Japanese customs, human relationships in Japan, and comparisons between Japanese culture and the students' own. Teachers can easily adapt this activity to students at the high school level by changing the content of discussions and the level of speaking, reading, and writing practices.

References

Houston, Jeanne Wakatsuki and James D. Houston. *Farewell to Manzanar*. New York: Bantam Books, 1973.

Jorden, Eleanor H. with Richard D. Lambert, 1991. *Japanese Language Instruction in the United States: Resources, Practice, and Investment Strategy*. National Foreign Language Center Monograph Series.

Kuroyanagi, Tetsuko. *Madogiwa no Totto-chan*. Tokyo: Kodansha International, 1982.

Natsume, Soseki. *Botchan*. Rutland, Vermont: Charles E. Tuttle Company, 1968.

Wardell, Steven. *Rising Sons and Daughters*. Cambridge, Massachusetts: Plympton Press International, 1995.

Standards for Learning Portuguese

*A project of the
American Association of Teachers
of Spanish and Portuguese*

K–16 TASK FORCE ON STANDARDS FOR LEARNING PORTUGUESE

Nancy Anderson, Princeton, NJ
Rosario Cantú, Health Careers High School, San Antonio, TX
José M. Díaz, Hunter College High School, New York, NY
Inés García, Texas Education Agency, Austin, TX
Gail Guntermann, Arizona State University, Tempe, AZ
Nancy Humbach, Miami University, Oxford, OH
Judith Liskin-Gasparro, University of Iowa, Iowa City, IA
Donna R. Long, The Ohio State University, Columbus, OH
Frank Medley, Jr. (Team Leader), West Virginia University, Morgantown, WV
Myriam Met, Montgomery County Public Schools, Rockville, MD
Marilyn Pavlik (ex-officio), Lyons Township Schools, LaGrange, IL
Alvaro Rodríguez, MB Lamar High School and University of St. Thomas, Houston, TX
Paul Sandrock, Wisconsin Department of Public Instruction, Madison, WI
Lynn A. Sandstedt, American Association of Teachers of Spanish and Portuguese, Greeley, CO
Martie Semmer, Summit School District RE-1, Frisco, CO
Carmen C. Tesser (Chair), University of Georgia, Athens, GA
Guadalupe Valdés, Stanford University, Stanford, CA

Standards for Learning Portuguese

REVIEWERS FOR STANDARDS FOR LEARNING PORTUGUESE

Maria Barbosa
University of Iowa
Iowa City, IA

Elizabeth Ginway
University of Florida
Gainesville, FL

Lyris Wiedemann
Stanford University
Palo Alto, CA

Ana Maria Carvalho
University of Arizona
Tucson, AZ

Margo Milleret
University of New Mexico
Albuquerque, NM

Table of Contents

STANDARDS FOR LEARNING PORTUGUESE		**408**
INTRODUCTION		**409**
PORTUGUESE IN THE WORLD		**410**
PORTUGUESE IN THE UNITED STATES		**410**
PORTUGUESE IN SCHOOLS		**411**
COMMUNICATION	**Goal 1**	**411**
CULTURES	**Goal 2**	**412**
CONNECTIONS	**Goal 3**	**417**
COMPARISONS	**Goal 4**	**420**
COMMUNITIES	**Goal 5**	**425**
SAMPLE LEARNING SCENARIOS		**427**
Flags		427
As araras: Macaws		428
A varinha mágica		429
Iberia		430
Portuguese in the World		431

Standards for Learning Portuguese

CONNECTIONS — GOAL THREE
Connect with Other Disciplines and Acquire Information

Standard 3.1 Students reinforce and further their knowledge of other disciplines through Portuguese.

Standard 3.2 Students acquire information and recognize the distinctive viewpoints that are only available through the Portuguese language and its many cultures.

COMMUNICATION — GOAL ONE
Communicate in Portuguese

Standard 1.1 Students engage in conversations, provide and obtain information, express feelings and emotions, and exchange opinions.

Standard 1.2 Students understand and interpret spoken and written Portuguese on a variety of topics.

Standard 1.3 Students present information, concepts, and ideas in Portuguese to an audience of listeners or readers on a variety of topics.

COMPARISONS — GOAL FOUR
Develop Insight into the Nature of Language and Culture

Standard 4.1 Students demonstrate understanding of the nature of language through comparisons between Portuguese and English and/or Spanish.

Standard 4.2 Students demonstrate understanding of the concept of culture through comparisons between the cultures studied and their own.

CULTURES — GOAL TWO
Gain Knowledge and Understanding of Portuguese Speaking Cultures

Standard 2.1 Students demonstrate an understanding of the relationship between the practices and perspectives of Luso-Brazilian cultures.

Standard 2.2 Students demonstrate an understanding of the relationship between the products and perspectives of the different Luso-Brazilian cultures.

COMMUNITIES — GOAL FIVE
Participate in Communities at Home and Around the World

Standard 5.1 Students use Portuguese both within and beyond the school setting.

Standard 5.2 Students show evidence of becoming life-long learners by using Portuguese for personal enjoyment and enrichment.

Introduction

The study of Portuguese offers learners the opportunity to communicate, to learn, and to function appropriately in the Portuguese language and in Luso-Brazilian communities. It encourages students to make comparisons and connections and to interact with the community, at home and throughout the world, in an increasingly proficient manner. These standards encourage schools to consider long sequences of language study, beginning in the elementary grades, in order for learners to develop greater proficiency, in exactly the same manner as we encourage them to begin early and continue throughout their school careers the study of language arts, mathematics, science, and social studies.

Guiding principles in the development of this document

It is not the intention of this document to reiterate nor repeat the contents of *Standards for Foreign Language Learning*, but rather to tailor it to the study of Portuguese language, literature, and culture. **This document is not intended to be used as a curriculum, nor is it a syllabus.** It is a guide for the preparation of programs, curricula, courses, or syllabi, as shown in the diagram on page 28 of the generic document. Those who use these standards as a guideline for developing curricula, will find that they present a new way of envisioning Portuguese programs unlike any structure that we have used up to now. Writers of state frameworks, curriculum planners, and school administrators are encouraged to use the Portuguese and the generic standards as references, as they envision ways of meeting the needs of learners, communities, and ultimately, the nation, with regard to the study of Portuguese.

Every learner has a unique motivation for studying a given language; however, the organizing principles of this document, as wellas of the generic standards, outline two major areas: the five Cs (communication, cultures, connections, comparisons, and communities), and the "weave" of curricular elements (the language system, cultural knowledge, communication strategies, critical thinking skills, learning strategies, other subject areas, and technology), and the Portuguese language system itself.

These content standards are based on the vision of an ideal program, in which Portuguese instruction begins in early childhood at the kindergarten level and continues uninterrupted throughout the high school and college years. After finishing their formal education, learners maintain their Portuguese skills by applying them in professional and personal settings. Along with each of the content standards in this document, there are sample progress indicators for learners of Portuguese at grades four, eight, twelve, and sixteen, that provide language-specific examples of achievable outcomes. At each level, the indicators include and build upon those of the preceding levels. Following the Standards, a section of learning scenarios features classroom activities for the teaching and learning of Portuguese at various levels.

Although the spirit of the AATSP Standards is visionary, the reality of Portuguese education in the United States today is quite different. Compared to other Western European languages, very few high schools in the country offer Portuguese; even fewer schools offer Portuguese before the high school level. The vast majority of learners of Portuguese will begin their formal study of the language in one of the 206 post-secondary institutions that offer some kind of Portuguese language instruction. (Data from the Center for Advanced Research on Language Acquisition, University of Minnesota). Almost half of these institutions are located in areas of the country where one finds large populations of Portuguese and/or Brazilian immigrants. For example, 31 of the institutions are in California, 21 are in New York, 23 are in the New England states, and 28 are in the Southeast/Gulf region. It should also be noted that of the 206 institutions that offer Portuguese language at the post-secondary level, only a fraction of them offer courses beyond the second year (intermediate language instruction).

PORTUGUESE IN THE WORLD

Portuguese is spoken by nearly 190 million people who are spread over four different continents. In Europe, Portuguese is the official language of Portugal. It is the official language of Brazil with its 160 million people. In Africa, it is spoken in Angola, Cape Verde, Guine-Bissau, São Tomé e Príncipe, and Mozambique. In Asia it is spoken in Macau. Portuguese is the third most spoken European language in the world (first is English, second Spanish, third Portuguese).

The language known today as Portuguese is a romance language that evolved from Latin. It spread to other parts of the world during the era of European expansion and exploration. In each area of the world where the Portuguese presence became permanent, the language has adapted to the environment and to the indigenous languages of the area. Although an analogy could be drawn between Portuguese from Portugal and British English, compared to Portuguese spoken in Brazil and English spoken in the United States, the development of Portuguese—especially in Brazil—has distanced itself from its origins. Moreover, we find a great deal of difference between spoken (informal) and written (formal) Portuguese, especially in Brazil. Modern technology and media have brought the languages of Portugal and Brazil closer, but the differences are more than trivial.

Teachers of Portuguese have studied in many different areas of the Portuguese-speaking world and reflect heritage knowledge from diverse communities. Whether they belong to the Portuguese communities of Santa Clara, California, or Mystic, Connecticut, or whether they are part of the ever growing Brazilian communities in Miami, in Boston, and in New York, they bring to their teaching the knowledge of their own particular variety of Portuguese. If students are lucky to be in a Portuguese and/or Brazilian heritage area where Portuguese is offered in the schools, they will have the opportunity to learn about the different modalities of the language by participating in community activities. It is imperative that Portuguese programs encourage students to explore the Internet, videos, and audiotapes so that they may become more familiar with the different forms of Portuguese spoken in different areas of the world.

PORTUGUESE IN THE UNITED STATES

The largest concentrations of people of Portuguese descent in the United States live in two areas of the country: California and the New England states. The largest concentrations of people of Brazilian descent in the United States live in Miami, Boston, and New York City (in this order). The Brazilian magazine *Veja* in 1996 called Miami "the fastest growing Brazilian city in the world." Brazilian immigration is relatively recent, while Portuguese immigration dates back to the late 1700s and 1800s. Many Portuguese immigrants were from fishing communities in the Azores. Many Brazilian immigrants come from middle-class backgrounds. The differences in the populations of heritage language speakers are as varied as the groups themselves. These populations find themselves in a constant search for identity within the terminology applied by the United States government. The politically charged term "latino" is rejected by many Portuguese speakers, as is the term "hispanic." The term "ibero-american," also politically charged among Spanish-speakers for emphasizing the colonial presence, has been used to describe Portuguese speakers from Portugal and/or Brazil. In general, most Portuguese speakers like to be identified with their country of origin. Brazilians, moreover, often identify themselves by the region of the country or city from which they originated (*gaúcho*, *carioca*, *paulista*, etc.). Lusophone heritage speakers, concentrated particularly in the California Bay area and in the Northeast of the United States, have a rich culture that is kept alive through community activities, heritage museums and festival celebrations.

PORTUGUESE IN SCHOOLS

Except for areas of the country where there is a presence of Portuguese speakers, virtually no pre-college Portuguese is available to students. With the growing importance of Brazil in the world market, and its impact in the political stability of South America, we expect to see more programs established in different areas of the country.

Throughout the document, some of the sample progress indicators are purposefully ordered to demonstrate developmental sequencing from one grade range to another. It is important to note that the progress indicators at the earliest levels are subsumed at the higher levels. Whether they are specifically stated in this document or not, each of the progress indicators for earlier levels should be mastered at the more advanced levels. The entry point for many Portuguese learners, as stated above, is the post-secondary level. Therefore, the challenge for teachers and learners of Portuguese is to develop the communicative proficiency of the student in a shorter and, at times, less realistic manner.

This document addresses briefly the needs of Spanish speakers who learn Portuguese, since many of the Portuguese learners in post-secondary settings have some background in Spanish. Most are interested in Latin America (both Spanish-speaking and Portuguese-speaking).

Communication *Goal One*
Communicate in Portuguese

Effective communication in Portuguese includes understanding and expressing oneself orally and in writing in situations that may be either planned and predictable or spontaneous. Thus, students must be able to participate appropriately in a range of contexts and in a variety of levels of formality (i.e., registers). They must be able to interact in communicative exchanges, either face-to-face or via technology; interpret what they observe, hear, read, and view, both in real-life interactions and in the media; and present information, concepts, and ideas orally, visually, and in writing.

The capacity to communicate requires not only an awareness of the linguistic code to be used, but also an understanding of the cultural context within which meaning is encoded and decoded. As an example, the word "bread" can be rendered into Portuguese "*pão*," but the images produced by the words might be quite different, depending upon the cultural community in which the word is used. Linguistically, one can know how to say "*desculpe*," but unless one knows when to use the term, the message conveyed may be quite different from the message intended. The better one speaks the language, the more one is expected to be aware of the cultural nuance embedded in the message conveyed. The mutual dependence of language and culture to produce meanings results in a close relationship among all of the goals. For instance, the insights highlighted in Goal Four build upon the cultural knowledge of Goal Two to enhance the communicative ability of Goal One.

Students may enter the Portuguese classroom with a variety of experiences in language and cultures. Some may be interested in Latin America in general and already know Spanish and now wish to learn more about the other geographical half of Latin America. Some may have participated in an immersion experience or a bilingual education program. For others, Portuguese may be the language of the community or the home, or may have been used to communicate informally with friends and/or family members. Still others may have had brief experiences or informal encounters through an isolated unit of instruction in an earlier grade.

All learners, regardless of their prior experience, have the capacity to improve, and must have the opportunity to build upon and expand their communicative skills. Students of Portuguese, regardless of their initial levels of functional ability in the language, can then improve their personal awareness and linguistic capabilities within an ever-expanding cultural context throughout their study of the language and cultures.

STANDARD 1.1 Students engage in conversations, provide and obtain information, express feelings and emotions, and exchange opinions.

This standard focuses on interpersonal communication. Many students begin the study of Portuguese with a desire to interact effectively with speakers of the language community. Others are already fluent Spanish speakers and wish to learn the differences between the two languages and the cultural reflections that these differences display.

Students who come from Portuguese-speaking backgrounds or who have had prior experience with the language may have already acquired the linguistic ability to communicate within their own communities. However, they may lack the broader knowledge of the language and its cultures necessary to adapt their skills to interact effectively with speakers from other cultural communities and in situations requiring varied levels (registers) of formality.

Students who come into Portuguese from a Spanish-speaking background may already have the linguistic facility to communicate (often in *portuñol*) but will lack the ability to communicate in Portuguese without much Spanish interference. For these students, emphasis on pronunciation in Portuguese is important.

Sample Progress Indicators, Grade 4

- Students give and follow simple instructions in order to participate in age-appropriate classroom and/or cultural activities (e.g., *Bom dia, Entre, vamos conversar*).

- Students ask and answer questions about very familiar topics (e.g., family, school events, celebrations) in person or via short letters, e-mail, audio, or video tapes.

- Students engage in common classroom interactions (e.g., providing their names and addresses, exchanging greetings and leave-takings, using culturally appropriate gestures and oral expressions).

- Students exchange descriptions of people and tangible products of the culture (e.g., *O sítio do Pica-Pau Amarelo* and common children's sayings that come from literary products—*Ciranda, cirandinha . . .*) with other members of the class.

- Students share their likes and dislikes with each other and with the class.

Sample Progress Indicators, Grade 8

- Students give and follow directions for participating in age-appropriate cultural activities and investigating the function of products of the cultures of the Portuguese speaking world (e.g., *Para que a gente usa uma figa? O que é um fado?*)

- Students exchange information about personal events, memorable experiences, and other school subjects with peers and/or members of one or more of the cultures. (e.g., school sports, parties, travel).

- Students compare, contrast, and express preferences about the information gathered regarding events experienced, and other school subjects. (e.g., *Eu gosto mais de futebol do que de basquete porque eu jogo mais.*).

Sample Progress Indicators, Grade 12

- Students use the language to exchange, support, and discuss their opinions and individual perspectives with peers and/or other Portuguese-speakers on a variety of topics dealing with contemporary and historical issues (e.g., discuss the *Tratado de Tordesillas, as missões portuguesa*s).

- Students use the language to share their analyses and personal reactions to expository and literary texts with peers and/or other speakers of Portuguese (e.g., *As lendas brasileiras*; the novels of Lygia Bojunga Nunes).

- Students discuss, orally and in writing, current or past events that are of significance in the Portuguese-speaking world or that are being studied in another subject (e.g., *Mercosur*; the European Union).

- Students use the language in group activities in which they develop and propose solutions to issues and problems that are of concern to members of their own cultures and to the cultures of the Portuguese-speaking world (e.g., *a selva amazônica, a música popular*).

Sample Progress Indicators, Grade 16

- Students use Portuguese in a professional experience or internship related to their field of study.

- Students exchange points of view on global topics (e.g., *a educação no Brasil; a ecologia; a política*).

- Students use Portuguese to discuss some aspects of their field of study with other speakers (e.g., *as diferenças entre o português e o espanhol; o português na medicina*).

- Students use Portuguese orally and in writing to communicate with people already employed in their field of study (e.g., *cartas pedindo emprego; entrevistas para o trabalho; opiniões sobre um texto literário*).

- Students read Portuguese language texts of a literary or non-literary nature and analyze cultural content in the text.

- Students use Portuguese to search for a job in their fields of study.

STANDARD 1.2 Students understand and interpret written and spoken Portuguese on a variety of topics.

Students must be able to interact with a wide range of texts that they hear and read. Beyond assigning literal meaning to a language sample, learners must be able to recognize and interpret the text at the cultural, non-literal or figurative level. Texts encompass formal and informal language samples including both literary and non-literary materials (e.g., magazines, newspapers, *romances, poesia, crônicas, lendas*). As the learners' skills improve, they should be introduced to a variety of textual sources, levels of formality, and regional variations.

Students who begin their formal study of Portuguese with a greater degree of aural comprehension because of their previous knowledge of Spanish, have the opportunity to develop greater skills in reading, interpreting, and decoding textual messages. Indeed, further reading—an "easy" skill in Portuguese for the speaker of Spanish—will contribute to the development of authentic cultural skills. Because of the higher levels of linguistic and cultural control, Spanish-speakers learning Portuguese should build upon and expand their communicative skills as they interact linguistically and culturally with more diverse and less familiar texts that come from the Portuguese-speaking world.

Sample Progress Indicators, Grade 4

- Students comprehend main ideas in developmentally appropriate oral narratives in the language (e.g., fairy tales from Western tradition; the children's literary tradition in Monteiro Lobato, personal anecdotes).

- Students identify people and objects in their environment or from other school subjects, based on oral and written descriptions in the language (e.g., school supplies, classroom vocabulary).

- Students comprehend brief written messages and short personal notes in the language on familiar topics (e.g., *A minha mãe é professora*; *Esta é a minha casa*).

- Students interpret gestures, intonation, and other visual or auditory clues in the language (e.g., video clips of Portuguese-language, age-appropriate programming).

Sample Progress Indicators, Grade 8

- Students identify the principal characters and comprehend the main ideas and themes in age-appropriate literary texts and other textual products from the Portuguese cultures (e.g., *Narizinho, Saci Pererê, O Negrinho do Pastoreio; Veja, Jornal de Letras*).

- Students comprehend information and messages in the language related to other school subjects (e.g., short texts from social studies, health, general science).

- Students understand announcements and messages connected to daily activities in Portuguese-speaking cultures (e.g., advertisements in magazines and newspapers, television commercials).

- Students use knowledge acquired in other settings and from other subject areas to comprehend spoken and written messages in the languages (e.g., mathematical word problems in Portuguese; metric system).

Sample Progress Indicators, Grade 12

- Students demonstrate an understanding of the main ideas and significant details of live and recorded discussions, short lectures, and presentations in Portuguese on current or past events from another class (e.g., Portuguese language newscasts, interviews).

- Students demonstrate an increasing understanding of the cultural nuances of meaning in written and spoken Portuguese as expressed by speakers of the language in formal and informal settings (e.g., interpret the actions and reactions of characters in a *telenovela*; begin to understand humor and irony in textual materials).

- Students begin to understand puns and other manipulations of the language.

- Students demonstrate an understanding of primary resource materials that relate to their fields of study or the subjects they are studying (encyclopedias, periodicals, web sources, etc.).

- Students demonstrate an increased understanding of details of authentic oral and written textual sources (e.g., *tu, você, o senhor, a senhora, a professora, a Carmen*, as different forms of address).

Sample Progress Indicators, Grade 16

- Students demonstrate the ability to distinguish between materials that state unsupported personal opinion of the author and factually-supported personal opinions.

- Students analyze authentic literary texts written in Portuguese (e.g., main plot, subplot, characters, and basic contextual references in the text).

- Students demonstrate the ability to read and derive information from all written materials related to their field of study (e.g., note-taking for subsequent presentation; documentation of resources).

STANDARD 1.3 Students present information, concepts, and ideas to an audience of listeners or readers on a variety of topics in Portuguese.

In the beginning stages, learners' performance capabilities may be limited largely to memorized phrases. They must move from memorized material to creative use of language in order to focus on presentation skills. Learners with prior experiences in Portuguese can be made aware of the conventions of purposeful writing, strategies and organization of composition, more formalized public speaking, etc., appropriate to the cultures. Students with a background in Spanish can be made aware of basic differences in the two languages.

Sample Progress Indicators, Grade 4

- Students prepare illustrated stories about activities or events in their environment and share them with an audience such as the class (e.g., *uma festa de aniversário, uma viagem*).

- Students use the language to give presentations to the students of another classroom (e.g., *canções típicas, peças curtas*).

- Students tell or retell familiar stories.

- Students use the language to write short notes to peers in other Portuguese speaking cultures.

Sample Progress Indicators, Grade 8

- Students make presentations for a school-related event (e.g., PTA meetings, short plays).

- Students prepare tape- or video-recorded messages to share locally or with school peers and/or members of the Portuguese-speaking community on topics of personal interest.

- Students prepare summaries of texts that they have read.

Sample Progress Indicators, Grade 12

- Students perform scenes and/or recite poems or excerpts from short stories connected to a topic from other disciplines.

- Students create stories and poems, short plays, or skits based on personal experiences.

- Students select and analyze creative and artistic expressions of Portuguese-speaking cultures from literary genres or from the visual and performing arts.

- Students analyze and present basic differences between Spanish and Portuguese based on texts and on interviews with Spanish and Portuguese speakers.

Sample Progress Indicators, Grade 16

- Students present a play in Portuguese.

- Students present their literary research findings to their classmates or in a conference-like atmosphere.

- Students design, develop, and use desktop publishing software for use in their fields of study (e.g., creating brochures, prospectuses).

- Students prepare a formal research-based analysis of some aspect of their fields of study, including perspectives from the United States and from another culture (e.g., relative importance of discipline; regulation or certification of practitioners).

- Students conduct and publish interviews in a student newsletter.

- Students collect oral histories and present them orally or in writing.

Cultures *Goal Two*
Gain Knowledge and Understanding of Portuguese-Speaking Cultures

Speakers of Portuguese share a common cultural heritage and also represent diverse cultures. These diverse cultures may be geographically identifiable and may also be further shaped by population characteristics such as gender, age, socio-economic status, and religion. Students should have a range of learning experiences that reflect the richness of cultures encompassed in the Portuguese-speaking world and, particularly, those they may encounter in their local community.

Students need to understand the perspectives, practices, and products of the Portuguese-speaking world. The term "perspectives" is used here to refer to what Portuguese speakers think and do from their own point of view. The term "practices" refers to the knowledge of "what to do when and where and how to interact within a Portuguese cultural context." Finally, the term "products" ranges from aesthetic expressions to more popular products that combine aesthetic expression with utilitarian purposes, such as *artesanatos*. Linguistic fluency alone does not guarantee successful cultural interactions. Goal Two prepares students to identify key cultural perspectives and culturally appropriate behaviors. Goal Two emphasizes the fact that students are learning the when and why of communication through the study of Luso-Brazilian cultures.

STANDARD 2.1 Students demonstrate an understanding of the relationship between the practices and perspectives of Luso-Brazilian cultures.

This standard emphasizes the importance of understanding the practices and perspectives of Luso-Brazilian cultures. One cannot effectively communicate using the Portuguese language, nor interact within the Luso-Brazilian cultures without being aware of the relationship between the practices and perspectives that define and describe the speakers of Portuguese.

Sample Progress Indicators, Grade 4

- Students use appropriate gestures and oral expressions for greetings, leave-takings, and common classroom interactions.

- Students participate in age-appropriate cultural activities such as games, songs, birthday celebrations and other observances of a personal or social nature within a Portuguese-speaking community (e.g., *Festa de aniversário, Coelinho da páscoa*).

- Students observe, identify, and/or discuss simple patterns of behavior or interaction in various settings such as school, family, and the community within the context of Portuguese speakers (e.g., *Dia da criança*).

Sample Progress Indicators, Grade 8

- Students use appropriate verbal and nonverbal behavior for daily activities among peers and adults (e.g., two kisses or three when greeting?).

- Students rethink common fairy tales, short stories, and short plays from a different character's point of view.

- Students analyze and discuss experiences of being a Spanish or English speaker learning Portuguese.

Sample Progress Indicators, Grade 12

- Students interact in a variety of cultural contexts that reflect both peer-group and adult activities within the different Luso-Brazilian cultures.

- Students analyze different cultural practices that either coincide with or may be contrasted to some of their own cultural practices. (e.g., celebration of Christmas in the summer; Carnival; Afro-Brazilian religions).

- Students participate in real or simulated age-appropriate cultural occurrences related to special events or personal occasions (Carnival).

- Students analyze and discuss various Luso-Brazilian patterns of behavior typical of the diversity in Luso-Brazilian communities (e.g., Bar Mitzvah in a Luso-Brazilian culture).

- Students analyze different texts, including literary, and are able to perceive the cultural context embedded in each.

Sample Progress Indicators, Grade 16

- Students demonstrate the ability to interact appropriately in most social and job-related situation with Portuguese speakers.

- Students identify, examine, and interpret cultural perspectives and points of view in socially approved behavioral patterns (e.g., gender roles; unwritten codes of conduct).

- Students understand cultural patterns expressed in written text—literary and non-literary (e.g., Saramago compared to Jorge Amado).

- Students identify, analyze and discuss Luso-Brazilian patterns of behavior typical of their possible future co-workers (e.g., through chat-room conversations with Portuguese-speaking students).

STANDARD 2.2 Students demonstrate an understanding of the relationship between the products and perspectives of the different Luso-Brazilian cultures.

The products from Luso-Brazilian cultures, whether tangible novels, *artesanatos*, music, or intangible such as sociocultural mores, are essential in the learning of Portuguese. A true understanding of Portuguese speakers is imbedded in the "what" of cultural products: food, clothing, political and social institutions, as interwoven with the "why" or the perspectives that surround these products. Appropriate interaction with Portuguese speakers includes the ability to demonstrate an understanding of these relationships.

Sample Progress Indicators, Grade 4

- Students identify and observe tangible products from Portuguese-speaking cultures such as toys, dress, types of dwellings, and foods (e.g., *doce de leite, brigadeiros, fios de ovos, pilchas*).

- Students identify and experience expressive products of Portuguese speakers such as children's songs, selections from children's literature, and legends (*Araras*).

- Students recognize common themes, ideas, or perspectives of groups of Portuguese speakers (e.g., *Churrasco, Banda de Pife, Fado*).

Sample Progress Indicators, Grade 8

- Students search for, investigate, and identify the functions of the most common *artesanatos* described in their books.

- Students experience (read, listen to, observe, perform) expressive products of the Portuguese-speaking world (e.g., stories, poetry, music, paintings, dance, and drama).

- Students identify, discuss, and analyze a Portuguese-speaking community and its themes, ideas, and perspective (e.g., discussion of the film "Mystic Pizza").

Sample Progress Indicators, Grade 12

- Students experience, discuss, and analyze expressive products of the culture, including selections from various literary genres and the fine arts (e.g., *novelas, samba, fado, saudade*).

- Students identify, analyze, and evaluate themes, ideas, and perspectives related to the products being studied (e.g. use of chat rooms and the Internet to explore different ideas with Portuguese speakers from other parts of the world).

- Students identify, discuss, and analyze intangible products of culture such as political institutions, voting procedures, democracy.

- Students use linguistic patterns appropriately within the Portuguese speaking culture and are sensitive to the underlying meaning and importance of these patterns.

- Students who have a background in Spanish use appropriate Portuguese phrases and culturally sound expressions in conversations

Sample Progress Indicators, Grade 16

- Students can act in a culturally correct manner in most contexts showing sensitivity to and understanding of the meanings that are implied by behaviors.

- Students demonstrate an understanding of the "unwritten rules of behavior" (norms of respect; "small talk" before discussion of business issues).

- Students participate appropriately in discussion with Portuguese speakers about themes, ideas, and perspectives related to their field of study or job.

- Students study and participate appropriately in discussions with Portuguese speakers about literary, social, economic, and political topics (e.g., social classes and how they are depicted in film, literature, economics).

Connections *Goal Three*
Connect with Other Disciplines and Acquire Information

Students of Portuguese—both beginners and heritage background learners—have unique opportunities to use their growing language skills for communicative purposes that go beyond personal survival topics. Students of Portuguese who bring to their studies a solid knowledge of Spanish, will need to develop the additional communication tools necessary for successful participation in a variety of activities with Portuguese speakers within their communities.

STANDARD 3.1 Students reinforce and further their knowledge of other disciplines through Portuguese.

All academic disciplines, or content areas, share a common core. Students deepen and enhance their understanding of concepts when they have the opportunity to learn them in both English and Portuguese. For example, young children learn how to tell time better when they can practice telling time in both languages. When students are learning content areas that refer specifically to the Portuguese speaking world, the content and the language skills will be reinforced by carrying out readings, discussions, and presentations in Portuguese.

Sample Progress Indicators, Grade 4:

- Students demonstrate in Portuguese an understanding about concepts learned in other subject areas (e.g., colors for map reading, telling time, animals, insects).

- Students talk about simple facts from other disciplines in Portuguese (e.g., *dois mais dois são quatro; O Brasil fica na América do Sul*).

- Students comprehend short, age-appropriate videos in Portuguese.
- Students present short, factual oral reports in Portuguese.

Sample Progress Indicators, Grade 12

- Students acquire information from a variety of sources written in Portuguese about a topic being studied in a range of school subject (e.g., religious holidays).
- Students combine information from other school subjects with information available in Portuguese (e.g., a report on John Phillip Souza's Portuguese roots).

Sample Progress Indicators, Grade 16

- Students use Portuguese to explore viewpoints about other academic disciplines on issues that are available in the Portuguese language (e.g., newspaper articles; contemporary painting; current film; current literary works).
- Students regularly read and apply information available only in Portuguese to communicate in oral and written forms with Portuguese speakers about a variety of topics (e.g., Portuguese language literary criticism; non-translated literary pieces; socio-political essays, economic and political essays).
- Students obtain and use information available only in Portuguese related to their field of study (e.g., information about immigrants' places of origin).
- Students use resources available through electronic means only in Portuguese (e.g., chat rooms, e-mail, Internet).

STANDARD 3.2 Students acquire information and recognize the distinctive viewpoints that are available only through the Portuguese language and its many cultures.

Successful participation in Portuguese-speaking communities requires that students know how to acquire information and recognize viewpoints from print and non-print media that are only available in Portuguese. Also, note that the ability to access and to process information available only in Portuguese contributes to students' becoming better informed citizens of the United States and of the world. Frequently, English translations of information originating in Portuguese, either do not exist or distort original meanings. Decisions about what is translated or not into English often involve political and social implications. As international technology continues to progress, more and more information in Portuguese will become available and easily obtained.

Sample Progress Indicator, Grade 4

- Students read, listen to, and talk about age-appropriate school content, folk tales, short stories, poems and songs written for native speakers of Portuguese (e.g., *A Vitória régia*).

Sample Progress Indicators, Grade 8

- Students use sources intended for same-age speakers of Portuguese to prepare reports on topics of personal interest, or those with which they have limited previous experience (e.g., *A copa do mundo*).

- Students use sources about the United States intended for same-age speakers of Portuguese and analyze different perspectives on contemporary issues of concern and /or interest (e.g., age appropriate magazines written in Portuguese).

Sample Progress Indicators, Grade 12

- Students prepare reports and cultural presentations by comparing information contained in Portuguese-only sources to the same type of information in English language sources (e.g., obituary announcements; wedding or anniversary announcements).

- Students use Portuguese to access viewpoints on issues written in Portuguese and compare these to the same issues in English language texts (e.g., newspaper accounts for the U.S. President's trip to another continent; two short-stories about the same topic).

Sample Progress Indicators, Grade 16

- Students analyze and interpret information available in Portuguese and in English related to their field of study (e.g., end-of-the-century predictions for their field).

- Students read and analyze literary and non-literary texts available only in Portuguese and comprehend the cultural and socio-political messages imbedded in such texts (e.g., subtle messages in TV commercials).

- Students discuss literary and non-literary topics within a Portuguese context. (e.g., the literary canon in Brazil).

Comparisons   *Goal Four*
Develop Insights into the Nature of Language and Culture

The purpose of language is communication. All languages are systems that have evolved for the primary purpose of communication. Although all languages share some characteristics, each is unique in the ways it is used to carry out specific tasks and functions. More than anything else, language reflects specific cultures and societal values. A comparison between English and Portuguese demonstrates both similarities and differences.

Students come to the Portuguese classroom with a variety of language backgrounds. In pre-college programs, many such students are heritage learners or native speakers of Portuguese. In post-secondary programs, the vast majority of Portuguese students have a background in Spanish. Teachers must acknowledge the vast differences among students and use these differences as a starting point for making observations about the nature of language as well as about the cultural content of languages.

STANDARD 4.1 Students demonstrate understanding of the nature of language through comparisons between Portuguese and English and/or Spanish.

This standard focuses on helping students understand how to learn a language, how to use a language, and to embrace the concept of the lifelong language learner. Students should become aware of the similarities and differences between Spanish and Portuguese and be able to observe the culture content of such differences.

Sample Progress Indicators, Grade 4

- Students cite and use examples of words that are the same in Portuguese, Spanish, and English, and talk about what words mean.

- Students realize that cognates enhance comprehension of spoken and written Portuguese and demonstrate that awareness by identifying commonly occurring cognates in the language.

- Students learn of the existence of idiomatic expressions in Portuguese and in English and talk about how idiomatic expressions work in general.

Sample Progress Indicators, Grade 8

- Students recognize grammatical gender in Portuguese, and reflect that awareness in their spoken and written language.

- Students hypothesize about the relationship between English and Portuguese based on cognates and notice patterns that exist (e.g., *educação*-education; *nação*-nation).

- Students demonstrate awareness that Portuguese has some sounds that are not part of the English language nor are they part of the Spanish language, and that such sounds must be articulated in communication (e.g., *vô/vó*).

Sample Progress Indicators, Grade 12

- Students recognize that some words that appear to be the same may have the same or different meanings between English and Portuguese (e.g., *assistir, atender, introduzir*).

- Students demonstrate an awareness that there are phrases and idioms that do not translate directly from English to Portuguese, and vice versa. (e.g., *matar aula; colar*).

- Students hypothesize about the evolution of language based on their awareness of cognates and idioms (e.g., etymological changes in words).

- Students observe and discuss sentence word order and hypothesize on how this may or may not reflect the ways in which cultures organize information and view the world (e.g., *um grande amigo, uma pessoa grande*).

Sample Progress Indicators, Grade 16

- Students compare Portuguese dialects (vocabulary, sound systems, structures).

- Students comprehend different dialects represented in literary and non-literary texts.
- Students use different registers appropriately.

STANDARD 4.2 Students demonstrate understanding of the concept of culture through comparisons between the cultures studied and their own.

The impact of culture on language is immense. Many times, the decisions of whether to use a particular gesture, vocabulary item, or phrase is determined culturally, not grammatically. Linguistic accuracy alone is not an indicator of cultural accuracy.

Sample Progress Indicators, Grade 4

- Students compare and practice several patterns of behavior and language use in different cultural settings (e.g., home, different types of greetings).
- Students demonstrate an awareness that gestures are an important part of communication and that gestures have different meanings in different cultural contexts (e.g., gestures for pointing, OK sign.)
- Students compare tangible cultural products (e.g., toys: *peteca*, musical instruments: *cavaquinho*, food: *feijoada*).
- Students learn rhymes, songs, folktales that differ from English-speaking cultural norms.

Sample Progress Indicators, Grade 8

- Students compare and contrast verbal and non-verbal behavior within particular activities in Luso-Brazilian cultures and their own (e.g., table manners).
- Students begin to comprehend their own cultural norms by comparing their activities with those of Luso-Brazilian cultures (e.g., dating customs, TV programs).
- Students speculate on why certain products originate in and/or are important to particular cultures (e.g., *figa* vs. rabbit's tail).
- Students read age-appropriate literary and non-literary texts in Portuguese and compare them to similar texts in English for cultural cues (*A varinha mágica*).

Sample Progress Indicators, Grade 16

- Students compare and contrast cultural institutions (e.g., government, education, religion) between Luso-Brazilian cultures and what they know about U.S. culture.
- Students demonstrate appropriate language and cultural practices while actively engaged in a professional or social setting (e.g., different cultural expectations in different situations; cultural taboos).
- Students are comfortable decoding cultural messages in literary and non-literary texts (e.g., Yayá García's African roots).

Communities *Goal Five*
Participate in Multilingual Communities at Home and Around the World

Goal Five focuses on the application of Portuguese to communities beyond the classroom. Such applications may be primarily personal in nature (travel, self-enrichment); academic (literary-drama, dance), or professional (business, diplomacy, politics). These activities may be spontaneous and self-motivated or required and monitored by the teacher.

STANDARD 5.1 Students use Portuguese both within and beyond the school setting.

Within the school setting, there are opportunities for students to interact with classmates, younger students, older students, and keypals in other schools, communities, and countries. When learners have opportunities to apply Portuguese skills to real-life activities, they become more motivated to excel. In areas of the country where Portuguese-speaking populations congregate, students will have the opportunity to use their newly acquired Portuguese language skills in the community. Although large Portuguese speaking communities are scarce in the United States, students may participate in chat rooms and other opportunities in cyberspace. In addition, travel abroad to a Portuguese speaking area of the world will greatly enhance students' proficiency in Portuguese.

Sample Progress Indicators, Grade 4

- Students convey spontaneous personal messages to Portuguese speakers via telephone (e.g., when contacted by the community).

- Students seek a pen pal or keypal from a Portuguese speaking community in the world (via Internet or more standard forms of correspondence).

- Students interact in Portuguese appropriately in set and "scripted" situations (greetings, leave-takings, birthday parties).

- Students read simple stories in Portuguese and are able to summarize the main idea in Portuguese (*A varinha mágica, Arara*).

Sample Progress Indicators, Grade 8

- Students discuss preferences in Portuguese with peers in the Portuguese speaking community.

- Students interact with Portuguese speaking members of their local community to learn how they use the language in different cultural settings.

Sample Progress Indicators, Grade 12

- Students communicate issues of personal interest to members of the Portuguese-speaking community through direct contact or through the Internet.

- Students participate in a career exploration or school-to-work project that uses Portuguese language skills and/or an understanding of the Portuguese-speaking community.

- Students read about the Luso-Brazilian community in Portuguese and present this information to others.

- Students gather information that is applicable to their field(s) of study from the Portuguese-speaking communities.

Sample Progress Indicators, Grade 16

- Students participate in an internship or study program in the United States or abroad that requires knowledge of Portuguese language.

- Students study in a Portuguese-speaking area of the world.

- Students take leadership roles in the Portuguese speaking communities at home and abroad.

- Students participate in community activities that reflect Luso-Brazilian traditions and celebrations.

- Students read literary and non-literary texts that reflect Luso-Brazilian communities and discuss their findings with colleagues.

STANDARD 5.2 Students show evidence of becoming life-long learners by using Portuguese for personal enjoyment and enrichment.

As already seen in other sections of this document, Portuguese is an avenue to gathering information and establishing interpersonal relations. By developing their skills in Portuguese, students can access information as they continue to learn throughout their lives. Moreover, they may begin to use Portuguese in non-school related settings merely for the enjoyment of speaking another language (e.g., in children's games; in e-mail correspondence; and in reading).

Sample Progress Indicators, Grade 4

- Students enjoy watching age-appropriate television shows in Portuguese and listening to Luso-Brazilian music (*O sítio do pica-pau amarelo* and its commonly addressed issues).

- Students learn to play culturally associated instruments (*cavaquinho, reco-reco*).

- Students learn to play culturally authentic games (e.g., *Peteca, tabuada*).

Sample Progress Indicators, Grade 8

- Students read Portuguese language materials (magazines, age-appropriate novels, poems, newspapers) for personal enjoyment outside the regularly assigned classwork.

- Students listen to, sing, and play music from Luso-Brazilian cultures for personal entertainment.

- Students participate in cultural and social events within the Portuguese-speaking community.

Sample Progress Indicators, Grade 12

- Students consult the World Wide Web as well as print media for Luso-Brazilian cultural and Portuguese-language items of personal interest outside the school environment.
- Students establish relationships with native speakers of Portuguese.
- Students practice their linguistic survival skills in Portuguese-speaking environments at home and abroad.

Sample Progress indicators, Grade 16

- Students refine their world view through intellectual activities such as attending seminars, lectures, and conferences in Portuguese.
- Students maintain relationships with speakers of Portuguese.
- Students feel self-reliant in traveling in Portuguese-speaking countries.
- Students read daily Portuguese-language newspapers to keep up with sociopolitical developments in the Luso-Brazilian world.
- Students plan and host events for Portuguese-speaking colleagues and friends.
- Students read literary and non-literary texts available only in Portuguese for personal pleasure.

Learning Scenarios

FLAGS

Students in a Portuguese FLES program are learning to identify colors in Portuguese. The teacher takes advantage of the daily raising of the U.S. flag to introduce cultural concepts and reinforce the vocabulary of colors. Students name the different colors of flags from the United States, Brazil, Portugal, Mozambique, and Macau. The teacher then brings airmail envelopes from these countries and students identify the country by naming the colors again. After practicing in groups, students take turns saying, "*Esta é a bandeira do Brasil. Ela é verde, amarela, azul e branca,*" etc. After each student has had a chance to feature one of the flags and identify the country, the teacher asks them about other flags—school, city, state, community, and group flags. Finally, in small groups, the students draw flags. In each group, students take turns being the "holder of the crayons" and distribute

TARGETED STANDARDS
1.1 Interpersonal Communication
1.2 Interpretive Communication
1.3 Presentational Communication
2.2 Products of Culture
3.2 Acquiring Information
4.2 Cultural Comparisons

each crayon when asked, "*Eu quero o amarelo*," etc. The teacher begins to explain the idea of cultural symbols. Students notice that the colors of the flag are symbols. They see the same symbol reflected in the envelopes. As a follow-up activity, students design flags for their class and describe them in Portuguese.

Reflection

1.1 Students work collaboratively in groups.

1.2 Students understand the symbolic message of the colors as well as the words themselves.

1.3 Students present their flag to the class.

2.2 Students learn that each culture (whether country, community group, etc.) has an identifiable symbol that represents it.

3.2 Students acquire basic information in Portuguese.

4.2 Students begin to compare different symbols by their colors.

In this activity, students use critical thinking skills to compare and contrast the information encoded in the colors of the flags. More advanced students who are learning about the different countries of the world can compare the countries that speak English and the colors of their flags *vis-a-vis* the flag of Great Britain. Students may look at the flags of the world and hypothesize about the language spoken in each of the countries. In addition, students can look at the flags from Portuguese speaking countries and make a chart based on frequency of colors. Connections with social studies classes may include map reading, connections with the Portuguese empire and its influence in the development of Portuguese-speaking countries today.

> **TARGETED STANDARDS**
> 1.2 Interpretive Communication
> 1.3 Presentational Communication
> 2.1 Practices of Culture
> 3.1 Making Connections
> 3.2 Acquiring Information

AS ARARAS: MACAWS

During story time in Grade 1 or 2, the teacher reads *As araras* by Mary França and Eliardo França (São Paulo: Atica, 1987—ISBN 85 08 01737—16 pp. picture book). The teacher shows several pictures of brightly colored macaws and writes the word ARARA on the chalkboard. She reads the story again and asks students about the colors, the sounds, and the size of the birds. The students, in small groups, look at a copy of one page of the book and identify the words they know. By the pictures and the words that they are able to identify, they figure out what part of the story is depicted in "their page." They take turns retelling the story. At the end of the group activity, the teacher arranges the group in the correct "order" and calls on each child to advance the story by concentrating on the portion discussed in the group. Then the teacher gives out pictures of macaws to be colored. When students finish coloring the pictures, each takes a turn describing it: "*A minha arara é verde e azul.*"

Reflection

1.2 Students read and interpret a book written for Brazilian children.

1.3 Students retell the story in small groups and to the class.

2.2 Students are aware of the importance of these birds in Brazil.

3.1 Students connect this lessons with colors, sizes, regions of Brazil.

3.2 Students receive their information from a book that, by its nature, cannot be translated.

This scenario is appropriate for the early grades and can be adapted for later grades. More advanced students can do some map study of the parts of the world where the macaw is an indigenous bird. They may also compare the size of the macaw with that of its "relatives" such as the more common parrot. Assessment can be achieved in several different ways. First, the students retell the story. Then, the students will be able to make comparisons of sizes and colors. Finally, the teacher may assess the level of speaking proficiency during all of the tasks. In addition, in grade four, students may also write a short paragraph describing the macaw.

A VARINHA MÁGICA

This scenario may be used in a conversational Portuguese class whether in the 8-12 or post-secondary setting. The unit may take one class period (for the more advanced students) or several class days. During this unit, students read and discuss *A varinha mágica*, by Alvaro Cardoso Gomes (São Paulo: FTD, 1992; ISBN 85-322-0732-4; 21pp.). This book is part of the growing list of books written for Brazilian adolescents. As pre-reading activities, the teacher asks students if they could re-arrange their world, how would it look? Would their friends have different names? If they were granted three wishes, what would they be? The teacher reads the entire story, or the part that will be discussed during the particular lesson. Students then divide into groups and taking a page at a time (or a paragraph at a time) take turns reading to each other. After each passage, they discuss what they would do in the situation (each page is filled with questions facing the young protagonist). Students negotiate meaning for the slang words that they find. They also take turns acting out the dialogues. After the group activity, the teacher asks each group to tell the class one thing that was particularly interesting to them. Then the teacher asks each group to describe someone like the young protagonist. Back in groups, students discuss the making up of words and the changes that occur when words are used "incorrectly" to describe animals. More advanced students discuss how language develops from use and from manipulation of meaning. At the end of several readings of the short text, students take turns making up a story that involves the young protagonist.

> **TARGETED STANDARDS**
> 1.1 Interpersonal Communication
> 1.2 Interpretive Communication
> 1.3 Presentational Communication
> 2.2 Products of Culture
> 3.1 Making Connections
> 4.1 Language Comparisons
> 4.2 Cultural Comparisons

Reflection

1.1 Students use Portuguese in their small group discussions.

1.2 Students understand what they read and what they hear from others.

1.3 Students present information based on their group discussions.

2.2 Students discuss books written for young people and what this particular text tells them about Brazilian culture.

3.1 Students talk about myths, myth-making, how to use the dictionary.

4.1 Students learn about how words evolve into a language and compare this concept to the development of English words and their meaning.

4.2 Students learn about slang and what words mean within different cultural settings.

This activity is appropriate when the student is already literate in Portuguese. Although the book is designed for children, adolescents and college age students are able to grasp the playfulness of manipulating the language. For an assessment, teachers should ask students to describe in Portuguese some ways that words are created. They may, for example, describe how English language vocabulary is changing due to the technological revolution. Another follow-up/assessment activity may involve the writing of a children's story that will be shared with the class. The students themselves may become judges of the stories and describe why they think story A "works" better than story B.

TARGETED STANDARDS
1.1 Interpersonal Communication
1.3 Presentational Communication
4.1 Language Comparisons
4.2 Cultural Comparisons

IBERIA

In a large metropolitan high school, the Portuguese teacher and the Spanish teacher plan an activity involving both groups of students. Both teachers present materials on Iberia and its first inhabitants. Students do some research on the two countries (Portugal and Spain and their histories). In groups in each of the classes, they sift through the information gathered and discuss the differences and similarities between the two countries. They discuss political organizations, social institutions, and indigenous populations. Each group then presents to its class (either in Spanish or Portuguese) the information found. At the end of the term, the classes meet together and each student gives a short presentation to the students in the other class. The presentations are in the target language and students use visual aids and the teacher as "an interpreter." Students then take another class period together to discuss, in English, their experience during the activity and what they learned about the two different languages.

Reflection

1.1 Students gather information and discuss it in Portuguese or Spanish.
1.3 Students present information to class peers and to students of the other language.
4.1 Students compare Spanish, Portuguese, and English.
4.2 Students discuss the context of the development of Spanish and Portuguese and their cultural reflections.

This scenario is particularly useful for the Portuguese learner who is also a Spanish speaker or has had some Spanish previously. The working together of the two groups not only bridges the gap that normally divides them, but also provides the speaker of the "other" language with insights into pronunciation, culture, and language.

PORTUGUESE IN THE WORLD

Students in a conversation and composition class in a rural research university develop a unit on Portuguese in the World. The teacher divides the class into groups and each group takes one of the Portuguese-speaking areas of the world. One group is assigned the Luso-Brazilian communities in the United States. Each group is to find, through the Internet or print sources, current material about their area. In addition, they are to try to make contact with a Portuguese speaker from that part of the world. (Students have already been using chat rooms through the Internet). Students are encouraged to interview professors in other fields (Political Sciences, Ecology, Social Work) and obtain their views on Portuguese speakers of their assigned population. Each week, students must write a "progress report" on the group's activities and produce a two-page newspaper. Twice during the term, students "produce" a news program that is videotaped. Each group takes turns being responsible for the production. Each class day begins with "breaking news" from members of the groups. Students are encouraged to have something new to report to the class as often as possible. At the end of the term, each group presents a retrospective view of their work. These presentations bring about much discussion on previously held ideas about each of the world areas; how these ideas changed (or were reinforced during the course of the term); how easy or difficult it was to find resources for the project; and comparisons among the groups and between the Portuguese speaking groups and their own English-speaking community.

TARGETED STANDARDS
1.1 Interpersonal Communication
1.2 Interpretive Communication
1.3 Presentational Communication
2.1 Practices of Culture
3.1 Making Connections
4.2 Cultural Comparisons
5.1 School and Community
5.2 Lifelong Learning

Reflections

1.1 Students conduct all class activities in Portuguese.
1.2 Students read material about their assigned "community" and interpret material presented by classmates.
1.3 Students present information to each other in a variety of ways—written, performed, through the Internet.
2.1 Students learn the relationship between the practices of the Portuguese speaking communities and their particular cultural context.
3.1 Students use knowledge acquired in other fields as well as their contacts with other professors in the development of the activities for this scenario.
4.2 Students reflect on their findings in comparison with their own cultural context.
5.1 Students communicate with Portuguese speakers in their community and in the world (through the Internet).
5.2 Students make acquaintances and friends through chat rooms and continue their conversations after the class activity has ended.

Students who participated in this scenario engaged in reflection as well as in learning the new material. At the end of the term, they put together a "book" that included not only their findings, but also their reflections about their discoveries. Students were actively engaged in the process and development of the course from the beginning to the end.

Standards for Russian Language Learning

A Project of the American Council of Teachers of Russian/ American Council for Collaboration in Education and Language Study

AUTHORS

Ruth Edelman, Tenafly High School, NJ
Peter Merrill, Phillips Academy, Andover, MA
Jane Shuffelton, Brighton High School, Rochester, NY

CONSULTANT

Thomas Garza, University of Texas, Austin

REVIEWERS

Thomas R. Beyer, Jr., Middlebury College, VT
Roald Sagdeev, University of Maryland, College Park
Thomas Welch, Jessamine High School, Nicholasville, KY
John Webb, Hunter College High School, New York, NY

RUSSIAN REPRESENTATIVE, BOARD OF DIRECTORS, COLLABORATIVE PROJECT FOR NATIONAL STANDARDS IN FOREIGN LANGUAGE LEARNING

Dan E. Davidson, ACTR, Washington, DC and Bryn Mawr College, PA

Standards for Russian Language Learning

a project of ACTR/ACCELS

Table of Contents

STANDARDS FOR RUSSIAN LANGUAGE LEARNING	**436**
INTRODUCTION: THE STATUS OF RUSSIAN LANGUAGE LEARNING IN THE US TODAY	**437**
The international context: Russia in transition	437
The national context	437
Goals, standards, and sample progress indicators	438
Russian language learning and national goals	439
Heritage learners	441
COMMUNICATION — Goal 1	**442**
CULTURES — Goal 2	**447**
CONNECTIONS — Goal 3	**449**
COMPARISONS — Goal 4	**452**
COMMUNITIES — Goal 5	**456**
FOLLOW-UP QUESTIONS	**459**
SAMPLE LEARNING SCENARIOS	**463**
Art	463
Geography	464
Greetings	464
Letter Writing	465
Map Game	466
Opinion Poll	467
Real Estate	468
Russian Culture in the US	479
Skits	470
Social History in the Lyrics of Igor' Tal'kov	471
Stalin	471
Telephone Book	472
Theater	473

Standards for Russian Language Learning

COMMUNICATION — Goal 1
Communicate in Russian

"Communication is at the heart of second language study, whether the communication takes place face-to-face, in writing, or across centuries through the reading of literature."

Standard 1.1: Students engage in conversation, provide and obtain information, express feelings and emotions, and exchange opinions in Russian.

Standard 1.2: Students understand and interpret written and spoken language on a variety of topics in Russian.

Standard 1.3: Students present information, concepts, and ideas to an audience of listeners or readers on a variety of topics in Russian.

CULTURES — Goal 2
Gain Knowledge and Understanding of Other Cultures

"Through the study of other languages, students gain a knowledge and understanding of the cultures that use that language and, in fact, cannot truly master the language until they have also mastered the cultural contexts in which the language occurs."

Standard 2.1: Students demonstrate an understanding of the relationship between the practices and perspectives of Russian culture.

Standard 2.2: Students demonstrate an understanding of the relationship between the products and perspectives of Russian culture.

CONNECTIONS — Goal 3
Connect with Other Disciplines and Expand Knowledge

"Learning language provides connections to additional bodies of knowledge that may be unavailable to the monolingual English speaker."

Standard 3.1: Students reinforce and further their knowledge of other disciplines through Russian.

Standard 3.2: Students acquire information and recognize the distinctive viewpoints that are only available through Russian and its cultures.

COMPARISONS — Goal 4
Develop Insight into the Nature of Language and Culture

"Through comparisons and contrasts with the language being studied, students develop insight into the nature of language and concept of culture and realize that there are multiple ways of viewing the world."

Standard 4.1: Students demonstrate understanding of the nature of language through comparisons of Russian and their own language.

Standard 4.2: Students demonstrate understanding of the concept of culture through comparisons of Russian culture and their own culture.

COMMUNITIES — Goal 5
Participate in Multilingual Communities at Home and Around the World

"Together, these elements enable the student of language to participate in multilingual communities at home and around the world in a variety of contexts and in culturally appropriate ways."

Standard 5.1: Students use Russian both within and beyond the school setting.

Standard 5.2: Students show evidence of becoming life-long learners by using Russian for personal enjoyment and enrichment.

Introduction
The Status of Russian Language Learning in the United States

THE INTERNATIONAL CONTEXT: RUSSIA IN TRANSITION

Today's adults grew up thinking of Russian as the language of the principal enemy of the United States. The dramatic changes now occurring in that country challenge us to update our views in order to keep pace with vast, ongoing shifts in the world's political and economic spheres. Even after the breakup of the Soviet Union, Russia remains the world's largest country in terms of area (70% larger than Canada, its nearest rival) and sixth largest in population. In addition to being a working language of the United Nations, Russian is an important second language in Eastern Europe, as well as Northern and Central Asia.

Vast natural wealth and huge emerging markets make Russia and its neighbors an area of great economic interest. As international trade increases, the demand for knowledge of Russian and of the region also increases. At the same time, political volatility in the former Soviet republics —important crossroads between Asia and Europe—makes this region significant for geopolitical reasons. It is vital that the United States broaden its base of citizens knowledgeable about this part of the world as we enter the 21st century. Knowledge of the Russian language is a prerequisite for anyone wishing to take part in or simply understand the politics and economies of this region where Russian remains the principal means of communication.

As compelling as reasons associated with money and power might be, the study of any foreign language is also important for the insights that learners gain into a culture different from their own. Russian daily life and cultural institutions have been profoundly influenced by these recent political and economic changes. From a historical perspective, Russia is the land that brought us some of the greatest literature and music of the nineteenth and twentieth centuries. Russian scholars have played important roles in the physical and human sciences. From Prokofiev to Pavlova, Gagarin to Gordeeva, Tchaikovsky to Chekhov, Russia and its people have had, and will continue to have, a substantial influence on the modern world.

THE NATIONAL CONTEXT

Educational reform in the United States took off in a new direction in 1989 when state and national leaders reached consensus on six national education goals for public schools. In 1994 Congress passed Goals 2000: Educate America Act, endorsing those goals and expanding Goal Three to include foreign languages in the core curriculum.

The publication in January 1996 of *Standards for Foreign Language Learning: Preparing for the 21st Century* was the culmination of three years' work by the language profession in developing foreign language standards. The standards include suggestions from

> ... the decisions that the United States and Russia make ... will determine what happens in our world.
> Hillary Rodham Clinton, in Novosibirsk, November 16, 1997

> ... cross-cultural communication is a national issue in the same way that economic competitiveness, national security, education, and healthcare are.
> David E. Maxwell & Richard D. Brecht, "America's Descent into Monolingualism" in *Christian Science Monitor,* November 15, 1996

the volunteer reviewers and language educators in the field. While four national modern language groups wrote the proposal and the Federal government funded it, the project successfully produced a collaborative document containing a vision for the entire foreign language profession.

Simultaneous with the efforts to develop national standards in foreign languages and other disciplines, there has been a great deal of work in many other spheres and at other administrative levels. At the national level, the National Council of Organizations of Less Commonly Taught Languages has developed language learning frameworks for many languages, including the "Language Learning Framework for Russian," to encourage curriculum development that facilitates movement by students across programs. A challenge for the profession in the near future will be to integrate the "Language Learning Framework for Russian" with the *Standards for Russian Language Learning*. Around the country, states and districts have been working to design more detailed standards to meet local needs and have begun the process of translating standards into curriculum.

The present document recasts the so-called generic foreign language standards to address issues specifically related to the teaching of Russian. This document is still very general, however, and is not a description of a curriculum. Rather, its purpose is to set the broadest parameters, here called goals and standards, within which curriculum development can proceed (with or without the prior development of state or local standards). It will be the task of teachers and administrators to develop specific curricula and assessment tools that meet their local needs within the general framework provided by the standards.

The intended role of this document is to serve as a bridge from the so-called "generic standards" found in *Standards for Foreign Language Learning* to more concrete, language-specific standards. It is not intended to be used as a stand-alone document, but rather as a companion to the generic standards from which it flows. There has been no attempt to duplicate here everything of interest in that document, and anyone designing or assessing foreign language curriculum is encouraged to make use of the materials available there.

GOALS, STANDARDS, AND SAMPLE PROGRESS INDICATORS

The goals and standards in *Standards for Foreign Language Learning* are visionary and describe a K-12 foreign language program in a core curriculum for all students and languages. Five broad **goals** define the principal questions which our profession believes are needed to shape foreign language learning experiences. These goals, the "Five Cs," are: Communication, Cultures, Connections, Comparisons, and Communities. These goals should serve as guiding questions as teachers, administrators and communities evaluate, develop, and elaborate foreign language programs.

Within these goals, eleven (**content**) **standards** address more specifically what it is that students should know and be able to do. Each of these standards may be seen as defining a particular area within which students will develop knowledge and abilities. This document intentionally does not contain performance standards. How well each student is able to perform within various content areas is not specified.

Some of what happens in various Russian language programs and classrooms already reflects the standards. However, *Standards for Russian Language Learning* will not be implemented in all programs overnight; rather, they provide a map for future curriculum devel-

---

The key to successful communication: Knowing how, when, and why to say what to whom.

from "Introduction"
Standards for Foreign Language Learning

opment and redesign. As teachers develop new units, as communities discover new needs, it is hoped that the standards will frame their activities.

In order to provide concrete examples of how student performance might demonstrate progress within these content standards, the framework that has been developed makes use of **sample progress indicators** (**SPI**). The SPIs are explicitly not standards; they are not meant to be normative in any way, but, as the name implies, samples of standard-appropriate activities that help in the process of curriculum design and in the assessment of student progress within a particular standard. SPIs have to do with the implementation of standards, and the applicability of an SPI in a particular setting depends on whether it defines an activity that can be realistically achieved at some level of performance by all students in that grade (specifically: 4th, 8th, 12th).

When the national standards were developed, it was decided to define SPIs at grades 4, 8 and 12 in order to align with standards in the other subject areas, all the while recognizing that many schools simply do not have K-12 programs. The Standards Task Force also considered it wise to develop SPIs for grades K-12 because this is the ideal, and to do anything less would be to shortchange the profession, particularly since it is hoped that the standards will guide the profession into the 21st century. When teachers are using the standards to develop curriculum for beginning programs in high schools, where most Russian programs exist, they are urged to study the SPIs for grades 4 and 8 and use them as guides for creating age-appropriate curriculum.

RUSSIAN LANGUAGE LEARNING AND NATIONAL GOALS

The twentieth century has been characterized by an important relationship between the United States and the Russian-speaking world. While the first, and largest, part of the century offered little occasion for contact between students of Russian and Russians overseas, the end of the century sees increased possibilities in many domains. Exchange programs for students, work in banking and commerce, international cooperation in science and environmental projects, issues in civil society and modern health management programs all allow meaningful opportunities to use Russian. The five goals at the heart of the Standards framework aim to promote learning that will allow American students to participate in the world of the twenty-first century.

Communication in Russian will be the foundation for interaction of American students with speakers of Russian in the worlds of business, the arts, the sciences, and the many other areas of mutual interest that will characterize the twenty-first century. A graduate student who began studying Russian in high school may find herself interning in the Moscow office of a multinational corporation, in Novosibirsk working on a project at the Siberian Academy of Sciences, or in Kyrgyzstan working on water management policy in the new republics of Central Asia where Russian remains the *lingua franca*. Ideally, all students will have opportunities for authentic communication with native speakers throughout their language learning experience.

The ability to interact with Russian speakers and Russian language materials will involve understanding the assumptions and world view that people raised in Russian **culture** bring to their language use. The tradition of Russia's cultural heritage will also be open to students of Russian when they can read and discuss literature and history, and when they can understand Russian opera, film, or theater. Seventh graders performing the story "The

> An important part of my message ... is the need for new thinking about Russia, because we are dealing with a fundamentally new Russia.
>
> Secretary of State Madeleine K. Albright, in Moscow, May 2, 1997

Turnip" to an American audience have shared a sense of the importance of folk tales in Russian culture for the underlying values and perspectives they embody.

At the same time, language study can enable students to understand the political relations between Russians and Americans that have dominated the twentieth century. The **connection** with material they learn in social studies courses will enable them to make better sense of Russian and American history. A senior using the World Wide Web for an American history project on American-Soviet relations during World War II may find material in Russian as a source.

Students' comprehension of Russian cultural concepts will bring fresh understanding of aspects of American culture as they make **comparisons**. For example, when they are invited to a home in their own community where Russian is spoken, they will be served a traditional Russian meal. They will also be comparing language systems. The process of learning to function in a language with a different alphabet, very different vocabulary, and radically different language structures will give students insight into the nature of their own language. Elementary school students learning the Cyrillic alphabet will see that not all languages are written the same way as English. Older students may broaden their perspectives to consider the nature of language systems in general.

Strong school programs will prepare students to carry their Russian knowledge into the **community**. First-year Russian students in high school may teach their friends and their parents to count in Russian just because it's fun. More advanced students volunteering in a American hospital may be called on to interpret on a basic level a physician's questions and a patient's complaints. As they continue to learn, they will also seek occasions to involve themselves in the many facets of the Russian-speaking world such as negotiating prices in a Russian store.

Language study involves more than the formal language system, as the national standards indicate. As we look at the separate goals, we see clearly that they blend into an integral whole. Teachers do not teach one of the goals in isolation any more than students use language for only one purpose at a time. It is the combination that makes language interaction meaningful. It is also important to remember that fluency in Russian requires many years of study. Teaching/learning for communication must be seen as a long-term process that should always be a central organizing principle in any program. Students need long-sequence programs, beginning in elementary school, to integrate the complex aspects of Russian.

As we think about the five goal areas together, we see that one of the strong points about the national standards is that they take the teaching of a foreign language beyond the realm of the traditional setting for foreign language learning—the foreign language classroom—where the focus is primarily on communication and the language itself. By encouraging foreign language teachers to take the study of language beyond classroom walls the standards encourage us to make links with other disciplines, to consider the fundamental connection of language to culture and human behaviors, and to involve the learner in the actual marketplace.

A word on implementation is in order. The final section of this document contains a group of sample learning scenarios. As they begin to reframe their teaching, teachers will find that different parts of the curriculum lend themselves to standards-based orientation more readily than others. Advanced courses may be an easier place to try out a relatively lengthy standards-based module, while the introductory level may at first be most susceptible to shorter activities. As teachers and students become acquainted with changes in focus and format, new ideas will emerge and the curriculum can evolve as all the participants gain a deeper understanding of what is involved in successfully integrating the various aspects of the five C's.

HERITAGE LEARNERS

The presence of heritage learners is a new reality in many Russian programs and promises to continue in the twenty-first century. The term should not be taken to signify a homogenous group of students. Heritage learners range all the way from the completely literate student who arrives at age fifteen having read all the classics of Russian literature to the one who was born in the United States, has never learned the Cyrillic alphabet, and knows little grammar. In the first case, the school may place the recent arrival in a Russian class for comfort until she is confident enough to take courses in English. In the second case, the student has needs that are just as complex as the non-heritage learner. Some of those needs are the same as for non-heritage learners, while other needs present distinct challenges to teachers and programs. In between are students who came to the United States at varying ages and with varying levels of linguistic and cultural competency. They are also just as varied as any other group of students in terms of their motivation, study habits, and aspirations.

Programs for these students will involve the same five goals that are central to all K-12 students. For truly literate Russian speakers, some of the standards and sample progress indicators might be adjusted to accommodate their language level. For instance, at grade 12 they might reasonably be reading and analyzing full-length novels, interviewing Russian speakers in the community in depth as part of long research projects, or carrying out research in Russian sources for history class. Heritage learners bring to the classroom a set of expectations different from other students. They may assume that their perceived advantage in vocabulary, and listening and speaking skills guarantees them good grades with little effort. Depending on their background, they may have strong structural competency, with or without the formal terminology to describe it. They may, on the other hand, have ingrained problems in structure or vocabulary that includes numerous anglicisms and overuse of diminutives.

Programs need to approach the heritage learners both in terms of what they bring to the classroom and what they need to correct, maintain, and increase their skills. Teachers need to confront the question of the effect on other learners if the heritage learners are added to a traditional class, or are in classes where they predominate. Some schools might have programs that include classes just for the heritage students, on all the different levels that correspond to their needs. In many schools, however, they will probably continue to be blended into traditional classes.

Communication
Communicate in Russian

Goal One

In recent decades, the foreign language teaching profession has come to embrace a view of its role as focused primarily on the development of communicative competence. While this terminology may sound uncontroversial and the appropriateness of the concept self-evident, communicative competence has not always been the goal of the foreign language profession. Many teachers were learners in an era in which vocabulary acquisition and grammatical accuracy were the unchallenged goals of foreign language programs and many of our teaching tools reflect this fact. The reorientation of our profession to the promotion of communicative competence is, thus, a change that requires teachers to examine carefully their practices and materials.

In *Standards for Foreign Language Learning* this goal is addressed in terms of communicative modes. These modes are defined using two parameters: one-way and two-way communication and productive and receptive skills. The interpersonal mode concerns two-way, interactive communication, the interpretive mode addresses receptive skills (one-way), and the presentational mode has to do with productive skills (one-way). Standards 1.1, 1.2, and 1.3 therefore represent a significant assertion regarding the structure of how to teach and acquire communicative competence.

In reading the sample progress indicators that follow each standard, it is important to keep in mind the nature of the SPIs. They do not carry with them any presuppositions about how well the activities that they describe are performed. They are perhaps best viewed as suggestions about objectives that fit with the standards, and directions—regarding both content and pedagogical approach—in which planning might try to move a curriculum. It is also not intended that the entire collection of SPIs must be part of every curriculum. While it may be possible in some languages and in some programs to address several of the SPIs at a given grade level, individual programs must set realistic goals for their students and teachers. Implementation of these standards will presumably take place gradually as curriculum redesign is experimented with and evaluated. A very reasonable first step might be to focus on a few progress indicators according to the needs and possibilities of a program and evaluate the success of each change as it is implemented, presumably over the course of several years.

STANDARD 1.1 Students engage in conversations, provide and obtain information, express feelings and emotions, and exchange opinions in Russian.

This standard addresses the interpersonal mode of communication. It is not by happenstance that this standard is the first; its placement accords well with the belief widely shared among foreign language teachers that helping students to acquire the ability to participate in two-way communication lies at the heart of our professional responsibility. As suggested above regarding the general goal of communication, however, this standard implies a great deal beyond the acquisition of vocabulary and the mastery of grammar. Programs that have been influenced by the so-called proficiency movement, on the other hand, may be more accustomed to thinking about and designing a curriculum that accords with this component of a standards-based approach.

Sample Progress Indicators, Grade 4

- Students follow simple instructions in order to participate in age-appropriate classroom activities (e.g., simple commands to listen, repeat, go to the board).
- Students ask and answer simple questions about topics such as family, school, and hometown.
- Students share likes and dislikes with each other and the class.
- Students exchange descriptions of people, places and tangible products of Russian culture such as foods, types of dwellings, and seasons with each other and the members of the class.
- Students exchange essential information such as greetings, leave-taking, and common classroom interactions using culturally appropriate gestures and oral expressions (e.g., привет 'hi,' Что на завтра 'What's (due) for tomorrow;' and perhaps standing when the teacher enters the room).

Sample Progress Indicators, Grade 8

- Students follow and give simple instructions and directions for participating in age-appropriate classroom activities (e.g., preparing skits, working in reading groups, doing cooperative research). They ask and respond to questions for clarification.
- Students exchange information on topics such as personal events, subjects in school, likes and dislikes, extracurricular activities and seasons with peers, teachers and/or native Russian speakers.
- Students, compare, contrast, and express opinions and preferences about the information gathered regarding events, subjects in school, likes and dislikes, extracurricular activities and seasons.
- Students acquire goods and information orally.
- Students raise and discuss issues and problems related to the school or community through group work (e.g., peer relationships, cafeteria food, volunteering at senior center).

Sample Progress Indicators, Grade 12

- Students discuss, orally or in writing, their reactions to material they have read on Russian culture, history, or significant events (e.g., the October Revolution, Stalinism, holidays, the life and poetry of Akhmatova).
- Students exchange commentary on issues and problems that are of concern to them and to Russians (e.g., future plans, economy, violence, roles of women and men).
- Students share their reactions with classmates, with heritage learners in the Russian program, with pen pals or electronic pen pals in Russia. They compare reactions to films such as *Kolya*, current popular music, painters of the Russian avant-garde.

- Students use interactive technology (e.g., e-mail, interactive television links) to exchange perspectives and opinions on a variety of topics of interest such as school, travel, music, and politics.
- Students discuss their understanding of Russian practices and perspectives (e.g., on family life, free time, school, jobs) or products (e.g., clothes, food, technology) with heritage learners who are their classmates.

STANDARD 1.2 Students understand and interpret written and spoken language on a variety of topics in Russian.

Standard 1.2 addresses the interpretive—one-way, receptive—mode of communication. The written component of this standard has long been at the center of foreign language instruction. This standard may, however, require that teachers devote more attention to their students' understanding of spoken Russian. The variety of topics considered within a Russian program can be broadened appreciably as students gain in proficiency and as they mature. Clearly this standard can intersect in very interesting ways with each of the other goal areas.

Sample Progress Indictors, Grade 4

- Students comprehend main ideas and identify the principal characters in developmentally appropriate oral texts such as songs, poems, tales, cartoons, and other texts based on familiar themes (e.g., "Очи чёрные," "Вакса-Клякса," "Ладушки," "Ну, погоди!").
- Students identify people and objects in their environment, or from other school subjects, based on oral description.
- Students comprehend brief, written messages and short personal notes on familiar topics such as family, school, and hometown.
- Students comprehend the principle message contained in media such as posters and advertisements (e.g., Soviet-era posters with messages of the type Миру мир or newer posters addressing problems such as alcohol and drug abuse).

Sample Progress Indicators, Grade 8

- Students comprehend information and messages related to other school subjects (e.g., Russian names and phrases in science and social studies).
- Students understand announcements and messages connected to daily activities in Russian culture (e.g., understanding the cost of something in a store or which stop to get off on the metro).
- Students understand some aspects of topics from other subjects and products of Russian culture as presented on TV, radio, video, or in live presentations.
- Students identify the principal characters and comprehend the main ideas in selected literary texts such as children's stories, poems, folk tales, and anecdotes (e.g., stories and poems by Lifshits, Marshak, Tolstoy, Zaxoder).

- Students use knowledge acquired in other settings and from other subject areas to comprehend spoken and written messages in Russian.

Sample Progress Indicators, Grade 12

- Students demonstrate an understanding of the main ideas and significant details of presentations and discussions of events or issues that they are studying (e.g., Russian avant-garde artists or personal narratives of Russian visitors).

- Students demonstrate an understanding of the principal elements of written material in the form of e-mail or other print media on topics of immediate or historical importance (e.g., the political situation, reports on the economy, simple narratives of victims of Soviet-era repression, letters from pen pals).

- Students demonstrate an increasing understanding of the cultural nuances of meaning in written and spoken Russian as expressed in formal and informal settings. For example, they notice the use of terms of endearment in film, or songs such as "Миленький ты мой" or folktales such as "Терем, теремок," "Каша из топора", or "Колобок."

- Students can relate the main plot and describe the characters of short authentic literary texts, or describe the events in brief excerpts from longer texts such as Natalya Baranskaya's *Неделя как неделя*, Viktoria Tokareva's *Старая собака*, or Vladimir Gilyarovsky's *Москва и москвичи*. Advanced heritage learners can read longer texts in their entirety and write longer analyses of them. For example, they can read and appreciate classic and modern prose (Tolstoy, Bulgakov, I. Grekova, Ginzburg), history (*Страницы истории*), and poetry (Pushkin, Akhmatova, Tsvetaeva).

STANDARD 1.3 Students present information, concepts, and ideas to an audience of listeners or readers on a variety of topics in Russian.

Moving beyond conversation-oriented skills, the development of proficiency in the presentational mode of this standard is a valuable life-skill as well as an important foreign language-specific mode of communication. In this vein, it is important for teachers to discuss not simply organization and linguistic accuracy, but also issues that bear on making an effective presentation—demonstrated enthusiasm and involvement, for example. As with each of the other standards relating to communication, there is a wealth of potential for interaction with the other C's. It is perhaps tautological to point out that communication presupposes content, but careful thought by the teacher as to the nature of this content can bear fruit if the other C's are used as a framework for course and curriculum design.

Sample Progress Indicators, Grade 4

- Students prepare illustrated stories on topics such as themselves, family, school, and hometown and share these stories with an audience such as the class.

- Students dramatize songs, short anecdotes, or poetry for members of other elementary classes.

- Students give short oral presentations about people and things at home and in their school environment and exchange information with another language class.

- Students tell or retell stories orally or in illustrated written form.

- Students tell in Russian about products and/or practices of their own culture to each other and other members of the class.

Sample Progress Indicators, Grade 8

- Students present short plays and skits, recite selected poems, and perform songs in Russian for the class, other classes, and school-related events (e.g., "Парус," "Я вас любил," "Калинка," "Катюша").

- Students prepare tape- or video- recorded messages to share in class, with school peers, and/or with native Russian speakers on topics of personal interest.

- Students prepare short paragraphs on topics such as personal experiences, school, home life, extra-curricular activities to share with classmates and/or native Russian speakers.

- Students prepare a brief oral or written summary of the main idea and characters in selected pieces of age-appropriate literature in Russian such as children's stories and poems, cartoons, and folktales.

Sample Progress Indicators, Grade 12

- Students prepare and present in Russian a substantive oral and written presentation on a topic in Russian culture (e.g., an artist, composer, scientist, historical figure or event) as a final course project.

- Students perform scenes from plays, recite poems, or relate folktales that are familiar to Russian speakers (e.g., Chekhov's *Чайка*, Tsvetaeva's "Только девочка," or the folktale "Кощей бессмертный").

- Students prepare pieces in Russian of creative writing or short articles for a student publication or for a joint e-mail project with a Russian school. Topics might include original poetry, personal narratives, surveys on gender roles, statistics on use of free time.

- Students present summaries in Russian of material they have researched on the Internet or other media sources on a topic of interest (e.g., Lenin, song lyrics, sites of interest in sister cities).

Cultures

Goal Two

Gain Knowledge and Understanding of Other Cultures

To understand a culture is to understand how its practices and products relate to one another and to the perspectives of the members of that culture. In talking with Russians about their daily life (their practices), a student may come to understand that families serve different functions in that culture, that there are different expectations associated with friendship, that individualism has different connotations in the two cultures, or that prestige is associated with very different sets of professions. Examining a popular magazine might lead to observations concerning differences in clothing, advertisements, or seats in school (products) which correlate with different perspectives in these spheres of life. Viewing a culture through its practices and products induces students to examine a wide range of topics from a different set of perspectives. Practices range from intensely personal to small-group to societal; products can be tangible or intangible and reflect so-called "high culture" or daily life.

STANDARD 2.1 Students demonstrate an understanding of the relationship between the practices and perspectives of Russian culture.

Whether on the playground or in the foreign language classroom, helping a student understand another person's perspective is perhaps one of the most difficult tasks that a teacher faces. In the foreign language classroom these different perspectives are not isolated phenomena, but are part of a web of interconnected interpretations of events, behaviors, and beliefs. A discussion about Russian attitudes towards marriage cannot avoid the topic of housing, for example.

The difficulty posed by the inherent complexity of culture is compounded for language teachers in that there is no agreed upon grammar of culture parallel to the reasonably well developed and shared sense of grammar of language that guides us in our approach to the linguistic side of language acquisition. As the profession implements this standard, it will be important for us to share not only particular activities that have proven successful, but also to maintain an ongoing conversation regarding the development of a shared general framework for our approach to Russian culture and its practices.

Sample Progress Indicators, Grade 4

- Students observe and identify simple patterns of behavior or interaction in settings such as school and family (e.g., noticing that Russian schoolchildren traditionally stand when a teacher enters the room).

- Students use appropriate gestures and simple oral expressions for greetings and leave-takings (e.g., the formal vs. informal ways of saying "hello" and "goodbye" in Russian).

- Students participate in age-appropriate Russian cultural activities (such as games, songs, birthday celebrations, and stories read in class).

Sample Progress Indicators, Grade 8
- Students recognize, identify and discuss Russian patterns of behavior or interaction in settings such as school, family and community (e.g., in classroom behavior, the particular way young Russian schoolchildren raise their hands in class; or in the relationship of the family at home, the way children relate to their grandparents who often live with the family).

- Students use appropriate gestures and oral expressions for simple activities (e.g., making phone calls, gift-giving, using transportation).

- Students learn about and participate in age-appropriate Russian cultural practices (e.g., games, sports, folk and contemporary music, and holiday celebrations).

Sample Progress Indicators, Grade 12
- Students compare attitudes and expectations in Russia and the US regarding cooperative learning, both in and out of the classroom, including views as to what constitutes cheating.

- Students discuss dating patterns among Russian teenagers by e-mail with Russian pen pals.

- Students learn about and discuss the process by which young Russians make career decisions.

- In discussions with Russian émigrés living in their community, students learn about Russian superstitions and when they are likely to pop up in day-to-day life.

STANDARD 2.2 Students demonstrate an understanding of the relationship between the products and perspectives of Russian culture.

The introduction of realia—of real Russian products—into the language learning context is a superb approach to opening a conversation that can lead to interesting observations about connections between products and perspectives. The student дневник "diary," for example, has no parallel in American schools, and can easily open the door to long and interesting discussions about many aspects of the Russian education system. American students may have a difficult time understanding such a different system and the physical artifact provides a tangible indication of how such a system might work.

Sample Progress Indicators, Grade 4
- Students observe and identify tangible products of Russian culture such as souvenirs, types of buildings, clothes, and food.

- Students encounter expressive products of Russian culture such as children's songs, folk tales, and types of artwork enjoyed or produced by their peer group in Russian culture.

- Students produce types of artwork representative of Russian culture, such as nature scenes, foods, and activities, and compare them with similar artwork done by Russian students.

- Students recognize themes, ideas, and perspectives as they relate to products of Russian culture. For example, students discuss the concept of Russian "Tea" and the significance of the samovar.

Sample Progress Indicators, Grade 8

- Students read, listen to, observe, and/or perform expressive products of Russian culture (e.g. children's stories and poems, songs, short skits, and dance).

- Students identify and look for products and representatives of Russian culture (e.g., athletes, musicians, dancers, foods, technology) found in their homes, school, and society.

- Students identify and discuss themes, ideas, and perspectives related to the products being examined. For example, students discuss the important contributions to society made by Russian athletes, musicians, artists, and scientists.

Sample Progress Indicators, Grade 12

- Students examine advertising in print media and on television and ask Russian pen pals whether the values that seem to be in evidence in the media reflect the values they hold.

- Students watch a video about a Russian teenager's birthday party and make observations about the people in attendance and their activities and interests.

- Students interview émigrés about their favorite poems and poets and discuss the place of literature in Russian society.

- Students analyze the rations of cosmonauts for insights on Russian dietary habits.

Connections *Goal Three*
Connect with Other Disciplines and Acquire Information

When they are engaged in learning to communicate in Russian and in gaining insight into cultural perspectives, students make connections to other core subject areas such as social studies, the arts, science, mathematics, English, and technology. They bring to those other areas their Russian knowledge base and thus have opportunities for interdisciplinary learning. A student explains to his history class the semantic implications of the Russian name of Ivan the Terrible. Students might discuss the significant effect that the launching of Sputnik had on education in the United States in the 1950s and '60s. It is important to note that this goal does not imply one-way connectivity; teachers should also seek to use knowledge from other disciplines to enhance the study of Russian. For example, the American preoccupation with opinion polls has caught on in Russia, and students may find that their relative sophistication in interpreting such information is useful as they analyze data from a poll taken in Russia.

More advanced students may have occasion to use Russian to explore topics of interest in a variety of subject areas. Access to information through various media within and beyond the school setting helps clarify and enhance the language learning process as an integral part of the entire school and life experience.

One of the most profound ways to address this goal is by means of content-based instruction. Learning in another discipline through the medium of a foreign language is a highly effective way to deepen understanding in both disciplines simultaneously. The excitement surrounding the Internet provides an easy entrée for nudging students in the direction of connections. Visiting Russian web sites provides an immediacy to the topic and a sense of relevance to language learning that we could only dream about less than a decade ago.

STANDARD 3.1 Students reinforce and further their knowledge of other disciplines through the study of Russian.

As students encounter new material in textbooks, the material may seem sterile and its inclusion unmotivated. By approaching the same material from a different perspective, students can more easily appreciate its significance and purpose. What may have seemed like a random collection of facts in a presentation on pollution in a social studies course, for example, may be seen to stem from a coherent framework when it is reified by a second perspective—when a Russian class discusses the Aral Sea. From relatively concrete topics such as the metric system to more abstract topics like the relationships between physical geography and invasion patterns or weather patterns, this connection-oriented standard can play a significant role in students' intellectual growth by deepening their understanding of systems and patterns across disciplines.

Sample Progress Indicators, Grade 4

- Students learn vocabulary in Russian on topics studied in other subject areas such as family, weather, nature, seasons, animals, or geography.

- Students look at a variety of sources (pictures, maps, videos) related to topics in other subject areas and identify items in Russian.

- Students use numbers in Russian to enhance their knowledge of math and science facts.

Sample Progress Indicators, Grade 8

- Students acquire vocabulary in Russian to reinforce their studies of topics in history, geography, science, math, or the arts. For example, students learn the origins of words like "Kremlin" and "Red Square" which enhances their knowledge of history.

- Students seek out short articles and advertisements, in print or on television in

Russian on topics being studied in other classes. These topics might include scientific discoveries, space travel, or famous historical figures.

- Students comprehend short videos in Russian that relate to other areas such as social studies, science, technology, or the arts.

Sample Progress Indicators, Grade 12

- Students integrate their knowledge of Russian culture through school activities in art and music. One example might be the student who brings to a rehearsal of a piece of Russian music her understanding of the contributions of Russian composers to the history of world music.

- Students demonstrate and augment their knowledge of Russia as they study topics in history, geography, economics, and government.

- Students demonstrate understanding of the Russian sociopolitical foundations for terminology used in the social sciences.

STANDARD 3.2 Students acquire information and recognize the distinctive viewpoints that are available only through knowledge of Russian language and culture.

While standard 3.1 is concerned with the effective reinforcement of learning in other disciplines that can be contributed by a foreign language program, standard 3.2 addresses the next step: the acquisition of "new" knowledge through Russian; that is, knowledge that becomes available to the learner only through the use of Russian. A middle school social studies project paper may include information from Russian-language materials; a high school science paper may be informed by an approach to research that is characteristically Russian; a report on space exploration might discuss different philosophies concerning modeling and certainty that permeate the space programs in the US and Russia.

This standard "goes beyond" the culture standards in that it involves a kind of analysis that transcends understanding the cultural system. This standard encourages students to understand consequences, and in this sense is a bridge to the fourth C: Comparisons.

Sample Progress Indicators, Grade 4

- Students listen to folktales, stories, and poems in Russian that illustrate various cultural and historical practices (e.g., folktales such as "Два Ивана", poems by Marshak).

- Students listen to and sing songs in Russian on topics such as birthdays and other celebrations (e.g., the Russian birthday song "Крокодил Генф").

- Students find Russian pictures and souvenirs to enhance their exploration of other topics. For example, students look at souvenirs such as matrioshkas and samovars and find pictures of various types of Russian art such as icons and works by artists such as Repin, Kandinsky, Chagall.

Sample Progress Indicators, Grade 8

- Students acquire information about Russian folklore, holidays, school life, and family customs through a variety of sources (e.g., short stories, folktales, conversations with native speakers).

- Students use a variety of sources (e.g., newspapers, magazines, videos, e-mail, Internet) to recognize Russian perspectives as they relate to other areas such as history, literature, the arts, science, or technology.

Sample Progress Indicators, Grade 12

- Students read, observe, and listen to a variety of sources intended for Russian speakers of their age on topics of interest. Music, the Internet, films, literature, and other media provide information in Russian that they can compare to information available in English.

- Students demonstrate comprehension of Russian perspectives or practices and products that have been factors in world history, literature, and the arts (e.g., icons, the Stanislavsky method, or the name of Petrograd/Petersburg).

- Students relate their knowledge of Russian folklore, holidays, school life, and family customs to practices in other cultures. In English class, for example, grade 10 students might present information on Russian folklore as it bears on their readings, while in a World Religions course grade 12 students might present information on Russian Orthodox holidays.

Comparisons   *Goal Four*

Develop Insight into the Nature of Language and Culture

This goal focuses on the way students compare Russian language and culture with American English and its cultures. The extent to which English-language structures differ from those of Russian makes students reflect on the nature and possibilities of language in general. Detailed analysis of Russian word order, for example, might help a student come to a better understanding of paragraph structure in English.

Similarly, as students discover that different cultures have different ways of life, they may become more receptive to unfamiliar ways of doing things and not immediately judge them good or bad, right or wrong. In so doing, they deepen their understanding of the systematic nature of culture as it relates to practices and products. The education systems of Russia and America are substantially different from one another. Learning what takes place in the course of their counterparts' education in Russia may provide new perspectives on issues that seem as diverse as career choice and social policy.

STANDARD 4.1 Students demonstrate understanding of the nature of language through comparisons of Russian and their own language.

It is common to hear Russian teachers complain about the fact that their beginning students seem not to possess even a rudimentary understanding of grammar—even in their native language. This is clearly a place of opportunity for Russian teachers to jump in and fill the gap. If any part of the standards system is second nature for the Russian teaching profession, it is perhaps the possibilities for comparative analysis of language structures underlined by standard 4.1. How often have we heard students exclaim, "So that's what a direct object is!" In like fashion, as students come to a fuller understanding of the case system, they are in a better position to understand what their English teacher means when she marks an instance of faulty parallelism.

Sample Progress Indicators, Grade 4

- Students listen to and recognize similarities and differences in the Russian and English alphabets.

- Students look at and recognize the similarities and differences of the letters of the Russian and English alphabets (e.g. size, appearance, number of letters).

- Students recognize that there are some words in Russian that sound similar and have the same meaning as in English, such as "taxi" and "radio".

- Students compare ways of saying "hello" and "goodbye" in Russian and in English.

- Students are aware of the similarities and differences in first names in Russian and in English (e.g., Cathy and Katya vs. Igor).

Sample Progress Indicators, Grade 8

- Students are aware that there are words in Russian that have the same meaning as in English (cognates such as metro, mama).

- Students demonstrate an awareness that Russian has grammatical gender where English does not and the role that plays in expression.

- Students demonstrate an awareness that there are certain grammatical points in English that do not exist in Russian (e.g., no verb "to be" in the present tense, no articles).

- Students demonstrate an awareness in Russian of formal and informal forms in Russian when addressing different people.

Sample Progress Indicators, Grade 12

- Students recognize some Russian words with Indo-European roots that are similar to English (брат 'brother,' сестра 'sister,' видеть 'to see,' cf. 'video'). They discuss the ways in which languages develop and are related.

Standards for Russian Language Learning

- Students recognize the importance of word order in English, realizing that English does not change noun forms to indicate grammatical function (direct object).

- Students consider the difficulties that English presents to speakers of Russian (articles, tenses).

- Students of several foreign languages realize the relationship between the relative number of cognates with English in Russian and the other language they study. They accept the impact of this factor on the longer sequence of time required to learn Russian.

- The limits of possibility in language structure become evident as students realize that an alphabet may present letters in a different order, but people can't change the order in which they count things.

- Students question the way languages evolve over time and understand that both English and Russian continue to add vocabulary, modify usage, and reinterpret the norms of formal use.

STANDARD 4.2 Students demonstrate understanding of the concept of culture through comparisons of Russian culture and their own culture.

A direct consequence to the Cultures goal, addressing standard 4.2 is almost unavoidable once students have begun to understand even the most basic cultural differences. The challenge for many language teachers lies in their own sense of inadequacy as culture teachers. Trained in language study, linguistics or literary analysis, many teachers feel ill-prepared to address the issues surrounding a productive comparison of cultures. We have less experience with the process of the acquisition of culture knowledge, and some may be fearful that their students will become stuck at the stage where they focus on what they perceive to be "weird" in Russian culture. Alternatively, language teachers may launch into presentations that include culture but not feel that they know how to structure their presentations or which topics to include. This vital topic will require in the future the kind of intensive attention that linguistics and literature have enjoyed in the past.

Sample Progress Indicators, Grade 4

- Students recognize the different ways in which Russians and Americans celebrate holidays and birthdays. (e.g., types of foods, songs, gifts).

- Students observe similarities and differences in Russian and American activities (e.g., playing sports, eating meals, spending free time).

- Students observe and compare Russian and American toys, souvenirs, games.

Sample Progress Indicators, Grade 8

- Students discuss and compare simple patterns of behavior and interaction both at home and at school.

- Students discuss the similarities and differences in the cultural practices involved in Russian holidays, celebrations, and birthdays (e.g., the differences in Easter and Christmas celebrations based on different religious traditions).

- Students observe the similarities and differences in Russian contemporary culture (especially teenage culture) by watching television and looking at newspapers and magazines.

- Students are aware of the similarities and differences in cultural perspectives as expressed in Russian songs, folktales, and children's poetry (e.g., students compare Russian and American birthday songs, look for similarities and differences in works of children's authors such as Kornei Chukovsky and Dr. Seuss).

Sample Progress Indicators, Grade 12

- Students compare the place of automobiles in teenage culture in Russia and the U.S. by examining such things as television and print advertising, teenage driving and the American preoccupation with getting a license, driver education courses, alternative forms of transportation, and the acceptance of seat belts, stop signs, and other rules.

- Students recognize the relative preoccupation with hygiene in American culture as compared to Russian culture.

- Students observe a society going through the process of dramatic political and economic change and the effects on people's outlook. They speculate on the way Russian teenagers feel about the future compared to the way they see their own lives.

- Students look at the definition of "American" and "Russian" in the context of the breakup of the Soviet Union.

- Students identify and analyze cultural perspectives reflected in Russian poetry, folk tales, songs, and short stories. They encounter the immense respect for poetry in Russian culture and reflect on American equivalents.

- Students recognize the importance of terms of endearment (ласкательные формы) and proverbs as reflecting Russian cultural perspectives. They consider American use of nicknames and sayings in daily conversation. At the same time, some heritage learners may have to relearn a great deal of standard (non-diminutive) vocabulary.

- Students examine the definition of "American" and "Russian" by considering, for example, information on birth certificates and other documents, hyphenated terms such as "Korean-American," bilingual education and the existence of non-Russian schools in the NIS, Russians in the other republics, and how heritage learners define their identity.

- Students discuss the way Russians and Americans view the world as citizens in countries with vast geographical space. At the same time, they recognize the effect of wars and invasions on the Russian psyche compared to the relative freedom from war on American territory.

Communities
Goal Five
Participate in Multilingual Communities at Home and Around the World

Expanding knowledge of Russian enriches the student's life beyond the classroom and beyond grade 12. Understanding Russian language and culture opens the way to appreciation of myriad aspects of the wider community. Combined with personal interests in other fields, Russian allows opportunities for professional and individual development. The news and other media, the arts, sciences and political life, contacts with native speakers in the community and in travel, telecommunications, are some of the many venues for integrating language study with daily life.

Unless the study of Russian begins early, in grades below high school, students will not have developed enough vocabulary resources to undertake major research projects, read and analyze long classic literary texts or engage in complex discussions with native speakers by grade 12. Nonetheless, from the beginning of their Russian career they will be alert to instances of Russian cultural, historical, political, and linguistic references they encounter beyond the classroom. When they overhear émigrés conversing in the supermarket, for instance, they will be eager to try to understand some of the conversation and even try out their conversational skills. When political and economic events in Russia appear on the evening news, they will help their families understand the geography or the history involved. If they become captivated by the study of Russian, they will go on to develop areas of personal enrichment that involve the language and culture at the postsecondary level. They will want to spend a college term or year in the culture, do research projects of interest, go on to advanced study and professional lives that integrate their language skills and other interests.

STANDARD 5.1 Students use Russian both within and beyond the school setting.

This standard represents an important way to bring life and immediacy to the learning of Russian as a supplement to classroom work, but at the same time requires that Russian teachers, already stretched by the demands of maintaining a program for a less commonly taught language, find ways to stretch themselves still further. Finding Russian émigrés and setting up situations for students to interact with them, arranging field trips to Russian films or traveling exhibits from Russia, or establishing contacts with a family services program for émigrés that will allow community service projects are all wonderful ways to help students realize that learning Russian is not simply a classroom exercise. Each of these also requires a great deal of time to initiate and maintain, and it will be important for teachers to integrate these valuable activities into their program in ways that are effective but not exhausting.

Sample Progress Indicators, Grade 4
- Students sing Russian songs for others in the school or community.

- Students draw pictures of aspects of Russian culture to show to others.
- Students present information about Russian language and culture to others.
- Students use the Russian words for "hello" and "goodbye" and other courtesy phrases with other Russian speakers.

Sample Progress Indicators, Grade 8
- Students participate in class discussions with others who speak Russian on topics such as the weather, likes and dislikes, and daily activities.
- Students sing Russian songs and perform short Russian skits for others in the school or community.
- Students expand their interest in and knowledge of Russian using the Internet and e-mail.
- Students engage in simple conversations with Russian speakers in the community (e.g. talking about themselves, their town, asking simple questions).

Sample Progress Indicators, Grade 12
- Students engage in classroom discussion with invited members of the community who have had experience in Russia, for example veterans, gulag survivors, school graduates working in Russia.
- Students use Russian to help Russian speakers they encounter in the community—in after-school jobs, church or temple functions, volunteer work —in situations such as giving directions, explaining prices, aiding with bus routes.
- Students converse with heritage speaker students in the school and enjoy language club activities with them (e.g., dinners, films, club meetings). Students welcome new Russian speakers to the school and help them understand the local culture.
- Students carry their interest and knowledge of Russian into research for other school courses as they look for information on the web, participate in e-mail projects, compare pieces of literature.

STANDARD 5.2 Students show evidence of becoming lifelong learners by using Russian for personal enjoyment and enrichment.

An important vehicle for addressing this standard is role modeling. We cannot require that students enjoy anything; we can show them what it is that we enjoy and why. We can bring literature, events, people to their attention and hope that their curiosity has been sufficiently piqued to want to read, participate in, go to meet—that is, to take advantage of the opportunities surrounding, of which they might not have been aware. Many teachers are already in the habit of pointing out and encouraging kids to be involved with what is, in fact, a new facet of their world. Linking learning to life is perhaps one of the most overlooked aspects of teaching the whole student.

Sample Progress Indicators, Grade 4

- Students watch Russian cartoons and musical events (e.g., "Кот Леопольд," "Чебурашка").

- Students listen to and sing Russian songs (e.g., "Бумажный солдат," "Пропала собака").

- Students play Russian games (e.g., Гуси, гуси; Городки).

- Students know Russian sports and entertainment figures.

Sample Progress Indicators, Grade 8

- Students acquire vocabulary to talk about topics of personal interest.

- Students sing Russian songs and listen to Russian music (both classical and contemporary).

- Students watch Russian television programs such as sports matches and musical events.

- Students gather information on a variety of Russian topics such as famous people, historical events, and scientific achievements using the Internet.

- Students learn Russian sports cheers.

Sample Progress Indicators, Grade 12

- Students are alert to news from Russia and they share with family and friends knowledge of Russian holidays, traditions, economic and political factors, and history.

- Students know Russian songs, folk tales, classical music, art and recognize references to them in the media (e.g., the story behind a famous opera). Students might recognize a Russian tune they have heard and sing the words.

- Students engage in cultural events and social activities with Russian themes (Russian club activities, films, sister city events)

- Students maintain relationships with Russian speakers (e.g., exchange students, pen pals, heritage learners, neighbors).

- Students seek information on postsecondary institutions that have Russian programs.

Follow-up Questions

While more specific than the volume on generic language standards on which this volume is based, this document will, nevertheless, raise questions having to do with interpretation and application of the document by an intentionally broad audience. The following information, presented in a question-and-answer format, is designed to anticipate some of the possible questions that may arise in the minds of various readers:

Why do these standards include grades K-8 where there are very few Russian programs?
The goals and standards represent a picture of an ideal situation in American education, a vision of where we would like to be rather than where we are. While some programs begin in early grades, the usual practice at the moment sees students enrolling in secondary programs, often as 13-year-old learners. Given the length of time required to learn Russian, study beginning in early grades is a desirable goal to allow more students to reach the progress indicators at grade 12 and continue to postsecondary programs with strong skills. Also, since the generic standards for foreign language education are based on the K-12 model in all the other disciplines, the Russian standards conform to this model.

If students typically don't start Russian before high school, how can they get to the same levels as the other languages? How can the same goals and standards apply to Russian as the other languages?
First, the standards and progress indicators are not proficiency assessments. They are descriptors of what students will be doing, not measures of how well they will be performing. At the same time, given the fact that students begin Russian later and given the extra length of time required in Russian, the progress indicators for Russian are not exactly the same as in other languages. A student who begins Russian in grade 9 or even grade 7 typically cannot read and analyze in Russian one of the longer nineteenth century Russian novels by grade 12, even in the ideal program.

Where is the language content? When am I supposed to teach the accusative case and what exactly are they supposed to know by the end of grade 12?
The standards are content standards in the broad sense. They do not prescribe specific topics for particular levels, nor do they define language learning in terms of structures to be mastered. They are not a curriculum. They are descriptors of activities that students and teachers will engage in both in and beyond the classroom, based on the overarching goals of communication, culture, etc. *Standards for Foreign Language Learning* contains a very useful metaphor for approaching this question: the "weave of curricular elements" (p. 28). Knowledge of the language system is one of the strands of this weave which also contains other important strands such as critical thinking skills, learning strategies, and the five C's of the standards. The comparison with weaving is highly appropriate since the design of an integrated, multi-level curriculum—especially one that spans elementary, middle and high school education—must encompass a vast array of types of knowledge.

How will a program based on these goals and standards prepare students who want to continue into more traditional postsecondary programs? What will happen when students who began the study of Russian in a K-12 program want to move on to college courses where communicative skills are valued, but where other advanced level linguistic and cognitive skills— for example, a specific theoretical knowledge of Russian grammatical structures—may be expected?

While these Standards do not directly address the issue of articulation across programs, they are part of a continuing national dialogue on language learning and its components. The discussion involved how best to prepare students all the way from K-12 through the undergraduate college level and beyond. Pre-college programs that reflect a focus on the five C's, on the goals and standards of this document and the generic *Standards* document, will produce Russian students who enter college programs with certain habits of language learning and use. They will bring with them expectations about Russian programs that teachers in postsecondary programs will want to acknowledge and accommodate. To maintain these students in their courses, to encourage them in a variety of interests, college programs will need to recognize both the strengths and the needs that students will bring. For example, secondary school graduates may not know rules for participle formation, or be able to analyze hard and soft adjective endings, but they may be adept at creating videos that demonstrate their ability to speak about topics such as the weather in Russian. They may not know the vocabulary necessary to appreciate Pushkin, but they may have the linguistic and cultural skills to negotiate a telephone call in Russian or shop in a Russian store. Postsecondary programs will want to maintain and encourage these students as lifelong learners by building on the strengths that they bring and supplying the other features of language study that they will need. For more detailed discussion of this issue, see the Language Learning Framework for Russian (cited above) available at the ACTR website (http://www.actr.org) or at the National Foreign Language Center website (http://www.councilnet.org).

This, however, may be viewed as a short-term answer. Work has already begun on extending the standards, and especially the SPIs, from K-12 to K-16 with the hope of addressing the question of articulation in a more uniform fashion. Some of the language-specific documents in this volume contain such SPIs, and it is the intent of the professional organizations involved in the development of the language-specific standards that the next edition of the standards will pertain to K-16 programs across the board.

What about the native speakers? Can you tell me more about how these standards will help me to serve them in our local Russian program?

One approach that is sometimes suggested—and that we do not recommend—is simply that the way to treat heritage learners is to persuade them to drop the course, forbid them to take Russian, or deny them certain portions of coursework. Testing may be revised for them so that they are not allowed to take the oral parts of exams, and thus can never get an "easy A". Such an approach makes the teacher's life simpler, but certainly does nothing to help serve the students' needs or maintain programs.

Where heritage learners are blended with and sometimes even predominate over non-heritage students, one immediate concern to teachers must be that of attitude and the affective atmosphere in the classroom. It does not help to have the teacher constantly trying to prove linguistic or cultural superiority over native speakers who assume they know everything better. Even in cases where the teacher is right, the classroom becomes a battleground where time is lost in skirmishes over all sorts of issues. With even the most helpful and non-confrontational Russian speakers in the room, non-heritage students may feel at a disadvantage, and the teacher may need a variety of strategies to reassure them.

One of the many complexities in working with these students is the question of their own perceived identity. Initial Russian 1 lessons may include as a conversation question, "Are you Russian? Are you American?" The answers from a class that includes heritage learners are very revealing. They do not necessarily and neatly fall into the distinction Guadelupe Valdes makes about Spanish speakers. It is not always the case that only the recent émigrés see themselves as "Russian" and those who have been here longer see themselves as "American." Sometimes students who have been here eight or nine years still identify themselves as "Russian," while others claim to be "American" and still others claim the label "Russian/American" or simply say, "I don't know." One can only imagine the effect of this ambivalence on their perceptions of a course in the language. This complex sense of community in the classroom, however, can be used to mirror parallel complexities in the surrounding local community and in the world at large. Homogeneity in the classroom leads to students' inability to cope with situations that diverge from their experience. Heritage learners, therefore, can help in substantial ways as teachers try to model complex communities, while at the same time developing a deeper sense of their own identity.

What other positive contributions can heritage learners bring to the class? They confirm by personal example and story the reality of cultural information, vocabulary, and structures that appear in textbooks and other material—two more of the five C's: culture and communication. Often, particular cultural references will elicit a wealth of individual stories and details that make the material real for non-heritage learners. When a group of high school freshmen are eager to share their memories of New Year's celebrations, or bring their collection of calendars illustrating cartoon characters, the whole class can benefit. They confirm that semantic distinctions such as синий, голубой are in fact real and give similar affirmation to vocabulary use that the textbook or teacher presents.

The needs of heritage learners sometimes seem difficult to meet because they are different than the needs of traditional learners. From the perspective of the standards, however, these different difficulties can be used to help all learners approach the fourth C: comparisons. Every teacher of heritage students knows the difficulty in helping them spell correctly words they have only heard and spoken, so that "o/a" and "e/i" distinctions are extremely challenging. While this can be the moment to point out to non-heritage students that it will actually be easier for them to learn to spell correctly, such a response does nothing to counter the heritage speaker's tendency to misspell. Some structural concepts that are so brand new, almost alien, to non-natives, such as inflection, may also turn out to be even more difficult for heritage learners to find the will to master. If they have been blithely speaking Russian with no attention to cases or adjective/noun agreement, they may resist the notion that these features involve rules that must be learned, or even find it nearly impossible to grasp these concepts. If they have been convinced by Russian-American usage that бэкпэк, 'backpack,' is a Russian word, they may resist learning another one, but they need to. Similarly, in certain aspects of culture they will be also learning from the same entrance plateau as non-natives. When the class studies the geography, history, art, music, literature, or film of Russia, the heritage students may have just as much to learn as anyone else. They have major needs in these areas, especially if they aspire to use their linguistic skills in future careers where a knowledge of these cultural areas would be assumed by native speakers. Each instance where the heritage learner encounters difficulties presents the teacher with an opportunity to address the question of comparisons, linguistic or cultural.

Special programs to address the needs of heritage learners, programs that recognize their varying levels of competence and their particular problems, such as ingrained spelling difficulties, will help where such are available. Teachers would also benefit from help with strategies for teaching heritage learners and access to material designed especially for them. The Russian field might consider collaborating with other languages to share experience and research in this area. We need the heritage learners in a time of decreasing enrollment, and they need us to find ways to help them maintain, remediate, and increase their Russian in all the Standards. The 5 Cs of the Standards suggest some approaches to this issues that are as beneficial to heritage learners as they are to traditional learners.

Sample Learning Scenarios

ART

Students in Russian 3 in Brighton High School (Rochester, NY) have been learning about Russian art and artists. They have found information about Russian painters of the nineteenth and twentieth centuries and have made oral reports in Russian to their classmates. Their classmates have taken notes, filling in information on a teacher-prepared form that includes each painter's date and place of birth, style of

> **TARGETED STANDARDS**
> 1.2 Interpretive Communication
> 1.3 Presentational Communication
> 2.2 Products of Culture
> 3.1 Making Connections
> 3.2 Acquiring Information
> 4.2 Cultural Comparisons

painting, and titles of well-known paintings. They have learned vocabulary related to painting and have seen slides and art books that illustrate the work of Russian artists. The school art teacher has visited the class to analyze some of the paintings. Now they are looking at a series of slides of Russian avant-garde paintings with a list of titles in Russian. In trying to match the titles with the paintings they are drawing on Russian vocabulary and knowledge of cultural practices and products (samovars, Easter food, the Caucusus mountains, the Kremlin) to make their decisions. Students then write about the painting they find most appealing. The unit on Russian art coincides with the opening of an exhibit of art by contemporary artists from Russia at the local art museum. In cooperation with the museum's education division, one of the artists from Moscow visits the class and shows slides of his own work. Upon hearing that the class has been studying the Russian avant-garde, he relates his personal art education, including the influence of American art on his work

Reflections

1.2 Students take notes in Russian on their classmates' reports on Russian painters.
1.3 Students present oral reports on Russian painters.
2.2 Students relate Russian cultural perspectives to the subjects of paintings.
3.1 Students apply the ability to analyze works of art to Russian paintings.
3.2 Students understand titles and subjects of avant-garde paintings through knowledge of Russian.
4.2 In learning about the life and training of a Russian artist, students compare his career paths with artists in the U.S.

An exciting component of this scenario is the potential to link language, art, and history. For students who find it difficult to learn history as merely a collection of dates and events, the possibility of reinforcing those connections with particular art works or genres will be an added benefit. This scenario is also elegant for its flexibility of scope. With little difficulty, it could be extended to review color words as well as an almost infinite range of general vocabulary.

GEOGRAPHY

TARGETED STANDARDS
1.1 Interpersonal Communication
1.2 Interpretive Communication
1.3 Presentational Communication
2.1 Cultural Practices
3.1 Making Connections
3.2 Acquiring Information

Mrs. Husen teaches a Russian 2 class in a three-year public residential high school in Illinois, a math and science academy for gifted and talented students. Her class meets four times a week, in two seventy-minute periods and two forty-five minute periods. Her students have studied one year using teacher-prepared material on a variety of topics. In the unit on geography they have learned vocabulary such as names of Russian cities and rivers, landscape features, and have had practice hearing statistics about Russia. They have also read a text prepared by the teacher on the geography of Russia and have viewed a documentary film about Lake Baikal.

Working in pairs, students choose one of the former Soviet republics to research. They present their research orally to their classmates and prepare questions for the class to answer. The unit concludes with peer evaluations of the presentations and self-evaluation for comparison.

Reflection

1.1 Students read Russian text and also acquire information from their classmates' oral reports.
1.2 Students understand Russian text and hear Russian oral reports.
1.3 Students present oral reports to the class.
2.1 Students discuss some of the factors of Russian geography and history that have affected the way Russians view the world.
3.1 Students make statistical analyses in Russian and apply knowledge of geography to the unit on Russia and the former republics.
3.2 Students acquire information in Russian that will enhance their study of European history, economics, environmental studies.

If this unit includes discussion comparing the newly researched information on the former republics with their knowledge of American geography and history, or with their studies in environmental issues, the scenario offers many possibilities for further learning. If students are encouraged to use Internet or other media sources in Russian for their research, they are expanding their knowledge further, and using Russian to acquire information that they might not find in English. A similar unit on different geographical areas within Russia itself would offer rich possibilities.

GREETINGS

TARGETED STANDARDS
1.1 Interpersonal Communication
1.2 Interpretive Communication
1.3 Presentational Communication
2.1 Cultural Practices
3.1 Making Connections
4.1 Language Comparisons
4.2 Cultural Comparisons

Students at the Summit School in Winston-Salem, NC, are first exposed to Russian in the fifth grade in order to select the language they will study full-time beginning in sixth grade. One of the early units in sixth grade focuses on greetings. Having been introduced to the very basic greetings in the fifth grade, students in sixth grade first study a handout about the nature of greetings and forms of address (the lack of "Mr." or "Ms.," etc.) and a simple breakdown between formal and informal situations. They then view a series of pictures involving pairs and groups of people of various ages and occupations and identify, in English, whether the situation calls for a formal or informal exchange. When they become comfortable with these distinctions (including the difference between "formal" and "plural"), they brainstorm all the greetings they can remember. They then compile a list, with teacher supplementation, of formal greetings and their informal counterparts, where applicable. Writing practice is an important part of the curriculum at this grade level, so students must each write out the list for themselves, and as a group they type it up on the computer to practice word processing in Russian.

After becoming comfortable with greetings and goodbyes, students are introduced to the nature of Russian names, particularly patronymics. They learn the basics of patronymic formation, as well as some common Russian names and nicknames. They then reexamine the pictures used earlier to identify formal vs. informal, and this time they select names for the characters, based on their relative situations. Finally, in pairs, they develop brief dialogues to accompany each picture, and act them out.

As a conversation practice activity, they have a party. Each student chooses an identity and comes to the party as that person. The person should be someone famous (they will have already studied some basic words for professions and nationality, and read a bit about some famous Russians such as Yuri Gagarin, Ivan Pavlov, Anna Akhmatova). One student is the host, and as each new student comes to the door, the previous one greets them formally and introduces them to the other guests.

Reflection
1.1 Students learn to greet and take leave in Russian and to present new "guests" at the party.
1.2 Students listen to introductions of famous Russians.
1.3 Students word process a reference list.
2.1 Students learn about the formal/informal distinction in Russian.
3.1 In selecting famous Russians, students make connections with other disciplines.
4.1 Students learn that social distinctions are reflected in the grammar of Russian.
4.2 Students learn that Russian and English differ in the encoding of information about social relationships.

While the formal/informal distinction in Russian is not particularly difficult to understand at an intellectual level, it is very difficult to develop a feeling for what this distinction means in action. By exploring its manifestations in numerous types of speech settings, students can see that it pervades the linguistic system more deeply than just a few verb forms. Names of all types are a related form of complexity that is addressed in this scenario.

LETTER WRITING

A project in writing letters and notes involves students from beginning through advanced levels of Russian, grades 8 through 12, in Iowa. Mr. Watzke's students correspond with each other in Russian, with Russian speakers in the local community, and with pen pals in Kislovodsk. They write about themselves, about school and community events. Letter writing is both a form of assessment for the course

> **TARGETED STANDARDS**
> 1.1 Interpersonal Communication
> 1.3 Presentational Communication
> 2.1 Cultural Practices
> 5.1 School and Community
> 5.2 Lifelong Learning

Standards for Russian Language Learning

and a preparation for the school exchange trip to Kislovodsk, at least for the students who will travel. A classroom mailbox allows students to deposit notes and letters to classmates or to students in other classes, correspondence which the teacher delivers weekly. Some students also have pen pals in the community and a chance to practice their Russian skills with native speakers, retired adults who are glad to encourage the study of Russian. Letters are also exchanged with pen pals in Kislovodsk. A class bulletin board and scrapbook display some of the notable letters, postcards, and pictures that students receive. Students extend their writing activities in the form of journal entries and short stories based on information from the letters they receive. In connection with social studies classes on the middle school level, they exchange cultural information they have learned from their pen pals in Russia.

Reflection

1.1 Students provide information, express feelings, and exchange opinions with their pen pals in Russian.
1.3 Students create short stories based on information received through correspondence.
2.1 Students understand relationships between Russian practices and perspectives reflected in letters they receive.
5.1 Students use Russian beyond the classroom.
5.2 Students continue the pen pal relationship into the following school year.

If there were an e-mail connection, the correspondence might take on another dimension and provide more frequent contact with the students in Kislovodsk. In addition to pen pals letters, writing activities could take the form of class or individual projects on topics of interest. The native speakers in the community might be invited to address the classes in person, or students might find ways to develop the contacts further in community outreach or service activities.

MAP GAME

> **TARGETED STANDARDS**
> 1.2 Interpretive Communication
> 3.1 Making Connections
> 3.2 Acquiring Information
> 4.1 Language Comparisons
> 5.2 Lifelong Learning

Each eighth grade class at Northern University Middle School, a small school within a laboratory school in Cedar Falls, Iowa, takes a four-and-a-half week exploratory language segment in the three languages offered at Northern University High School: Russian, French, and Spanish. The purpose of this is to expose the students to each language so that they may better choose the language they would most like to take when they enter high school next year. Most of the students have had Spanish since the first grade, and this is their first contact with a second foreign language. The eighth grade is broken into three groups of approximately 18 students each, and each group takes the exploratory courses separately from the other groups.

Upon entering Russian, most students have fear about a language that they think is "going to be too hard." Students learn to read and write both the printed and cursive forms of the Russian alphabet during this course, and almost all of them find that this is not as difficult as they had previously thought. New words focus heavily on cognate and/or international words, as well as on things related to family, city words, classroom objects, sports, etc.

Another way to help students realize that Russian isn't that hard is by playing the "map game." Using world maps purchased in Russia, students sit in groups of two or three to a table. The teacher calls out the names of different countries, which the students then have to be able to find. Students quickly realize that they understand the names of about 90% of the world's countries in Russian! This is also an excellent way to review place location and geography, especially since many students have a difficult time finding these places on an English-language map!

Reflection

1.2 Students understand and interpret written and spoken language on a variety of topics in Russian.

3.1 Students reinforce and further their knowledge of other disciplines through Russian.

3.2 In the course of learning to read words in Russian, students learn more about geography than they know from their English-based learning.

4.1 Students demonstrate understanding of the nature of language through comparisons of Russian and their own language.

5.2 Students acquire information about the world that can serve as part of their core knowledge of geography for the rest of their lives.

Especially in high school, extending students' knowledge of geography is an important service to their general education. Done in conjunction with history and social science courses, the map game can be a focal point in multidisciplinary learning. This rich activity can be expanded by having students choose an area in which to become an expert and give a presentation, thus addressing Standard 1.3.

OPINION POLL

Mr. Doyle teaches in a technical high school on Staten Island, New York, in a magnet school for gifted students. His school is unusual in requiring three years of Russian for all students. His second year class of sophomores uses an opinion poll from "*Chas Pik*," a Saint Petersburg publication that has a web site. The poll compares Russian students and parents on the question of what they like and dislike about school. In his introduction, Mr. Doyle asked his class if they thought Russian children and parents would have the same reactions to school. The class did its own oral poll on what students like most and least about school, with new vocabulary on the board as questions arose about how to express opinions in Russian. The class was then able to read the Russian poll downloaded from the web site and note how many answers were the same or similar. Next the class was asked to write in Russian five positive things about school and five things that they don't like. They also asked their parents to name likes and dislikes. Sample answers were written on the board the next day, leading to discussion about the similarities and differences.

> **TARGETED STANDARDS**
> 1.1 Interpersonal Communication
> 2.1 Cultural Practices
> 4.2 Cultural Comparisons
> 5.1 School and Community

Reflection

1.1 Students exchange information about opinions.

2.1 Students learn about perspectives on school life and learning in Russia.

4.2 Students compare attitudes about school in Russia and the United States.

5.1 Student discussion reflects community attitudes in both countries and brings this information into the classroom.

This activity offers a fine occasion for involving parents in the language learning process, sharing opinions, cultural perspectives and comparisons. The use of authentic material on a subject of universal interest to students (school) provides a setting for building vocabulary and cultural awareness. Students may not otherwise be aware how much material is available in Russian on the web, and could follow this scenario with more opportunities to use, or search for, Russian web sites. They might also propose other topics for surveys, and conduct polls with other groups of students, either in the school where everyone is studying Russian, or with other classes in the US or Russia via the web.

REAL ESTATE

> **TARGETED STANDARDS**
> 1.1 Interpersonal Communication
> 1.2 Interpretive Communication
> 1.3 Presentational Communication
> 5.1 School and Community

A second- and third-year, mixed-level class in a large public high school in Anchorage, AK, spends part of several class periods on a variety of activities related to the theme of home. In one activity, students bring in newspaper ads and describe houses to try to persuade their classmates to buy them. Students listen to each presentation, take notes, and then move about the classroom trying to match their notes with the pictures of the various houses that are displayed on a bulletin board.

As a follow-up activity, students prepare their own home plans in Russian as a homework assignment. They label the different parts and special features of the house. Working in groups in class, each group selects one plan to sell to the rest of the class. Each member of the group shares the responsibility of describing the house in Russian. As other students hear the presentations, they fill in a chart of features they like or don't like about each house.

Another related activity, "House Tour," has students giving tours of celebrity's houses. They stroll about the classroom, indicating where various parts of the imaginary house are located. The teacher and class are paid participants in the tour and must react in Russian to features they see.

A further activity has students work to create a blueprint of a room or apartment. Using a blueprint form created with a computerized program such as HyperStudio, students label areas and draw furnishings as they listen to the teacher or another student describe the room.

As a final activity, "Moving Time," half the class prepares a description of a home they would like to move into, while the other half prepares a description of a home they would like to sell or rent. Students then move around the classroom trying to find potential matches.

Reflection

1.1 Students interact in their discussion of reactions to real estate presentations.
1.2 In both oral and written formats, students receive information about real estate.
1.3 Students present information both orally and in writing.
5.1 By bringing advertisements into class, students integrate real-world information into their classwork.

This activity could readily be expanded to include cross-cultural comparisons regarding housing and living patterns in Russia (Standards 2.1, 2.2, 4.2). The nature of family units, who is at home most/least, and so on, would be natural topics to learn about and to compare with situations in the students' region (Standards 2.1, 4.2).

RUSSIAN CULTURE IN THE US

Some of the students in a third-year Russian class in a Dallas high school have begun to express frustration that their knowledge of Russian does not extend much past the textbook, i.e., largely an understanding of basic grammar rules and vocabulary. Though their teacher tries to maintain a "four-skills" approach in his classes, he admits that the textbook and related materials used in the course do not offer much context for using the language.

> **TARGETED STANDARDS**
> 1.1 Interpersonal Communication
> 1.2 Interpretive Communication
> 2.2 Products of Culture
> 3.1 Making Connections
> 3.2 Acquiring Information
> 5.1 School and Community
> 5.2 Lifelong Learning

The teacher suggests that students explore the use of Russian in other parts of the US, asking his students for suggestions to locate such communities or institutions. Perhaps, he suggests, some of these sites might provide useful relevant information on the current status and use of Russian outside the classroom within their own state and country. He suggests that the students use resources on the Internet to locate these sites. The teacher gives his students a modified course in using the Internet, using a Russian-language guide to computers as a source for basic lexicon and terminology.

Using the World Wide Web, the students identify and explore sites that contain relevant content about Russian-speaking communities and related cultural events in Texas and other states. Since many of the sites are in Russian, students work in small groups to pool their language skills and try to understand the content of the various sites, using the full context of the material in the site -- graphics, sound, format, etc. Students work together, using all available reference materials, to identify those sites that will best offer opportunities to use and expand their knowledge of Russian beyond the confines of the textbook. Even in their groups, however, some of the sites contain material referring to specific cultural entities and persons that they cannot recognize or identify. The teacher provides enough information about these topics to lead the students to sources to find out more about them. Once the students have identified several appropriate sites, the teacher asks them to contact individuals connected to the various sites by e-mail and request information and/or realia on the particular entities mentioned in the website. For example, one of the sites mentioned an exhibition of Catherine the Great in Houston. Since the students had begun to study the great tsarina in their classes, they knew about her biography and some facts about her reign. They are interested in finding out more about the interest in Catherine among Americans in Houston today. They ask the contact person at the site to send them any materials on the exhibition that were available in either English or Russian.

Reflections

1.1 Students use Russian while on-line.
1.2 Students use websites to obtain information.
2.2 Students relate Russian cultural products and perspectives based on the information given on the various sites.
3.1 Students use information from history classes and computers in working with the language on the websites.
3.2 Students gain knowledge of Russian cultural entities throughout the United States.

5.1 Students use the Internet to access Russian-language sites outside of school.

5.2 Developing interest in the language and culture throughout the U.S., students learn how to access such information.

Although it may once have seemed counterintuitive, this is a clear example of ways in which technology can play a substantial role in deepening students' understanding of culture. The connections that are made on the Internet provide a framework on which students can begin to organize their expanding knowledge of history, music, art, politics. By linking their new knowledge of things Russian with places and events in the US that may be more familiar to them, the connections are more real and, perhaps, more lasting.

> **TARGETED STANDARDS**
> 1.1 Interpersonal Communication
> 1.2 Interpretive Communication
> 1.3 Presentational Communication
> 2.2 Products of Culture
> 4.2 Cultural Comparisons
> 5.1 School and Community

SKITS

In the Tenafly, NJ, school system, the Tenafly Middle School and High School Russian classes, levels 1-5, organize a Russian evening for the Russian students and their parents. The event consists of catered Russian food and entertainment by the students themselves.

As part of this, the 7th grade first-year Russian class worked on and performed a Russian skit based on the story "The Turnip." A teacher from Russia, who was working at Tenafly Middle School at that time, adapted the story into a play. Each student was assigned a role with lines to learn. In class, both the classroom teacher and the teacher from Russia rehearsed with the students, helping them to understand the story and memorize their parts.

As Russian evening approached, the skit was staged and costumes and props were added. On the night of Russian evening, before performing the skit, one of the students gave a brief description of the story in English to help the parents who did not understand Russian. Afterwards, the class discussed their performance and other ideas that could be added in the future.

Reflection

1.1 Students engage in conversation, provide and obtain information.
1.2 Students understand and interpret written and spoken language.
1.3 Students present information, concepts, and ideas to an audience of listeners or readers.
2.2 Students demonstrate an understanding of the relationship between the products and perspectives of Russian culture.
4.2 Students demonstrate understanding of the concept of culture through comparison.
5.1 Students use Russian both within and beyond the school setting.

This rich scenario is a good example of ways to bring Russian to the community. It could easily be enhanced to address the standards even more deeply. Students could spend more time studying the importance of agriculture in Russian society and do oral reports (Standard 2.2). Students might look at additional folk literature in Russian and English to make comparisons (Standard 4.1) and compare the different ways of addressing people in Russian and in English (Standard 4.2). By performing the skit for other classes and other schools (i.e., elementary schools) and/or videotaping the skit to share with others, students could extend their use of Russian outside the classroom (Standard 5.1).

SOCIAL HISTORY IN THE LYRICS OF IGOR' TAL'KOV

The Russian Village of Concordia Language Villages offers an intensive summer language/culture experience for students in grades 9-12. As part of the four week language program, a learning scenario in Russian social history utilizes Russian/Soviet rock music to illustrate principles of glasnost'/perestroika and the realities of ethnic conflict in the former USSR. Students enjoy listening to Russian rock music and bring a high level of interest to this mode of language and culture learning. A class of advanced students listens to Igor' Tal'kov's song "Vojna" and completes listening and reading activities for language development. They also engage in activities that link the song with the context of Russian/Soviet social history. The song includes many cognates of geographical terms, and several repetitive phrases. As part of the scenario students will also work with a map in Russian to locate all the geographical locations mentioned in the song. They also discuss the nationalities and languages besides Russian spoken in the areas that the song refers to. They become aware of the importance of songs and their messages in Soviet/Russian culture. As extended activities, they use media sources and Internet to find further information about those places and to find out how the situation has changed in the former USSR since Talkov wrote the song in 1991.

TARGETED STANDARDS
1.2 Interpretive Communication
2.1 Cultural Practices
2.2 Products of Culture
3.1 Making Connections
3.2 Acquiring Information
5.1 School and Community

Reflection

1.2 Students understand and interpret the Russian they hear in songs.
2.1 Students demonstrate understanding of the relationship between Russian perceptions of social change and the expression of social issues.
2.2 Students understand the relationship between Russian songs and Russian cultural perspectives.
3.1 Students reinforce their knowledge of twentieth century geopolitical history through the work on the song.
3.2 Students recognize the distinctive viewpoints toward social change that are apparent in the song.
5.1 Students use Russian Internet sources to find information about areas affected by the breakup of the Soviet Union.

Songs are a particularly strong motivator for language students. Students might be asked to compare the expression of major political and social issues in the Talkov song with the content of American songs, for example songs from eras of strife and controversy such as the Vietnam War.

STALIN

Stimulated by viewing the award-winning film *Burnt by the Sun*, students in a fourth-level Russian class at Phillips Academy (Andover, MA) asked to do some reading of history written during the Soviet era. Since not all members of the class had studied Russian/Soviet history in depth, they read excerpts from two different history textbooks, both from the same Moscow publishing firm, written for Russian high school students. One textbook was published in 1983, before the breakup of the USSR, the other in

TARGETED STANDARDS
1.1 Interpersonal Communication
1.2 Interpretive Communication
1.3 Presentational Communication
2.1 Cultural Practices
3.1 Making Connections
3.2 Acquiring Information
4.1 Language Comparisons
5.2 Lifelong Learning

Standards for Russian Language Learning

1992 (after the breakup). The excerpts cover the same period of time—late 1920s, early 1930s—but could hardly be more different in their discussions of all that surrounded the push toward industrialization that characterized this period.

To help them process these difficult texts, students select twelve sentences or small segments of text from each textbook which they feel give an accurate flavor of the topics discussed and the language used in the different textbooks. They present a few of their selections to the class, making sure that classmates understand the language and historical references of each sentence. Based on their two sets of sentences, each student then writes a one to two page essay comparing salient features of these two very different perspectives on history.

Following the history readings, students read from two works of fiction. They read two short chapters of Rybakov's *Дети Арбата* (*Children of the Arbat*) in which a fictionalized Stalin is a central character. In these chapters, they can see some of the aspects of Stalin's character that fostered the development of the so-called "Personality Cult," the consequences of which are so evident in the contrastive history readings. Then, in a chapter of Dovlatov's *Наши* (*Ours*), students encounter characters who were children during Stalin's reign and see at a more personal level some of the effects of the cultural distortions deriving from this era.

Reflection

1.1 Students discuss text selections and explain vocabulary and history.
1.2 Students read Soviet- and post-Soviet-era history textbooks.
1.3 Students write essays comparing text selections.
2.1 Students learn how economic and political systems influence cultural practices.
3.1 Students reinforce and further their knowledge of history and economics.
3.2 Students observe different perspectives of history through authentic texts.
4.1 Students contrast the nature of vocabulary used to describe history used in different-era textbooks.
5.2 By understanding the nature of the Stalin's "Personality Cult," students are better able to understand the complex nature of political systems as they encounter them throughout their lives.

Reading authentic texts aimed at Russian students their own ages provides a valuable window for American students to understand the profound impact that Stalin had on all aspects of Soviet life from the 1920s on. The language of such texts is quite challenging, but by giving special attention to a limited number of sentences, the scope of the challenge can be managed to allow the activity to be used at different levels.

Discussion of McCarthy-era politics in the US would enrich the discussion of cultural distortions deriving from extremist politics based on fear, and would address Standard 4.2: Cultural Comparisons. Standard 5.1: School and Community could be addressed by having students interview émigrés who remember the Stalin era, either directly or from family conversations.

TARGETED STANDARDS
1.1 Interpersonal Communication
1.2 Interpretive Communication
1.3 Presentational Communication
2.1 Cultural Practices
2.2 Products of Culture
3.2 Acquiring Information
5.2 Lifelong Learning

TELEPHONE BOOK

The Maplewood School, a small public elementary school outside Albany, New York, has a long-standing Russian program for grades 4-8, recently integrated into grades 1-3. First and second grades have three 20-minute classes per week. The twenty-five students in Mrs. Einstein's second grade class learn the letters of the Cyrillic alphabet by making a telephone book. Mrs. Einstein has taped the

Russian spelling of her students' names to their desks as references. As each new letter in the Russian alphabet is presented, students try to find it in their names. They look forward to finding a letter, since it then gives them the opportunity to share their telephone number in Russian with the class. When the telephone book is completed, it becomes the first Russian reader for the class and also a prop for role-playing telephone conversations. Eventually, copies will be sent home for students to share with their families.

Reflection

1.1 Students role-play telephone conversations.
1.2 Students search for Cyrillic letters in their names.
1.3 Students share their telephone numbers with the class.
2.1 Students share telephone numbers, an important source of contact/information in many cultures.
2.2 Students are encouraged to think about the influence of the telephone on day-to-day life.
3.2 Students use Russian to acquire telephone numbers.
5.2 Students take their work home and use it in their daily life as they call friends.

This is an example of a learning scenario for an early grade that could be adapted to a beginning class in higher grades. Students might also learn about telephone manners in Russia and compare them to ways in which the telephone is used in their homes. Work with numbers in Russian will be enhanced if there are consequences to making mistakes (classmates will dial a wrong number, for instance). Real telephone numbers of real friends will also help set numbers more firmly in students' memories.

THEATER

Since Russian language and culture is offered in several Houston-area high schools, but only in one or two sections each, the instructor moves among the schools offering the course and tries to make optimal use of the scarce resources in the area for promoting the study of the language to her students. As she locates local sources of Russian culture, for example, she tries to find ways to use this material in all of her schools at several different levels of instruction. One such source was a Houston theater which was sponsoring workshops and a performance given by a visiting troupe of the Moscow Art Theater (MXAT).

TARGETED STANDARDS
1.1 Interpersonal Communication
1.2 Interpretive Communication
1.3 Presentational Communication
2.1 Cultural Practices
2.2 Products of Culture
3.1 Making Connections
3.2 Acquiring Information
4.2 Cultural Comparisons
5.1 School and Community
5.2 Lifelong Learning

After contacting the theater and making arrangements with the troupe director, the instructor was able to videotape a rehearsal session of the troupe as they prepared for the final performance during their Texas visit. The tape showed members of the troupe taking direction from the director and discussing various stagings and blockings for the performance. All of the interaction was, of course, in Russian. This videotape became the basis for a variety of classroom activities and instruction for the various groups in all of her schools.

None of the beginning-level students knew about the rich history of the MXAT, so after an introduction to the subject in English, students watched the videotape as the basis for guessing and deduction activities. They learned basic vocabulary for many of the items on stage, such as clothing and furniture. At the intermediate level, students listened for and indicated the words and particles that they recognized in the speech of the director and actors. They also speculated on the meaning of the various scenes based on literature that they were already familiar with (the play in rehearsal was Chekhov's *Seagull*). The advanced students used the video to work on forms of the imperative mood, as the director used this form regularly in talking to his actors. All groups received extensive commentary and supplementary materials on speech etiquette and behavior in Russian. Students were encouraged to notice the differences between the more familiar interaction among the actors during rehearsal and much more formal interaction of the actual performance. After working with the videotaped and supplementary materials for several days, all of the students attended the performance in Houston. Following the performance, the students were able to make many comparisons between the Moscow Art Theater and the types of American theater they were already familiar with. Students also returned to the videotape of the rehearsal and discussed the scenes being practiced in light of the final finished production. They compared the dress and behaviors of the cast members during rehearsal and during the play. Finally, all of the sections in the instructor's schools undertook various production projects based on what they had seen and learned using the theater-based materials. Each level worked on a project of appropriate scope and complexity. Students worked individually, in pairs, or in small groups to prepare and execute the final productions. The instructor helped each project with the language and level of cultural appropriateness for the miniproductions. For the two weeks that the students in all of the schools were working with the Russian theater materials, the students kept individual journals for their portfolios, as usual, noting in particular language-specific entities that they found most challenging or difficult, as well as the new lexical items, grammar, and cultural information that they learned at various stages of the project.

Reflection

1.1 Students use Russian while rehearsing scenes.
1.2 Students read and listen to the theater materials.
1.3 Students perform the various scenes or skits.
2.1 Students view first-hand the interaction of Russians in a culturally-marked situation.
2.2 Students relate Russian cultural products and perspectives based on the rehearsal and performance of the play.
3.1 Students apply information from history and literature classes.
3.2 Students gain knowledge of the Russian theater through performance.
4.2 Students compare the American and Russian theater experience.
5.1 Students use Russian outside of school at theatrical performances.
5.2 Developing interest in the language and culture through drama and theater stays with the students through life.

By linking study of video and texts with a project, this scenario addresses nearly the full range of the standards. It is an excellent demonstration of the way in which a focal activity can be extended to connect with learning of many different types.

Standards for Learning Spanish

a project of the American Association of Teachers of Spanish and Portuguese

SPANISH

K–16 TASK FORCE ON STANDARDS FOR LEARNING SPANISH

Nancy Anderson, Princeton, NJ
Rosario Cantú, Health Careers High School, San Antonio, TX
José M. Díaz, Hunter College High School, New York, NY
Inés García, Texas Education Agency, Austin, TX
Gail Guntermann (Chair)**,** Arizona State University, Tempe, AZ
Nancy Humbach, Miami University, Oxford, OH
Judith Liskin-Gasparro, University of Iowa, Iowa City, IA
Donna R. Long (Team Leader)**,** The Ohio State University, Columbus, OH
Frank Medley, Jr. (Team Leader)**,** West Virginia University, Morgantown, WV
Myriam Met, Montgomery County Public Schools, Rockville, MD
Marilyn Pavlik (ex-officio), Lyons Township Schools, LaGrange, IL
Alvaro Rodríguez, MB Lamar High School and University of St. Thomas, Houston, TX
Paul Sandrock, Wisconsin Department of Public Instruction, Madison, WI
Lynn A. Sandstedt, American Association of Teachers of Spanish and Portuguese, Greeley, CO
Martie Semmer, Summit School District RE-1, Frisco, CO
Carmen C. Tesser (Team Leader)**,** University of Georgia, Athens, GA
Guadalupe Valdés, Stanford University, Stanford, CA

Standards for Learning Spanish

BOARD OF REVIEWERS

Martha Dow Adams
Petal High School
Hattiesburg, MS

Marco A. Arenas
President, AATSP
Windsor, CT

Susan Bacon
University of Cincinnati
Cincinnati, OH

Lauren Bearden
Columbus High School
East
Columbus, MS

George Blanco
University of Texas
Austin, TX

Paula Brandenburg
Lausanne Collegiate School
Memphis, TN

Fé Brittain
Pima Community College
Tucson, AZ

James Crapotta
Barnard College
New York, NY

Gisela M. Diez
Roncalli High School
Carmel, IN

Sister Rosalie Ferrari
Merion Mercy Academy
Merion Station, PA

Anne Fountain
Peace College
Raleigh, NC

T. Bruce Fryer
University of South
Carolina
Columbia, SC

Eileen W. Glisan
Indiana University of
Pennsylvania
Indiana, PA

Audrey Heining-Boynton
University of North
Carolina
Chapel Hill, NC

Delia L. Montesinos
University of Texas
Austin, TX

Dorothy Rissell
State University
of New York
Buffalo, NY

José Suárez
Clemson University
Clemson, SC

Elizabeth Welles
Association of Depts. of
Foreign Languages and
Modern Language
Association
New York, NY

Carol Wilkerson
Kennesaw State University
Kennesaw, GA

Table of Contents

STANDARDS FOR LEARNING SPANISH — **478**

INTRODUCTION: WHAT IS THE *STANDARDS FOR LEARNING SPANISH* DOCUMENT? — **479**

THE SPANISH LANGUAGE IN THE SCHOOL, THE COMMUNITY, AND THE WORLD — **480**

COMMUNICATION   **Goal 1** — **483**

CULTURES   **Goal 2** — **488**

CONNECTIONS   **Goal 3** — **492**

COMPARISONS   **Goal 4** — **496**

COMMUNITIES   **Goal 5** — **499**

SAMPLE LEARNING SCENARIOS — **502**

La Independencia	502
Birds Beyond Borders/*Aves sin fronteras*	503
The Tale of the Corn/*La leyenda del maíz*	505
Planning to Study in Spain	508
Housing: Scale Drawings for Cultural Comparisons	509
Apartment Hunting in San José, Costa Rica	510
Los estereotipos y el prejuicio	511
Volcanoes	512
Abuelitos Adoptivos	512
Interview with Rigoberta Menchú	513
Language Variation Project	514
Spanish in the Community	515
Literary Theory and Interpretation	517

Standards for Learning Spanish

COMMUNICATION — GOAL ONE
Communicate in Spanish

Standard 1.1 Students engage in conversations, provide and obtain information, express feelings and emotions, and exchange opinions.

Standard 1.2 Students understand and interpret spoken and written Spanish on a variety of topics.

Standard 1.3 Students present information, concepts, and ideas in Spanish to an audience of listeners or readers on a variety of topics.

CULTURES — GOAL TWO
Gain Knowledge and Understanding of the Cultures of the World

Standard 2.1 Students demonstrate an understanding of the relationship between the practices and perspectives of Hispanic cultures.

Standard 2.2 Students demonstrate an understanding of the relationship between the products and perspectives of Hispanic cultures.

CONNECTIONS — GOAL THREE
Connect with Other Disciplines and Acquire Information

Standard 3.1 Students reinforce and further their knowledge of other disciplines through Spanish.

Standard 3.2 Students acquire information and recognize the distinctive viewpoints that are only available through the Spanish language and its cultures.

COMPARISONS — GOAL FOUR
Develop Insight into the Nature of Language and Culture

Standard 4.1 Students demonstrate understanding of the nature of language through comparisons between Spanish and English.

Standard 4.2 Students demonstrate understanding of the concept of culture through comparisons between Hispanic cultures and their own.

COMMUNITIES — GOAL FIVE
Participate in Communities at Home and Around the World

Standard 5.1 Students use Spanish both within and beyond the school setting.

Standard 5.2 Students show evidence of becoming life-long learners by using Spanish for personal enjoyment and enrichment.

Introduction

WHAT IS THE *STANDARDS FOR LEARNING SPANISH* DOCUMENT?

In 1996, *Standards for Foreign Language Learning: Preparing for the 21st Century* defined content standards in foreign language education–what students should know and be able to do–in grades four, eight, and twelve. They serve as a gauge for excellence, as states and local districts carry out their responsibilities for foreign language curriculum in the schools. The purpose of *Standards for Learning Spanish* is to tailor the foreign language standards to the teaching and learning of Spanish, by providing sample progress indicators and learning scenarios that describe stages of progress and activities for learning that are specific to Spanish. Although this document will serve as a reference and can provide guidance to writers of state frameworks and curriculum writers, as well as administrators at the district and school levels, it is not itself intended as either a curriculum or a syllabus.

Readers will notice that the vision of language learning for the twenty-first century has been expanded in this document by the inclusion of sample progress indicators and learning scenarios for post-secondary Spanish students. As language instruction starts in the early grades and continues through long articulated sequences, students will arrive at college ready to undertake advanced courses that focus more on high-level intellectual content and far less on language skill development. The baccalaureate-level progress indicators and learning scenarios presuppose this population of students.

Organizing principles

The 5 C's. This document has adopted the major organizing principles of the *Standards for Foreign Language Learning*: a) the five C's (Communication, Cultures, Connections, Comparisons, and Communities); and b) the "weave" of curricular elements (the language system, cultural knowledge, communication strategies, critical thinking skills, learning strategies, other subject areas, and technology). A major tenet of the document holds that although every learner has a unique motivation for studying a given language, those organizing principles apply to all school-based language learning.

What is "communication"? The ability to use language in a variety of culturally-appropriate communicative tasks is the most basic goal of most learners, yet communication is understood in a variety of ways. The approach taken by the Foreign Language Standards task force identifies three modes of communication that link language and underlying culture: interpersonal, interpretive, and presentational. (See figure 6, Framework of Communicative Modes, in *Standards for Foreign Language Learning*, for a graphic presentation of the definitions, skill paths, and cultural and linguistic knowledge involved in these three modes of communication.)

... TO COMMUNICATE, TO LEARN, AND TO FUNCTION APPROPRIATELY IN HISPANIC COMMUNITIES

Individual variation. Many factors intervene to affect the levels of knowledge and ability that learners attain. Individual learner characteristics, such as aptitude, motivation, and knowledge of other foreign languages, may contribute to the speed of language acquisition. Similarly, situational factors such as program goals and expectations, the quality of the facilities, and preparation of teachers may foster or limit student achievement. Finally, multiple entry points into a school's or district's Spanish program will also lead to considerable variation in student knowledge and performance. Students who move into a district as adolescents or who begin to study Spanish in high school as a second foreign language will almost always be at a different level from their peers who have been studying Spanish since kindergarten.

Given the foregoing variables, the issue of articulation is of paramount importance in the Spanish standards project. The progress indicators and learning scenarios provided in this document can be adapted to different age groups and types of learners and, in addition, can be used as guides to create high-quality instructional programs of shorter duration.

Format of this document. Each section of this document follows the same format: a) the one-line Standard statement taken directly from the generic Standards, b) a brief discussion of the standard with reference to Spanish, and c) sample progress indicators for learners of Spanish at grades four, eight, twelve, and at the conclusion of four years of college, assuming that Spanish study starts in kindergarten. The document concludes with a set of learning scenarios that features classroom activities submitted by AATSP members.

Sample progress indicators. The sample progress indicators provide specific examples of achievable outcomes. Because we assume an articulated sequence of instruction, each group of indicators builds upon those of the preceding levels; it is important to note that the progress indicators at the earliest levels are subsumed at the higher levels. The following example shows this progression.

Goal 5
Students perform in Spanish for a school or community event

Grade 4	Grade 8	Grade 12	Grade 16
Perform a simple skit for foreign language week	Write and perform a simple skit for a Cinco de mayo celebration	Write and/or perform a one-act play in a regional contest	Present a Lope de Vega play for the community

THE SPANISH LANGUAGE IN THE SCHOOL, THE COMMUNITY, AND THE WORLD

The study of Spanish offers learners the opportunity to communicate, to learn, and to function appropriately in Hispanic communities. It encourages them to make comparisons and connections and to interact with the community, at home and throughout the world, in an increasingly proficient manner. The standards encourage schools to consider long sequences of language study, beginning in the elementary grades, so that learners may develop greater proficiency. This is the approach that is taken with the study of language arts, mathematics, science, and social studies, all of which students begin early and continue throughout their school careers.

There are a plethora of linguistic and cultural opportunities in the United States for learners of Spanish as a second language. No longer is it the case that most learners first hear Spanish when they enter the classroom. Many visit countries where Spanish is spoken. Others have grown up in communities where they interact often with speakers of Spanish. Still others have spoken Spanish at home. Increasingly, music, films, and foods produced in the United States for the general population feature the Spanish language and cultural phenomena from the Spanish-speaking world.

Spanish in the world. Spanish is spoken by nearly 400,000,000 people who are spread over four continents. In Europe, Spanish is one of the several national languages of Spain (including the Canary Islands and the Balearic Islands), and it is the official language of over twenty nations in North, Central, and South America. Spanish was the first European language to arrive on our shores and is widely spoken in the United States. Spanish is spoken on the African continent in Ceuta, Melilla, Morocco, and Equatorial Guinea. In Asia, Spanish has a historical presence in the Philippines.

The language today known as Spanish, or e*spañol*, is a romance language that evolved from Latin. Spanish is still known in many areas of the world--including parts of the Americas--by its original name, *castellano*, the language spoken in the Spanish province of old Castile.

Spanish, like English, spread from Europe to other areas of the world. Peninsular, or European, Spanish is analogous to British English, and the Spanish of the Americas is analogous to U.S. and Canadian English. Like the speakers of English in the British Isles, North America, Australia, and South Africa, residents of different areas of Spain speak different varieties of peninsular Spanish, and there are many different varieties of Spanish spoken in the Americas. As is the case in the United States, where one can often recognize speakers from Boston or the deep South by their "regional accents," one can generally identify the different sounds and cadences of the Spanish of the various regions of the world where it is spoken. Nevertheless, all varieties of Spanish are mutually comprehensible.

Teachers of Spanish have lived, studied, and traveled in many areas of the Spanish-speaking world and, understandably, they bring to their teaching their own particular variety of Spanish. This diversity of background and experience works to students' benefit, since learners may hear several regional varieties of Spanish and learn about different countries or regions of the Spanish-speaking world as they move through the grades. In addition, many teachers deliberately use resources from numerous parts of the Spanish-speaking world in an effort to provide learners with a broader perspective on the many linguistic and cultural variations that exist in modern Spanish.

Spanish speakers in the United States. Although the largest concentrations (about 74%) of the more than 22,000,000 people of Latin American and Spanish descent in the United States live in the United States/Mexico border area, Florida, and the New York metropolitan area, every state of the Union counts Spanish speakers among its population. Since Spanish speakers have been immigrating to what is now the United States for over 400 years, it is not surprising that some of the current residents are fluent speakers of Spanish while others speak their heritage language very little or not at all. Figure 1 of *Standards for Foreign Language Learning*, p. 19, provides a glimpse of the variety in home language backgrounds among such learners.

▼

... ALL VARIETIES OF SPANISH ARE MUTUALLY COMPREHENSIBLE

Standards for Learning Spanish

There is no widespread agreement about the use of a generic term to refer to this demographic group because it is characterized by many diverse cultural, ethnic, and racial backgrounds. Terms such as Hispanic, Latino/Latina, and "Spanish" are ever-changing and sometimes politically motivated. Such terms may refer to any individual of Latin American or Spanish descent.

Spanish in US schools. The importance of Spanish in the world and the growing presence of Spanish speakers and Hispanic cultures in the United States have, in large part, inspired the visionary spirit of this document. In contrast to the vision of long, articulated sequences of instruction expressed here, however, the reality of Spanish education in the United States today is quite different. Even when a long sequence of instruction is available, such programs are scarce, articulation is uneven, and learners enter at various points. The majority of learners still begin their study of Spanish at the high school level. Fewer learners start at the middle school and elementary levels, and a small percentage wait until the college years. Many schools do not have programs that are appropriate for heritage learners.

On the positive side, developments in the methodologies for teaching foreign languages continue to push the creation of curricula toward a more proficiency-based approach. Textbooks and other pedagogical materials reflect the market demand to teach for proficiency in listening, speaking, reading, and writing, and prepare learners to interact effectively with Hispanic communities. Learners and their parents have the right to expect that the course of study will provide ample opportunities to develop fluency and a knowledge of the culture. With expanded travel, greater access to technology, and the increasing mobility of society, learners have many opportunities to interact with peers or other community members, local or global, whose first language is Spanish.

Opportunities to learn Spanish. National and international demographic trends make the study of Spanish a particularly exciting and fast-moving area. No longer are languages studied only by the college bound. Over sixty school districts have implemented immersion programs in which English-speaking children study all subjects in Spanish, beginning in kindergarten. Still other districts have established programs in which Spanish language courses comprise a key part of the curriculum from the elementary grades on. Some schools have developed special Spanish courses for heritage speakers, in which their advanced listening and speaking skills are complemented by the study of culture. Many institutions at the secondary and tertiary levels have developed professional programs and courses for these and other students, in business, medical, and legal Spanish. Bilingual education programs, too, can nurture and enrich the Spanish skills of heritage learners while enabling them to become proficient in English.

Although the teaching of Spanish has a relatively short history in the United States, having begun only at the turn of the century, today more than 4,000,000 learners in grades K-12 and more than 600,000 at the post-secondary level are studying Spanish. Enrollments have increased by almost fifteen percent at the college level and by nearly fifty percent in grades K-12 during the past ten years. It is clear that the relevance of the study of Spanish has been widely recognized and that study of the language is increasing over the entire educational spectrum.

> ... THE GROWING PRESENCE OF SPANISH SPEAKERS AND HISPANIC CULTURES IN THE UNITED STATES ...

INTRODUCTION TO GOALS

Readers of the Spanish Standards may find it helpful to refer to the generic Standards document included in this volume. It is important to keep in mind that both the *Standards for Foreign Language Learning* and these *Standards for Learning Spanish* envision language learning as it best serves students of the twenty-first century: articulated sequences of instruction that begin when children start school and continue throughout their educational careers, and that situate language learning as a core element of the school curriculum as well as a valuable component of personal and professional adult life.

Communication — *Goal One*
Communicate in Spanish

In our rapidly shrinking, interdependent world of the twenty-first century, the ability to communicate in Spanish is becoming increasingly important. Effective communication includes the ability to understand and express oneself orally and in writing in situations that may be either planned and predictable or spontaneous and unpredictable. Thus, students must be able to participate appropriately in a range of social relationships and in a variety of contexts. They must be able to interact in communicative exchanges, either face-to-face or via technology; interpret what they observe, hear, read, and view, both in real-life interactions and in the media; and present information, concepts, and ideas orally, visually, and in writing.

The capacity to communicate requires not only an awareness of the linguistic code to be used, but also an understanding of the cultural context within which meaning is encoded and decoded. As an example, the word "house" can be rendered into Spanish as "*casa*," but the images produced by the word might be quite different, depending upon the cultural community in which the word is used. Linguistically, one can know how to say "*gracias*," but unless one knows when to use the term, the message conveyed may be quite different from the message intended. The better one speaks the language, the more one is expected to be aware of the cultural nuance embedded in the message conveyed. This mutual dependence of language and culture to produce meaning results in a close relationship among all of the goals. For instance, the insights highlighted in the Goal Four section build upon the cultural knowledge described under Goal Two to enhance the communicative abilities of Goal One.

Students may enter the classroom with a range of previous experiences with Spanish language and cultures. Some may have participated in a Foreign Language in the Elementary School (FLES) or immersion experience or a bilingual education program. For others, Spanish may be the language of the community or of the home, or it may have been used to communicate informally with friends and/or family members. Still others may have had brief experiences or informal encounters through an isolated unit of instruction in an earlier grade, through having watched television programs like *Sesame Street,* or as a result of

> ... MUTUAL DEPENDENCE OF LANGUAGE AND CULTURE TO PRODUCE MEANING...

some other incidental exposure. In addition, some students may have a home language other than English, which may influence how and what they learn.

All learners, regardless of their prior experience, have the capacity to improve, and must have the opportunity to build upon and expand their communicative skills, gaining the ability to comprehend the varieties of Spanish that are common worldwide. Students of Spanish, whatever their initial levels of functional ability in the language, can then improve their personal awareness and linguistic capabilities in an increasing range of cultural contexts and using a variety of media to communicate.

ALL LEARNERS ...

MUST HAVE THE

OPPORTUNITY TO ...

EXPAND THEIR

COMMUNICATIVE

SKILLS ...

STANDARD 1.1 Students engage in conversations, provide and obtain information, express feelings and emotions, and exchange opinions.

This standard focuses on interpersonal communication. Many students begin the study of Spanish with a desire to interact effectively with speakers of the language community. In general, native speakers are reasonably tolerant of novice learners with respect to the cultural and linguistic appropriateness of their communicative efforts. As learners' skills improve, however, there is a rising expectation that their Spanish will be increasingly appropriate linguistically and culturally.

Students who come from Spanish-speaking backgrounds or who have had prior experience with the language may have already acquired the linguistic ability to communicate within their own communities. However, they may lack the broader knowledge of the language and its cultures necessary to adapt their skills to interact effectively with speakers from other cultural communities and in situations requiring varied levels of formality (registers).

Sample Progress Indicators, Grade 4

- Students ask and answer questions about very familiar topics, such as family, school events, and celebrations, in person or via short letters, e-mail, audio, or videotapes.
- Students engage in common classroom interactions, such as greeting each other and the teacher and taking their leave; stating needs and preferences; and expressing gratitude and appreciation, using culturally appropriate gestures and oral expressions. (For example, for saying goodbye, they add polite expressions like ¡*Qué gusto de verte!* or ¡*Que te/le vaya bien*! and they use appropriate gestures.)
- Students exchange descriptions of people and tangible products of the culture, including toys, dress, types of dwellings, and foods, with other members of the class.
- Students share their likes and dislikes with each other and with the class.

Sample Progress Indicators, Grade 8

- Students extend, accept, and refuse invitations, formal and informal, oral and written, using expressions and behavior appropriate to varied situations.
- Students use expressions for managing conversations—that is, they can show interest in what others say (¡*Qué interesante!*; ¡*No me digas!*; ¿*De veras?*), take the floor (*Sí, y…*; *Sí, pero un momento…*; *Yo digo que…*); and ask for help or check comprehension (¿*Cómo se dice…?*; ¿*Comprende/s?*)

- Students exchange information about personal events, memorable experiences, and other school subjects with classmates and/or peers in Spanish-speaking communities. They then use these data to compare, contrast, and express opinions and preferences.
- Students use Spanish to acquire goods, services, or information orally and/or in writing.
- Students use Spanish in group activities such as "town meetings" and advice columns in which they develop and propose solutions to issues and problems related to the school or community.

Sample Progress Indicators, Grade 12

- Students use expressions appropriately for managing conversations, taking into account the speakers and their relationships and other aspects of the situation; that is, they can interrupt, apologize, express agreement and disagreement, according to appropriate rules of politeness.
- Students use Spanish to exchange and support their opinions and individual perspectives with peers and/or other Spanish-speakers on a variety of topics dealing with contemporary and historical issues.
- Students use Spanish to share their analyses and personal reactions to expository and literary texts with peers and/or other speakers of Spanish, such as the battle between man and nature in the short stories of Horacio Quiroga, or the emotions expressed in *Las coplas* of Jorge Manrique.
- Students use Spanish in group activities in which they develop and propose solutions to issues and problems that are of concern to members of their own cultures and to the cultures of the Spanish-speaking world, such as deforestation and loss of rain forests, ecotourism, or the maintenance/loss of the Spanish language in the United States.

Sample Progress Indicators, Grade 16

- Students use Spanish to discuss some aspects of their field of study such as major Spanish language skills required and employment opportunities, with other speakers of Spanish.
- Students use Spanish orally and in writing to communicate with people already employed in their field of study by writing letters of inquiry for positions and/or participating in simulated job interviews.
- Students use Spanish in a professional experience or internship related to their field of study.
- Students exchange points of view on global topics such as poverty, education, politics, ecology, or other topics of personal interest.

STANDARD 1.2 Students understand and interpret written and spoken Spanish on a variety of topics.

Students must be able to interact with a wide range of texts that they hear and read. Beyond assigning literal meaning to a language sample, learners must be able to recognize and interpret the text at the cultural or figurative level. Text types encompass oral and written, formal and informal, language samples including both literary and non-literary materials (for example, lectures and content-based texts in academic disciplines, literature in many

> STUDENTS USE SPANISH APPROPRIATELY FOR MANAGING CONVERSATIONS ...

genres, audiovisual media, and other print and non-print items produced by and for native speakers of Spanish). As the learners' skills expand, they should be introduced to a variety of textual sources, levels of formality, and regional variations.

Students who begin their formalized study of Spanish with a high degree of oral comprehension have the opportunity to develop greater skill in reading and interpreting. Because of their higher levels of linguistic and cultural control, they should build upon and expand their communicative skills as they interact linguistically and culturally with more diverse and less familiar texts that come from authentic sources, and that are age appropriate and of high interest to the learners. Oral and written language samples should reflect the diversity found among national and regional Spanish-language communities and incorporate the colloquial usage, linguistic patterns, dialectical variations, and lexicon common to those groups.

... INTERPRET TEXTS AT THE CULTURAL OR FIGURATIVE LEVEL.

Sample Progress Indicators, Grade 4

- Students comprehend main ideas and identify the principal characters in developmentally-appropriate oral narratives in Spanish, such as personal anecdotes, well-known fairy tales, and other narratives based on familiar themes.
- Students identify people and objects in their school and home or those from other school subjects, based on oral and written descriptions in Spanish.
- Students comprehend the principal message contained in various Spanish-language media such as illustrated texts, posters, and advertisements.
- Students interpret gestures, intonation, and other visual or auditory clues in Spanish-language visual media such as videos, films, and television programs.

Sample Progress Indicators, Grade 8

- Students identify the principal characters and comprehend the main ideas and themes in age-appropriate Spanish language literary texts.
- Students understand announcements as found in advertisements, magazines, newspapers, or television commercials.
- Students understand the main themes and significant details of writings on topics from other subjects and products of the cultures as found in newspapers, magazines, e-mail, the Internet, the World Wide Web or other printed sources in Spanish.
- Students use knowledge acquired in other settings and from other subject areas to comprehend spoken and written messages in Spanish, such as using the metric system or understanding time expressed using the 24-hour clock.

Sample Progress Indicators, Grade 12

- Students demonstrate an understanding of the main ideas and significant details of live and recorded discussions, short lectures, and presentations in Spanish on current or past events that are reported in Spanish-language media.
- Students demonstrate an understanding of the principal elements of non-fiction articles such as those found in newspapers, magazines, and e-mail, on topics of current and historical importance to Spanish speakers.
- Students demonstrate an increasing understanding of the cultural nuances of meaning in written and spoken Spanish as expressed by speakers of the language in

formal and informal settings such as a *telenovela* or an editorial published in a Spanish language newspaper.

- Students analyze the main plot, subplot, characters, (their descriptions, roles, and significance to the story) in authentic literary texts written in Spanish.

Sample Progress Indicators, Grade 16

- Students demonstrate an increased understanding of details of authentic oral and written textual sources, such as plays on words, social satire, and slapstick comedy, demonstrating sensitivity to stylistic features such as word choice and level of formality.

- Students demonstrate an awareness of the cultural basis of humor.

- Students demonstrate the ability to distinguish between materials that state unsupported personal opinion of the author and factually-supported personal opinions.

- Students use textual evidence to support interpretations of literary or journalistic works such as cultural perspective and stylistic conventions.

- Students demonstrate the ability to derive information from written material related to their fields of study in tasks such as note-taking for subsequent presentation or documentation of resources.

STANDARD 1.3 Students present information, concepts, and ideas to an audience of listeners or readers on a variety of topics in Spanish.

> ... MOVE FROM MEMORIZED MATERIAL TO CREATIVE USE OF LANGUAGE ...

In the beginning stages, novice learners' performance capabilities may be limited largely to memorized phrases. They must move from memorized material to creative use of language in order to focus on presentation skills. Learners with prior experiences with Spanish, such as heritage language learners, students in intensive elementary school programs, and students with extended residence abroad, building upon their stronger oral base, can be made aware of the conventions of purposeful writing, strategies and organization of composition, more formalized public speaking, appropriate to the cultures. All learners must meet the cultural expectations regarding the different ways in which information, concepts, and ideas may be presented.

Sample Progress Indicators, Grade 4

- Students prepare illustrated stories about activities or events in their environment and share them with an audience orally or in writing.

- Students give presentations in Spanish to students in another classroom, dramatizing songs, short anecdotes, or poetry commonly known by peers in Hispanic cultures..

- Students tell or retell familiar stories in Spanish, both orally and in writing.

- Students tell or write peers in Hispanic cultures about products and/or practices of their own culture, such as typical celebrations, family events, or foods.

Sample Progress Indicators, Grade 8

- Students perform short plays and skits, recite selected poems and anecdotes, or sing songs at a school board or PTA meeting, or at another school-related event.
- Students prepare tape or video recorded messages on topics of personal interest to share locally or with school peers and/or members of the Spanish-speaking community, using culturally appropriate behavior or typical gestures.
- Students prepare stories or brief written reports about Hispanic sports or political figures in the media, their own personal experiences, or their other school subjects to share with classmates and/or members of the Spanish-speaking communities.
- Students prepare a written summary for a school magazine of the plot and characters in selected pieces of age-appropriate literature written in Spanish.

Sample Progress Indicators, Grade 12

- For a public audience, students perform scenes and/or recite poems or excerpts from short stories connected to a topic from other disciplines such as world history, geography, the arts, or mathematics.
- Students select and analyze creative and artistic expressions of Spanish-speaking cultures from the visual and performing arts.
- Students summarize the content of an excerpt from the Hispanic media in order to discuss the topics via e-mail with other speakers of Spanish.
- Students prepare a research-based analysis of a current event or issue such as the World Cup finals or immigration, from the perspective of both U.S. and Hispanic cultures.

Sample Progress Indicators, Grade 16

- Students prepare a formal, research-based written analysis of some aspect of their field of study, including perspectives from the United States and from a culture where Spanish is spoken, such as the certification of practitioners or international copyright law. They make extensive use of Spanish-language sources.
- Students collect oral histories and present them orally or in writing.
- Students present a play, write poems, and/or write short stories.
- Students use desktop publishing software to develop brochures, prospectuses, or scientific reports for use in their fields of study.

STUDENTS ACQUIRE A PERSPECTIVE FROM WHICH TO EXAMINE AND ANALYZE THEIR OWN CULTURE MORE OBJECTIVELY

Cultures *Goal Two*
Gain Knowledge and Understanding of Spanish-Speaking Cultures

Speakers of Spanish share a common cultural heritage and also represent diverse cultures. These diverse cultures may be geographically identifiable and may also be further shaped by factors such as gender, age, socio-economic status, and religion. Students should have a range of learning experiences that reflect the richness of cultures encompassed in the Spanish-speaking world and, particularly, those they may encounter in their local community.

Students need to understand the perspectives, practices, and products of the Spanish-speaking world. The term "perspectives" is used here to refer to the worldview, attitudes, and belief systems that frame what Spanish speakers think and do. The term "practices" is used here to represent the knowledge of "what to do when and where, and how to interact within a Hispanic cultural context." Practices are exemplified in the everyday life, the social observances and behaviors in the diverse cultures of Spanish-speakers. "Products" range from aesthetic expressions often identified with literature, art, and music, to those that combine aesthetic expressions and utilitarian purposes, such as *artesanías*, folk tales, folk art, pottery, and musical instruments, to functional objects used in everyday life. Social, political, economic, and cultural institutions may be viewed as both cultural practices and products. The mutually-influential relationships among perspectives, practices, and products are illustrated in the graphic below.

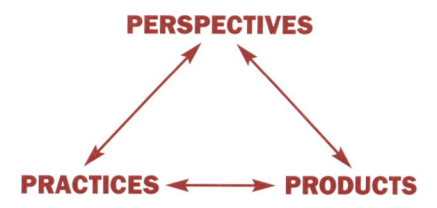

PERSPECTIVES

PRACTICES ⟷ PRODUCTS

… A BASIS FOR INTERPRETING EVENTS IN THE MODERN WORLD …

Traditionally, knowledge of cultural products and practices has been the primary focus of culture instruction. However, such knowledge is incomplete unless students understand how cultural perspectives drive and are, in turn, shaped by products and practices. Further, cultural perspectives are critical for developing communication skills that allow students to exchange meanings effectively, accurately, and appropriately with native speakers. It is possible and necessary not only to make students aware of the role that cultural perspectives play in language and life, but also to teach students useful strategies to discover perspectives through their interactions with the cultures, culture bearers, cultural products, and cultural practices. Heritage learners have a unique opportunity to explore contrasts in perspectives and practices of diverse members of their communities.

Linguistic fluency does not guarantee successful cultural interactions. Students of Hispanic communities who represent a variety of background knowledge, including heritage speakers from in United States, will benefit from a deeper understanding of the relationships among cultural perspectives and culturally appropriate behaviors. Goal 2 prepares students to identify key cultural perspectives, products, practices, and concepts and to select, synthesize, and interpret them in ways that result in sensitive and meaningful interactions. Goal 2 emphasizes the fact that students are learning the when and why of communication through the study of Hispanic culture.

STANDARD 2.1 Students demonstrate an understanding of the relationship between the practices and perspectives of Hispanic cultures.

One cannot effectively communicate using the Spanish language, nor interact within Spanish-speaking cultures, without being aware of the relationship between the practices and perspectives that define and describe the Hispanic community. This standard focuses on the need for awareness and understanding of Hispanic cultural behaviors within families, within the classroom, and within the community, as an important element in the learning of the Spanish language as a system. The following progress indicators relate to learning experiences based on the cultures of Spanish speakers.

Sample Progress Indicators, Grade 4

- Students use appropriate gestures and oral expressions for greetings, leave-takings, and common classroom interactions such as addressing the teacher formally and their classmates informally and accompanying greetings with a kiss on the cheek, an *abrazo*, or a handshake.

- Students participate in age-appropriate cultural activities such as games, songs, birthday celebrations and dramatizations appropriate to the Hispanic community, identifying appropriate songs for each celebration, and describing holiday practices, typical foods, gift-giving traditions, and other practices that reflect Hispanic cultures.

- Students observe, identify, and/or demonstrate simple patterns of behavior or interaction in various settings such as school, family, and the community, recognizing who speaks first, who addresses whom first, and forms of address that demonstrate politeness, respect, and consideration for others.

Sample Progress Indicators, Grade 8

- Students learn about and participate in age-appropriate cultural practices such as leading games, taking turns, playing sports, and attending musical, dance, and dramatic performances.

- Students participate in real or simulated age-appropriate cultural occurrences related to special events or personal occasions, such as saint's days and birthday celebrations, and graduation exercises within the context of Hispanic cultures.

- Students observe, analyze, and discuss patterns of behavior, such as going out in groups instead of in couples, that are typical of their peer group within the Hispanic communities.

Sample Progress Indicators, Grade 12

- Students interact in a variety of cultural contexts that reflect both peer-group and adult activities within different cultures by role playing and using appropriate verbal and nonverbal cues in different activities, such as shopping, planning an itinerary, or applying for a job.

- Students identify, analyze, and discuss various Hispanic patterns of behavior or interaction related to cultural perspectives that are typical of the diversity in Hispanic cultures, such as weddings, funerals, personal events, independence day observances, and national ceremonial events.

- Students identify, examine, and discuss connections between cultural perspectives and socially approved behavioral patterns related to dating, pursuing university studies, establishing one's independence, and maintaining close family relationships.

- Students analyze, discuss, compare and contrast experiences of heritage and non-heritage learners as they relate to family gatherings, friendships and *noviazgos*, celebrations of national and/or ethnic heritage, and other events common to Hispanic communities.

Sample Progress Indicators, Grade 16

- Students interact appropriately in *tertulias* and other social activities with Spanish speakers who are among their peer groups.

- Students interact appropriately, in Spanish, in cultural contexts related to their chosen field of study, such as the medical and legal professions, academia, business and clerical jobs, and community service-related work.

- Students identify, analyze, and discuss ways in which perspectives influence patterns of behavior in the workplace of both heritage and non-heritage workers.

- Students identify, analyze, and support or challenge positions that reflect current issues and events that affect the Hispanic community, such as the English Only movement, or the changes in economic patterns that threaten traditional ways of life.

- Students act in a culturally correct manner in most contexts, showing sensitivity to and understanding of the meanings that are implied by patterns of behavior such as appropriate table manners and norms of respect within different social situations, or "small talk" before discussion of business issues.

STANDARD 2.2 Students demonstrate an understanding of the relationship between the products and perspectives of the different Hispanic cultures.

> ... THE RELATIONSHIP BETWEEN THE "WHAT" AND THE "WHY"

Development of an awareness of the products from Hispanic cultures, whether tangible, as are *artesanías*, or intangible, as are sociocultural mores, is essential to effective communication in Spanish. A true understanding of the cultures of Spanish speakers means, among other things, understanding the relationship between the "what" of cultural products (food, clothing, *artesanías*, political institutions), as it is interwoven with the "why," or the perspectives that surround these products. Effective interaction with Spanish speakers requires the ability to understand relationships between the "what" and the "why." The following progress indicators relate to learning experiences based on perspectives—"viewpoints"— that define and describe products from Hispanic communities.

Sample Progress Indicators, Grade 4

- Students observe, identify and/or describe tangible products from Spanish-speaking cultures such as toys (*papaletas, títeres*), traditional and contemporary dress (*las molas de San Blas, los huipiles de Guatemala*), types of dwellings (*palacios, casas, chosas*), and staple foods (*arroz, frijoles* in Central America).

- Students identify, experience, hear, or read about expressive products of Spanish speakers such as children's songs (*Que llueva, que llueva, la Virgen de la Cueva…*), selections from children's literature, traditional poetry and rhymes (*Acerín, Acerán, los maderos de San Juan*), popular children's stories, and folklore (Aztec legends).

- Students recognize common themes, ideas, or perspectives of groups of Spanish speakers, such as friendships and individual and family responsibilities.

Sample Progress Indicators, Grade 8

- Students search for, investigate, and identify the function of *artesanías*, which might include hand painted ceramics, *serapes*, baskets, jewelry, *molinillos* for making hot cholocate, and wooden and stone carvings.
- Students experience (read, listen to, observe, perform) expressive products of Spanish-speakers, such as stories, poetry, music, paintings, dance, and drama.
- Students identify, discuss, and analyze a selected Hispanic community and its themes, ideas, and perspectives related to the products being studied (for example, for Peru, *arpilleras* and weavings made from the wool of the alpaca).

Sample Progress Indicators, Grade 12

- Students experience, discuss, and analyze expressive products of the culture, such as selections from various literary genres, the fine arts, architecture, *artesanías* (e.g., *tapices, tejidos*), and useful everyday objects.
- Students identify, analyze, and evaluate themes, ideas, and perspectives related to the products being studied, such as Mexico's literature and murals of social protest, national symbols and emblems (the eagle and serpent), and for modern times, the Mexico City subway system.
- Students explore the relationships among the products, practices, and perspectives of Spanish speakers as indicated in formal documents such as the Spanish Constitution of 1978; in political cartoons; and in product advertising unique to the region being studied, such as the Maja health and beauty care products of Spain.

Sample Progress Indicators, Grade 16

- Students participate appropriately in discussions with Spanish speakers about institutions and their themes, ideas, and perspectives related to their field of study or job, such as customer relations, new product development, and marketing strategies within a business.
- Students participate appropriately in discussions with Spanish speakers about literary, social, economic, political, and other topics that might be controversial, such as social classes and the extent to which they are depicted realistically in film, literature, and the news media.
- Students identify, discuss, and analyze such intangible products of Hispanic cultures as social, economic, and political institutions (the monarchy in Spain; the political party structure of Mexico; the educational system of Costa Rica) and explore relationships among these institutions and the perspectives of the people.

Connections   *Goal Three*
Connect with Other Disciplines and Acquire Information

All students of Spanish—from beginners to more advanced learners and learners with heritage backgrounds—have unique opportunities to use their growing language skills for communicative purposes that go beyond personal survival or literary topics. The number of Spanish speakers and Hispanic communities in the United States allows students access to resources on topics and in disciplines that have not traditionally been included in Spanish classrooms. Students now have opportunities to interact with native speakers who are in the medical profession, legal profession, academe, and community-service positions, to explore ideas and viewpoints on a range of current issues that are relevant to Spanish-speaking communities.

Print and non-print resources developed for and by native speakers in the United States further increase the resources through which learners of Spanish may access information on a broad range of issues and topics. Moreover, many students will want to use Spanish for academic purposes, as they pursue their chosen career, and as they interact with community members. Students may want to use Spanish in their study of content areas across the grades, as they research academic literary and non-literary topics, in the workplace, and in Hispanic communities.

Students will need to have developed the communication tools necessary for successful participation in such activities. Inclusion of a range of issues and topics drawn from disciplines across the curriculum is likely to facilitate the development of the language skills students need. Finally, using Spanish for acquiring information in various disciplines reinforces awareness of the applicability of these languages for pursuing varied personal and career goals.

STANDARD 3.1 Students reinforce and further their knowledge of other disciplines through Spanish.

All academic disciplines, or content areas, share a common core of skills and processes, such as higher order thinking and the use of reading strategies. Students deepen and enhance their understanding of concepts when they have the opportunity to learn them in both English and Spanish. For example, young children learn about the rain forest better when they practice the concepts in English and Spanish.

For students to increase their knowledge of other subjects they need to be able to process content-related information that is available only in Spanish. Moreover, the availability of increasing amounts of Spanish language material via the Internet makes knowing Spanish an indispensable tool for students.

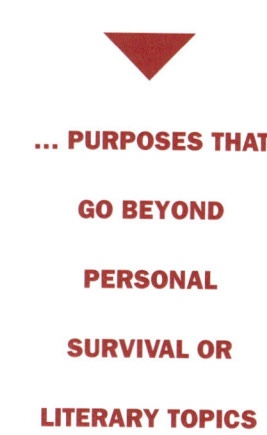

Sample Progress Indicators, Grade 4

- Students demonstrate in Spanish an understanding about concepts learned in other subject areas, such as the categorization of animals by their habitats; this may include concepts from other subject areas, such as weather, mathematics, measurements, and geography.
- Students use their understanding of weather maps and temperature charts to select cities or countries in South America that they would like to visit.
- Students apply their knowledge of the metric system when role-playing a shopping trip to an authentic *mercado*.

> ... PURPOSES THAT GO BEYOND PERSONAL SURVIVAL OR LITERARY TOPICS

Sample Progress Indicators, Grade 8

- Through research projects, students expand on topics learned in other school subjects as they relate to the Spanish-speaking world, such as geographical information, historical facts and concepts, and ecological developments.

- Students comprehend articles or short videos in Spanish on topics being studied in other classes, such as current sports events, volcanic eruptions and other natural disasters, and national patriotic celebrations (e.g., independence day in various countries).

- Students present oral or written reports in Spanish on topics being studied in other classes.

Sample Progress Indicators, Grade 12

- Students acquire information from a variety of sources written in Spanish about a topic being studied in a range of school subjects; for example, they use an essay on European architecture of the sixteenth century and an Internet tour of the Prado Museum as they study the Renaissance in an interdisciplinary unit.

- Students combine information from other school subjects with information available in Spanish to complete activities in the Spanish classroom, as when they research early nineteenth century American writings on the settlement of the Southwest, as well as writings by *Tejanos* and *Mexicanos* of the period.

- Students discuss topics from other school subjects in Spanish, including political and historical concepts, worldwide social issues, environmental issues, and current events. Examples: global warming and conservation of resources.

Sample Progress Indicators, Grade 16

- Students obtain and use information available in Spanish related to their field of study; for example, students read reactions of Spaniards to the "euro" and its impact on the Spanish economy.

- Students use Spanish language resources available through electronic means, such as chat rooms, e-mail, and the Internet, to gather information in Spanish on the work and knowledge base of professionals in their own fields of study.

- Students successfully combine information acquired in Spanish and in English to meet the needs of their fields of study, as when an international business student prepares a prospectus for a new international business venture using data gathered from different sites around the world.

▼

… BECOMING BETTER INFORMED CITIZENS OF THE UNITED STATES AND OF THE WORLD.

STANDARD 3.2 Students acquire information and recognize the distinctive viewpoints that are available only through the Spanish language and its many cultures.

Successful participation in Spanish-speaking communities requires that students know how to acquire information and recognize viewpoints from print and non-print media that is only available in Spanish. The ability to access and to process information available only in Spanish contributes to students' becoming better informed citizens of the United States and of the world. Information and viewpoints related to mathematics, science, and especially social studies, are at times nonexistent via English translations. Translations, when available, may also be inaccurate or misleading in cultural perspective. Decisions about what is or is not translated into English often have political and social implications.

As international technology continues to progress, more and more information in Spanish will become available and easily obtained.

Sample Progress Indicators, Grade 4

- Students read, listen to, and talk about the cultural bases of age-appropriate school content, folk tales, short stories, poems, and songs written for native speakers of Spanish, such as a science lesson from a Grade 4 textbook; *La leyenda de Popocatépetl*; or the song *De colores*.

Sample Progress Indicators, Grade 8

- Students use sources intended for same-age speakers of Spanish to prepare reports on topics of personal interest, or those with which they have limited previous experience. For example, a tennis enthusiast reports on magazine articles on Gabriela Sabatini.

- Students use sources about the United States intended for same-age speakers of Spanish and analyze different perspectives on contemporary issues of concern and/or interest (e.g., articles on U.S. celebrities and famous persons from Hispanic countries in the United States; news reports on current events in the United States; television commercials that advertise U.S.-made products for local consumption in other countries).

Sample Progress Indicators, Grade 12

- Students use a variety of sources intended for same-age speakers of Spanish to prepare reports on topics of personal interest, or those with which they have limited previous experience, and compare these to information obtained on the same topics written in English (e.g., obituary announcements from several different countries' newspapers—easily obtained through the Internet).

- Students use Spanish to access viewpoints on issues available only through Spanish print and non-print media and compare them to print and non-print media coverage of the same topics written in the United States for an English-speaking audience (e.g., newspaper accounts of an election or of the effects of *El Niño* in Peru vs. the United States; the media treatment of *el Día de la Raza* vs. Columbus Day).

Sample Progress Indicators, Grade 16

- Students use information available only in Spanish, acquired through electronic or other means, in comparisons with information on the same topics available in English, and analyze the different perspectives and/or biases shown in the sources. For example, the English Only movement, conditions of migrant workers, indigenous movements and human rights, bilingual education.

- Students regularly apply information available only in Spanish to communicate in oral and written forms with Spanish speakers about a variety of topics relevant to their field of study. For example, prospective teachers in the United States gather views from teachers in Spain on accountability issues.

- Students use Spanish to explore viewpoints about other academic disciplines on issues such as global warming, South American national boundary conflicts, or practices related to business negotiations.

Comparisons — Goal Four
Develop Insights into the Nature of Language and Culture

ABOVE ALL ELSE, LANGUAGE REFLECTS CULTURE

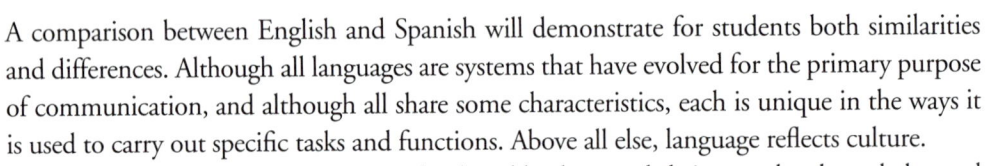

A comparison between English and Spanish will demonstrate for students both similarities and differences. Although all languages are systems that have evolved for the primary purpose of communication, and although all share some characteristics, each is unique in the ways it is used to carry out specific tasks and functions. Above all else, language reflects culture.

Students from varied language and cultural backgrounds bring to class knowledge and abilities which teachers can use as a starting point for making observations about the diverse ways in which languages and cultures meet the needs of their people.

STANDARD 4.1 Students demonstrate understanding of the nature of language through comparisons between the language studied and their own.

This standard focuses on helping students understand how to learn a language and how to use it for communicative purposes, while embracing the concept of the life-long language learner. Heritage learners of Spanish should demonstrate an awareness of similarities between their native language and English, as well as differences among varieties of Spanish. All students develop understanding that each variety of a language is valid for purposes of the community it serves.

Sample Progress Indicators, Grade 4
- Students cite and use examples of words that are borrowed in Spanish and in English, and they hypothesize about why languages might need to borrow words. Some examples of Spanish-English borrowing are *jonrón, jogging, camping, patio, enchilada, rodeo.*
- Students realize that cognates enhance comprehension of spoken and written Spanish, and they demonstrate that awareness by identifying commonly occurring cognates in the language, such as words ending in *-ción, -ero, -tad, -dad, -mente.*
- Students are aware of the existence of idiomatic expressions in English and in Spanish, and explain how idiomatic expressions work in general (e.g., t*omar el pelo* - to pull one's leg; *llover a cántaros* - to rain buckets).
- Students demonstrate an awareness of formal and informal forms of language (registers) and try out expressions of politeness (e.g., for responding to being called upon in class, and for addressing adults formally but addressing peers informally), comparing the expressions to those found in their first language.

Standards for Learning Spanish

- Students report differences and similarities between the sound and writing systems of their own language and Spanish (b/v, h, ll, ñ, r, rr; location of letters in alphabetical listings).

Sample Progress Indicators, Grade 8

- Students hypothesize about the relationship between English and Spanish based on their awareness of cognates (*la reata* - lariat; *montaña* - mountain; *educación* - education; *universidad* - university; *estudiante* - student) and the similarity of idioms (*de tal palo, tal astilla* - a chip off the old block).
- Students demonstrate an awareness of ways of expressing respect and communicating status differences in their own language and in Spanish, such as *señor, señorita, señora* - Mr., Miss, Mrs., Ms./Sir, Ma'am; *Maestra/Maestro*; and the familiar and formal forms of verbs.
- Students demonstrate awareness that English and Spanish have sound distinctions that they must master to communicate meaning (*pero-perro; continuo-continúo-continuó*).

Sample Progress Indicators, Grade 12

- Students recognize that some words that appear to be the same may have different meanings between English and Spanish (*embarazar* is not embarrass; *introducir* is not always introduce; *molestar* is to bother; *realizar* is to realize a goal or dream).
- Students demonstrate an awareness that there are phrases and idioms that do not translate directly from Spanish to English or vice-versa, such as *tomar una decisión* or *hacer pedazos* in Spanish; to rain cats and dogs or to eat like a horse in English.
- Students analyze elements of Spanish, such as time and tense, and comparable linguistic elements in English, and conjecture about how languages use forms to express time and tense relationships (e.g., auxiliary verbs; verb endings as tense markers).
- Students compare the writing systems of English and Spanish. They also examine other writing systems and report about the nature of those writing systems (logographic, syllabic, alphabetic).

Sample Progress Indicators, Grade 16

- Students hypothesize about the evolution of language based on their awareness of cognates, similarities among idioms (e.g., "*Pájaro en mano…*" and "A bird in the hand…") and etymological changes in words (*Vuestra merced* - *Usted*).
- Students investigate the ways in which languages in contact influence each other, such as Arabic words in Spanish (*alfombra, almohada*); Spanish words in English (patio, plaza, corral); and code-switching (*Vamos al mall; ¿Dónde está mi lunch?*)
- Students compare terminology and structure in the presentation of material related specifically to their field of study (e.g., technical vocabulary) and hypothesize about the cultural implications for this usage.

STUDENTS DEVELOP A GREATER UNDERSTANDING OF THE STRUCTURE AND VOCABULARY OF ENGLISH

STANDARD 4.2 Students demonstrate understanding of the concept of culture through comparisons between the cultures studied and their own.

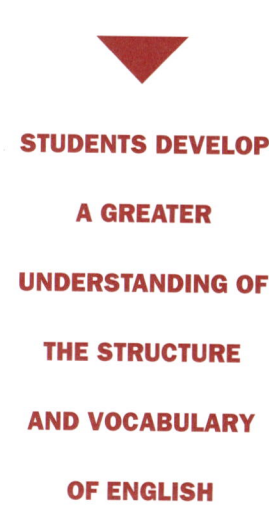

The impact of culture on language use is immense. Many times, the decision of whether to use a particular gesture, vocabulary item, or phase is determined culturally, not grammatically. The grammatically accurate use of *Yo quiero…* to express a wish or desire may not be as effective as more softened forms, such as *Quisiera….* Likewise, a student may ask a question with linguistic accuracy but ask it in a social context that renders the question inappropriate. For example, asking a person's age or marital status may be done accurately in a grammatical sense, but considered inappropriate or impertinent from a cultural perspective.

STUDENTS BECOME AWARE THAT THEY, TOO, HAVE A CULTURE

Sample Progress Indicators, Grade 4

- Students demonstrate an awareness that gestures are an important part of communication and that gestures may differ between English and Spanish, for example, for pointing out things and people; for showing how tall someone is; for asking someone to "come here."

- Students compare and contrast tangible products of Hispanic cultures and their own, for example, *fútbol* - football; *marimba* - xylophone; *leyendas*; team cheers (*A la bi, a la ba, a la sim, bum, ba*); children's rhymes (*Tortillas, tortillas, para mamá…*); and songs (*Arroz con leche*; *Naranja dulce*).

Sample Progress Indicators, Grade 8

- Students contrast verbal and non-verbal behavior within particular activities in Hispanic cultures and their own, such as table manners and saying "*Buen provecho*"; and behavior for private parties (time of arrival, how long to stay, hostess gifts).

- Students demonstrate an awareness that they, too, have a culture, by comparing sample daily activities in Hispanic cultures and their own (e.g., mealtimes as family events including *sobremesa*; dating customs in both cultures; the influence of sports heroes and other cultural icons on aspects of daily life in the United States).

- Students speculate on why certain products are important to cultures by analyzing selected products from Hispanic cultures and their own (*calaveras* - jack-o-lanterns; *tortilleras* - bread machines; *colectivos*, *busetas* - buses vs. automobiles).

- Students hypothesize about the relationship between cultural perspectives and expressive products such as music, visual arts, performing arts, and appropriate forms of literature by analyzing selected products from Hispanic cultures and their own (*artesanías*; folk songs and dances; Becquer's *Rimas*).

Sample Progress Indicators, Grade 12

- Students hypothesize about the relationship between cultural perspectives and practices, such as work schedules, by analyzing selected conventions from Hispanic cultures and their own (length and frequency of vacations; the *almuerzo* and *siesta* vs. *jornada única* and carrying a lunch to the office).

- Students identify variations in rhythms instrumentation as reflections of local resources and history (*el güiro* in Puerto Rico, *el cuatro* in Venezuela, *el charango* and *la flauta* in the Andean region, *la marimba* in Central America).

- Students compare themes and styles of age-appropriate literary works written for English speakers and Spanish speakers (José Larra's *Artículos de costumbres* [selected items]; Amado Nervo, *Una esperanza*; Anderson Imbert, *Microcuentos*; Quevedo's *Poderoso caballero es don Dinero*).

- Students compare the social acceptability of words, idioms, and vocal inflections in English and in Spanish (e.g., *idiota; estúpido; ¡Dios mío!*; diminutives and terms of endearment like *tío, hijita, mi corazón, amorcito, mi reina*).
- Students analyze crosscultural misunderstandings to discover their bases and suggest remedies (e.g., stereotypes; concept of family; standards of entertainment; standards of dress; concept of friendship; importance of individual rights vs. the interests of the group).

Sample Progress Indicators, Grade 16

- Students compare and contrast cultural institutions, such as government, schools, and religion, between Hispanic countries and the United States.
- Students demonstrate appropriate language and cultural practices while actively engaged in a professional or social setting when these are different from U.S. practices (engaging in small talk vs. "getting down to business"; observing social protocol in a business context; recognizing the "must-do's" and taboos of the host culture).
- Students compare and contrast various types of original texts and their English translations in terms of literal and figurative meaning.
- Students compare and contrast conventions in poetry, such as meter, rhyme, and free verse, and discourse style and organizational patterns in selected literary forms in English and Spanish.

Communities *Goal Five*
Participate in Multilingual Communities at Home and Around the World

Goal Five focuses on using Spanish as a means of communicating with other Spanish speakers in schools, in the local community, in the United States, and abroad. Such applications may be primarily personal in nature (making friendships, travel, self-enrichment) or professional (education, business, politics). These activities may be spontaneous and self-motivated, or required and monitored by the teacher.

STANDARD 5.1 Students use the language both within and beyond the school setting

Within the school setting, there are opportunities for students to interact with classmates, younger students, older students, and keypals in other schools, communities, and countries. When students have opportunities to apply the Spanish skills that they learn in the classroom to real-life activities, they become more motivated to excel. Because of the large Spanish-speaking population in the United States, many students can participate in Hispanic communities in their own cities. Students can also familiarize themselves with specific cultures, as well as improve their Spanish proficiency, by traveling or participating in study abroad programs. With the ever-increasing access to technology, students may also participate in Spanish-speaking communities in cyberspace.

WHEN STUDENTS ... APPLY WHAT THEY LEARN ... TO REAL-LIFE ACTIVITIES, THEY BECOME MOTIVATED ...

Sample Progress Indicators, Grade 4

- Students convey messages to Spanish speakers in person and by telephone, letters, e-mail, audio cassettes, and videotapes.
- Students name professions that benefit from proficiency in Spanish: *policía, bombero/bombera, enfermero/enfermera*, and the like.
- Students write and illustrate simple stories in Spanish and present them for school (Parents' Night, PTA) or community (International Festival, *Festival latino*) functions.
- Students perform skits and songs in Spanish for school and community celebrations like Foreign Language Week or *Cinco de mayo*.

Sample Progress Indicators, Grade 8

- Students talk about favorite activities (*deportes, pasatiempos, música*) in Spanish with peers in the Spanish-speaking community.
- Students interview Spanish-speaking members of their local community to learn how they use Spanish in their various fields of work.
- Students describe family, school, and community activities for a Spanish-speaking keypal.
- Students visit Spanish language sites on the Internet to prepare poster sessions about Spanish-speaking countries for a community display.

Sample Progress Indicators, Grade 12

- Students participate in a school-to-work project, such as volunteering at a senior citizen center, that requires proficiency in Spanish and/or an emerging understanding of the Spanish-speaking community.
- Students use community resources to research a cultural or linguistic topic related to the Spanish-speaking community, for example, identifying businesses that cater to a Spanish-speaking clientele.
- Students write a newsletter about their school for peers in a Spanish-speaking country.

Sample Progress Indicators, Grade 16

- Students shadow members of the Spanish-speaking community at their work places in order to learn occupation-specific vocabulary, expressions, and protocol. In the health care professions, for example, they might learn *yeso, dosis, camilla,* and how to interview a patient.
- Students socialize with peers in the Spanish-speaking community at dances, parties, and other events that reflect Hispanic traditions and celebrations.
- Students participate in internship programs in Spanish-speaking countries.
- Students volunteer as tutors for Spanish-speaking children or as conversation partners for members of the Spanish-speaking community.

STANDARD 5.2 Students show evidence of becoming life-long learners by using Spanish for personal enjoyment and enrichment

Spanish is an avenue to gathering information and establishing interpersonal relations. By developing their skills in Spanish, students can acquire information as they continue to learn throughout their lives. Within the United States, there are many communities where Spanish is spoken, providing students with opportunities to maintain and enhance their language skills after leaving school. Major cable television networks, as well as many local radio and television stations, provide Spanish language programming for their audiences. Spanish language newspapers and magazines are widely available in the United States on newsstands and by subscription. Films from Europe and Latin America can be rented at video stores almost everywhere. For the older student, many clubs have Latino Nights featuring salsa, merengue, and other forms of popular Latin music and dance. Local festivals highlight the many cultures represented by the Spanish language. Travel opportunities to Spanish-speaking countries and communities within the U.S. are readily available to students of Spanish.

Sample Progress Indicators, Grade 4

- Students read materials in Spanish (*cuentos infantiles*, children's web pages, *leyendas*), view children's programs in Spanish on cable television, and listen to music from Spanish-speaking countries for personal enjoyment.
- Students learn to play culturally-associated instruments, such as the guitar, accordion, maracas, and drums.
- Students play culturally-authentic games, such as *Dominó, Cola del diablo,* or *La gallina ciega*.
- Students establish friendships with children in the local Spanish-speaking community.

Sample Progress Indicators, Grade 8

- Students read authentic materials (*Tú* magazine, *microcuentos y leyendas*, teen novels like *Hermanas*) for personal enjoyment.
- Students listen to, sing, and play music from Spanish-speaking countries for personal entertainment.
- Students participate in Spanish Club activities.

Sample Progress Indicators, Grade 12

- Students continue to learn more about personal interests by consulting various Spanish references, such as Spanish websites on the Internet, *periódicos y revistas*, and Spanish-Spanish dictionaries.
- Students enhance their Spanish skills and knowledge of a particular culture by participating in supervised homestay programs in Spanish-speaking countries or Hispanic communities in the U.S.
- Students maintain relationships with members of the local Hispanic communities.

Sample Progress Indicators, Grade 16

- Students use diverse Spanish language references to research topics of professional interest (*manuales, atlas, documentos, diccionarios de ideas afines*).
- Students read popular literature from the Spanish-speaking world, such as the works of Gabriel García-Márquez and Isabel Allende.

> TRAVEL OPPORTUNITIES … ARE READILY AVAILABLE TO STUDENTS OF SPANISH

- Students plan and host events like *tertulias, fiestas de cumpleaños*, and *meriendas* for Spanish-speaking friends.
- Students participate in intellectual activities and cultural events, such as attending *conferencias* and theater performances in Spanish.
- Students seek opportunities to maintain or improve their Spanish skills by attending conversation hours and volunteering in the Spanish-speaking community.

Learning Scenarios

Learning scenarios were written or adapted by the following contributors: **Martha Dow Adams**, Petal High School, Petal, MS and the University of Southern Mississippi, Hattiesburg, MS; **Jeannette Borich**, Ankeny Community Schools, Ankeny, IA; **Susan Graham**, Joliet Center High School, Joliet, IL; **Nancy Humbach**, Miami University, Oxford, OH; **Donna Kleinman**, Logan School, Denver, CO; **Judith Liskin-Gasparro**, University of Iowa, Iowa City, IA; **Melvy Jensen**, Mt. Vernon High School, Fairfax County Public Schools, Fairfax, VA; **Donna R. Long**, The Ohio State University, Columbus, OH; **Mary McCorkle**, Mobridge High School, Mobridge, SD; **Frank W. Medley, Jr.**, West Virginia University, Morgantown, WV; **Myriam Met**, Montgomery County Public Schools, Rockville, MD; **Janet Norden**, Baylor University, Waco, TX; **Mary Lynn Redmond**, Wake Forest University, Winston-Salem, NC, for NNELL (National Network for Early Language Learning); **Martie Semmer**, Summit School District RE-1, Frisco, CO; **Jill Surprenant**, Nantucket High School, Nantucket, MA.

> **TARGETED STANDARDS**
> 1.1 Interpersonal Communication
> 1.2 Interpretive Communication
> 1.3 Presentational Communication
> 2.1 Practices of Culture
> 3.2 Acquiring Information
> 4.1 Language Comparisons
> 5.1 School and Community

LA INDEPENDENCIA

Fifth graders at Las Alturas Elementary School studied the American Revolution in their Social Studies class. The Spanish teacher, Señor Medina, worked with the fifth-grade teacher to develop a unit on the independence movements of Latin American countries. Students studied the revolutionary heroes of the Spanish-speaking countries in the Americas, as well as the dates of their independence from Spain. Working in pairs, the students used the World Wide Web and materials from the school library to make posters about these heroes, which were displayed during Parents' Night. Each poster displayed the name of the country, a drawing of the national flag, the date of independence, and information about the patriots of the independence movement. From the Internet, students obtained maps of the capital cities of the Latin American countries and identified streets that were named for the revolutionary heroes. Repeating the same activity with maps of Washington, DC and Philadelphia (the first US capital), they searched for streets named for heroes of the Revolutionary War. Students also studied the formation of *apellidos* in connection with the names of Latin American patriots. As a final project, students shared information via e-mail with peers in their sister school in Chile about typical Independence Day celebrations in their respective countries.

Reflection

1.1 Learners communicate by e-mail with peers in a Spanish-speaking country.
1.2 Learners study the concept of independence.
1.3 Learners make posters for Parents' Night.
2.1 Learners compare and contrast streets named for revolutionary heroes in the US and Latin America.
3.2 Learners acquire information from print and non-print sources.
4.1 Learners compare and contrast last names in the US and Latin America.
5.1 Learners present their poster sessions at Parents' Night.

In this activity, learners use critical thinking skills to compare and contrast information about their own language and culture with the Spanish language and Latin American culture. More advanced learners could plan a celebration to celebrate the Independence Day of a Spanish-speaking country that is significant in their own community. Leaders of the community could be invited to the celebration. The domain of music could be included by having learners study the words and melodies of national anthems of Spanish-speaking countries. History would also be a natural connection with the project, as learners relate US history with Latin America (Treaty of Guadalupe-Hidalgo, Spanish-American War, Chamizal Treaty, etc.).

BIRDS BEYOND BORDERS/*AVES SIN FRONTERAS*

Elementary school students of Spanish in a small private school in Denver and in a rural district in the mountains of Colorado are participating in an international education program sponsored by the Colorado Bird Observatory. Students are linked with peers in the western Mexican state of Michoacán. Birds Beyond Borders is a science-related project, in which they focus on songbirds that migrate between Colorado and Michoacán. Students exchange information regarding observations of songbirds, their habitat, the environmental dangers that affect them, and the practices of humans in Colorado and Michoacán that threaten the existence of songbirds as part of healthy ecosystems. Teachers from Colorado visit their sister school in Mexico and teachers from the sister schools have visited Colorado.

TARGETED STANDARDS
1.1 Interpersonal Communication
1.2 Interpretive Communication
1.3 Presentational Communication
2.1 Practices of Culture
2.2 Products of Culture
3.1 Making Connections
3.2 Acquiring Information
4.1 Language Comparisons
4.2 Cultural Comparisons
5.1 School and Community
5.2 Lifelong Learning

Teachers use props, visuals demonstrations, simulations, and gestures to introduce concepts and unfamiliar vocabulary. To practice new vocabulary and concepts, they use TPR (Total Physical Response), TPR storytelling strategies, Gouin series (activities performed in sequence and described by students), active listening, reading and writing activities, interactive pair activities, and graphing.

Language use begins to emerge during subthemes based on concrete experiences, such as students constructing the school yard habitat or bird-banding at a local lake. Through Gouin series students first pantomime the steps of the hands-on activity as the teacher says the steps in Spanish; students then say the steps in Spanish as they perform the actions. Through an adaptation of TPR storytelling, the teacher and students create mini-stories activated through the language experience approach based on content and vocabulary of the Gouin series. When all of the vocabulary has been internalized through the various techniques, students dramatize, illustrate, tell, and retell learned content knowledge in the form of a story. Students are now ready to conduct research in Spanish on songbirds and factors that affect their survival, using books, maps, and field guides provided by teachers. Students from both countries exchange written information with their sister classes. Colorado students present dramatizations, stories, songs, narrations of the school yard habitat, etc. for the visiting teachers from Mexico.

The sister classrooms maintain a regular exchange of information through letters, projects, drawings, photographs, video and audio cassettes, and small cultural gifts throughout the school year. Mexican students have sent their sister classes in Colorado cultural products such as foods and bark paintings. Community volunteers, both native and non-native speakers of Spanish, come into classrooms to help children read the letters they receive.

Students learn to understand and interpret the written language; they compare and contrast the English and Spanish language systems; they compare and contrast the formats of social letters from both cultures. They have both direct contact with their sister schools during teacher visits as well as indirect contact through correspondence with students in their sister school.

Reflection

1.1 Students converse with visiting Mexican teachers. Students engage in communication with classmates in pair activities.

1.2 Students read and interpret letters and written projects from sister classes in Mexico.

1.3 Students perform in videos and write letters in Spanish to their sister classes.

2.1 Students gain awareness of cultural practices in Mexico from letters, student projects, videos, and visiting teachers from Mexico.

2.2 Students learn firsthand of the cultural products in Mexico from the gifts they receive.

3.1 Students further their knowledge of other disciplines. Science: students design and create a schoolyard habitat for winter birds; students keep a log of birds and their observed behaviors in the schoolyard habitat and in the field. Social Studies: students learn and reinforce geography as they follow bird migration paths using maps. Art: students have the opportunity to make *amates* or bark paintings. Language Arts: students read and create poems, letters and stories. Math: students determine distances that birds migrate.

3.2 Students increase their awareness of the plight of migratory birds in Mexico and the environmental factors that impact birds by reading the posters that the Mexican students send during an exchange protesting specific practices that occur in Mexico, information that is not available in English.

4.1 Students observe through Spanish speech and writing that there are differences and similarities with English. Students become aware there are both different and similar forms of communication.

4.2 Students become aware through videos, letters, and teacher visits that everyday life in Mexico is different from and yet also similar to life in their community in Colorado.

5.1 Students experience Mexico through the exchange of letters, videos, and gifts. Students experience the bilingual/international quality of their local community through interaction with local teaching staff and volunteers.

5.2 Students show evidence of lifelong learning by communicating in Spanish outside the classroom setting with speakers of Spanish. Students show evidence of a desire for lifelong learning by indicating the wish to meet their Mexican classmates and to continue an exchange.

Birds Beyond Borders is a project that can incorporate all of the standards. This learning scenario is an example of an integrated curricular unit in which students make connections among the disciplines using a common theme. There are many additional options for expansion into other content areas. This project, which affords all elementary school children the opportunity to communicate with children their own age from Mexico, brings their language study to life, especially in terms of the Communication and Cultures goals. Students see an immediate use and meaningful application of Spanish as they participate in learning opportunities in cooperation with students in another country through shared environmental issues. Students feel empowered to do what they can to help protect important habitat and share their knowledge with the community. Projects of this nature are more easily accessible than ever before. For many international projects, technology can play a key role in order to enhance Standard 3.2, although in this case technology is not available in the Mexican schools that participate in this project. Other projects offer myriad additional authentic learning experiences for children using the World Wide Web and e-mail.

All students—including students with special needs, students who are learning Spanish as a third or fourth language—in all FLES program models can succeed in these learning activities. Since the purpose is for each student to reach his/her potential in Spanish, each student, regardless of whether he or she is a heritage learner or is learning Spanish as a second language, will greatly benefit from projects such as Birds Beyond Borders. Obviously, heritage learners and other students who have an extensive background in Spanish will derive more from this project than students who have had minimal contact with the language. This and similar projects can be adapted to middle school and high school levels from beginning through advanced proficiency levels.

THE TALE OF THE CORN/
LA LEYENDA DEL MAÍZ

In their second grade class, students have been learning to talk about food in Spanish. One series of lessons, described in this scenario, is designed to help students understand the important role of corn in Mexican life. Students listen to and read an authentic legend, *La leyenda del maíz*. In class meetings prior to hearing the legend, students participate in pre-reading activities that will facilitate their understanding of the story.

> **TARGETED STANDARDS**
> 1.2 Interpretive Communication
> 2.2 Products of Culture
> 3.1 Making Connections
> 3.2 Acquiring Information
> 4.1 Language Comparisons
> 4.2 Cultural Comparisons

Students make posters and collages that show foods they like. In anticipation of the story, the teacher ensures that corn is one of the foods that students know they may include in their collage.

Students make bar graphs to indicate how many students have eaten certain foods in the last few days, one of which is corn.

Students are directed to ask their parents to identify food items in their own homes that are made primarily from corn. Students may bring product packages, advertisements, or their own drawings to class to illustrate the information they gather. From this information and the previous activities students discover whether or not corn is a significant part of their diet.

Students figure out what would happen if they could not get a food that is important in their diet (perhaps even corn).

The teacher tells or reads *La leyenda del maíz* using a combination of many or all of the following strategies: TPR Storytelling, pantomime, physical gestures, and visuals. A simplified version of the story follows:

LA LEYENDA DEL MAIZ

Quetzalcoatl está triste: los indios de México tienen hambre.
Quetzalcoatl sabe que en la montaña las hormigas rojas guardan el maíz.
Quetzalcoatl vuela a la montaña. En la montaña las hormigas rojas guardan el maíz.
Quetzalcoatl les dice: "Por favor, un poco de maíz. Los indios tienen hambre."
Las hormigas rojas le dicen: "Quetzalcoatl, ¿este maíz es para los indios o para los dioses?"
Quetzalcoatl responde: "Es para los indios. Tienen hambre."
Las hormigas rojas responden: "¡No es para los indios, no! Es para los dioses."
Entonces, otra vez, Quetzalcoatl está triste.
Quetzalcoatl piensa y piensa. "¡Me convierto en una hormiga negra!"
Y Quetzalcoatl se convierte…¡en una hormiga negra!
Quetzalcoatl les dice a las hormigas rojas: "¡por favor…por favor!"
Las hormigas le responden, "sí", y le dan maíz.
Y Quetzalcoatl está contento; él es de muchos colores—rojo, amarillo, azul y de color café.
¡La hormiga negra se convierte en Quetzalcoatl! y vuela a los indios.
Los indios cultivan el maíz. Hacen tortillas del maíz.
Ahora, ¿tienen hambre los indios? ¡NO! y están contentos.

The folktale highlights the importance of corn in the Mexican diet and culture. In class meetings subsequent to the reading of the story, the teacher introduces students to different products made from corn, particularly the tortilla. Students compare the use of corn in the Mexican culture as compared to the use of corn in their own. One activity to help students discover the frequency of "corn" in Mexican cuisine is to have students scan authentic recipes and menus for the word and tally the number of times it appears as an ingredient or as a menu item. Students compare the information to that which they generated in the pre-reading activities.

Additional follow-up activities include the following:
- Students locate the mountain ranges of Mexico on a map.
- Students read along as the teacher re-reads the story aloud, using big books, sentence strips, or the overhead projector. More able learners are encouraged to identify cognates.
- Students act out the story (or use puppets) as the teacher retells it.

Reflection

1.2 Students become active listeners as they demonstrate understanding of *La leyenda del maíz* through actions, pantomiming, etc.

2.2 Students learn about the importance of corn in the daily living of the Mexican people past and present.

3.1 Students make the geography connection when they learn the location of mountains in Mexico.

3.2 Students have accessed and acquired the story of a folk tale that is best understood and interpreted when told in Spanish.

4.1 Students identify the cognates of this folk tale: *montañas, indios, colores, no, contento, contentos. Tortilla* is a borrowed word.

4.2 Students compare the use of the *tortilla de maíz* in the Mexican culture with the use of the "corn muffin" in the students' culture.

This is an appropriate learning scenario for all beginning students—including students with special learning needs and students who are studying Spanish as a third or fourth language—in all FLES program models and for beginning students at all levels. Students are presented with ample opportunities to internalize the language of *La leyenda del maíz* before they are expected to produce spoken language. For Standard 3.1, another connection can be made with language arts and art. The class can make a big book. Every student gets a blank page except for one sentence printed on that page. The students draw a picture depicting the sentence on that particular page. Before the class big book is bound, the class can practice putting in order the pages, which are the sentences that tell the story.

For Standard 3.2, students might access the World Wide Web or exchange e-mail for more information on corn or other folk tales. Also, Mexico is not the only Spanish-speaking country in which corn plays a significant role. Students might consider researching the role of corn in other countries, plus how corn arrived in Spain. For Standard 4.2, the class may explore other ways, besides the tortilla, in which corn is used in Mexico as compared to the use of corn, the corn muffin, in the United States. If there are students whose home language is not English, the class can also learn how corn is used in that culture. Students could also examine the practices that have evolved as a result of Mexico's historically being an agricultural economy, which would address Standard 2.1. Students could also prepare tortillas for their parents or other classes; this activity would address Standard 5.1.

Heritage learners can advance their language skills by reading the original story. Then, they might write and paraphrase the story in Spanish or write a journal entry. The teacher can then select misspelled words that might serve as spelling words for the heritage learners. Also, heritage learners can record on an audio cassette *La leyenda del maíz* for listening by the other students in the class. Even though students will not understand all the words, they can act out the words and phrases that they learned in the simplified version.

PLANNING TO STUDY IN SPAIN

TARGETED STANDARDS
1.1 Interpersonal Communication
1.2 Interpretive Communication
1.3 Presentational Communication
2.1 Practices of Culture
2.2 Products of Culture
3.1 Making Connections
3.2 Acquiring Information
4.2 Cultural Comparisons
5.1 School and Community

Students in an Illinois middle school planned a trip to Spain to study in a Spanish language school. First, they were given the web site of a school and a list of decisions to make about the information found there, in relation to their trip: class schedules, the cost in U.S. dollars, excursions they would take, and what further information they would need in order to make an effective plan. They sought other Spanish web sites and shared information that they found on topics like weather, sports, money, entertainment, school life, and food. In small groups, students drew Venn diagrams comparing the United States and Spain on one of the topics.

Each student prepared a trip plan and compared this plan to those of classmates, noting further possibilities gleaned from the interaction. They then wrote letters to their prospective host families, after studying appropriate cultural etiquette and register. A checklist prepared in a full-class brainstorming session was used by students to evaluate the content and quality of their own letters, which were then revised as necessary.

Students discussed what clothes and other items they would need, and made lists of what to pack and other things to do to get ready to travel. They compared their lists and revised their plans after further thought and discussion. Finally, on their "return," students pretended to be reporters for the school paper; each student interviewed one classmate and wrote an article about his or her experiences.

At each step, students helped create rubrics to assess the completeness and quality of their efforts. They and their teacher carried out the evaluations separately.

Reflection

1.1 Students share information found on the Internet, and discuss and compare their plans at each step in the process.
1.2 Students collect information found on the Internet.
1.3 Students write articles for others to read.
2.1, 2.2 Students find information on many aspects of living and studying in Spain.
3.1 Students convert money from *pesetas* to dollars and collect information on topics such as weather, geography, and history.
3.2 Students discover information that they did not expect, such as the non-existence of the term and the institution of "middle school" in Spain.
4.2 Students compare aspects of student life in Spain with that of the United States.
5.1 Students use Spanish web sites to find information that was written with Spanish readers in mind.

In this unit, middle school students used Spanish web sites to find information pertinent to planning a trip to Spain to study. At higher levels, or as a follow-up to this unit, classes could conduct e-mail and other exchanges with counterparts in other countries, both in English and in Spanish. The students themselves could provide much of the necessary information for each other, answering questions that arise in the process; compare and contrast their schools and lives; and discuss schedules, exams, dress (uniforms), etc. They could also prepare videotapes and other materials to exchange through the mail. Students in both countries would experience information and perspectives that would not be readily available from other sources.

HOUSING: SCALE DRAWINGS FOR CULTURAL COMPARISONS

Sr. Olivero knows that students in his eighth-grade class are expected to apply ratios and proportions to making scale drawings on their final exam in math. To help his Spanish students be successful on the exam, he integrates math into his unit on the house and home.

> **TARGETED STANDARDS**
> 1.1 Interpersonal Communication
> 1.2 Interpretive Communication
> 3.1 Acquire Information
> 4.2 Culture Comparisons
> 5.1 School and Community

Students began by measuring the classroom in meters. In groups, they used their measurements to draw a scale representation of the classroom. With this experience as preparation, Sr. Olivero selected advertisements for apartments in Sevilla, Spain that are representative of typical dwellings. Groups of students developed tables to show various combinations of widths and lengths that would result in the listed total number of square meters.

Then Sr. Oliveros selected advertisements for middle-sized apartments in the local community and gave these to groups of students. Students first converted the apartment size measurements from square feet to square meters and then developed tables of the various widths and lengths that would result in the appropriate size in square meters.

Students then prepared a chart to compare the size of apartments in their local community to those in Sevilla. To expand students' understanding, Sr. Oliveros then led the class in a discussion about the relative size of apartments in the two places and other culturally-based similarities and differences. He then had students use the Internet to locate data on the percent of households living in apartments vs. single-family dwellings in Sevilla and in the local community.

Reflection

1.1 Students share information and help each other to produce their scale drawings.
1.2 Students read apartment advertisements and interpret them by representing the information in them in scale drawings.
3.1 Students learn about housing patterns in a city in Spain.
4.2 Students learn about the diversity of housing patterns in the two cultures.
5.1 Students learn about housing patterns in their own community.

   This learning scenario links concepts of mathematics and sociology to the learning of Spanish. Students both bring to and take away from this learning scenario information and skills rooted in the other disciplines. Through drawings and discussion, students learn about housing patterns in their own communty and in a city of the Spanish-speaking world.

TARGETED STANDARDS
1.1 Interpersonal Communication
1.2 Interpretive Communication
3.1 Making Connections
4.2 Cultural Comparisons

APARTMENT HUNTING IN SAN JOSE, COSTA RICA

Taking the roles of partners in a real estate agency in San José, Costa Rica, students worked in groups of two to create a display of two different apartment floor plans, including available options, that they were planning to offer for rent at an upcoming simulated housing fair in San José. Each pair also prepared a map to illustrate the location of the building with respect to business, shopping, and tourist areas of San José, as well as a one-page flyer listing the agency's address and phone number, along with information about the apartments. Finally, each group prepared an ad for the real estate section of a tourist publication; the ads were pasted onto a single document and copies were made for the housing fair.

The next stage of the activity took place at the housing fair. Half of the students continued to act as real estate agents, while the other half assumed the role of tourists or business people from the U.S. who were interested in renting apartments in San José. Each potential tenant read the ads and, after deciding which apartments might best fit his or her needs, visited those displays, perused the flyers, and asked questions about location, floor plans, features, price, etc. Each potential tenant entered key information about four apartments onto a form provided by the teacher.

At the conclusion of the housing fair, "tenants" wrote paragraphs to the teacher, appending the forms they had filled out, explaining which apartment they had chosen and why. "Real estate agents" wrote reports to their absent partners describing the event and giving information on the apartments that were rented.

In a follow-up activity, students examined real estate ads from the newspapers of several capital cities of Latin America that they found on the Internet and recorded the rental prices and sizes of various apartments. They also determined the exchange rates for the national currencies and computed the rental prices in U.S. dollars. They then gathered rental information on apartments in their community and two large cities in other parts of the U.S. Finally, they researched information on average income in each area.

Reflection

1.1 Students talk with each other while setting up their booths for the housing fair. They also talk with each other in their roles as agent and potential tenant at the housing fair.

1.2 Students present information about apartments in San José and produce written reports about their experiences at the housing fair.

3.1 Students use their math skills to calculate Latin American housing costs in U.S. dollars and to compute the percentage of income spent on housing.

4.2 Students get a sense of the cost of housing in Latin American capital cities and compare those amounts to housing costs in the U.S. They also become aware of the role of housing costs in the context of total income.

Students developed skills in working collaboratively, in asking and answering questions, and in describing and summarizing information to put into practice vocabulary and structures they had learned in their math classes. They also acquired information on housing costs and average income in other parts of the world that might be applied to social studies classes.

LOS ESTEREOTIPOS Y EL PREJUICIO

Students initiate this unit by discussing stereotypes found in their own communities, e.g., athletes, cheerleaders, blondes, redheads. The teacher leads a discussion that leads students to begin to realize that people are more alike than different, using a Venn diagram to categorize similarities and differences. Before beginning the question of stereotypes for Hispanic people, the teacher assesses attitudes, encouraging students to write about their feelings on issues of immigration, undocumented workers, and

> **TARGETED STANDARDS**
> 1.1 Interpersonal Communication
> 1.2 Interpretive Communication
> 1.3 Presentational Communication
> 2.1 Practices of Culture
> 3.1 Acquiring Information
> 4.1 Language Comparisons
> 4.2 Cultural Comparisons
> 5.1 School and Community
> 5.2 Lifelong Learning

maquiladoras. A number of readings, chosen for the students' level of comprehension, lead them into a study of issues. Readings such as *La sandía*, by Anderson Imbert; *La mariposa* (Denevi); *Juan Darién* (Quiroga); works by Francisco Jiménez (*Capas de cartón, Mariposa*) illustrate the emotions of the issues in question. Spanish speakers visit the classroom and students interview them. Students also find information via the Internet. Several films, shown either in complete or edited versions, culminate the unit. Examples are *El norte, The Ballad of Gregorio Cortez, La familia*. Finally, students are asked to write again, in a journal, their thoughts and reflections of a possible change in attitude as a result of the unit. The teacher acts as a facilitator, without expressing opinions, in order to encourage students to form their own opinions. The teacher brings the unit to a close by focusing again on the problems of prejudice and stereotypes in the school and community.

Reflection

1.1 Students discuss in Spanish a variety of stereotypes in their own society, and interview native speakers on attitudes and emotions toward the issues.
1.2 Students demonstrate an understanding of the issues, following readings and after viewing films.
1.3 Students role-play and present reports on materials they collect.
2.1 Students interpret cultural behaviors that might impede understanding of a culturally diverse population.
3.1 Students research issues in books and via the Internet.
4.1, 4.2 Students compare languages, translations, and sources of misunderstandings, and make comparisons between Spanish and English.
5.1 Students find opportunities to employ their Spanish to obtain further information.
5.2 Students complete the unit, having attained a greater level of understanding of the source of cultural conflicts.

As a follow-up to this unit, students can prepare presentations for class, based on interviews or independent research, on issues related to the farm workers, or immigration problems in their area. If possible, volunteer opportunities in areas where immigrant populations are located might provide further exposure to the issues. Assessment strategies include observations of students at work, journals and other writing, oral and written reports, participation in classroom discussions, and group work with both individual and group assessments.

TARGETED STANDARDS
1.1 Interpersonal Communication
1.2 Interpretive Communication
1.3 Presentational Communication
2.1 Practices of Culture
3.1 Making Connections
3.2 Acquiring Information
5.1 School and Community
5.2 Lifelong Learning

VOLCANOES

Students prepare a study of volcanoes—the various types, and how and why they function as they do. They research the information and present it in groups to the class, make model volcanoes, and discuss or write about events in history that resulted from volcanic eruptions. Because a great number of volcanoes exist in Spanish-speaking countries, there are a number of legends regarding them. Students read them, act them out, or tell them. Examples are *Popocatéptl e Ixtaccíhuatl*, *Paricutín* (both in Mexico) and *Imbabura* (Ecuador). Students also research the agricultural benefits of volcanic soil (e.g., coffee), volcanic stone and glass (obsidian), folklore relating to the volcanoes, as well as the practical issues of living near an active volcano such as *Popocatéptl* and the abundant information that is available on evacuations, using the ash as fertilizer, health issues, etc. The teacher works closely with the earth science teacher, and the collaboration is a joint project in both languages.

Reflection

1.1 Students discuss in Spanish the nature of volcanoes.
1.2 Students read and interpret information from legends and scientific resources.
1.3 Students present information to class and/or discuss their projects.
2.1 Students interpret cultural beliefs and practices relating to volcanoes.
3.1 Students incorporate their knowledge of earth science into this project.
3.2 Students acquire new information from a variety of sources.
5.1 Students interview (via the Internet or in person) people who have knowledge and experience with volcanoes. Students in Latin class may also collaborate on this unit, using Vesuvius and Pompeii as a comparison.
5.2 Students carry away a greater understanding of the force of volcanic action and its impact on population.

TARGETED STANDARDS
1.1 Interpersonal Communication
1.2 Interpretive Communication
1.3 Presentational Communication
3.1 Making Connections
3.2 Acquiring Information
4.1 Language Comparisons
4.2 Cultural Comparisons
5.1 School and Community
5.2 Lifelong Learning

ABUELITOS ADOPTIVOS

Ninth graders at Alta Vista High School were studying US history. Because their area of the United States has a significant Hispanic/Latino population, the Spanish teacher, Señorita Villareal, worked cooperatively with the history teacher, Ms. Wooten, to design an oral history project. Señorita Villareal's students "adopted" volunteers from the nearby Alderete Senior Center as *abuelitos* for the project. Using their knowledge of imperfect and preterit, they prepared simple questions about adolescent life in the past (clothing, school, activities, responsibilities, etc.). Then they visited the Senior Center and interviewed their *abuelitos*. They discovered that some of the *abuelitos* lived their entire lives in the community, while others emigrated to the United States from Cuba and other Spanish-speaking countries. Next, students studied the local newspaper archives for additional information about their *abuelitos'* era. Using this information, they wrote reports in which they compared and contrasted their own lives with those of their *abuelitos* at the same age. Using Spanish phrases that they studied in class, the students wrote thank-you notes to their *abuelitos* and invited them to visit Alta Vista High. On *el Día de los Abuelos*, the abuelitos spent the day with their *nietos*, attending classes and eating lunch in the school cafeteria. In Señorita Villareal's class, they related anecdotes from their youth, which Señorita Villareal videotaped with their permission. When the local shopping mall celebrated Education Week, the class members created a display based on the information and materials that they gathered. Several of the students maintained the relationships that they established with their *abuelitos* by talking with them on the telephone, visiting their homes, and helping them with errands.

Reflection

1.1 Students conduct interviews with senior citizens.
1.2 Students compare and contrast their own lives with those of others, based on oral and written sources.
1.3 Students develop a display based on the information that they have gathered.
3.1 Students further their knowledge of local history.
3.2 Students understand different perspectives on life in the past.
4.1 Students understand the concept of aspect and how it influences the past tense.
4.2 Students compare and contrast life in the United States with life in Mexico.
5.1 Students explore community resources and venues for displaying their knowledge.
5.2 Students develop relationships with Spanish speakers that will last over time.

In this scenario, students use their ability to communicate in Spanish outside of the school environment. Critical thinking skills are utilized in comparing and contrasting the past with the present, as well as in negotiating meaning in real-life conversations. This activity could be used in any grade. Younger students could learn games and songs from their abuelitos, which they could perform at a school assembly. Older students could develop a multimedia presentation with photographs, video, music, and other information for a civic event or the school library. Heritage students could develop their presentational skills by creating a program for the local cable channel or radio station.

INTERVIEW WITH RIGOBERTA MENCHÚ (SPANISH FOR HERITAGE LEARNERS)

Hispanic students at Mount Vernon High School in Fairfax County, VA were working on a unit, "*La mujer*," focusing on various aspects of women's life in society. The students watched a video interview of Nobel Prize Laureate Rigoberta Menchú, held at a local university. This interview gave the students an opportunity to see how people live and interact with their local community. This video also provided insights into the economic and sociopolitical aspects of Guatemalan society. Before viewing the video, the class had a short discussion of famous women around the world, and the characteristics of these women. They then shared their previous knowledge of ancient civilizations of the New World. The students were also asked to search the Internet for information on

> **TARGETED STANDARDS**
> 1.1 Interpersonal Communication
> 1.2 Interpretive Communication
> 2.1 Practices of Culture
> 3.2 Acquiring Information
> 4.2 Cultural Comparisons

the geography, the economic and sociopolitical structure, the languages spoken, and other cultural aspects of Guatemala. After viewing the video, students wrote a response to the film in which they summarized the salient points of the interview, their personal reactions, and the new information and perspectives they gained from it. Finally, they wrote questions for further study.

Reflection

1.1 Students provided their opinions on the traditional roles of women in many Spanish-speaking countries, and the changes occurring at the present time.

1.2 The video gave students a sense of the strength of Rigoberta Menchú, and they gained an understanding of the struggles that she and others have endured.

2.1 Through the video and the Internet research, students saw many sociopolitical aspects of highly stratified societies.

3.2 Accessing web sites from Latin America gave students the opportunity to read directly in Spanish and obtain valuable information that was not available in English. Students learned about the interview process and the use of formal language.

4.2 Students were able to draw comparisons between their respective cultural backgrounds and those represented on the video and obtained from the Internet.

The video format consisted of an interview posing questions in English with a translator providing them in Spanish for Ms. Menchú. This arrangement allowed students to see the value and importance of bilingualism, since the interpreter was highly proficient in both English and Spanish. In her presentation, Ms. Menchú provided many insights into the character of Guatemalan indigenous culture, thus giving students an excellent opportunity to reflect on their own cultures, U.S. culture, and the culture represented by Ms. Menchú.

TARGETED STANDARDS
1.1 Interpersonal Communication
1.2 Interpretive Communication
1.3 Presentational Communication
2.1 Practices of Culture
2.2 Products of Culture
3.1 Making Connections
3.2 Acquiring Information
4.1 Language Comparisons
4.2 Cultural Comparisons
5.1 School and Community
5.2 Lifelong Learning

LANGUAGE VARIATION PROJECT

Students in a college-level introductory course in Hispanic Linguistics studied language variation in the Hispanic/Latino community and abroad. To begin the project, the class members hypothesized possible categories of lexical variation in the Spanish-speaking world, such as food items, household appliances, and technological terms. Sources of variation, such as age, gender, and geographical location, were also hypothesized. The professor divided the class into groups of four, and each group selected one of the categories for investigation. During the next week, group members determined ten specific lexical items to be investigated. The technology group, for example, chose personal applications of technology: beeper, laptop computer, fax modem, caller ID, voice mail, automatic teller machine, electronic key card, scanner, remote control, and home security system. During the second week, students wrote paraphrases in Spanish for each lexical item, for example: *aparato que se usa para localizar a una persona*. Next, members of the group identified informants within the local Hispanic/Latino community and websites on the Internet that were used as sources of linguistic data. The next four weeks were spent on data collection. Students interviewed and tape-recorded native informants, identifying them by gender, age, and country of origin. They also consulted the previously identified websites, copying specific examples of the items in context and identifying their sources and countries of origin.

Data organization and analysis was the next stage of the project. Students transcribed the tape-recorded language samples and organized all materials item by item. Sources of language variation were tabulated and compared with the groups' initial hypotheses. The groups then drew conclusions and made recommendations for future research. Using a template designed by their professor, each group prepared a handout describing the results of their investigation. Results of the research projects were presented at a summary "conference" that consisted of the class members and other interested students and faculty members.

Reflection

1.1 Students speak Spanish in the classroom and with native informants.
1.2 Students analyze linguistic data.
1.3 Students make a handout showing the results of their investigation and present them in a summary "conference".
2.1 Students discover whether items common to their culture are also used in the Spanish-speaking world.
2.2 Students discover how products reflect aspects of culture such as age, gender, and geographical location.
3.1 Students use maps to identify geographical zones of the Spanish-speaking world: North America, Central America, Caribbean, Andean region, Southern Cone, Iberian Peninsula, West Africa.
3.2 Students acquire information for their research through native informants and authentic resources.
4.1 Students compare variation in their own language with language variation in the Spanish-speaking world.
4.2 Students acquire research skills that will be useful to them in other courses.
5.1 Students consult with members of the Hispanic/Latino community in the course of their investigation.
5.2 Students acquire research skills that will be useful to them in the future.

As a result of this activity, students have become much more aware of and attentive to variation in the Spanish language. Their success in doing the research project encouraged the students to enroll in a more advanced Hispanic linguistics course, in which they were able to apply the research techniques that they had previously learned.

SPANISH IN THE COMMUNITY

In an advanced Spanish conversation course at a large midwestern university, students interacted with and prepared independent projects about the Hispanic/Latino community in their city. The professor's primary goal was having students practice their speaking and listening skills outside of class. As one means to this end, she had arranged for her students to have Spanish-speaking conver-

TARGETED STANDARDS
1.1 Interpersonal Communication
1.3 Presentational Communication
5.1 School and Community
5.2 Lifelong Learning

Standards for Learning Spanish

sation partners who were members of an adult English as a Second Language course sponsored by the public schools. Every week, the students met with their partners for at least one hour and conversed for half of that time in Spanish and the other half in English, allowing both students to benefit from one-on-one language practice with a native speaker. In class, the students brainstormed about possible themes for their independent projects and each student selected a topic of personal interest.

One student secured a volunteer position with the city health department. One morning each week, she assisted a prenatal counselor who advised Spanish-speaking women about nutrition, immunizations, and other important issues. Another student decided to use his conversation partner's family, who had recently arrived in the city, as his project by helping them acclimate to their new home. Among the other projects selected were an annotated survey of local restaurants in which Spanish was spoken, a review of local dance clubs that featured Latino music, and a directory of civic organizations, social clubs, and service groups based in the Hispanic/Latino community. Students interviewed members of the Spanish-speaking community in order to gather information for their projects. Written reports were prepared in forms appropriate to the topic: directories, annotated bibliographies, narratives, etc. The project culminated in a poster session to which the students and faculty of the Spanish Department were invited. At the poster session, each student had a small table at which he/she presented a visual display (posters and other materials) of his/her project. Participants stopped by each booth to hear about the students' experiences and ask questions about the projects.

At the end of the course, the professor had her students complete an evaluation of the out-of-class activities. The majority of the students reacted enthusiastically to these experiences and many planned to continue their relationships with their conversation partners and other Spanish-speaking individuals that they had met while preparing their projects. Results of a pretest of speaking skills at the beginning of the course and a final oral examination revealed that the majority of the students enrolled in the course had indeed improved their speaking skills.

Reflection

1.1 Students interact with conversation partners and other members of the Spanish-speaking community.
1.3 Students present their final projects at a poster session.
5.1 Students use their oral language skills to get information for their projects.
5.2 Students establish mutually helpful contacts with the Spanish-speaking community that will enable them to improve their language skills and cultural information.

This activity primarily emphasizes communication (Goal 1). The professor capitalized on opportunities within the local Spanish-speaking community to provide extended oral language practice with native speakers for her students. In the process of utilizing these contacts, the students were also able to tap into Goal 5 (Participate in Multilingual Communities at Home and Around the World). A serendipitous outcome was that several students who attended the poster session became interested in taking the course and forming their own relationships with the Hispanic/Latino community.

LITERARY THEORY AND INTERPRETATION

Students in an Introduction to Literary Theory and Interpretation course in Spanish have been learning about various approaches to literary texts. For each of the approaches they have studied, they have interpreted one or more short texts (short stories, poems, essays). They have also kept journals, which they used to summarize and reflect on their reading.

> **TARGETED STANDARDS**
> 1.1 Interpersonal Communication
> 1.2 Interpretive Communication
> 1.3 Presentational Communication
> 2.2 Cultural Products
> 3.1 Making Connections
> 3.2 Acquiring Information
> 4.2 Cultural Comparisons

This learning scenario, which is the culminating project of the course, involves both individual work and small group collaboration. The instructor formed groups of four students and assigned to each group a text by a Latin American or Spanish writer who is still actively engaged in his or her craft. The students in each group read the text assigned to the group, wrote about it in their journals, and sent their journal entries to the other group members via e-mail for comments and discussion. The groups participated actively in their respective discussions because all of the students were eager to understand their text as well as possible in anticipation of the next stage of the project.

The task for the next stage was for each student to write an interpretation of the group's text from a particular critical stance. Since each group had to produce four interpretations from four different perspectives, the members of each group first met to negotiate their interpretive stances: feminist, Marxist, queer theory, reader response, etc. Each student then wrote an interpretive paper five to seven pages in length. The students read the papers of the other group members and worked collaboratively both on the content of their groups' papers and on sentence-level editing. The papers were then turned in to the instructor for further feedback.

After receiving the papers with the instructor's comments, the group members met again to reduce each paper to two to three pages and produce a packet of interpretations plus a cover letter to the author of the text, explaining the project and inviting the author's response to their work. (The instructor was able to provide the groups with electronic or postal addresses.)

For the final stage of the project, the members of each group presented a report to the class, which included a summary/description of the text, a brief interpretation according to the critical perspectives of the group members, and a description of the reaction of the author, if available.

The final product submitted to the instructor included the materials sent to the author and the author's response (from the group as a whole), as well as the revised version of the interpretive paper (from the individual student).

Reflection

1.1 Students communicate with each other orally and in writing at various stages of the project.
1.2 Students read and interpret literary texts. They also read and interpret the papers of their fellow group members, as well as the letter they receive from the author of the text they have worked on.

1.3 Students present the results of their work at various stages to the members of their group, to the rest of the class, to the instructor, and to the author of the literary text.

2.2 Students work intensively with a literary text, which is a product of both an individual writer and the culture in which the writer and the text are situated.

3.1 Students learn about literary theory through their in-depth study of a literary text.

3.2 By interpreting a literary text from various perspectives, students become aware of the culturally-based nature of the interpretive act. Such literary elements as relationships between characters, the ordering of events, and the selection of metaphors take on meaning according to the interpretive stance of the reader.

4.2 Students experience something of the Hispanic literary world by corresponding with a contemporary writer.

This scenario engages undergraduate students of literature in the process of literary criticism and provides them with a multi-faceted introduction to the Hispanic literary world. The multiple stages of the project ensure that all students remain active and involved at all times, and the design of the group collaboration both depends on and supports individual effort. Students maintain contact with the instructor but also work independently. The individual-plus-group design guarantees that all students read, write, speak, and listen to spoken Spanish while dealing with intellectual content of a high level. Due to the fact that their work has at least four audiences--the other members of the small group, the whole class, the instructor, and the author of the literary text on which they have worked--they become aware of the role of task, audience, and context in presentational discourse.

Standards for Foreign Language Learning in the 21st Century

3rd Edition: Revised including Arabic Standards

MAIL OR FAX YOUR ORDER TO:
National Standards Report
P.O. Box 1897
Lawrence, KS 66044 USA
Phone: (785) 843-1235
Fax: (785) 843-1274

COMMUNICATION
COMMUNITIES
CULTURES
COMPARISONS
CONNECTIONS

CREDIT CARD
Call for Fastest Service
1-800-627-0629
(U.S. and Canada Only)

Standards for Foreign Language Learning in the 21st Century includes the updated text of the original Standards for Foreign Language Learning: Preparing for the 21st Century, plus nine new sections devoted to standards for specific languages:

| Arabic | Chinese | Classic | French | German |
| Italian | Japanese | Portuguese | Russian | Spanish |

This latest version of the foreign language standards was fully-funded by the National Standards in Foreign Language Education Collaborative Project, and all proceeds from its sale will be used to provide professional development and other programs that will assist in the implementation of standards across the United States.

SHIPPING ADDRESS:

Full Name:

School/Company:

Address:

City, State, Zip Code:

Country:

ORDER INFORMATION

Standards for Foreign Language Learning _____ copies x $27.50 $ _____
(Price includes UPS shipping in U.S.)

Special Shipping Fees For Single Copies Only:
  For information on ordering multiple copies call (785) 843-1221
  Delivery (UPS Ground Trac) to Canada $12.00 $ _____
  Airmail Delivery to Mexico $15.00 $ _____
  Airmail Delivery elsewhere outside the U.S. $30.00 $ _____
  Overnight (DHL) delivery (U.S. only) $18.00 $ _____
                                          TOTAL = $ _____

PAYMENT INFORMATION (Please check method of payment)
❏   Check or postal money order (in US$ drawn on US Bank made payable to: National Standards in Foreign Language Education). Price includes delivery within the US.

❏   Credit Card   ❏ MasterCard   ❏ Visa   ❏ American Express

Credit Card Number _____ Exp. Date _____

Signature: _____

Purchase Order # (institutions only) _____